U0949551

东莞统计年鉴

DONGGUAN STATISTICAL YEARBOOK

2015

(总第25期 NO.25)

东 莞 市 统 计 局
国家统计局东莞调查队 编

Compiled by

Dongguan Municipal Bureau of Statistics

Survey Office of the National Bureau of Statistics in Dongguan

图书在版编目（CIP）数据

东莞统计年鉴. 2015 / 东莞市统计局, 国家统计局东莞调查队编.
-- 北京：中国统计出版社，2015.8
ISBN 978-7-5037-7527-7

Ⅰ. ①东…
Ⅱ. ①东… ②国…
Ⅲ. ①统计资料-东莞市-2015-年鉴
Ⅳ. ①C832.653-54

中国版本图书馆 CIP 数据核字（2015）第 185418 号

东莞统计年鉴-2015

作　　者/ 东莞市统计局　国家统计局东莞调查队
责任编辑/ 陈越月
装帧设计/ 冯　坚
出版发行/ 中国统计出版社
地　　址/ 北京市丰台区西三环南路甲 6 号
邮政编码/ 100073
电　　话/ 邮购（010）63376909　书店（010）68783171
网　　址/ http://csp.stats.gov.cn
印　　刷/ 东莞市本色印刷有限公司
经　　销/ 新华书店
开　　本/ 890mm×1240mm　1/16
字　　数/ 1200 千字
印　　张/ 31.5 印张
版　　别/ 2015 年 8 月第 1 版
版　　次/ 2015 年 8 月第 1 次印刷
定　　价/ 350.00 元

如有印装差错，由本社发行部调换。

编者说明

一、《东莞统计年鉴—2015》（以下简称年鉴）是一部反映东莞国民经济和社会发展情况的资料性年刊，本书收录了东莞2014年大量的统计数据以及主要指标的历年数据，旨在全面系统地反映东莞在经济和社会方面的发展变化。

二、全书分三部分。第一部分，概述，含中英文统计公报、政府工作报告；第二部分，统计资料，具体分为综合、人口与劳动力、农业、工业、固定资产投资与建筑业、运输邮电、国内贸易、价格指数、对外经济贸易与旅游、财政、金融与保险、人民生活、社会事业、能源、镇街主要指标、村（居）委会主要指标、历年国民经济和社会发展主要指标、东莞与全国、全省、三角洲城市及港澳台主要指标比较等17部分；第三部分，基本单位情况。

三、本年鉴资料大部分来自政府统计部门和调查队的各种统计报表、抽样调查资料，部分来自中央省属单位和市属各主管部门的统计资料。

四、本年鉴部分历史数据已根据第三次经济普查进行了调整，在此之前公布的数据凡与本年鉴数字不符的均以本年鉴为准。

五、年鉴统计表中的符号说明："#"表示其中主要项；"空格"表示该项统计指标数据不详或无该项数据。

六、今年本年鉴新增加了中国香港、中国澳门特别行政区和中国台湾省主要社会经济指标。

本年鉴在编辑出版过程中，得到省统计局、有关部门和镇街的大力支持，在此我们表示衷心感谢。限于我们的水平，本书难免有疏漏之处，敬请批评指正，以帮助我们进一步改进年鉴编辑工作，更好地为广大读者服务。

《东莞统计年鉴—2015》
编委会和编辑出版人员

目　　录

CONTENTS

第一部分　概述

Part One　Outline

第二部分　统计资料

Part Two　Statistics

一、综　合

General Survey

二、人口与劳动力
Population and Labor Force

三、农　业
Agriculture

四、工业
Industry

五、固定资产投资与建筑业
Investment in Fixed Assets and Construction

六、运输邮电

Transport, Postal and Telecommunication Services

七、国内贸易

Domestic Trade

八、价格指数
Price Indices

九、对外经济贸易与旅游
Foreign Trade and Tourism

十、财政、金融与保险
Finance, Banking and Insurance

十一、人民生活
People's Living Conditions

十二、社会事业
Social Undertakings

十三、能源
Energy

十四、镇街主要指标
Main Indicators of Towns

十五、村（居）委会主要指标
Main Indicators of Villagers'（Neighborhood）Committees

十六、历年国民经济和社会发展主要指标
Main Indicators of National Economy and Social Development over Years

十七、东莞与全国、全省、三角洲城市及港澳台主要指标比较
Comparison of Main Indicators between Dongguan and China, Guangdong Province, the Cities of the Pearl River Delta Hong Kong Macao Taiwan

第三部分 基本单位情况
Part Three Basic Units

生产总值

地区生产总值（亿元）

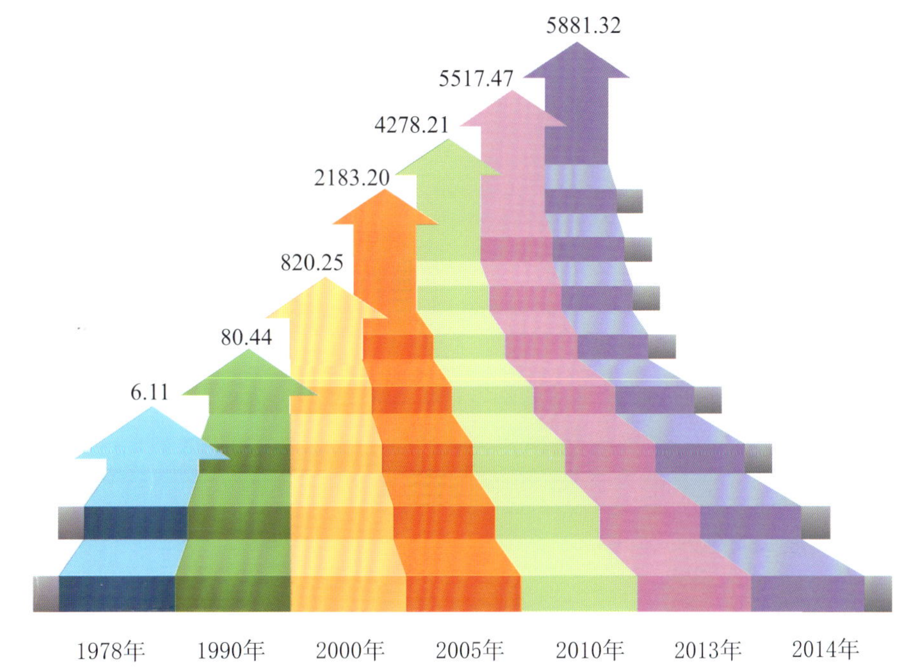

地区生产总值构成（%）

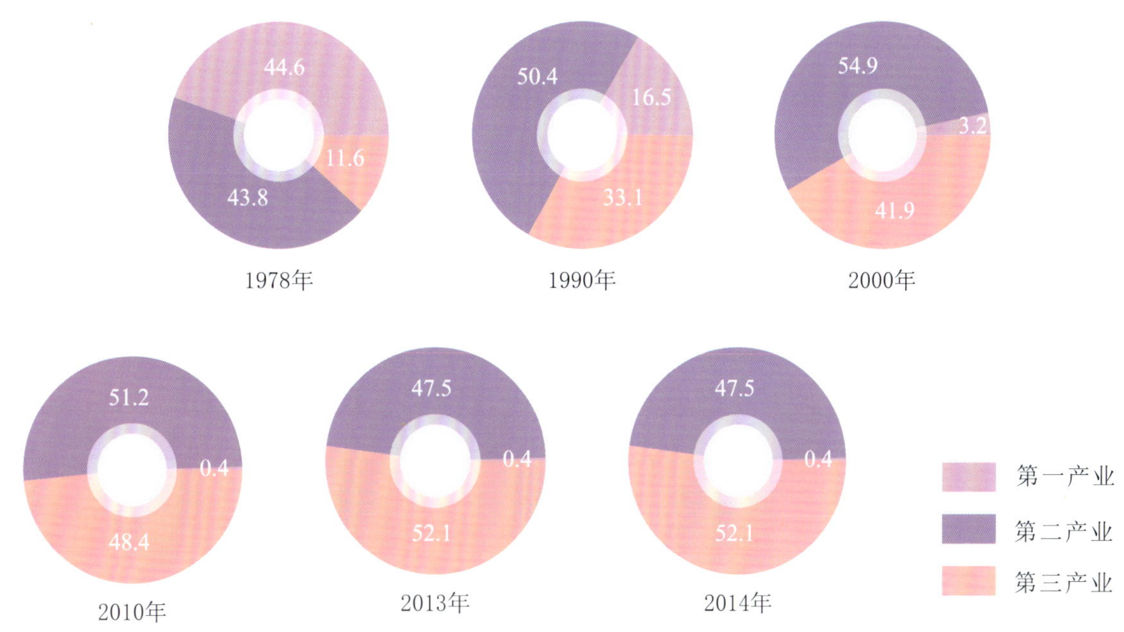

人口与劳动力

人口与劳动力（万人）

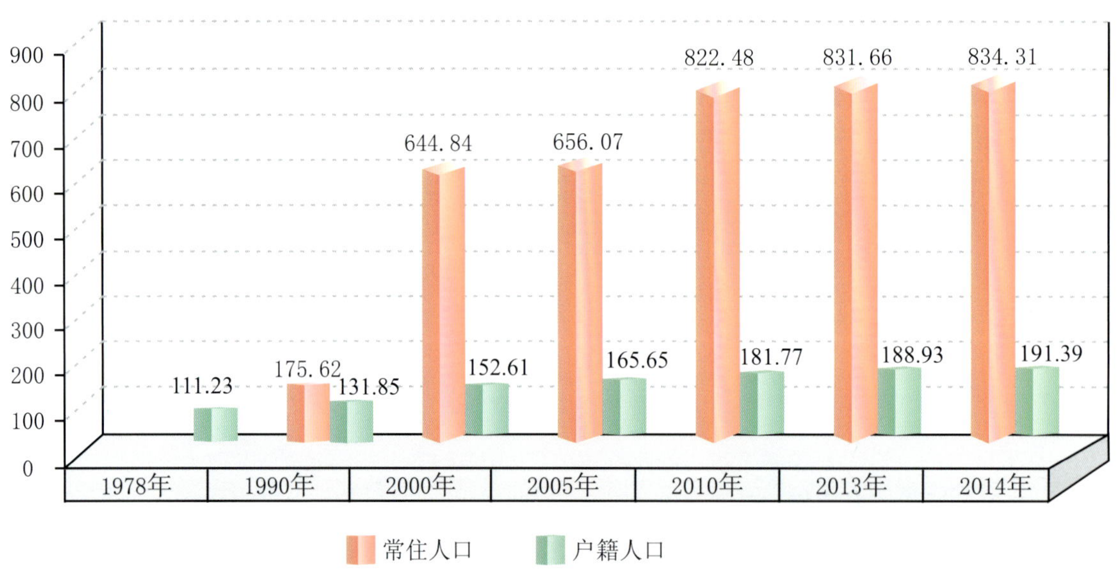

全社会从业人员（万人）

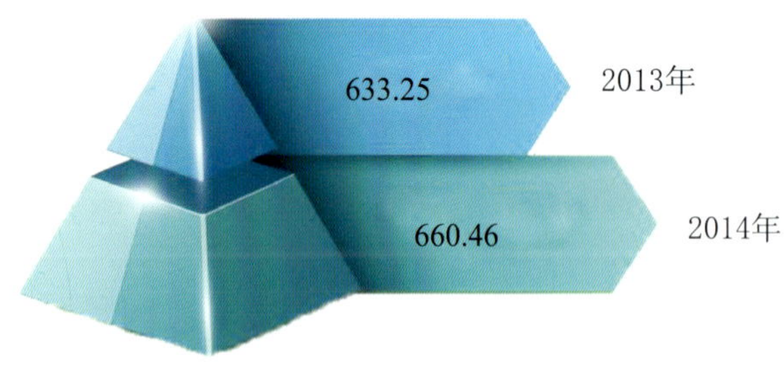

城镇非私营单位在岗职工年平均工资（元）

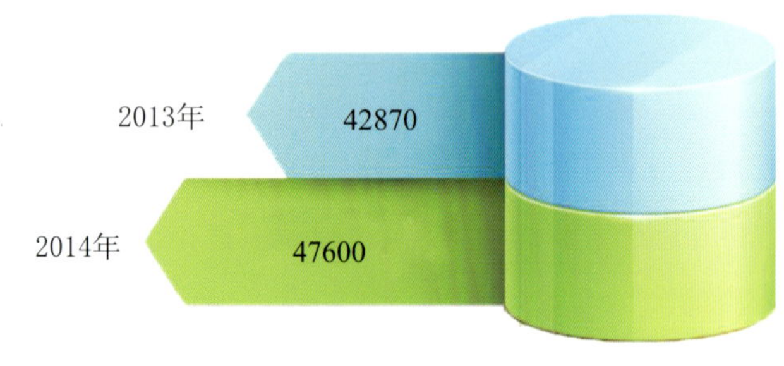

农业

农、林、牧、渔业总产值（亿元）

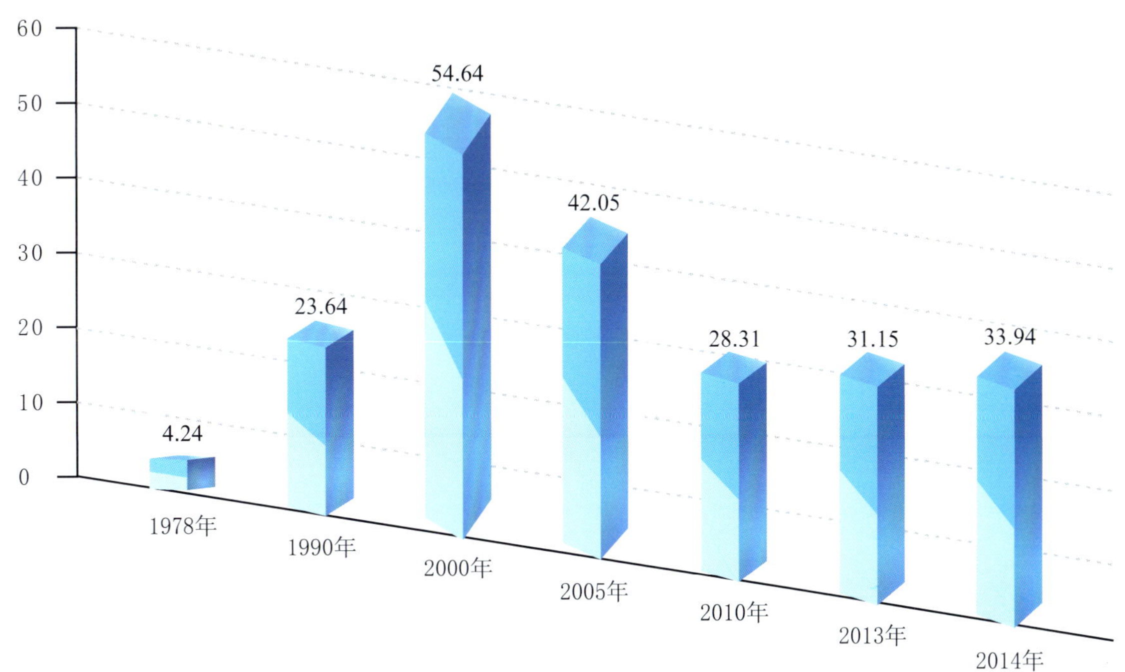

农、林、牧、渔业增加值（亿元）

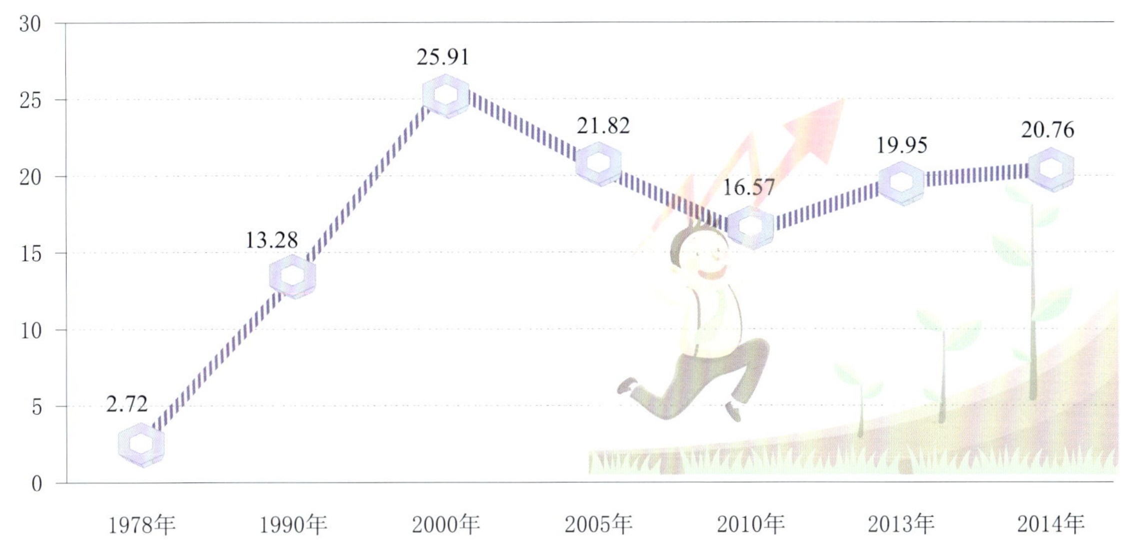

工业

规模以上工业增加值（亿元）

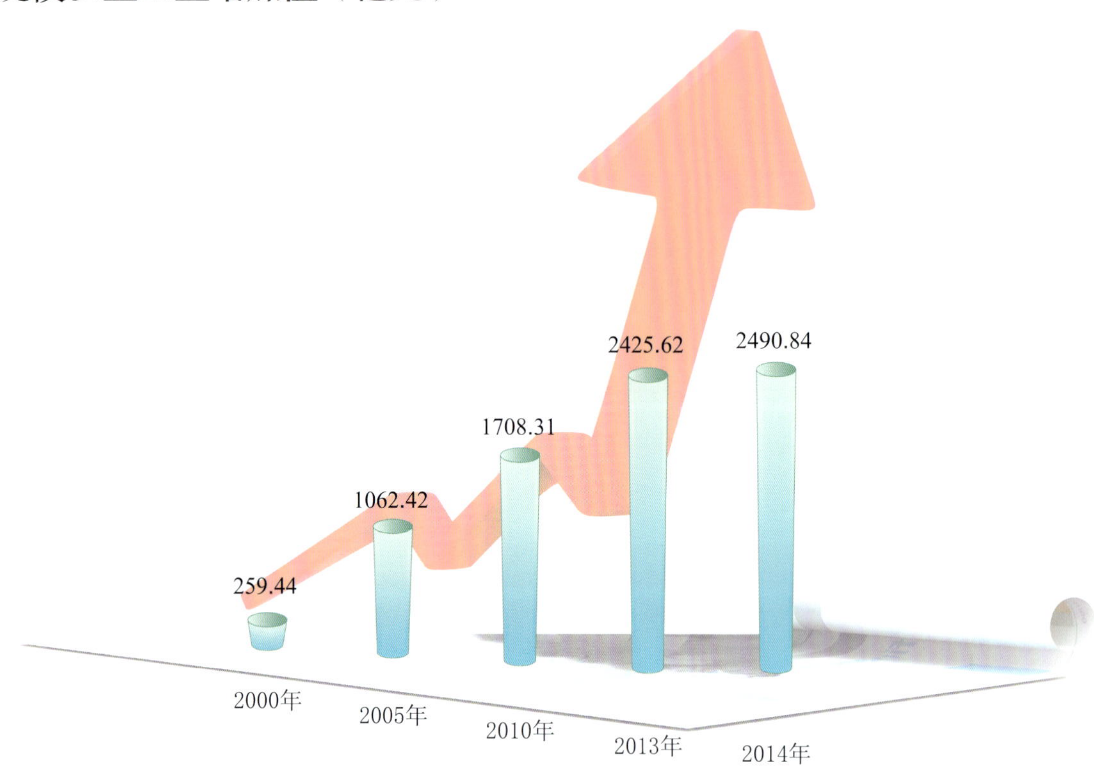

规模以上工业增加值构成（%）

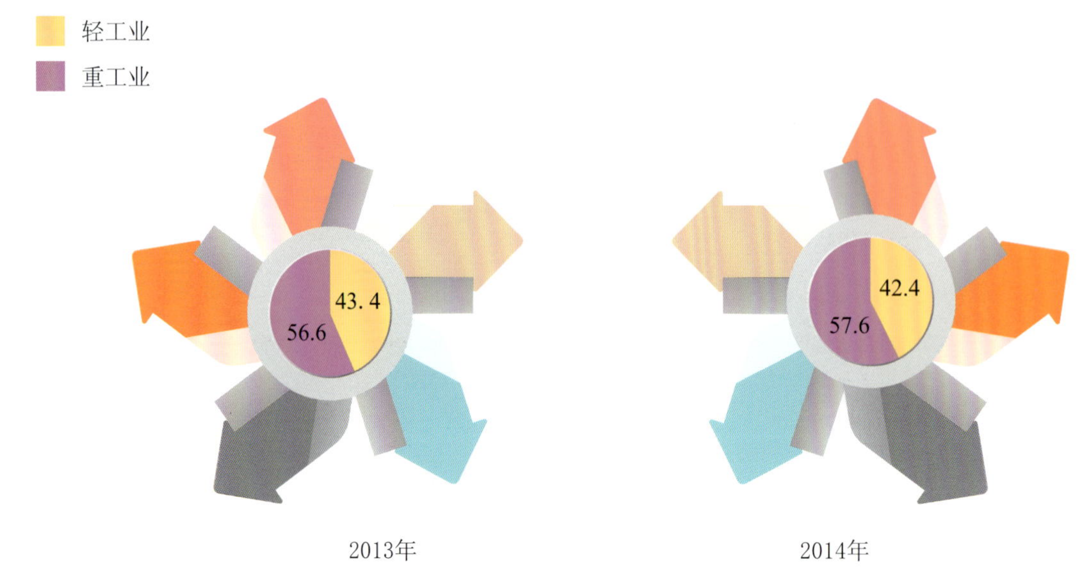

固定资产投资

固定资产投资总额（亿元）

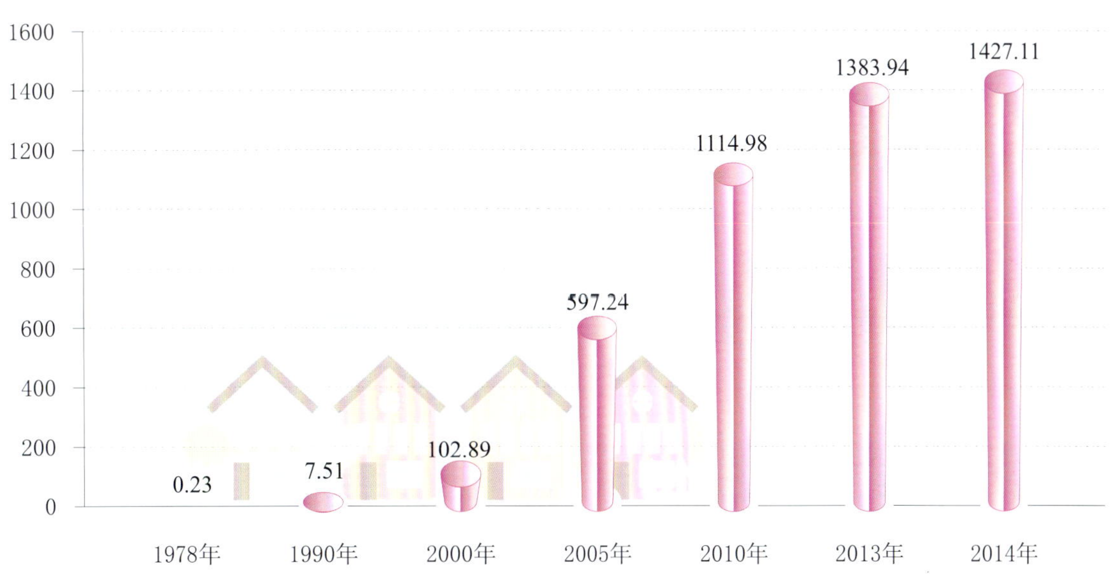

房地产开发投资总额（亿元）

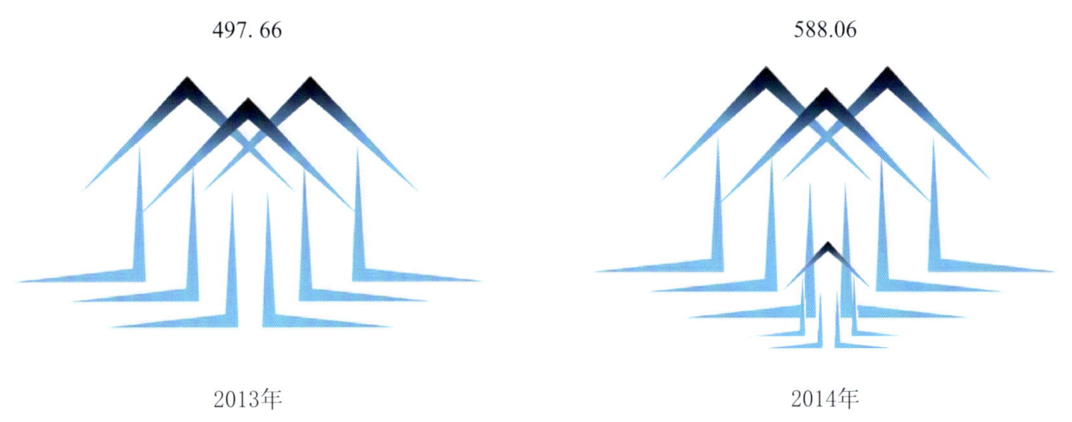

运输邮电

货物、旅客运输量

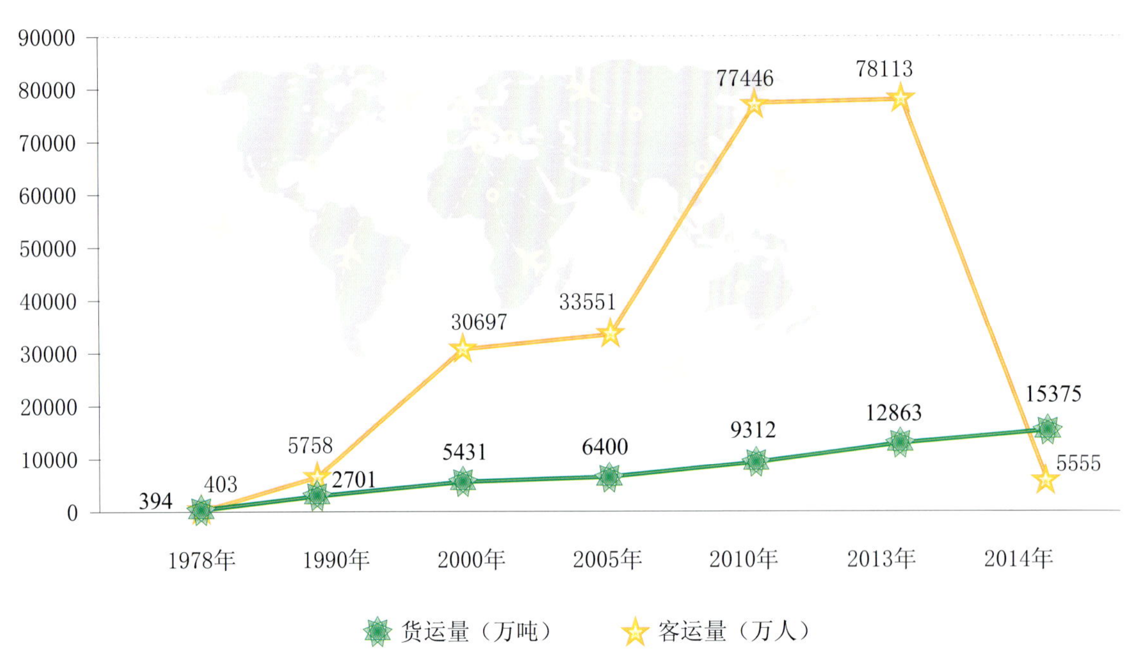

注：2014年客运量和旅客周转量不含城市客运量，数据与往年不可比。

本地电话用户、移动电话用户（万户）

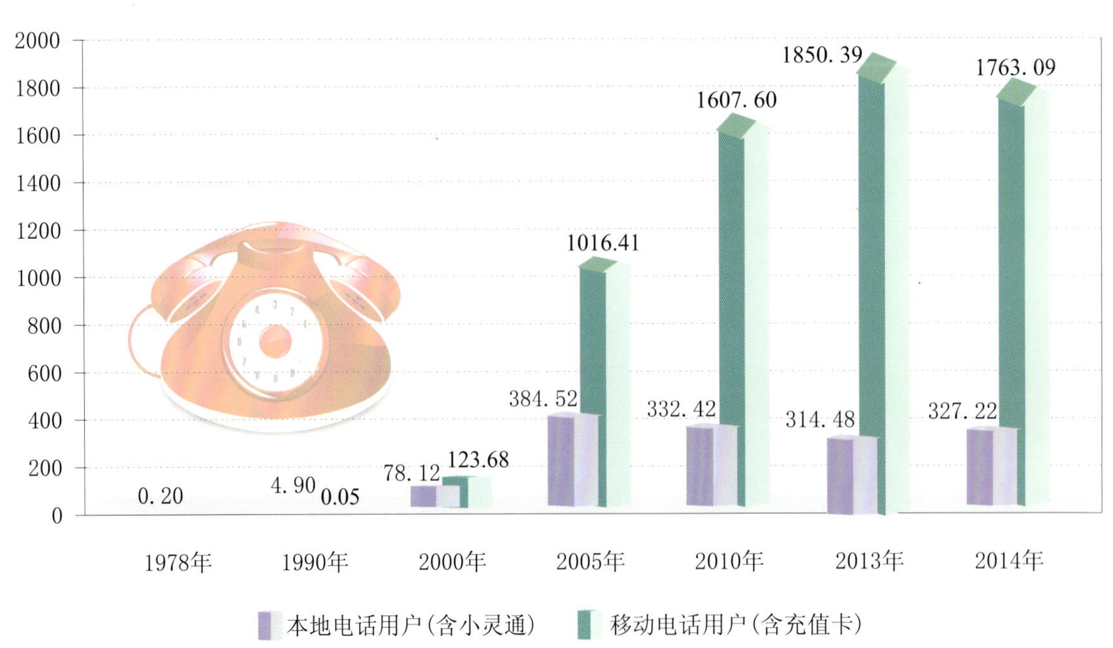

国内贸易

社会消费品零售总额（亿元）

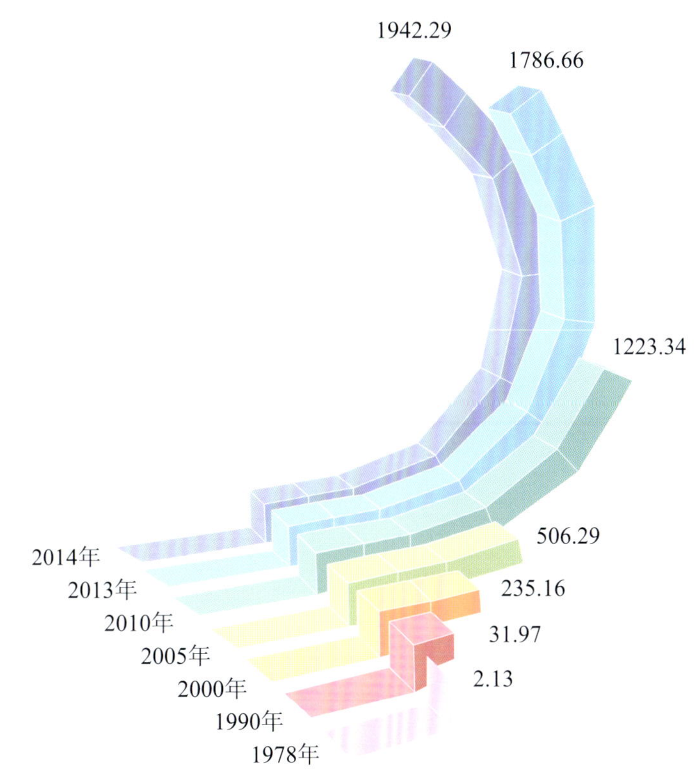

批发和零售、住宿和餐饮

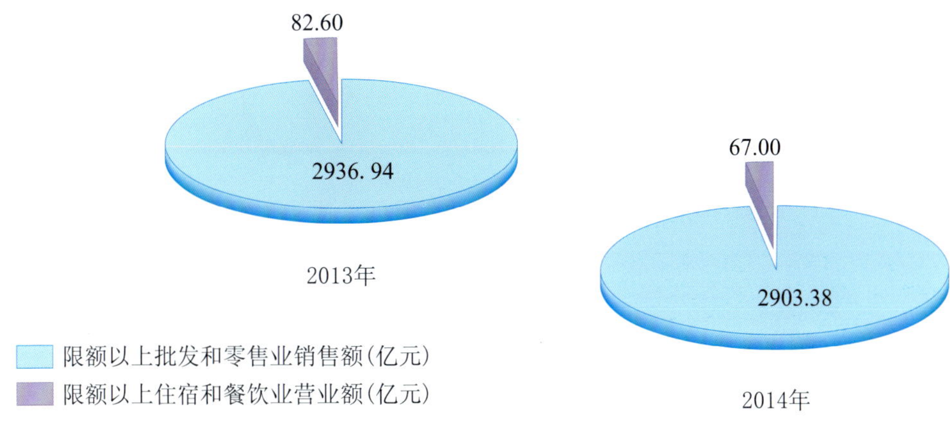

价格指数

居民消费价格总指数(以上年为100)

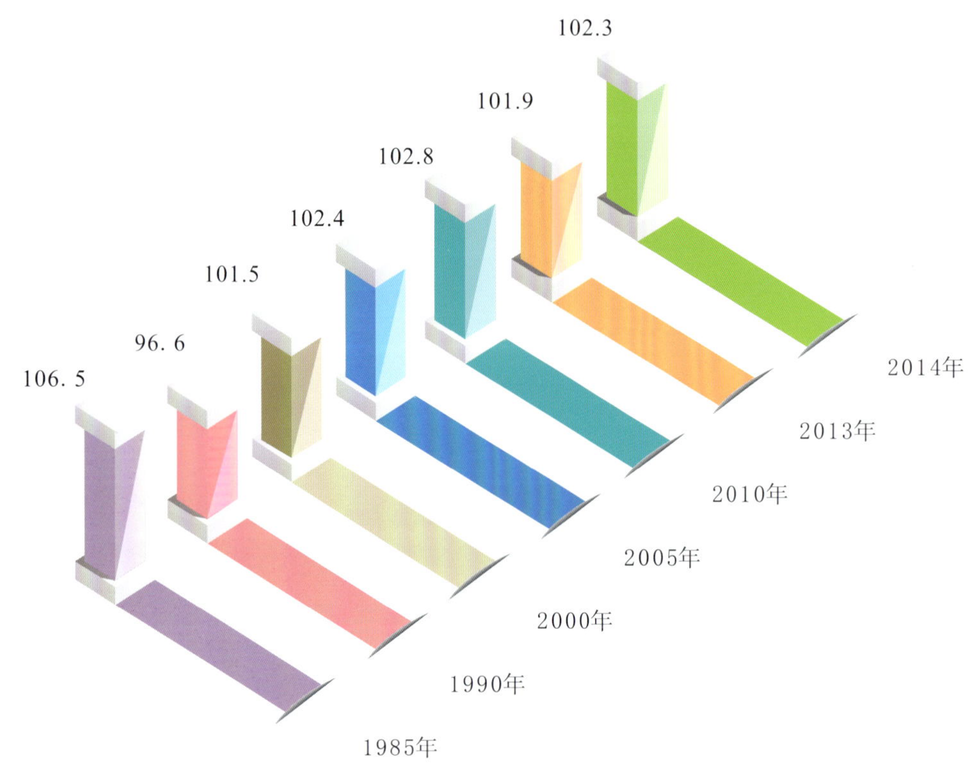

工业生产者出厂价格指数(以上年为100)

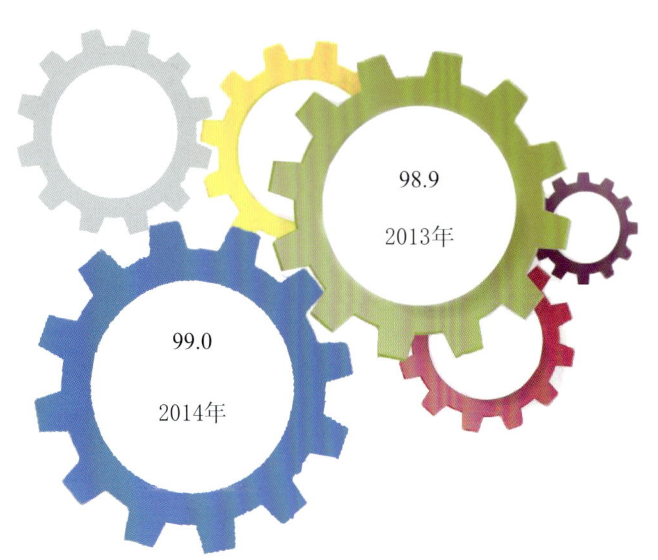

对外经济贸易与旅游

进口总额、出口总额(亿美元)

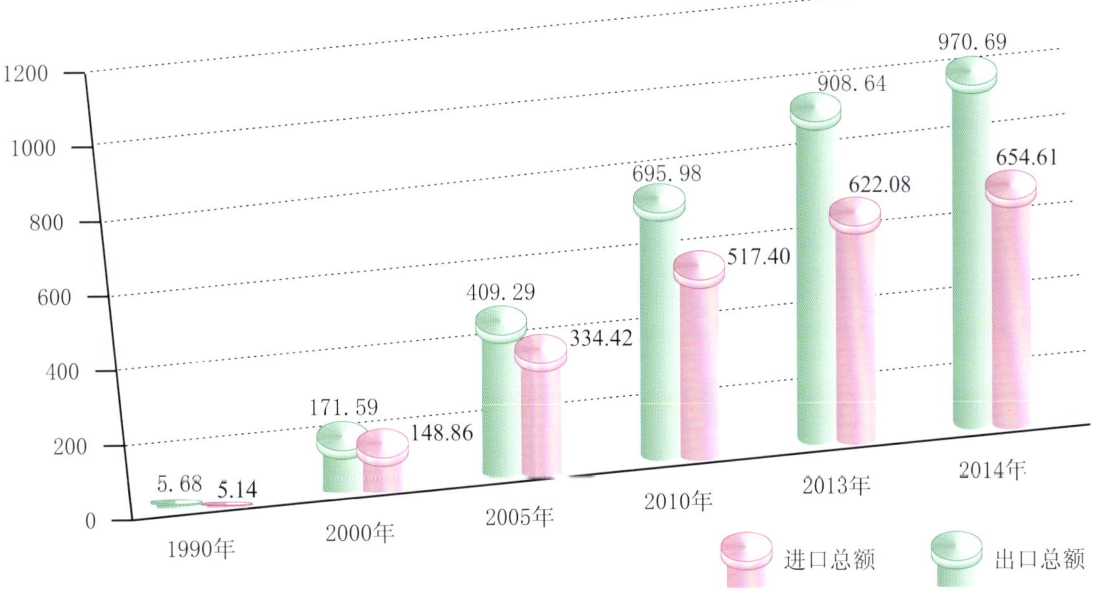

当年实际利用外资(亿美元)

全年接待国内外旅游人数(万人次)

财政、金融

来源于东莞的财政收入 (亿元)

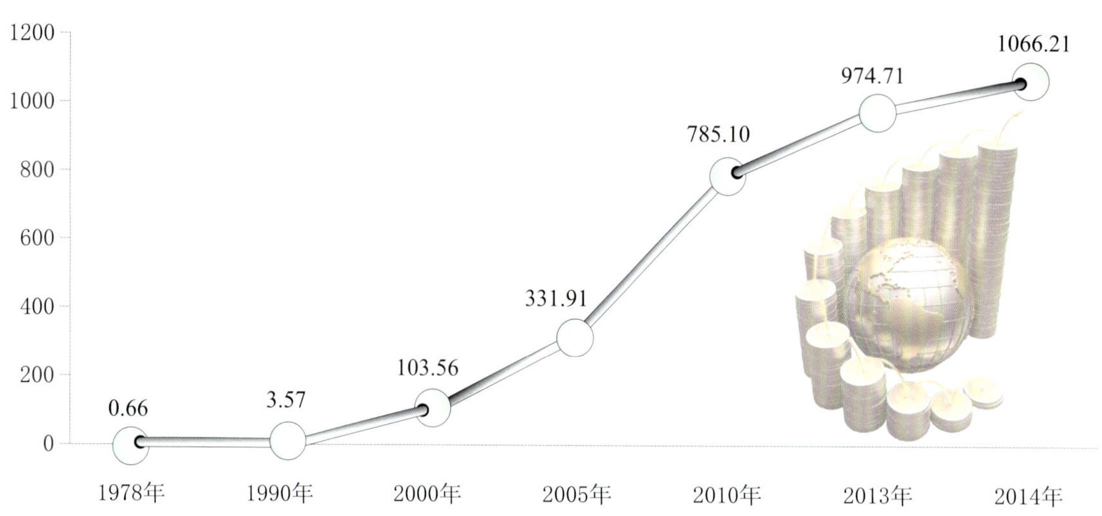

各项人民币存、贷款余额 (亿元)

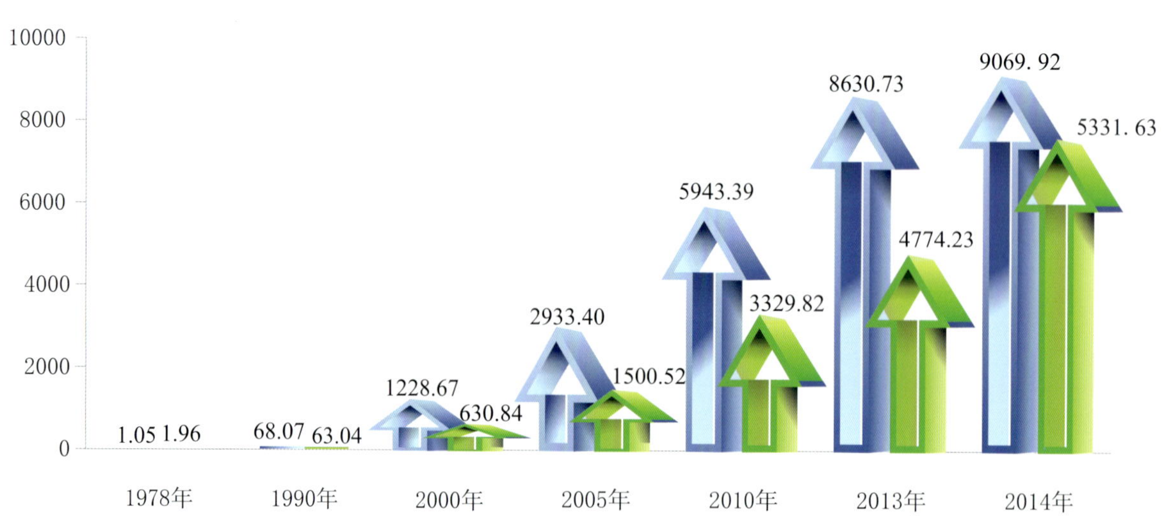

人民生活

2014年人民生活（元）

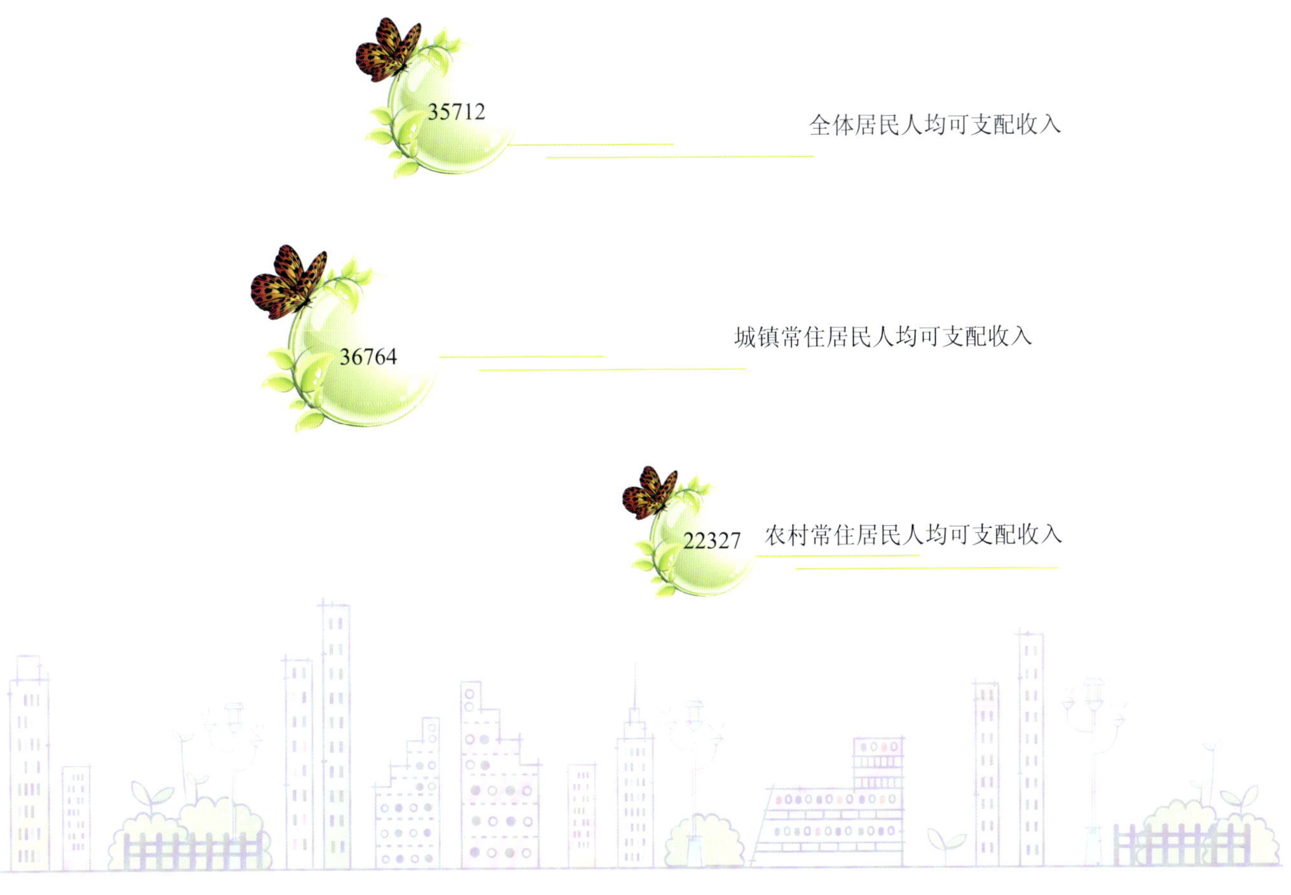

社会事业

绿地面积（万平方米）

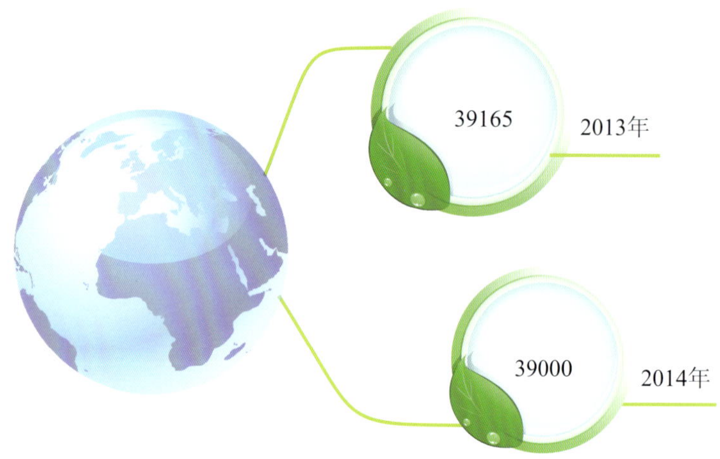

专利申请量（件）

专利授权量（件）

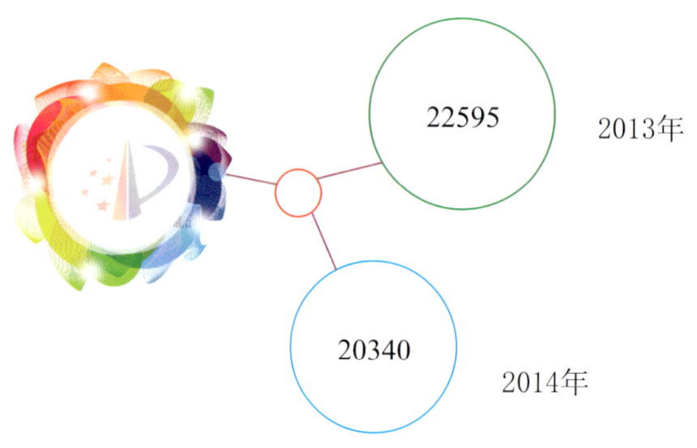

社会事业

卫生事业机构床位数(张)

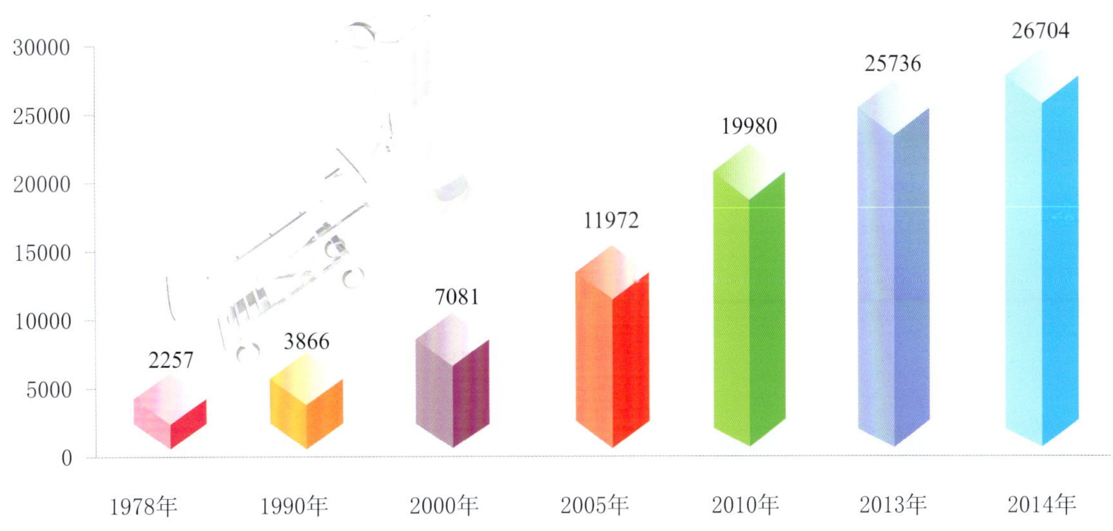

执业(助理)医师(人)

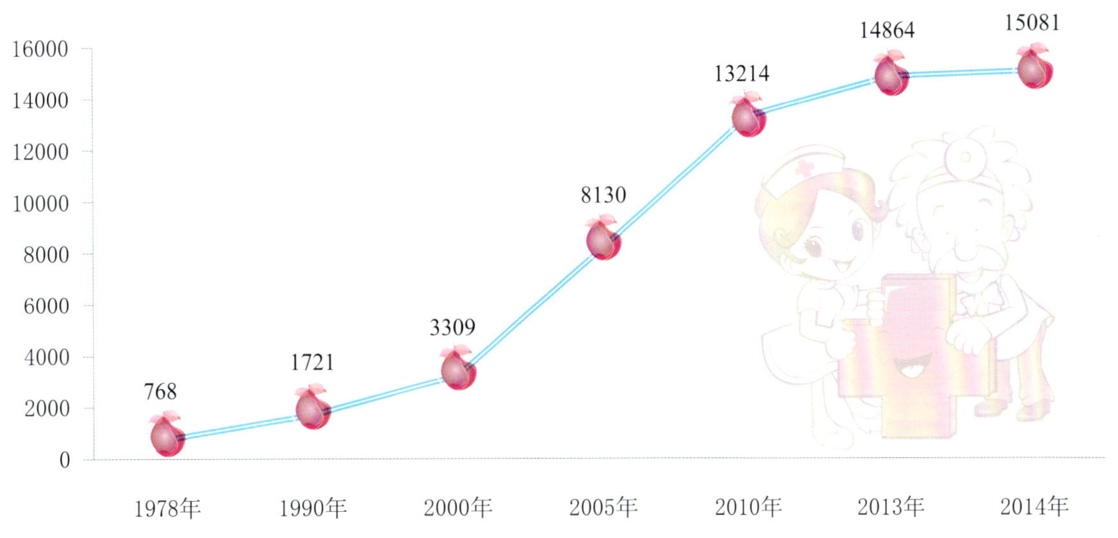

社会事业

各类学校(所)

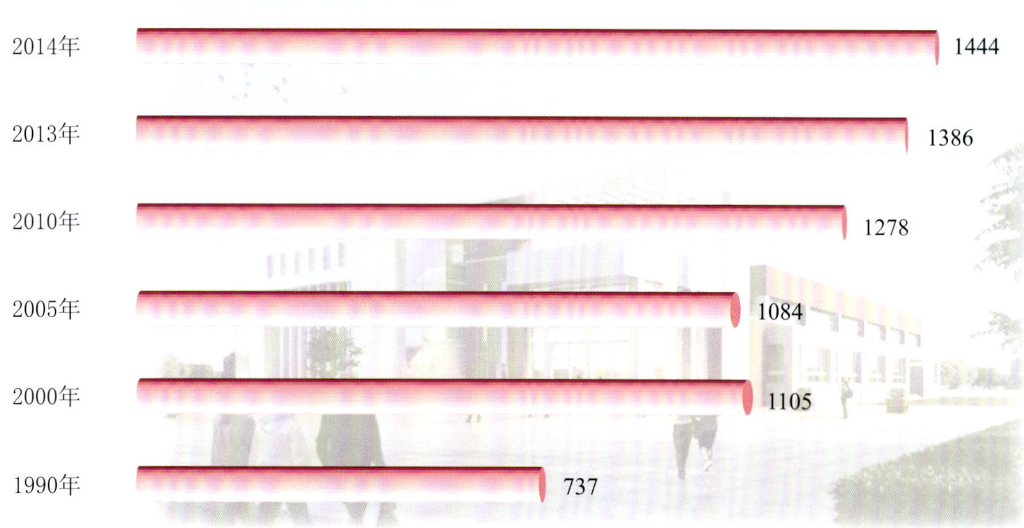

各类学校在校学生(万人)

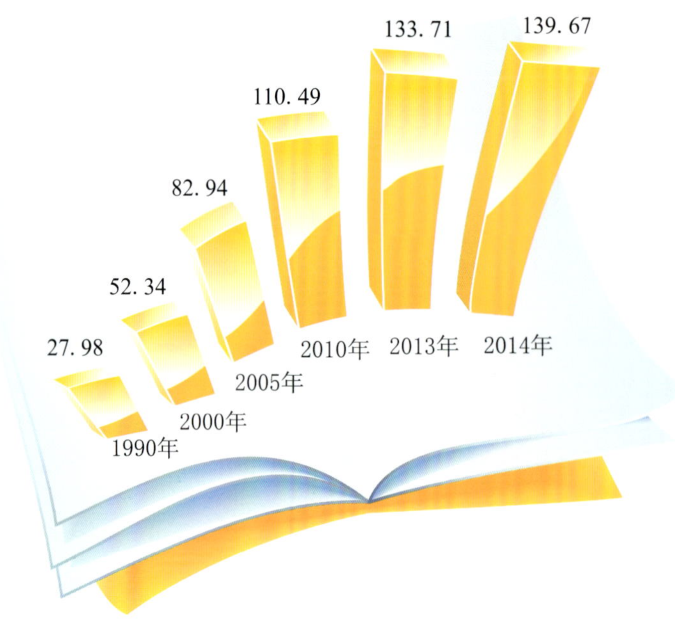

能源

单位生产总值能耗上升或下降(±%)

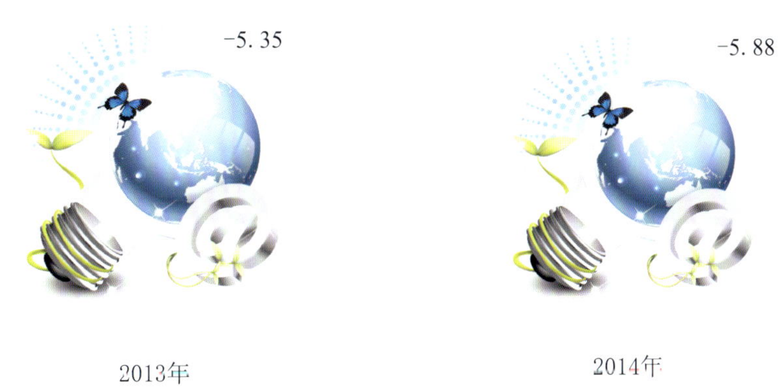

规模以上工业综合能源消费量(万吨标准煤)

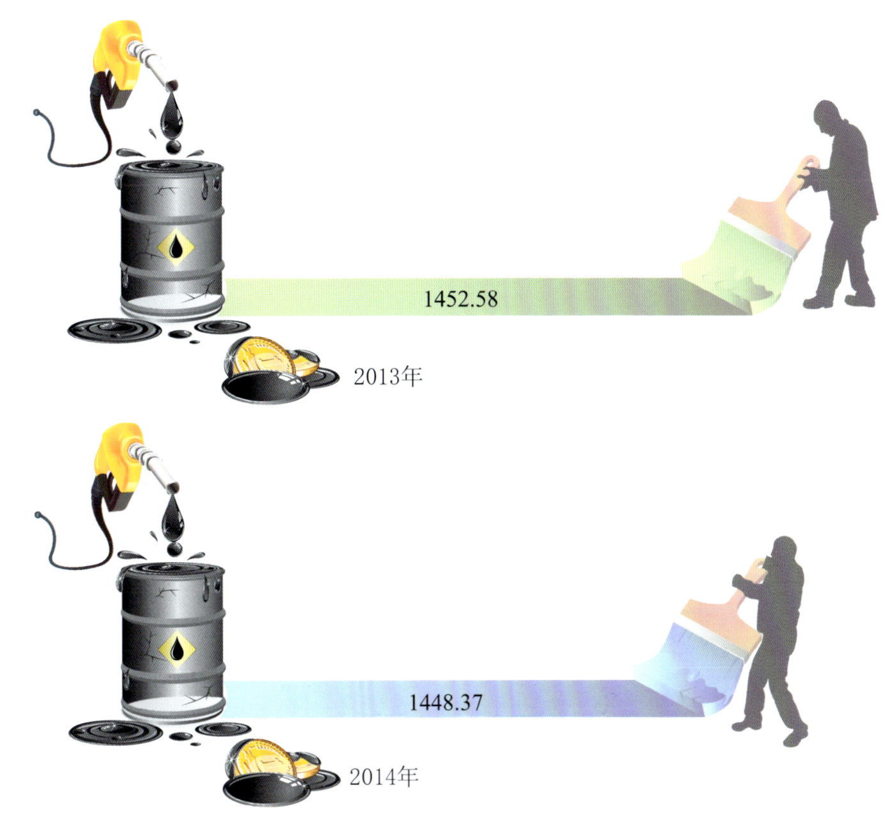

第一部分　概　述

Part One　Outline

2014 年东莞市国民经济和社会发展统计公报

2014 年是全面贯彻落实党的十八届三中、四中全会精神，全面深化改革的起始之年，也是东莞推动高水平崛起的攻坚之年，在市委、市政府的坚强领导下，全市上下紧紧围绕“稳增长、调结构、促改革、惠民生”的核心任务，着力优环境、抓改革、促转型，牢牢把握发展大势，奋力激发市场活力，着力培育创新动力，全市经济在“新常态”下保持平稳运行，社会保持和谐稳定。

一、综合

初步核算，2014 年东莞生产总值（GDP）5881.18 亿元，比上年增长 7.8%。分产业看，第一产业增加值 20.84 亿元，增长 2.5%；第二产业增加值 2697.90 亿元，增长 9.2%；第三产业增加值 3162.44 亿元，增长 6.3%。三大产业比例为 0.3：45.9：53.8。人均地区生产总值 70604 元，增长 7.4%。

在现代产业中，规模以上先进制造业增加值 1219.54 亿元，增长 13.9%；现代服务业增加值 1845.79 亿元，增长 7.6%。

在第三产业中，交通运输、仓储和邮政业增长 2.9%，批发和零售业增长 4.8%，住宿和餐饮业下降 4.5%，金融业增长 9.0%，房地产业增长 3.2%，其他服务业增长 10.9%。

图一　2008-2014 年地区生产总值及增长速度

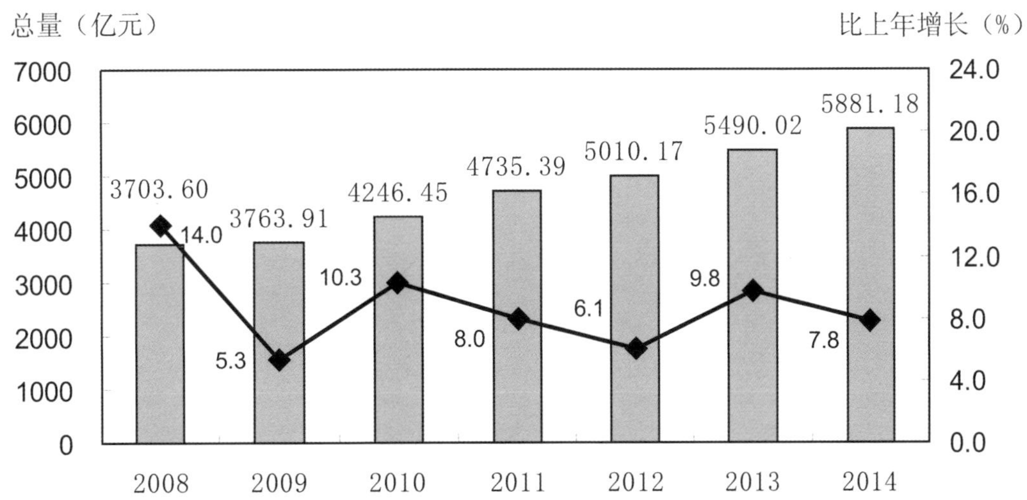

年末，全市工商登记总数 62.93 万户，同比增长 11.0%。其中企业工商登记 20.89 万户，增长 20.7%；个体户登记 41.96 万户，增长 6.8%。私营企业登记户数增长较快，增长 24.9%。从新登记注册情况看，2014 年，全市工商新登记 114278 户，增长 7.6%；新登记企业 45633 家，增长 41.6%。

全年居民消费价格总水平比上年上涨 2.3%。其中居住类上涨 0.8%，娱乐教育文化用品及服务类上涨 1.7%，衣着类上涨 0.3%，食品类上涨 6.0%，医疗保健和个人用品类上涨 0.3%，烟酒类上涨 0.4%，交通和通信类下降 1.7%，家庭设备用品及维修服务类上涨 1.3%。此外，全年商品零售价格上涨 1.2%。

工业生产者出厂价格下降1.0%。

图二 2008-2014年居民消费价格总指数(上年=100)

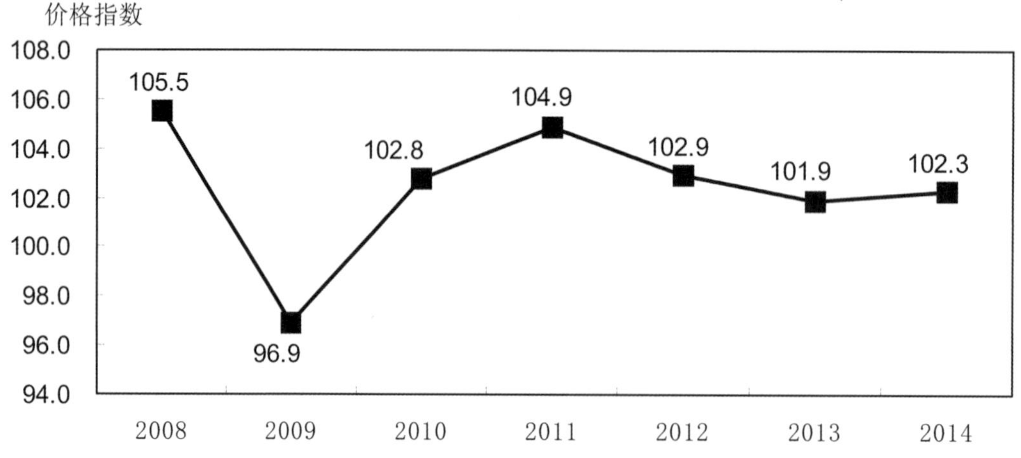

表一 2014年价格变动情况

类　　别	价格指数（上年=100）	比上年升降幅度（%）
居民消费价格指数	102.3	2.3
食　品	106.0	6.0
其中：粮食	103.0	3.0
肉禽及其制品	104.3	4.3
油脂	97.2	-2.8
蛋	105.3	5.3
菜	99.3	-0.7
水产品	109.8	9.8
烟　酒	100.4	0.4
衣　着	100.3	0.3
家庭设备用品及维修服务	101.3	1.3
医疗保健和个人用品	100.3	0.3
交通和通信	98.3	-1.7
娱乐教育文化用品及服务	101.7	1.7
居　住	100.8	0.8
商品零售价格指数	101.2	1.2
工业生产者出厂价格指数	99.0	-1.0

全年来源于东莞的财政收入1066.21亿元，比上年增长9.4%。市公共财政预算收入455.21亿元，增长11.2%。市公共财政预算支出457.68亿元，增长2.9%。其中，一般公共服务支出39.53亿元，公共安全支出53.69亿元，教育支出118.94亿元，社会保障和就业支出28.96亿元。全年全市税收总额1237.04亿元，增长14.0%。

年末城镇实有登记失业人数1.20万人，全年失业人员安置就业人数0.83万人，城镇登记失业率为2.26%。

二、农业

2014年全市农林牧渔业总产值33.94亿元，比上年增长（按可比价计算，下同）1.0%。其中农业产值20.35亿元，增长6.6%，占农林牧渔业总产值的59.9%；林业产值0.36亿元，下降1.6%，占1.1%；牧业产值4.51亿元，下降11.6%，占13.3%；渔业产值7.73亿元，下降4.1%，占22.8%。全年农作物总播种面积36.61万亩，其中水果种植面积19.83万亩。全年粮食产量1.24万吨；水产品总产量7.27万吨；蔬菜产量39.05万吨，增长2.1%；生猪出栏20.82万头，下降10.4%；家禽出栏428.14万只，下降7.4%。

2014年新增23家农民专业合作社、广东省名牌产品（农业类）9个。目前，全市共有农民专业合作社144家、农业龙头企业19家（其中省级以上10家，国家级3家）、有效期内的省级农业类名牌产品达47个（含林业、渔业）。

三、工业和建筑业

全年全市规模以上工业实现增加值2593.54亿元，比上年增长8.8%。在规模以上工业中，重工业增加值1482.63亿元，增长11.8%，占57.2%；轻工业增加值1110.91亿元，增长5.0%，占42.8%。

全年全市规模以上五大支柱产业完成增加值1803.81亿元，增长10.6%；四个特色产业完成增加值249.66亿元，增长4.0%。

全年高技术制造业增加值增长16.3%，其中，医药制造业增长9.2%，电子及通信设备制造业增长19.8%，电子计算机及办公设备制造业增长0.1%，医疗设备及仪器仪表制造业下降6.2%。

全年先进制造业增加值增长13.9%，其中，装备制造业增长14.4%，钢铁冶炼及加工业增长22.7%，石油及化学制造业增长5.4%。装备制造业中，汽车制造业增长13.8%，船舶制造业和环境污染防治专用设备制造业分别增长10.9%和8.5%；钢铁冶炼及加工业中，钢压延加工增长22.7%；石油及化学行业中，石油加工、炼焦及核燃料加工业增长10.8%，化学原料及化学制品制造业增长7.4%，橡胶制品业下降5.5%。

全年优势传统产业增加值增长4.0%，其中,纺织服装业增长4.9%，食品饮料业下降5.0%，家具制造业增长1.2%，建筑材料增长11.9%，金属制品业增长12.6%，家用电力器具制造业下降7.2%。

规模以上工业综合经济效益指数为148.7%，实现利润总额331.86亿元。

表二　2014年规模以上工业主要产品产量

产品名称	计量单位	产量	增长（%）
啤酒	千升	379694	−1.7
果汁和蔬果类饮料类	吨	7085	−98.8
服装	万件	143997	11.1
轻革	万平方米	365.49	−18.0
人造板	万立方米	33.33	−0.8
人造板表面装饰板	万平方米	747.52	−0.2
复合木地板	万平方米	8.32	−72.1

续上表

产品名称	计量单位	产量	增长（%）
家具	万件	5596.20	−5.0
纸浆（原生浆及废纸浆）	万吨	39.84	−2.7
机制纸及纸板（外购原纸加工除外）	万吨	1545.59	26.6
塑料制品	万吨	123.44	−0.4
水泥	万吨	821.34	179.4
瓷质砖	万平方米	2591.47	9.1
平板玻璃	万重量箱	3654.29	11.3
卫生陶瓷制品	万件	154.12	−2.0
金属集装箱	万立方米	652.32	13.0
数码照相机	万台	29.69	−32.1
模具	万套	7.72	−53.5
太阳能热水器	万平方米	16.82	11.3
灯具及照明装置	万套（万台、万个）	26603.31	8.0
电子计算机整机	万台	184.92	15.4
打印机	万台	89.83	−2.2
电话单机	万部	3916.82	0.7
移动通信手持机（手机）	万台	20286.37	51.5
数字激光音、视盘机	万台	5166.90	43.6
电视接收机顶盒	万台	51.34	−8.2
集成电路	万块	13846	−11.0
电子元件	亿只	10936.42	6.0
印制电路板	万平方米	1887.19	8.1
汽车仪器仪表	万台	58.87	20.5
光学仪器	万台（万个）	98.97	−7.5
眼镜成镜	万副	5814.62	9.1
自来水生产量	亿立方米	16.67	−1.3

全年全市建筑业实现增加值 91.35 亿元，比上年增长 3.3%。建筑企业完成总产值 195.84 亿元，增长 8.1%；施工面积 1102.92 万平方米，增长 39.5%；竣工面积 505.87 万平方米，增长 29.1%。建筑企业按施工产值计算的全员劳动生产率为 30.7 万元 / 人，增长 7.3%。

四、固定资产投资

全年固定资产投资 1427.11 亿元，比上年增长 10.0%。按登记注册类型分，国有经济投资 209.33 亿元，增长 18.9%；集体经济投资 92.79 亿元，下降 22.8%；民营经济投资 949.68 亿元，增长 10.9%；外商及港澳台商投资 223.47 亿元，下降 6.2%。

图三　2008—2014年固定资产投资增长速度

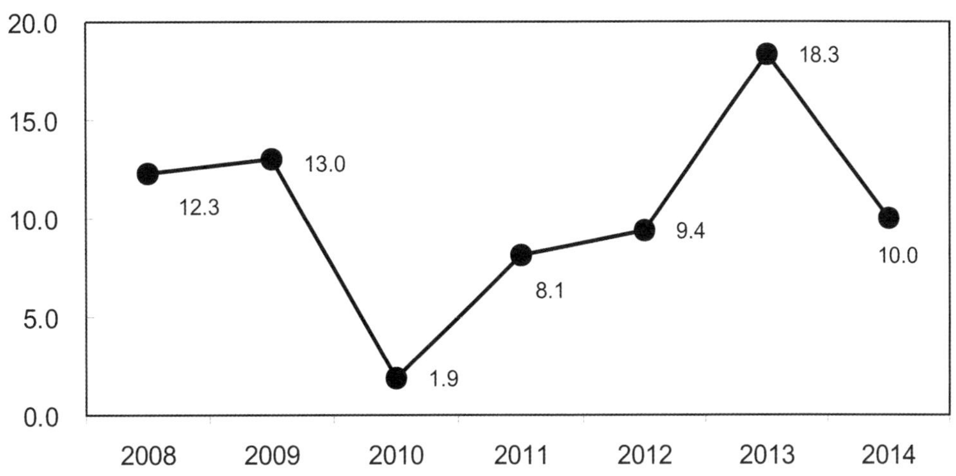

从产业投向看，投资集中在第二、三产业。第二产业投资397.45亿元,其中制造业投资351.33亿元；第三产业投资1029.39亿元。全年完成投资5000万元以上项目414个，共完成投资601.80亿元。

表三　2014年分行业固定资产投资情况

行　业	投资额（万元）	增长（%）
总　计	14271099	10.0
农、林、牧、渔业	2739	-75.0
制造业	3513278	0.04
电力、热力、燃气及水生产和供应业	455356	13.6
建筑业	1800	-71.6
交通运输、仓储和邮政业	1711835	14.4
信息传输、软件和信息技术服务业	382470	94.5
批发和零售业	210904	2.2
住宿和餐饮业	57950	-16.3
金融业	92650	3.3
房地产业	6676809	16.5
租赁和商务服务业	78341	29.9
科学研究和技术服务业	230777	14.3
水利、环境和公共设施管理业	584002	5.1
居民服务、修理和其他服务业	6349	-22.0
教育	126408	-47.1
卫生和社会工作	56507	4.4
文化、体育和娱乐业	63913	-40.2
公共管理、社会保障和社会组织	14945	-43.2

全年完成房地产开发投资 588.06 亿元，增长 18.2%。商品房施工面积 3585.66 万平方米，增长 26.3%；竣工面积 264.94 万平方米，下降 26.9%；新建商品房网上签约销售面积 665.05 万平方米，下降 20.7%，其中商品住宅销售面积 558.74 万平方米，下降 25.4%。全年新建商品房网上签约销售额 644.13 亿元，下降 16.9%，其中商品住宅销售额 511.28 亿元，下降 22.1%。

五、国内贸易

全年全市批发和零售业实现增加值 588.68 亿元，增长 4.8%；住宿和餐饮业实现增加值 179.96 亿元，下降4.5%。

全年社会消费品零售总额 1615.29 亿元，比上年增长 8.7%。分行业看，批发零售贸易业零售额 1491.81 亿元，增长 9.4%；住宿餐饮业零售额 123.48 亿元，下降0.1%。

在限额以上批发和零售业中，食品、饮料、烟酒类零售额增长 3.2%；服装鞋帽、针、纺织品类下降 1.4%；日用品类增长 4.3%；汽车类增长 6.9%。

图四　2008－2014 年社会消费品零售总额及增长速度

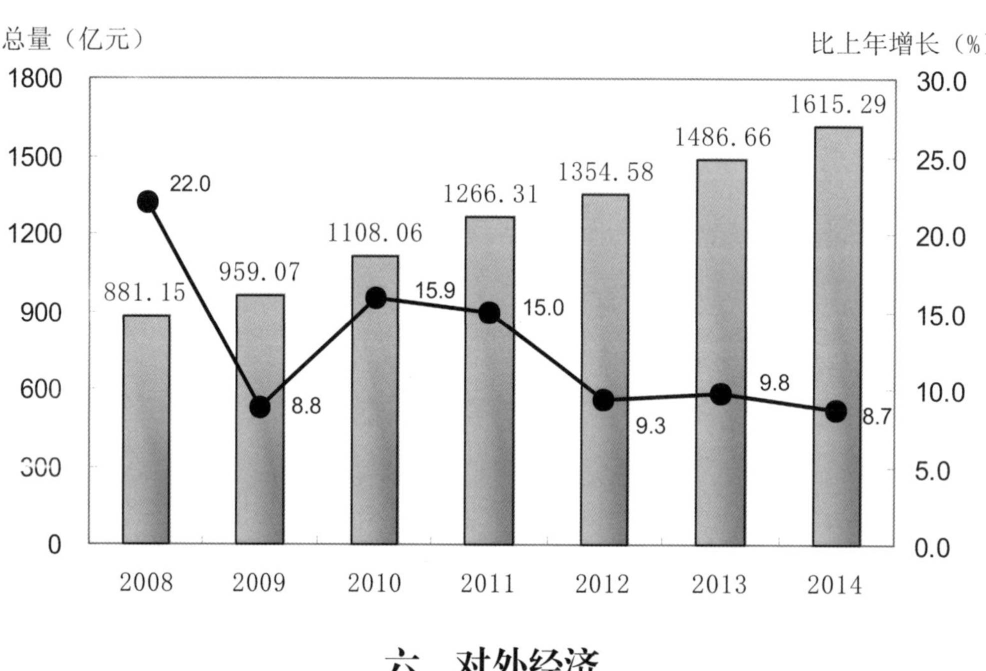

六、对外经济

全年全市进出口总额 1625.30 亿美元，比上年增长6.2%。其中进口 654.61 亿美元，增长 5.2%；出口 970.69亿美元，增长 6.8%。

按贸易方式分，一般贸易出口 268.77 亿美元，增长33.9%；加工贸易出口 657.50 亿美元，下降 3.7%；其他出口 44.42 亿美元，增长 77.7%。

按出口的地区分，对亚洲出口 516.68 亿美元，增长4.1%；对北美洲出口 237.32 亿美元，增长 3.4%；对欧洲出口 159.22 美元，增长 16.0%；对拉丁美洲出口 32.05亿美元，增长 17.0%；对大洋洲出口 13.36 亿美元，增长23.3%。

全年机电产品出口 696.25 亿美元，增长 5.8%，占出口总额的 71.7%；高新技术产品出口 365.24 亿美元，增长 8.7%，占 37.6%。

表四　2014 年主要商品出口情况

商品名称	金额（万美元）	增长（%）
机电产品（包括本目录已具体列名的机电产品）	6962482	5.8
高新技术产品	3652375	8.7
自动数据处理设备及其部件	797628	7.1
服装及衣着附件	596005	4.7
电话机	575031	98.5
家具及其零件	440795	11.2
自动数据处理设备的零件	406763	2.9
静止式变流器	361863	−2.6
鞋类	308832	3.5
电线和电缆	239765	5.6
玩具	225640	12.8
箱包及类似容器	222882	3.4
通断保护电路装置及零件	219286	4.1
灯具、照明装置及类似品	194056	14.0
塑料制品	186052	11.5
打印机(包括多功能一体机)	177195	16.3
纺织纱线、织物及制品	161603	5.8
电视、收音机及无线电讯设备的零附件	129735	−2.6
印刷电路	96172	8.3
眼镜及其零件	85998	19.4
液晶显示板	82633	0.8
二极管及类似半导体器件	82321	61.9

全年全市新签外商直接投资项目 465 宗，合同外资金额 43.15 亿美元，增长 6.8%。实际利用外资 45.29 亿美元，增长 15.0%。其中电子及通信设备制造业实际利用外资 9.00 亿美元，增长 7.7%；专用设备制造业实际利用外资 2.39 亿美元，下降 17.4%。

表五　2014 年分行业利用外资情况

行业名称	合同外资金额（万美元）	增长（%）	实际利用外资（万美元）	增长（%）
总计	431459	3.1	452919	15.0
制造业	312867	−0.2	362095	13.3
纺织业	10988	71.4	12886	84.8
纺织服装、鞋、帽制造业	23754	128.0	8597	-7.7
家具制造业	1991	−45.5	5074	213.8
通用设备制造业	9130	−28.9	13548	12.0
专用设备制造业	24716	26.6	23876	-17.4
电气机械及器材制造业	16518	−50.7	26795	0.8
通信设备、计算机及其他电子设备制造业	69623	−8.3	90002	7.7
金属制品业	28623	48.9	32290	132.0
塑料制品业	22943	−18.6	31676	-1.6
文教体育用品制造业	4957	−32.2	7967	-1.4
造纸及纸制品业	19867	104.0	19416	102.5
其他制造业	79757	−7.9	89968	3.8
交通运输、仓储和邮政业	17306	0.5	11491	36.8
批发和零售业	49567	−4.7	41864	-13.1

七、交通、邮电和旅游

全年全市交通运输、仓储和邮政业实现增加值158.39亿元，增长 2.9%。

截至 2014 年底，全市公路通车里程 5144.9 公里，公路密度 208.7 公里 / 百平方公里，继续位居全省前列。年末全市机动车保有量（民用）165.14 万辆，增长 6.8%。其中汽车保有量 155.96 万辆，增长 12.3%。

全年公路货物运输量 10915 万吨，货物周转量 75.52 亿吨公里；水路货物运输量 4460 万吨，货物周转量372.48 亿吨公里。全年公路运输完成客运量 5524 万人，旅客周转量 85.26 亿人公里；水路运输完成客运量 31.00 万人，旅客周转量 2004 万人公里。全年港口旅客吞吐量31.32 万人次，货物吞吐量 12900 万吨。

表六　2014 年客　(货)　运量、周转量

指　　标	单　位	数　值	增长（%）
客运量	万人	5555	−1.5
# 公路	万人	5524	−1.5
旅客周转量	亿人公里	85.46	−1.4
# 公路	亿人公里	85.26	−1.5
货运量	万吨	15375	4.7
# 公路	万吨	10915	−0.7
货物周转量	亿吨公里	448.01	2.9
# 公路	亿吨公里	75.52	5.6

全年完成邮电业务收入 169.46 亿元，比上年下降 3.6%。邮政发送信函 4369 万件，邮政特快专递 88 万件，邮政汇款金额 122.16 亿元。年末全市固定电话用户(含小灵通、公共电话) 327.21 万户，比上年增加 5.22 万户；移动电话用户 1763.09 万户，减少 87.30 万户。全年长途电话通话时长 248.76 亿分钟，年末互联网用户204.86 万户，比上年减少 11.25 万户；宽带接入用户195.89 万户，减少 11.65 万户。

图五　2008-2014 年年末电话用户数

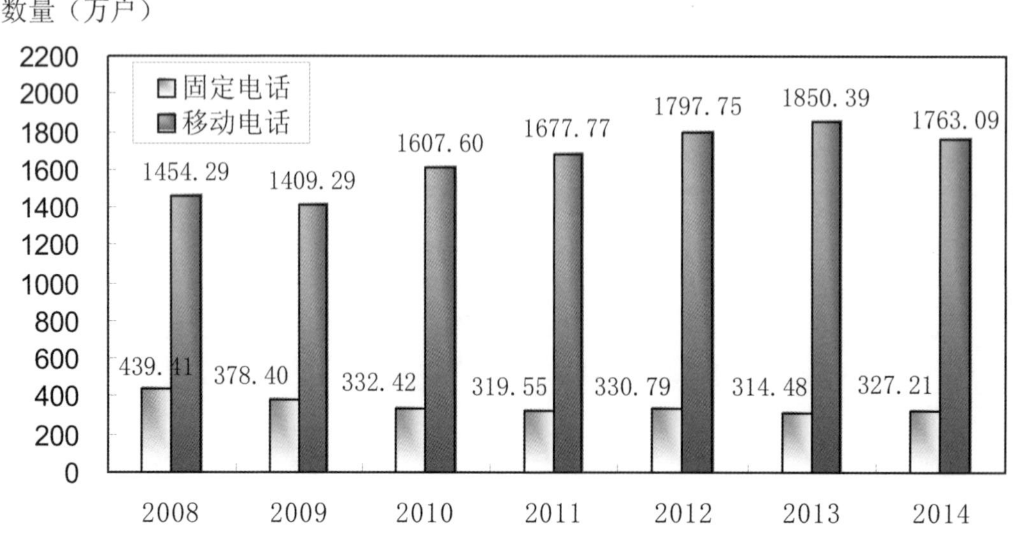

年末全市有星级酒店 63 家，其中五星级酒店 21 家。全市有旅行社 76 家，全年接待国际及港澳台游客 356.21万人次，下降 14.8%。其中接待外国游客 122.18 万人次，下降 11.6%；接待港澳台游客 234.03 万人次，下降16.4%。国际旅游外汇收入 15.75 亿美元，增长 8.6%。全年接待国内游客 2434.77 万人次，增长 1.1%。国内旅游总收入 374.60 亿元，增长 8.1%。全年东莞组团外出旅游 150.88 万人次，下降 6.3%。其中，国内旅游 131.40万人次，下降 8.4%；出境旅游 19.48 万人次，增长10.9%。

八、金融

全年全市金融业实现增加值 266.85 亿元，增长9.0%。

年末全市有各类金融机构 129 家，其中银行类机构37 家（含 1 家代表处），保险类机构 52 家，证券期货类机构 40 家。年末全市金融机构各项人民币存款余额9069.92 亿元，比年初增长 5.1%。其中城乡居民储蓄存款余额 4606.79 亿元，增长 2.9%。各项人民币贷款余额 5331.63 亿元，增长 11.7%。在个人消费贷款余额中，个人住房按揭贷款余额 1182.98 亿元，增长 18.8%；个人汽车消费贷款余额 5.48 亿元，增长 0.8%。

图六　2008－2014 年城乡居民储蓄存款余额及其增长速度

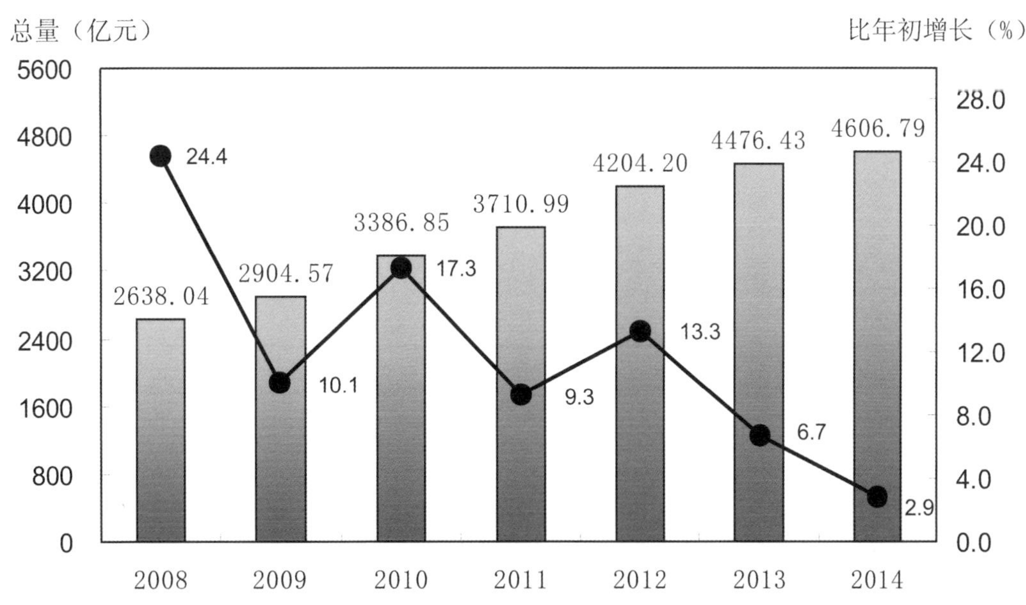

全年股票总成交额 12723.86 亿元，同比增长 54.3%。年末保证金余额 161.89 亿元，增长 145.3%。

全年全市各类保险保费收入 258.00 亿元，同比增长 24.6%。其中财产险保费收入 84.88 亿元，增长 18.5%；人寿险保费收入 173.12 亿元，增长 27.7%。全年保险赔款与给付金额 70.27 亿元，综合赔付率为 27.2%。

九、科技和教育

全年新增国家高新技术企业 80 家，235 家企业拟通过认定，总数预计达 755 家，位居省内地级市首位。全市专利申请量和授权量分别为 28431 件和 20336 件。其中，发明专利申请量为 6913 件，同比增长 7.11%，占专利申请总量的 24.31%；发明专利授权量为 1624 件，同比增长 8.63%，排全省第 3 位；PCT 专利申请量为 299 件，排全省第 3 位。科技资源加快集聚。新建东莞同济大学研究院和东莞前沿技术研究院 2 家新型研发机构；成功举办 2014 中国（东莞）国际科技合作周；全市新增7个省创新科研团队立项，引进总数达到 22 个，居全省第三；新引进 8 个市级创新科研团队，团队立项资助6200 万元；国家可持续发展实验区申报工作稳步推进。科技金融结合得到加强。推动出台《东莞市创新财政投入方式，促进科技金融产业融合发展工作方案》，启动科技保险试点，专利质押融资累计贷款 1.12 亿元。

年末，全市有幼儿园 881 所，同比增加 54 所，其中，省、市一级幼儿园 276 所，比上年增加 139 所。全市有小学 320 所，在校学生 68.73 万人，本市户籍学龄儿童入学率达 100%，小学毕业生升学率达 100%。全市有初中 172 所（不含完全中学），在校学生 20.66 万人，本市户籍适龄少年初中入学率 100%，初中毕业生升学率 98.4%。全市高中阶段学校共有 65 所，其中普通高中（含完中和多层次学校高中部）40 所，在校生 7.81 万人，中职学校 25 所（含技工学校 3 所），在校生 6.44 万人。全市有普通高等院校 6 所，在校学生 6.99 万人。全年普通高等院校共招收本科、专科学生 2.28 万人，毕业生 1.3 万人。

表七　教育情况

指　标	招生（万人）	增　长（%）	在校生（万人）	增　长（%）	毕业生（万人）	增　长（%）
普通本专科	2.28	9.7	6.99	14.8	1.3	11.7
成人本专科	0.66	−8.7	1.75	1.3	0.51	−35.1
中等职业技术教育	2.45	−0.4	6.44	6.1	1.75	12.4
普通高中	2.67	2.7	7.81	1.3	2.52	3.4
初中	7.54	1.7	20.66	2.7	5.75	6.5
小学	12.50	−1.7	68.73	4.3	8.67	2.4
学前教育	12.62	14.2	29.05	4.6	7.75	−8.1

十、文化、卫生和体育

年末全市有群众艺术馆 1 个，文化站 33 个，公共图书馆 641 个，博物馆 33 个，艺术表演场所 13 个，电影放映单位 60 个，网吧 1136 间。全市有公共广播节目 63 套，公共电视节目 36 套。全年共发行报纸 4403.69 万份，其中《东莞日报》3266.27 万份；各类杂志 70.83 万册，电影放映 62 万场次，观众 1102.37 万人次。

年末全市有医疗机构 2156 个，其中，三级甲等医院 7 所，门诊、诊所、医务室、卫生站、社区卫生服务机构等基层医疗机构 2070 个。全市卫生技术人员 4.31 万人，医疗机构病床 2.67 万张。全年诊疗总人数下降 4.9%。

全年全市运动员共获得 124 枚金牌、134 枚银牌、111 枚铜牌。其中夺得全国赛金牌 8 枚；广东省赛金牌 113 枚、银牌 100 枚、铜牌 92 枚。全年举办全市全民健身活动 333 次，参加人数 18.87 万人次。全市有各类体育运动场地 13860 个（座），其中体育场 516 个，体育馆 166 座，灯光篮球场 5316 个，足球场 102 个，健身路径 1384 条，室外游泳池 353 个，室内游泳池 56 个，室外羽毛球场 1378 个。全市有体育彩票发行网点 979 个，销售总额 15.09 亿元，体彩公益金 10956 万元。

十一、人民生活

2014 年东莞居民收入保持平稳增长态势，全年东莞居民人均可支配收入 35712 元，名义增长 8.7%。

从城乡划分来看，农村常住居民可支配收入增速快于城镇居民。按新口径测算，2014 年东莞城镇常住居民人均可支配收入 36764 元，名义增长 8.6%；全年东莞农村常住居民人均可支配收入 22327 元，名义增长 9.0%。

从收入构成来看，东莞居民人均工资性收入 27928 元，占人均可支配收入的 78.2%；人均财产净收入 6242 元，占人均可支配收入的 17.5%。

十二、社会保障

全市五大险种参保总人次为 2748.28 万人次，比上年增长 6.7%。基本医疗保险 615.69 万人次，失业保险 392.59 万人次，工伤保险 492.28 万人次。全年社会保险基金总收入 287.05 亿元，保险基金总支出 131.22 亿元，年末保险基金累计余额 887.78 亿元。

年末全市有收养类福利事业单位 37 个，其中社会福利院 1 个，社会福利中心 1 个，敬老院 34 个，敬老院供养老人 1603 人。社会福利事业单位收养 2724 人，全年社会救济 2.1 万人。全市居民最低生活保障支出 10404 万元，自然灾害生活救助支出 467 万元，慈善基金结余 2.35 亿元。全市纳入“五保户”对象有 854 人，“五保户”费用支出 2123 万元。

十三、人口、资源和环境

年末全市户籍人口 191.39 万人。全年出生人口 2.14 万人，出生率为 11.2‰；死亡人口 1.03 万人，死亡率为 5.37‰；人口自然增长率为 5.83‰。年末全市常住人口 834.31 万人，其中城镇常住人口 740.95 万人。人口城镇化率为 88.81%。

全年雨日天数 174 天，日照时数 1959 小时，平均气温 22.9 摄氏度，相对湿度 74%，降水量 1936 毫米。

年末全市森林公园达 19 个，新增森林公园配套设施一批。林业用地面积 80.37 万亩，生态公益林 32.96 万亩，林木积蓄量 282.90 万立方米，林木总生长量 12.75 万立方米。

年末全市建成区土地面积 922.02 平方公里，公共管理与公共服务用地面积 45.60 平方公里。森林覆盖率为 36%。城市建成区绿地率为 44.5%，绿化覆盖率为 47.5%，城市人均公园绿地面积 17.3 平方米；全市已建成公园 1210 个，面积 1.45 万公顷。

注：1. 本公报中 2014 年数据为初步统计数，统计图中 2008–2013 年数据为年报数，最后统计数据以《东莞统计年鉴–2015》为准。

2. 地区生产总值、各行业增加值、农业总产值绝对数按当年价格计算，增长速度按可比价格计算。

3. 从 2011 年起，规模以上工业统计口径由年主营业务收入 500 万元调整为 2000 万元及以上的工业法人企业；固定资产投资项目统计起点由计划总投资50万元提高到500万元，增速为可比口径。

4. 五大支柱产业包括电子信息制造业、电气机械及设备制造业（包括电气机械及器材制造业，仪器仪表制造业，通用设备制造业，专用设备制造业，铁路、船舶、航空航天和其他运输设备制造业以及汽车制造业）、纺织服装鞋帽制造业（包括纺织业，纺织服装、服饰制造业，皮革、毛皮、羽毛及其制品和制鞋业）、食品饮料加工制造业（包括食品制造业,酒、饮料和精制茶制造业,农副产品加工业）、造纸及纸制品业。

   四个特色产业包括玩具及文体用品制造业、家具制造业、化工制品制造业（包括化学原料及化学制品制造业，石油加工、炼焦业及核燃业）、包装印刷业。

   先进制造业包括装备制造业、钢铁冶炼及加工制造业、石油及化学制造业。

   高技术制造业包括医药制造业、航空、航天器及设备制造业、电子及通信设备制造业、医疗仪器设备及仪器仪表制造业、信息化学品制造业。

5. 根据《广东省人民政府办公厅关于开展全省城乡一体化住户调查的通知》（粤办函〔2013〕561号）要求，全省自2014年起正式启动分市县城乡一体化住户调查改革工作。由于城乡一体化住户调查的统计范围、口径和方法不同，一体化住户调查数据与原城镇居民人均可支配收入和农村居民人均纯收入等老口径数据不可比。

   ①可支配收入的指标内涵大幅收窄。

   ②调查范围和对象扩大影响城镇居民收入数据。

   ③城乡居民组别调整影响城乡居民收入数据。

6. 阅读本公报时，请注意统计指标的时间、口径和计算方法等。

7. 资料来源:本公报中城镇实有登记失业人数及失业人员安置就业人数、城镇登记失业率数据来自市人力资源局；新增农民专业合作社、龙头企业及省级农业类名牌产品数来自市农业局；进出口、利用外资数据来自市外经贸局；公路通车里程、交通运输、公路、水路相关数据来自市交通运输局；邮电业务收入、邮政发送信函、电话用户等数据来自市邮政、电信、移动等相关运营商；星级酒店及旅游情况来自市旅游局；年末各类金融机构数据来自金融工作局；人民币存贷款余额来自市人民银行；股票总成交额及年末保证金余额数据来自证券期货业协会；保险保费及赔款与给付来自市保险行业协会；国家高新技术企业家数、专利申请和授权量以及科研成果奖等数据来自市科学技术局；教育数据来自市教育局；艺术馆、文化站、博物馆、公共图书馆、公共广播节目、报纸杂志等数据来自市文化广电新闻出版局；卫生医疗机构等数据来自市卫生局；运动员获得奖牌、健身活动、体育彩票发行情况来自市体育局；社会保障数据来自市社会保障局；福利单位、敬老院等数据来自市民政局；户籍人口数据来自市公安局；出生和死亡人口等相关数据来自市卫生和计划生育局；气象数据来自市气象局；森林公园、林业用地、生态公益林、林木积蓄量等数据来自市林业局；建成区及公共管理与公共服务用地面积来自市城乡规划局；建成区绿地率、绿化覆盖率、人均公园绿地面积及公园数据来自市城市综合管理局。

Statistical Communiqué of Dongguan Economic and Social Development 2014

2014 is a brand new start for Dongguan to fully implement the initial of 18th Party Congress with its 3rd and 4th Plenary Session and comprehensively deepen reforms, as well as the crucial year to vigorously promote the High -Level -Rise development strategy. Under the strong leadership of municipal CPC and government, our city strived to complete the core mission of stabling economic growth, adjusting industrial structure, promoting social reform and benefiting public livelihood, by means of improving environment, deepening reform and fastening transition. By firmly grasping the trend of development, Dongguan spares no effort to stimulate market vitality, cultivate creativity power, and stabilize economy together with society harmonic under New Normal.

Ⅰ. Outlook

After preliminary accounting, in 2014 Dongguan's GDP had increased to 588.12 billion yuan, up by 7.8% from the previous year, with the scale proportion of the three major industrial sectors standing at 0.3: 45.9: 53.8.The added value of the primary industry was 2.08 billion yuan, up by 2.5%. The secondary and tertiary industries increased to 269.79 billion and 316.24 billion yuan, up by 9.2% and 6.3% respectively over the same period. The per capita GDP realized 70.60 thousand yuan, up by 7.4% over the previous year.

In the modern industry, the added value of industrial manufacturing enterprises above the designated size was 121.95 billion yuan, up by 13.9%, and the modern service industry rose by 7.6%, reaching 184.58 billion yuan.

In tertiary industry, the growth rate of added-value rose by 2.9% in sectors of transport, storage and post, and 4.8% in wholesale and retail trade, 9.0% in financial service, as well as 3.2% in real estate development and 10.9% in other services. At the same time, lodging and catering services decreased by 4.5%.

At the end of the year, the city's total number of industrial and commercial registrations reached 629.3 thousand, increased by 11.0%, including 208.9 thousand enterprises and 419.6 thousand sole proprietors which increased by 20.7% and 6.8% respectively. Particularly, private-own enterprises had been seen a rapid growth of 24.9%. When it comes to new registrations, in 2014 there were 114278 new industrial and commercial registrations, increased by 7.6%, of which 45633 ones are enterprises, up by 41.6%.

Figure 1: Dongguan GDP & Growth Rates 2008-2014

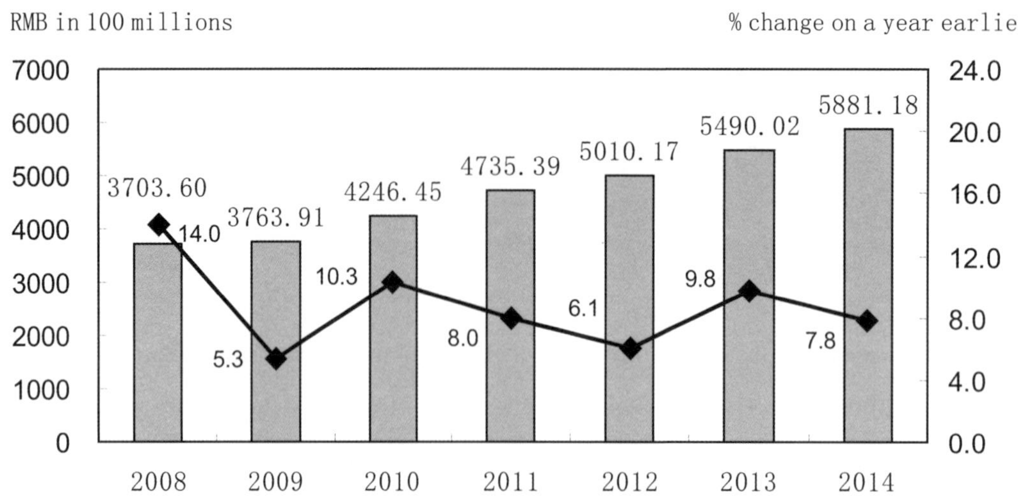

The overall Consumer Price Index (CPI) of Dongguan increased 2.3% throughout last year. In detail, housing index rose 0.8%. Recreational, educational and cultural goods and services index had risen 1.7%. Apparel index had increased 0.3%. Food index rose 6.0%, medical care and personal goods index increased 0.3%, tobacco and alcohol index rose 0.4%, and household furnishings and supplies index increased 1.3%, while the transportation and communication index decreased 1.7%. Moreover, Retail Price Index (RPI) saw an increase of 1.2%, while Producer Price Index (PPI) declined 1.0%.

Figure 2: Dongguan Yearly Changes of CPI in 2008-2014

(Index in preceding year is 100)

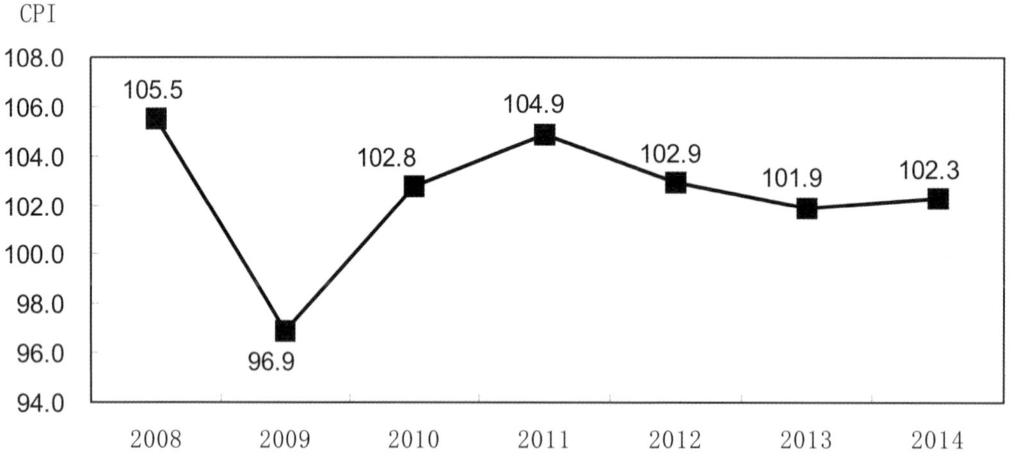

Table 1: CPI Changes in 2014

(Index in preceding year is 100) Number in %

Item	CPI	Changes
General CPI level	102.3	2.3
Food	106.0	6.0
-Grain	103.0	3.0

Continue to the above-mentioned

Item	CPI	Changes
-Meat poultry and related products	104.3	4.3
-Oil-bearing crops	97.2	-2.8
-Poultry eggs	105.3	5.3
-Vegetables	99.3	-0.7
-Aquatic products	109.8	9.8
Tobacco & Liquor	100.4	0.4
Clothing	100.3	0.3
Household facilities, articles and maintenance services	101.3	1.3
Medical, health and personal articles	100.3	0.3
Transportation and telecommunications	98.3	-1.7
Recreation, education, culture articles and services	101.7	1.7
Housing	100.8	0.8
Retail price index	101.2	1.2
Producer price index	99.0	-1.0

In 2014, Dongguan's fiscal revenue reached 106.62 billion yuan, up by 9.4% over the previous year. The municipal public budget revenue was 45.52 billion yuan, up by 11.2%. The public budget expenditure amounted to 45.77 billion yuan, up by 2.9%, of which 3.95 billion yuan were appropriated for general public services, 5.37 billion for public security, 11.89 billion for education, as well as 2.90 billion for social insurances and employment. Overall, the taxes collected in the whole year were 123.70 billion yuan, up by 14%.

By the end of 2014, the urban unemployed had amounted to 12 thousand, while 8300 job placements had been created. The urban registered unemployment rate was kept at 2.26%.

Ⅱ. Agriculture

In 2014, the gross output value of farming, forestry, animal husbandry and fishery reached 3.39 billion yuan, up by 1.0% at comparable prices. In detail, the output value of farming accounted for 59.9% (2035 million yuan, up by 6.6%). Forestry constituted 1.1% (36 million yuan, down by 1.6%). Animal husbandry accounted for 13.3% (451 million yuan, down by 11.6%). Fishery constituted 22.8% (773 million yuan, down by 4.1%). The total planted areas for agriculture reached 24.4 thousand hectares, including 13.2 thousand hectares for planting fruit. The crops' annual output was total 12.4 thousand tons. The production of fishery was 72.7 thousand tons, and the vegetable farming 390.5 thousand tons with an increase of 2.1%. Besides, 208.2 thousand heads of hogs and 4.28 million heads of poultry were slaughtered, down by 10.4% and 7.4% respectively on year.

During 2014, Dongguan added 23 new farmer cooperatives and 9 brand products in agriculture. So far, there had been 144 farmer cooperatives, 19 leading agricultural enterprises (including 10 provincial level and 3 national level corporations), and 47 provincial agricultural brand products within the term of validity.

Ⅲ. Manufacturing and Construction

In 2014, the added values of industrial sectors above designated size reached a total of 259.35 billion yuan, up by 8.8%. Heavy industry contributed 57.2%, equal to 148.26 billion yuan, up by 11.8%, the other 42.8% was generated by light industry, equal to 111.09 billion yuan, up by 5.0%.

The added values of 5 pillar industries in Dongguan economy reached 180.38 billion yuan, up by 10.6%, together with 24.97 billion yuan from 4 characteristic industries which increased by 4.0%.

In general, the high-tech manufacturing industries increased by 16.3% in terms of added value. For instances, pharmacy increased by 9.2%, electronic and communications equipment up by 19.8%, computer and office equipment up by 0.1%, while medical equipment and instruments decreased by 6.2%.

The added value of advanced manufacturing industries rose by 13.9%, along with increasing of 14.4% in equipment manufacturing, 22.7% in iron and steel industry, and 5.4% in petroleum and chemical industry. With regard of the equipment manufacturing, automobile manufacturing industries saw a 13.8% increase, the added values of ship and pollution control device manufacturing had increased by 10.9% and 8.5% respectively. In iron and steel sector, the added value from steel rolling and processing industries declined by 22.7%. In petroleum and chemical industry, the added value saw a 10.8% growth in the field of petroleum refining and nuclear-fuel processing. The chemical materials and commodity -chemicals manufacturing rose by 7.4%, while the rubber and plastic products manufacturing decreased by 5.5%.

The added value of traditional advantageous industries increased 4.0%. In detail, the textile and garment sector increased by 4.9%, the food and beverage sector declined by 5.0%, the household furniture sector increased by 1.2%, the architectural material sector rose by 11.9%. The metal products sector grew up by 12.6%, and the household appliances sector decreased by 7.2%.

The comprehensive economic efficiency index was 148.7%. The industries above the designated size had a total profit of 33.19 billion yuan.

Last year, the annual added value in construction business was 9.14 billion yuan, up by 3.3% on year. The total output values of construction contractors were 19.58 billion yuan, up by 8.1%, with 11.03 million m^2 floorage under construction, increased by 39.5%, and 5.06 million m^2 completed, increased by 29.1%. Based on the total output values by contractors, the output per worker in construction sector was calculated to be 307000 yuan, up by 7.3%.

Table 2: Output and Growth Rates of Major Products by Manufacturing Companies above Designated Size in 2014

Items	Unit	Quantity	Increase over 2013 (%)
Beers	1000 L	379694	-1.7
Fruit and vegetable beverage	1 millions Tons	70.85	-98.8
Garments	10000 Pcs	143997	11.1
Light leathers	10000 Sqm	365.49	-18.0
Wood-based panels	10000 Sqm	33.33	-0.8
Decorated surfaces on wood-based panel	10000 Sqm	747.52	-0.2
Solid wood-flooring	10000 Sqm	8.32	-72.1
Furniture	10000 Pcs	5596.20	-5.0
Pulp	10000 Tons	39.84	-2.7
Machine-made paper & paperboards	10000 Tons	1545.59	26.6
Plastic products	10000 Tons	123.44	-0.4
Cement	10000 Tons	821.34	179.4
Porcelains	10000 Sqm	2591.47	9.1
Glass plates	10000 Weight Boxes	3654.29	11.3
Sanitary pottery	10000 Pcs	154.12	-2.0
Metal containers	10000 Sqm	652.32	13.0
Digital cameras	10000 Sets	29.69	-32.1
Moulds	10000 Sets	7.72	-53.5
Solar water heaters	10000 Sqm	16.82	11.3
Lighting equipment	10000 Sets	26603.31	8.0
Computers	10000 Sets	184.92	15.4
Printers	10000 Sets	89.83	-2.2
Fixed phones	10000 Sets	3916.82	0.7
Mobile phones	10000 Sets	20286.37	51.5
DVD players	10000 Sets	5166.90	43.6
TV set-top box	10000 Sets	51.34	-8.2
Integrated circuits	10000 Sets	13846	-11.0
Electronic components	1 billion Pcs	1093.64	6.0
Printed circuit boards	10000 Sqm	1887.19	8.1
Vehicle instruments	10000 Sets	58.87	20.5
Optical instruments	10000 Sets	98.97	-7.5
Glasses	10000 Sets	5814.62	9.1
Tap water	1million Cbm	1667	-1.3

Ⅳ. Investment in Fixed Assets

The total investment in fixed assets reached 142.71 billion yuan in 2014, up by 10% on year. In terms of registration category, the state-own enterprises accounted for 20.93 billion yuan, up by 18.9% on year. The collective-own enterprises constituted 9.28 billion yuan, down by 22.8%. The private scoter accounted for 94.97 billion yuan, up by 10.9%. Foreign investment, besides Hong Kong, Macau and Taiwan, declined to 22.35 billion yuan, down by 6.2%.

Figure 3: Investment in Fixed Assets and Its Growth 2008—2014

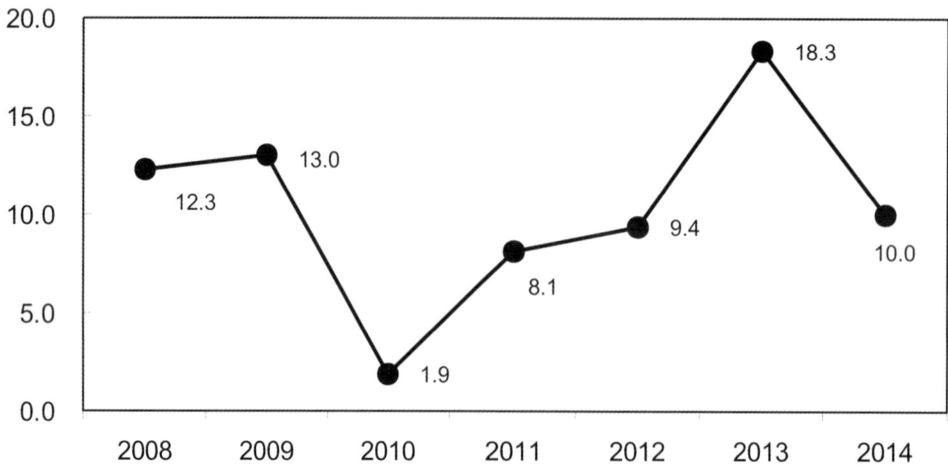

In regard to the investment direction, the capital mainly flew into the secondary and tertiary industries during 2014. The fixed asset investment in secondary industry was 39.75 billion yuan, including 35.13 billion yuan in manufacturing, and 102.94 billion yuan in tertiary industry. Throughout last year, 414 above-50-million-yuan investment projects had been completed, in total 60.18 billion yuan in value.

Table 3: Fixed Assets Investments in Sectors 2014

Sectors	Capital (in ten-thousand yuan)	Increase over 2013 (%)
Total	14271099	10.0
Farming, forestry, animal husbandry and fishery	2739	-75.0
Manufacturing	3513278	0.04
Production and supply of electric power, heat, gas and water	455356	13.6
Construction industry	1800	-71.6
Transport, storage and postal services	1711835	14.4
Information transmission, computer services and software	382470	94.5
Wholesale and retail trade	210904	2.2
Hotel and catering services	57950	-16.3
Finance	92650	3.3
Real estate	6676809	16.5
Leasing and business services	78341	29.9
Scientific research and technical services	230777	14.3
Water conservancy, environment and public facilities Management	584002	5.1
Resident services, repairing and other services	6349	-22.0
Education	126408	-47.1
Health care, social work	56507	4.4
Culture, sports and recreation	63913	-40.2
Public administration, social security and social Organization	14945	-43.2

The investment in real estate development reached 58.81 billion yuan, increased by 18.2%. The gross floor area of condominiums constructions was 35.86 million m^2, up by 26.3%, and gross floor area of completed condominiums was 2.65 million m^2, down by 26.9%. The sale area of newly-built condominium after online sign-up registration was 6.65 million m^2, down by 20.7%, of which residential condominium accounted for 5.59 million m^2, down by 25.4%. The sales value in total was 64.41 billion yuan, down by 16.9%, including 51.13 billion yuan from residential condominium which was 22.1% less than that of last year.

Ⅴ. Domestic Trade

The total added value of wholesale and retail trade was 58.87 billion yuan in 2014, up by 4.8% over the previous year, and that of lodging and catering sector reached 18.00 billion yuan, down by 4.5%.

The gross retail sales of Dongguan reached 161.53 billion yuan, up by 8.7%. In terms of sectors, the wholesale and retail trade was total 149.18 billion yuan, up by 9.4%, and the lodging and catering amounted to 12.35 billion yuan, down by 0.1%.

Among enterprises above designated size in wholesale and retail trades, in terms of sales value, food, beverages, tobacco and liquor increased by 3.2%. Clothing, shoes, hats and textiles decreased by 1.4%. Daily necessities increased by 4.3%. Vehicles increased by 6.9%.

Figure 4: Retail Sales of Consumer Goods and Its Growth 2008—2014

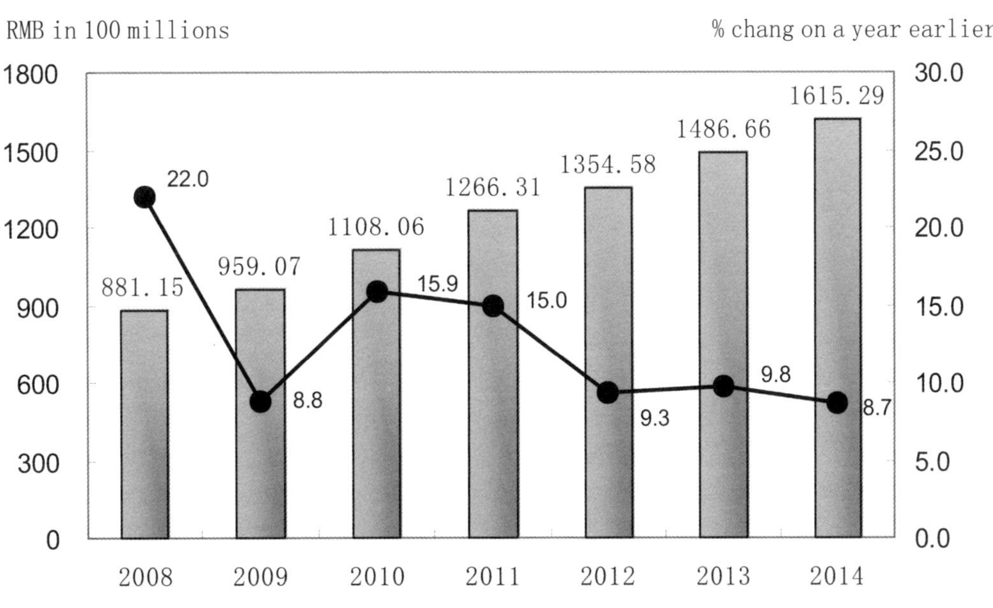

VI. Foreign Trade

The total value of imports and exports in 2014 reached 162.53 billion USD, up by 6.2% on year.

The import value reached 65.46 billion USD, up by 5.2%, and the export value was 97.07 billion USD, up by 6.8%.

From the angle of category, the export value of general merchandises increased by 33.9% to 26.88 billion USD. The export value of labor-intensive products reached 65.75 billion USD, decreased by 3.7%. In addition, other trading goods rose by 77.7% to 4.42 billion USD.

From the angle of export region, Asia amounted to 51.67 billion USD, up by 4.1%, North America 23.73 billion USD, up by 3.4%, European Union 15.92 billion USD, up by 16.0%, Latin America 3.21 billion USD, up by 17.0%, Oceania 1.34 billion USD, up by 23.3%.

Electromechanical products took up 71.7% of the gross export and reached 69.63 billion USD, up by 5.8% over 2013. The hi-tech products occupied 37.6% which increased by 8.7% to 36.52 billion USD.

Table 4: Values and Growth Rates of Major Export Merchandises in 2014

Numbers in million USD

Commodities	Value	Increase over 2013 (%)
Electromechanical products (including relevant products listed as below)	69624.82	5.8
Hi-tech products	36523.75	8.7
Automatic data processing machines and components	7976.28	7.1
Garments and relevant accessories	5960.05	4.7
Telephones	5750.31	98.5
Furniture and components	4407.95	11.2
Parts of automatic data processing machines	4067.63	2.9
Static converters	3618.63	-2.6
Shoes	3088.32	3.5
Wires or cables	2397.65	5.6
Toys	2256.40	12.8
Traveling supplies and cases	2228.82	3.4
Electric apparatus for switching or protecting electrical circuits	2192.86	4.1
Lamps, lighting fixtures and similar products	1940.56	14.0
Plastic products	1860.52	11.5
Printers (including the MFP)	1771.95	16.3
Spinning yarn, fabric and products	1616.03	5.8
Televisions, radios and wireless telecommunication equipment′s parts	1297.35	-2.6
Printed circuit	961.72	8.3
Glasses and parts	859.98	19.4
The liquid crystal display panel	826.33	0.8
Diodes and similar semiconductor devices	823.21	69.1

There were 465 newly-added foreign investment projects during 2014. The total capital on contracts of foreign direct investment saw a 6.8% increase to 4.32 billion USD. The utilized capital increased by 15.0% to 4.53 billion USD, of which the capital of electronic and communicational equipment manufacturing increased by 7.7% to 900 million USD, together with specialized machinery manufacturing decreasing by 17.4% to 239 million USD.

Table 5: Utilized Foreign Capitals in Sectors, 2014

Numbers in million USD

Sectors	Capital on contrasts	Increase over 2013 (%)	Capital Utilized	Increase over 2013 (%)
In total	4314.59	3.1	4529.19	15.0
Manufacturing	3128.67	−0.2	3620.95	13.3
Textile	109.88	71.4	128.86	84.8
Garments, shoes and hats	237.54	128.0	85.97	−7.7
Furniture	19.91	−45.5	50.74	213.8
General−purpose machineries	91.30	−28.9	135.48	12.0
Special−purpose machineries	247.16	26.6	238.76	−17.4
Electric machineries and equipment	165.18	−50.7	267.95	0.8
Communication equipment, computers and other electronic equipment	696.23	−8.3	900.02	7.7
Metal products	286.23	48.9	322.90	132.0
Plastics products	229.43	−18.6	316.76	−1.6
Stationery and sport commodities	49.57	32.2	79.67	−1.4
Papers and paper−made products	198.67	104.0	194.16	102.5
Others	797.57	−7.9	899.68	3.8
Transportation, storage and postal industry	173.06	0.5	114.91	36.8
Wholesale and retail trade	495.67	−4.7	418.64	−13.1

Ⅶ. Transportation, Post, Telecommunication and Tourism

The added value of the transport, storage and post sectors amounted to 15.84 billion yuan last year, up by 2.9%.

By the end of 2014, the total length of highway and expressway in Dongguan had reached 5144.9 kilometers. The highway density was 208.7 kilometers per hundred kilometers^2, ranking top among cities in Guangdong. The total number of vehicles (for civil use) in Dongguan had increased by 6.8% to 1.65 million, including 1.56 million cars with 12.3% growth.

Over the same period, the freight volume by land was 109.15 million tons, and the freight turnover is equaled to 7.55 billion ton−kilometers. The freight volume by water was 44.60 million tons, and the turnover was 37.25 billion ton− kilometers. The total volume of passengers by land was 55.24 million person−times, with a turnover of 8.53 billion person−kilometers. The total volume of passengers by water was 310 thousand person−times, with a turnover of 20.04 million person−kilometers. The seaports in Dongguan handled 313.2 thousand passengers and 129 million tons of cargo in total.

Table 6: Volume and Turnover of Handled Cargo and Passengers 2014

Indicators	Unit	Volume	Increase over 2013 (%)
Passengers	million	55.55	−1.5
# by land	million	55.24	−1.5
Turnover	billion person−km	8.55	−1.4
# by land	billion person−km	8.53	−1.5
Cargos	million tons	153.75	4.7
# by land	million tons	109.15	−0.7
Turnover	billion ton−km	44.80	2.9
# by land	billion ton−km	7.55	5.6

Post and telecommunication industries had revenue of 16.95 billion yuan, down by 3.6%. In postal industry, 43.69 million single mails were delivered last year, including 880 thousand express mails. The wire transfer through Dongguan Post Office reached 12.22 billion yuan in total. There had been 3.27 million landline subscribers (including PHS users) , increasing customers by 52.2 thousand. In contract, the mobile phone users reduced 873 thousand to 17.63 million. The total duration of long distance call was 24.88 billion minutes. The internet users was 2.05 million, reducing by 112.5 thousand totally, of which the wideband subscribers were 1.96 million, 116.5 thousand less than those of 2013.

Figure 5: Number of Phone Subscribers, 2008-2014

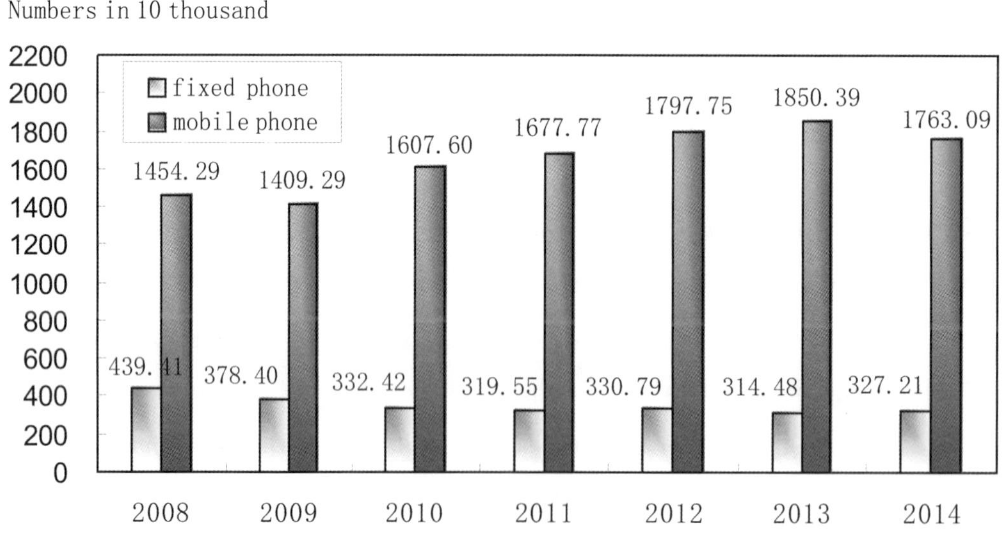

By the end of 2014, Dongguan processed 63 star−rated hotels, among which 21 hotels were five−star ranking. There were 76 travel agencies, receiving 3.56 million visitors from abroad, down by 14.8%, of which 2.34 million passengers came from Hong Kong, Macao and Taiwan, down by 16.4%, and the other 1.22 million tourists were from foreign countries worldwide, down by 11.6% . The international tourists generated revenue of 1.58 billion USD, up by 8.6%, and the domestic visitors, equivalent to 24.35 million and up by 1.1%, also contributed 37.46 billion yuan, an increase of 8.1% on year. The passengers traveling in groups from Dongguan dropped by 6.3%, equivalent to 1.51 million, of which there were 1.31 million passengers having a tour in mainland, down by 8.4%, and 194.8 thousand traveling overseas up by 10.9%.

Ⅷ. Financial Service

In 2014, the added value of finance was 26.69 billion yuan, up by 9.0%.

At the end of 2014, Dongguan had 129 financial institutions, including 37 depositary institutions (including 1 representative office) , 52 contractual institutions, and 40 investment institutions. The total savings in all financial institutions in Dongguan had been reaching 906.99 billion yuan, up by 5.1% over 2013, of which 460.68 billion was contributed by households both in urban and rural areas, increasing by 2.9%. The total number of loans in all financial institutions reached 533.16 billion yuan at the end of year, up by 11.7%. On consumer debt, the mortgage loans rose 18.8% to 118.30 billion yuan, in addition to 548 million yuan of car loans, up by 0.8%.

Figure 6: Saving Deposits of Urban and Rural Households and Its Growth, 2008—2014

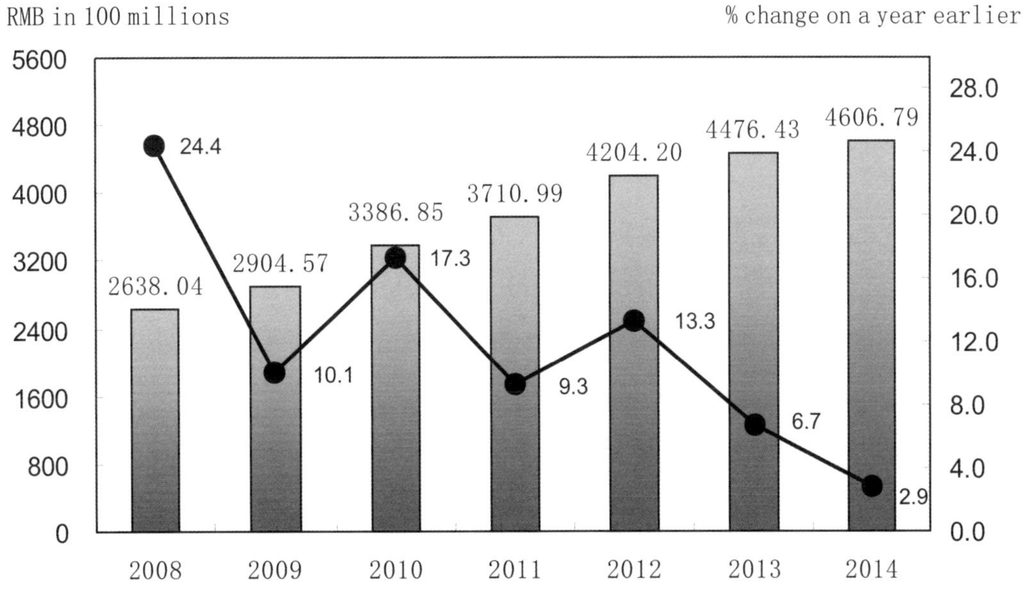

RMB in 100 millions

% change on a year earlier

Year	RMB in 100 millions	% change on a year earlier
2008	2638.04	24.4
2009	2904.57	10.1
2010	3386.85	17.3
2011	3710.99	9.3
2012	4204.20	13.3
2013	4476.43	6.7
2014	4606.79	2.9

The turnover of stock market increased to 1272.39 billion yuan up by 54.3%. The balance of guarantee fund totaled 16.19 billion yuan, up by 145.3%.

The revenue of insurance companies in Dongguan amounted to 25.80 billion yuan, up by 24.6%. The revenue could be divided into two parts, one is property insurance, reaching 8.49 billion yuan and up by 18.5%, and the other is life insurance, equivalent to 17.31 billion yuan and up by 27.7%. The total compensation in 2014 reached 7.03 billion yuan, with a compensation rate of 27.2% for all claims.

Ⅸ.Technology and Education

Together with 80 newly added enterprises and 235 to be licensed, the total number of National High-Tech Enterprises was expected to exceed 755, ranked the top among the prefecture-level cities of Guangdong. There were 28431 patent applications and 20366 were licensed in 2014. Among them 6913 were inventory patent applications, an increase of 7.11% compared to 2013, accounting for 24.31% of the total applications. And 1624 inventory patents were licensed, with an increase of 8.63%, ranked 3rd in Guangdong. The number of PCT applications was 299 and ranked 3rd in Guangdong. Scientific and technological resources are gathering at a fast pace. 2 new research and develop institutes: Institute of Dongguan Tongji University and Advanced Technology Research Institute of Dongguan were established. China (Dongguan) International Science and Technology Cooperation Week 2014 had been successfully held. With 7 provincial-level innovation and scientific-research team projects newly approved, there were 22 teams as a whole, ranking 3rd in Guangdong. Another 8 city-level innovation and scientific-research team projects were introduced with a research funding of 62 million yuan. The process of applying for National Sustainable Development Experimental Area was moving on steadily. Cooperation between technology and finance was strengthened. The Work Proposal to Innovate the Fiscal Investment and Promote the Development of Technology-Finance Industry was published. Technology-Insurance pilot programs were set up, and the patent backed loan added up to 112 million yuan.

By the end of the year, there were 881 kindergartens, 54 more than that of 2013. Of these 276 were first-level in Dongguan and even Guangdong, increased by 139 over last year. And there were 320 primary schools with 687.3 thousand pupils in Dongguan, with 100% school-aged children (local residents) enrollment rate and primary school graduation rate. Also, there were 172 middle schools (schools that combine middle and high school were not included) with 206.6 thousand students, with 100% school-aged students (local residents) enrollment rate and 98.4% graduation rate. And there were 65 high schools as a whole in Dongguan, including 40 traditional schools (including comprehensive schools that combine middle and high school, as well as multi-level schools with high school department) with 78.1 thousand students and 25 vocational schools with 64.4 thousand students. In terms of higher education, 69.9 thousand students were studying in 6 universities or colleges in Dongguan. In 2014, 22.8 thousand students enrolled in these colleges or universities while 13 thousand graduated with diplomas.

Table 7: Education Situation in 2014

Indicators	Enrollment (in thousands)	Increase over (%)	Total students (in thousands)	Increase over (%)	Graduates (in thousands)	Increase over (%)
Higher education, full time	22.8	9.7	69.9	14.8	13.0	11.7
Higher education, remote	6.6	−8.7	17.5	1.3	5.1	−35.1
Vocational middle schools	24.5	−0.4	64.4	6.1	17.5	12.4

Continue to the above-mentioned

Indicators	Enrollment (in thousands)	Increase over (%)	Total students (in thousands)	Increase over (%)	Graduates (in thousands)	Increase over (%)
Senior middle schools	26.7	2.7	78.1	1.3	25.2	3.4
Junior middle schools	75.4	1.7	206.6	2.7	57.5	6.5
Primary schools	125.0	−1.7	687.3	4.3	86.7	2.4
Kindergartens	126.2	14.2	290.5	4.6	77.5	−8.1

Ⅹ. Culture, Health and Sports

By 2014, there had been 1 public art center, 33 cultural stations, 641 libraries, 33 museums, 13 performing arts venues, 60 theatres and 1136 internet cafes around Dongguan. In addition, 63 public radio programs and 36 television programs were available for the citizens. Last year, 44.04 million newspapers had been printed and distributed, including Dongguan Daily of 32.66 million publications for a whole year. Furthermore, 708.3 thousand magazines had been published, and movies been broadcast by 620 thousand times in theatres with 11.02 million audience in total as well.

Moreover, there were 2156 medical care institutions, including 7 AAA hospital, and 2070 primary health care facilities, such as outpatient departments, clinics, dispensary, health stations, infirmaries and community medical care institutions, with 43.1 thousand medical staff and 26.7 thousand hospital beds. The number of patients in need of treatment had decreased by 4.9%.

In the past calendar year, athletes registered in Dongguan won 124 gold, 134 silver and 111 bronze medals, including 8 gold medals in national competitions, 113 gold medals, 100 silver medals and 92 bronze medals in provincial games. 333 sport activities for fitness have been held, attracting 188.7 thousand participants totally. There were 13.86 thousand sports venues, including 516 stadiums, 166 gymnasiums, 5316 floodlit basketball courts, 102 football courts, 1384 fitness trails, 353 outdoor and 56 indoor swimming pools, and 1378 outdoor badminton courts. There were 979 sport lottery retailers in Dongguan having generated 1.51 billion yuan in sales, and raising a prize fund over 109.56 million yuan.

Ⅺ.Resident Income

In 2014, the income of Dongguan citizens maintained a stable growth. The average annual disposable income per citizen was 35712 yuan, a nominal growth of 8.7%.

The growth rate of average annual disposable income of rural residents is faster than that of urban resident. Calculating in new caliber, the average annual disposable income per urban resident was 36764 yuan with a nominal growth of 8.6%, while the average annual disposable income per rural resident was 22327 yuan, with a nominal growth of 9.0 %.

In income structure, the average wage income of Dongguan citizens was 27928 yuan, accounting for 78.2% of total disposable income, and the average property income was 6242 yuan, accounting for 17.5%.

Ⅻ. Social security and Safety production

The coverage by five major type insurances was 27.48 million person–times, up by 6.7%. In detail, 6.16 million bought basic medical insurance, 3.93 million chose unemployment insurance, and 4.92 million people purchased injury insurance. The total revenue of social insurance fund was 28.71 billion yuan, and the total expenditures were 13.12 billion yuan. By the end of 2014, accumulative balance of the insurance fund had reached 88.78 billion yuan.

By the end of 2014, there were 37 welfare institutions for adoption in Dongguan, including 1 social welfare house, 1 social welfare center, and 34 nursing houses receiving 1603 elderly residents. There were 2724 people provided with foster care and 21 thousand with social assistance by social welfare institutions. The expenditures of residents' lowest–standard living allowance were 104.04 million yuan, and the social relief spending for natural disasters was 4.67 million yuan. The balance of charity fund was 235 million yuan. There were 854 people registered in the list of "Five–Guaranteed Households" , which cost 21.23 million yuan of public budget last year.

ⅩⅢ. Demographics, Climate and Environment

At the end of 2014, there were 1.91 million Dongguan local residents. The birth rate was 11.2‰, equivalent to 21.4 thousand infants born, meanwhile the death rate was 5.37‰ for 10.3 thousand deaths. Thus, the growth rate of population was 5.83‰. The inhabitants of Dongguan reached 8.34 million, of whom 7.41 million were urban residents. The urbanization rate reached a record of 88.81%.

There were 174 rainy days and 1959 hours of sunshine over the year. The average temperature was 22.9°C, and the average relative humidity was 74% throughout the year with the average rainfall of 1936 millimeters.

As of 2014, the number of forest parks amounted to 19, in which the facilities had been greatly added and improved. Furthermore, the forest planning areas covered 535.80 km^2 with 219.73 km^2 of natural woods which supplied with 2.83 million m^3 of timber in potential. The growth rate of trees was 127.5 thousand m^3.

At the end of 2014, urban areas in Dongguan covered 922.02 km^2, which contained 45.60 km^2 for government and public facilities. The forest coverage rate was 36%. The greening rate of Dongguan was 47.5%, particularly 44.5% only around urban areas, with an average of 17.3 m^2 per person in terms of greening land. There had been 1210 parks in Dongguan covering an area of 145 km^2 as a whole.

政府工作报告

REPORT ON THE WORK OF THE GOVERNMENT

——2015年1月28日在东莞市第十五届人民代表大会第五次会议上

东莞市人民政府市长　袁宝成

各位代表：

现在，我代表市人民政府，向大会报告2014年政府工作，对2015年工作提出建议，请予审议。并请政协各位委员和其他列席人员提出意见。

2014年工作回顾

“看似寻常最奇崛，成如容易却艰辛。”一年来，全市上下在上级和市委的正确领导下，以党的十八届三中、四中全会精神为指导，积极应对各种不利因素的影响，聚力改革攻坚、项目攻坚、效能攻坚，扎实做好各项工作，较好地推进了市第十五届人大四次会议确定的年度目标任务。

在经济下行压力加大的一年里，我们以多管齐下的积极举措，保障了经济发展稳中有进。面对外部需求不振、国家政策收紧、结构调整阵痛等因素的叠加，出台有力措施扶持实体经济、稳定外贸增长、促进商贸和房地产等产业健康发展，努力推动在平稳发展基础上加快转型升级。预计全市生产总值5881亿元，同比增长7.8%，快于全国平均水平0.4个百分点。市一般公共预算收入455.2亿元，增长11.2%。人民币存款余额突破9000亿元。规模以上工业企业内销比重首次超过外销。海博会、加博会、国际科技合作周等重要活动成功举办。新型研发机构建设、电机能效提升、节能减排等工作得到上级高度肯定。在社科院发布的蓝皮书中，东莞城市综合经济竞争力排全国第12位。福布斯2014中国城市创新力排行榜上，东莞居第11位。

在改革发展任务艰巨的一年里，我们以先行先试的争先意识，实现了关键领域改革的良好开局。200多项改革陆续铺开，在全国率先形成系统化的商事制度后续监管模式，率先发出跨境电商货物通关第一票，率先推行外商投资“多证联办”，率先启动项目投资建设直接落地改革，社会投资项目审批时间缩短三分之二。东莞获批国家新型城镇化综合试点城市，顺利通过全国质量强市示范城市验收，争取了一批先行先试改革项目，争取了更多的政策红利。重大项目超过七成动工，一批项目建设速度创下新纪录，为城市经济发展注入了强大动能。在北京师范大学发布的2014中国地方政府效率排行榜上，我市在全国54个重点城市中排名第一。

在深层矛盾接连爆发的一年里，我们以及时果敢的应对处置，倒逼了社会治理水平提升。面对长期积累社会问题的集中凸显，我们痛定思痛，沉着应对，以“扫黄”歼灭战为抓手铲除不健康产业生态，以处置“裕元事件”为契机完善社保、公积金缴存机制，以应对“丐帮”失实报道为切入点加强流浪乞讨未成年人救助，全方位改进城市管理、权益保护、公共安全等方面的不足，努力把问题暴露带来的压力，转化成倒逼整改、长效治理的动力，促进了社会治理法治化水平全面提升。

在深入开展群众路线教育实践活动的一年里，我们以对“四风”问题的坚决整治，促进了作风改进和民生改善。八项规定、三严三实等要求全面落实，一批形式主义、官僚主义、享乐主义和奢靡之风问题得到集中整改，切实解决服务群众“最后一公里”问题，密切联系群众日益成为机关新风尚。十件实事圆满完成，扶贫、公交等民生工程扎实推进，城市社区居家养老实现全覆盖，基本养老金连续提升，普通高考总录取率等四项高考指标实现全省“三连冠”，医保满意度居珠三角首位，村组资产负债率降至历史新低，群众在发展中得到更多实惠。

一年来，我们主要抓了以下工作：

——*着力扶持以先进制造业为核心的实体经济发展*。出台50条措施扶持实体经济。开展千干扶千企活动，积极缓解企业融资难、用工难等问题。先进制造业增加值增长13.9%，占规模以上工业的47%，比2013年提高2.4个百分点。新增规模以上工业企业145家。规模以上工业企业内销比重提高到52%。百亿元企业达10家，五百亿元企业实现零突破。一批战略性新兴产业初具规模，智能手机年出货量2.3亿部，占全球的17.7%。从事云计算应用的企业超2000家。物联网及相关产业年产值680亿元。东莞成为第二个国家级两化深度融合暨智能制造试验区。新增境内外上市企业7家，总数达29家。新增全国股转系统挂牌企业15家、区域性股权交易中心挂牌企业近200家，均居全省地级市第一。实体经济质量效益进一步提升。

——*以超常规力度解决“三率”问题，促进重大产业项目建设全面提速*。坚持每月会诊督促重大项目建设，落实市领导包干、“五个一”、明白卡、销号制等制度，全力推进重大项目建设。全市新开工重大项目45个、总投资576亿元。截至2013年底的156个重大项目开工率从年初的42.9%提高至71.8%。一批项目建设投产速度创下新纪录，大朗三星项目从签约到投产仅用8个月，松山湖记忆科技总部提前7个月开工。累计24个项目建成投产，一批项目逐渐释放产能。组团赴东南亚、南美、日本、以色列、土耳其等地开拓市场、加强招商。新引进一批总投资558亿元的重大项目，发展后劲不断增强。

——*加快重大平台和重要基础设施建设*。水乡特色发展经济区管委会获省批准成立，挂影洲中心涌等8个示范片区和基础项目开工，水乡大道改造等工程竣工。粤海银瓶合作创新区上升为省级战略，首个产业项目动工，总投资100亿元的环普工业园项目签约。东莞港区集装箱达288万标箱，增幅连续三年保持全国超百万标箱港口第一位。东莞保税物流中心（B区）进入全国B型保税区四强。松山湖高新区主要经济指标增长25%以上，辐射带动作用不断增强。生态产业园引资106亿元。长安新区完成总体规划编制。松山湖高新区与生态产业园、长安镇与长安新区实行统筹发展。省市重要基础设施项目建设超额完成年度目标，带动全社会固定资产投资1427亿元，增长10%。地铁2号线车站全部封顶，隧道全线贯通。虎门二桥正式动工，东部快速改造完工。东莞篮球中心正式投入使用，市民艺术中心、工人文化宫完工。建成110千伏以上输变电工程15项。4G网络基本实现全覆盖。

——*以新型研发机构、“机器换人”等为抓手，增强科技创新能力*。大学创新城一期工程基本竣工。全市新型研发机构增至23家，居全省第三。启动“机器换人”行动计划，市财政连续三年、每年安排2亿元对企业进行资助。设立机器人产业基地和创投基金。成立新能源汽车联盟。新引进省创新科研团队7个，总数22个，在全省均排第三位。新增国家高新技术企业80家、企业研发机构657家，总数分别达755家和1593家。发明专利授权量居全省第三。350多家企业开展电机能效提升，年节电量超2.6亿千瓦时。散裂中子源首台设备安装成功。预计研发经费支出增长12%，占

GDP 比重 2.1%，连续六年提升。

——深入推进商事制度、项目投资、外商服务管理等改革。积极探索电商集群注册、住所信息申报、加强协同监管等商改新举措，市场主体达 63 万户。大力推动项目投资审批体制改革，探索直接落地改革试点，社会投资项目落地时间从 18 个月压减至 7 个月。推行外商投资市场准入“多证联办”改革，企业仅用 3、4 个工作日即可领齐相关证照。深化审批制度改革，行政审批和日常管理事项累计压减幅度分别达 68.1%、67.5%。深化政府机构改革，调整理顺物价、商贸、卫生、计生等职能，政府工作部门压缩调整为 32 个。社会信用体系建设加快推进。医疗、公交、户籍等民生领域改革进一步深化。

——成功举办海博会等大型展会，对外开放取得新成绩。圆满举办省委省政府交办的首届 21 世纪海上丝绸之路博览会，开辟了广东及东莞与沿线国家交流合作的重要平台。加博会、漫博会、台博会、国际科技合作周等影响力不断扩大。构建开放型经济四大体系，实施加工贸易增效计划，出台稳定外贸增长 37 条措施。全市进出口总额 1625.3 亿美元，增长 6.2%，增速在全国外贸总额前五名城市中排第一位。承办中国（广东）——马来西亚经贸合作交流会。推动成立中英低碳产业园。与罗马尼亚布里扎市、捷克奥帕瓦市和德国乌波塔尔市结为友好城市。

——扶持电子商务等新兴业态发展。成功创建国家电子商务示范城市。全市电商主体达 5.4 万户，电商交易额增长 26%，阿里巴巴网络收货量和发货量分别居全国第七和第二。与阿里巴巴牵头成立的菜鸟网络签约，建设中国智能骨干网节点项目和华南区域 O2O 体验式购物中心项目。四成多中小企业应用电子商务。在海关总署支持下，率先启用跨境电商服务平台、建设跨境电商公共监管仓，规划建设一批跨境电商园区，东莞速卖通跨境电商交易额升至全国第七。成立城市共同配送标准联盟，获准设立清溪保税物流中心（B 型）。东城万达、长安万科等城市综合体相继开业，商业生态环境进一步完善。社会消费品零售总额 1615 亿元，增长 8.7%。

——加大节能减排与生态建设力度。推进国家节能减排财政政策综合示范城市建设，全面启动三年总投资 350 亿元的示范项目建设计划。启动水乡“两高一低”企业整治与退出。推进土地生态利用，整合盘活土地近 5 万亩。实施大气污染防治行动。超额完成黄标车淘汰任务，环保限行范围进一步扩大。投放 4547 辆清洁能源公交车和出租车。PM2.5 年均值比上年削减 6.3%，优良空气天数占全年 70.2%。推进 8 个污水处理厂扩容工程建设，在石马河、茅洲河等实施河长制。完成 18 条内河涌整治。东江水库联网一期工程基本完工。大力创建国家生态城市和国家森林城市，新建改建各类公园 33 个。

——铁腕整治涉黄涉毒等违法犯罪行为，提升社会治理水平。开展“扫黄”歼灭战，全面清剿涉黄违法行为，坚决铲除保护伞，加强娱乐场所长效管理，有效净化了社会风气。严打涉毒涉众型犯罪，开展“六大专项”及“两抢一盗”打击整治行动，刑事案件破案数上升 11.8%。加强劳资纠纷处置，涉及 30 人以上的劳资突发事件、欠薪逃匿和劳资信访案件分别下降 58.7%、73.2%和 50%。完善医疗纠纷第三方化解机制，医闹事件下降 38%。狠抓安全生产、食品安全、消防安全等专项整治，全年未发生重特大安全事故。

——强化土地监管、财政绩效管理和政府性债务控制。进一步加强依法用地管理，积极配合开展土地审计，着力整改突出问题，规范耕地保护和土地出让管理。完善财政管理制度，加强财政绩效评价，首次公开市本级“三公”支出决算，全面公开 300 多个行政事业单位“三公”支出预算，试点公开 64 个市直部门“三公”支出决算。加强政府性债务管控，全面统计核查镇街政府性债务。

全市村组资产负债率下降 1.8 个百分点。

——**切实抓好社会民生建设和十件实事**。投入 252.3 亿元发展民生事业，向社会承诺的十件实事圆满完成。开办东莞外国语学校。调增中职学校工科学位 4000 个。积分制入学公办学位增加 11.6%。向民办学校学生发放补助 6.7 亿元。积极争创全国文明城市"三连冠"。成功入选国家公共文化服务标准化试点。音乐剧《妈妈再爱我一次》获全国"五个一工程"奖，莞产音乐剧影响力不断扩大。入围当当网评比的"非直辖城市图书消费十大城市"，超过 13 个省成为全国购书记录最多的地级市。亚运会、亚残运会东莞健儿再创夺金新纪录。连续第十年提高基本养老金标准。启动社保跨镇街双定点就医机制。台心医院正式开业。推行家庭医生式服务。发放就业补贴 3.2 亿元。创业贷款增长 13 倍。加强流浪乞讨未成年人综合救助保护。向困难群体发放各类补助金 10.5 亿元。市区内涝整治应急三期工程顺利完成。妥善应对"3·30"大暴雨、登革热等疫情灾害。

——**加强对口帮扶与区域协作工作**。推进市内"双到"帮扶，欠发达村年纯收入平均增长 26%。携手共建深莞惠"3+2"经济圈。深入推进穗莞合作。东莞韶关帮扶合作进入新阶段，"一中心七组团"平台初步形成，引进 125 个总投资达 317 亿元项目。东莞揭阳"双到"扶贫工作顺利开展。援疆援藏、对口帮扶广西河池、重庆巫山等工作扎实开展。国防动员、统计审计、人口计生、外事侨务、工青妇幼、民族宗教、档案方志、科普法普、法制、气象、打私等工作有效推进。

——**扎实开展群众路线教育实践活动**。紧紧围绕"为民务实清廉"主题，针对排查出的 31 个方面问题和收集的 1 万多条意见建议，全面落实整改，构建长效机制，着力解决政府系统"四风"问题。聘请第三方明查暗访机关服务质量，试点推进社会评议科长活动。撤销 56 个市级议事协调机构。清理近九成创建达标活动。加强依法行政。村（社区）法律顾问实现全覆盖。扩大政府购买公共服务范围。开通 12345 政府服务热线。加快网上办事大厅建设，新推动 1599 项事项上网办理，努力打通服务群众"最后一公里"。

各位代表！过去一年，全市上下负重前行，克难奋进，经受了严峻考验，迈出了坚实步伐。这些成绩的取得，离不开中央、省委省政府和市委的正确领导，离不开市人大、市政协与各民主党派的监督支持，离不开全市人民、驻莞部队、武警官兵的实干奋进和港澳台同胞、海外侨胞、国际友人的共同努力。在此，我代表市政府，向所有参与、支持和关心东莞经济社会发展的各界人士，表示衷心的感谢和崇高的敬意！

与此同时，我们也清醒看到，东莞资源环境约束趋紧、核心竞争力不强等深层次矛盾还未有效破解，仍然面临不少问题和隐忧：一是部分指标完成不理想。生产总值、消费等与年度增长目标有一定距离，工业投资等增长较慢。二是招商引资势头有所放缓，产能释放尚需时日。新引进重大项目还不够多，已投产项目释放产能的规模效应还不够强。三是公共安全问题仍较突出。各类治安案件及食品安全、生产消防等方面事故时有发生。四是民生热点问题有待加力解决。入学、入户、公交、医疗等公共服务与群众要求还有一定差距。五是政府效能还需进一步提高。一些干部干事创业激情减弱，一些部门审批手续仍较繁琐，提升行政效能还需付出更大努力。针对这些问题，我们将采取积极措施，认真加以解决。

新常态下的新东莞

在新一轮改革发展的关键时刻，习近平总书记提出了中国经济发展进入新常态的重要论断，并深刻阐述了其内涵和特征。新常态是对中国经济新航道、新格局的科学阐释，外在表现为增速放缓与质量提升，实质是经济发展新旧增长动力的转换、新旧发展路径的替代、新旧竞争优势的演化、新旧空间组织的重构以及新旧产业结构的调整过程。这对东莞实现高水平崛起具有重大的现实指导意义。我市作为中国改革开放精彩而生动的缩影，对外开放早、改革起步早、经济发展快，与此相应碰到各种新形势、新情况、新问题也比较早。可以说经济新常态的系列特征在东莞表现得更为深刻明显。具体体现在以下趋势性变化上：

从经济增速看，正逐步从高速增长切换为追求更有质量、效益和后劲的中高速新挡位。这个过程与国际金融危机冲击期、转型升级阵痛期等交叉叠加。近六年来我市有五年“个位数增长”。传统粗放的高速增长已无法再持续，而高效率、低成本、可持续的中速增长成为全市经济发展的新阶段、新目标。

从市场格局看，正逐步从高度外向依赖转为内外两个市场两种资源并重。过去东莞以外资为主、以出口为主、以引进来为主，既成就了开放型经济的特色和优势，也带来了外向依赖过高、经济风险过大的隐患。经过多年努力，全市外向依存度从最高峰的433.8%下降到170.4%，规模以上工业企业内销比重首次超过外销；民营企业纳税额超过六成，外资和民营“比翼齐飞”、出口和内销“两分天下”、引进来和走出去“双轮并驱”的格局已经初步奠定。

从区域协调看，正逐步从镇街小组团向区域大组团一体化发展。随着水乡统筹步伐加快和经济区整合力度加大，随着超3000亿重大项目的平衡布局和市内“双到”扶贫的深入推进，东莞以镇街为单元的小组团格局，正演变为以经济区为主导的大组团格局，行政区划限制被逐步打破，各自为政、重复建设、资源浪费等问题将会有效破解，欠发达镇村的“造血”功能在持续增强，全市一盘棋和区域一体化的协调发展局面正加快形成。

从产业形态看，正逐步从简单的加工贸易向以新技术、新产品、新业态、新模式为特征的“四新”经济方向发展转变。作为东莞经济的发家之本和重要主体，加工贸易在企业形态、技术、品牌等方面的转型升级成效明显，服装、家具等传统优势产业的核心竞争力稳步增强。同时，更多生产要素向“四新”经济集聚，大量新技术广泛应用，智能手机、机器人等新产业初具规模，电子商务、现代物流等新业态、新模式生机蓬勃，国家高新技术企业总数已稳居全省地级市第一位，经济发展正稳步迈入创新驱动的新阶段。

从发展路径看，正逐步从“多轮驱动”向市镇统筹转变。伴随着土地统筹和招商统筹力度的加大，以及利益分配机制的完善，尽管基层仍存在“卖土地、建厂房、收租金”的路径依赖和冲动，但统筹发展的共识不断强化。以往“村村点火”的放养式、多主体、低层次的传统模式，正逐步被“市镇统筹、三级分利”的新模式所替代，镇村集体经济也从以收租为主、存在债务风险的状况，朝着多元投资、增资减债的方向迈出坚实步伐。全市发展层次持续提升。

从改革红利看，正逐步从改革开放的“首创”红利向新一轮全面深化改革的“增创”红利转变。过去30多年，东莞能在没有太多优惠政策的情况下脱颖而出，凭借的是敢为人先精神和招商“一条龙服务”等首创举措。在以往红利衰减式微的新形势下，东莞以自我革命的勇气，又一次在商事制度、项目投资审批等改革中尝到了甜头。全市正掀起新一轮改革攻坚的热潮，不少莞版改革正在逐步增创和释放出新的红利。

从人力资源看，正逐步从“成本洼地”向“人才高地”转变。随着人口红利逐步消减，东莞早期在“孔雀东南飞”背景下形成的劳动力“洼地”效应已全面消退，“求工难”已演变为“招工难”，而且与周边中心城市相比，非但没有人才引进的成本优势，反倒会因为城市配套不完善、人文环境不理想等加重成本。种种新形势倒逼我们必须在政策扶持、工作环境、生活配套等方面下功夫，以待遇引人、以真情待人、以事业留人，努力建设“人才高地”。

从竞争优势看，正逐步从传统的区位和先发优势向激烈竞争下综合新优势转变。随着发展形势的不断变化，我市曾经引以为傲的地理区位等优势已逐步淡化甚至被超越。其他城市数倍于东莞的土地资源优势，北上广深等中心城市和自贸区的“磁吸效应”，制造订单的“去中国化”趋势等，都将是东莞“成长的烦恼”。同时，完善的产业配套成为当前东莞最大的优势，加上良好的经济基础、系统的产业扶持政策，以及近年来着力打造政府服务“加一”和综合成本“减一”的法治化国际化营商环境，东莞正在逐步形成一种新的综合竞争优势。

以上这些趋势性变化，既是东莞发展新常态的外在特征，又是内在动因。新常态为东莞创造了新机遇，也带来了新挑战。如果应对得好，东莞经济将步入平稳健康发展、质量效益提升的新轨道，一幅令人憧憬的新东莞蓝图将在不久的将来成为现实；如处理不好就可能掉入“城市发展陷阱”。我们必须趋利避害，扬长避短，顺势而为，乘势而上，更好地适应新常态、建设新东莞。

适应新常态、建设新东莞，要求我们树立新思维，把握新形势、凝聚新共识。新常态是提质增效的调整，是发展后劲的积蓄。要把思想和行动统一到中央的科学判断上来，深刻认识到东莞发展新常态不可逆转、不容回避。要看清并且承认新趋势、新情况、新问题，不能仍然想着过去铺摊子、卖土地、建厂房的粗放型高速发展模式，那样即使暂时把速度抬上去了也不会持久，相反会使发展中的矛盾和问题进一步积累、激发直至总爆发。要树立和强化新思维，更加注重创新驱动发展，更加注重经济结构战略性调整，更加注重生态建设和富民强市，努力追求实实在在、质量效益提升的经济发展。尤其要通过锐意改革，破除路径依赖，破解发展难题，增创新的发展红利，同时运用法治手段，巩固和深化改革成效，把创新举措转化成工作常态和长效机制，防止体制复归。

适应新常态、建设新东莞，要求我们保持平常心，摒弃“换挡焦虑”、强化“底线意识”。不是经济增速高一点形势就“好得很”，也不是速度下来一点形势就“糟得很”。经济发展速度有升有降是正常的。要认清增速已经换挡的事实，彻底走出高速纠结，摆脱“经济何时才能恢复到危机前速度”等困惑，充分认识到突破资源瓶颈就是构建产业新格局的机遇，战胜复杂经济形势就是赢得城市竞争的机遇，化解深层矛盾就是提升发展水平的机遇，进一步坚定信心，增强发展定力。同时，切实增强忧患意识和责任意识，看到合理经济增速对于促进就业增收、保持投资信心、强化财力保障等的重要意义，采取有力措施确保平稳增长，避免大起大落，努力实现化危为机、逆境突破，推动经济行稳致远。

适应新常态、建设新东莞，要求我们发扬钉钉子精神，坚持主动作为、注重踏实干事。新常态意味着固有发展路径和利益格局的深刻调整，伴随着深层次矛盾和问题的集中爆发，面临着项目引进和用地制约、产能扩张和节能减排、民间投资渠道窄与实体经济融资难等两难困境，一些改革难题亟待攻坚突破，一批重大项目亟需加速建设，招商引资、加工贸易转型、科技金融产业“三融合”等工作的每一步都必须付出巨大努力。必须提振与新常态相适应的干部作风和精神面貌，进一步增强钉钉子的实干精神，破除“乱作为、不作为”现象，抓好决策部署的贯彻落实，抓好目标任务的分解落实，通过一件一件的具体工作、一年一年的务实成效，久久为功，稳步实现长远发展目标，推动东莞在新常态轨道上坚定迈进。

2015年工作安排

2015年是“十二五”的收官之年。展望新的一年，世界部分地区经济增速会略有回升，但总体复苏疲弱态势难有明显改观，经济下行压力仍然很大，外部环境仍然错综复杂，诸多不确定因素将对东莞经济产生较大影响。与此同时，我国经济增长总体处于合理区间，依法治国方针、重大改革举措、“一带一路”战略、新型城镇化等，将创造新的发展红利，激发更多的内需动力，开拓更广阔的外部市场，为我市高水平崛起带来了新机遇。今年政府工作的总体要求是：**认真贯彻落实党的十八届三中四中全会、中央经济工作会议、省委十一届四次全会和市委十三届五次全会精神，深入贯彻习近平总书记系列重要讲话精神，以建设“国际制造名城、现代生态都市”为目标，着力加强依法行政，推进重点领域改革，在加快转型升级、强化创新驱动上出实招，在做强制造产业、加速“三重”建设上下功夫，在深化开放型经济体系建设、提升对内对外开放水平上求突破，在创新社会治理、发展民生事业上求实效，注重防范化解风险，更好地适应新常态，努力推动全市经济社会发展行稳致远。**

综合考虑各方面因素，今年全市发展的主要预期目标是：**生产总值增长8%左右，人均生产总值增长7.5%，市一般公共预算收入增长10%，固定资产投资总额增长12%，社会消费品零售总额增长10%，进出口总额增长5%；先进制造业、高技术制造业增加值占规模以上工业增加值比重分别达47%和37%；研发经费支出占生产总值比重2.3%以上；发明专利授权量增长10%；城市居民人均可支配收入、农村居民人均纯收入分别增长8%和8.5%，居民消费价格涨幅控制在3%左右；全面完成省“十二五”节能减排任务目标。**

围绕以上目标要求，重点做好几方面工作：

一、以法治思维引领改革发展，提高依法行政和创新发展能力

党的十八届四中全会作出了全面推进依法治国的重大战略部署。我们必须增强法治思维和创新意识，根据今年市委一号文的要求，将法治贯穿到改革发展的方方面面，使之成为政府工作的指南针和温度计，成为攻坚突破的助推器和保险杠。

*深入推进依法行政，提升法治化、国际化营商环境。*实行重大行政决策听证和专家咨询论证制度。严格行政处罚自由裁量标准。推行行政机关负责人出庭应诉制度。继续争取地方立法权。加强财政预决算、招投标、“三公”经费等重点领域的信息公开。加快建设企业信用系统。实行重点企业“一对一”挂钩服务，建立企业大数据综合服务平台，搭建“企业问题池”。深入落实系列减负政策，让东莞成为税费收取最透明、综合营商成本最低的城市之一。

*深化重点领域改革，争创莞版改革更多亮点。*推进外商投资管理服务改革，在所有企业实行“多证联办”。深化商事制度改革，继续在便利化登记和后续监管两端发力。落实项目投资改革举措，推广直接落地改革试点经验。稳妥发展混合所有制经济，全面深化国企新一轮改革。在公共基础设施项目投资领域，加快实行政府与社会资本合作（PPP）模式。推动全国农村综合改革示范点建设，完善集体资产交易和监管机制，深化股权制度改革。推进城乡土地生态利用制度综合改革，开展不动产统一登记和土地承包经营权确权。探索实施镇街排污总量指标有偿调配制度。

*大力推进行政权力清单化、行政审批标准化。*编制部门权责清单，实现审批事项一单尽收，赋予唯一代码，凡不在清单上的审批事项，一律不得保留。率先在项目投资领域推行行政审批标准化，逐步覆盖所有审批领域，核减并明确每个审批事项所需资料、流程和办理时限。推动能上网审批事项尽可能上网，实行全程大数据管理，着力提高网上办理率和办结率。

加强政府自身建设，以问题为导向推动作风持续改善。巩固群众路线教育实践活动成果，将改进会风文风、杜绝铺张浪费等经验做法制度化。针对居住证办理、户籍变更等常办事项，开展专项督查，解决擅自增设环节、中介变相收费等问题。积极开展第三方评估，扩大暗访和作风评议范围，深入整治“庸懒散拖”，倒逼机关作风改善。严格执行八项规定，加强政府系统廉政建设，打造为民务实清廉的法治政府。

二、实施东莞制造2025战略，建设中国制造样板城市

当前，全球制造业正在迈入数字化、网络化、智能化的新时代。我们必须坚定制造业强市方向，按照今年市政府一号文的要求，大力实施东莞制造2025战略，推进智能制造、服务型制造、创新制造、优质制造、集群制造、绿色制造“六大工程”，努力将东莞建设成为中国制造样板城市。

掀起制造业智能化改造热潮。加快实施“机器换人”计划，选择一批重点项目示范带动智能化改造。在模具、服装等传统行业推动数控一代机械产品运用。引导企业加快实施电机能效提升和注塑机节能伺服技术改造。预留用地指标，优先解决投资强度每亩500万元以上的技改项目，对拆除重建、加层等符合条件的技改项目，新增建筑面积不再征收土地出让金。

推动制造业“扩链强链”。依托智能手机省市共建基地，推动全产业链集聚发展。依托机器人产业基地和“机器换人”庞大市场，引进培育机器人龙头企业，加快形成集群优势。依托省数控一代示范镇建设，整合科研机构、装备制造企业和应用单位资源，培育和完善数控产品产业链。依托服装、家具、五金模具等专业镇，用好专业市场、品牌展会、行业创新平台等资源，推动传统优势产业占据上下游高附加值链。

打造制造业的“东莞质量”和“东莞标准”。推进质量强市建设，推动检测和认证业创新发展，将东莞建成华南地区重要检测基地。鼓励企业参与标准制定，规划重点行业标准路线图，抢占智能机械手、新能源汽车、智能手机等行业制高点。开展工业产品质量专项整治，加强质量监督抽查。加快工业设计等生产性服务业发展，提高“东莞制造”的品牌含金量。

进一步加大对金融业发展的支持力度，推动民营资本与先进制造业深度融合。整合金融资源，通过境内外上市、股权融资等，扩大企业直接融资比例。引导民间资本参与或设立产业基金、创投基金，投资制造业项目和技术。探索建立新型民营股权投资基金。建立先进制造业项目大数据资源库，定期举办对接活动，推动资本与项目在碰撞融合中迸发出制造业发展新活力。大力推行设备融资租赁，为急需设备更新的中小企业提供融资服务支持。

三、大力发展新技术、新产品、新业态、新模式，增强创新驱动发展能力

加强新型研发机构和科技企业孵化器建设。加快大学创新城二、三期工程建设。与北京航空航天大学等国内外知名院校加强合作，进一步推动新型研发机构进驻并发挥作用。加快散裂中子源项目建设，发展关联配套产业。实施孵化器“双提升”与“全覆盖”行动，加快香市科技园等大型孵化器建设。促进科技创新服务业发展。鼓励开展各类股权众筹与创客路演活动。

加快发展电子商务、配送物流和港口经济。引导更多专业镇建立电商平台，鼓励企业用好第三方电商推动线上线下融合发展。鼓励企业收集用户需求，生产个性化产品，打造互联网工厂。全面推行电商企业集群注册。完善跨境电商公共服务平台功能，构筑跨境电商专业园区体系。推进全国城市共同配送试点。以虎门港为载体，打造保税加工、现代物流、临港产业三位一体的综合性开放平台。

促进城市商务商贸功能进一步完善。全面启动南城国际商务区北区开发，引进一批企业总部和高端服务业。结合轨道交通TOD开发，探索以空中连廊等方式促进商贸资源整合，推动中央商圈和各镇成熟商圈功能强化、布局优化。探索建立新型商业购销平台和物流集散中心。完善厚街作为全市会展核心镇的功能，提升会展产业集中度。

加快旅游业发展和酒店业转型升级。突出"项目强市、旅游富民"，出台旅游业发展规划，深入挖掘莞香旅游资源，重点打造虎门销烟、明清古村落、岭南水乡等精品线路，力争引进若干个旅游大项目，打响东莞古迹游、水乡游、会展游、工业游等"十大旅游"品牌。通过"异业同盟"等手段加快酒店业转型升级，提升东莞酒店业品牌形象。

四、构筑对内对外开放新格局，提高开放型经济核心竞争力

建设海上丝绸之路先行市。依托 "一带一路"战略，继续办好海博会，积极拓展与东盟、非洲、南美等地区的经贸文化合作，探索与沿线国家共建产业园区，推动企业加快走出去步伐。加快台湾高科技园、两岸生物产业基地、中以产业园、中英低碳产业园等建设。主动对接融入广东自贸区。

加快转变外经贸发展方式。推进国家加工贸易转型升级试点城市建设，深入实施加工贸易增效计划。探索建设国际贸易"单一窗口"。以区域通关一体化为契机，推动物流跨区域整合和功能延伸。大力发展服务贸易和服务外包。强化加博会、漫博会、台博会、国际科技合作周等品牌展会对产业转型升级的带动作用。

多层次、全方位、多渠道主动出去招商。建立招商引资"项目源"大数据。围绕机器人、智能手机、电子商务等产业，瞄准重点地区登门招商。充分发挥莞商和在莞商会作用，加强以商引商。鼓励和帮扶现有企业增资扩产。在美国硅谷建立商务代表处，探索设立国际合作引导基金，力争将东莞打造为"硅谷先进制造中心"。

集聚境内外优秀人才，营造进得来、留得下、用得好的最佳人才环境。进一步放宽人才入户限制，创新人才引进机制，探索实行企业自评人才入户。研究引进高端退休"银色人才"。加强技能人才培养，推行中职教育校企深度融合的现代学徒制，加强重点企业的订单式人才培养和引进。完善城市生活配套和公共服务供给，让人才更愿意留在东莞。

五、按照"建设一批、投产一批、储备一批"的要求，让重大项目成为经济结构战略性调整的强力引擎

落实"五个一"、明白卡、销号制等制度，加速重大产业项目落地开花结果。建立重大项目建设"问题池"，加大市镇领导挂钩督导力度。对征地拆迁难、管线迁改慢等共性问题进行集中会审，对个性问题及时协调解决，对推而不动、无法开工的坚决取消重大项目资格、收回土地指标。重点推动中集物流等总投资 605.8 亿元的项目动工，加快华为终端总部、步步高研发生产基地等建设，力争年内投产重大项目 13 个，新增产值 346.4 亿元。

全力加强土地等资源要素保障。力争统筹连片土地 3 万亩，盘活存量土地、处置闲置土地 1.3 万亩，形成"熟地"目录，强化招商用地保障。鼓励金融机构加大对重点项目的信贷投放力度。加快完善项目水电气等基础设施及周边生活配套，协助解决员工子女读书等问题，全方位优化投产项目的跟踪服务。

完善重大项目引进和管理机制，形成项目储备梯队。健全绩效考核与奖励机制，掀起重大项目引进新热潮。全市一盘棋优化重大项目布局，建立重大项目统筹流转和利益共享机制，实行镇街（园区）共建"飞地招商"税收分成。推广凤岗利用分散厂区承接重大项目的做法。对未完全满足既定条件、但对我市产业发展具有战略性意义的重大项目，实行"一事一议"认定。

六、以国家新型城镇化综合试点为契机，打造现代生态都市

*强化“产城融合”理念，以重大平台引领“一中心四组团”格局完善。*依托市区、松山湖、生态园打造中心组团，完善功能配套，强化城市中心区辐射带动。加快松山湖大道沿线开发。依托水乡打造西北组团，启动水乡新城建设，推进疏港大道延长线等路网工程。依托虎门、长安和长安新区打造西南组团，完善虎门港码头设施和航线，争取长安新区上升为省级战略，对接湾区经济。依托塘厦、清溪、凤岗等打造东南组团，建设现代产业发展集聚区。依托“一区一镇”打造东北组团，加快银瓶创新区建设和招商，强化常平镇辐射带动，建设产城融合发展示范区。

*做好步入城市地铁时代的各项准备工作。*加快轨道交通建设，全面建成2号线，开通运营莞惠城际轨道常平至惠州段，启动有轨电车试验段建设。完善地铁站点周边及东莞火车站、虎门白沙站、东莞东站等交通枢纽功能配套，统筹开发地上地下空间，建设一批高开发强度、多功能复合的城市综合体。加快城市更新改造，优先安排成片改造用地指标，抓好5个示范片区项目，鼓励“工改工”和新型工业楼宇建设。严格查处违法用地和违建行为。

*加快电力设施、信息网络等基础建设。*打好电网规划建设大会战，力争投产110千伏及以上输变电工程19项，进一步强化电力保障。超前建设光纤、基站等通信设施，实现重点公共区域WiFi全覆盖。启动深圳外环高速东莞段、环莞快速路三期等工程，加快虎门二桥等项目建设，推动石大公路大修等项目建成通车。圆满完成省下达我市的高速公路建设任务。

*打造山清水秀的宜居城乡。*积极创建国家生态市、森林城市、水生态文明城市。推进美丽幸福村居建设。加强“小山小湖”保护利用，建成不少于100个社区公园。发展现代农业，加快高标准基本农田建设。推进植物园二期工程。完善森林公园配套。推进节能减排财政政策综合示范城市建设。推广河长制、涌长制。加快挂影洲中心涌水环境综合整治。加快污水处理厂改扩建及次支管网工程，力争石马河、茅洲河水质进一步改善。深入开展大气污染防治行动。把环保限行区域扩大到全市，淘汰全部黄标车。加快水乡“两高一低”企业整治和退出。加大环境监察执法力度。加强东江及联网水库水源保护，实施安全饮用水工程。

*有序加快农业转移人口市民化进程。*加快制定人口发展规划，依法确定合理的人口迁入条件和规模。优化积分制入户政策。增加10%积分入学学位供给。建立与居住年限等挂钩的基本公共服务提供机制，探索制定“同城共享”批次清单，让居住证持有人逐步享有与户籍人口同等的基本公共服务。完善政府向社会组织购买服务机制，为市民提供更好公共服务。

七、积极创新社会治理，营造安定和谐、文明有序的发展环境

*严打各类违法犯罪，时刻绷紧“安全弦”。*保持对涉黄涉赌行为的高压严打态势，强化娱乐场所长效管理。严打涉毒涉黑、“两抢一盗”等犯罪。每个镇街完成1—2个治安重点区域或行业整治。加强刑事侦查队伍能力建设。加快公安指挥中心及情报平台、第二看守所第三监区配套工程建设。发挥视频监控在治安管理中的作用。深化出租屋及流动人口管理服务。严格落实安全生产工作责任制，强化隐患排查整改，加强应急救援演练，开展消防安全、食品安全、极端天气安全等专项整治，切实维护群众生命财产安全。推进和谐劳动关系示范区创建工程，力争企业参与率达70%。健全工会律师团工作机制。完善劳资纠纷预警与应急处置机制，严厉打击欠薪逃匿犯罪行为。加强医患纠纷第三方调解。

*推进交通大整治和“微治理”。*开展为期一年的交通大整治，抓好镇际村际公路等建设，完善路政管养，明晰行车指引，清拆标牌违建，做好绿化美化，改善过镇过村公路脏乱差堵现象。开展交

通拥堵路段“微治理”，通过增划转弯车道、增设中间护栏、查处占道通行、优化路口交通组织等精细化手段，为市民提供安全顺畅的通行环境。

开展社区网格化管理试点，创新基层社会治理。整合村级政务服务中心、综合服务中心和综治信访维稳工作站等，打造统一的综合服务管理平台。选取若干镇村作为试点，划分网格作为基本治理单元，整合综治维稳、城市管理、公共安全、市场监管、自治管理等队伍，在网格内实行“一组多能、一员多职”。加强网格内信息采集和上传，推动网格管理员和各职能部门共享一个系统、一套数据，切实提高基层管理效能。

八、带着对群众的真挚感情，切实办好民生社会事业

着力解决医疗卫生、公共交通、垃圾处理等群众关注的热点问题。加快市人民医院分院、市儿童医院等建设。在公立医院实行医药分开，所有药品零差价销售。优化公立医院绩效考核。提高社区卫生服务水平。整合跨镇公交资源，优化完善公交线网，提高群众公交满意度。加强出租车承包管理，严肃查处违规经营行为。推进“数字城管”建设。加快麻涌、横沥等环保热电厂改造建设，完善生活垃圾处理生态补偿机制。进一步加强内涝整治。推进家禽集中屠宰、生鲜上市。

办好十件实事，带动民生社会事业全面发展。创建省推进教育现代化先进市。提高公办中学经费标准，对民办学校教师发放从教津贴。推进民办学校标准化建设。构建慕课创新教育平台，选取若干学校开展翻转课堂、在线教育等新型教学试点。完善异地中考政策，取消民办学校小升初考试。推进社保扩面征缴，争取让全市社会养老保险退休人员悉数进入全省统筹。低保标准提高至每人每月610元。为户籍老年人购买意外伤害险。非莞籍老人纳入免费乘公交范围。推动残疾人事业发展。完善12345热线功能。促进就业创业。加大市内扶贫力度。加强对口帮扶韶关、揭阳和援疆援藏工作。加快深莞惠“3+2”经济圈建设。进一步深化穗莞合作。积极争创全国双拥模范城“八连冠”。

以贴近群众为宗旨，促进文化文艺事业百花齐放。实施文化惠民工程，创建国家公共文化服务标准化试点城市。大力弘扬优秀传统文化，挖掘重大历史题材，推进电视剧《袁崇焕》拍摄。完善基层文化设施配套。设立专项资金扶持民办博物馆发展。深化全国文明城市创建工作，培育践行社会主义核心价值观，强化未成年人思想道德教育和法治教育。

以高水平承办苏迪曼杯为契机“办赛事、办城市”。努力办好我市承办的首个重要国际体育赛事。全力做好赛事接待、环境布置和绿化美化工作，展现整洁有序、清新亮丽的城市形象。以赛事宣传为切入点，进一步创新城市营销，运用更加符合网络新时代特点的各种渠道和手段，加强城市整体包装推广，全面改善和提升东莞城市形象。

各位代表，2015年是“十二五”规划的收官之年，也是“十三五”发展的谋划之年。“十三五”是我国实现第一个百年目标、全面建成小康社会的关键时期，也是东莞加快转型升级、实现高水平崛起的决胜时期，编制好“十三五”规划具有重大而深远的意义。各级各部门必须强化全局意识，树立战略思维，准确把握东莞发展的阶段特征和时代要求，科学编制全市“十三五”规划纲要，以及科技、交通、教育等18项重点专项规划和各镇街、园区的“十三五”规划，确保各项规划的前瞻性、科学性和可操作性，注重与城乡总体规划、土地利用总体规划等规划的融合，注重各级各类规划的无缝衔接，精心编制好全市未来五年发展的总纲领、路线图和时间表。

各位代表！我们正处在变革与奋进的时代。唯有积极投身新一轮改革开放的伟大实践，才能让东莞再立潮头、再谱新篇。让我们紧密地团结在以习近平同志为总书记的党中央周围，在中共东莞市委的坚强领导下，团结和带领全市人民，主动适应新常态，奋力建设新东莞，在高水平崛起的征程上阔步向前！

名词注解：

多证联办：指对企业登记注册类的多类证照实行网上联办，包括营业执照、组织机构代码证、国税登记证、地税登记证、社会保险登记证、新设外商投资企业外汇信息登记、财政登记证、海关报关单位注册登记证等。

全国股转系统：是专门为国内非上市的中小企业股份转让提供的交易平台，主要解决中小企业股份转让及融资问题。

区域性股权交易中心：指为特定区域内的企业提供股权、债券的转让和融资服务的私募市场，俗称"四板"市场。

"五个一"、明白卡、销号制制度：指我市推出的重大项目引进和建设机制。"五个一"指"一个项目、一个领导、一个班子、一条龙服务、一个月检查"制度；明白卡、销号制指每个项目都办一个卡，存在问题逐条列出来，每解决一个问题打一个勾，所有问题解决了就销号。

电商集群注册：指以企业作为集群注册托管公司，允许多家电商企业将地址登记为该托管公司的住所，以托管公司出具的托管证明代替住所证明办理工商登记，组成企业集群。

中英低碳产业园：指东莞与英国共建的产业园，位于清溪镇，主要接纳英国科研机构和低碳企业项目落户。

速卖通：是阿里巴巴旗下面向全球市场打造的在线交易平台，被广大卖家称为国际版"淘宝"。

"两高一低"企业：指高污染、高能耗、低效益企业。

公安"六大专项"行动：指涉毒、涉黄赌、涉食药假、涉电信诈骗及银行卡、涉车、涉枪等六大打击整治行动。

深莞惠"3+2"经济圈：指深莞惠经济圈扩容，汕尾、河源两市加入经济圈，参与经济圈建设，承接经济圈辐射。

一中心七组团："一中心"指在韶关主城区规划建设约5平方公里的莞韶城，做大做强韶关中心城区；"七组团"指东莞7个镇街与韶关7个县（市）"一对一"结对帮扶。

城市发展陷阱：根据"中等收入陷阱"引申出来的一个概念，是指当一座城市发展到一定程度，原有的发展红利就会逐步消减甚至消失，如果不能有效转变发展方式，就可能会面临掉入陷阱的危险，城市发展出现停滞甚至倒退。

2015年市委、市政府一号文：市委一号文指《中共东莞市委关于全面深化法治东莞建设的实施意见》（东委发〔2015〕1号）；市政府一号文《关于实施"东莞制造2025"战略的意见》（东府〔2015〕1号）。

PPP模式：即Public—Private—Partnership的字母缩写，指政府与社会资本合作参与公共基础设施建设或提供某种公共服务的模式。

融资租赁：指企业购买设备等实物时，由第三方金融机构出资，企业向第三方支付实物租金的新型融资方式。

孵化器"双提升"与"全覆盖"行动："双提升"指提升孵化器的管理能力与盈利能力，"全覆盖"指每个镇街（园区）至少完成一个孵化器建设。

股权众筹：指募资人通过平台集合众多个人投资者小额投资，以支持其创业经营或其他社会事业的新型融资模式。

创客路演：指有创意的创业者，直接面对投资机构或投资者进行演示、争取投资的推介活动。

互联网工厂：指运用互联网连接生产消费环节，实现信息快速流通，具备大规模定制生产能力的新型工厂。

轨道交通TOD开发：即公共交通导向开发，指在站点周边步行5-10分钟半径内，建设集工作、商业、文化、教育、居住等为一体的高密度城区的土地开发模式。

空中连廊：指在地面以上，连接道路周边建筑物及其它城市设施，以步行为主要方式的公共交通系统。

"十大旅游"品牌：即会展游、体育游、乡村游、生态游、水乡游、古迹游、文化游、工业游、健康游、休闲游。

异业同盟：指为实现规模效应和增加额外收益，不同行业或同行业不同层次的商业主体进行资源共享的商业联合体或合作模式。

国际贸易"单一窗口"：指建立一个大数据共享的政府信息平台，投资企业或进出境商品电子数据只需提交一次，就能达到所有相关管理部门的审批要求。

银色人才：即已退休的高端人才。

熟地：指经过征地拆迁和市政基础设施投入，达到"七通一平"，可直接用于建设的土地。

"飞地招商"税收分成：指园区、镇街招引的项目落户在其他园区或镇街，项目产生的效益由招商主体与落户地共享的招商机制。

慕课教育：英文"MOOC"的音译，指运用网络开放课程，进行大规模远程授课的教育模式。

翻转课堂：指课堂外提前运用网络视频等进行授课，课堂上师生面对面交流和完成作业的教学模式。

2015年市政府十件实事

一、加强市民安全保障。投入40845万元，加强防范宣传和守法教育，建立健全医院救治绿色通道，加大刑事技术设备投入，组建刑事技术助理员队伍，提升现场证据发现和提取率，实现命案发案率同比下降5%，破案率达93%以上；加大重点区域及路面监控设备的投入，推动出租屋安防设施的安装，加强研判专班和基层技术队伍建设，提升批量破案效能，实现入室盗抢案件发案率同比下降3%，破案率同比上升3%以上。

二、均衡教育资源配置。投入119306万元，提高对义务教育阶段民办学校学生财政补助标准(包含教科书补助)，小学生每年每人补助金额从1050元提高到1250元，初中生每年每人补助金额从1730元提高到2130元；提供新莞人子女积分制入学（含符合优惠政策新莞人子女入学）学位23830个，同比增长10%；设立民办教育专项资金，加大民办教育扶持力度，提高民办教育教学质量。

三、强化食品安全监管。投入31150万元，加大食品安全监管力度，在全市80%以上的镇街和园区配备食品快检室，对问题食品进行快速抽样检测，及时发现和制止食品制假售假行为；对现有80%以上的食品安全量化C级中小学校食堂进行改造升级，提升食品安全量化等级至B级以上标准，推动我市学校食堂食品安全保障水平整体提升；强化食品安全监管，提高食品抽检频次，全年抽检蔬菜生产环节不少于15万批次，牛猪不少于53万批次，水产品样本不少于5580批次，生产环节不少于2000批次，流通环节不少于1800批次，餐饮服务环节不少于1000批次，定期发布不合格食品抽检信息；整合莞城、东城、南城、万江4街道的生猪定点屠宰场，建成市中心定点屠宰场，加快我市生猪定点屠宰现代化建设，提高肉食质量卫生安全水平。

四、改善大气环境质量。投入105398万元，实施6项大气污染专项整治行动，加强空气质量监测，力争全市大气质量优于2014年。引导水乡经济区不少于33家“两高一低”造纸企业退出；对全市21个大型煤炭堆场和9个干散货码头的扬尘进行整治；基本完成全市“黄标车”淘汰工作任务；完成400家餐饮服务单位的油烟污染整治；强化对430家挥发性有机化合物重点排放企业的监管；淘汰整治100台高污染禁燃区外高污染燃料锅炉；完成石龙镇、厚街镇及生态园3个空气质量监测子站的建设。

五、提升交通服务能力。投入33680万元，对女性满65周岁以上、男性满70周岁以上的非莞籍老年人实行免费乘公交政策，惠及约4.6万人；对东莞巴士公司投放运营的跨镇公交线路实行降低20%票价优惠，逐步推行城市公共交通低票价政策；新增和更新500辆清洁能源或新能源公交车，新开通跨镇公交里程达1000公里以上；实施莞深高速南段改造提速，实现全线提速至120公里/小时；整治市区繁忙路段，完成环城南路台心医院和光明隧道等11个路口或路段整治，改善交通秩序。

六、提高民生保障水平。投入24008万元，提高全市最低生活保障标准，从510元/人/月提高至610元/人/月；提高全市离退休人员养老保险待遇；提高村（社区）退休人员基本养老金最低保障线至每人每月680元，与企业退休人员待遇水平持平，惠及约1.6万人；在全市所有公立医院实施医药分开，取消药品加成，实行全部药品零差价销售，减轻群众医药费用负担；提高社区卫生服务水平，实现全市开展家庭医生式服务的社区卫生服务机构达40%以上。

七、优化公共文化服务。投入3489万元，开展文化演出，惠及约30万人；组织文化培训，惠及约 1.2 万人；组织放映公益电影 9900 场；扶持业余粤剧团队发展，活跃群众文化活动；举办东莞市千场家庭教育大讲堂进村（社区）活动，完成讲座 1500 场，惠及约 30 万人；进一步开展普及性应急救护培训，完成培训约 5 万人；开展“送法上门”活动 6500 次，增强群众守法意识和安全防范常识。

八、完善配套体育设施。投入 9750 万元，进一步打造全国篮球城市，全市每个镇街各选取 3 个篮球场共 96 个进行升级改造，免费对市民开放；在各镇街、村（社区）群众生活密集的公共场所，更换 205 套全民健身器材，方便群众参与体育锻炼；增加群众性体育场地，建成茶山镇体育馆。

九、打造便民服务平台。投入 2013 万元，实施教育信息惠民工程，完善和推广“微课掌上通”平台应用，为全市所有中小学（幼儿园）学生家长提供免费公益性家校沟通服务；建成全市智能公交管理平台，实现市民实时查询公交路况信息；建成突发事件预警信息发布平台，通过微博、微信和手机智能终端等渠道，为公众提供突发事件实时预警信息；建成东莞市空气质量预报预警系统，为公众提供全市空气质量预报预警信息；升级完善社保公共服务平台，为参保人提供网上、微信和手机社保服务，方便市民查询社保信息。

十、救助帮扶困难群众。投入 15063 万元，完成市社会福利中心的改扩建工程，为全市孤残儿童智慧康复增加 900 个床位；新增 5000 名符合条件的老人家庭安装使用“平安铃”，使全市享受居家养老“平安铃”服务的人群覆盖面达 80%，惠及约 1.2 万人；实施“银龄安康行动”，为本市 60 周岁以上五保户、低保户老年人，以及 75 周岁以上户籍老年人购买 2015 年老年人意外伤害综合保险，惠及约 8.7 万人；推动和帮扶 8000 名登记失业人员实现就业；帮扶东莞生源困难家庭高校毕业生就业，实现 100%就业；为 10000 名残疾人免费体检，建立健全个人健康档案。

第二部分　统计资料

Part Two　Statistics

一、综　合

General Survey

1-1 东莞行政区划（2014年）

Divisions of Administrative Areas in Dongguan (2014)

镇街	村（居）委会		
	个数		名称
合计	村委会	350	
	社区居委会	247	
莞城	社区居委会	8	东正 市桥 北隅 西隅 罗沙 博厦 兴塘 创业
石龙	村委会	7	西湖 忠维 林屋 蒲溪 新维 王屋洲 黄家山
	社区居委会	3	中山东 中山西 兴龙
虎门	社区居委会	30	虎门寨 东方 则徐 大宁 树田 白沙 沙角 怀德 博涌 镇口 村头 新联 九门寨 居岐 金洲 南面 北栅 小捷滘 北面 陈村 东风 武山沙 黄村 南栅 龙眼 宴岗 赤岗 路东 新湾 民泰
东城	社区居委会	23	岗贝 花园新村 东泰 温塘 桑园 周屋 余屋 鳌峙塘 峡口 柏洲边 上桥 下桥 樟村 梨川 堑头 主山 石井 同沙 光明 牛山 立新 火炼树 星城
万江	社区居委会	28	万江墟 万江 石美 莫屋 拔蛟窝 黄粘洲 蚬涌 谷涌 小享 滘联 上甲 新村 新谷涌 共联 水蛇涌 大莲塘 牌楼基 严屋 大汾 流涌尾 金泰 曲海 坝头 胜利 官桥滘 简沙洲 新和 新城
南城	社区居委会	18	鸿福 宏远 胜和 元美 亨美 三元里 篁村 新基 周溪 袁屋边 白马 石鼓 蛤地 西平 雅园 水濂 新城 宏图
中堂	村委会	15	潢涌 三涌 湛翠 凤冲 袁家涌 吴家涌 鹤田 中堂 一村 东向 蕉利 槎滘 下芦 马沥 四乡
	社区居委会	5	中心 斗朗 红锋 东泊 江南
望牛墩	村委会	21	李屋 望东 扶涌 赤滘 五涌 下漕 上合 聚龙江 望联 洲湾 洲涡 杜屋 寮厦 芙蓉沙 官桥涌 横沥 福安 石排 官洲 朱平沙 锦涡
	社区居委会	1	望牛墩
麻涌	村委会	13	麻一 麻三 麻四 大步 东太 新基 川槎 鸥涌 华阳 南洲 大盛 漳澎 黎滘
	社区居委会	2	麻涌 麻二
石碣	村委会	14	石碣 唐洪 黄泗围 西南 单屋 梁家村 沙腰 刘屋 水南 四甲 鹤田厦 涌口 横滘 桔洲
	社区居委会	1	城中
高埗	村委会	18	冼沙 卢溪 宝莲 塘厦 草墩 护安围 保安围 三联 横滘头 低涌 朱磡 新联 欧邓 芦村 高埗 凌屋 上江城 下江城
	社区居委会	1	新创
道滘	村委会	13	南城 南丫 闸口 大鱼沙 小河 永庆 北永 昌平 厚德 九曲 大罗沙 大岭丫 蔡白
	社区居委会	1	兴隆
洪梅	村委会	9	洪屋涡 新庄 梅沙 氹涌 黎洲角 夏汇 尧均 乌沙 金鳌沙
	社区居委会	1	洪梅
沙田	村委会	16	中围 和安 大流 泥洲 杨公洲 福禄沙 阇西 民田 先锋 西大坦 穗丰年 大泥 齐沙 稔洲 义沙 西太隆
	社区居委会	2	横流 滨港
厚街	社区居委会	24	竹溪 厚街 珊美 宝屯 三屯 陈屋 赤岭 河田 寮厦 汀山 环冈 大迳 新围 桥头 南五 新塘 涌口 双岗 溪头 沙塘 宝塘 下汴 白濠 湖景
长安	社区居委会	13	长盛 涌头 霄边 咸西 锦厦 新安 乌沙 新民 沙头 上沙 厦岗 厦边 上角

1-1 续表

(2014年)

镇街	村（居）委会		
	个数		名称
寮步	村委会	20	西溪 凫山 石龙坑 石步 良边 富竹山 塘唇 向西 霞边 上屯 下岭贝 竹园 上底 药勒 刘屋巷 浮竹山 陈家埔 井巷 小坑 长坑
	社区居委会	10	寮步 塘边 横坑 岭厦 新旧围 缪边 牛杨 泉塘 坑口 良平
大岭山	村委会	21	太公岭 大塘朗 下高田 连平 鸡翅岭 马蹄岗 金桔 大沙 百花洞 大塘 水朗 杨屋 矮岭冚 颜屋 大片美 梅林 元岭 大岭 新塘 旧飞鹅 大环
	社区居委会	2	大岭山 农场
大朗	村委会	16	高英 洋乌 洋坑塘 松柏朗 黎贝岭 松木山 犀牛陂 水平 宝陂 石厦 杨涌 沙步 新马莲 佛子凹 蔡边 水口
	社区居委会	12	大朗 佛新 巷头 巷尾 大井头 屏山 竹山 求富路 长塘 黄草朗 圣堂 长富
黄江	社区居委会	7	新市 田美 三新 梅塘 宝山 北岸 长龙
樟木头	社区居委会	10	圩镇 樟罗 百果洞 樟洋 石新 柏地 官仓 裕丰 金河 樟新
清溪	村委会	20	浮岗 上元 清厦 铁松 铁场 谢坑 青皇 大埔 长山头 三中 九乡 三星 渔樑围 厦坭 大利 土桥 重河 松岗 罗马 荔横
	社区居委会	1	清溪
塘厦	社区居委会	22	塘厦 三局 林村 石潭埔 四村 振兴围 大坪 莆心湖 平山 诸佛岭 桥陇 龙背岭 石鼓 田心 横塘 蛟乙塘 凤凰岗 莲湖 沙湖 石马 清湖头 塘新
凤岗	村委会	11	雁田 官井头 油甘埔 凤德岭 塘沥 黄洞 竹塘 竹尾田 三联 五联 天堂围
	社区居委会	1	凤岗
谢岗	村委会	11	黎村 窑山 南面 大龙 大厚 赵林 稔子园 五星 曹乐 谢岗 谢山
	社区居委会	1	泰园
常平	村委会	31	岗梓 塘角 苏坑 袁山贝 金美 还珠沥 朗贝 桥沥 卢屋 九江水 朗洲 陈屋贝 司马 霞坑 漱旧 漱新 黄泥塘 元江元 横江厦 沙湖口 白石岗 松柏塘 上坑 木棆 下墟 板石 田尾 白花沥 桥梓 麦元 土塘
	社区居委会	2	常平 新民
桥头	村委会	11	田头角 李屋 朗厦 岗头 屋厦 禾坑 邓屋 邵岗头 东江 山和 石水口
	社区居委会	6	莲城 田新 桥头 大洲 迳联 岭头
横沥	村委会	16	石涌 隔坑 半仙山 田头 田坑 横沥 村头 长巷 田饶步 六甲 村尾 水边 新四 山厦 月塘 张坑
	社区居委会	1	恒泉
东坑	村委会	14	东坑 坑美 角社 塔岗 黄麻岭 初坑 凤大 黄屋 寮边头 长安塘 新门楼 井美 彭屋 丁屋
	社区居委会	2	草塘 骏达
企石	村委会	19	铁岗 深巷 湖美 博夏 上洞 江边 旧围 清湖 东平 上截 下截 东山 莫屋 杨屋 新南 南坑 铁炉坑 企石 霞朗
	社区居委会	1	宝石
石排	村委会	18	石排 下沙 福隆 庙边王 沙角 黄家壆 赤坎 向西 水贝 田寮 横山 埔心 谷吓 塘尾 李家坊 田边 中坑 燕窝
	社区居委会	1	太和
茶山	村委会	16	上元 茶山 下朗 横江 增埗 卢边 寒溪水 南社 塘角 博头 冲美 粟边 孙屋 超朗 京山 刘黄
	社区居委会	2	茶山圩 茶溪
松山湖	社区居委会	4	松山湖 东部 北部 南部
生态园	社区居委会	1	生态产业园区

1-2 历年东莞行政区划

Divisions of Administrative Areas in Dongguan over Years

单位：个

年份	镇街	村(居)委会		
			村委会	社区居委会
1978	33	526	496	30
1979	33	531	501	30
1980	33	545	515	30
1981	34	554	524	30
1982	34	561	531	30
1983	34	561	531	30
1984	34	542	512	30
1985	33	546	516	30
1986	33	560	530	30
1987	34	580	537	43
1988	33	582	542	40
1989	33	583	544	39
1990	33	583	543	40
1991	33	586	546	40
1992	33	590	549	41
1993	33	590	549	41
1994	33	592	551	41
1995	33	592	551	41
1996	33	593	552	41
1997	33	594	551	43
1998	32	594	551	43
1999	32	593	546	47
2000	32	675	546	129
2001	32	678	546	132
2002	32	678	546	132
2003	32	616	487	129
2004	32	596	440	156
2005	32	596	404	192
2006	32	596	394	202
2007	32	591	386	205
2008	32	591	383	208
2009	32	598	383	215
2010	32	599	383	216
2011	32	594	350	244
2012	32	595	350	245
2013	32	597	350	247
2014	32	597	350	247

注：2013年起，虎门港社区居委会并入沙田镇。

1-3 主要年份户数、人口与自然资源

Number of Households, Population and Natural Resources in Main Years

项　目	单 位	1978年	1990年	1995年	2000年	2005年	2010年	2013年	2014年
户　数									
年末户籍总户数	万户	24.82	32.73	36.43	41.40	46.50	53.05	55.03	55.88
#非农业户	万户	4.37	8.91	10.06	11.44	18.90	27.08	28.54	29.19
人口与劳动力									
年末常住人口	万人		175.62	336.45	644.84	656.07	822.48	831.66	834.31
年末户籍人口	万人	111.23	131.85	143.65	152.61	165.65	181.77	188.93	191.39
#非农业人口	万人	18.49	30.87	35.38	39.61	65.84	92.09	97.34	99.17
人口密度(常住人口)	人/平方公里		712	1365	2616	2662	3343	3381	3392
人口密度(户籍人口)	人/平方公里	451	535	583	619	672	739	768	778
全社会从业人员	万人					388.13	626.25	633.25	660.46
第一产业	万人					13.65	6.05	5.93	5.67
第二产业	万人					250.04	476.94	482.37	450.94
第三产业	万人					124.45	143.26	144.95	203.85
城镇登记失业率	%				0.60	1.29	1.70	2.17	2.26
土　地									
土地面积	平方公里	2465	2465	2465	2465	2465	2460	2460	2460
年末耕地面积	万亩	118.39	88.26	70.86	66.33	50.29	57.69	56.09	55.42
人均耕地面积	亩	1.06	0.67	0.49	0.43	0.30	0.32	0.30	0.29
建成区面积	平方公里			82.48	147.68	620.31	798.48	902.95	922.02
#城区建成区面积	平方公里				28.13	108.10	91.65	111.98	115.61
气　候									
年降水量	毫米	1748.3	1602.9	1664.8	2019.3	1837.6	2165.9	2087.2	1935.6
年平均气温	摄氏度	21.9	22.8	22.4	23.2	22.7	22.4	22.8	22.9
极端最高气温	摄氏度	35.7	37.8	36.2	37.0	37.4	36.1	36.4	36.8
极端最低气温	摄氏度	2.7	4.3	6.7	5.6	1.8	1.9	6.1	3.9
年日照时数	小时	1958.8	1910.2	1935.7	2059.5	1736.3	1699.7	1830.0	1958.8
森　林									
有林地面积	万亩		83.48	91.48	92.16	89.23	87.30	79.29	79.76
林木蓄积量	万立方米		167.18	123.02	136.11	175.38	255.82	262.82	282.90
森林覆盖率	%		31.4	29.7	30.6	33.1	36.7	37.3	37.4
水资源									
大陆海岸线总长度	公里	61.4	61.4	61.4	115.9	92.1	97.2	97.2	97.2
海水养殖可养面积	万亩	5.0	5.0	5.5	2.6	16.9	2.0	0.9	0.9
淡水养殖可养面积	万亩	30.0	30.0	28.0	14.3	30.7	10.0	8.5	12.9

注：1. 土地面积数据来源于市国土局，不包括海域面积。
2. 人均耕地面积按户籍人口计算。
3. 大陆海岸线从2000年起以咸水为界定。
4. 常住人口2006-2010年数据，根据东莞市第六次全国人口普查数据结果重新修订，下同。

1-4 历年土地与自然资源
Land and Natural Resources over Years

年 份	土地面积 (平方公里)	气候				
		年降水量 (毫米)	年平均气温 (摄氏度)	极端最高气温 (摄氏度)	极端最低气温 (摄氏度)	年日照时数 (小时)
1978	2465	1748.3	21.9	35.7	2.7	1958.8
1979	2465	2007.1	21.9	36.5	2.9	1991.4
1980	2465	1434.7	22.3	37.7	3.3	2157.1
1981	2465	2394.9	22.1	35.6	3.2	1792.2
1982	2465	1454.1	22.1	37.5	3.8	1754.1
1983	2465	1947.1	21.8	35.8	3.3	1909.7
1984	2465	1444.5	21.5	35.9	3.1	1749.2
1985	2465	1678.0	21.8	35.8	4.2	1671.7
1986	2465	1665.2	22.2	35.9	3.0	2098.1
1987	2465	1908.8	22.9	37.0	4.3	1816.6
1988	2465	1735.0	22.0	37.0	7.0	1836.5
1989	2465	1567.2	22.5	37.6	5.2	1926.0
1990	2465	1602.9	22.8	37.8	4.3	1910.2
1991	2465	1219.6	23.0	36.6	1.2	1968.8
1992	2465	1827.1	22.3	37.0	4.5	1854.5
1993	2465	2393.6	22.5	35.6	3.0	1965.7
1994	2465	1809.1	23.0	38.2	5.4	1828.6
1995	2465	1664.8	22.4	36.2	6.7	1935.7
1996	2465	1547.4	22.7	37.1	3.4	2036.0
1997	2465	2074.0	22.8	36.3	6.1	1558.1
1998	2465	1844.5	23.6	36.5	5.6	1699.0
1999	2465	1614.5	23.3	37.8	3.1	2015.8
2000	2465	2019.3	23.2	37.0	5.6	2059.5
2001	2465	2042.6	23.3	36.6	6.6	1978.2
2002	2465	1557.4	23.6	36.7	4.5	2046.9
2003	2465	1416.7	23.0	36.1	3.8	2268.7
2004	2465	1705.8	22.8	38.0	3.5	2192.9
2005	2465	1837.6	22.7	37.4	1.8	1736.3
2006	2465	2412.0	22.7	36.8	4.7	1616.4
2007	2465	1806.9	22.9	35.9	6.7	1876.7
2008	2465	2710.9	22.2	36.8	4.8	1879.3
2009	2465	1881.6	22.8	36.3	5.3	1967.8
2010	2460	2165.9	22.4	36.1	1.9	1699.7
2011	2460	1298.6	22.1	36.2	3.2	2120.1
2012	2460	1838.6	22.6	36.7	4.1	1708.7
2013	2460	2087.2	22.8	36.4	6.1	1830.0
2014	2460	1935.6	22.9	36.8	3.9	1958.8

注：土地面积数据由市国土资源局提供，不包括海域面积，下同。

1-4 续表

年 份	森 林			水 资 源		
	有林地面 积(万亩)	林木蓄积 量(万立方米)	森 林覆盖率(%)	大陆海岸线总长度(公里)	海水养殖可养面积(万亩)	淡水养殖可养面积(万亩)
1978				61.4	5.0	30.0
1979	44.4	110.3	14.7	61.4	5.0	30.0
1980				61.4	5.0	30.0
1981				61.4	5.0	30.0
1982				61.4	5.0	30.0
1983				61.4	5.0	30.0
1984	76.6	160.5	21.9	61.4	5.0	30.0
1985	78.3	156.0	28.6	61.4	5.0	30.0
1986	82.4	157.8	30.0	61.4	5.0	30.0
1987	83.9	183.9	34.5	61.4	5.0	30.0
1988	84.3	169.1	34.7	61.4	5.0	30.0
1989	80.9	164.8	31.1	61.4	5.0	30.0
1990	83.5	167.2	31.4	61.4	5.0	30.0
1991	85.0	169.2	31.6	61.4	5.0	29.0
1992	86.3	169.8	31.3	61.4	5.5	29.0
1993	87.3	168.9	31.9	61.4	5.5	28.0
1994	86.1	116.8	28.3	61.4	5.5	28.0
1995	91.5	123.0	29.7	61.4	5.5	28.0
1996	91.9	115.7	29.9	61.4	5.5	28.5
1997	93.5	121.1	29.9	61.4	5.7	28.7
1998	93.4	126.0	30.1	61.4	5.7	28.7
1999	92.2	120.4	30.1	115.9	4.8	28.7
2000	92.2	136.1	30.6	115.9	2.6	14.3
2001	93.3	146.0	31.2	116.0	2.8	12.9
2002	93.8	155.0	31.7	115.9	4.1	11.7
2003	93.3	165.1	32.2	92.1	4.2	10.4
2004	93.3	165.1	33.0	92.1	4.0	10.0
2005	89.2	175.4	33.1	92.1	16.9	30.7
2006	88.9	194.4	33.5	92.1	16.6	30.5
2007	89.1	215.1	35.5	92.1	16.9	30.7
2008	88.6	227.9	36.2	97.2	2.5	15.0
2009	90.1	241.4	36.5	97.2	2.0	10.0
2010	87.3	255.8	36.7	97.2	2.0	10.0
2011	87.4	273.0	36.9	97.2	1.1	10.0
2012	87.6	291.0	37.1	97.2	1.1	10.0
2013	79.3	262.8	37.3	97.2	0.9	8.5
2014	79.8	282.9	37.4	97.2	0.9	12.9

1-5 主要年份国民经济主要指标

Main Indicators on National Economy in Main Years

项　　目	单位	1978年	1990年	1995年	2000年	2005年	2010年	2013年	2014年
国民经济核算									
地区生产总值	亿元	6.11	80.44	296.29	820.25	2183.20	4278.21	5517.47	5881.32
第一产业	亿元	2.72	13.28	21.43	25.91	20.55	16.57	19.55	20.35
第二产业	亿元	2.68	40.53	166.97	450.71	1227.86	2191.78	2622.67	2794.42
第三产业	亿元	0.71	26.63	107.89	343.64	934.78	2069.86	2875.25	3066.55
农村经济									
农林牧渔业总产值	亿元	4.24	23.64	42.69	54.64	42.05	28.31	33.15	33.94
农村集体经营总收入	亿元		7.18	41.23	77.50	120.57	143.38	162.97	171.47
年末耕地面积	万亩		88.26	70.86	66.33	50.29	57.69	56.09	55.42
工　业									
规模以上工业企业指标									
工业增加值	亿元		12.25	64.99	259.44	1062.42	1708.31	2425.62	2490.84
主营业务收入	亿元	2.69	47.27	275.84	988.91	3912.15	7708.17	10830.33	11890.43
年末固定资产原值	亿元	0.78	14.29	60.14	728.85	1856.09	3216.25	4038.04	4213.37
年末固定资产净值	亿元	0.51	11.95	46.26	470.19	1105.26	1783.69	2155.87	2140.63
流动资产合计	亿元	0.26	1.74	21.28	529.82	1873.28	3788.83	5315.55	5699.74
资产总额	亿元		13.51	52.98	1122.60	3345.33	6001.71	8103.32	8582.98
负债总额	亿元				563.04	1858.09	3525.30	4823.75	5070.29
资产负债率	%				50.2	55.5	58.7	59.5	59.1
利税总额	亿元				84.10	183.10	469.59	596.95	610.73
综合效益指数	%				114.0	119.9	130.3	141.1	145.0
能源消费									
单位GDP能耗上升或下降	±%						-2.02	-5.35	-5.88
规模以上工业综合能源消费量	万吨标准煤					1203.77	1496.06	1452.58	1448.37

注：1. 2005年以前地区生产总值采用全国第一次经济普查资料修订的数据；2005-2008年采用第二次经济普查资料修订的数据；2009-2013年采用第三次经济普查资料修订的数据；2013年起，三次产业分类依据国家统计局2012年制定的《三次产业划分规定》，下同。

2. 规模以上工业企业1997年及以前为独立核算企业口径，1998-2005年为全部国有及年销售收入500万元以上非国有企业口径，2006-2010年为年主营业务收入500万元及以上口径，2011年起为年主营业务收入2000万元及以上口径，下同。

3. 2005年以前工业相关数据采用第一次经济普查资料修订的数据，2008年采用第二次经济普查资料修订的数据，下同。

1-5 续表 1

项目	单位	1978年	1990年	1995年	2000年	2005年	2010年	2013年	2014年
运输邮电									
公路通车里程	公里	1259	1325	2327	2518	2871	4751	5002	5145
#高速公路	公里				89	154	217	335	335
旅客周转量	亿人公里	0.94	32.22	44.62	100.19	118.53	129.07	155.98	85.46
水　运	亿人公里	0.43	0.15	0.19	0.14	0.33	0.20	0.20	0.20
公　路	亿人公里	0.51	32.07	44.43	100.05	118.20	128.87	155.78	85.26
货物周转量	亿吨公里	1.51	18.47	26.46	40.47	42.48	109.03	432.28	448.01
水　运	亿吨公里	1.42	11.25	13.66	15.86	15.23	57.95	363.89	372.48
公　路	亿吨公里	0.09	7.22	12.80	24.60	27.25	51.08	68.39	75.52
港口货物吞吐量	万吨	293	233	201	746	2280	5657	11187	12900
邮政业务收入	亿元						6.32	8.86	10.82
电信业务收入	亿元						149.02	166.92	158.64
局用交换机容量	万门		6.98	52.29	103.13	286.25	365.02	295.26	363.83
年末移动电话交换机总容量	万户			4.80	154.20	1059.10	1657.00	2646.40	2033.00
本地电话用户(含小灵通)	万户	0.20	4.90	31.58	78.12	384.52	332.42	314.48	327.22
移动电话用户(含充值卡)	万户		0.05	4.77	123.68	1016.41	1607.60	1850.39	1763.09
#充值卡	万户				42.71	839.58	1433.56	1282.05	1165.96
互联网用户	万户			0.05	13.78	52.90	153.92	216.11	204.86
供用电									
总供电量	亿千瓦时	1.64	18.01	68.00	178.03	415.66	556.89	617.20	655.72
#网供	亿千瓦时	1.64	11.18	38.48	134.91	342.26	547.33	606.15	645.05
全社会用电量	亿千瓦时		18.01	68.00	179.66	419.83	562.00	622.51	660.99
#工业用电	亿千瓦时				136.79	337.43	159.37	453.80	482.95
固定资产投资									
固定资产投资总额	亿元	0.23	7.51	63.14	102.89	597.24	1114.98	1383.94	1427.11
#房地产开发	亿元			8.52	11.25	144.43	298.99	497.66	588.06
房地产开发当年房屋施工面积	万平方米					1160.20	2060.54	2837.95	3585.66
房地产开发当年房屋竣工面积	万平方米					132.90	296.59	264.94	410.35
商品房销售面积	万平方米					321.90	511.25	803.09	643.65
商品房销售额	亿元					119.40	373.77	728.07	626.65
新增固定资产	亿元					173.30	577.86	655.07	728.70
固定资产交付使用率	%					29.0	51.8	47.3	51.1
国内贸易									
批发和零售业商品销售总额	亿元	7.49	43.41	155.69	279.19	824.82	2877.33	4377.68	4806.69
社会消费品零售总额	亿元	2.13	31.97	113.01	235.16	506.29	1223.34	1786.66	1942.29

注：1. 2006年起公路通车里程含专用公路和村道，与往年数据不可比，下同。
2. 2014年客运量和旅客周转量不含城市客运量，数据与往年不可比，下同。
3. 2005年以前国内贸易相关数据采用第一次经济普查资料修订的数据，2005-2008年采用第二次经济普查资料修订的数据，2009-2013年采用第三次经济普查资料修订的数据，下同。

1-5 续表 2

项　　目	单 位	1978年	1990年	1995年	2000年	2005年	2010年	2013年	2014年
城　镇	亿元						1129.10	1668.44	1808.39
乡　村	亿元						94.24	118.22	133.89
物价指数(以上年价格为100)									
商品零售物价总指数	%	100.4	94.9	109.7	100.1	103.0	103.2	100.6	101.2
居民消费价格总指数	%		96.6	113.9	101.5	102.4	102.8	101.9	102.3
消费品价格指数	%		94.9	109.7	100.1	103.0	102.8	101.8	102.6
服务项目价格指数	%		111.0	128.9	112.8	100.4	102.6	102.1	101.4
对外经济贸易、旅游									
进出口总额(海关口径)	亿美元		10.82	153.91	320.45	743.72	1213.38	1530.72	1625.30
进口总额	亿美元		5.14	75.92	148.86	334.42	517.40	622.08	654.61
出口总额	亿美元		5.68	77.99	171.59	409.29	695.98	908.64	970.69
#一般贸易	亿美元			2.32	2.09	17.55	95.41	200.78	268.77
来料加工装配	亿美元			43.46	83.43	161.17	195.54	107.02	110.27
进料加工	亿美元			32.02	85.84	230.43	394.62	575.83	547.23
其他	亿美元			0.19	0.22	0.14	10.40	25.00	44.42
新签利用外资协议(合同)数	宗					773	869	506	465
合同外资金额(新口径)	亿美元					29.80	25.97	40.41	43.15
实际利用外资(新口径)	亿美元					14.68	27.32	39.38	45.29
全年接待旅游人数	万人次		125	89	291	1156	2251	2826	2791
#国际及港澳台旅游者	万人次		27	27	106	169	327	418	356
旅游外汇收入	万美元				7617	28189	67592	144981	157493
财政、金融									
来源于东莞的财政收入	亿元	0.66	3.57	18.01	103.56	331.91	785.10	974.71	1066.21
市公共财政预算收入	亿元			11.56	30.47	103.97	277.84	409.29	455.21
市公共财政预算支出	亿元	0.18	2.28	12.42	33.61	117.04	289.83	444.66	457.68
金融机构各项人民币存款余额	亿元	1.05	68.07	383.68	1228.67	2933.40	5943.39	8630.73	9069.92
金融机构各项人民币贷款余额	亿元	1.96	63.04	254.85	630.84	1500.52	3329.82	4774.23	5331.63
人民生活									
全市职工平均工资	元						16108	30067	36057
城镇在岗职工平均工资	元	474	3552	9682	14051	28253	46576	42870	47600
城镇常住居民人均可支配收入	元		2508	9588	14142	22882	35690	46594	36764
城镇常住居民人均消费性支出	元		2038	9220	12529	21768	25733	33251	27071
农村常住居民人均可支配收入	元	149	1542	4769	8484	13076	20486	27214	22327
城乡居民人民币储蓄存款余额	亿元	0.54	45.51	232.97	672.07	1728.28	3386.85	4476.43	4606.79

注：1. 2013年起，将原属于乡镇企业且符合城镇非私营单位条件的“四上”企业纳入城镇单位从业人员及工资统计的范围，下同。

2. 全年接待旅游人数和旅游外汇收入2002年起是旅游局口径，与往年数不可比。

3. 按照国家统计局的统一部署，自2012年12月起正式启动城乡住户调查一体化改革工作。在经历了为期一年的过渡期后，从2014年起正式发布全体居民人均可支配收入和消费支出指标。新口径指标将城市居民人均可支配收入和人均消费性支出改为城镇常住居民人均可支配收入和人均消费支出，农民人均纯收入改为农村常住居民人均可支配收入，与往年数不可比，下同。

1-6 主要年份国民经济和社会发展主要比例与效益指标

Main Indicators on National Economy and Social Development in Main Years

项　　目	单 位	1990年	1995年	2000年	2005年	2010年	2013年	2014年
户籍人口								
出生率	‰	17.07	17.59	12.11	10.62	10.90	11.79	11.20
死亡率	‰	4.76	4.84	4.59	4.60	4.68	4.61	5.37
自然增长率	‰	12.31	12.75	7.52	6.02	6.23	7.18	5.83
人口性别比(男/女)	%	97.1	100.4	102.4	103.1	103.1	102.9	102.8
地区生产总值中三次产业比重								
第一产业	%	16.5	7.2	3.2	0.9	0.4	0.4	0.4
第二产业	%	50.4	56.4	54.9	56.2	51.2	47.5	47.5
第三产业	%	33.1	36.4	41.9	42.8	48.4	52.1	52.1
全员劳动生产率	元/人				59743	71440	87258	90922
(按全社会从业人员、增加值计算)								
第一产业	元/人				14238	24017	32679	35095
第二产业	元/人				50634	51883	54451	59882
第三产业	元/人				86154	122110	198732	175833
农　业								
农林牧渔业总产值结构								
农　业	%	54.9	45.7	39.6	25.5	52.3	57.1	59.9
林　业	%	1.8	2.1	0.7	0.4	1.0	1.1	1.1
牧　业	%	19.2	30.0	41.4	57.7	19.6	15.8	13.3
渔　业	%	13.3	16.1	14.9	14.9	24.0	23.1	22.8
农林牧渔服务业	%				1.5	3.0	2.9	2.9
工　业								
规模以上工业企业效益								
固定资产利税率	%	8.5	10.7	11.5	9.9	26.3	27.7	28.5
资金利税率	%	6.3	7.7	7.5	5.5	7.8	8.0	7.8
产值利税率	%	5.4	10.0	9.2	4.6	6.1	5.4	5.0

1-6　续表 1

项　　目	单 位	1990年	1995年	2000年	2005年	2010年	2013年	2014年
建筑业								
技术装备率	万元/人		0.37	0.43	0.68	1.02	0.88	0.95
产值利税率	%		3.9	5.4	7.5	8.1	8.7	8.2
劳动生产率(按总产值计算)	元/人	18636	42766	60849	108136	218076	286159	265845
固定资产投资								
固定资产投资相当于地区生产总值比例	%	9.3	17.0	12.5	27.4	26.3	25.2	24.3
全社会房屋建筑面积竣工率	%	45.2	34.1	60.7	22.5	20.7	10.5	11.9
财　政								
来源于东莞的财政收入相当于地区生产总值比例	%	4.4	6.1	12.6	15.2	18.5	17.8	18.1
市公共财政预算支出相当于地区生产总值比例	%	2.8	4.2	4.1	5.4	6.5	8.1	7.7
外经外贸								
利用外资结构								
外商直接投资	%	41.2	63.6	66.0	75.2	86.4	97.7	98.0
外商其他投资	%	58.8	36.4	34.0	24.8	13.6	2.3	2.0
实际利用外资额相当于协议规定外商投资额比例	%	80.6	31.9	89.7	78.9	103.0	96.9	104.0
进出口总额比例								
进口总额	%	47.5	49.3	46.5	45.0	42.6	40.6	40.3
出口总额	%	52.5	50.7	53.6	55.0	57.4	59.4	59.7
#一般贸易	%		3.0	1.2	4.3	13.7	22.1	27.7
来料加工装配	%		55.7	48.6	39.4	28.1	11.8	11.4
进料加工	%		41.1	50.0	56.3	56.7	63.4	56.4
其他	%		0.2	0.2		1.5	2.7	4.5
交通运输								
货运量中各种运输方式比例								
公　路	%	58.2	55.7	63.3	71.7	82.0	71.2	71.0
水　运	%	41.8	44.3	36.7	28.3	18.0	28.8	29.0

1-6 续表 2

项目	单位	1990年	1995年	2000年	2005年	2010年	2013年	2014年
金融								
各项人民币存款相当于生产总值比例	%	84.6	129.5	149.8	134.5	140.0	157.2	154.2
各项人民币贷款相当于生产总值比例	%	78.4	86.0	76.9	68.8	78.4	87.0	90.7
各项人民币存款余额中主要存款比例								
#单位存款	%					40.4	41.2	41.9
财政性存款	%	1.2	2.2	0.3	0.9	0.8	1.2	1.5
储蓄存款	%	66.9	60.7	54.7	58.9	57.0	51.9	50.8
各项人民币贷款余额中主要贷款比例								
#短期贷款	%	90.5	64.6	84.2	48.9	37.1	42.7	38.3
中长期贷款	%	2.1	10.8	7.4	46.7	59.1	53.1	57.2
科技、教育、文化、卫生								
科教文卫事业费占财政支出比例	%	28.7	24.5	25.8	17.8	27.9	34.9	36.3
学龄儿童入学率	%	99.9	100.0	100.0	100.0	100.0	100.0	100.0
小学毕业生升学率	%	95.4	99.2	99.8	99.9	100.0	100.0	100.0
初中毕业生升学率	%	44.1	85.4	90.3	94.1	97.9	98.4	98.4
普通高中毕业生升学率	%	31.2	64.9	70.5	96.5	95.1	95.4	98.4
每一教师负担学生数								
普通高等学校	人		13.7	20.1	15.4	17.6	20.6	22.2
职业技术学校	人	20.6	21.8	19.0	18.2	20.3	22.8	22.5
普通中学	人	20.7	21.1	22.4	19.8	17.7	16.9	16.6
小学	人	24.0	24.2	34.3	27.5	23.3	24.7	24.0
人民生活								
城镇常住居民消费结构								
食品类	%	63.5	39.5	32.3	27.7	33.9	35.2	33.3
衣着类	%	4.7	6.6	3.9	5.9	6.6	6.9	6.1
其他	%	31.8	53.9	63.8	66.4	59.5	57.9	60.6

1-7 国民经济主要指标分月变化情况（2014年，累计绝对数）

Main Indicators on National Economy by Month
(2014, Accumulative Figures in Value Terms)

项　　目	单位	1 月	1-2 月	1-3 月	1-4 月	1-5 月	1-6 月
规模以上工业增加值	亿元		308.87	512.13	691.08	977.49	1210.97
#国有经济	亿元		17.17	25.17	34.63	43.79	4.09
外资型经济	亿元		212.17	343.17	463.35	652.05	807.64
#民营企业	亿元		86.40	155.21	208.51	309.60	385.62
#五大支柱产业	亿元		212.81	362.03	485.23	688.41	854.13
#四个特色产业	亿元		32.28	50.99	68.94	88.77	109.97
规模以上工业销售产值	亿元		1551.12	2582.18	3490.54	4464.68	5520.49
规模以上工业产品出口交货值	亿元		740.44	1264.08	1706.23	2187.89	2687.74
规模以上工业产品产销率	%		99.3	97.1	97.0	97.3	97.0
规模以上工业企业主营业务收入	亿元		1572.52	2537.45	3484.53	4474.44	5511.32
规模以上工业企业利润总额	亿元		28.22	52.84	84.76	110.87	139.93
固定资产投资总额	亿元		133.63	237.76	347.65	450.41	566.88
#房地产开发	亿元		69.13	101.33	151.85	197.83	240.96
来源于东莞的财政收入	亿元	139.10	216.70	281.08	382.33	459.70	541.80
市公共财政预算收入	亿元	39.88	78.60	116.87	150.16	184.37	228.89
市公共财政预算支出	亿元	33.45	46.10	91.87	107.03	209.39	238.60
金融机构各项人民币存款余额	亿元	8224.56	8330.45	8704.57	8474.15	8560.14	8941.33
#城乡居民储蓄存款余额	亿元	4189.36	4223.45	4459.85	4257.57	4302.05	4580.57
金融机构各项人民币贷款余额	亿元	4836.46	4872.25	4905.92	4955.63	5015.38	5057.77
进出口总额(海关口径)	亿美元	128.44	214.90	340.45	474.31	611.50	744.15
#出口总额	亿美元	78.86	126.50	199.72	276.67	356.41	433.84
新签项目宗数	宗	38	59	97	148	176	220
合同规定外商投资额	亿美元	3.04	6.93	10.53	13.64	17.67	22.87
实际利用外资	亿美元	3.05	5.59	9.79	13.18	17.50	22.14
社会消费品零售总额	亿元		264.62	399.45	524.33	652.47	793.49
居民消费价格总指数	%	103.4	103.1	102.9	102.8	102.9	103.0
服务项目价格指数	%	105.6	103.7	103.0	102.6	102.5	102.2
总供电量	亿千瓦时	39.40	73.14	123.89	174.42	232.12	294.90
全社会用电量	亿千瓦时	39.81	73.92	125.13	176.08	234.28	297.59
邮电业务收入	亿元	14.97	28.71	44.89	60.75	74.36	88.70

注：物价指数以上年同期为100；各项指标1-12月累计不等于年报数。

1-7 续表

(2014年，累计绝对数)

项　　目	单位	1-7 月	1-8 月	1-9 月	1-10 月	1-11 月	1-12 月
规模以上工业增加值	亿元	1435.64	1661.77	1911.18	2124.82	2341.84	2593.54
#国有经济	亿元	4.79	0.29	0.34	0.38	0.43	0.45
外资型经济	亿元	956.90	1106.85	1273.30	1411.83	1552.98	1715.83
#民营企业	亿元	456.20	511.65	584.99	650.66	718.53	801.13
#五大支柱产业	亿元	1004.45	1158.55	1329.26	1475.85	1625.20	1803.81
#四个特色产业	亿元	133.94	158.21	184.56	204.98	225.63	249.66
规模以上工业销售产值	亿元	6522.56	7559.71	8690.21	9664.95	10671.15	11797.08
规模以上工业产品出口交货值	亿元	3160.70	3662.78	4212.50	4684.05	5168.66	5657.72
规模以上工业产品产销率	%	97.2	97.6	97.8	97.8	98.0	97.8
规模以上工业企业主营业务收入	亿元	6521.32	7532.79	8595.90	9599.54	10595.90	11671.06
规模以上工业企业利润总额	亿元	167.87	201.24	238.27	260.01	294.55	331.86
固定资产投资总额	亿元	697.68	842.25	1035.09	1128.15	1243.30	1427.11
#房地产开发	亿元	293.18	357.06	428.64	464.85	518.80	588.06
来源于东莞的财政收入	亿元	681.21	747.19	820.32	921.92	997.96	1066.21
市公共财政预算收入	亿元	261.38	293.69	335.11	376.15	408.35	455.21
市公共财政预算支出	亿元	273.52	305.45	337.53	362.31	395.36	463.77
金融机构各项人民币存款余额	亿元	8710.05	8717.25	8872.82	8815.94	8857.42	9069.92
#城乡居民储蓄存款余额	亿元	4385.14	4407.07	4510.71	4468.99	4474.32	4606.79
金融机构各项人民币贷款余额	亿元	5075.38	5112.56	5156.88	5208.76	5262.42	5331.63
进出口总额(海关口径)	亿美元	886.65	1029.13	1170.77	1312.22	1468.23	1625.30
#出口总额	亿美元	518.78	605.62	692.01	776.79	875.07	970.69
新签项目宗数	宗	263	300	341	385	422	465
合同规定外商投资额	亿美元	26.42	29.84	32.74	35.75	38.82	43.15
实际利用外资	亿美元	28.34	32.06	35.04	37.73	38.84	45.29
社会消费品零售总额	亿元	926.81	1062.48	1197.54	1333.37	1471.00	1615.29
居民消费价格总指数	%	102.9	102.7	102.6	102.5	102.4	102.3
服务项目价格指数	%	102.0	101.8	101.6	101.5	101.4	101.4
总供电量	亿千瓦时	365.21	433.30	496.90	553.23	604.07	655.72
全社会用电量	亿千瓦时	368.46	437.08	501.16	557.89	609.06	660.99
邮电业务收入	亿元	103.11	117.43	130.86	53.39	61.48	69.33

1-8 国民经济主要指标分月变化情况（2014年，比上年同期增长）

Main Indicators on National Economy by Month (2014, Compare with Same Period of Preceding Year %)

项　　目	单位	1 月	1-2 月	1-3 月	1-4 月	1-5 月	1-6 月
规模以上工业增加值	%		6.5	8.0	7.9	7.9	8.2
#国有经济	%		10.5	4.9	6.4	7.2	7.7
外资型经济	%		4.3	5.9	4.8	3.2	3.8
#民营企业	%		13.9	15.5	18.2	23.6	24.1
#五大支柱产业	%		7.5	9.7	9.2	9.7	10.3
#四个特色产业	%		5.1	4.1	3.5	2.4	2.9
规模以上工业销售产值	%		7.1	14.5	11.4	10.3	11.4
规模以上工业产品出口交货值	%		4.1	9.9	6.0	4.7	5.5
规模以上工业产品产销率	%		-0.9	-1.4	-1.6	-0.8	-0.8
规模以上工业企业主营业务收入	%		10.4	12.3	11.7	11.5	12.5
规模以上工业企业利润总额	%		14.0	17.5	28.9	25.8	30.3
固定资产投资总额	%		19.7	19.7	16.0	15.5	15.5
#房地产开发	%		11.4	18.2	25.6	21.1	14.8
来源于东莞的财政收入	%	34.0	20.6	21.7	24.0	21.5	20.8
市公共财政预算收入	%	11.2	10.9	14.8	13.2	12.5	14.1
市公共财政预算支出	%	42.1	-10.9	11.6	-4.0	43.6	33.7
金融机构各项人民币存款余额	%	-4.7	-3.5	0.9	-1.8	-0.8	3.6
#城乡居民储蓄存款余额	%	-6.4	-5.7	-0.4	-4.9	-3.9	2.3
金融机构各项人民币贷款余额	%	1.3	2.1	2.8	3.8	5.1	5.9
进出口总额(海关口径)	%	-1.5	1.4	3.4	5.2	5.3	5.6
#出口总额	%	3.2	1.0	3.3	4.9	5.3	5.3
新签项目宗数	%	-33.3	-28.0	-19.2	-16.4	-22.1	-17.6
合同规定外商投资额	%	-32.6	-5.9	6.6	7.4	7.5	8.3
实际利用外资	%	5.3	12.1	15.3	15.4	16.4	16.8
社会消费品零售总额	%		3.8	8.0	8.0	8.3	8.5
居民消费价格总指数	%	3.4	3.1	2.9	2.8	2.9	3.0
服务项目价格指数	%	5.6	3.7	3.0	2.6	2.5	2.2
总供电量	%	-14.1	2.5	3.5	3.8	3.9	4.8
全社会用电量	%	-14.0	2.6	3.6	3.8	3.9	4.7
邮电业务收入	%	6.5	5.2	5.8	6.6	3.6	2.3

注：存贷款增速为比年初增长，下同。

1-8 续表

(2014年，比上年同期增长)

项　　目	单位	1-7 月	1-8 月	1-9 月	1-10 月	1-11 月	1-12 月
规模以上工业增加值	%	8.6	8.6	9.0	9.1	8.8	8.8
#国有经济	%	6.0	33.0	31.3	36.4	35.3	24.4
外资型经济	%	4.5	4.5	4.5	4.0	3.5	3.7
#民营企业	%	23.7	22.8	23.9	25.1	24.4	23.7
#五大支柱产业	%	10.5	10.7	11.0	11.1	10.6	10.6
#四个特色产业	%	3.6	3.7	4.7	4.0	3.9	4.0
规模以上工业销售产值	%	11.6	11.1	11.1	10.5	9.7	9.1
规模以上工业产品出口交货值	%	6.4	6.1	6.2	5.8	4.8	3.9
规模以上工业产品产销率	%	-0.8	-0.2	0.1	0.1	0.1	-0.3
规模以上工业企业主营业务收入	%	11.9	11.0	10.5	10.2	9.2	8.3
规模以上工业企业利润总额	%	27.6	27.1	26.2	12.8	9.8	10.2
固定资产投资总额	%	15.0	14.8	13.6	11.2	11.0	10.0
#房地产开发	%	14.8	20.9	23.6	20.3	18.3	18.2
来源于东莞的财政收入	%	24.7	20.7	18.2	10.9	13.4	9.4
市公共财政预算收入	%	12.2	11.1	12.3	13.6	11.8	11.2
市公共财政预算支出	%	29.4	29.5	26.8	21.7	19.3	2.9
金融机构各项人民币存款余额	%	0.9	1.0	2.8	2.1	2.6	5.1
#城乡居民储蓄存款余额	%	-2.0	-1.6	0.8	-0.2	-0.1	2.9
金融机构各项人民币贷款余额	%	6.3	7.1	8.0	9.1	10.2	11.7
进出口总额(海关口径)	%	5.6	5.1	4.7	4.2	5.2	6.2
#出口总额	%	5.4	5.2	4.9	4.2	5.7	6.8
新签项目宗数	%	-16.0	-18.7	-16.0	-11.3	-11.3	-8.1
合同规定外商投资额	%	8.5	3.0	1.8	3.1	4.3	6.8
实际利用外资	%	16.5	14.2	12.0	11.2	11.5	15.0
社会消费品零售总额	%	8.5	8.5	8.6	8.6	8.6	8.7
居民消费价格总指数	%	2.9	2.7	2.6	2.5	2.4	2.3
服务项目价格指数	%	2.0	1.8	1.6	1.5	1.4	1.4
总供电量	%	6.1	6.5	7.0	7.0	6.5	6.2
全社会用电量	%	6.0	6.5	7.0	7.0	6.5	6.2
邮电业务收入	%	1.2	0.3	-0.9	19.9	23.6	25.9

1-9 历年地区生产总值

Gross Domestic Product over Years

年 份	地区生产总值（万元）	第一产业	第二产业	第三产业	人均地区生产总值（元）
1978	61122	27235	26781	7106	553
1979	66233	26460	29244	10528	593
1980	72199	26323	33290	12586	643
1981	91131	32772	42980	15379	802
1982	114322	37257	58137	18927	991
1983	130340	39847	68962	21531	1115
1984	159632	45671	78091	35869	1350
1985	226033	61475	116584	47973	1885
1986	300167	81416	135735	83016	2462
1987	392859	98236	177249	117373	3170
1988	554583	118888	282771	152924	4408
1989	609202	126568	279724	202910	4768
1990	804401	132787	405290	266325	6173
1991	959073	134523	503220	321330	5095
1992	1108922	144115	592701	372106	5038
1993	1570491	143953	873114	553424	5850
1994	2170341	174796	1194928	800616	6357
1995	2962892	214306	1669723	1078863	7421
1996	3617502	248645	1994826	1374031	8444
1997	4485981	256388	2432816	1796777	9747
1998	5579964	259437	3056779	2263749	11265
1999	6672386	257863	3670519	2744004	12494
2000	8202530	259087	4507072	3436372	13679
2001	9918905	260968	5405092	4252845	15268
2002	11869374	248791	6488109	5132474	18131
2003	14525186	228165	7981954	6315068	22174
2004	18060258	227087	10160382	7672789	27554
2005	21831961	205546	12278624	9347791	33287
2006	26279791	120089	15065985	11093717	39173
2007	31600489	118991	17546573	13934924	45057
2008	37036004	148251	19016068	17871685	50471
2009	37858259	147877	18360096	19350286	49273
2010	42782106	165719	21917828	20698558	53193
2011	47719336	178776	24175357	23365203	57913
2012	50392120	187556	24446097	25758468	60907
2013	55174708	195518	26226700	28752490	66440
2014	58813173	203493	27944169	30665510	70605

注：人均地区生产总值1990年及以前按户籍人口计算，1991年起按常住人口计算，与以前年份不可比。

1-10 历年地区生产总值指数

Indices of Gross Domestic Product over Years

年份	地区生产总值指数(上年=100)	第一产业	第二产业	第三产业	人均地区生产总值指数(上年=100)	人均地区生产总值指数与地区生产总值指数之比
1979	99.5	86.5	107.0	146.4	98.6	0.991
1980	102.7	90.3	117.3	113.9	102.0	0.993
1981	116.6	115.0	122.1	110.8	115.4	0.989
1982	116.9	105.3	131.0	117.6	115.1	0.985
1983	110.4	104.8	115.7	111.3	108.9	0.987
1984	114.2	109.0	107.0	140.9	112.9	0.988
1985	132.3	118.9	144.5	132.7	130.5	0.986
1986	126.1	111.9	110.3	174.7	124.0	0.983
1987	122.5	111.6	127.7	126.0	120.5	0.984
1988	115.7	90.6	143.7	103.0	114.0	0.985
1989	107.1	99.8	106.2	113.7	105.5	0.985
1990	123.2	104.4	127.6	128.0	120.8	0.980
1991	117.5	103.1	121.5	118.6	108.8	0.926
1992	108.3	100.0	112.6	105.1	92.6	0.855
1993	127.9	79.4	139.2	129.0	104.8	0.820
1994	122.5	107.2	124.7	122.3	96.3	0.786
1995	127.4	110.5	135.1	116.8	108.9	0.855
1996	117.5	109.4	115.5	123.5	109.5	0.932
1997	119.6	104.5	119.8	121.8	111.3	0.931
1998	121.8	100.9	122.1	124.5	113.1	0.929
1999	119.7	102.3	120.6	120.3	111.0	0.928
2000	119.7	99.8	120.7	120.0	106.6	0.891
2001	119.9	103.0	121.6	118.9	110.7	0.923
2002	120.5	97.6	122.6	119.1	119.6	0.992
2003	120.5	90.2	122.3	119.7	120.4	0.999
2004	121.0	90.0	125.6	115.8	120.9	0.999
2005	119.5	102.3	120.0	119.3	119.4	0.999
2006	119.2	58.9	121.9	117.1	116.6	0.978
2007	118.3	89.9	114.8	123.3	113.1	0.957
2008	114.0	110.6	106.1	124.0	109.0	0.956
2009	105.3	102.3	100.3	110.8	100.6	0.955
2010	110.3	101.6	117.1	103.7	105.4	0.956
2011	108.0	100.5	107.4	108.7	105.4	0.976
2012	106.1	100.0	106.1	106.2	105.7	0.996
2013	109.8	100.1	111.9	107.7	109.4	0.996
2014	107.8	102.8	109.1	106.3	107.4	0.996

1-11　历年地区生产总值产业构成

Composition of Gross Domestic Product over Years

单位：%

年　份	地区生产总　值	第一产业	第二产业	第三产业
1978	100.0	44.6	43.8	11.6
1979	100.0	40.0	44.2	15.9
1980	100.0	36.5	46.1	17.4
1981	100.0	36.0	47.2	16.9
1982	100.0	32.6	50.9	16.6
1983	100.0	30.6	52.9	16.5
1984	100.0	28.6	48.9	22.5
1985	100.0	27.2	51.6	21.2
1986	100.0	27.1	45.2	27.7
1987	100.0	25.0	45.1	29.9
1988	100.0	21.4	51.0	27.6
1989	100.0	20.8	45.9	33.3
1990	100.0	16.5	50.4	33.1
1991	100.0	14.0	52.5	33.5
1992	100.0	13.0	53.5	33.6
1993	100.0	9.2	55.6	35.2
1994	100.0	8.1	55.1	36.9
1995	100.0	7.2	56.4	36.4
1996	100.0	6.9	55.1	38.0
1997	100.0	5.7	54.2	40.1
1998	100.0	4.7	54.8	40.6
1999	100.0	3.9	55.0	41.1
2000	100.0	3.2	54.9	41.9
2001	100.0	2.6	54.5	42.9
2002	100.0	2.1	54.7	43.2
2003	100.0	1.6	55.0	43.5
2004	100.0	1.3	56.3	42.5
2005	100.0	0.9	56.2	42.8
2006	100.0	0.5	57.3	42.2
2007	100.0	0.4	55.5	44.1
2008	100.0	0.4	51.3	48.3
2009	100.0	0.4	48.5	51.1
2010	100.0	0.4	51.2	48.4
2011	100.0	0.4	50.7	48.9
2012	100.0	0.4	48.5	51.1
2013	100.0	0.4	47.5	52.1
2014	100.0	0.4	47.5	52.1

1-12 各行业增加值项目（2014年）

Composition of Value-added by Industry (2014)

单位：万元

项 目	增加值	劳动者报酬	生产税净额	固定资产折旧	营业盈余
地区生产总值	58813173	29956920	7826004	8983481	12046768
#农林牧渔业	207558	195517		12041	
工业	27089969	16986965	2867379	3054444	4181181
建筑业	913538	542733	147616	52061	171128
交通运输、仓储和邮政业	1996868	1047423	164778	481940	302727
交通运输和仓储业	1863032	943625	159895	473156	286355
邮政业	133837	103798	4883	8784	16372
信息传输、软件和信息技术服务业	1559616	155543	125188	278896	999990
批发和零售业	7352571	3297006	2789047	185429	1081089
住宿和餐饮业	1472305	1078979	114841	226357	52128
金融业	3708027	832952	398458	58508	2418109
#货币金融服务	3105897	638834	295410	49638	2122015
房地产业	4457653	434514	915423	2256568	851147
房地产开发经营业	1902364	171820	878697	45404	806442
物业管理业	214719	165341	20564	8959	19856
房地产中介服务业	64031	40087	5784	779	17381
自有房地产经营活动	2243970	35769	5940	2198436	3825
其他房地产业	32569	21497	4438	2991	3643
租赁和商务服务业	4065826	1016164	162872	1383468	1503323
科学研究和技术服务业	602632	300701	36914	79553	185464
水利、环境和公共设施管理业	174280	91468	8680	44875	29257
居民服务、修理和其他服务业	881987	704709	37482	53690	86106
教育	1346201	1050869	10299	256412	28620
卫生和社会工作	1019583	766153	15198	114716	123516
文化、体育和娱乐业	266327	146140	30746	56458	32983
#娱乐业	71750	50473	9382	8868	3027
公共管理、社会保障和社会组织	1698231	1309083	1083	388065	
#第一产业	203493	191539		11954	
第二产业	27944169	17490728	3009128	3100720	4343593
第三产业	30665510	12274653	4816876	5870807	7703174

1-13 主要年份支出法地区生产总值

Gross Domestic Product by Expenditure Approach in Main Years

项目	1995年	2000年	2005年	2010年	2013年	2014年
支出法地区生产总值(万元)	2962892	8202530	21831961	42782106	55174708	58813173
最终消费	1502524	4342481	11201390	22984391	29213545	32646496
资本形成总额	1210079	2369818	7148513	12757774	15143838	16790616
货物和服务净出口	250290	1490232	3482058	7039941	10817325	9376061
资本形成率(投资率)(%)	40.8	28.9	32.7	29.8	27.4	28.5
最终消费率(消费率)(%)	50.7	52.9	51.3	53.7	52.9	55.5

1-14 主要年份资本形成总额及构成

Gross Capital Formation and Its Composition in Main Years

项目	1995年	2000年	2005年	2010年	2013年	2014年
资本形成总额(万元)	1210079	2369818	7148513	12757774	15143838	16790616
固定资产形成总额	884671	1775228	6115306	10513989	14357408	15765320
存货增加	325407	594590	1033207	2243785	786430	1025296
比重(资本形成总额=100)						
固定资产形成总额	73.1	74.9	85.5	82.4	94.8	93.9
存货增加	26.9	25.1	14.5	17.6	5.2	6.1

1-15 主要年份最终消费支出及构成

Final Consumption Expenditure and Its Composition in Main Years

项目	1995年	2000年	2005年	2010年	2013年	2014年
最终消费(万元)	1502524	4342481	11201390	22984391	29213545	32646496
居民消费	1262972	3752814	9798031	19852461	24844424	27685082
政府消费	239552	589666	1403359	3131930	4369121	4961414
比重(最终消费=100)						
居民消费	84.1	86.4	87.5	86.4	85.0	84.8
政府消费	15.9	13.6	12.5	13.6	15.0	15.2

1-16 全市企业和个体工商户登记注册年末实有数量（2005-2014年）

Enterprises and Self-employed Individuals Registered at Year-end (2005-2014)

单位：户

项　　目	2005年	2006年	2007年	2008年	2009年	2010年	2011年	2012年	2013年	2014年
工商登记户数合计	353266	403403	476125	504988	505521	518544	506113	540171	567209	629333
#内资企业	13898	12953	13401	13074	12493	12439	12820	13264	14050	14424
#国有	1977	1554	1404	1313	1141	1058	1014	1005	925	890
集体	6478	4989	4487	3385	2899	2180	1968	1846	1706	1549
有限责任公司	1606	1468	1493	7017	7886	7649	8271	8767	9719	10239
外商投资企业	7675	7695	7973	9437	9748	10113	11240	11974	11867	11932
#中外合资	1013	822	718	860	1206	1120	1197	1243	462	449
中外合作	482	379	307	218	197	179	177	167	103	99
“三来一补”企业	9552	8206	7417	6552	5748	4906	4047	3231	2362	1715
私营企业	29017	38282	48955	63241	74229	88650	104689	122703	144794	180829
个体工商户	293124	336267	398379	412674	403284	402405	373265	388932	392901	419584

注：本表数据来源于市工商局。

1-17　个体工商户情况（2014年）

Statistics on Self-employed Individuals (2014)

项　　目	户　数（户）	从业人员（人）	资金数额（万元）	其中城镇		
				户　数（户）	从业人员（人）	资金数额（万元）
合　　计	419584	986697	1098675	210929	493300	514046
农、林、牧、渔业	361	1083	4700	106	325	763
工　业	70500	276378	318675	24462	94522	106874
建筑业	506	1263	2208	263	625	1000
交通运输、仓储和邮政业	2175	5626	8327	1099	2847	3862
信息传输、软件和信息技术服务业	888	1399	945	546	835	518
批发和零售业	276663	523909	546132	147883	298056	282744
住宿和餐饮业	33315	93286	117812	17606	50898	65122
房地产业	28	55	56	21	41	38
租赁和商务服务业	3976	8618	11396	2112	4590	5889
居民服务、修理和其他服务业	27915	68164	77018	15018	36551	40281
卫生和社会工作	37	80	112	28	58	58
文化、体育和娱乐业	530	1775	6262	305	1080	3923
其他行业	2690	5061	5033	1480	2872	2976

注：本表数据来源于市工商局。

1-18 私营工商企业基本情况（2014年）

Basic Statistics on Private Industrial & Commercial Enterprises (2014)

项目	户数（户）	投资者人数（人）	雇工人数（人）	注册资本（万元）	其中：1. 独资企业 户数（户）	投资者人数（人）	雇工人数（人）	注册资本（万元）
合计	180829	331855	1025379	28377133	95775	186683	561865	19320507
农、林、牧、渔业	656	1091	8262	139666	254	461	2752	71388
工业	68569	130613	422752	7986807	27988	53525	169801	3584185
建筑业	8244	14378	45796	2017123	4834	9395	29549	1569509
交通运输、仓储和邮政业	3295	5861	16405	576639	1668	3405	9440	377278
信息传输、软件和信息技术服务业	3338	5786	18980	485618	2099	4070	12252	384248
批发和零售业	57257	100579	303433	5706896	33683	63746	193397	3861877
住宿和餐饮业	2244	3489	15604	265921	1196	2168	9273	169357
房地产业	4026	7535	20210	1238696	2261	4790	12178	858512
租赁和商务服务业	18631	36598	94188	7014502	12423	26448	68149	6116702
居民服务、修理和其他服务业	5602	8742	30806	470124	2737	5086	16021	272182
卫生和社会工作	35	64	374	27764	27	53	143	17479
文化、体育和娱乐业	1924	3388	12487	209389	1459	2725	9917	168218
其他行业	7008	13731	36082	2237989	5146	10811	28993	1869571

1-18 续表

项目	2. 合伙企业 户数（户）	合伙人数（人）	雇工人数（人）	注册资本（万元）	3. 有限责任公司 户数（户）	投资者人数（人）	雇工人数（人）	注册资本（万元）
合计	1047	3189	6947	2509180	170543	318638	945383	24868429
农、林、牧、渔业	66	161	1021	4794	346	665	1713	99460
工业	304	725	2471	18539	63975	125205	380912	7543838
建筑业	1	3	5	25	8207	14352	45590	2016858
交通运输、仓储和邮政业	3	8	12	95	3263	5822	16292	572006
信息传输、软件和信息技术服务业	144	304	865	13792	2437	4732	12842	405174
批发和零售业	74	157	301	3208	55358	98246	297521	5586374
住宿和餐饮业	72	172	701	15353	1672	2840	9436	209483
房地产业	2	9		41	4015	7513	20176	1221662
租赁和商务服务业	260	1249	945	2436412	18008	34867	92122	4459142
居民服务、修理和其他服务业	66	207	444	3628	4862	7914	24871	449056
卫生和社会工作					35	64	374	27764
文化、体育和娱乐业	32	76	128	2198	1517	2940	8127	181779
其他行业	23	118	54	11096	6848	13478	35407	2095833

注：本表数据来源于市工商局。

1-19 历年总供用电

Gross Electricity Supply over Years

单位：万千瓦时

年　份	总供电量	#网供	全社会用电量	#工业用电	照明用电
1978	16375	16376			1741
1979	19271	19271			2338
1980	21659	21569			3372
1981	22247	22247			4650
1982	26871	26351			6272
1983	31527	31527			8052
1984	32617	28566			9484
1985	38183	33907			9934
1986	39305	35100			10204
1987	64258	45129			16657
1988	94842	66295			22347
1989	120861	76762			26139
1990	180142	111800	180142		39677
1991	240471	139841	240471		56504
1992	320003	180902	320003		25578
1993	436231	242205	436231		103583
1994	585763	393312	585763		110357
1995	680030	384764	680004		125135
1996	800300	506062	800300		153093
1997	949296	612907	948296		180583
1998	1094816	724758	1094818		221750
1999	1327788	973427	1343746	1017261	261629
2000	1780290	1349134	1796578	1367883	337044
2001	2077248	1649458	2091668	1616179	584700
2002	2585474	2219054	2598555	2004227	392879
2003	3216468	2846679	3235342	2499705	424869
2004	3728441	3196454	3758498	2822014	527332
2005	4156629	3422603	4198289	3374306	652514
2006	4644506	3676492	4720112	3735651	759384
2007	5078933	4167125	5154025	4061784	859851
2008	5073489	4423085	5141578	3962669	935510
2009	4888467	4318868	4955750	3673716	1011494
2010	5568902	5473261	5619996	4262339	1070692
2011	5793482	5699321	5860652	4351290	1196914
2012	6005828	5911793	6042842	4429317	1274923
2013	6172030	6061530	6225139	4537990	1338917
2014	6557176	6450483	6609853	4829488	1473307

1-20 历年国民经济主要指标人均水平

The Per Capita Level of Main National Economic Indicators over Years

年　份	人均地区生产总值（元）	人均地方财政收入（元）	人均出口总　额（美元）	人均消费品零售额（元）	人均固定资产投资额（元）	人　均用电量（千瓦时）	年末人均储蓄存款余额（元）
1978	553	60	36	192	21		49
1979	593	59	48	224	15		64
1980	643	60	69	281	21		104
1981	802	60	81	354	33		178
1982	991	70	94	417	157		238
1983	1115	73	102	447	157		328
1984	1350	72	110	625	254		520
1985	1885	93	146	781	589		761
1986	2462	132	191	1004	945		1068
1987	3170	163	216	1214	1145		1519
1988	4408	215	253	1959	1315		1965
1989	4768	250	273	2116	392		2529
1990	6173	274	436	2454	576		2592
1991	5095	236	879	1943	732	1280	3074
1992	5038	263	1217	2073	883	1496	3580
1993	5850	385	1318	2615	1345	1791	4131
1994	6357	277	1548	3070	5074	2111	5130
1995	7421	366	2468	3577	1998	2152	6924
1996	8444	268	2553	3489	1879	2224	8300
1997	9747	278	2774	3564	1608	2314	9758
1998	11265	324	2799	3753	1650	2509	10740
1999	12494	344	2851	3806	1662	2528	10890
2000	13679	503	2834	3884	1700	2968	10422
2001	15268	693	2923	4244	1932	3220	12212
2002	18131	845	3626	4907	2926	3971	15297
2003	22174	1030	4275	5645	4876	4939	18788
2004	27554	1261	5369	6506	6940	5734	21836
2005	33287	1585	6240	7719	9106	6401	26343
2006	39173	1922	7062	8934	10516	7036	29364
2007	45057	2658	8588	10301	11994	7349	29577
2008	50471	2851	8931	12008	12869	7007	35146
2009	49273	3009	7180	12482	14239	6450	36950
2010	53193	3455	8653	13777	13863	6988	41179
2011	57913	3799	9506	15368	13099	7113	44956
2012	60907	4307	10282	16372	14267	7304	50700
2013	66440	4929	10942	17902	16665	7496	53825
2014	70605	5465	11653	19392	17132	7935	55217

注：1. 人均指标1991年以前按户籍人口计算，1991年起按常住人口计算；时点数按年末人口计算，时期数按年平均人口计算。
2. 人均指标2006-2010年数据，根据东莞市第六次全国人口普查数据结果重新修订，下同。

主要统计指标解释

Explanatory Notes on Main Statistical Indicators

国内（地区）生产总值 指按市场价格计算的一个国家（或地区）所有常住单位在一定时期内生产活动的最终成果。国内（地区）生产总值有三种计算方法，即生产法、收入法和支出法。三种方法分别从不同的方面反映国内（地区）生产总值及其构成。

增加值 指常住单位生产过程创造的新增价值和固定资产的转移价值。它可以按生产法计算，也可以按收入法计算，按生产法计算，它等于总产出减去中间投入；按收入法计算，它等于劳动者报酬、生产税净额、固定资产折旧和营业盈余之和。

劳动者报酬 指劳动者因从事生产活动所获得的全部报酬，包括劳动者获得的各种形式的工资、奖金和津贴，既包括货币形式的，也包括实物形式的，还包括劳动者所享受的公费医疗和医药卫生费、上下班交通补贴和单位支付的社会保险费、住房公积金等。对于个体经济来说，其所有者所获得的劳动报酬和经营利润不易区分，这两部分统一作为劳动者报酬处理。

生产税净额 指生产税减生产补贴后的差额。生产税指政府对生产单位从事生产、销售和经营活动以及因从事生产活动使用某些生产要素（如固定资产、土地、劳动力）所征收的各种税、附加费和规费。生产补贴与生产税相反，指政府对生产单位的单方面转移支付，因此视为负生产税，包括政策性亏损补贴、价格补贴等。

固定资产折旧 指一定时期内为弥补固定资产损耗按照规定的固定资产折旧率提取的固定资产折旧，或按国民经济核算统一规定的折旧率虚拟计算的固定资产折旧。它反映了固定资产在当期生产中的转移价值。各类企业和企业化管理的事业单位的固定资产折旧是指实际计提的折旧费；不计提折旧的政府机关、非企业化管理的事业单位和居民住房的固定资产折旧是按照统一规定的折旧率和固定资产原值计算的虚拟折旧。

营业盈余 指常住单位创造的增加值扣除劳动者报酬、固定资产折旧和生产税净额后的余额。它相当于企业的营业利润加上生产补贴，但要扣除从利润中开支的工资和福利等。

三次产业 第一产业：指农、林、牧、渔业（不含农、林、牧、渔服务业）；第二产业：指采矿业（不含开采辅助活动），制造业（不含金属制品、机械和设备修理业），电力、热力、燃气及水生产和供应业，建筑业；第三产业：指服务业，是指除第一产业、第二产业以外的其他行业。第三产业包括：批发和零售业，交通运输、仓储和邮政业，住宿和餐饮业，信息传输、软件和信息技术服务业，金融业，房地产业，租赁和商务服务业，科学研究和技术服务业，水利、环境和公共设施管理业，居民服务、修理和其他服务业，教育，卫生和社会工作，文化、体育和娱乐业，公共管理、社会保障和社会组织，国际组织，以及农、林、牧、渔业中的农、林、牧、渔服务业，采矿业中的开采辅助活动，制造业中的金属制品、机械和设备修理业。

发展速度 用以反映社会经济发展程度的相对指标，根据两个时期发展水平的对比而得。由于比较的标准时期不同，发展速度可分为定基发展速度和环比发展速度两种。

增长速度 发展速度 - 1（或 100%）就是增长速度。即增长速度=发展速度 - 1（或 100%）。

平均每年增长速度　我国计算平均增长速度有两种方法，一种是习惯上经常使用的“水平法”，又称几何平均法，是以间隔最后一年的水平同基期水平对比来计算平均每年增长（或下降）的速度；另一种是“累计法”又称代数平均法或方程法，是以间隔年内各年水平的总和同基期水平对比来计算平均每年增长（或下降）的速度。具体计算方法，可参照中国财经出版社出版的《平均增长速度查对表》。

在一般正常情况下，两种方法计算的平均每年增长速度比较接近，但在经济发展不平衡出现大起大落时，两种方法计算的结果差别较大。

本《年鉴》内所列的平均每年增长速度都是用水平法计算的。从某年到某年平均增长速度的年份，均不包基期年在内。如 1981-2014 年平均每年增长速度，是以 1980 年为基期，2014 年为报告期，年份从 1981 年算起，共 34 年。

二、人口与劳动力
Population and Labor Force

2-1 历年总人口数与人口密度

Total Population and Density over Years

单位：万人

年份	户籍人口	按性别分		按农业、非农业分		外来暂住人口	常住人口	人口密度（人/平方公里）
		男	女	农业人口	非农业人口			
1949	68.24	32.87	35.37	56.29	11.95			
1952	71.68	34.53	37.15	58.69	12.99			
1957	77.48	37.50	39.98	62.52	14.96			
1962	79.64	38.07	41.57	64.42	15.22			
1965	86.46	41.83	44.63	70.28	16.18			
1970	98.56	47.91	50.65	81.26	17.30			
1975	107.94	52.70	55.24	90.37	17.57			
1978	111.23	54.34	56.89	92.74	18.29			451
1979	112.04	54.45	57.59	92.86	19.18			455
1980	112.70	54.43	58.27	92.87	19.83			457
1981	114.46	55.36	59.10	94.08	20.38			464
1982	116.19	56.28	59.91	95.32	20.87			471
1983	117.59	57.05	60.54	96.36	21.23			477
1984	118.95	57.80	61.15	96.47	22.48			483
1985	120.85	58.84	62.01	95.36	25.49			490
1986	123.01	59.95	63.06	96.53	26.48	15.62		499
1987	124.86	61.02	63.84	97.20	27.66	25.29		507
1988	126.76	62.09	64.67	97.96	28.80	36.89		514
1989	128.76	63.27	65.49	98.82	29.94	47.19		522
1990	131.85	64.96	66.89	100.99	30.86	65.59	175.62	712
1991	133.65	66.10	67.55	101.79	31.86	80.58	200.01	811
1992	136.06	67.55	68.51	103.35	32.71	114.48	227.78	924
1993	138.92	69.20	69.72	105.18	33.74	121.70	259.41	1052
1994	141.40	70.64	70.76	106.85	34.55	139.09	295.43	1198
1995	143.65	71.97	71.68	108.27	35.38	142.18	336.45	1365
1996	145.25	72.92	72.33	109.11	36.14	143.32	383.17	1554
1997	147.12	74.04	73.08	110.15	36.97	144.68	436.38	1770
1998	148.77	74.99	73.78	110.93	37.84	199.11	496.97	2016
1999	150.82	76.18	74.64	112.09	38.73	244.81	565.98	2296
2000	152.61	77.22	75.39	113.00	39.61	254.72	644.84	2616
2001	153.89	77.94	75.95	113.52	40.37	457.82	654.43	2655
2002	156.19	79.14	77.05	115.17	41.02	433.65	654.84	2657
2003	158.96	80.65	78.31	102.09	56.87	440.45	655.25	2658
2004	161.97	82.25	79.72	100.49	61.48	486.95	655.66	2660
2005	165.65	84.07	81.58	99.81	65.84	584.98	656.07	2662
2006	168.31	85.43	82.88	97.89	70.42	586.76	685.66	2782
2007	171.26	87.00	84.26	97.59	73.67	557.80	717.02	2909
2008	174.86	88.88	85.98	98.06	76.80	552.50	750.60	3045
2009	178.73	90.78	87.95	97.27	81.46	429.96	786.08	3189
2010	181.77	92.27	89.50	89.68	92.09	411.47	822.48	3343
2011	184.77	93.76	91.01	90.31	94.46	413.62	825.48	3356
2012	187.02	94.92	92.10	91.05	95.96	416.74	829.23	3371
2013	188.93	95.83	93.10	91.59	97.34	434.68	831.66	3381
2014	191.39	97.02	94.37	92.21	99.17	415.86	834.31	3392

注：1. 人口密度1990年以前户籍人口计算，1990年起按常住人口计算。
2. 常住人口2006-2010年数据，根据东莞市第六次全国人口普查数据结果重新修订，下同。

2-2 主要年份户籍人口与劳动力指标

Main Indicators of Household Population and Labor in Main Years

指　　标	单 位	1990年	1995年	2000年	2005年	2010年	2013年	2014年
年末户籍人口	人	1318526	1436525	1526090	1656541	1817709	1889306	1913879
#农业人口	人	1009857	1082703	1130002	998159	896789	915868	922138
人口性别比(女性人口=100)	%	97.1	100.4	102.4	103.1	103.1	102.9	102.8
人口密度	人/平方公里	535	583	619	672	739	768	778
人口出生率	‰	17.1	17.6	12.1	10.6	10.9	11.8	11.2
人口死亡率	‰	4.8	4.8	4.6	4.6	4.7	4.6	5.4
人口自然增长率	‰	12.3	12.8	7.5	6.0	6.2	7.2	5.8
人口净迁移率	‰	1.9	1.9	2.2	16.4	12.0	4.1	7.7
城镇本年新登记的失业人员	人		6536	6524	7080	3207	7289	9143
城镇失业人员安置就业人数	人			5683	6088	3796	7213	8343

2-3 历年户籍人口自然变动情况

Changes of Household Population over Years

年 份	出 生		死 亡		自然增长	
	人 数（人）	出生率（‰）	人 数（人）	死亡率（‰）	人 数（人）	自然增长率（‰）
1978	20728	18.73	5451	4.92	15277	13.81
1979	26931	24.13	5755	5.13	21176	19.00
1980	27428	24.41	5747	5.10	21681	19.31
1981	24828	21.86	6016	5.29	18812	16.57
1982	21991	19.07	5681	4.93	16310	14.14
1983	19573	16.74	6100	5.21	13473	11.53
1984	18380	15.54	5841	4.94	12539	10.60
1985	18432	15.37	5439	4.54	12993	10.83
1986	20049	16.44	5955	4.88	14094	11.56
1987	19962	16.11	5502	4.44	14459	11.67
1988	21077	16.75	5863	4.66	15214	12.09
1989	23457	17.06	5966	4.67	17491	12.39
1990	22238	17.07	6208	4.76	16030	12.31
1991	23771	17.91	6070	4.57	17701	13.34
1992	26040	19.31	6485	4.81	19555	14.50
1993	25270	18.38	6833	4.97	18437	13.41
1994	24152	17.88	6319	4.51	17833	13.37
1995	25312	17.59	6898	4.84	18414	12.75
1996	24635	17.05	7333	5.08	17302	11.97
1997	24106	16.50	6448	4.41	17658	12.09
1998	22563	15.31	6553	4.45	16010	10.86
1999	21673	14.55	6460	4.34	15213	10.22
2000	18260	12.11	6923	4.59	11337	7.52
2001	17083	11.16	6344	4.14	10739	7.01
2002	16029	10.35	6873	4.44	9156	5.91
2003	16204	10.34	7346	4.69	8858	5.65
2004	17312	10.86	7814	4.90	9498	5.96
2005	17301	10.62	7497	4.60	9804	6.02
2006	16819	10.14	7103	4.28	9716	5.86
2007	17482	10.39	7418	4.41	10064	5.98
2008	18382	10.77	7752	4.54	10630	6.23
2009	18584	10.67	7587	4.36	10997	6.31
2010	19509	10.90	8367	4.68	11142	6.23
2011	19884	10.92	8728	4.79	11156	6.13
2012	24712	13.32	9684	5.22	15028	8.10
2013	22222	11.79	8693	4.61	13529	7.18
2014	21383	11.20	10253	5.37	11130	5.83

2-4 历年户籍人口迁移变动情况

Changes of Household Migration over Years

年 份	迁 入		迁 出		总迁移		净迁移	
	人 数 (人)	迁入率 (‰)	人 数 (人)	迁出率 (‰)	人 数 (人)	总迁移率 (‰)	人 数 (人)	净迁移率 (‰)
1978	10148	9.2	13179	11.9	23327	21.1	-3031	-2.7
1980	13345	11.9	28624	25.5	41969	37.4	-15279	-13.6
1985	19205	16.0	15636	13.0	34841	29.1	3569	3.0
1990	13485	10.4	11061	8.5	24546	18.8	2424	1.9
1991	12628	9.5	12531	9.4	25159	19.0	97	0.1
1992	14622	10.8	11168	8.3	25790	19.1	3454	2.5
1993	10801	7.9	4886	3.6	15687	11.4	5915	4.3
1994	10127	7.2	6406	4.6	16533	11.8	3721	2.7
1995	10312	7.2	7675	5.4	17987	12.6	2637	1.9
1996	9273	6.4	11508	8.0	20781	14.4	-2235	-1.6
1997	10284	7.0	9469	6.5	19753	13.5	815	0.6
1998	12400	8.4	11253	7.6	23653	16.0	1147	0.8
1999	15049	10.0	11497	7.6	26546	17.6	3552	2.4
2000	15618	10.2	12314	8.1	27932	18.3	3304	2.2
2001	15968	10.4	11099	7.2	27067	17.6	4869	3.2
2002	20214	12.9	8033	5.1	28247	18.1	12181	7.8
2003	27143	17.1	7173	4.5	34316	21.6	19970	12.6
2004	29621	18.3	7618	4.7	37239	23.0	22003	13.6
2005	43026	26.0	15798	9.5	58824	35.5	27228	16.4
2006	30710	18.2	11442	6.8	42152	25.0	19268	11.4
2007	26940	15.7	4847	2.8	31787	18.6	22093	12.9
2008	33595	19.2	5974	3.4	39569	22.6	27621	15.8
2009	36387	20.4	7381	4.1	43768	24.5	29006	16.2
2010	28534	15.7	6651	3.7	35185	19.4	21883	12.0
2011	28623	15.5	7425	4.0	36048	19.5	21198	11.5
2012	20698	11.1	8326	4.5	29024	15.5	12372	6.6
2013	18812	10.0	11035	5.8	29847	15.8	7777	4.1
2014	25530	13.3	10748	5.6	36278	19.0	14782	7.7

2-5　历年外来暂住人口与外来劳动力

Temporary Residents and Labor over Years

单位：人

年　份	外来暂住人口总计	按性别分		按省内省外分						
		男　性	女　性	本　省	外　省					
						#湖南省	四川省	广　西 自治区	湖北省	江西省
1986	156222									
1987	252895									
1988	368913									
1989	481850									
1990	655902			333180	322722					
1991	805790			360379	445411					
1992	1144753	440500	704253	494278	650475					
1993	1217010	529096	687914	370770	846240					
1994	1390884	547435	843449	380790	1010094	257348	227793	139137	66189	60638
1995	1421754	581304	840450	371816	1023510	253574	223727	149478	84727	67562
1996	1433157	606524	826633	305821	1106749	232329	223315	137933	90528	79730
1997	1446830	554193	892637	298510	1130981	243384	227077	140483	89140	83272
1998	1991122	850266	1140856	402267	1569963	330241	294149	183734	143662	118685
1999	2448134	1084492	1363642	504722	1921206	391491	387730	236936	173787	149000
2000	2547221	1155277	1391944	485889	2041959	377257	319039	240923	196697	157323
2001	4578163	2138218	2439945	731931	3826830	718295	622166	442904	359872	294740
2002	4336453	1973316	2363137	722894	3593034	685311	555569	394088	389735	294086
2003	4404467	2198324	2206143	665549	3720408	663487	591145	432738	443603	339518
2004	4869462	2347115	2522347	747804	4096599	812976	581272	483329	490063	329715
2005	5849785	2746833	3102952	1036417	4747692	844053	642170	574634	514760	376526
2006	5867555	2775718	3091837	1012637	4807064	875904	617644	556961	531987	367094
2007	5577988	2666292	2911696	986062	4551507	816688	553907	497438	521529	355798
2008	5525022	2657712	2867310	1012341	4468505	828779	533496	488226	517519	353738
2009	4299615	2093055	2206560	889160	3367565	604891	441758	396425	391650	269133
2010	4114745	2010869	2103876	791665	3275768	587153	411005	405051	353414	252936
2011	4136177	2054179	2081998	900560	3194930	571601	370717	387198	350490	264965
2012	4167396	2072592	2094804	940956	3183488	587921	387226	398858	352191	236544
2013	4346839	2186786	2160053	949443	3356719	629746	387979	438718	380395	258666
2014	4158580	2103624	2054956	927905	3189809	570631	350809	441886	356586	252054

2-5 续表

单位：人

年份			外来劳动力	工业	农业	商业	服务业
	港澳台	国外					
1986			104091	87154	9849	2509	4579
1987			180285	154842	13110	4181	8152
1988			292499	260237	16911	5797	9554
1989			405287	365840	19893	7763	11791
1990			572044	518971	25576	10793	16704
1991			701982	633400	25838	17945	24799
1992			1071048	874149	62324	88087	46488
1993			1126813	933147	40177	88524	64965
1994	21213	2703	1241814	1069478	52146	39869	80321
1995	23729	2699	1265368	1084860	54714	52965	72829
1996	18094	2493	1276626	1084330	64732	61092	66472
1997	16048	1291	1307279	1114235	57214	67242	68588
1998	17557	1335	1831939	1577922	68143	100041	85833
1999	20664	1542	2161487	1609539	113324	282938	155686
2000	17547	1826	2448415	2043270	88195	187015	129935
2001	17975	1427	4496771	3681099	174936	283277	357459
2002	18856	1669	4260142	3573355	127584	300642	258561
2003	16986	1524	4327312	3753904	85109	278632	209667
2004	21700	3359	4733903	4078400	98272	315021	242210
2005	59798	5878	5534248	4676454	107933	420810	329051
2006	44653	3201	5669798	4820388	124942	412180	312288
2007	36321	4098	5389490	4480800	102519	460114	346057
2008	37329	6847	5303008	4227211	97597	560345	417855
2009	35630	7260	4134581	3361306	74982	430183	268110
2010	37665	9647	3912274	3191436	92451	402786	225601
2011	31731	8956	3947135	3277984	82025	358941	228185
2012	34069	8883	3979414	3278448	85557	390327	225082
2013	33505	7172	4127952	3431195	93051	397091	206615
2014	32932	7934	3893258	3243831	63386	377854	208187

2-6 主要年份城镇在岗职工年末人数

Number of Employed Persons in Urban Areas at Year-end in Main Years

单位：人

项　　目	1985年	1990年	1995年	2000年	2005年	2010年	2013年	2014年
合　　计	122951	131631	178724	164080	188579	226268	2398215	2342549
第一产业	2432	2053	620	476	483	625	575	28
第二产业	64525	72993	110885	76153	80596	87136	2001324	1956590
工　业	60571	68508	105782	68354	79359	84992	1968085	1922112
采矿业			130	62	59	52		
制造业			99194	62790	71569	77544	1959091	1913403
电力、热力、燃气及水的生产和供应业			6458	5502	7731	7396	9047	8808
建筑业			5103	7799	1237	2144	33239	34478
第三产业	55994	56585	67219	87451	107500	138507	396316	385931
交通运输、仓储和邮政业						6427	28764	29681
信息传输、软件和信息技术服务业						2535	7914	7523
批发和零售业						6215	62297	59595
住宿和餐饮业						739	40225	30490
金融业	2270	4291	9487	13945	16584	20706	28018	28372
房地产业	1551	2529	73	387	427	488	22836	23152
租赁和商务服务业						2270	43709	37048
科学研究和技术服务						1984	10584	12378
水利、环境和公共设施管理业						654	2144	1968
居民服务、修理和其他服务业						105	12767	14250
教育						26138	35732	35988
卫生和社会工作						26859	44534	44480
文化、体育和娱乐业						1711	7468	6923
公共管理、社会保障和社会组织	5854	7887	9711	15733	28542	41676	49194	53904
国际组织								

注：1.2012年起城镇在岗职工含劳务派遣人员。
　　2.2013年起，将原属于乡镇企业且符合城镇非私营单位条件的“四上”企业纳入城镇单位从业人员及工资统计的范围，下同。

2-7 历年分行业城镇在岗职工人数

Numbers of Employers by Sector in Urban Areas over Years

单位：人

年 份	年末城镇在岗职工人数合计	第一产业	第二产业	#工业	第三产业
1978	81971	2875	41179	38729	37917
1979	96807	3051	44905	42251	48851
1980	98587	2637	47374	44737	48576
1981	106626	2897	52638	50370	51091
1982	114119	2133	56391	52418	55595
1983	115926	1978	58139	53246	55809
1984	117627	1933	59129	54916	56565
1985	122951	2432	64525	60571	55994
1986	132744	2252	73922	65674	56570
1987	136666	2359	76393	69985	57914
1988	127098	2702	69385	64631	55011
1989	131039	2397	73042	68738	55600
1990	131631	2053	72993	68508	56585
1991	145873	2083	84992	79389	58798
1992	154712	2043	89713	82611	62956
1993	176578	1933	107296	92212	67349
1994	160872	621	95378	83322	64873
1995	178724	620	110885	105782	67219
1996	174964	497	98061	91228	76406
1997	164987	616	82513	76619	81858
1998	164047	779	80510	70499	82758
1999	163917	583	76905	68860	86429
2000	164080	476	76153	68354	87451
2001	164226	444	76181	69260	87601
2002	164209	431	75384	68348	88394
2003	165978	522	73357	72118	92099
2004	175415	565	78003	76786	96847
2005	188579	483	80596	79359	107500
2006	199878	483	84618	83328	114777
2007	205640	487	81448	79949	123705
2008	207234	459	77982	76563	128793
2009	225990	477	94365	92943	131148
2010	226268	625	87136	84992	138507
2011	246083	966	82164	80648	162953
2012	250225	925	85582	82647	163718
2013	2398215	575	2001324	1968085	396316
2014	2342549	28	1956590	1922112	385931

2-8 主要年份国有单位分行业年末城镇在岗职工人数

Number of Employed Persons in Urban State-owned Units at Year-end by Sector in Main Years

单位：人

指　　标	1985年	1990年	1995年	2000年	2005年	2010年	2013年	2014年
合　　计	56534	63469	71165	78216	94902	121690	151894	153894
按企业、事业、机关单位分								
企业	40201	43538	38022	31988	20401	20348	34405	31793
事业	11362	13072	23147	31506	46382	60310	70402	69835
机关	4971	6859	9996	14722	28119	41032	47087	52266
按国民经济行业分								
第一产业	2264	1956	712	476	483	625	575	28
第二产业	22373	22877	17363	11658	4442	4888	8671	10723
工　业	20919	19390	14610	10119	3471	3638	517	657
采矿业	423	72	130	62	59	52		
制造业	19625	16912	12908	6611	1217	981	517	657
电力、热力、燃气及水的生产和供应业	871	2406	1572	3446	2195	2605		
建筑业	1454	3487	2753	1539	971	1250	8154	10066
第三产业	31897	38571	53090	66082	89977	116177	142648	143143
交通运输、仓储和邮政业					3381	2182	5396	5167
信息传输、软件和信息技术服务业					2243	2275	985	1122
批发和零售业					1582	1790	2884	2279
住宿和餐饮业								
金融业	943	2215	5634	7343	9401	9319	14206	13076
房地产业	138	149	44	98	244	329	10	16
租赁和商务服务业					676	1437	1506	476
科学研究和技术服务					1496	1928	1272	1071
水利、环境和公共设施管理业					484	542	706	790
居民服务、修理和其他服务业					95	105	126	125
教育					23301	26138	27467	27087
卫生和社会工作					17134	26795	36877	36382
文化、体育和娱乐业					1398	1661	1942	1568
公共管理、社会保障和社会组织	4971	6859	9563	15372	28542	41676	49194	53904
国际组织								

2-9 主要年份集体单位分行业年末城镇在岗职工人数

Number of Employed Persons in Urban Collective-owned Units at Year-end by Sector in Main Years

单位：人

指　　标	1985年	1990年	1995年	2000年	2005年	2010年	2013年	2014年
合　计	63383	58749	64923	50592	44251	35106	57342	47310
按企业、事业、机关单位分								
企业	58258	54671	63194	49257	43200	34245	53661	44318
事业	4062	3050	1581	974	1051	861	804	219
机关	1063	1028	148	361				
按国民经济行业分								
第一产业	168	97	33					
第二产业	39858	41795	52334	34958	32778	23765	33137	25914
工　业	37358	40979	49984	28698	32527	22879	25493	19902
采矿业		433						
制造业		40458	48600	27268	30772	21497	22980	17803
电力、热力、燃气及水的生产和供应业		88	1384	1430	1755	1382	2513	2099
建筑业	2500	998	2350	6260	251	886	7644	6012
第三产业	23357	16857	12556	15634	11473	11341	24205	21396
交通运输、仓储和邮政业					3446	3543	814	116
信息传输、软件和信息技术服务业					45	40		
批发和零售业					2078	1818	1845	1560
住宿和餐饮业					307	289	1044	736
金融业	1327	2076	3844	3437	4184	4533	6456	6182
房地产业			29	289	183	159	872	795
租赁和商务服务业					843	677	8359	7701
科学研究和技术服务					16	56	2131	1731
水利、环境和公共设施管理业					237	112	109	116
居民服务、修理和其他服务业							255	5
教育								
卫生和社会工作					92	64	2257	2371
文化、体育和娱乐业					42	50	63	83
公共管理、社会保障和社会组织	1063	1028	148	361				
国际组织								

2-10 主要年份其他所有制单位分行业年末城镇在岗职工人数

Number of Employed Persons in Urban Other Ownership Units at Year-end by Sector in Main Years

单位：人

指　　标	1985年	1990年	1995年	2000年	2005年	2010年	2013年	2014年
合　计	3034	9413	42636	35272	49426	69472	2188979	2141345
按企业、事业、机关单位分								
企业	2312	9413	42597	35272	49426	69472	2182611	2134781
事业	722		39					319
机关								
其他							6368	6245
按国民经济行业分								
第一产业								
第二产业	2294	8321	41188	29537	43376	58483	1959516	1919953
工　业	2294	8321	41188	29537	43361	58475	1942075	1901553
采矿业		48						
制造业		8273	37686	28911	39580	55066	1935594	1894943
电力、热力、燃气及水的生产和供应业			3502	626	3781	3409	6534	6709
建筑业					15	8	17441	18400
第三产业	740	1092	1448	5735	6050	10989	229463	221392
交通运输、仓储和邮政业					412	702	22554	24398
信息传输、软件和信息技术服务业					240	220	6929	6401
批发和零售业					1530	2607	57568	55756
住宿和餐饮业					678	450	39181	29754
金融业			9	3165	2999	6854	7356	9114
房地产业	722						21954	22341
租赁和商务服务业					191	156	33844	28871
科学研究、技术服务业							7181	9576
水利、环境和公共设施管理业							1329	1062
居民服务、修理和其他服务业							12386	14120
教育							8265	8901
卫生和社会工作							5400	5727
文化、体育和娱乐业							5463	5272
公共管理、社会保障和社会组织								
国际组织								

2-11 工业、建筑业企业年末城镇在岗职工人数（2013-2014年）

Number of Urban Employed Persons in Industrial and Construction Enterprises at Year-end (2013-2014)

单位：人

指　　标	2013年	2014年
工业总计	1968085	1922112
按经济类型分		
国有经济单位	517	657
城镇集体经济单位	25493	19902
其他各种经济单位	1942075	1901553
按工业行业分(大类)		
非金属矿采选业		
农副食品加工业	4605	4572
食品制造业	12570	11865
酒、饮料和精制茶制造业	7130	7647
烟草制品业		
纺织业	39598	34065
纺织服装、服饰业	112517	99449
皮革、毛皮、羽毛及其制品和制鞋业	224659	196973
木材加工和木、竹、藤、棕、草制品业	3289	1224
家具制造业	54851	59477
造纸和纸制品业	43400	39881
印刷和记录媒介复制业	37151	36248
文教、工美、体育和娱乐用品制造业	154316	152047
石油加工、炼焦和核燃料加工业	198	214
化学原料和化学制品制造业	18185	15783
医药制造业	2458	2623
化学纤维制造业	868	1197
橡胶和塑料制品业	139292	151018
非金属矿物制品业	13549	13799
黑色金属冶炼和压延加工业	4367	3896
有色金属冶炼和压延加工业	7090	6412
金属制品业	75927	95426
通用设备制造业	71884	74786
专用设备制造业	35514	37055
汽车制造业	17304	17409
铁路、船舶、航空航天和其他运输设备制造业	7183	8056
电气机械和器材制造业	196469	195627
计算机、通信和其他电子设备制造业	607059	581360
仪器仪表制造业	55219	52683
其他制造业	12331	12462
废弃资源综合利用业	55	50
电力、热力生产和供应业	3826	3448
燃气生产和供应业	911	928
水的生产和供应业	4310	4432
建筑业总计	33239	34478
国有经济单位	8154	10066
城镇集体经济单位	7644	6012
其他各种经济单位	17441	18400

2-12 按经济类型分行业城镇在岗职工人数及构成（2014年）

Employed Persons in Urban Areas by Registration Status and Sector (2014)

项　　目	合　计	国有经济单位	城镇集体经济单位	其他经济单位
合　计(人)	2342549	153894	47310	2141345
第一产业	28	28		
第二产业	1956590	10723	25914	1919953
工　业	1922112	657	19902	1901553
采矿业				
制造业	1913403	657	17803	1894943
电力、热力、燃气及水的生产和供应业	8808		2099	6709
建筑业	34478	10066	6012	18400
第三产业	385931	143143	21396	221392
交通运输、仓储和邮政业	29681	5167	116	24398
信息传输、软件和信息技术服务业	7523	1122		6401
批发和零售业	59595	2279	1560	55756
住宿和餐饮业	30490		736	29754
金融业	28372	13076	6182	9114
房地产业	23152	16	795	22341
租赁和商务服务业	37048	476	7701	28871
科学研究和技术服务	12378	1071	1731	9576
水利、环境和公共设施管理业	1968	790	116	1062
居民服务、修理和其他服务业	14250	125	5	14120
教育	35988	27087		8901
卫生和社会工作	44480	36382	2371	5727
文化、体育和娱乐业	6923	1568	83	5272
公共管理、社会保障和社会组织	53904	53904		
国际组织				
各项比重(%)				
第一产业				
第二产业	83.52	6.97	54.77	89.66
工　业	82.05	0.43	42.07	88.80
采矿业				
制造业	81.68	0.43	37.63	88.49
电力、燃气及水的生产和供应业	0.38		4.44	0.31
建筑业	1.47	6.54	12.71	0.86
第三产业	16.47	93.01	45.23	10.34
交通运输、仓储和邮政业	1.27	3.36	0.25	1.14
信息传输、软件和信息技术服务业	0.32	0.73		0.30
批发和零售业	2.54	1.48	3.30	2.60
住宿和餐饮业	1.30		1.56	1.39
金融业	1.21	8.50	13.07	0.43
房地产业	0.99	0.01	1.68	1.04
租赁和商务服务业	1.58	0.31	16.28	1.35
科学研究和技术服务	0.53	0.70	3.66	0.45
水利、环境和公共设施管理业	0.08	0.51	0.25	0.05
居民服务、修理和其他服务业	0.61	0.08	0.01	0.66
教育	1.54	17.60		0.42
卫生和社会工作	1.90	23.64	5.01	0.27
文化、体育和娱乐业	0.30	1.02	0.18	0.25
公共管理、社会保障和社会组织	2.30	35.03		
国际组织				

主要统计指标解释

Explanatory Notes on Main Statistical Indicators

人口数 指一定时点、一定地区范围内的有生命的个人的总和。年度统计的年末人口数是指每年 12 月 31 日 24 时的人口数。

常住人口 指实际居住在某地区半年以上的人口，应抱括：1.居住在本乡、镇、街道，并已在本乡、镇街道办理常住户口登记的人；2.已在本乡、镇 、街道居住半年以上，常住户口在本乡、镇 、街道以外的人；3.在本乡、镇 、街道居住不满半年，但已离开常住户口登记地半年以上的人；4.居住在本乡、镇 、街道，常住户口待定的人；5.原住本乡、镇、街道，人口统计（或登记）时在国外工作或学习的人。

户籍人口 指公民依照《中华人民共和国户口登记条例》在公安户籍管理机关登记了常住户口的人。这类人口不管其是否外出，也不管外出时间长短，只要在某地注册有常住户口，则为该地区的户籍人口。

外来暂住人口 指户口登记地在外县、市，目前在本市暂住的人口。

性别比 反映两性人口之间比例的指标。指在总人口中或在各年龄人口中，男性人数与女性人数之比。通常用每 100 个女性人口相应有多少男性人口表示。

出生率（又称粗出生率） 指在一定时期内（通常为一年）平均每千人所出生的人数的比率，一般用千分率表示。

死亡率（又称粗死亡率） 指在一定时期内（通常为一年）一定地区的死亡人数与同期平均人数（或期中人数）之比，一般用千分率表示。

人口自然增长率 指在一定时期内（通常为一年）人口自然增加数（出生人数减死亡人数）与该时期内平均人口数（或期中人数）之比，一般用千分率表示。

总迁移率 是反映人口迁移变动总规模的相对指标，是某地区一定时期内（通常为一年）迁入人数及迁出人数之和与同时期平均人口数之比，一般用千分率表示。

净迁移率 是反映人口迁移变动的相对指标之一，是某地区一定时期内（通常为一年）迁入与迁出相抵销后的余额与同时期平均人口数之比，一般用千分率表示。

在岗职工 指在本单位工作且与本单位签订劳动合同，并由单位支付各项工资和社会保险、住房公积金的人员，以及上述人员中由于学习、病伤产假等原因暂未工作，仍由单位支付工资的人员。

三、农　业

Agriculture

3-1 主要年份农业指标

Main Indicators of Agriculture in Main Years

指　标	单　位	1978年	1980年	1985年	1990年	1995年	2000年
乡镇从业人员	人	467757	478599	544734	598911	639985	727328
第一产业	人	390585	368322	283425	269460	202138	189349
第二产业	人	51422	94576	167116	228114	283050	362666
第三产业	人	25750	15701	94193	101337	154797	175313
年末耕地面积	亩	1183926	1177400	966725	882602	708595	663304
农业机械总动力	千瓦	248760	354250	667750	1003980	795120	586063
水利建设总投资	万元	413	927	886	5428	16900	35550
化肥施用量(实物量)	吨	113296	100776	150083	235836	124263	103570
农药施用量	吨	4276	3382	2951	3453	1924	1836
农村用电量	万千瓦时	5667	7355	14365	82545	406327	1312931
农林牧渔业总产值	万元	42394	41943	91244	236412	426901	546383
主要农产品产量							
粮　食	吨	532308	529381	488705	494259	227441	204136
糖　蔗	吨	508976	447318	526033	538712	233803	49359
花　生	吨	14157	29015	20963	13411	3724	1960
水　果	吨	26457	23688	189350	282410	243231	129367
水产品	吨	30900	25471	32641	68508	74778	95076
肉　类	吨	26920	27652	33298	62191	97572	179032
#猪　肉	吨	22790	23461	25759	40130	68649	149648
禽　蛋	吨	425	398	2424	6906	5431	4367
森林覆盖率	%			28.6	31.4	29.2	30.6

注：本表乡镇从业人员含部分外来从业人员，下同。

3-1 续表

指　标	单　位	2005年	2010年	2013年	2014年
乡镇从业人员	人	830705	878912	951610	927522
第一产业	人	110612	72856	59340	56786
第二产业	人	447207	448637	472365	444716
第三产业	人	272886	357419	419905	426020
年末耕地面积	亩	502937	576883	560884	554163
农业机械总动力	千瓦	229297	367988	418422	431884
水利建设总投资	万元	59437	78308	89161	89326
化肥施用量(实物量)	吨	52749	41445	32347	29441
农药施用量	吨	1090	819	723	716
农村用电量	万千瓦时	2970738	3950486	4511168	4746936
农林牧渔业总产值	万元	420496	283092	331545	339364
主要农产品产量					
粮　食	吨	20004	12482	12435	12406
糖　蔗	吨	450	800		
花　生	吨	114	115	241	211
水　果	吨	151255	75540	61144	62475
水产品	吨	67381	76268	74526	72660
肉　类	吨	171737	28830	22829	20068
#猪　肉	吨	159169	22339	16965	14844
禽　蛋	吨	1355	386	1057	1130
森林覆盖率	%	33.1	36.7	37.3	37.4

注：1. 2010年起，农业机械总动力数据采用农业局统计口径，下同。
　　2. 2011年起，农村用电量数据采用供电局统计口径，下同。

3-2 主要年份农村经济比例和效益指标

Main Indicators of Proportions and Efficiency in Rural Economy in Main Years

指　　标	单　位	1990年	1995年	2000年	2005年	2010年	2013年	2014年
各产业乡镇从业人员比例								
第一产业	%	45.0	31.6	26.0	13.3	8.3	6.2	6.1
第二产业	%	38.1	44.2	49.9	53.8	51.0	49.6	47.9
第三产业	%	16.9	24.2	24.1	32.9	40.7	44.2	45.9
劳动生产条件								
平均每一农业人口用电量	千瓦时	826	3778	11666	29762	44051	49256	51478
每亩耕地农业机械总动力	瓦特	1138	1122	884	455	638	746	779
平均每亩耕地化肥施用量	公斤	267	175	156	105	72	58	53
平均每亩耕地农药施用量	公斤	3.91	2.72	2.77	2.17	1.42	1.29	1.29
增加值率								
农林牧渔业增加值率	%		57.8	56.9	51.9	58.5	60.2	61.2
劳动生产率(平均每个劳动力创造或生产的)								
农林牧渔业总产值	元/人	3977	6737	7828	5062	3221	3484	3659
农林牧渔业增加值	元/人		3892	4453	2627	1886	2096	2238
粮食产量	吨/人	0.83	0.36	0.29	0.02	0.01	0.01	0.01
蔬菜(含菜用瓜)产量	吨/人	0.75	0.88	0.94	0.55	0.45	0.40	0.42
糖蔗产量	吨/人	0.91	0.37	0.07				
水果产量	吨/人	0.48	0.38	0.19	0.18	0.09	0.06	0.07
畜牧总肉产量	吨/人	0.10	0.15	0.26	0.21	0.03	0.02	0.02
#猪　肉	吨/人	0.07	0.11	0.21	0.19	0.03	0.02	0.02
水产品产量	吨/人	0.12	0.12	0.14	0.08	0.09	0.08	0.08

注：平均每亩耕地化肥施用量按化肥施用实物量计算。

3-3 主要年份农村集体(经联社、经济社两级)资产负债及收益分配

Assets, Liabilities and Income Distribution of Rural Collective Economy in Main Years

单位：亿元

指　　标	2005年	2010年	2013年	2014年
资产负债情况				
资产总额	929.60	1228.20	1316.64	1375.90
负债总额	221.56	292.15	256.37	242.92
资产负债率(%)	23.83	23.79	19.47	17.66
净资产	708.04	936.05	1060.27	1132.98
收益分配情况				
经营总收入	120.57	143.38	162.97	171.47
#直接经营收入	12.83	14.39	15.33	14.20
物业出租收入	77.02	91.65	107.23	114.17
协作服务款	13.07	7.51	7.83	7.74
结汇收入		3.52	1.36	1.03
农业发包及上交收入	3.17	2.09	2.48	2.39
投资收益	5.07	7.07	8.46	9.11
其他收入	9.40	17.15	20.28	22.83
经营总费用	48.05	66.45	69.12	67.67
#直接经营费用	6.46	8.59	8.31	7.42
租赁费用	24.05	32.62	35.97	36.46
经营税金		1.90	2.47	2.93
管理费用	9.34	12.46	12.41	12.39
其他支出	7.92	10.89	9.96	8.47
经营纯收入	72.52	76.93	93.85	103.80
收益分配总额	64.57	92.79	104.63	107.43
可弥补分配的收益总额	3.29	15.79	21.94	21.10

3-4 历年农产品人均拥有量

Per Capita Possession of Agricultural Products over Years

单位：公斤

年 份	粮 食		#稻 谷		蔬 菜(含菜用瓜)	
	按总人口	按农业人口	按总人口	按农业人口	按总人口	按农业人口
1949	312	378	304	368		
1952	379	463	364	444		
1957	373	463	337	419		
1962	414	514	392	486		
1965	513	632	502	618		
1970	463	562	451	546		
1975	473	565	452	539		
1980	471	570	462	558	111	134
1985	408	510	397	497	260	330
1990	379	495	368	480	337	440
1995	160	211	148	196	388	515
1996	168	224	155	207	411	548
1997	169	225	155	207	436	582
1998	167	224	151	203	450	603
1999	165	222	149	200	443	597
2000	135	181	121	163	431	582
2001	83	113	71	97	459	623
2002	34	54	27	43	418	653
2003	19	30	13	20	352	549
2004	19	30	8	12	329	530
2005	12	20	7	12	278	461
2006	6	10	4	8	212	364
2007	6	10	4	7	200	351
2008	7	12	3	6	224	399
2009	7	12	4	7	224	412
2010	7	14	5	10	216	438
2011	7	14	5	10	211	431
2012	7	14	4	9	207	425
2013	7	14	3	7	203	418
2014	6	13	3	5	204	423

注：本表按户籍人口计算。

3-4 续表

单位：公斤

年 份	水 果		猪 肉		水产品	
	按总人口	按农业人口	按总人口	按农业人口	按总人口	按农业人口
1949					5	6
1952					5	6
1957					5	7
1962					8	10
1965	53	66			12	14
1970	71	87			17	20
1975	34	41			20	24
1980	21	26	21	25	23	27
1985	158	197	21	27	27	34
1990	218	283	31	40	53	69
1995	171	226	48	64	52	70
1996	143	190	58	77	56	76
1997	113	151	68	91	63	84
1998	77	103	84	112	65	88
1999	91	122	87	117	63	84
2000	85	115	97	131	61	82
2001	98	132	109	148	58	79
2002	121	190	106	165	53	82
2003	92	143	85	133	48	74
2004	108	175	79	128	44	71
2005	91	152	96	159	41	68
2006	83	143	18	31	28	48
2007	77	135	9	15	28	48
2008	58	104	10	18	41	74
2009	51	94	11	20	41	75
2010	42	84	12	25	42	85
2011	40	82	10	21	42	87
2012	35	71	10	21	41	85
2013	32	67	9	19	39	81
2014	33	68	8	16	38	79

3-5 主要年份基层组织情况

Basic Statistics on Rural Grassroots Units in Main Years

指　　标	单位	1990年	1995年	2000年	2005年	2010年	2013年	2014年
农村基层组织								
镇街政府	个	33	33	32	32	32	32	32
社区居委会、村委会	个	583	594	593	596	599	597	597
镇街户籍总户数	户	327344	364273	414007	465008	530497	550274	558833
#农业户	户	238221	263669	299576	275988	259691	264923	266943
镇街户籍总人口	人	1318526	1436525	1526090	1656541	1817709	1889306	1913879
#农业人口	人	1009857	1082703	1130002	998159	896789	915868	922138
乡镇从业人员	人	598911	639985	727328	830705	878912	951610	927522
按性别分								
男性	人	289258	315892	364866	427840	475996	509024	496671
女性	人	309653	324093	362462	402865	402916	442586	430851
按行业分								
农、林、牧、渔业	人	269460	190061	174201	110612	72856	59340	56786
工业	人	194485	254999	335545	414017	416197	437802	409355
建筑业	人	33629	28051	27121	33190	32440	34563	35361
交通运输、仓储和邮政业	人	29005	40032	31291	40619	40124	46187	48949
信息传输、软件和信息技术服务业	人				16889	31432	42534	45712
批发和零售业	人				65051	82662	94621	96807
住宿和餐饮业	人				32953	48728	58519	59730
其他行业	人				117374	154473	178044	174822

3-6 历年耕地面积

Area of Cultivated Land over Years

单位：亩

年　份	年末实有耕地面积	当　年新增面积	当　年减少面积	粮食占用耕地面积
1949	1398338			1260357
1952	1445016			1283151
1957	1435861			1199575
1962	1214417	15405	75905	1053985
1965	1199611	4142	11473	956906
1970	1203350	11359	8818	944903
1975	1193180	1246	6402	922916
1978	1183926	288	6515	874967
1979	1182292	120	1754	896347
1980	1177400	177	5069	856824
1981	1159963	279	17716	824166
1982	1146458	1086	14591	834028
1983	1121311	216	25363	837642
1984	1077659	664	44316	784763
1985	966725	1655	112589	691895
1986	889780	2350	79295	624471
1987	887369	1986	22271	618066
1988	877308	12374	22435	609332
1989	885694	13885	5499	626334
1990	882602	6991	10083	621564
1991	878980	962	4584	614994
1992	845159	100	33921	532296
1993	753746	6319	97732	391736
1994	718144	11169	46771	382238
1995	708595	12227	21776	394913
1996	674588	6270	40277	391610
1997	663013	6350	17925	382890
1998	663045	156	124	376133
1999	663122	1684	1607	381933
2000	663304	1632	1450	354980
2001	643648	4410	24066	255771
2002	500694		150	116989
2003	492433	1922	10183	81939
2004	489448	625	3610	85988
2005	502937	291	4302	76037
2006	491535		11403	34366
2007	483740		7795	32314
2008	479260	375	4855	40795
2009	516623	9	1212	41561
2010	576883	65649	5362	41922
2011	571850		5033	41461
2012	564267	12181	19621	41282
2013	560884	67	3421	41115
2014	554163	5	6326	41263

3-7 历年耕地面积变动情况

Changes of Cultivated Land over Years

单位：亩

年份	当年增加耕地面积	#新开荒	围海造田	当年减少耕地面积	#国家基建占用	种果占用	鱼塘占用
“六五”时期累计	3900	1152		214575	6687	148244	33462
1981	279	91		17716	1275	7577	4507
1982	1086	215		14591	505	3345	8073
1983	216	135		25363	788	19590	2152
1984	664	148		44316	1122	31072	7694
1985	1655	563		112589	2997	86660	11036
“七五”时期累计	33250	2507	600	38017	9587	9138	2698
1986							
1987							
1988	12374	1199		22435	6971	5379	1871
1989	13885	651	100	5499	1433	330	151
1990	6991	657	500	10083	1183	3429	676
“八五”时期累计	30777	569	150	204784	5339	101880	44542
1991	962	95	150	4584	1463	430	57
1992	100	5		33921	1090	17435	3154
1993	6319	270		97732	808	64790	19032
1994	11169	139		46771	645	16031	16162
1995	12227	60		21776	1333	3194	6137
“九五”时期累计	16092	443	175	61383	2824	26550	9637
1996	6270	194	19	40277	532	16382	5597
1997	6350			17925	797	10168	4027
1998	156		156	124	85		
1999	1684	148		1607	128		
2000	1632	101		1450	1282		13
“十五”时期累计	7248			42311	3114	14531	5704
2001	4410			24066	1406	14434	5704
2002				150			
2003	1922			10183	1587		
2004	625			3610	121		
2005	291			4302		97	
“十一五”时期累计	66033	23627		30627			
2006				11403			
2007				7795			
2008	375			4855			
2009	9			1212			
2010	65649	23627		5362			
“十二五”时期累计							
2011				5033			
2012	12181	138		19621			
2013	67	67		3421			
2014	5	4		6326			

3-8 历年乡镇从业人员（按性别、产业分）

Towmship Employees over Years (by Sex and Industry)

单位：人

年 份	合 计	按性别分		按产业分		
		男	女	第一产业	第二产业	第三产业
1978	467757			390585	51422	25750
1979	468059			373438		
1980	478599	227496	251103	368322	94576	15701
1981	484346	231033	253313	367225		
1982	502066	239398	262668	360387	106294	35385
1983	512240	262608	249632	305715	145787	60738
1984	526766	253922	272844	248406	178527	99833
1985	544734	260439	284295	283425	167116	94193
1986	557048	265132	291916	277085	187920	92043
1987	571077	272044	299033	269984	204802	96291
1988	582425	281299	301126	270357	216508	95560
1989	589920	281420	308500	273377	215634	100909
1990	598911	289258	309653	269460	228114	101337
1991	601467	286328	315139	261271	232797	107399
1992	612142	298997	313145	239845	253218	119079
1993	625571	311208	314363	219230	267438	138903
1994	627366	313942	313424	200833	245562	180971
1995	639985	315892	324093	202138	283050	154797
1996	639492	316928	322564	206543	286166	146783
1997	643671	320844	322827	208030	284919	150722
1998	661604	329713	331891	205300	297418	158886
1999	668473	333136	335337	207432	300506	160535
2000	727328	364866	362462	189349	362666	175313
2001	743662	377491	366171	174786	383363	185513
2002	754294	384417	369877	151487	394770	208037
2003	851484	439406	412078	130930	486298	234256
2004	798954	412687	386267	119347	434172	245435
2005	830705	427840	402865	110612	447207	272886
2006	847361	445915	401446	92819	460758	293784
2007	837283	446755	390528	85246	441523	310514
2008	842933	451325	390608	82059	436029	324845
2009	870156	468137	402019	77502	447662	344992
2010	878912	475996	402916	72856	448637	357419
2011	913251	490951	422300	58767	465239	389245
2012	944317	506083	438234	60062	476215	408040
2013	951610	509024	442586	59340	472365	419905
2014	927522	496671	430851	56786	444716	426020

注：本表乡镇从业人员包含部分外来从业人员，下同。

3-9 历年乡镇从业人员（按主要行业分）

Towmship Employees over Years (by Main Sectors)

单位：人

年 份	合 计	#农 业	工 业	建筑业	交通运输、仓储和邮政业	住宿和餐饮业批发和零售业
1978	467757	390585	46651	4771	2515	2441
1979	468059	373438	85306			
1980	478599	368322	94576			
1981	484346	367225	87204			
1982	502066	360387	92860	13434	15580	3158
1983	512240	305715	124791	20996	8129	5916
1984	526766	248406	147324	31203	15804	12808
1985	544734	283425	133685	33431	20142	16970
1986	557048	277085	150136	37784	25049	18417
1987	571077	269984	167354	37448	25832	20919
1988	582425	270357	181234	35274	27280	21698
1989	589920	273377	183107	32527	28491	21582
1990	598911	269460	194485	33629	29005	22652
1991	601467	261271	201152	31645	29787	25813
1992	612142	239845	222722	30496	32777	29991
1993	625571	219230	236994	30444	39612	33629
1994	627366	200833	245562	28425	39479	35798
1995	639985	202138	254999	28051	40032	36974
1996	639492	206543	258227	27939	41092	40166
1997	643671	208030	258432	26487	37375	37702
1998	661604	205300	271099	26319	36939	38880
1999	668473	207432	273914	26592	37323	39284
2000	727328	189349	335545	27121	31291	48088
2001	743662	174786	357527	25836	32153	50512
2002	754294	151487	361418	33352	34919	57997
2003	851484	130930	451920	34378	35517	62978
2004	798954	119347	398596	35576	38406	83901
2005	830705	110612	414017	33190	40619	98004
2006	847361	92819	427500	33258	43295	102259
2007	837283	85246	406910	34613	41687	113141
2008	842933	82059	402895	33134	40827	117545
2009	870156	77502	413929	33733	40299	123631
2010	878912	72856	416197	32440	40124	131390
2011	913251	58767	431269	33970	41074	138379
2012	944317	60062	441850	34365	43527	146476
2013	951610	59340	437802	34563	46187	153140
2014	927522	56786	409355	35361	48949	156537

3-10 历年农林牧渔业总产值及指数

Gross Output Value and Indices of Agriculture over Years

年份	农林牧渔业总产值(万元)	农业	#粮食	水果	林业	牧业	渔业	农林牧渔服务业
农林牧渔业总产值								
1978	42394	29425	21006	1404	312	5665	3149	
1980	41943	28054	17178	1570	238	6313	2878	
1985	91244	57684	19986	1913	759	12652	6219	
1986	122988	79251	18869	34831	2425	18078	8940	
1987	148414	90502	21593	39295	2330	23324	11930	
1988	203685	109531	29776	33939	4732	36915	26500	
1989	221079	117464	35488	30276	4316	45313	28495	
1990	236412	129032	34543	44268	4324	45405	31449	
1991	242587	130986	30256	44250	4038	47839	32640	
1992	271293	148412	28551	56967	5307	57163	38026	
1993	284539	130666	18519	39505	5489	78919	46737	
1994	347451	158315	22426	44798	6735	101117	60263	
1995	426901	194921	29030	59567	8850	128089	68547	
1996	497161	213018	33620	55763	9149	155112	86992	
1997	514373	232721	35329	53483	4383	176254	81573	
1998	536047	220614	34338	29852	5472	193404	93090	
1999	537442	236429	35549	47159	5640	197474	75495	
2000	546383	216318	19893	46423	3649	226293	81118	
2001	559280	228740	12895	48496	5309	245444	72132	
2002	536729	224452	5680	49790	2346	242928	67003	
2003	490206	209739	3377	54346	1414	203477	67276	8300
2004	441912	163246	3489	46992	2247	199912	67272	9235
2005	420496	107174	4194	35130	1746	242534	62639	6403
2006	212632	116110	2232	29801	3101	50638	31968	10815
2007	199782	114389	2446	27434	3238	38354	33562	10239
2008	255307	129962	3326	22551	3585	53221	60296	8243
2009	253077	131924	3170	22986	2232	49982	60642	8297
2010	283092	148151	3389	22804	2937	55499	67958	8547
2011	306621	160161	3562	28917	2109	63758	71450	9143
2012	320083	169305	3349	25163	1675	63278	76427	9398
2013	331545	189296	2923	27508	3626	52378	76620	9625
2014	339364	203503	2505	28591	3579	45138	77288	9856

注：绝对值按当年价格计算，指数按可比价格计算；从2003年起新增农林牧渔服务业，下同。

3-10 续表

年 份	农林牧渔业总产值(%)	农业	#粮食	水果	林业	牧业	渔业	农林牧渔服务业
指数(1978=100)								
1978	100.0	100.0	100.0	100.0	100.0	100.0	100.0	
1980	98.0	100.3	98.1	89.0	65.6	81.4	88.3	
1985	138.9	131.3	84.6	719.8	154.2	130.7	127.5	
1986	174.6	158.0	78.8	1159.9	677.2	183.5	166.7	
1987	186.4	160.1	80.0	1354.9	416.9	194.9	241.0	
1988	182.1	143.5	79.8	959.0	476.4	215.1	262.2	
1989	181.9	138.0	84.5	784.5	372.4	225.4	288.4	
1990	195.3	150.6	85.7	1005.4	320.6	238.5	316.2	
1991	199.5	149.4	77.3	961.8	286.4	262.1	335.9	
1992	211.3	163.7	60.0	1255.3	325.7	289.3	356.7	
1993	175.5	115.7	32.9	720.2	281.8	320.1	332.3	
1994	188.4	123.9	32.8	905.8	235.5	364.3	382.1	
1995	207.8	132.8	36.8	1022.0	337.0	410.4	407.0	
1996	216.3	122.6	39.3	791.4	312.7	465.1	467.4	
1997	225.0	129.1	40.0	835.4	167.7	532.0	540.4	
1998	227.3	103.6	39.9	407.7	225.3	612.8	659.7	
1999	242.8	140.2	39.9	981.4	297.4	616.2	686.0	
2000	243.3	111.5	32.9	593.1	214.9	697.5	769.6	
2001	246.3	111.8	20.5	634.6	233.4	750.0	766.0	
2002	263.2	150.9	8.5	1336.5	124.5	730.2	652.5	
2003	209.7	105.7	4.6	654.3	62.1	600.5	666.2	100.0
2004	213.5	118.0	3.3	899.9	123.9	563.1	647.9	108.0
2005	222.2	107.7	2.2	861.4	171.4	662.2	653.8	72.9
2006	121.0	108.3	2.4	683.1	246.6	155.2	590.7	121.2
2007	105.6	102.7	2.3	667.9	261.7	93.6	584.9	111.5
2008	118.3	106.0	3.9	520.6	286.3	109.5	899.5	84.2
2009	122.2	109.4	4.3	507.1	178.9	116.9	929.2	84.8
2010	126.2	107.6	4.6	415.3	205.2	132.2	982.2	84.8
2011	126.1	111.2	4.7	425.7	144.5	121.1	983.2	86.1
2012	126.9	108.8	4.3	352.1	111.7	125.1	1034.3	86.1
2013	125.1	111.2	3.7	353.2	240.5	107.2	1022.9	86.1
2014	126.4	118.5	3.1	362.0	236.7	94.8	981.0	86.1

3-11 历年农林牧渔业增加值

Added Value of Agriculture over Years

单位：万元

年份	农林牧渔业增加值	农业	林业	牧业	渔业	农林牧渔服务业
1978	27235	18903	200	3639	2023	
1980	26323	17606	149	3962	1806	
1985	61475	38864	511	8524	4190	
1986	81416	52463	1605	11967	5918	
1987	98236	59904	1542	15438	7897	
1988	118888	63932	2762	21547	15468	
1989	126568	67248	2471	25942	16313	
1990	132787	72474	2429	25503	17664	
1991	134523	72636	2239	26528	18100	
1992	144115	78839	2819	30366	20200	
1993	143953	66106	2777	39926	23645	
1994	174796	79645	3388	50870	30317	
1995	214306	97851	4443	64301	34411	
1996	248645	106537	4576	77576	43507	
1997	256388	115999	2185	87853	40660	
1998	259437	106773	2648	93604	45054	
1999	257863	113438	2706	94747	36222	
2000	259087	102575	1730	107305	38465	
2001	260968	106733	2477	114528	33658	
2002	248791	104041	1087	112605	31058	
2003	228165	96676	658	94708	31313	4810
2004	227087	84939	1155	102730	34569	3694
2005	218212	82306	1162	97864	34412	2468
2006	123936	83612	1913	17938	16011	4462
2007	118991	82374	1997	13586	16810	4224
2008	148250	93585	2212	18851	30202	3400
2009	147877	94998	1378	17703	30375	3423
2010	165719	106684	1812	19658	34040	3525
2011	178777	115332	1301	22583	35789	3772
2012	187556	121950	1033	22413	38282	3878
2013	199488	136350	2237	18552	38379	3970
2014	207558	146584	2208	15988	38714	4065

注：绝对值按当年价格计算。

3-12 历年农作物播种面积

Total Sown Area of Farm Crops over Years

单位：亩

年 份	农作物总播种面积	#粮食	#稻谷	薯类	大豆	甘蔗	花生	蔬菜(含菜用瓜)
1978	2859494	2072184	1715230	66400	36764	131200	155021	68743
1979	2585334	1937441	1676936	62537	37993	110580	185434	63959
1980	2436118	1756854	1624873	49665	39261	92397	232541	58550
1981	2267521	1606926	1525072	48999	32143	131453	264903	63768
1982	2204381	1600137	1511345	57188	35450	125787	217612	82982
1983	2193087	1635344	1530918	71430	32029	110684	152335	119370
1984	2165276	1576777	1468801	77105	31718	98449	173198	153636
1985	1950081	1395692	1293847	70997	28982	96627	159918	139795
1986	1791221	1257126	1174464	54993	31469	67920	152214	159100
1987	1795990	1250934	1165554	57850	28471	63655	130292	184744
1988	1792952	1236359	1151493	55368	27929	69694	113882	208930
1989	1834039	1284184	1199979	55964	26200	85238	101077	211217
1990	1848814	1286028	1194153	61281	26444	85977	97808	229532
1991	1791266	1226573	1138043	60107	22785	90137	85537	238418
1992	1561497	963947	889074	51273	20688	76184	67897	318193
1993	1068053	551155	499223	34449	12843	43720	39062	361826
1994	1009468	536191	482051	32615	7542	36346	25344	367122
1995	1078363	598547	527594	43346	7058	28521	24779	379362
1996	1083418	628347	559499	37989	8276	32620	20805	363331
1997	1082610	624091	560506	32629	8190	41427	18490	369113
1998	1101826	624383	558668	34799	7028	48602	16824	385151
1999	1088854	626481	558508	36329	5597	31641	14305	388173
2000	986022	527689	465616	31754	5290	7566	11969	407304
2001	854229	338467	283351	31214	3947	4610	9405	465659
2002	634205	148184	112388	18265	1983	3193	4746	445447
2003	509504	84782	54970	11154	1550	1879	2823	380252
2004	462244	81207	31108	24683	816	868	1544	350412
2005	410648	62084	34356	9390	1006	950	574	315537
2006	333854	34366	25159	4100	183	575	556	241070
2007	320500	32314	19534	5330	253	1676	340	236490
2008	352222	40352	18781	4381	443	2330	586	287618
2009	370740	41421	18629	5047	140	4144	838	306270
2010	369257	41922	26124	3192		2944	713	300622
2011	366840	41461	26412	4247	418	2395	456	297537
2012	372455	41282	23675	8044	901	2434	930	303778
2013	367808	41115	17974	12484	1088	1733	1025	303783
2014	366082	41263	13713	17035	1242	1050	1152	304555

注：2010年及以前年份，粮食数据不含大豆，下同。

3-13 历年农作物产量

Total Output of Farm Crops over Years

单位：吨

年 份	粮食	#稻谷	薯类	大豆	甘蔗	花生	蔬菜（含菜用瓜）
1978	532308	501074	6458	1948	511492	14157	135603
1979	535342	516263	6568	1982	366424	19100	127918
1980	529381	518591	5432	2245	449907	29015	124859
1981	447540	439534	6318	1722	678160	35506	132846
1982	543349	532998	8430	2162	707764	29930	123117
1983	561246	548073	11345	1875	553174	19662	168878
1984	558216	545548	10946	1980	569225	23076	230454
1985	488705	476399	10304	1771	556983	20963	314539
1986	455243	443760	9422	2050	382608	20056	427138
1987	462830	451032	10058	1920	378094	17019	414261
1988	460929	448923	9950	1965	420391	15119	412436
1989	487648	474476	11052	2023	528463	13746	410879
1990	494259	479350	12452	2184	557102	13411	444377
1991	473663	458425	12998	1838	619884	11510	446204
1992	368083	354298	11070	1763	543657	9323	523806
1993	202097	192018	7366	1035	343133	5594	572376
1994	202356	189688	7929	668	313851	3678	537442
1995	227441	210876	10758	647	246707	3724	557807
1996	243204	224469	11271	806	285732	3120	597732
1997	246901	227163	11487	811	354420	2879	641403
1998	247194	223938	13916	758	411555	2588	668753
1999	247287	223403	14580	566	242773	2204	668822
2000	204136	183485	9730	610	54095	1960	658196
2001	128366	109881	9920	426	33387	1556	706775
2002	53732	42508	5420	244	20224	865	653272
2003	30500	20423	3415	215	8019	395	560523
2004	30374	12230	9803	138	4763	216	532116
2005	20004	11941	2733	147	4433	114	460204
2006	10040	7548	1314	31	3167	99	356347
2007	9864	6467	1732	48	10834	73	342703
2008	11902	6007	1381	95	15286	130	391192
2009	11912	6560	1437	19	23044	113	400335
2010	12482	8768	668		15952	115	392904
2011	12890	9137	888	53	14239	78	389014
2012	12476	8357	1609	162	13032	281	386603
2013	12435	6450	3171	145	9452	241	382619
2014	12406	4965	4674	186	5369	211	390484

3-14 主要年份农作物播种面积、亩产及总产量

Sown Area, Yield Per Acreage and Total Output of Farm Crops in Main Years

单位：亩、公斤、吨

指　　标	1978年			1985年			1990年		
	播种面积	亩产	总产量	播种面积	亩产	总产量	播种面积	亩产	总产量
粮食作物	2072184	257	532308	1395692	350	488705	1286028	384	494259
按品种分									
稻谷	1715230	292	501074	1293847	368	476399	1194153	401	479350
旱粮	290554	85	24776	30848	65	2002	30594	80	2457
薯类	66400	97	6458	70997	145	10304	61281	203	12452
大豆	36764	53	1948	28982	61	1771	26444	83	2184
按季节分									
春收				30978	131	4042	33352	174	5790
夏收	1127790	248	279552	649856	377	244755	614059	399	244890
#早稻	814852	309	251907	620409	389	241413	587821	410	241018
秋收	944394	268	252757	714858	336	239907	638617	381	243579
#晚稻	900378	277	249167	673438	349	234985	606332	393	238332
经济作物				306406			209120		
#甘蔗	131200	3899	511492	96627	5765	556983	85977	6480	557102
糖蔗	130676	3895	508976	91884	5725	526033	83246	6471	538712
果蔗	524	4802	2516	4743	6525	30950	2731	6734	18390
油料作物				160186	131	20974	97808	137	13411
#花生	155021	91	14157	159918	131	20963	97808	137	13411
其他作物				219001			327222		
#蔬菜(含菜用瓜)	68743	1973	135603	139795	2250	314539	229532	1936	444377

3-14 续表 1

单位：亩、公斤、吨

指 标	1995年			2000年			2005年		
	播种面积	亩产	总产量	播种面积	亩产	总产量	播种面积	亩产	总产量
粮食作物	598547	380	227441	527689	387	204136	62084	322	20004
按品种分									
稻谷	527594	400	210876	465616	394	183485	34356	348	11941
旱粮	27607	210	5807	30319	360	10921	18338	291	5330
薯类	43346	248	10758	31754	306	9730	9390	291	2733
大豆	7058	92	647	5290	115	610	1006	146	147
按季节分									
春收	17880	224	4008	20787	287	5966	9665	312	3019
夏收	282978	388	109914	245110	392	96015	23286	306	7136
#早稻	255886	405	103592	225985	397	89729	14713	351	5164
秋收	297689	381	113519	261792	390	102155	29133	338	9850
#晚稻	271708	395	107284	239631	391	93756	19643	345	6777
经济作物	62092			35221			18011		
#甘蔗	28521	8650	246707	7566	7150	54095	950	4666	4433
糖蔗	26488	8827	233803	6775	7285	49359	55	8182	450
果蔗	2033	6347	12904	791	5987	4736	895	4450	3983
油料作物	24779	150	3724	11969	164	1960	574	199	114
#花生	24779	150	3724	11969	164	1960	574	199	114
其他作物	410666			417822			329547		
#蔬菜(含菜用瓜)	379362	1470	557807	407304	1616	658196	315537	1458	460204

3-14 续表 2

单位：亩、公斤、吨

指 标	2010年			2013年			2014年		
	播种面积	亩产	总产量	播种面积	亩产	总产量	播种面积	亩产	总产量
粮食作物	41922	298	12482	41115	302	12435	41263	301	12406
按品种分									
稻谷	26124	336	8768	17974	359	6450	13713	362	4965
旱粮	12606	242	3046	9569	279	2669	9273	278	2581
薯类	3192	209	668	12484	254	3171	17035	274	4674
大豆				1088	133	145	1242	150	186
按季节分									
春收	5202	221	1150	5158	275	1421	5576	287	1601
夏收	17948	306	5501	17300	309	5348	16940	297	5034
#早稻	12017	330	3965	8751	360	3147	5923	369	2183
秋收	18772	311	5831	18657	304	5666	18747	308	5771
#晚稻	14107	340	4803	9223	358	3303	7790	357	2782
经济作物	14084			17549			15638		
#甘蔗	2944	5418	15952	1733	5454	9452	1050	5113	5369
果蔗	2844	5328	15152	1733	5454	9452	1050	5113	5369
油料作物	713	161	115	1025	235	241	1152	183	211
#花生	713	161	115	1025	235	241	1152	183	211
其他作物	313251			309144			309181		
#蔬菜(含菜用瓜)	300622	1307	392904	303783	1260	382619	304555	1282	390484

3-15 主要年份农机总动力、水利、化肥、农药及农村用电量

Basic Statistics on Total Power of Agricultural Machinery, Water Conservancy, Consumption of Chemical Fertilizers and Pesticides, and Electricity Consumed in Rural Areas in Main Years

指　　标	单 位	1978年	1990年	1995年	2000年	2005年	2010年	2013年	2014年
农业机械总动力	千瓦	248760	1003980	795120	586063	229297	367988	418422	431884
#耕作机械	千瓦	42550	157910	83482	51848	16386	24079	25904	25828
排灌机械	千瓦	104050	178280	112392	91745	36251	99716	116350	123142
收获机械	千瓦	6180	84130	54722	51084	969	2280	616	766
运输机械	千瓦	16930	322950	397735	184949	41678	12463	15195	19747
水利建设总投资	万元	413	5428	16900	35550	59437	78308	89161	89326
化肥施用实物量	吨	113296	235836	124263	103570	52749	41445	32347	29441
氮肥	吨	86371	84642	43441	30214	14439	10214	7732	6764
磷肥	吨	23164	52483	28939	23939	10967	8055	6554	5773
钾肥	吨	3761	26131	16915	14606	6403	5030	3973	3759
复合肥	吨		39098	34968	34811	20940	18146	14088	13145
农药施用量	吨	4276	3453	1924	1836	1090	819	723	716
农村用电量	万千瓦时	5667	82545	406327	1312931	2970738	3950486	4511168	4746936
平均每一农业人口用电量	千瓦时		826	3778	11666	29762	44051	49256	51478

注：农业机械总动力数据从2010年起采用农业局统计口径，数据与往年不可比，下同。

3-16 历年水果面积及产量

Planted Area and Output of Fruits over Years

年 份	年末实有水果面积(亩)	#香(大)蕉	荔 枝	水 果总产量(吨)	#香(大)蕉	荔 枝
1978	93245	18828	46678	26457	18867	4959
1979	91021	17977	46697	23346	12165	8667
1980	88444	15582	46743	23688	10894	7884
1981	97468	18042	48230	46909	25513	15599
1982	114730	28439	50669	58196	40872	7042
1983	159260	39749	63349	77225	42079	20724
1984	235311	66506	84183	105851	69186	14714
1985	407416	125998	115428	189350	133503	19304
1986	609347	171168	168820	307743	210439	18577
1987	609569	158874	175366	363085	222826	17439
1988	548482	99256	176979	263710	126655	7699
1989	476598	54867	164782	221418	69410	6165
1990	452729	54185	160355	282410	73555	16994
1991	440442	56481	154456	343155	85702	6201
1992	420661	81331	139584	344751	97986	22972
1993	360130	86299	117557	271346	80982	717
1994	325336	67595	121236	264875	92072	12703
1995	322876	62351	142370	243231	86466	23324
1996	326291	59822	159403	206276	77768	14804
1997	319556	57583	188220	165016	80355	22572
1998	310873	46377	208899	114106	78978	2885
1999	285514	48975	198144	136317	82169	35218
2000	297618	71454	189862	129367	108913	9107
2001	275428	86578	156019	150115	132292	7059
2002	209924	76764	109948	189343	135209	45339
2003	199634	82024	95812	146414	130688	9012
2004	183375	84812	80115	175389	150669	18312
2005	176845	75452	83357	151255	123986	21026
2006	173470	73493	81395	139582	124601	8615
2007	163448	66904	80313	131571	116833	10107
2008	178337	64141	94953	101541	86817	8498
2009	177281	52761	103364	91544	75341	10240
2010	170536	47420	100136	75540	60236	8266
2011	167667	42874	101458	73866	55291	11032
2012	178746	36661	118158	64916	51883	6333
2013	194327	34951	133793	61144	46701	7910
2014	198288	31704	140915	62475	43439	11500

3-17 历年林业生产

Basic Statistics on Forestry Production over Years

年 份	林业用地面积(亩)	#杉	松	桉	当年育苗面积(亩)	当年幼林抚育面积(亩)	当年四旁植树(万株)
1978	700570	63994	541492	49008	485	32900	44
1979	705764	67104	543210	50439	880	14900	30
1980	740052	70665	568729	56272	316	9500	15
1981	743697	67236	584674	49994	133	12500	12
1982	698715	63730	535072	52925	500	11945	19
1983	769893	67423	574171	56724	361	40464	17
1984	739402	66107	552721	58092	501	106982	16
1985	761460				801	120000	150
1986	706823	61438	510042	60581	33231	210540	22
1987	714664	57824	526254	75498	1728	53759	35
1988	729896	59351	512451	90998	3667	70275	37
1989	691944	53293	490370	103887	2101	64950	58
1990	709240	47054	484397	133706	3464	56647	54
1991	709306	44432	459015	148127	609	53827	63
1992	662919	39326	422527	149944	762	60764	49
1993	628612	36213	400816	144346	677	28511	57
1994	1016138	43815	382482	129473	2492	28127	34
1995	1015223	43661	360591	125133	4273	25130	48
1996	1014972	9654	248288	115878	699	21000	133
1997	1014954	8843	235410	113928	823	23745	218
1998	1014876	8367	222147	112005	387	36000	417
1999	1009965	10890	221585	133500	506	29863	522
2000	1009037	29940	526797	280618	625	47145	425
2001	1007298	9678	189930	133464	705	45000	357
2002	900335	8265	187665	138525	516	46500	98
2003	890877	6540	66206	105666	420	38910	147
2004	980942				255	60000	625
2005	934700	3086	2860	100145	195	61005	253
2006	930162	3716	60890	162125	15	25320	480
2007	926760	3870	62363	149440	255	43320	600
2008	923097	3873	59864	145340	255	49571	610
2009	921000	3719	58375	143690	610	56545	60
2010	909900	3719	56987	142971	285	37278	18
2011	905370	3719	56801	141945	345	41085	22
2012	902927	2934	41480	99353	360	35790	19
2013	902148	3719	56433	144674	390	39920	309
2014	803735	1091	10821	101783	885	39810	316

3-18 历年畜牧业生产及产品产量

Production of Animal Husbandry and Output of Livestock Products over Years

年份	耕牛年末存栏量(头)	羊年末存栏量(头)	生猪饲养量(头)	生猪存栏量(头)	生猪出栏量(头)	三鸟饲养量(万只)	三鸟出栏量(万只)	畜牧总肉量(吨)	#猪肉	禽蛋总产量(吨)
1978	53004		1018060	672919	345141	428	219	26920	22790	425
1979	50595		995408	626435	368973	379	187	29209	25647	367
1980	53385		799568	501380	298188	420	209	27652	23461	444
1981	58619		703659	449638	254021	476	252	28011	23387	1284
1982	64067		791518	526106	265412	568	309	33037	27374	679
1983	69117		842198	489887	352311	630	370	35695	28872	1256
1984	70992		784473	458804	325669	652	369	33260	26301	1899
1985	62763		790505	471268	319237	832	414	33298	25759	2424
1986	62874		812102	428545	383557	940	655	43302	30920	5159
1987	58577		781957	396082	385875	1235	862	46120	32588	5478
1988	54723		811945	402035	409910	1400	1020	56125	35067	6734
1989	52713		846598	407317	439281	1565	1136	58563	38270	7109
1990	48760	1559	870782	410875	459907	1592	1188	62191	40130	6906
1991	44121	1396	930377	420919	509458	1806	1336	68844	44702	5924
1992	32259	1068	981698	448586	533112	1889	1419	67983	45492	5845
1993	18688	783	982084	404352	577732	2185	1647	76562	49470	4990
1994	14219	863	1089793	434904	654889	2334	1730	85448	57920	5521
1995	12207	1593	1250597	469355	781242	2501	1881	97572	68649	5431
1996	12945	1806	1407080	490161	916919	2418	1851	116058	83404	5862
1997	12675	2391	1772892	619114	1153778	2608	1863	128992	99300	6295
1998	10522	2159	2217247	776851	1440396	2291	1742	153513	123874	4738
1999	6811	1508	2573310	900285	1673025	2228	1667	159889	130494	4742
2000	5550	1675	2894126	967056	1927070	2362	1784	179032	149648	4367
2001	4618	1851	3255780	1079397	2176383	2226	1683	198423	168353	4441
2002	2919	1931	3075523	927477	2148046	1962	1557	188774	165344	4052
2003	1727	1789	2525252	742101	1783151	1652	1282	154615	135344	3597
2004	1024	1936	2444990	785289	1659701	1396	1048	146184	128286	3435
2005	827	998	2487962	214120	2273842	1314	1072	171737	159169	1355
2006	82	242	530959	110396	420563	485	312	34891	30199	371
2007	399	415	292234	88648	203586	525	341	20257	14862	361
2008	55		454117	195016	259101	758	574	24052	17946	106
2009	94		464727	183904	280823	767	576	25457	19095	515
2010	224	60	511356	174933	336423	761	591	28830	22339	386
2011	200	50	455875	176805	279070	706	547	26010	19074	643
2012	28	80	428781	142454	286327	733	577	26726	19570	842
2013	25	30	298476	65977	232499	576	448	22829	16965	1057
2014	25	1335	285531	77291	208240	528	408	20068	14844	1130

3-19 历年水产品产量及养殖面积

Output and Cultured Area of Aquatic Products over Years

年份	水产品产量(吨)	海水产量			淡水产量			养殖面积(亩)		
		海水产量	捕捞	养殖	淡水产量	捕捞	养殖		海水养殖	淡水养殖
1978	30900	23307	23307		7593		7593	89040		89040
1979	22309	13878	13878		8431		8431	94916		94916
1980	25471	17069	17069		8402		8402	95549		95549
1981	24905	15669	15669		9236		9236	104069		104069
1982	27695	16120	16120		11575		11575	112586		112586
1983	30292	17330	17330		12962		12962	116943		116943
1984	32465	18025	18025		14440		14440	119456		119456
1985	32641	15422	15214	208	17219		17219	131350	5301	126049
1986	46534	28439	25918	2521	18095		18095	138651	16078	122573
1987	65679	45214	42793	2421	20465		20465	163225	15036	148189
1988	68087	44111	42926	1185	23976	182	23794	137966	9670	128296
1989	62306	37189	35372	1817	25117	1194	23923	123090	10350	112740
1990	68508	41002	38423	2579	27506	2177	25329	136174	19286	116888
1991	69025	39906	37209	2697	29119	2147	26972	131849	18446	113403
1992	73164	42429	38033	4396	30735	2590	28145	134558	20400	114158
1993	64973	33745	28192	5553	31228	3120	28108	143696	25855	117841
1994	67420	31284	24059	7225	36136	2565	33571	144869	26583	118286
1995	74778	32132	24637	7495	42646	2084	40562	162609	27795	134814
1996	81067	33363	25471	7892	47704	1940	45764	172656	27791	144865
1997	91901	35407	26704	8703	56494	5157	51337	184889	30326	154563
1998	96872	33618	24319	9299	63254	3146	60108	192381	29223	163158
1999	94023	31332	24257	7075	62691	2747	59944	167880	19440	148440
2000	95076	33234	24180	9054	61842	3135	58707	167841	25695	142146
2001	89599	30877	23726	7151	58722	2285	56437	155720	27928	127792
2002	82361	30800	23474	7326	51561	2762	48799	142167	26696	115471
2003	75756	30151	22826	7325	45605	2121	43484	126660	27097	99563
2004	71526	29289	22382	6907	42237	3078	39159	125116	25652	99464
2005	67381	28319	21622	6697	39062	1783	37279	102023	23530	78493
2006	47059	21152	15256	5897	25907	1062	24845	71745	6345	65400
2007	47292	21637	15992	5645	25655	857	24797	71100	5925	65175
2008	72282	21297	14322	6975	50985	512	50473	137718	17559	120159
2009	73323	19034	13205	5829	54289		54289	129136	4197	124939
2010	76268	19300	13257	6043	56968	1563	55405	132960	4147	128813
2011	78229	17816	12255	5561	60413	1801	58612	118676	3473	115203
2012	76967	17131	11664	5467	59836	1513	58323	131640	10175	121465
2013	74526	14672	10783	3889	59854	1494	58360	144005	9395	134610
2014	72660	13838	9386	4452	58822	1442	57380	137818	9114	128704

3-20 主要农产品产量与最高年份比较（2014年）

Output of Main Agricultural Products in Comparison with Peak Year (2014)

指　　标	单位	2014年	建国以来最高年份		
			年　份	产　量	2014年为最高年份的(%)
粮食总产量	吨	12406	1977	563463	2.2
#稻　谷	吨	4965	1973	548073	0.9
#早　稻	吨	2183	1983	279723	0.8
晚　稻	吨	2782	1984	279898	1.0
大　豆	吨	186	1954	2790	6.7
经济作物					
#甘　蔗	吨	5369	1982	707764	0.8
花　生	吨	211	1981	35506	0.6
其他作物					
#蔬　菜(含菜用瓜)	吨	390484	2001	706775	55.2
水果总产量	吨	62475	1987	363085	17.2
#香(大)蕉	吨	43439	1987	222826	19.5
荔　枝	吨	11500	2002	45339	25.4
水产品	吨	72660	1998	96872	75.0
生猪年末存栏量	头	77291	2001	1079397	7.2
生猪年出栏头数	头	208240	2005	2273842	9.2
猪肉产量	吨	14844	2001	168353	8.8
三鸟饲养量	万只	528	2000	2362	22.4
三鸟出栏量	万只	408	2000	1784	22.9
禽蛋产量	吨	1130	1989	7109	15.9

主要统计指标解释

Explanatory Notes on Main Statistical Indicators

耕地面积 指可以用来种植农作物、经常进行耕锄的田地，包括熟地、当年新开荒地、连续撂荒未满三年的耕地和当年的休闲地(轮歇地)，还包括以种植农作物为主并附带种植桑树、茶树、果树和其他林木的土地，以及沿海、沿湖地区已围垦利用的“海涂”、“湖田”等面积。不包括属于专业性的桑园、茶园、果园、果木苗圃、林地、芦苇地、天然或人工草地面积。

农作物播种面积 指实际播种或移植有农作物的面积。凡是实际种植有农作物的面积，不论种植在耕地上还是种植在非耕地上，均包括在农作物播种面积中。在播种季节基本结束后，因遭灾而重新改种和补种的农作物面积，也包括在内。

粮食产量 指全社会的产量。包括国有经济经营的、集体统一经营的和农民家庭经营的粮食产量，还包括工矿企业办的农场和其他生产单位的产量。粮食除包括稻谷、小麦、玉米、高粱、谷子及其他杂粮外，还包括薯类和豆类。其产量计算方法，豆类按去豆荚后的干豆计算；薯类(包括甘薯和马铃薯，不包括芋头和木薯)1963年以前按每4公斤鲜薯折1公斤粮食计算，从1964年开始改为按5公斤鲜薯折1公斤粮食计算。城市郊区作为蔬菜的薯类(如马铃薯等)按鲜品计算，并且不作粮食统计。其他粮食一律按脱粒后的原粮计算。

水产品产量 指人工养殖的水产品和天然生长的水产品的捕捞量。包括海水的鱼类、虾蟹类、贝类和藻类以及内陆水域的鱼类、虾蟹类和贝类，不包括淡水生植物。

猪、牛、羊肉产量 指当年出栏并已屠宰、除去头蹄下水后带骨肉(即胴体重)的重量。

期初(末)畜禽存栏头(只)数 指报告期初(末)农村各种合作经济组织和国营农场、农民个人、机关、团体、学校、工矿企业、部队等单位以及城镇居民饲养的大牲畜、猪、羊、家禽等畜禽的存栏数。

农林牧渔业总产值 指以货币表现的农、林、牧、渔业全部产品的总量，它反映一定时期内农业生产总规模和总成果。农业总产值的计算方法通常是按农林牧渔业产品及其副产品的产量分别乘以各自单位产品价格求得；少数生产周期较长，当年没有产品或产品产量不易统计的，则采用间接方法匡算其产值；然后将四业产品产值相加即为农业总产值。

农业机械总动力 指主要用于农、林、牧、渔业的各种动力机械的动力总和。包括耕作机械、排灌机械、收获机械、农用运输机械、植物保护机械、牧业机械、林业机械、渔业机械和其他农业机械〔内燃机按引擎马力折成瓦(特)计算、电动机按功率折成瓦(特)计算〕。不包括专门用于乡、镇、村、组办工业、基本建设、非农业运输、科学试验和教学等非农业生产方面用的动力机械与作业机械。

四、工　业

Industry

4-1 主要年份工业主要指标

Main Indicators of Industry in Main Years

指　　标	单位	1998年	2000年	2005年	2010年	2013年	2014年
全市工业企业单位数	个	16406	16975	21868	38273	67332	80567
全市工业增加值	万元	2906904	4304525	11732288	21094155	25426000	27089969
规模以上工业:							
企业单位数	个	1500	1663	4505	5899	5361	5377
年末固定资产原值合计	万元	6257040	7288486	18560858	32162507	40380407	42133715
年末固定资产	万元	4392164	4701886	11052566	17836928	22485283	22510815
年末流动资产	万元	3798813	5298239	18732801	37888251	53155504	56997425
年末资产总额	万元	9267121	11225950	33453291	60017098	81033203	85829774
年末负债总额	万元	4752964	5630399	18580908	35252952	48237524	50702946
所有者权益	万元	4514157	5595551	14872383	24750103	32549280	34499225
工业增加值	万元	1687134	2594352	10624190	17083110	24256174	24908441
主营业务收入	万元	6399088	9889058	39121487	77081695	108303294	118904336
利税总额	万元	447544	841047	1830988	4695854	5969517	6107314
#利润总额	万元	255715	503589	1243516	3523632	3137479	3659798
全员劳动生产率(按增加值计算)	元/人	26688	36101	53340	60854	91121	96964
综合效益指数	%	94.1	114.0	119.9	130.3	141.1	145.0

注：1. 2005年以前数据根据东莞市第一次经济普查取得，2008年数据根据第二次经济普查取得，下同。
2. 规模以上工业企业1997年及以前年份为独立核算工业企业口径，1998-2005年为全部国有工业及年销售收入500万元以上非国有工业企业口径，2006-2010年为年主营业务收入500万元及以上工业企业口径，2011年起为年主营业务收入2000万元及以上的工业企业口径,下同。

4-2 历年工业企业单位数（按经济成份分）

Number of Industrial Enterprises over Years (by Ownership)

单位：个

年 份	全市工业企业单位数	国有	集体企业	外资企业	其他类型企业
1949	1	1			
1952	23	20	3		
1957	262	76	186		
1962	280	57	223		
1965	260	61	199		
1970	220	57	163		
1975	324	61	263		
1978	1290	64	1226		
1979	1250	63	1187		
1980	1293	64	1229		
1981	1479	64	1415		
1982	1862	66	1796		
1983	1964	68	1896		
1984	2329	69	2109		151
1985	4187	73	2990	79	1045
1986	5949	81	4263	89	1516
1987	8106	74	5123	175	2734
1988	8408	72	5424	241	2671
1989	8757	76	5835	323	2523
1990	9892	78	6165	525	3124
1991	10094	77	6404	758	2855
1992	11639	72	6400	936	4231
1993	12449	75	7129	1412	3833
1994	14086	45	7185	2193	4663
1995	15215	70	9345	2841	2959
1996	15326	40	8958	2381	3947
1997	16857	41	9949	2379	4488
1998	16406	29	8814	2511	5052
1999	16877	29	10325	3358	3165
2000	16975	23	10184	3610	3158
2001	18094	20	9978	4791	3305
2002	21313	19	198	11737	9359
2003	21935	19	200	11927	9789
2004	22156	13	211	10872	11060
2005	21868	10	220	12234	9404
2006	22447	10	211	12461	9765
2007	22587	16	151	12569	9851
2008	26372	35	484	7611	18242
2009	31160	26	313	7580	23241
2010	38273	21	262	7864	30126
2011	46413	20	215	8676	37502
2012	57808	20	254	8965	48569
2013	67332	17	222	9151	57942
2014	80567	16	194	8911	71446

注：本表来源于市工商局，2002年起集体企业不包括“三来一补”企业。

4-3 主要年份工业企业单位数（按不同类型分）

Number of Industrial Enterprises in Main Years (by Ownership)

单位：个

指　　标	1998年	2000年	2005年	2010年	2013年	2014年
全市企业单位数	16406	16975	21868	38273	67332	80567
轻工业	14389	14440	12651	20651	35519	41774
重工业	2017	2535	9217	17622	31813	38793
在总计中:						
(一)规模以上工业企业	1500	1663	4505	5899	5361	5377
按轻重工业分						
轻工业	1082	1124	2569	3183	2828	2788
重工业	418	539	1936	2716	2533	2589
按登记注册类型分						
国有	29	16	5	10	5	2
集体	204	248	162	151	39	32
私营	24	44	621	1159	1226	1266
联营	5	6	2	5	1	
股份合作	9	6	1	2		
股份有限公司	6	3	18	20	43	50
外商投资	134	201	820	1321	1133	1091
港澳台商投资	1082	1119	2481	2564	1990	1914
其他	7	20	395	667	924	1022
按企业规模分						
大型企业	16	28	39	84	244	249
中型企业	27	19	579	1327	1812	1721
小型企业	1457	1616	3887	4488	3237	3307
微型企业					68	100
(二)规模以下工业企业	14906	15312	17363	32374	61971	75190

注：2011年起采用新的企业规模划分标准，共分大型、中型、小型、微型四类企业规模，下同。

4-4 历年工业增加值

Value-added of Industry over Years

年　份	工业增加值	
	绝对值（万元）	增速（%）
1986	105398	
1987	142357	25.8
1988	250456	51.4
1989	272185	6.4
1990	391840	30.6
1991	483441	21.8
1992	566316	13.7
1993	828934	38.5
1994	1107729	24.3
1995	1541922	35.3
1996	1878517	16.2
1997	2307863	20.1
1998	2906904	22.2
1999	3495304	20.7
2000	4304525	20.9
2001	5170314	22.0
2002	6218553	23.0
2003	7571849	21.4
2004	9680128	26.5
2005	11732288	20.2
2006	14416864	22.0
2007	16818293	15.0
2008	18192243	6.4
2009	17544607	0.1
2010	21094155	18.0
2011	23397456	8.1
2012	23664869	6.4
2013	25426000	12.1
2014	27089969	9.3

注：本表工业增加值绝对值为当年价，增速按可比价计算。

4-5 规模以上工业企业单位数（2014年）

Number of Industrial Enterprises above Designated Size (2014)

单位：个

项目	工业单位数	按登记注册类型分		
		内资企业	港澳台商投资企业	外商投资企业
总计	5377	2372	1914	1091
按轻重工业分				
轻工业	2788	1264	1065	459
重工业	2589	1108	849	632
按企业规模分				
大型企业	249	46	121	82
中型企业	1721	468	837	416
小型企业	3307	1792	936	579
微型企业	100	66	20	14
按工业行业分(大类)				
煤炭开采和洗选业				
石油和天然气开采业				
黑色金属矿采选业				
有色金属矿采选业				
非金属矿采选业				
开采辅助活动				
其他采矿业				
农副食品加工业	47	35	5	7
食品制造业	33	17	12	4
酒、饮料和精制茶制造业	15	7	5	3
烟草制品业				
纺织业	132	50	63	19
纺织服装、服饰业	388	248	121	19
皮革、毛皮、羽毛及其制品和制鞋业	336	118	142	76
木材加工和木、竹、藤、棕、草制品业	28	15	9	4
家具制造业	259	160	53	46
造纸和纸制品业	202	135	56	11
印刷和记录媒介复制业	115	45	55	15
文教、工美、体育和娱乐用品制造业	252	65	139	48
石油加工、炼焦和核燃料加工业	4	1	3	
化学原料和化学制品制造业	173	94	45	34
医药制造业	10	7	1	2
化学纤维制造业	12	5	5	2
橡胶和塑料制品业	567	213	237	117
非金属矿物制品业	113	69	30	14
黑色金属冶炼和压延加工业	32	12	9	11
有色金属冶炼和压延加工业	68	34	19	15
金属制品业	328	144	126	58
通用设备制造业	227	103	71	53
专用设备制造业	194	90	64	40
汽车制造业	54	18	11	25
铁路、船舶、航空航天和其他运输设备制造业	24	12	5	7
电气机械和器材制造业	588	239	224	125
计算机、通信和其他电子设备制造业	980	352	334	294
仪器仪表制造业	86	25	39	22
其他制造业	53	16	23	14
废弃资源综合利用业	2	2		
金属制品、机械和设备修理业	2		1	1
电力、热力生产和供应业	13	5	7	1
燃气生产和供应业	6	2		4
水的生产和供应业	34	34		

4-6 规模以上工业增加值（2014年）

Value-added of Industrial Enterprises above Designated Size (2014)

单位：万元

项 目	工业增加值	按登记注册类型分		
		内资企业	港澳台商投资企业	外商投资企业
总 计	24908441	8215313	9885027	6808101
按轻重工业分				
轻工业	10557001	3277722	4987944	2291335
重工业	14351440	4937591	4897083	4516766
按企业规模分				
大型企业	11000739	3419731	4136997	3444011
中型企业	8445261	2233772	3939528	2271962
小型企业	5353196	2473676	1799762	1079758
微型企业	109245	88134	8741	12370
按工业行业分(大类)				
煤炭开采和洗选业				
石油和天然气开采业				
黑色金属矿采选业				
有色金属矿采选业				
非金属矿采选业				
开采辅助活动				
其他采矿业				
农副食品加工业	171121	124782	16777	29562
食品制造业	288857	46147	85185	157524
酒、饮料和精制茶制造业	196119	31416	52415	112289
烟草制品业				
纺织业	451515	95125	214020	142370
纺织服装、服饰业	1380061	774505	523763	81793
皮革、毛皮、羽毛及其制品和制鞋业	1340784	261010	732225	347549
木材加工和木、竹、藤、棕、草制品业	33775	19930	8067	5778
家具制造业	581842	297704	158968	125171
造纸和纸制品业	1103784	355900	707331	40553
印刷和记录媒介复制业	462680	109428	259166	94086
文教、工美、体育和娱乐用品制造业	929540	175375	610215	143949
石油加工、炼焦和核燃料加工业	53395	33071	20324	
化学原料和化学制品制造业	485836	172196	174897	138744
医药制造业	90028	72927	1197	15903
化学纤维制造业	16244	9646	5343	1255
橡胶和塑料制品业	1512368	361272	750594	400502
非金属矿物制品业	419133	156562	207244	55327
黑色金属冶炼和压延加工业	89181	36928	28436	23818
有色金属冶炼和压延加工业	248294	89439	91251	67605
金属制品业	1003294	330203	505309	167782
通用设备制造业	905041	208969	366584	329488
专用设备制造业	570342	201628	267781	100933
汽车制造业	363273	51531	41778	269964
铁路、船舶、航空航天和其他运输设备制造业	180739	38802	107881	34056
电气机械和器材制造业	2143225	601468	1010738	531019
计算机、通信和其他电子设备制造业	7348930	1929631	2382014	3037285
仪器仪表制造业	479892	53506	198090	228296
其他制造业	120570	24944	68512	27114
废弃资源综合利用业	3502	3502		
金属制品、机械和设备修理业	1458		1044	414
电力、热力生产和供应业	1745444	1432354	287879	25211
燃气生产和供应业	76554	3792		72762
水的生产和供应业	111620	111620		

4-7 规模以上工业企业主要财务指标（2014年）

Main Financial Indicators of Industrial Enterprises above Designated Size (2014)

单位：万元

指标	全市总计	按登记注册类型分			按轻重工业分	
		内资企业	港澳台商投资企业	外商投资企业	轻工业	重工业
企业单位数(个)	5377	2372	1914	1091	2788	2589
年末资产						
流动资产合计	56997425	20831109	21366648	14799669	23753603	33243822
#产成品存货	4497513	1511150	1816496	1169867	2086919	2410594
固定资产净值	21406326	7646561	9028462	4731303	8091514	13314813
年末资产总额	85829774	31709490	33263674	20856611	34398256	51431518
年末负债及所有者权益						
年末负债总额	50702946	21705303	18202678	10794965	19678218	31024727
所有者权益合计	34499225	9557983	14938313	10002929	14584835	19914390
损益及分配						
主营业务收入	118904336	43689148	40556604	34658585	43500996	75403340
主营业务成本	105700718	38217568	36260809	31222341	38234133	67466585
主营业务税金及附加	387342	146341	134376	106624	168864	218479
主营业务利润	12816276	5325238	4161418	3329619	5098000	7718276
销售费用	2520762	1061394	803875	655493	1344938	1175824
管理费用	6126715	2022373	2383992	1720350	2519417	3607298
财务费用	390434	261803	137361	-8730	159551	230884
#利息支出	547864	301230	190767	55867	205987	341878
利税总额	6107314	2740947	1844152	1522215	2274739	3832575
#利润总额	3659798	1568120	1094460	997218	1270633	2389165
亏损企业亏损总额	601184	67773	366442	166969	182090	419094

4-8 规模以上工业企业主要指标（2014年）

Main Indicators of Industrial Enterprises above Designated Size (2014)

单位：万元

项　　目	企业单位数(个)	#亏损企业	工业销售产值	工　业增加值	全部从业人员平均人数(人)
总　计	5377	691	118842699	24908441	2568832
按轻重工业分					
轻工业	2788	369	43338392	10557001	1346002
重工业	2589	322	75504308	14351440	1222830
按企业规模分					
大型企业	249	17	56765195	11000739	876716
中型企业	1721	251	35498348	8445261	1188273
小型企业	3307	395	24818117	5353196	498680
微型企业	100	28	1761038	109245	5163
按工业行业分(大类)					
煤炭开采和洗选业					
石油和天然气开采业					
黑色金属矿采选业					
有色金属矿采选业					
非金属矿采选业					
开采辅助活动					
其他采矿业					
农副食品加工业	47	6	3378038	171121	8280
食品制造业	33	3	910143	288857	15616
酒、饮料和精制茶制造业	15	4	912557	196119	10707
烟草制品业					
纺织业	132	20	1673128	451515	53276
纺织服装、服饰业	388	38	4860214	1380061	179692
皮革、毛皮、羽毛及其制品和制鞋业	336	45	3487891	1340784	245933
木材加工和木、竹、藤、棕、草制品业	28	7	163983	33775	4455
家具制造业	259	33	2382547	581842	88402
造纸和纸制品业	202	13	5437596	1103784	61770
印刷和记录媒介复制业	115	9	1394830	462680	46003
文教、工美、体育和娱乐用品制造业	252	38	3225876	929540	187716
石油加工、炼焦和核燃料加工业	4		216810	53395	212
化学原料和化学制品制造业	173	18	2956973	485836	24891
医药制造业	10	2	200906	90028	3082
化学纤维制造业	12	1	100376	16244	2294
橡胶和塑料制品业	567	75	5691116	1512368	189677
非金属矿物制品业	113	16	1646120	419133	32266
黑色金属冶炼和压延加工业	32	3	490871	89181	5345
有色金属冶炼和压延加工业	68	10	766491	248294	8799
金属制品业	328	34	3294775	1003294	113672
通用设备制造业	227	26	5639803	905041	97455
专用设备制造业	194	28	1825364	570342	59254
汽车制造业	54	9	1397345	363273	21529
铁路、船舶、航空航天和其他运输设备制造业	24	5	707242	180739	11922
电气机械和器材制造业	588	66	8953446	2143225	256918
计算机、通信和其他电子设备制造业	980	146	47953226	7348930	734775
仪器仪表制造业	86	15	1586594	479892	57439
其他制造业	53	7	428076	120570	17700
废弃资源综合利用业	2		18669	3502	140
金属制品、机械和设备修理业	2		4863	1458	97
电力、热力生产和供应业	13	4	6435770	1745444	23847
燃气生产和供应业	6		405631	76554	900
水的生产和供应业	34	10	295431	111620	4768

4-8 续表 1

(2014年)

单位：万元

项目	年末资产合计	#流动资产合计	#产成品	固定资产合计	年末负债合计
总计	85829774	56997425	4497513	22510815	50702946
按轻重工业分					
轻工业	34398256	23753603	2086919	8579217	19678218
重工业	51431518	33243822	2410594	13931598	31024727
按企业规模分					
大型企业	35821212	22005660	1636955	11597499	20765159
中型企业	27668840	18890212	1644990	6702105	15676038
小型企业	20864406	15422716	1171198	4000519	13042051
微型企业	1475317	678837	44370	210691	1219698
按工业行业分(大类)					
煤炭开采和洗选业					
石油和天然气开采业					
黑色金属矿采选业					
有色金属矿采选业					
非金属矿采选业					
开采辅助活动					
其他采矿业					
农副食品加工业	2171740	1640941	111979	348963	1628829
食品制造业	1054079	702666	40513	266479	370541
酒、饮料和精制茶制造业	810938	428597	20509	333661	454097
烟草制品业					
纺织业	1651676	1205322	127865	396963	727332
纺织服装、服饰业	3724429	2992084	285069	468113	2399832
皮革、毛皮、羽毛及其制品和制鞋业	2139551	1662937	189596	359791	1337509
木材加工和木、竹、藤、棕、草制品业	139946	107752	13832	24890	102979
家具制造业	1770353	1380107	139129	261303	1039408
造纸和纸制品业	5601981	2734688	260103	2594992	2953882
印刷和记录媒介复制业	1414079	975687	48959	335715	682871
文教、工美、体育和娱乐用品制造业	2106953	1614587	222760	388645	1265966
石油加工、炼焦和核燃料加工业	201823	189428	13614	5953	174172
化学原料和化学制品制造业	2357008	1808504	124410	356676	1265193
医药制造业	362918	174800	7875	137686	127989
化学纤维制造业	60166	49382	4366	10575	40841
橡胶和塑料制品业	4230868	2956449	261066	971710	2422026
非金属矿物制品业	1925863	998126	79832	722012	1173724
黑色金属冶炼和压延加工业	346229	271369	28508	61094	205527
有色金属冶炼和压延加工业	713169	442709	46918	82974	620424
金属制品业	3240633	1933160	151318	1047252	1688292
通用设备制造业	3311292	2524805	186687	621876	2011157
专用设备制造业	1766954	1222237	122226	416875	926053
汽车制造业	1064236	672048	46320	290515	476358
铁路、船舶、航空航天和其他运输设备制造业	765405	553844	36669	161745	508749
电气机械和器材制造业	7349417	5611300	467411	1336789	4149133
计算机、通信和其他电子设备制造业	26845556	19570370	1364670	5446376	17318458
仪器仪表制造业	1047820	651277	62894	300758	475446
其他制造业	381431	249652	22422	112464	211295
废弃资源综合利用业	17825	11364	92	4998	8395
金属制品、机械和设备修理业	8644	6933	1046	1582	4493
电力、热力生产和供应业	5855800	1165433	7658	3980596	2992373
燃气生产和供应业	297157	72753	114	184612	136441
水的生产和供应业	1093837	416119	1084	476184	803163

4-8 续表 2

(2014年)

单位：万元

项目	主营业务收入	主营业务税金及附加	成本费用总额	本年应交增值税	亏损企业亏损总额
总计	118904336	387342	116790927	2054065	601184
按轻重工业分					
轻工业	43500996	168864	42721713	831920	182090
重工业	75403340	218479	74069214	1222145	419094
按企业规模分					
大型企业	56452290	166595	55278717	989944	84624
中型企业	35432813	131953	34808776	593191	179194
小型企业	25291666	84976	24839019	463270	153056
微型企业	1727567	3818	1864415	7661	184311
按工业行业分(大类)					
煤炭开采和洗选业					
石油和天然气开采业					
黑色金属矿采选业					
有色金属矿采选业					
非金属矿采选业					
开采辅助活动					
其他采矿业					
农副食品加工业	3899373	1508	4141015	21113	15194
食品制造业	921396	9313	844341	59563	860
酒、饮料和精制茶制造业	929347	15108	854836	41880	35564
烟草制品业					
纺织业	1645899	7603	1610765	23035	11044
纺织服装、服饰业	4683528	20042	4480957	127078	6038
皮革、毛皮、羽毛及其制品和制鞋业	3479444	17640	3488176	59336	14310
木材加工和木、竹、藤、棕、草制品业	159363	686	163970	3262	1302
家具制造业	2393009	11504	2356071	43640	15075
造纸和纸制品业	5441462	14572	5341249	153135	6207
印刷和记录媒介复制业	1384952	5534	1293011	33347	2536
文教、工美、体育和娱乐用品制造业	3217098	13147	3182020	30851	17137
石油加工、炼焦和核燃料加工业	215775	212	214730	1081	
化学原料和化学制品制造业	3086167	8683	2942900	53454	7462
医药制造业	194576	1705	169137	16504	1090
化学纤维制造业	102558	358	100276	1913	226
橡胶和塑料制品业	5697858	20414	5561027	107551	24976
非金属矿物制品业	1654320	7493	1597452	42277	25467
黑色金属冶炼和压延加工业	505868	926	487031	7127	484
有色金属冶炼和压延加工业	756412	1482	777285	8399	50676
金属制品业	3304746	11882	3225621	55417	18076
通用设备制造业	5630821	14184	5506791	51194	16921
专用设备制造业	1802068	8094	1737633	42206	10153
汽车制造业	1397218	5795	1295316	28228	5608
铁路、船舶、航空航天和其他运输设备制造业	684180	2096	686681	13187	1788
电气机械和器材制造业	8850881	32074	8572383	105492	31909
计算机、通信和其他电子设备制造业	47676484	116540	47310752	561736	238829
仪器仪表制造业	1570458	5362	1534423	18390	12288
其他制造业	422823	1935	421833	5627	3320
废弃资源综合利用业	18662	48	17710	401	
金属制品、机械和设备修理业	4863	21	4675	265	
电力、热力生产和供应业	6486147	28033	6235054	316346	19360
燃气生产和供应业	395255	1748	349609	9736	
水的生产和供应业	291327	1603	286195	11294	7285

4-8 续表 3

(2014年)

项目	利税总额(万元)	人均税收(元)	利润总额(万元)	人均利润(元)
总计	6107314	9528	3659798	14247
按轻重工业分				
轻工业	2274739	7460	1270633	9440
重工业	3832575	11804	2389165	19538
按企业规模分				
大型企业	3170298	13210	2012116	22951
中型企业	1700056	6117	973145	8190
小型企业	1404096	11047	853190	17109
微型企业	-167137	22304	-178653	-346025
按工业行业分(大类)				
煤炭开采和洗选业				
石油和天然气开采业				
黑色金属矿采选业				
有色金属矿采选业				
非金属矿采选业				
开采辅助活动				
其他采矿业				
农副食品加工业	66985	28099	43719	52801
食品制造业	146430	44112	77545	49657
酒、饮料和精制茶制造业	70582	53225	13594	12696
烟草制品业				
纺织业	84169	5760	53484	10039
纺织服装、服饰业	352787	8220	205082	11413
皮革、毛皮、羽毛及其制品和制鞋业	123294	3145	45954	1869
木材加工和木、竹、藤、棕、草制品业	4426	8890	466	1045
家具制造业	96924	6252	41659	4712
造纸和纸制品业	302226	27155	134491	21773
印刷和记录媒介复制业	155099	8592	115573	25123
文教、工美、体育和娱乐用品制造业	82252	2362	37904	2019
石油加工、炼焦和核燃料加工业	3278	60962	1986	93665
化学原料和化学制品制造业	191417	24972	129260	51930
医药制造业	47040	59081	28831	93547
化学纤维制造业	4446	9902	2174	9477
橡胶和塑料制品业	283911	6755	155785	8213
非金属矿物制品业	103908	15429	54124	16774
黑色金属冶炼和压延加工业	17606	15084	9543	17854
有色金属冶炼和压延加工业	-30018	11394	-40044	-45509
金属制品业	158629	5929	91235	8026
通用设备制造业	235602	6718	170137	17458
专用设备制造业	132395	8504	82004	13839
汽车制造业	148371	15803	114348	53113
铁路、船舶、航空航天和其他运输设备制造业	40626	12830	25331	21247
电气机械和器材制造业	449063	5364	311242	12114
计算机、通信和其他电子设备制造业	1928284	9243	1249108	17000
仪器仪表制造业	65039	4138	41268	7185
其他制造业	15421	4279	7847	4434
废弃资源综合利用业	1482	32071	1033	73757
金属制品、机械和设备修理业	454	29423	168	17330
电力、热力生产和供应业	738445	144955	392769	164704
燃气生产和供应业	64787	127670	53296	592182
水的生产和供应业	21956	27416	8884	18633

4-9 规模以上工业企业主要经济效益指标（2014年）

Main Indicators on Economic Benefit of Industrial Enterprises above Designated Size (2014)

项目	工业增加值率(%)	总资产贡献率(%)	资产负债率(%)	流动资产周转率(次/年)	成本费用利润率(%)	全员劳动生产率(元/人)	产品销售率(%)
总计	20.5	7.5	59.1	2.1	3.1	96964	97.9
按轻重工业分							
轻工业	23.8	7.0	57.2	1.9	3.0	78432	97.6
重工业	18.7	7.9	60.3	2.3	3.2	117363	98.2
按企业规模分							
大型企业	19.0	9.2	58.0	2.6	3.6	125477	98.2
中型企业	23.3	6.5	56.7	1.9	2.8	71072	97.8
小型企业	21.2	7.3	62.5	1.7	3.4	107347	98.3
微型企业	5.5	-9.7	82.7	2.6	-9.6	211592	89.1
按工业行业分(大类)							
煤炭开采和洗选业							
石油和天然气开采业							
黑色金属矿采选业							
有色金属矿采选业							
非金属矿采选业							
开采辅助活动							
其他采矿业							
农副食品加工业	5.1	3.5	75.0	2.5	1.1	206668	100.5
食品制造业	31.0	13.4	35.2	1.3	9.2	184975	97.8
酒、饮料和精制茶制造业	22.5	9.5	56.0	2.2	1.6	183169	104.5
烟草制品业							
纺织业	26.5	4.5	44.0	1.4	3.3	84750	98.2
纺织服装、服饰业	25.8	9.7	64.4	1.6	4.6	76801	90.8
皮革、毛皮、羽毛及其制品和制鞋业	37.9	6.0	62.5	2.1	1.3	54518	98.6
木材加工和木、竹、藤、棕、草制品业	20.2	4.1	73.6	1.5	0.3	75815	98.2
家具制造业	23.9	5.5	58.7	1.7	1.8	65818	98.0
造纸和纸制品业	19.5	6.7	52.7	2.0	2.5	178693	96.0
印刷和记录媒介复制业	33.1	11.1	48.3	1.4	8.9	100576	99.7
文教、工美、体育和娱乐用品制造业	28.2	4.2	60.1	2.0	1.2	49518	97.7
石油加工、炼焦和核燃料加工业	25.4	2.4	86.3	1.1	0.9	2518615	103.0
化学原料和化学制品制造业	16.1	8.6	53.7	1.7	4.4	195185	97.9
医药制造业	44.2	13.0	35.3	1.1	17.1	292108	98.5
化学纤维制造业	15.5	8.7	67.9	2.1	2.2	70810	95.6
橡胶和塑料制品业	26.1	6.9	57.3	1.9	2.8	79734	98.2
非金属矿物制品业	24.9	6.0	61.0	1.7	3.4	129899	97.9
黑色金属冶炼和压延加工业	17.4	5.3	59.4	1.9	2.0	166850	95.7
有色金属冶炼和压延加工业	31.2	-2.5	87.0	1.7	-5.2	282184	96.4
金属制品业	29.6	5.5	52.1	1.7	2.8	88262	97.3
通用设备制造业	15.9	7.2	60.7	2.3	3.1	92868	99.1
专用设备制造业	30.9	7.8	52.4	1.5	4.7	96254	99.0
汽车制造业	25.0	14.4	44.8	2.1	8.8	168737	96.2
铁路、船舶、航空航天和其他运输设备制造业	25.7	5.5	66.5	1.3	3.7	151601	100.4
电气机械和器材制造业	23.5	6.3	56.5	1.6	3.6	83421	98.2
计算机、通信和其他电子设备制造业	15.1	7.3	64.5	2.5	2.6	100016	98.2
仪器仪表制造业	29.3	6.3	45.4	2.4	2.7	83548	96.8
其他制造业	27.4	4.1	55.4	1.7	1.9	68119	97.4
废弃资源综合利用业	20.4	10.4	47.1	1.6	5.8	250133	108.8
金属制品、机械和设备修理业	30.0	5.2	52.0	0.7	3.6	150321	100.0
电力、热力生产和供应业	27.0	14.3	51.1	5.6	6.3	731934	99.6
燃气生产和供应业	18.9	23.1	45.9	5.5	15.2	850597	100.0
水的生产和供应业	36.4	4.6	73.4	0.7	3.1	234102	96.4

4-10 规模以上国有及国有控股工业企业主要经济指标（2014年）

Main Indicators of State-owned and State-holding Industrial Enterprises above Designated Size (2014)

项目	企业单位数（个）	#亏损企业	工业增加值（万元）	主营业务收入（万元）	亏损企业亏损总额（万元）
总计	26	4	1896640	7855199	14939
按轻重工业分					
轻工业	12	1	95183	1150973	4145
重工业	14	3	1801457	6704226	10795
按企业规模分					
大型企业	4		1443029	5859533	
中型企业	7	1	140296	824023	4145
小型企业	15	3	313315	1171643	10795
微型企业					
按销售收入分					
10亿元以上	7		1722973	7310353	
5-10亿元	5	1	115041	327410	1440
1-5亿元	7	2	50868	189974	10767
1亿元以下	7	1	7757	27462	2732
按工业行业分(大类)					
煤炭开采和洗选业					
石油和天然气开采业					
黑色金属矿采选业					
有色金属矿采选业					
非金属矿采选业					
开采辅助活动					
其他采矿业					
农副食品加工业	2		12338	887699	
食品制造业					
酒、饮料和精制茶制造业	2		6698	51875	
烟草制品业					
纺织业					
纺织服装、服饰业	1		4566	11868	
皮革、毛皮、羽毛及其制品和制鞋业					
木材加工和木、竹、藤、棕、草制品业					
家具制造业					
造纸和纸制品业					
印刷和记录媒介复制业	1		1377	7259	
文教、工美、体育和娱乐用品制造业	1		1175	4380	
石油加工、炼焦和核燃料加工业					
化学原料和化学制品制造业					
医药制造业					
化学纤维制造业					
橡胶和塑料制品业					
非金属矿物制品业					
黑色金属冶炼和压延加工业	1		11945	62068	
有色金属冶炼和压延加工业	1		1374	4578	
金属制品业					
通用设备制造业	1		17524	61405	
专用设备制造业					
汽车制造业					
铁路、船舶、航空航天和其他运输设备制造业	1		81629	276475	
电气机械和器材制造业	1		6465	16132	
计算机、通信和其他电子设备制造业	2	1	14582	50008	2732
仪器仪表制造业					
其他制造业					
废弃资源综合利用业					
金属制品、机械和设备修理业					
电力、热力生产和供应业	7	2	1686005	6292615	8062
燃气生产和供应业					
水的生产和供应业	5	1	50963	128838	4145

4-10 续表

(2014年)

项目	利税总额(万元)	人均税收(元)	利润总额(万元)	人均利润(元)
总计	803878	113140	444015	139597
按轻重工业分				
轻工业	70326	21686	56837	91378
重工业	733553	135371	387178	151318
按企业规模分				
大型企业	507260	115091	211671	82417
中型企业	59749	47652	39626	93833
小型企业	236870	232250	192719	1013776
微型企业				
按销售收入分				
10亿元以上	730677	139274	389568	159059
5-10亿元	39126	53370	27816	131271
1-5亿元	31858	15421	25000	56218
1亿元以下	2218	7834	1631	21772
按工业行业分(大类)				
煤炭开采和洗选业				
石油和天然气开采业				
黑色金属矿采选业				
有色金属矿采选业				
非金属矿采选业				
开采辅助活动				
其他采矿业				
农副食品加工业	22796	28618	21044	343859
食品制造业				
酒、饮料和精制茶制造业	2911	50299	1080	29681
烟草制品业				
纺织业				
纺织服装、服饰业	1496		1496	37393
皮革、毛皮、羽毛及其制品和制鞋业				
木材加工和木、竹、藤、棕、草制品业				
家具制造业				
造纸和纸制品业				
印刷和记录媒介复制业	1008	17163	850	92435
文教、工美、体育和娱乐用品制造业	305	13841	17	827
石油加工、炼焦和核燃料加工业				
化学原料和化学制品制造业				
医药制造业				
化学纤维制造业				
橡胶和塑料制品业				
非金属矿物制品业				
黑色金属冶炼和压延加工业	830	60600	467	77750
有色金属冶炼和压延加工业	170	5172	77	4272
金属制品业				
通用设备制造业	11074	37145	7976	95638
专用设备制造业				
汽车制造业				
铁路、船舶、航空航天和其他运输设备制造业	10001	29095	5008	29184
电气机械和器材制造业	1878	7126	1405	21120
计算机、通信和其他电子设备制造业	30892	12079	28041	118765
仪器仪表制造业				
其他制造业				
废弃资源综合利用业				
金属制品、机械和设备修理业				
电力、热力生产和供应业	710796	149243	372969	164768
燃气生产和供应业				
水的生产和供应业	9720	36537	3586	21355

4-11 规模以上国有及国有控股工业企业主要经济效益指标（2014年）

Main Indicators on Economic Benefit of State-owned and State-holding Industrial Enterprises above Designated Size (2014)

项　　目	工业增加值率(%)	总资产贡献率(%)	资　产负债率(%)	流动资产周转率(次/年)	成本费用利润率(%)	全员劳动生产率(元/人)	产　品销售率(%)
总　　计	25.5	13.5	53.1	4.7	5.9	596296	100.2
按轻重工业分							
轻工业	12.2	10.7	65.6	3.5	4.8	153028	101.5
重工业	27.1	13.9	51.5	5.0	6.1	704052	100.0
按企业规模分							
大型企业	24.8	12.1	54.1	8.9	3.7	561862	100.0
中型企业	18.8	8.2	52.3	2.0	5.0	332218	101.2
小型企业	35.6	24.5	49.3	1.9	18.2	1648161	100.4
微型企业							
按工业行业分(大类)							
煤炭开采和洗选业							
石油和天然气开采业							
黑色金属矿采选业							
有色金属矿采选业							
非金属矿采选业							
开采辅助活动							
其他采矿业							
农副食品加工业	2.4	9.9	56.2	5.7	2.4	201606	102.9
食品制造业							
酒、饮料和精制茶制造业	13.5	10.2	41.4	4.4	2.1	184000	107.5
烟草制品业							
纺织业							
纺织服装、服饰业	35.5	11.3	37.5	1.0	14.4	114149	95.0
皮革、毛皮、羽毛及其制品和制鞋业							
木材加工和木、竹、藤、棕、草制品业							
家具制造业							
造纸和纸制品业							
印刷和记录媒介复制业	19.1	12.0	28.4	2.0	12.0	149664	110.9
文教、工美、体育和娱乐用品制造业	28.1	8.5	7.1	10.4	0.1	56513	104.8
石油加工、炼焦和核燃料加工业							
化学原料和化学制品制造业							
医药制造业							
化学纤维制造业							
橡胶和塑料制品业							
非金属矿物制品业							
黑色金属冶炼和压延加工业	19.2	5.8	71.8	4.9	0.9	1990751	100.0
有色金属冶炼和压延加工业	27.5	3.2	52.0	1.3	1.6	76335	91.6
金属制品业							
通用设备制造业	30.6	28.8	44.0	2.1	14.9	210120	103.2
专用设备制造业							
汽车制造业							
铁路、船舶、航空航天和其他运输设备制造业	29.4	2.3	74.3	0.8	1.8	475691	99.4
电气机械和器材制造业	31.9	7.4	73.6	1.1	9.5	97222	85.9
计算机、通信和其他电子设备制造业	29.1	29.8	48.5	1.1	45.9	61760	99.7
仪器仪表制造业							
其他制造业							
废弃资源综合利用业							
金属制品、机械和设备修理业							
电力、热力生产和供应业	27.0	15.0	48.9	6.7	6.3	744833	100.0
燃气生产和供应业							
水的生产和供应业	36.8	6.4	79.5	1.2	2.8	303533	96.6

4-12 规模以上集体工业企业主要经济指标（2014年）

Main Indicators of Collective-owned Industrial Enterprises above Designated Size (2014)

项目	企业单位数（个）	#亏损企业	工业增加值（万元）	主营业务收入（万元）	亏损企业亏损总额（万元）
总计	32	12	112385	222670	8371
按轻重工业分					
轻工业	29	12	105864	212455	8371
重工业	3		6521	10215	
按企业规模分					
大型企业					
中型企业	6	3	64696	96203	5230
小型企业	26	9	47689	126467	3141
微型企业					
按销售收入分					
10亿元以上					
5-10亿元					
1-5亿元	5	1	66510	110130	3532
1亿元以下	27	11	45875	112540	4839
按工业行业分(大类)					
煤炭开采和洗选业					
石油和天然气开采业					
黑色金属矿采选业					
有色金属矿采选业					
非金属矿采选业					
开采辅助活动					
其他采矿业					
农副食品加工业					
食品制造业					
酒、饮料和精制茶制造业					
烟草制品业					
纺织业					
纺织服装、服饰业					
皮革、毛皮、羽毛及其制品和制鞋业	2	2	10887	31039	3558
木材加工和木、竹、藤、棕、草制品业					
家具制造业					
造纸和纸制品业					
印刷和记录媒介复制业	1		1254	3246	
文教、工美、体育和娱乐用品制造业	2	1	34841	41535	1672
石油加工、炼焦和核燃料加工业					
化学原料和化学制品制造业	1		160	2541	
医药制造业					
化学纤维制造业					
橡胶和塑料制品业	1		1204	4480	
非金属矿物制品业					
黑色金属冶炼和压延加工业					
有色金属冶炼和压延加工业					
金属制品业					
通用设备制造业					
专用设备制造业					
汽车制造业					
铁路、船舶、航空航天和其他运输设备制造业					
电气机械和器材制造业	1		12711	18433	
计算机、通信和其他电子设备制造业	2		6361	7674	
仪器仪表制造业					
其他制造业					
废弃资源综合利用业					
金属制品、机械和设备修理业					
电力、热力生产和供应业					
燃气生产和供应业					
水的生产和供应业	22	9	44967	113722	3141

4-12 续表

(2014年)

项　　目	利税总额(万元)	人均税收(元)	利润总额(万元)	人均利润(元)
总　计	6575	2701	885	420
按轻重工业分				
轻工业	6400	2865	720	363
重工业	175	80	165	1326
按企业规模分				
大型企业				
中型企业	-3607	43	-3685	-2027
小型企业	10182	19446	4570	15835
微型企业				
按销售收入分				
10亿元以上				
5-10亿元				
1-5亿元	3075	882	1670	1049
1亿元以下	3500	8343	-785	-1528
按工业行业分(大类)				
煤炭开采和洗选业				
石油和天然气开采业				
黑色金属矿采选业				
有色金属矿采选业				
非金属矿采选业				
开采辅助活动				
其他采矿业				
农副食品加工业				
食品制造业				
酒、饮料和精制茶制造业				
烟草制品业				
纺织业				
纺织服装、服饰业				
皮革、毛皮、羽毛及其制品和制鞋业	-3557	1	-3558	-7443
木材加工和木、竹、藤、棕、草制品业				
家具制造业				
造纸和纸制品业				
印刷和记录媒介复制业	184	7720	145	29000
文教、工美、体育和娱乐用品制造业	-133	4	-136	-153
石油加工、炼焦和核燃料加工业				
化学原料和化学制品制造业	62	1284	52	7068
医药制造业				
化学纤维制造业				
橡胶和塑料制品业	2364	40033	1639	90547
非金属矿物制品业				
黑色金属冶炼和压延加工业				
有色金属冶炼和压延加工业				
金属制品业				
通用设备制造业				
专用设备制造业				
汽车制造业				
铁路、船舶、航空航天和其他运输设备制造业				
电气机械和器材制造业	74	205		
计算机、通信和其他电子设备制造业	113	3	112	962
仪器仪表制造业				
其他制造业				
废弃资源综合利用业				
金属制品、机械和设备修理业				
电力、热力生产和供应业				
燃气生产和供应业				
水的生产和供应业	7470	20950	2631	11387

4-13 规模以上集体工业企业主要经济效益指标（2014年）

Main Indicators on Economic Benefit of Collective-owned Industrial Enterprises above Designated Size (2014)

项　　　目	工业增加值率(%)	总资产贡献率(%)	资　产负债率(%)	流动资产周转率(次/年)	成本费用利润率(%)	全员劳动生产率(元/人)	产　品销售率(%)
总　　计	41.7	2.6	76.0	1.0	0.4	53357	97.6
按轻重工业分							
轻工业	40.8	2.7	75.6	1.0	0.3	53407	97.5
重工业	63.8	0.9	85.5	2.0	1.6	52545	100.0
按企业规模分							
大型企业							
中型企业	46.5	-9.0	134.8	8.8	-3.6	35592	100.0
小型企业	36.6	3.8	70.2	0.6	3.7	165242	95.1
微型企业							
按工业行业分(大类)							
煤炭开采和洗选业							
石油和天然气开采业							
黑色金属矿采选业							
有色金属矿采选业							
非金属矿采选业							
开采辅助活动							
其他采矿业							
农副食品加工业							
食品制造业							
酒、饮料和精制茶制造业							
烟草制品业							
纺织业							
纺织服装、服饰业							
皮革、毛皮、羽毛及其制品和制鞋业	62.8	-121.8	833.2	20.2	-10.3	22776	100.0
木材加工和木、竹、藤、棕、草制品业							
家具制造业							
造纸和纸制品业							
印刷和记录媒介复制业	34.2	4.0	20.1	1.0	4.6	250857	100.0
文教、工美、体育和娱乐用品制造业	83.9	-0.8	80.6	7.1	-0.3	39112	100.0
石油加工、炼焦和核燃料加工业							
化学原料和化学制品制造业	6.3	5.0	46.4	2.7	2.1	21594	100.0
医药制造业							
化学纤维制造业							
橡胶和塑料制品业	26.4	25.3	50.7	0.9	58.5	66539	98.0
非金属矿物制品业							
黑色金属冶炼和压延加工业							
有色金属冶炼和压延加工业							
金属制品业							
通用设备制造业							
专用设备制造业							
汽车制造业							
铁路、船舶、航空航天和其他运输设备制造业							
电气机械和器材制造业	16.9	1.8	1.0	16.6		35377	100.0
计算机、通信和其他电子设备制造业	82.9	0.6	88.3	1.9	1.5	54507	100.0
仪器仪表制造业							
其他制造业							
废弃资源综合利用业							
金属制品、机械和设备修理业							
电力、热力生产和供应业							
燃气生产和供应业							
水的生产和供应业	38.4	3.2	71.7	0.6	2.4	194662	94.6

4-14 规模以上外商投资工业企业主要经济指标（2014年）

Main Indicators of Industrial Enterprises above Designated Size with Foreign Funds (2014)

项　　目	企业单位数（个）	#亏损企业	工业增加值（万元）	主营业务收入（万元）	亏损企业亏损总额（万元）
总　　计	1091	198	6808101	34658585	166969
按轻重工业分					
轻工业	459	88	2291335	10844048	65513
重工业	632	110	4516766	23814537	101456
按企业规模分					
大型企业	82	5	3444011	19506606	36493
中型企业	416	73	2271962	9585092	70112
小型企业	579	115	1079758	5490652	56623
微型企业	14	5	12370	76235	3741
按销售收入分					
10亿元以上	58	6	3188087	20717379	38471
5-10亿元	44	9	741118	2916375	21340
1-5亿元	363	56	1957107	7723325	58131
1亿元以下	626	127	921789	3301506	49027
按工业行业分(大类)					
煤炭开采和洗选业					
石油和天然气开采业					
黑色金属矿采选业					
有色金属矿采选业					
非金属矿采选业					
开采辅助活动					
其他采矿业					
农副食品加工业	7	2	29562	1001152	10545
食品制造业	4		157524	398261	
酒、饮料和精制茶制造业	3	2	112289	409215	8801
烟草制品业					
纺织业	19	3	142370	582892	663
纺织服装、服饰业	19	4	81793	259653	976
皮革、毛皮、羽毛及其制品和制鞋业	76	10	347549	1004656	2906
木材加工和木、竹、藤、棕、草制品业	4	2	5778	29853	939
家具制造业	46	10	125171	600703	10724
造纸和纸制品业	11	1	40553	152168	207
印刷和记录媒介复制业	15	1	94086	251515	83
文教、工美、体育和娱乐用品制造业	48	11	143949	445997	9183
石油加工、炼焦和核燃料加工业					
化学原料和化学制品制造业	34	5	138744	1130627	4696
医药制造业	2	1	15903	38234	787
化学纤维制造业	2		1255	8919	
橡胶和塑料制品业	117	19	400502	1504976	14463
非金属矿物制品业	14	5	55327	207957	13707
黑色金属冶炼和压延加工业	11	1	23818	148517	354
有色金属冶炼和压延加工业	15	5	67605	222998	2452
金属制品业	58	11	167782	688361	1613
通用设备制造业	53	12	329488	2588194	7510
专用设备制造业	40	3	100933	301729	1388
汽车制造业	25	4	269964	1026184	2769
铁路、船舶、航空航天和其他运输设备制造业	7	1	34056	133455	146
电气机械和器材制造业	125	16	531019	2106249	6053
计算机、通信和其他电子设备制造业	294	62	3037285	17972071	62076
仪器仪表制造业	22	5	228296	890308	3034
其他制造业	14	2	27114	110498	895
废弃资源综合利用业					
金属制品、机械和设备修理业	1		414	2266	
电力、热力生产和供应业	1		25211	65228	
燃气生产和供应业	4		72762	375750	
水的生产和供应业					

4-14 续表

(2014年)

项目	利税总额(万元)	人均税收(元)	利润总额(万元)	人均利润(元)
总计	1522215	7845	997218	14902
按轻重工业分				
轻工业	478252	6867	278616	9584
重工业	1043963	8596	718602	18986
按企业规模分				
大型企业	811855	8653	563640	19649
中型企业	460616	6416	277554	9728
小型企业	251972	9695	158785	16520
微型企业	-2228	5790	-2762	-29953
按销售收入分				
10亿元以上	910718	12645	640085	29908
5-10亿元	192499	10862	120435	18153
1-5亿元	329205	4879	212350	8866
1亿元以下	89793	4382	24348	1630
按工业行业分(大类)				
煤炭开采和洗选业				
石油和天然气开采业				
黑色金属矿采选业				
有色金属矿采选业				
非金属矿采选业				
开采辅助活动				
其他采矿业				
农副食品加工业	-4376	3683	-4831	-39114
食品制造业	80730	47661	47582	68414
酒、饮料和精制茶制造业	57851	114562	21764	69093
烟草制品业				
纺织业	30802	2959	26791	19760
纺织服装、服饰业	10547	6144	2227	1645
皮革、毛皮、羽毛及其制品和制鞋业	34416	2320	17793	2484
木材加工和木、竹、藤、棕、草制品业	585	12457	-325	-4450
家具制造业	5513	3623	-2042	-979
造纸和纸制品业	17238	17780	10702	29113
印刷和记录媒介复制业	38939	6202	34400	47007
文教、工美、体育和娱乐用品制造业	4133	1741	-714	-256
石油加工、炼焦和核燃料加工业				
化学原料和化学制品制造业	54040	32542	33011	51085
医药制造业	-370	767	-406	-8584
化学纤维制造业	504	8961	226	7294
橡胶和塑料制品业	72788	5338	45886	9105
非金属矿物制品业	-5568	10589	-10031	-23803
黑色金属冶炼和压延加工业	4044	16393	2406	24085
有色金属冶炼和压延加工业	1622	8523	-811	-2841
金属制品业	28701	7270	17951	12139
通用设备制造业	68245	5999	44596	11312
专用设备制造业	29180	10754	18968	19975
汽车制造业	121076	18419	95849	69983
铁路、船舶、航空航天和其他运输设备制造业	10637	7930	7346	17706
电气机械和器材制造业	108013	5688	73750	12244
计算机、通信和其他电子设备制造业	625936	7991	412568	15452
仪器仪表制造业	41016	3810	33727	17631
其他制造业	2505	5653	229	568
废弃资源综合利用业				
金属制品、机械和设备修理业	81	10564	40	10205
电力、热力生产和供应业	20978	211116	17516	1068018
燃气生产和供应业	62410	132423	51048	594970
水的生产和供应业				

4-15 规模以上外商投资工业企业主要经济效益指标（2014年）

Main Indicators on Economic Benefit of Industrial Enterprises above Designated Size with Foreign Funds (2014)

项目	工业增加值率(%)	总资产贡献率(%)	资产负债率(%)	流动资产周转率(次/年)	成本费用利润率(%)	全员劳动生产率(元/人)	产品销售率(%)
总计	19.3	7.3	51.8	2.4	2.9	101734	98.2
按轻重工业分							
轻工业	21.1	6.1	51.8	2.0	2.6	78819	99.0
重工业	18.5	7.9	51.7	2.6	3.1	119335	97.8
按企业规模分							
大型企业	17.3	8.1	52.2	2.8	3.0	120059	98.4
中型企业	23.0	7.0	52.6	2.1	2.9	79632	97.5
小型企业	19.6	6.0	49.4	1.8	3.0	112340	98.7
微型企业	15.0	-4.2	56.4	1.6	-3.6	134167	93.5
按工业行业分(大类)							
煤炭开采和洗选业							
石油和天然气开采业							
黑色金属矿采选业							
有色金属矿采选业							
非金属矿采选业							
开采辅助活动							
其他采矿业							
农副食品加工业	3.3	-0.3	59.4	3.8	-0.4	239365	99.5
食品制造业	39.9	12.4	23.0	1.0	13.9	226491	101.0
酒、饮料和精制茶制造业	28.1	18.0	48.3	2.1	6.8	356472	100.1
烟草制品业							
纺织业	24.4	2.6	32.1	1.1	4.8	105008	100.7
纺织服装、服饰业	31.0	6.4	60.8	2.1	0.9	60404	98.6
皮革、毛皮、羽毛及其制品和制鞋业	34.1	5.2	51.6	2.0	1.8	48517	97.9
木材加工和木、竹、藤、棕、草制品业	19.3	3.8	62.7	1.0	-1.1	79048	99.3
家具制造业	21.0	1.0	57.1	1.6	-0.3	60022	100.1
造纸和纸制品业	22.1	14.0	38.4	1.7	7.5	110319	84.6
印刷和记录媒介复制业	38.3	18.5	35.0	1.7	15.8	128568	102.0
文教、工美、体育和娱乐用品制造业	33.1	1.5	46.8	2.0	-0.2	51704	98.2
石油加工、炼焦和核燃料加工业							
化学原料和化学制品制造业	12.1	7.6	46.1	2.0	3.0	214707	97.3
医药制造业	36.3	-0.4	81.8	3.1	-1.0	336223	100.0
化学纤维制造业	13.8	7.2	54.0	1.6	2.6	40478	100.0
橡胶和塑料制品业	25.8	6.2	54.3	1.9	3.1	79466	97.8
非金属矿物制品业	24.3	-1.6	45.0	2.2	-4.5	131293	95.0
黑色金属冶炼和压延加工业	16.0	3.5	46.5	1.6	1.6	238417	97.8
有色金属冶炼和压延加工业	28.3	1.2	67.4	1.5	-0.4	236794	95.1
金属制品业	23.8	6.0	42.8	2.0	2.7	113458	99.2
通用设备制造业	12.8	5.3	61.1	2.6	1.8	83580	99.9
专用设备制造业	31.1	8.6	40.9	1.3	6.6	106290	95.6
汽车制造业	25.5	16.6	41.5	2.2	10.2	197111	97.6
铁路、船舶、航空航天和其他运输设备制造业	26.5	7.7	46.0	1.3	5.8	82083	104.0
电气机械和器材制造业	24.3	6.7	51.1	1.8	3.6	88162	98.0
计算机、通信和其他电子设备制造业	16.5	7.2	56.6	2.9	2.3	113757	98.0
仪器仪表制造业	24.3	8.4	44.0	3.0	3.9	119339	95.0
其他制造业	24.2	3.3	58.2	2.3	0.2	67347	100.6
废弃资源综合利用业							
金属制品、机械和设备修理业	18.3	1.8	81.6	0.5	1.8	106243	100.0
电力、热力生产和供应业	38.7	11.5	34.0	0.8	25.6	1537228	100.6
燃气生产和供应业	18.8	23.3	46.1	5.6	15.4	848044	100.0
水的生产和供应业							

4-16 规模以上港澳台商投资工业企业主要经济指标（2014年）

Main Indicators of Industrial Enterprises above Designated Size with Hong Kong, Macao and Taiwan Funds (2014)

项目	企业单位数（个）	#亏损企业	工业增加值（万元）	主营业务收入（万元）	亏损企业亏损总额（万元）
总计	1914	308	9885027	40556604	366442
按轻重工业分					
轻工业	1065	178	4987944	17739864	82130
重工业	849	130	4897083	22816739	284312
按企业规模分					
大型企业	121	10	4136997	18217619	45978
中型企业	837	135	3939528	13784646	76770
小型企业	936	156	1799762	7443729	66282
微型企业	20	7	8741	1110609	177413
按销售收入分					
10亿元以上	60	7	3331946	17437927	171683
5-10亿元	76	9	1334344	5043592	68908
1-5亿元	581	72	3386578	12078733	69680
1亿元以下	1197	220	1832159	5996352	56172
按工业行业分(大类)					
煤炭开采和洗选业					
石油和天然气开采业					
黑色金属矿采选业					
有色金属矿采选业					
非金属矿采选业					
开采辅助活动					
其他采矿业					
农副食品加工业	5		16777	577395	
食品制造业	12	3	85185	327822	860
酒、饮料和精制茶制造业	5	1	52415	344549	24941
烟草制品业					
纺织业	63	14	214020	753686	9850
纺织服装、服饰业	121	19	523763	1727737	3749
皮革、毛皮、羽毛及其制品和制鞋业	142	24	732225	1652059	7239
木材加工和木、竹、藤、棕、草制品业	9	3	8067	39190	195
家具制造业	53	10	158968	512765	3423
造纸和纸制品业	56	6	707331	3264888	4761
印刷和记录媒介复制业	55	7	259166	765174	2432
文教、工美、体育和娱乐用品制造业	139	23	610215	1728078	5784
石油加工、炼焦和核燃料加工业	3		20324	83812	
化学原料和化学制品制造业	45	6	174897	732358	2207
医药制造业	1	1	1197	4631	303
化学纤维制造业	5	1	5343	28082	226
橡胶和塑料制品业	237	39	750594	2828841	7369
非金属矿物制品业	30	6	207244	849952	9918
黑色金属冶炼和压延加工业	9	1	28436	169819	42
有色金属冶炼和压延加工业	19	3	91251	251371	47565
金属制品业	126	15	505309	1463895	14790
通用设备制造业	71	6	366584	2154441	5499
专用设备制造业	64	15	267781	863852	6077
汽车制造业	11	2	41778	143793	311
铁路、船舶、航空航天和其他运输设备制造业	5		107881	349480	
电气机械和器材制造业	224	33	1010738	4051040	20040
计算机、通信和其他电子设备制造业	334	52	2382014	13558799	157828
仪器仪表制造业	39	10	198090	465440	9254
其他制造业	23	4	68512	216005	2423
废弃资源综合利用业					
金属制品、机械和设备修理业	1		1044	2597	
电力、热力生产和供应业	7	4	287879	645054	19360
燃气生产和供应业					
水的生产和供应业					

4-16 续表

(2014年)

项目	利税总额(万元)	人均税收(元)	利润总额(万元)	人均利润(元)
总计	1844152	6106	1094460	8914
按轻重工业分				
轻工业	912406	5873	502014	7184
重工业	931746	6413	592447	11198
按企业规模分				
大型企业	946889	7381	628727	14586
中型企业	528174	3914	278588	4369
小型企业	540111	11323	363025	23212
微型企业	-171022	17728	-175880	-641896
按销售收入分				
10亿元以上	945648	13465	612657	24774
5-10亿元	222379	5032	139862	8530
1-5亿元	507099	4360	293310	5981
1亿元以下	169027	3691	48632	1491
按工业行业分(大类)				
煤炭开采和洗选业				
石油和天然气开采业				
黑色金属矿采选业				
有色金属矿采选业				
非金属矿采选业				
开采辅助活动				
其他采矿业				
农副食品加工业	2216	6822	1535	15378
食品制造业	50952	68318	22942	55956
酒、饮料和精制茶制造业	807	26095	-13767	-24649
烟草制品业				
纺织业	34477	5866	17006	5710
纺织服装、服饰业	100132	5700	50794	5868
皮革、毛皮、羽毛及其制品和制鞋业	48903	2444	16302	1222
木材加工和木、竹、藤、棕、草制品业	783	5537	-12	-83
家具制造业	27788	4756	16380	6829
造纸和纸制品业	196413	36472	86289	28578
印刷和记录媒介复制业	96248	10353	70306	28060
文教、工美、体育和娱乐用品制造业	42748	1530	22163	1647
石油加工、炼焦和核燃料加工业	2861	42486	1961	92481
化学原料和化学制品制造业	87322	27724	65370	82558
医药制造业	-273	2922	-303	-29388
化学纤维制造业	1184	8924	449	5444
橡胶和塑料制品业	137579	5984	77923	7816
非金属矿物制品业	68637	21741	43081	36649
黑色金属冶炼和压延加工业	7891	10881	5443	24190
有色金属冶炼和压延加工业	-41427	9412	-43708	-180315
金属制品业	52510	3375	31549	5080
通用设备制造业	112229	5381	92814	25722
专用设备制造业	48489	6342	28761	9245
汽车制造业	7745	5945	5219	12280
铁路、船舶、航空航天和其他运输设备制造业	12776	11992	6564	12672
电气机械和器材制造业	178564	3705	129384	9748
计算机、通信和其他电子设备制造业	349521	5013	193512	6218
仪器仪表制造业	6630	2679	-1953	-610
其他制造业	6929	2858	3661	3201
废弃资源综合利用业				
金属制品、机械和设备修理业	373	42103	128	22121
电力、热力生产和供应业	203146	475035	164668	2032937
燃气生产和供应业				
水的生产和供应业				

4-17 规模以上港澳台商投资工业企业主要经济效益指标（2014年）

Main Indicators on Economic Benefit of Industrial Enterprises above Designated Size with Hong Kong, Macao and Taiwan Funds (2014)

项目	工业增加值率(%)	总资产贡献率(%)	资产负债率(%)	流动资产周转率(次/年)	成本费用利润率(%)	全员劳动生产率(元/人)	产品销售率(%)
总计	23.6	5.9	54.7	1.9	2.8	80509	97.6
按轻重工业分							
轻工业	27.2	6.3	51.2	1.8	2.9	71384	97.9
重工业	20.8	5.6	57.7	2.0	2.6	92560	97.5
按企业规模分							
大型企业	22.0	7.1	52.6	2.3	3.5	95978	98.1
中型企业	27.9	4.6	53.2	1.7	2.1	61781	97.8
小型企业	23.8	8.8	57.6	1.5	5.0	115079	98.4
微型企业	0.7	-14.6	82.7	3.7	-14.2	31901	85.3
按工业行业分(大类)							
煤炭开采和洗选业							
石油和天然气开采业							
黑色金属矿采选业							
有色金属矿采选业							
非金属矿采选业							
开采辅助活动							
其他采矿业							
农副食品加工业	2.9	0.3	85.0	2.1	0.3	168109	99.8
食品制造业	25.6	17.4	36.1	1.7	7.6	207769	94.9
酒、饮料和精制茶制造业	17.8	1.5	57.7	1.9	-3.8	93849	112.9
烟草制品业							
纺织业	26.9	5.2	40.5	1.7	2.3	71855	97.4
纺织服装、服饰业	27.1	7.6	59.2	1.7	3.0	60507	95.0
皮革、毛皮、羽毛及其制品和制鞋业	42.8	4.8	66.7	2.0	1.0	54901	98.4
木材加工和木、竹、藤、棕、草制品业	19.4	1.7	74.8	0.9	0.0	56214	95.3
家具制造业	30.3	6.1	40.1	1.5	3.2	66272	97.6
造纸和纸制品业	20.9	6.0	45.6	1.9	2.7	234262	95.5
印刷和记录媒介复制业	33.2	10.6	46.0	1.3	9.8	103435	99.2
文教、工美、体育和娱乐用品制造业	34.3	3.5	61.8	1.7	1.3	45354	98.3
石油加工、炼焦和核燃料加工业	25.4	4.4	73.0	1.0	2.4	958669	106.0
化学原料和化学制品制造业	23.0	12.7	42.4	1.4	9.8	220885	97.2
医药制造业	25.8	-5.6	98.5	1.3	-6.2	116213	99.8
化学纤维制造业	17.6	6.5	56.6	1.6	1.6	64847	98.4
橡胶和塑料制品业	26.4	6.6	51.0	1.9	2.8	75287	98.6
非金属矿物制品业	24.2	6.9	60.7	1.8	5.4	176303	98.5
黑色金属冶炼和压延加工业	16.4	6.1	58.6	1.7	3.3	126382	98.7
有色金属冶炼和压延加工业	34.8	-11.5	116.1	2.4	-16.2	376447	98.7
金属制品业	33.6	3.5	46.8	1.6	2.2	81369	96.4
通用设备制造业	16.6	8.3	55.6	2.2	4.4	101595	98.3
专用设备制造业	30.4	6.7	42.5	1.7	3.4	86078	99.1
汽车制造业	28.1	7.5	24.7	2.4	3.8	98301	100.4
铁路、船舶、航空航天和其他运输设备制造业	30.0	2.6	71.4	0.9	1.9	208264	97.8
电气机械和器材制造业	24.6	5.6	55.8	1.7	3.3	76153	98.7
计算机、通信和其他电子设备制造业	16.8	4.1	58.2	2.4	1.4	76534	97.2
仪器仪表制造业	41.3	2.0	44.4	2.1	-0.4	61841	99.3
其他制造业	30.2	3.0	48.6	1.6	1.7	59909	94.3
废弃资源综合利用业							
金属制品、机械和设备修理业	40.2	8.8	20.6	1.0	5.2	179961	100.0
电力、热力生产和供应业	44.6	23.1	62.1	1.4	27.1	3554064	99.9
燃气生产和供应业							
水的生产和供应业							

4-18 规模以上私营工业企业主要经济指标（2014年）

Main Indicators of Private Industrial Enterprises above Designated Size (2014)

项目	企业单位数（个）	#亏损企业	工业增加值（万元）	主营业务收入（万元）	亏损企业亏损总额（万元）
总计	1266	97	3430443	18462090	25550
按轻重工业分					
轻工业	667	51	1560962	6357742	7583
重工业	599	46	1869481	12104348	17968
按企业规模分					
大型企业	17		1109618	8406748	
中型企业	237	18	943825	3946034	10089
小型企业	971	68	1314485	5813856	14343
微型企业	41	11	62515	295452	1119
按销售收入分					
10亿元以上	10		977231	8155452	
5-10亿元	18		268303	1214968	
1-5亿元	236	12	949691	4428816	10003
1亿元以下	1002	85	1235219	4662855	15547
按工业行业分(大类)					
煤炭开采和洗选业					
石油和天然气开采业					
黑色金属矿采选业					
有色金属矿采选业					
非金属矿采选业					
开采辅助活动					
其他采矿业					
农副食品加工业	15	1	41361	419985	157
食品制造业	11		21199	100603	
酒、饮料和精制茶制造业	3		19458	97864	
烟草制品业					
纺织业	18	1	38809	122063	6
纺织服装、服饰业	188	11	619687	2104113	1072
皮革、毛皮、羽毛及其制品和制鞋业	43	4	87580	275087	104
木材加工和木、竹、藤、棕、草制品业	7	1	9438	38855	93
家具制造业	88	9	135248	587773	898
造纸和纸制品业	71	3	143707	840272	634
印刷和记录媒介复制业	23	1	58832	178514	22
文教、工美、体育和娱乐用品制造业	33	1	48900	205782	378
石油加工、炼焦和核燃料加工业	1		33071	131963	
化学原料和化学制品制造业	40	3	62914	328517	497
医药制造业	2		5420	13040	
化学纤维制造业	4		8993	60540	
橡胶和塑料制品业	111	11	197335	738015	2413
非金属矿物制品业	33	2	73738	261684	153
黑色金属冶炼和压延加工业	6	1	10359	50736	88
有色金属冶炼和压延加工业	18		52813	170903	
金属制品业	78	5	124939	451000	810
通用设备制造业	53	5	92916	417293	1186
专用设备制造业	57	3	132114	400791	473
汽车制造业	2		3023	14351	
铁路、船舶、航空航天和其他运输设备制造业	6	3	22216	103220	197
电气机械和器材制造业	143	11	319090	1525121	2490
计算机、通信和其他电子设备制造业	185	20	1018109	8649031	13875
仪器仪表制造业	16		32165	106905	
其他制造业	9	1	13311	51528	2
废弃资源综合利用业	1		2594	12656	
金属制品、机械和设备修理业					
电力、热力生产和供应业					
燃气生产和供应业					
水的生产和供应业	1		1107	3886	

4-18 续表

(2014年)

项目	利税总额(万元)	人均税收(元)	利润总额(万元)	人均利润(元)
总计	966248	11734	598230	19073
按轻重工业分				
轻工业	429583	10278	251811	14559
重工业	536664	13523	346418	24623
按企业规模分				
大型企业	464831	19232	355573	62588
中型企业	253441	9180	140870	11488
小型企业	245063	10737	101962	7650
微型企业	2913	33171	-175	-1883
按销售收入分				
10亿元以上	431777	30264	332135	100879
5-10亿元	86751	8664	63804	24089
1-5亿元	255670	11207	141907	13980
1亿元以下	192049	8621	60384	3954
按工业行业分(大类)				
煤炭开采和洗选业				
石油和天然气开采业				
黑色金属矿采选业				
有色金属矿采选业				
非金属矿采选业				
开采辅助活动				
其他采矿业				
农副食品加工业	27794	26383	21523	90548
食品制造业	5686	14105	2371	10090
酒、饮料和精制茶制造业	9660	34557	5997	56575
烟草制品业				
纺织业	9247	7787	5909	13783
纺织服装、服饰业	213247	11283	142914	22928
皮革、毛皮、羽毛及其制品和制鞋业	16155	9128	5704	4982
木材加工和木、竹、藤、棕、草制品业	1322	11106	211	2105
家具制造业	25410	8048	9060	4460
造纸和纸制品业	31865	15772	12477	10151
印刷和记录媒介复制业	9258	5896	4581	5774
文教、工美、体育和娱乐用品制造业	8662	7560	2786	3584
石油加工、炼焦和核燃料加工业	417	54403	25	3486
化学原料和化学制品制造业	19103	21603	9611	21873
医药制造业	1377	23627	491	13088
化学纤维制造业	2668	11246	1442	13232
橡胶和塑料制品业	33302	10189	12709	6288
非金属矿物制品业	18845	10097	10762	13444
黑色金属冶炼和压延加工业	2517	20552	657	7256
有色金属冶炼和压延加工业	5858	17672	2786	16030
金属制品业	17817	8036	7043	5254
通用设备制造业	30884	15210	18282	22063
专用设备制造业	35697	10917	23356	20661
汽车制造业	387	8128	145	4852
铁路、船舶、航空航天和其他运输设备制造业	12534	33248	8338	66067
电气机械和器材制造业	83854	8248	55324	15994
计算机、通信和其他电子设备制造业	325061	14609	223051	31943
仪器仪表制造业	11407	15778	5866	16701
其他制造业	4903	12421	3499	30933
废弃资源综合利用业	43		43	4722
金属制品、机械和设备修理业				
电力、热力生产和供应业				
燃气生产和供应业				
水的生产和供应业	1270		1270	249078

4-19 规模以上私营工业企业主要经济效益指标（2014年）

Main Indicators on Economic Benefit of Private Industrial Enterprises above Designated Size (2014)

项目	工业增加值率(%)	总资产贡献率(%)	资产负债率(%)	流动资产周转率(次/年)	成本费用利润率(%)	全员劳动生产率(元/人)	产品销售率(%)
总计	18.0	8.5	73.7	2.0	3.2	109373	97.1
按轻重工业分							
轻工业	22.7	10.5	69.5	1.9	4.0	90250	93.8
重工业	15.3	7.4	76.2	2.1	2.8	132882	99.0
按企业规模分							
大型企业	12.7	10.8	78.0	2.4	4.1	195314	96.2
中型企业	23.2	9.1	64.8	1.9	3.7	76966	98.2
小型企业	22.0	6.3	75.0	1.8	1.8	98629	97.7
微型企业	21.2	1.2	89.6	1.3	-0.1	671487	100.9
按工业行业分(大类)							
煤炭开采和洗选业							
石油和天然气开采业							
黑色金属矿采选业							
有色金属矿采选业							
非金属矿采选业							
开采辅助活动							
其他采矿业							
农副食品加工业	9.9	8.9	79.1	1.9	4.5	174007	98.3
食品制造业	20.1	7.9	81.3	1.8	2.2	90209	95.9
酒、饮料和精制茶制造业	18.9	23.4	77.6	4.1	6.5	183565	98.4
烟草制品业							
纺织业	30.4	6.3	73.5	0.9	5.1	90527	95.8
纺织服装、服饰业	24.4	14.1	61.3	1.6	7.3	99416	86.2
皮革、毛皮、羽毛及其制品和制鞋业	32.2	10.7	55.1	3.0	2.1	76495	103.4
木材加工和木、竹、藤、棕、草制品业	23.6	6.4	87.3	2.6	0.5	94286	99.0
家具制造业	22.6	6.7	71.1	1.8	1.6	66572	96.9
造纸和纸制品业	16.9	8.2	75.1	2.4	1.5	116911	98.7
印刷和记录媒介复制业	33.3	8.8	73.6	2.2	2.6	74161	99.7
文教、工美、体育和娱乐用品制造业	24.0	10.1	83.2	2.7	1.4	62910	100.1
石油加工、炼焦和核燃料加工业	25.4	0.4	98.7	1.3	0.02		101.1
化学原料和化学制品制造业	18.2	5.6	66.5	1.2	3.0	143181	97.2
医药制造业	34.3	10.4	77.6	1.4	3.9	144530	80.3
化学纤维制造业	14.8	11.3	76.4	2.6	2.5	82501	98.7
橡胶和塑料制品业	26.0	7.0	76.3	2.1	1.8	97638	97.9
非金属矿物制品业	28.1	10.2	71.8	1.8	4.3	92115	98.3
黑色金属冶炼和压延加工业	19.6	7.9	68.0	2.2	1.3	114466	96.0
有色金属冶炼和压延加工业	30.6	8.2	67.7	2.4	1.7	303873	99.0
金属制品业	26.9	6.8	76.8	2.0	1.6	93197	96.4
通用设备制造业	21.7	10.0	68.8	1.6	4.6	112136	98.4
专用设备制造业	31.9	9.0	68.7	1.3	6.2	116873	96.7
汽车制造业	20.8	9.5	67.8	1.5	1.0	101447	98.8
铁路、船舶、航空航天和其他运输设备制造业	18.4	27.7	60.6	3.3	6.8	176034	102.0
电气机械和器材制造业	20.4	7.4	66.8	1.5	3.8	92249	96.6
计算机、通信和其他电子设备制造业	11.7	7.2	81.4	2.4	2.5	145802	99.6
仪器仪表制造业	30.0	10.6	42.5	1.3	5.8	91586	99.4
其他制造业	24.0	10.3	56.6	1.5	6.8	117690	101.4
废弃资源综合利用业	20.2	3.1	59.2	2.0	0.3	288211	98.7
金属制品、机械和设备修理业							
电力、热力生产和供应业							
燃气生产和供应业							
水的生产和供应业	28.5	12.2	47.4	1.7	49.4	217088	100.0

4-20 大中型工业企业主要经济指标（2014年）

Main Indicators of Large and Medium-sized Industrial Enterprises (2014)

项目	企业单位数（个）	#亏损企业	工业增加值（万元）	主营业务收入（万元）	亏损企业亏损总额（万元）
总计	1970	268	19446000	91885103	263818
按轻重工业分					
轻工业	1098	156	8099716	31659376	123771
重工业	872	112	11346284	60225727	140046
按企业规模分					
大型企业	249	17	11000739	56452290	84624
中型企业	1721	251	8445261	35432813	179194
按工业行业分(大类)					
煤炭开采和洗选业					
石油和天然气开采业					
黑色金属矿采选业					
有色金属矿采选业					
非金属矿采选业					
开采辅助活动					
其他采矿业					
农副食品加工业	8	2	52391	1612177	9437
食品制造业	10	1	254085	770836	253
酒、饮料和精制茶制造业	8	3	176565	827218	35000
烟草制品业					
纺织业	32	3	321721	1183433	6638
纺织服装、服饰业	148	16	1068647	3521623	2843
皮革、毛皮、羽毛及其制品和制鞋业	165	22	1105916	2775889	10700
木材加工和木、竹、藤、棕、草制品业	4	1	8710	46798	82
家具制造业	86	9	391791	1546366	6952
造纸和纸制品业	53	5	877986	4072632	5026
印刷和记录媒介复制业	44	2	285496	864099	522
文教、工美、体育和娱乐用品制造业	143	23	797372	2715680	12606
石油加工、炼焦和核燃料加工业					
化学原料和化学制品制造业	18	2	90860	471441	866
医药制造业	3	1	72978	150620	787
化学纤维制造业	2		6483	41890	
橡胶和塑料制品业	173	35	940634	3401300	15979
非金属矿物制品业	33	8	263135	958228	23230
黑色金属冶炼和压延加工业	5		25670	85976	
有色金属冶炼和压延加工业	4	2	13898	35577	1551
金属制品业	79	4	624062	1806425	5544
通用设备制造业	58	10	658847	4510667	10834
专用设备制造业	51	9	340055	1061420	3915
汽车制造业	19		298797	1121962	
铁路、船舶、航空航天和其他运输设备制造业	13		163488	617116	
电气机械和器材制造业	238	28	1676303	6195696	16963
计算机、通信和其他电子设备制造业	502	67	6894553	43644008	78961
仪器仪表制造业	47	11	422310	1361067	8641
其他制造业	16	3	71652	251416	2344
废弃资源综合利用业					
金属制品、机械和设备修理业					
电力、热力生产和供应业	4		1429932	5769240	
燃气生产和供应业	2		67775	352161	
水的生产和供应业	2	1	43887	112147	4145

4-20 续表

(2014年)

项目	利税总额(万元)	人均税收(元)	利润总额(万元)	人均利润(元)
总计	4870355	9129	2985261	14457
按轻重工业分				
轻工业	1798935	6965	1043892	9630
重工业	3071420	11520	1941368	19790
按企业规模分				
大型企业	3170298	13210	2012116	22951
中型企业	1700056	6117	973145	8190
按工业行业分(大类)				
煤炭开采和洗选业				
石油和天然气开采业				
黑色金属矿采选业				
有色金属矿采选业				
非金属矿采选业				
开采辅助活动				
其他采矿业				
农副食品加工业	18656	46478	2119	5957
食品制造业	135771	54441	70491	58787
酒、饮料和精制茶制造业	60968	52266	12027	12843
烟草制品业				
纺织业	73199	5405	52437	13651
纺织服装、服饰业	311919	8311	193911	13656
皮革、毛皮、羽毛及其制品和制鞋业	99497	2825	38307	1769
木材加工和木、竹、藤、棕、草制品业	874	2132	510	2987
家具制造业	75065	5747	40131	6601
造纸和纸制品业	256624	32264	120690	28646
印刷和记录媒介复制业	73676	4903	57146	16950
文教、工美、体育和娱乐用品制造业	67599	2008	33879	2018
石油加工、炼焦和核燃料加工业				
化学原料和化学制品制造业	33142	12538	22664	27120
医药制造业	41693	77789	26423	134605
化学纤维制造业	1887	11792	1064	15236
橡胶和塑料制品业	171733	5721	92924	6746
非金属矿物制品业	67648	14785	35226	16064
黑色金属冶炼和压延加工业	8332	16693	3888	14605
有色金属冶炼和压延加工业	212	8906	-1372	-7713
金属制品业	113728	5104	73300	9254
通用设备制造业	159123	4967	122644	16699
专用设备制造业	80113	7305	51658	13261
汽车制造业	128545	16212	102480	63739
铁路、船舶、航空航天和其他运输设备制造业	38280	12496	25610	25259
电气机械和器材制造业	373190	4824	275178	13544
计算机、通信和其他电子设备制造业	1836972	9265	1232317	18883
仪器仪表制造业	58728	3625	40048	7772
其他制造业	6951	3059	3387	2907
废弃资源综合利用业				
金属制品、机械和设备修理业				
电力、热力生产和供应业	513090	133983	209778	92666
燃气生产和供应业	58383	141563	47242	600276
水的生产和供应业	4756	37649	-847	-5689

4-21 大中型工业企业主要经济效益指标（2014年）

Main Indicators on Economic Benefit of Large and Medium-sized Industrial Enterprises (2014)

项目	工业增加值率(%)	总资产贡献率(%)	资产负债率(%)	流动资产周转率(次/年)	成本费用利润率(%)	全员劳动生产率(元/人)	产品销售率(%)
总计	20.7	8.0	57.4	2.3	3.3	94170	98.0
按轻重工业分							
轻工业	24.8	7.3	53.8	1.9	3.4	74721	97.3
重工业	18.5	8.5	59.8	2.6	3.3	115662	98.4
按企业规模分							
大型企业	19.0	9.2	58.0	2.6	3.6	125477	98.2
中型企业	23.3	6.5	56.7	1.9	2.8	71072	97.8
按工业行业分(大类)							
煤炭开采和洗选业							
石油和天然气开采业							
黑色金属矿采选业							
有色金属矿采选业							
非金属矿采选业							
开采辅助活动							
其他采矿业							
农副食品加工业	3.7	2.1	76.9	2.9	0.1	147249	104.1
食品制造业	32.3	14.4	32.6	1.2	10.1	211896	97.3
酒、饮料和精制茶制造业	22.8	9.5	54.4	2.2	1.6	188558	104.6
烟草制品业							
纺织业	26.5	4.9	37.9	1.4	4.6	83751	98.9
纺织服装、服饰业	25.9	10.9	59.4	1.5	5.8	75261	88.8
皮革、毛皮、羽毛及其制品和制鞋业	39.1	5.9	61.5	2.1	1.4	51059	98.5
木材加工和木、竹、藤、棕、草制品业	16.2	4.4	72.6	3.0	1.0	50994	97.5
家具制造业	24.9	5.8	55.7	1.6	2.7	64448	98.0
造纸和纸制品业	20.7	6.7	49.3	1.9	3.0	208389	95.2
印刷和记录媒介复制业	32.5	8.7	44.6	1.6	7.0	84679	99.6
文教、工美、体育和娱乐用品制造业	28.5	4.1	60.5	2.0	1.3	47490	97.7
石油加工、炼焦和核燃料加工业							
化学原料和化学制品制造业	18.5	7.7	44.5	1.7	5.0	108723	97.6
医药制造业	46.5	13.2	30.2	1.1	20.8	371770	100.3
化学纤维制造业	15.2	12.5	69.2	2.9	2.6	92884	98.4
橡胶和塑料制品业	27.3	7.0	55.0	2.1	2.8	68289	98.7
非金属矿物制品业	26.8	5.3	59.0	1.4	3.8	119994	96.5
黑色金属冶炼和压延加工业	29.4	13.4	63.8	1.7	4.7	96432	97.8
有色金属冶炼和压延加工业	47.5	1.4	60.8	1.8	-3.7	78124	115.1
金属制品业	33.1	6.0	46.4	1.8	4.2	78790	96.7
通用设备制造业	14.5	6.7	61.7	2.6	2.8	89706	99.2
专用设备制造业	31.0	8.1	48.1	1.6	5.1	87297	98.0
汽车制造业	25.6	16.6	38.0	2.3	10.0	185842	96.0
铁路、船舶、航空航天和其他运输设备制造业	26.0	5.5	66.4	1.2	4.2	161247	101.8
电气机械和器材制造业	26.0	7.3	51.1	1.7	4.6	82503	97.9
计算机、通信和其他电子设备制造业	15.5	8.1	65.7	2.6	2.9	105648	98.6
仪器仪表制造业	29.5	6.7	43.4	2.6	3.0	81961	96.2
其他制造业	27.6	3.1	50.5	2.0	1.4	61499	95.9
废弃资源综合利用业							
金属制品、机械和设备修理业							
电力、热力生产和供应业	24.9	12.6	49.5	10.1	3.8	631651	99.5
燃气生产和供应业	18.8	23.2	46.1	5.5	15.1	861181	100.0
水的生产和供应业	37.1	5.4	86.7	1.2	-0.7	294939	96.1

4-22 主要年份规模以上工业企业经济效益指标

Main Indicators on Economic Benefit of Industrial Enterprises above Designated Size in Main Years

项　　目	单位	1985年	1990年	1995年	2000年	2005年	2010年	2013年	2014年
产品销售率	%	85.6	94.7	98.7	99.8	99.5	99.9	98.4	97.9
成本费用利润率	%	6.5	1.5	5.0	5.4	3.3	4.8	3.0	3.1
产值利税率	%	6.9	6.4	9.8	9.2	4.6	6.1	5.4	5.0
资金利税率	%	9.0	6.3	6.9	7.5	5.5	7.8	8.0	7.8
销售利税率	%	8.2	6.7	9.1	9.2	4.7	6.1	5.5	5.1
每百元固定资产原值实现的产值	元	174.9	133.6	108.7	125.5	212.4	240.6	273.0	288.0
每百元固定资产原值实现的利税	元	14.2	8.5	10.7	11.5	9.9	14.6	14.8	14.5
每百元固定资产原值实现的利润	元	4.4	1.8	5.5	6.9	6.7	11.0	7.8	8.7
每百元流动资产实现的产值	元	210.2	247.8	169.4	178.6	216.3	204.3	207.4	212.9
每百元流动资产实现的利税	元	17.1	15.7	16.6	16.4	10.0	12.4	11.2	10.7
每百元流动资产实现的利润	元	4.9	3.3	8.6	9.8	6.8	9.3	5.9	6.4
亏损企业亏损面	%	7.2	11.1	25.9	31.3	30.1	16.2	13.6	12.9
全部流动资产周转天数	天	173.7	155.6	201.1	189.0	169.8	179.4	174.8	170.0
全员劳动生产率	元/人	2906	6439	13778	36101	53340	60854	91121	96964
人均利税	元	626	1519	5351	11703	9193	16728	22425	23775

注：由于1993年财务会计制度改革，本表中有关财务指标1993年起数据与往年不可比；全员劳动生产率1993年起按增加值计算，以前年份按净产值计算；1993年以前的流动资产按定额资金计算，下同。

4-23 主要年份规模以上国有经济工业企业经济效益指标

Main Indicators on Economic Benefit of State-owned and State-holding Industrial Enterprises above Designated Size in Main Years

项　　目	单位	1985年	1990年	1995年	2000年	2005年	2010年	2013年	2014年
产品销售率	%	89.6	102.0	100.8	98.3	100.0	99.8	100.0	100.2
成本费用利润率	%	8.0	-0.8	15.5	7.0	5.8	3.2	2.1	5.9
产值利税率	%	13.2	9.2	40.6	69.4	11.3	7.3	6.3	10.8
资金利税率	%	20.4	8.3	14.9	21.6	10.6	6.7	8.8	13.8
销售利税率	%	14.8	9.0	20.6	19.2	11.3	7.3	6.3	10.2
每百元固定资产原值实现的产值	元	142.9	85.5	61.1	63.4	105.0	79.0	82.5	76.5
每百元固定资产原值实现的利税	元	21.1	7.8	24.8	44.0	11.8	5.7	5.2	8.3
每百元固定资产原值实现的利润	元	9.6	-0.6	10.8	14.5	5.6	2.4	1.7	4.6
每百元流动资产实现的产值	元	445.1	397.8	96.3	73.4	443.4	794.5	1997.1	438.5
每百元流动资产实现的利税	元	65.7	36.4	39.1	50.9	50.0	57.7	126.7	47.4
每百元流动资产实现的利润	元	27.5	-2.4	17.0	16.7	23.8	24.6	40.5	26.2
亏损企业亏损面	%	9.9	16.7	20.9		20.0			15.4
全部流动资产周转天数	天	80.9	88.7	299.8	137.7	83.0	46.1	17.8	77.2
全员劳动生产率	元/人	3641	11253	73910	456736	2320312	405232	497858	596296
人均利税	元	1757	5325	55113	303960	1197862	144620	147376	252736

4-24 主要年份规模以上集体经济工业企业经济效益指标

Main Indicators on Economic Benefit of Collective-owned Industrial Enterprises above Designated Size in Main Years

项　　目	单位	1985年	1990年	1995年	2000年	2005年	2010年	2013年	2014年
产品销售率	%	85.1	92.2	98.0	97.0	100.5	97.4	98.7	97.6
成本费用利润率	%	5.9	3.3	5.2	2.7	3.3	9.7	0.9	0.4
产值利税率	%	9.3	6.9	9.0	5.1	5.8	10.4	3.3	2.4
资金利税率	%	15.1	9.7	6.0	2.9	3.2	9.7	2.6	1.7
销售利税率	%	11.0	7.5	8.7	5.2	5.8	10.7	3.3	3.0
每百元固定资产原值实现的产值	元	236.7	159.4	128.0	99.3	98.1	131.1	79.1	70.0
每百元固定资产原值实现的利税	元	22.1	11.0	11.5	5.0	5.7	13.6	2.6	1.7
每百元固定资产原值实现的利润	元	10.8	4.5	6.4	2.4	3.0	11.5	0.6	0.2
每百元流动资产实现的产值	元	509.0	225.7	179.5	113.8	157.7	214.9	155.4	124.0
每百元流动资产实现的利税	元	47.5	15.6	16.1	5.7	9.1	22.4	5.1	3.0
每百元流动资产实现的利润	元	23.2	6.4	9.0	2.8	4.8	18.8	1.2	0.4
亏损企业亏损面	%	6.6	8.8	12.8	18.6	25.9	22.5	33.3	37.5
全部流动资产周转天数	天	84.3	175.3	197.4	340.1	241.7	175.1	226.4	349.8
全员劳动生产率	元/人	2664	5437	5820	16344	28414	31412	45399	53357
人均利税	元	715	1058	1533	3135	5241	8428	3938	3121

4-25 主要年份大中型工业企业经济效益指标

Main Indicators on Economic Benefit of Large and Medium-sized Industrial Enterprises in Main Years

项　　目	单位	1985年	1990年	1995年	2000年	2005年	2010年	2013年	2014年
产品销售率	%	104.3	103.5	99.7	98.6	99.5	100.6	98.2	98.0
成本费用利润率	%	14.3	2.2	12.9	12.0	3.8	5.1	3.0	3.3
产值利税率	%	16.1	8.7	19.9	21.4	4.7	6.4	5.5	5.2
资金利税率	%	14.8	6.5	14.0	15.3	6.1	8.4	8.4	8.3
销售利税率	%	15.5	8.4	19.8	21.7	4.7	6.4	5.6	5.3
每百元固定资产原值实现的产值	元	106.0	87.1	112.8	98.4	229.8	221.6	266.5	286.6
每百元固定资产原值实现的利税	元	17.1	7.6	22.4	21.1	10.7	14.2	14.7	14.8
每百元固定资产原值实现的利润	元	11.5	1.7	13.1	13.0	8.4	10.9	7.7	9.1
每百元流动资产实现的产值	元	758.8	329.3	174.3	183.4	227.4	220.6	222.5	230.1
每百元流动资产实现的利税	元	122.4	28.6	34.6	39.2	10.6	14.2	12.3	11.9
每百元流动资产实现的利润	元	82.3	6.4	20.2	24.2	8.3	10.9	6.5	7.3
亏损企业亏损面	%		17.2	22.2	12.8	20.1	12.2	14.3	13.6
全部流动资产周转天数	天	46.1	107.1	209.5	210.2	160.8	164.8	163.3	157.8
全员劳动生产率	元/人	6202	16492	81787	280810	72657	66101	88423	94170
人均利税	元	2601	7883	52997	165448	11918	18679	21853	23585

4-26 主要年份规模以上港澳台商投资工业企业经济效益指标

Main Indicators on Economic Benefit of Industrial Enterprises above Designated Size with Hong Kong, Macao and Taiwan Funds in Main Years

项　　目	单位	1995年	2000年	2005年	2010年	2013年	2014年
产品销售率	%	99.6	100.8	99.4	99.7	98.0	97.6
成本费用利润率	%	2.1	4.6	3.2	5.4	2.6	2.8
产值利税率	%	4.9	6.6	4.0	6.3	5.0	4.4
资金利税率	%	3.8	5.4	4.6	7.6	6.4	6.1
销售利税率	%	4.9	6.5	4.1	6.3	5.1	4.5
每百元固定资产原值实现的产值	元	114.8	114.5	198.1	216.6	220.7	233.4
每百元固定资产原值实现的利税	元	5.6	7.5	8.0	13.6	11.0	10.3
每百元固定资产原值实现的利润	元	2.6	5.1	6.0	11.1	5.5	6.1
每百元流动资产实现的产值	元	165.2	182.2	192.3	189.1	189.6	196.1
每百元流动资产实现的利税	元	8.1	12.0	7.8	11.8	9.4	8.6
每百元流动资产实现的利润	元	3.7	8.1	5.8	9.7	4.7	5.1
亏损企业亏损面	%	46.4	36.1	35.1	20.2	18.6	16.1
全部流动资产周转天数	天	199.1	199.9	191.1	194.1	191.5	187.6
全员劳动生产率	元/人	17478	28933	41933	54793	74074	80509
人均利税	元	4232	7026	6244	14293	15304	15020

4-27 主要年份规模以上外商投资工业企业经济效益指标

Main Indicators on Economic Benefit of Foreign-funded Industrial Enterprises above Designated Size in Main Years

项　　目	单位	1995年	2000年	2005年	2010年	2013年	2014年
产品销售率	%	91.0	99.2	99.4	100.1	99.3	98.2
成本费用利润率	%	-2.6	4.7	2.8	4.4	3.4	2.9
产值利税率	%	-0.6	5.7	3.2	5.3	5.6	4.3
资金利税率	%	-0.5	7.4	4.1	7.5	10.1	7.8
销售利税率	%	-0.6	5.7	3.2	5.3	5.6	4.4
每百元固定资产原值实现的产值	元	155.45	231.22	285.20	286.90	366.78	356.3
每百元固定资产原值实现的利税	元	-0.87	13.08	9.20	15.30	20.40	15.3
每百元固定资产原值实现的利润	元	-1.90	10.26	7.60	12.10	11.96	10.1
每百元流动资产实现的产值	元	94.26	250.96	223.60	211.10	238.40	238.7
每百元流动资产实现的利税	元	-1.53	14.20	7.20	11.20	13.26	10.3
每百元流动资产实现的利润	元	5.53	11.14	5.90	8.90	7.77	6.7
亏损企业亏损面	%	38.2	31.3	34.5	18.8	17.5	18.1
全部流动资产周转天数	天	174	148	164	173	152	152.0
全员劳动生产率	元/人	3646	50318	70722	66212	102023	101734
人均利税	元	-700	13714	8288	16893	27351	22747

4-28 主要年份规模以上工业产品产量

Output of Main Industrial Products of Industrial Enterprises above Designated Size in Main Years

产品名称	单位	1985年	1990年	1995年	2000年	2005年	2010年	2013年	2014年
精制食用植物油	吨	5571	4431	6824	5180	181869	1135677	2632365	971703
饮料酒	千升	4034	2441	1720			493644	560442	379694
软饮料	吨		44061	71566	158599	861853	3142076	2088348	699822
棉　纱	吨		321	9902	3048	49383	11252	1825	3931
布	万米		82	31045	28139	65669	15794	10799	9988
服　装	万件	108	1835	112177	85635	70054	140556	127970	143997
#衬　衫	万件			2518	3624	2210	6372	10118	9135
西服套装	万件			205	1761	555	204	241	209
轻　革	万平方米		5	1076	378	1391	744	444	365
皮革鞋靴	万双	17	457	27184	23474	31942	43062	23888	18961
人造板	立方米		7100	40666		167088	266113	349044	333331
家　具	万件	815	8657	77501	151374	7974	7390	6360	5596
机制纸及纸板	万吨	3	11	34	62	408	933	1202	1546
中成药	吨		216	6268	2354	1759	2478	2791	2908
塑料制品	吨	3089	17335	624476	571900	1265865	3998208	1753307	1234390
#塑料薄膜	吨		1928	59128	71394	83954	134737	114880	125683
水　泥	万吨	41	140	283	435	305	249	250	821
砖	万块	159305	296962	252783		2903		2570	2726
卫生陶瓷制品	万件	561	480	2414	1860	5745	2426	524	154
耐火材料制品	吨	7600	9928	9144			62512	2261	1714
钢　材	吨	4678	1730	19690	14550	1087242	191656	273198	189485
铝　材	吨		881	3536	4080	61510	69933	56634	90227
输送机械	吨		8622	3736		33200		40741	8934
电动手提式工具	万台		1.89	471	357	6	1520	2098	2210
滚动轴承	万套	36	373	691	594	1333	4232	2846	18820
民用钢质船舶	载重吨	1916	841	3620	2894		18186	310379	123739

注：2000年以前家具的计量单位为“万元”，输送机械的计量单位为“吨”。

4-28 续表

产品名称	单位	1985年	1990年	1995年	2000年	2005年	2010年	2013年	2014年
交流电动机	万千瓦	23	19	43	87		193	178	1965655
变压器	千伏安				6730	816409	2980343	4346147	2356850
电力电缆	千米		15091	20694	61996	78266	383829	1625169	2878259
原电池及原电池组	万只	12354	7607	63237	69401	214507	417215	407740	383555
家用吸尘器	万台	0.13	7.35	483	67	464	428	277	191
家用电风扇	万台		106	474	436	964	2081	1268	940
房间空气调节器	台	31		26480	39582	4941		30721	42680
自行车	辆			95439	185608	885211	1014533	992655	980075
家用电冰箱	台			35336		19360		6585	
白炽灯泡	万只			5778	8560	45164	13198	6397	6329
灯具及照明装置	万件		87	42407	25135	14017	22819	22644	26603
电话单机	万部		17	877	1074	3651	4809	3637	3917
移动通信手持机(手机)	万部				619	639	1995	13928	20286
电子计算机整机	万台				27	180	44	996	185
彩色显像管	万只			210	394				
电子元件	亿只	0.14	2.05	72	104	4642	9185	17565	10936
显示器	万台						157	88	200
打印机	万台						57	225	90
硬盘存储器	万台						30	4792	249
半导体分立器件	亿只			248.48	3.23	220.32	404.44	451.36	505.34
彩色电视机	万台		1.04	81	134	135	536	696	547
组合音响	万台			1136	1572	2446	3637	4947	4306
照相机	万台		3	374	122	1355	210	73	30
表	万只		15	8514	954	1370	2168	1689	1881
钟	万只			1986	984	1193	3776	3069	2172
发电量	亿千瓦时	0.29	93	139	269	344	356	348	344
自来水生产量	万吨			21070	102083	94962	179639	155376	166730

4-29 规模以上五大支柱产业及四个特色产业主要经济指标（2014年）

Main Indicators of Five Pillar Industries & Four Characteristic Industries above Designated Size (2014)

项　　目	企业单位数(个)	#亏损企业	工业增加值(万元)	主营业务收入(万元)	亏损企业亏损总额(万元)
总　计	4109	522	19436976	98909559	448922
按轻重工业分					
轻工业	2295	297	9141381	38665748	157223
重工业	1814	225	10295595	60243811	291699
按企业规模分					
大型企业	226	17	8968549	48748877	84624
中型企业	1417	196	6908634	30124451	125532
小型企业	2389	285	3518240	18516394	102600
微型企业	77	24	41552	1519838	136166
按工业行业分(大类)					
五大支柱产业	3306	424	16923682	88612559	406713
电子信息制造业	980	146	7348930	47676484	238829
电气机械及设备制造业	1173	149	4642512	19935626	78666
纺织服装鞋帽制造业	856	103	3172360	9808870	31393
食品饮料加工制造业	95	13	656097	5750117	51619
造纸及纸制品业	202	13	1103784	5441462	6207
四个特色产业	803	98	2513293	10297001	42209
玩具及文体用品制造业	252	38	929540	3217098	17137
家具制造业	259	33	581842	2393009	15075
化工制品制造业	177	18	539231	3301942	7462
包装印刷业	115	9	462680	1384952	2536

4-29 续表

(2014年)

项　　目	利税总额(万元)	人均税收(元)	利润总额(万元)	人均利润(元)
总　计	4674822	8239	2893686	13386
按轻重工业分				
轻工业	1983215	7430	1107500	9397
重工业	2691607	9209	1786187	18167
按企业规模分				
大型企业	2481878	10063	1687109	21361
中型企业	1399189	5980	806629	8140
小型企业	916662	10205	532477	14145
微型企业	-122908	20915	-132528	-288105
按工业行业分(大类)				
五大支柱产业	4145852	8699	2567305	14148
电子信息制造业	1928284	9243	1249108	17000
电气机械及设备制造业	1071096	6477	744329	14753
纺织服装鞋帽制造业	560249	5340	304520	6359
食品饮料加工制造业	283997	43100	134858	38973
造纸及纸制品业	302226	27155	134491	21773
四个特色产业	528970	5835	326381	9400
玩具及文体用品制造业	82252	2362	37904	2019
家具制造业	96924	6252	41659	4712
化工制品制造业	194695	25276	131246	52283
包装印刷业	155099	8592	115573	25123

4-30 规模以上电子信息、电气机械及仪器仪表制造业主要指标（2011-2014年）

Main Indicators of Electronic Information, Machinery and Instrument Manufacturing above Designated Size (2011-2014)

指　　标	单位	2011年	2012年	2013年	2014年
企业单位数	个	1292	1373	1539	1066
#亏损企业单位数	个	231	239	224	161
工业增加值	亿元	633.84	775.11	976.71	782.88
主营业务收入	亿元	3754.40	4264.03	4944.96	4924.69
成本费用总额	亿元	3647.55	4180.21	4865.67	4884.52
#营业成本及销售费用	亿元	3476.10	3973.63	4627.66	4645.96
管理费用	亿元	171.69	198.47	230.54	237.00
财务费用	亿元	-0.24	8.12	7.47	1.56
利税总额	亿元	152.61	178.97	221.64	199.33
#利润总额	亿元	113.66	102.10	115.02	129.04
应交增值税	亿元	32.39	67.43	91.75	58.01
亏损企业亏损总额	亿元	16.72	17.88	26.70	25.11
企业资产总额	亿元	2390.82	2645.73	3089.40	2789.34
#流动资产	亿元	1622.67	1823.10	2225.10	2022.16
#应收帐款余额	亿元	663.92	729.51	904.43	798.44
产成品存货	亿元	141.08	161.77	155.21	142.76
企业负债总额	亿元	1406.50	1557.62	1945.82	1779.39
企业资产负债率	%	58.8	58.9	63.0	63.8
成本费用利润率	%	3.1	2.4	2.4	2.6

注：本表统计范围为规模以上计算机、通信和其他电子设备制造业、电气机械和器材制造业、仪器仪表制造业。

4-31 规模以上先进制造业企业主要经济指标（2014年）

Main Indicators of Advanced Manufacturing Enterprises above Designated Size (2014)

项目	企业单位数（个）	#亏损企业	工业增加值（万元）	主营业务收入（万元）	亏损企业亏损总额（万元）
总计	2239	272	11375070	64452944	313548
按企业规模分					
大型企业	140	11	5865982	36491259	45213
中型企业	639	80	3347586	15329431	62794
小型企业	1428	173	2154151	11370165	75209
微型企业	32	8	7351	1262088	130332
按工业行业分					
装备制造业	1977	247	10657575	60312395	305431
金属制品业	284	29	782091	2674744	17089
通用设备制造业	195	20	547563	2753230	11894
专用设备制造业	184	25	543283	1712043	9173
汽车制造业	54	9	363273	1397218	5608
铁路、船舶、航空航天和其他运输设备制造业	7	2	102442	340757	249
电气机械和器材制造业	337	34	1193270	5482097	20150
计算机、通信和其他电子设备制造业	866	122	6913297	44977194	230644
仪器仪表制造业	50	6	212356	975112	10625
船舶、航空航天器修理					
钢铁冶炼及加工	23	2	57166	399283	442
炼铁					
炼钢					
钢压延加工	23	2	57166	399283	442
铁合金冶炼					
石油及化学	239	23	660328	3741266	7675
石油和天然气开采业					
石油加工、炼焦及核燃料加工业	4		53395	215775	
化学原料和化学制品制造业	173	18	485836	3086167	7462
橡胶制品业	62	5	121097	439324	213

4-31 续表 1

(2014年)

项　　目	利税总额(万元)	人均税收(元)	利润总额(万元)	人均利润(元)	工业增加值率(%)
总　　计	2855700	8958	1871028	17022	17.3
按企业规模分					
大型企业	1593872	10079	1124335	24135	15.8
中型企业	756754	6538	480996	11405	21.0
小型企业	628534	11154	394921	18856	19.0
微型企业	-123460	26586	-129223	-596048	0.5
按工业行业分					
装备制造业	2630063	8606	1721083	16295	17.2
金属制品业	97159	4993	52666	5910	28.5
通用设备制造业	147378	8492	99476	17634	19.3
专用设备制造业	130424	8980	81386	14903	31.2
汽车制造业	148371	15803	114348	53113	25.0
铁路、船舶、航空航天和其他运输设备制造业	18794	22156	11289	33331	29.6
电气机械和器材制造业	227999	4697	160233	11105	21.4
计算机、通信和其他电子设备制造业	1819072	9608	1178865	17691	15.0
仪器仪表制造业	40866	8790	22820	11115	20.5
船舶、航空航天器修理					
钢铁冶炼及加工	9009	17661	5544	28259	14.1
炼铁					
炼钢					
钢压延加工	9009	17661	5544	28259	14.1
铁合金冶炼					
石油及化学	216628	17610	144400	35206	17.8
石油和天然气开采业					
石油加工、炼焦及核燃料加工业	3278	60962	1986	93665	25.4
化学原料和化学制品制造业	191417	24972	129260	51930	16.1
橡胶制品业	21933	5517	13154	8266	25.8

4-31 续表 2

(2014年)

项目	总资产贡献率(%)	资产负债率(%)	流动资产周转率(次/年)	成本费用利润率(%)	全员劳动生产率(元/人)	产品销售率(%)
总计	7.2	61.4	2.2	3.0	103484	98.1
按企业规模分						
大型企业	8.3	66.1	2.6	3.1	125920	98.8
中型企业	7.2	53.8	2.0	3.2	79374	97.2
小型企业	6.9	59.4	1.5	3.6	102853	98.6
微型企业	-11.0	73.5	3.0	-9.4	33908	85.6
按工业行业分						
装备制造业	7.1	61.8	2.3	2.9	100902	98.1
金属制品业	4.2	53.2	1.7	2.0	87759	96.9
通用设备制造业	7.6	61.9	1.9	3.7	97068	98.3
专用设备制造业	8.0	52.0	1.5	4.9	99486	99.5
汽车制造业	14.4	44.8	2.1	8.8	168737	96.2
铁路、船舶、航空航天和其他运输设备制造业	3.7	71.5	0.9	3.4	302455	98.4
电气机械和器材制造业	5.9	59.9	1.7	3.0	82701	98.2
计算机、通信和其他电子设备制造业	7.3	64.5	2.5	2.6	103747	98.2
仪器仪表制造业	7.3	47.7	2.5	2.4	103432	94.7
船舶、航空航天器修理						
钢铁冶炼及加工	3.4	58.4	1.9	1.4	291368	95.1
炼铁						
炼钢						
钢压延加工	3.4	58.4	1.9	1.4	291368	95.1
铁合金冶炼						
石油及化学	8.0	56.6	1.7	4.0	160993	98.0
石油和天然气开采业						
石油加工、炼焦及核燃料加工业	2.4	86.3	1.1	0.9	2518615	103.0
化学原料和化学制品制造业	8.6	53.7	1.7	4.4	195185	97.9
橡胶制品业	7.0	59.4	1.8	3.1	76100	96.7

4-32 规模以上高技术制造业企业主要经济指标（2014年）

Main Indicators of High-tech Manufacturing Enterprises above Designated Size (2014)

项目	企业单位数（个）	#亏损企业	工业增加值（万元）	主营业务收入（万元）	亏损企业亏损总额（万元）
总计	1116	169	8310251	52434962	257742
按企业规模分					
大型企业	127	9	5479989	35908974	38619
中型企业	438	70	2253083	11986873	52689
小型企业	531	83	615094	3441190	35896
微型企业	20	7	-37915	1097926	130537
按工业行业分					
信息化学品制造业	1		7783	114284	
医药制造业	10	2	90028	194576	1090
航空航天器制造业					
电子及通信设备制造业	840	134	6453508	42306604	234013
通信设备制造业	72	16	2102414	18529215	30023
雷达及配套设备制造业	2		6649	43610	
广播电视设备制造业	22	4	72321	292479	3121
电子器件制造业	125	27	745481	7294745	151479
电子元件制造业	412	53	2848569	12291666	37529
视听设备制造业	114	24	435633	2699290	8185
其他电子设备制造业	93	10	242442	1155599	3675
电子计算机及办公设备制造业	154	14	1148722	7810374	6646
计算机整机制造业	6		69791	170325	
计算机零部件制造业	87	5	656597	3995307	4243
计算机外围设备制造业	37	7	119527	898925	573
其他计算机制造业	10		49507	305323	
办公设备制造业	14	2	253300	2440493	1830
医疗设备及仪器仪表制造业	60	9	239415	1065137	11605
医疗仪器设备及器械制造业	10	3	27059	90025	980
仪器仪表制造业	50	6	212356	975112	10625
公共软件服务制造业					
其他	1		10430	34278	

4-32　续表 1

(2014年)

项　　目	利税总额(万元)	人均税收(元)	利润总额(万元)	人均利润(元)	工业增加值率(%)
总　　计	2219232	9125	1469190	17874	15.5
按企业规模分					
大型企业	1608346	10918	1136470	26295	15.0
中型企业	495708	6455	303930	10230	18.2
小型企业	239664	8992	158091	17427	17.7
微型企业	-124486	24934	-129301	-669605	-2.8
按工业行业分					
信息化学品制造业	5484	29442	5330	1025077	7.3
医药制造业	47040	59081	28831	93547	44.2
航空航天器制造业					
电子及通信设备制造业	1734245	10192	1106696	17973	14.9
通信设备制造业	893438	27803	591975	54597	11.3
雷达及配套设备制造业	2754	18847	1263	15971	15.3
广播电视设备制造业	7847	4826	2709	2545	25.0
电子器件制造业	98804	9562	28863	3946	9.8
电子元件制造业	561898	6061	368766	11574	22.5
视听设备制造业	109212	5696	70243	10267	15.7
其他电子设备制造业	60293	4880	42877	12014	21.0
电子计算机及办公设备制造业	268583	4399	204237	13963	14.3
计算机整机制造业	66230	34326	56228	192957	49.2
计算机零部件制造业	89849	3367	59519	6607	15.7
计算机外围设备制造业	28292	5063	18576	9681	12.3
其他计算机制造业	9667	2306	8089	11815	16.0
办公设备制造业	74544	4669	61826	22693	10.4
医疗设备及仪器仪表制造业	42837	7706	23437	9309	21.1
医疗仪器设备及器械制造业	1971	2913	618	1330	27.3
仪器仪表制造业	40866	8790	22820	11115	20.5
公共软件服务制造业					
其他	6443	10407	6050	160053	30.4

4-32　续表 2

(2014年)

项　　目	总资产贡献率(%)	资　产负债率(%)	流动资产周转率(次/年)	成本费用利润率(%)	全员劳动生产率(元/人)	产　品销售率(%)
总　　计	7.5	63.2	2.4	2.8	101104	98.2
按企业规模分						
大型企业	8.8	66.8	2.7	3.2	126791	98.9
中型企业	6.7	57.8	2.2	2.6	75836	97.5
小型企业	7.3	54.5	1.4	4.7	67806	98.7
微型企业	-12.8	69.7	3.6	-10.7	-196349	84.7
按工业行业分						
信息化学品制造业	11.5	17.8	2.9	4.9	1496716	95.4
医药制造业	13.0	35.3	1.1	17.1	292108	98.5
航空航天器制造业						
电子及通信设备制造业	7.4	65.1	2.5	2.6	104808	98.4
通信设备制造业	10.1	81.2	2.6	3.2	193901	99.3
雷达及配套设备制造业	14.3	39.8	2.4	3.0	84057	100.0
广播电视设备制造业	2.9	53.5	1.2	0.9	67933	97.6
电子器件制造业	3.2	58.1	3.1	0.4	101914	96.2
电子元件制造业	6.6	52.5	2.2	3.1	89402	98.1
视听设备制造业	6.9	64.3	2.2	2.6	63673	98.8
其他电子设备制造业	7.7	64.1	1.8	3.8	67930	99.3
电子计算机及办公设备制造业	7.0	60.4	2.7	2.7	78532	98.2
计算机整机制造业	28.6	21.7	1.1	44.1	239504	106.7
计算机零部件制造业	4.3	63.3	2.6	1.5	72889	97.0
计算机外围设备制造业	7.4	59.8	3.0	2.1	62289	96.8
其他计算机制造业	6.0	62.4	2.7	2.7	72315	99.2
办公设备制造业	7.4	63.2	3.1	2.6	92975	100.3
医疗设备及仪器仪表制造业	6.8	49.4	2.5	2.2	95097	94.4
医疗仪器设备及器械制造业	2.8	62.6	2.3	0.7	58255	90.4
仪器仪表制造业	7.3	47.7	2.5	2.4	103432	94.7
公共软件服务制造业						
其他	24.8	28.8	1.5	21.7	275928	100.0

4-33 规模以上IT制造业企业主要经济指标（2014年）

Main Indicators of IT Manufacturing Enterprises above Designated Size (2014)

项　　目	企业单位数(个)	#亏损企业	工业增加值(万元)	主营业务收入(万元)	亏损企业亏损总额(万元)
总　　计	1221	184	8400160	51144670	262632
按企业规模分					
大型企业	117	9	5115800	32832635	38619
中型企业	512	88	2619523	12887463	57961
小型企业	571	80	702622	4339687	33799
微型企业	21	7	-37786	1084886	132253
按工业行业分(小类)					
训练健身器材制造	2		4234	19740	
玩具制造	126	20	521501	1337184	9944
信息化学品制造	1		7783	114284	
照相机及器材制造	13	2	92184	365340	2500
复印和胶印设备制造	10	1	160949	1119598	1444
计算器及货币专用设备制造	4	1	92351	1320895	385
医疗诊断、监护及治疗设备制造	1		1063	3914	
微电机及其他电机制造	22		198241	775471	
电线、电缆制造	138	16	402871	2503630	10277
光纤、光缆制造	2		7329	33426	
锂离子电池制造	27	7	291811	714026	3256
镍氢电池制造	2	2	6151	39968	647
其他电池制造	16	2	90456	290850	498
计算机整机制造	6		69791	170325	
其他计算机制造	10		49507	305323	
通信系统设备制造	18	1	443499	2498691	3712
通信终端设备制造	54	15	1658915	16030524	26311
电视机制造	6	2	50880	474480	1620
音响设备制造	82	17	289982	1524782	5152
影视录放设备制造	26	5	94772	700029	1413
电子真空器件制造	1		961	7151	
集成电路制造	11	5	137806	850073	3222
光电子器件及其他电子器件制造	111	22	562812	6240327	148256
电子元件及组件制造	357	45	2575942	11296451	31467
印制电路板制造	55	8	272627	995215	6063
其他电子设备制造	93	10	242442	1155599	3675
电子测量仪器制造	5		10611	41693	
其他未列明制造业	22	3	62689	215683	2790

4-33 续表 1

(2014年)

项目	利税总额(万元)	人均税收(元)	利润总额(万元)	人均利润(元)	工业增加值率(%)
总计	2172274	8430	1433182	16348	16.1
按企业规模分					
大型企业	1543137	11137	1100281	27671	15.4
中型企业	502600	5391	297139	7797	19.7
小型企业	253104	8903	167166	17317	16.0
微型企业	-126567	34086	-131404	-926033	-2.9
按工业行业分(小类)					
训练健身器材制造	1058	6431	682	11660	21.1
玩具制造	27487	1409	11348	991	38.1
信息化学品制造	5484	29442	5330	1025077	7.3
照相机及器材制造	8636	3498	4301	3471	26.8
复印和胶印设备制造	48423	1964	45775	33948	14.4
计算器及货币专用设备制造	26121	7319	16051	11665	7.1
医疗诊断、监护及治疗设备制造	49	352	37	1078	25.8
微电机及其他电机制造	61165	3473	54316	27538	25.0
电线、电缆制造	65595	6847	31943	6499	15.7
光纤、光缆制造	3711	26457	2640	65183	16.2
锂离子电池制造	93077	4997	79827	30101	38.6
镍氢电池制造	-557	766	-647	-5512	14.8
其他电池制造	22755	27904	8803	17605	30.5
计算机整机制造	66230	34326	56228	192957	49.2
其他计算机制造	9667	2306	8089	11815	16.0
通信系统设备制造	90275	8633	48276	9924	17.7
通信终端设备制造	803163	43404	543699	90952	10.3
电视机制造	39185	8967	33947	58119	9.8
音响设备制造	43503	3413	26158	5147	18.9
影视录放设备制造	26524	13937	10137	8621	13.3
电子真空器件制造	85	836	72	4497	11.9
集成电路制造	42134	12579	30959	34848	16.2
光电子器件及其他电子器件制造	52703	9697	-5419	-904	8.6
电子元件及组件制造	526370	6247	344969	11881	22.1
印制电路板制造	35528	4150	23797	8420	25.9
其他电子设备制造	60293	4880	42877	12014	21.0
电子测量仪器制造	3447	6804	2655	22813	25.4
其他未列明制造业	10162	4517	6333	7472	28.2

4-33 续表 2

(2014年)

项　　目	总资产贡献率(%)	资产负债率(%)	流动资产周转率(次/年)	成本费用利润率(%)	全员劳动生产率(元/人)	产品销售率(%)
总　计	7.4	64.1	2.4	2.8	95817	98.4
按企业规模分						
大型企业	9.1	67.7	2.6	3.4	128656	99.2
中型企业	6.2	58.8	2.1	2.3	68735	97.6
小型企业	6.9	58.3	1.5	3.9	72788	98.7
微型企业	-13.2	69.6	3.7	-11.0	-266286	84.3
按工业行业分(小类)						
训练健身器材制造	11.3	60.8	2.4	3.6	72381	98.5
玩具制造	2.8	65.5	1.6	0.9	45521	98.4
信息化学品制造	11.5	17.8	2.9	4.9	1496716	95.4
照相机及器材制造	3.2	42.6	2.1	1.2	74384	99.2
复印和胶印设备制造	10.6	52.9	3.1	4.3	119363	100.2
计算器及货币专用设备制造	4.6	72.1	3.0	1.2	67116	100.4
医疗诊断、监护及治疗设备制造	0.8	45.0	0.6	1.0	30910	85.9
微电机及其他电机制造	12.6	46.0	2.2	7.3	100507	99.3
电线、电缆制造	4.4	68.7	1.7	1.3	81966	97.7
光纤、光缆制造	10.6	66.7	1.2	8.6	180975	87.5
锂离子电池制造	9.3	47.2	1.0	12.6	110034	95.5
镍氢电池制造	-0.7	79.1	1.5	-1.5	52442	96.5
其他电池制造	9.8	56.6	1.9	3.1	180912	99.1
计算机整机制造	28.6	21.7	1.1	44.1	239504	106.7
其他计算机制造	6.0	62.4	2.7	2.7	72315	99.2
通信系统设备制造	11.2	77.5	5.3	2.0	91165	99.7
通信终端设备制造	10.0	81.6	2.4	3.3	277508	99.2
电视机制造	11.4	83.7	1.8	6.7	87108	96.7
音响设备制造	4.9	56.6	2.4	1.8	57063	99.3
影视录放设备制造	7.1	64.3	2.2	1.5	80602	99.1
电子真空器件制造	4.3	68.1	6.3	1.0	60415	100.0
集成电路制造	7.4	59.0	2.0	3.8	155117	99.7
光电子器件及其他电子器件制造	2.4	59.5	3.4	-0.1	93904	95.7
电子元件及组件制造	7.0	53.6	2.3	3.2	88715	98.1
印制电路板制造	3.6	44.9	1.8	2.4	96457	98.0
其他电子设备制造	7.7	64.1	1.8	3.8	67930	99.3
电子测量仪器制造	19.6	57.0	3.1	6.8	91160	98.5
其他未列明制造业	4.8	53.8	1.8	2.9	73961	95.8

主要统计指标解释

Explanatory Notes on Main Statistical Indicators

工业 指从事自然资源的开采，对采掘品和农产品进行加工和再加工的物质生产部门。具体包括：对自然资源的开采，如采矿、晒盐、森林采伐等（但不包括禽兽捕猎和水产捕捞）；对农副产品的加工、再加工，如粮油加工、食品加工、轧花、缫丝、纺织、制革等；对采掘品的加工、再加工，如炼铁、炼钢、化工生产、石油加工、机器制造、木材加工等，以及电力、自来水、煤气的生产和供应等；对工业品的修理、翻新，如机器制造设备的修理、交通运输工具（包括小卧车）的修理等。

轻工业 是指主要提供生活消费品和制作手工工具的工业。按其所使用的原料不同，可分为两大类：以农产品为原料的轻工业，是指直接或以农产品为基本原料的轻工业，主要包括食品制造、饮料制造、烟草加工、纺织、缝纫、皮革和毛皮制作、造纸以及印刷等工业；以非农产品为原料的轻工业，是以工业品为原料的轻工业，主要包括文教体育用品、化学药品制造、合成纤维制造、日用化学制品、日用玻璃制品、日用金属制品、手工工具制造、医疗器械制造、文化和办公用机械制造等工业。

重工业 是指为国民经济各部门提供物质技术基础的主要生产资料的工业。按其生产性质和产品用途，可以分为下列三类：采掘（伐）工业，是对自然资源的开采，包括石油开采、煤炭开采、金属矿开采等工业；原材料工业，指向国民经济各部门提供基本材料、动力和燃料的工业，包括金属冶炼及加工、炼焦及焦炭化学、化学原料、水泥、人造板以及电力、石油和煤炭加工等工业；加工工业，是指对工业原材料进行再加工制造的工业，包括装备国民经济各部门的机械设备制造工业、金属结构、水泥制造等工业，以及为农业提供的生产资料如化肥、农药等工业。

资产总额 是指企业拥有或控制的能以货币计量的经济资源，包括各种财产、债权和其他权利。资产按其流动性（即资产的变现能力和支付能力）划分为：流动资产、长期投资、固定资产、无形资产、递延资产和其他资产，即为企业资产负债表中的资产总计项。

流动资产 是企业资产的重要组成部分，通常是指一年内或超过一年的一个营业周期内可以变现或耗用的资产。其特点是在企业的生产经营或者业务活动中不断地在生产循环中周转，不断改变其形态。其价值一次性消耗、转移或者实现。包括：货币资金、短期投资、应收票据、应收账款、预付账款、其他应收款、存货、待摊费用、待处理流动资产损失、一年内到期的本期债券投资及其他流动资产。

固定资产原价 是指企业在建造、购置、安装、改建、扩建、技术改造某项固定资产时实际支出的全部货币总额。它一般包括买价、包装费、运杂费和安装费等。

固定资产合计 包括固定资产净值、固定资产清理、在建工程、待处理固定资产净损失所占用的资金合计。

固定资产净值 是指固定资产原价减去历年已提折旧额后的净额。

负债 是指企业所承担的能以货币计量，将以资产或劳务偿付的债务。其偿还形式可以用货币，也可以用资产或提供劳务的方式进行。包括流动负债、长期负债和递延税款贷项等，即为企业资产负债表的负债合计项。

实收资本 是指企业实际收到的投资人投入的资本。包括有国家资本、集体资本、法人资本、个人资本、外商资本、港澳台资本等。

主营业务收入 是企业在销售商品、提供劳务及让渡资产使用权等日常活动中所产生的收入。

主营业务税金及附加 是指企业日常活动应负担的税金及附加，包括营业税、消费税、城市维护建设税、资源税、土地增值税和教育费附加等。

主营业务成本 是指企业因销售商品、提供劳务或让渡资产使用权等日常活动而发生的实际成本。

营业利润　是企业生产经营活动所取得的利润，包括主营业务利润和其他业务利润。

利润总额　是指企业在一定时期内生产经营活动的最终的财务成果，是企业的收入减去有关成本与费用后的差额，收入大于相关的成本费用，企业就盈利，反之则亏损。包括营业利润、补贴收入、投资净收益、营业外收支净额、以前年度损失调整。

应交增值税　是指企业按税法规定，从事货物销售或提供加工、修理修配劳务等增加货物价值的活动本期应交纳的税金，即企业在报告期应交的增值税额。计算公式为：

应交增值税 = 销项税额-(进项税额-进项税额转出)-出口抵减内销产品应纳税额-减免税款+出口退税

从业人员平均人数　从业人员指企业工作并取得劳动报酬的全部人员数。包括在岗职工、再就业的离退休人员、民办教师及在企业工作的外方人员和港澳台方人员、兼职人员、借用的外单位人员和第二职业者。不包括离开本单位但仍保留劳动关系的职工。而从业人员平均人数指报告期内每天平均拥有的从业人员人数。其计算公式为：

月平均人数=报告月内每天实有人数之和÷报告月日历日数

季平均人数=季内各月平均人数之和÷3

年平均人数=全年各月平均人数之和÷12

资产利税率　是在一定时期内已实现的利润、税金总额与同期的资产总额之比。计算公式：

$$\text{资产利税率（\%）}=\frac{\text{报告期累计实现利税总额}}{\text{资产总额}}\times 100\%$$

资产利税率反映每单位（通常是每万元）资产所提供的利税金额。它是考察和评价部门或企业资金运用的经济效益，分析资金投入效果的主要分析指标。

产值利税率　是报告期已实现的利润、税金总额（包括利润总额、产品销售税金及附加和应交增值税）占同期全部工业总产值的百分比，计算公式为：

$$\text{产值利税率（\%）}=\frac{\text{利税总额}}{\text{工业总产值（现价）}}\times 100\%$$

工业经济效益综合指数　是现行综合评价工业经济效益总体水平及工业经济运行质量的指数，它是以若干项代表性经济效益指标，分别除以各项指标的标准值，再乘以各自的权数，加总后除以总权数求得。其计算公式为：

$$\text{工业经济效益综合指数}=\Sigma\left(\frac{\text{某项经济效益指标报告期数值}}{\text{该项指标标准值}}\times\text{权数}\right)\div\text{总权数}$$

上式总权数为 100。

工业产品销售率　是反映工业产品已实现销售的程度，是分析工业产销衔接情况、研究工业产品满足社会需求的指标。计算公式是：

$$\text{产品销售率（\%）}=\frac{\text{现价工业销售产值}}{\text{现价工业总产值}}\times 100\%$$

总资产贡献率　是指企业一定时期内全部资产获利能力，是企业经营业绩和管理水平的集中体现，是评价和考核企业盈利能力的核心指标。计算公式为：

$$总资产贡献率（\%）=\frac{利润总额+税金总额+利息支出}{平均资产总额}\times100\%\times\frac{12}{累计月数}$$

注：税金总额为主营业务税金及附加与应交增值税之和，平均资产总额为期初、期末资产总计的算术平均值。

资本保值增值率　是反映企业净资产变动状况的一个重要指标，是企业发展能力的集中体现。是指期末所有者权益总额与期初所有者权益总额的比率。计算公式为：

$$资本保值增值率（\%）=\frac{期末所有者权益}{期初所有者权益}\times100\%$$

所有者权益等于资产总计减负债总计。

资产负债率　是指反映企业经营风险的大小，反映企业利用债权人提供的资金从事经营活动的能力。计算公式为：

$$资产负债率（\%）=\frac{负债总额}{资产总额}\times100\%$$

资产及负债均为报告期期末数。

流动资产周转率　是指一定时期内流动资产完成的周转次数，反映投入工业企业流动资金的周转速度，一般以一年内周转多少次表示。计算公式为：

$$流动资产周转率（次）=\frac{产品销售收入}{流动资产平均余额}\times\frac{12}{累计月数}$$

成本费用利润率　是指工业企业投入的生产成本及费用的经济效益，同时也反映企业降低成本所取得的经济效益。计算公式为：

$$成本费用利润率（\%）=\frac{利润总额}{成本费用总额}\times100\%$$

注：成本费用总额为产品销售成本、销售费用、管理费用、财务费用之和。

全员劳动生产率　是指反映企业的生产效率和劳动投入的经济效益。一般用平均每人一年创造的工业增加值表示。计算公式为：

$$全员劳动生产率（元/人）=\frac{工业增加值}{全部职工平均人数}\times\frac{12}{累计月数}$$

五、固定资产投资与建筑业

Investment in Fixed Assets and Construction

5-1 主要年份固定资产投资与建筑业主要指标

Main Indicators of Investment in Fixed Assets and Construction in Main Years

项　　目	单　位	1990年	1995年	2000年	2005年	2010年	2013年	2014年
固定资产投资总额	万元	75052	631355	1028914	5972443	11149822	13839352	14271099
#国有单位	万元	50658	106935	197658	686333	1479886	1760188	2093340
私营个体经济	万元				1027969	2077250	3330613	3392863
港澳台投资经济	万元		10281	130501	1246450	1326063	1460423	1174881
外商投资经济	万元		230409	92699	507322	938943	1106367	1059862
新增固定资产	万元				1732967	5778616	6550663	7287028
固定资产交付使用率	%				29.02	51.83	47.33	51.06
房屋竣工面积	万平方米				696.99	686.22	440.73	585.53
房屋面积竣工率	%				21.6	20.7	10.5	11.9
固定资产计划总投资	万元				13905355	45000174	58764749	63967273
固定资产投资建设周期	年				2.32	4.04	4.25	4.48
固定资产投资资金来源	万元	50100	480875	1047861	6717711	18550102	23172687	23601295
#国家预算内资金	万元	3600	10858	10490	536	130717	443253	318547
国内贷款	万元	2900	27439	122561	651723	1882278	2276020	2569988
利用外资	万元	17000	194486	207444	940432	1400920	1307812	742196
自筹资金	万元	25400	163090	587176	3901138	8390847	8503501	9488464
房地产开发投资	万元		85163	112498	1444277	2989853	4976593	5880630
房地产开发当年房屋施工面积	万平方米		160.74	315.45	1160.17	2060.54	2837.95	3585.66
房地产开发当年房屋竣工面积	万平方米		76.78	103.20	132.88	296.59	264.94	410.35
#住宅	万平方米		68.36	77.97	115.23	256.09	191.31	317.50
商品房销售面积	万平方米		25.42	63.21	321.85	511.25	803.09	643.65
#住宅	万平方米		20.49	51.02	297.19	469.90	723.96	556.22
建筑企业(单位)个数	个	8	8	99	361	431	503	536
建筑企业平均人数	人	6803	22200	64300	79965	57473	73648	76814
建筑企业总产值	万元	12678	94941	404493	843540	1220569	1881265	2042058
劳动生产率(按总产值计算)	元/人	18636	42766	60849	108136	218076	286159	265845
建筑业房屋施工面积	万平方米	66.30	278.72	1218.00	1234.98	733.44	790.43	1102.92
建筑业房屋竣工面积	万平方米	29.95	94.99	53.76	707.77	311.94	391.89	505.87

注：1. 本表固定资产投资资金来源1990年前是国有单位数，1995年以后是城镇集体以上单位数；1995年固定资产投资含沙角C厂完成的126374万元，2005年起是全社会固定资产投资单位数。
2. 从2011年起，固定资产投资统计起点由计划投资50万元提高到计划投资500万元，下同。

5-2 历年固定资产投资

Total Investment in Fixed Assets over Years

单位：万元

年 份	固定资产投资总额	#民营	#外资	#港澳台	#房地产开发
1978	2319				
1979	1641				
1980	2395				
1981	3756				
1982	18102				
1983	18370				
1984	30050				
1985	70600				
1986	115173				
1987	141856				
1988	165459				
1989	50135				
1990	75052				
1991	137464				
1992	188824				
1993	327630		62600		52110
1994	1407621		1038599		78392
1995	631355		240690		85163
1996	676185		259705		86258
1997	658941		69055		86662
1998	769953		91719	35868	95451
1999	883201		188036	116708	104411
2000	1028914		146887	96112	112498
2001	1254945		224812	181822	148544
2002	1915741		466569	213458	268350
2003	3193889		888664	619193	551184
2004	4548691		1094045	716611	1144195
2005	5972443		1753772	1246450	1444277
2006	7054511	2410417	2297486	1584104	1642398
2007	8412074	2841860	2356983	1136955	2094187
2008	9443426	3240949	2710398	1469186	2714197
2009	10940753	4279669	2038232	1114631	2776623
2010	11149822	4847208	2265006	1326063	2989853
2011	10793144	4438880	2228117	1460388	3733062
2012	11803493	6662441	2942143	1891724	3773210
2013	13839352	8835235	2566790	1460423	4976593
2014	14271099	9496756	2234743	1174881	5880630

注：1994、1995、1996年全社会投资总额分别含沙角C厂投资额956758万元、126374万元、102760万元。

5-3 按登记类型和行业分的固定资产投资（2014年）

Total Investment in Fixed Assets by Registration Status and Sector (2014)

单位：万元

项　　目	全市合计	城镇	#房地产	农村
合　　计	14271099	12148097	5880630	2123002
按登记注册类型分				
内资	12036356	10480883	5333634	1555473
国有	1206405	1188978		17427
集体	926457	593743	179944	332714
股份合作	1286			1286
国有联营				
集体联营	173	173		
国有与集体联营	14640	14640		
其他联营				
国有独资公司	886935	886935	29844	
其他有限责任公司	4807553	4358843	3431531	448710
股份有限公司	487854	390248	71641	97606
私营	3270646	2693055	1601725	577591
其他	312190	253923	18949	58267
个体经营：个体户	112873	95645		17228
个人合伙	9344	4700		4644
港澳台商投资	1174881	783518	332904	391363
#合资经营	234191	225744	119837	8447
合作经营	95243	95243	92668	
独资	803453	428281	120399	375172
股份有限公司	39450	34250		5200
外商投资	1059862	883696	214092	176166
#合资经营	235115	220265	126944	14850
合作经营	17353	17353	16062	
独资	741210	587575	66299	153635
股份有限公司	64989	57893	4787	7096
按国民经济行业分				
第一产业	2739	684		2055
第二产业	3974500	2600389		1374111
制造业	3513278	2160415		1352863
电力、热力、燃气及水的生产和供应业	455356	439974		15382
建筑业	1800			1800
第三产业	10293860	9547024	5880630	746836
交通运输、仓储和邮政业	1711835	1563838		147997
信息传输、软件和信息技术服务业	382470	380670		1800
批发和零售业	210904	128568		82336
住宿和餐饮业	57950	16776		41174
金融业	92650	86250		6400
房地产业	6676809	6488590	5880630	188219
租赁和商务服务业	78341	9695		68646
科学研究和技术服务业	230777	221677		9100
水利、环境和公共设施管理业	584002	463684		120318
居民服务、修理和其他服务业	6349	3549		2800
教育	126408	74534		51874
卫生和社会工作	56507	56507		
文化、体育和娱乐业	63913	43076		20837
公共管理、社会保障和社会组织	14945	9610		5335

5-4 固定资产投资主要指标（2014年）

Main Indicators of Total Investment in Fixed Assets (2014)

单位：万元

项目	计划总投资	本年完成投资	建筑工程	安装工程	设备工器具购置	其他费用
合计	32065866	8390469	4926459	410193	2267438	786379
按登记注册类型分						
内资	27469673	6702722	4408716	378389	1203569	712048
国有	6014849	1206405	899283	112036	110110	84976
集体	3557825	746513	678433	19280	24105	24695
股份合作	102286	1286	1286			
国有联营						
集体联营	2075	173	173			
国有与集体联营	110632	14640	13140		1500	
其他联营						
国有独资公司	3813258	857091	374657	61826	192326	228282
其他有限责任公司	7026045	1376022	815028	83486	302113	175395
股份有限公司	1114290	416213	269907	4230	123884	18192
私营个体	4574460	1791138	1134775	91360	433533	131470
其他	1153953	293241	222034	6171	15998	49038
港澳台商投资	2700097	841977	228899	14808	567788	30482
外商投资	1896096	845770	288844	16996	496081	43849
按国民经济行业分						
第一产业	3456	2739	2739			
第二产业	10656736	3974500	1581916	137302	1965697	289585
制造业	8552935	3513278	1334299	114855	1826620	237504
电力、热力、燃气及水的生产和供应业	2098935	455356	242351	22347	138677	51981
建筑业	2100	1800	1200	100	400	100
第三产业	21405674	4413230	3341804	272891	301741	496794
交通运输、仓储和邮政业	10560037	1711835	1266770	8910	72004	364151
信息传输、软件和信息技术服务业	833121	382470	58453	171174	144627	8216
批发和零售业	584529	210904	171366	4735	15292	19511
住宿和餐饮业	181518	57950	36839	5607	6900	8604
金融业	404282	92650	90987	28		1635
房地产业	2464908	796179	721577	33826	5045	35731
租赁和商务服务业	291795	78341	56103	12588	9598	52
科学研究和技术服务业	1241946	230777	179581	13936	1780	35480
水利、环境和公共设施管理业	3326909	584002	551087	8038	16736	8141
居民服务、修理和其他服务业	31326	6349	4549		600	1200
教育	823783	126408	114548	6633	876	4351
卫生和社会工作	294891	56507	24101	5952	23440	3014
文化、体育和娱乐业	228689	63913	51408	1154	4843	6508
公共管理、社会保障和社会组织	134140	14945	14435	310		200
按建设性质分						
新建	24947343	5520990	4128164	213850	477953	701023
扩建	2130928	556528	281389	128323	131200	15616
改建和技术改造	3097353	897762	463307	67188	306535	60732
单纯建造生活设施	26523	12336	8609	772	2415	540
迁建	120440	65668	44990	60	12408	8210
恢复	2500	258				258
单纯购置	1740779	1336927			1336927	

注：本表不含房地产开发投资。

5-4 续表 1

(2014年)

单位：万元

项目	本年新增固定资产	本年施工房屋面积(万平方米)	本年竣工房屋面积(万平方米)	本年资金来源合计	#上年末结余资金
合计	4970435	1325.20	175.17	10808145	1185329
按登记注册类型分					
内资	3650146	1040.11	159.84	7979934	554749
国有	559364	42.17	1.50	1448077	130272
集体	638663	191.11	38.06	935189	144657
股份合作	1286	0.62		1286	
国有联营					
集体联营				86	
国有与集体联营				15540	
其他联营					
国有独资公司	268311			904544	6888
其他有限责任公司	687407	221.41	38.50	1707788	81862
股份有限公司	215672	59.22	3.18	509019	5158
私营个体	1122014	505.37	74.47	2157327	180598
其他	157429	20.22	4.13	301078	5314
港澳台商投资	655667	161.05	3.43	1463743	298271
外商投资	664622	124.04	11.91	1364468	332309
按国民经济行业分					
第一产业	2739			2739	
第二产业	2987910	774.41	100.90	5469781	694791
制造业	2690664	768.94	100.71	4747422	474907
电力、热力、燃气及水的生产和供应业	293180	4.46	0.19	716493	219884
建筑业		0.04		1800	
第三产业	1979786	550.78	74.27	5335625	490538
交通运输、仓储和邮政业	359121	89.93	11.25	1949743	139113
信息传输、软件和信息技术服务业	335965	42.95		452396	18891
批发和零售业	179142	36.95	10.38	235623	16547
住宿和餐饮业	43070	28.16	0.87	61724	4795
金融业	12594	4.09	1.18	106953	3386
房地产业	368341	223.91	31.77	944767	67766
租赁和商务服务业	24816	0.05		134012	3666
科学研究和技术服务业	45888	57.73	7.44	290170	47668
水利、环境和公共设施管理业	425991	20.20	0.60	745184	145172
居民服务、修理和其他服务业	2218	0.85	0.85	7567	250
教育	88350	31.28	3.66	218156	540
卫生和社会工作	49497	9.38	6.00	81563	24668
文化、体育和娱乐业	31465	3.58	0.28	86762	15426
公共管理、社会保障和社会组织	13328	1.72		21005	2650
按建设性质分					
新建	2512788	1136.62	157.52	7185558	642917
扩建	488442	85.08	9.30	960745	302158
改建和技术改造	699090	86.87	4.78	1013700	82121
单纯建造生活设施	10350	1.84		54334	25072
迁建	70831	14.78	3.58	67037	
恢复	258			258	
单纯购置	1188676			1526513	133061

5-4 续表 2

(2014年)

单位：万元

项目	本年资金来源					
	#本年资金来源小计	国家预算内资金	国内贷款	利用外资	自筹资金	其他资金来源
合计	9622816	318547	948900	732735	7261497	361137
按登记注册类型分						
内资	7425185	318547	815697	19811	6003680	267450
国有	1317805	241728	14189	700	1010853	50335
集体	790532	66551	3300	3370	663534	53777
股份合作	1286				1286	
国有联营						
集体联营	86		86			
国有与集体联营	15540				15540	
其他联营						
国有独资公司	897656		334345		542478	20833
其他有限责任公司	1625926	2678	310912		1176318	136018
股份有限公司	503861		47700		453417	2744
私营个体	1976729	7590	105165	15741	1844490	3743
其他	295764				295764	
港澳台商投资	1165472		129006	298866	649963	87637
外商投资	1032159		4197	414058	607854	6050
按国民经济行业分						
第一产业	2739				2739	
第二产业	4774990	2320	201834	639136	3782251	149449
制造业	4272515	320	201313	635093	3338276	97513
电力、热力、燃气及水的生产和供应业	496609	2000	521	4043	438109	51936
建筑业	1800				1800	
第三产业	4845087	316227	747066	93599	3476507	211688
交通运输、仓储和邮政业	1810630	202915	563167	56725	836057	151766
信息传输、软件和信息技术服务业	433505		7000	500	425752	253
批发和零售业	219076	100	6000	9215	203761	
住宿和餐饮业	56929		7200	2800	46929	
金融业	103567				100237	3330
房地产业	877001	21049	31256	12719	805228	6749
租赁和商务服务业	130346		2000	2413	125933	
科学研究和技术服务业	242502	32500	32943	9227	163834	3998
水利、环境和公共设施管理业	600012	49708			525133	25171
居民服务、修理和其他服务业	7317				7317	
教育	217616	6155	97500		106423	7538
卫生和社会工作	56895				49285	7610
文化、体育和娱乐业	71336	3300			65347	2689
公共管理、社会保障和社会组织	18355	500			15271	2584
按建设性质分						
新建	6542641	254616	888802	188312	4960076	250835
扩建	658587	16373		16213	622194	3807
改建和技术改造	931579	45769	12659	48265	798690	26196
单纯建造生活设施	29262	1789	17123	2855	6600	895
迁建	67037			6482	60555	
恢复	258				258	
单纯购置	1393452		30316	470608	813124	79404

5-5 固定资产投资分类情况（2014年）

Basic Statistics on Total Investment in Fixed Assets by Type (2014)

单位：万元

项 目	计 划总投资	自开始建设累计完成投资	本年完成投资	#住宅	本年新增固定资产
固定资产投资总额	32065866	20914684	8390469	59708	4970435
#基础设施	15285267	9898486	2808575	1300	1258802
#基础产业	15476911	10027230	2906667	1300	1341210
#城市建设	7131475	5102763	1038070		326126
#原材料	341650	230889	175990	320	143751
#能源	1713822	848975	398431		282670
#工业合计	10658436	7025017	3972700	8965	2987910
#工业九大产业	6702860	4393415	2482693	8965	1817321
#电子信息业	3029484	1984464	904375	2855	656847
电气机械及专用设备	1526302	1009848	603887		461882
石油及化学	156431	101592	80538	320	66987
纺织及服装	304858	244773	218304	1000	149397
食品饮料	965242	526005	312941	4790	225388
建筑材料	191028	133855	96875		79387
森工造纸	280669	221016	156064		120430
医药	128700	83598	32084		2400
汽车	120146	88264	77625		54603

注:本表不含房地产开发投资。

5-6 房地产开发主要指标

Main Indicators of Real Estate Development

项 目	单位	2005年	2006年	2007年	2008年	2009年	2010年	2013年	2014年
本年土地购置面积	万平方米	45	73	58	70	92	136	98	174
本年完成投资额	万元	1444277	1642398	2094187	2714197	2776623	2989853	4976593	5880630
#住宅	万元	1197154	1475181	1860580	2213498	2513852	2504525	3676823	4184338
资金来源	万元	1632570	2120240	2900238	4049833	4281021	6533564	8824494	9032094
#国内贷款	万元	114755	292488	446710	1079194	544169	1271530	1560931	1621088
利用外资	万元	2075	10140		27053	105397	75182	53617	9461
自筹资金	万元	867824	677095	905912	1067823	1840753	2025670	1684408	2226967
房屋施工面积	万平方米	1160	1438	1522	1998	2334	2061	2838	3586
#住宅	万平方米	890	1229	1371	1681	2050	1687	2044	2598
房屋竣工面积	万平方米	133	166	137	478	310	297	265	410
#住宅	万平方米	115	114	112	395	268	256	192	318
商品房屋销售额	万元	1193991	1612449	2949939	2885975	3530040	3737742	7280663	6266493
#住宅	万元	1091095	1460425	2736729	2461024	3342466	3341485	6325059	5092691
商品房屋销售面积	万平方米	322	382	573	512	600	511	803	644
#住宅	万平方米	297	353	541	468	579	470	724	556

5-7 房地产开发企业主要经济指标（2014年）

Main Indicators of Real Estate Enterprises (2014)

单位：万元

项　　目	资产总计	负债总计	主营业务收入	主营业务税金及附加	利润总额
合　　计	29331977	23854473	6159272	1568947	768658
按登记注册类型分					
#内源型经济	26475600	21947269	5522599	1512101	686054
#民营经济	25743780	21365848	5192717	1486292	601326
#国有经济	412634	300269	157630	21317	53404
集体经济	781163	655639	94528	11745	1647
私营个体经济	6436209	5629797	1334104	143095	140516
外源型经济	2856378	1907204	636673	56846	82604
#港澳台商投资	1536009	859738	462623	40419	82047
外商投资	1320369	1047466	174050	16428	557
按控股情况分					
国有控股	706980	550042	314199	23093	84682
集体控股	1221653	1084030	95159	12151	-3231
私人控股	15484941	13105697	3016339	1200307	255944
港澳台控股	1569393	901691	462623	40419	82342
外商控股	1311825	1036892	189732	19143	307
其他控股	9037185	7176121	2081219	273835	348613
按资质等级分					
一级	3337332	1936196	422281	88983	68273
二级	4536300	3932537	917162	93755	165469
三级	3961841	3106259	883695	90733	181713
四级	6968703	5677251	2202680	227907	300776
暂定	8677322	7967020	1523787	1040233	59263
其他	1850480	1235209	209668	27336	-6836

5-8 房地产开发投资情况（2013-2014年）

Investment in Real Estate Development (2013-2014)

项　　目	2013年		2014年	
	房地产开发投资（万元）	#住宅	房地产开发投资（万元）	#住宅
合　　计	4976593	3676823	5880630	4184338
内资	4445746	3330975	5333634	3807888
国有	53169	18486		
集体	93819	61866	179944	139892
国有独资公司	46907	46661	29844	21217
其他有限责任公司	2572086	2032290	3431531	2409643
私营独资	103105	59446	20637	19735
私营有限责任公司	1487895	1029987	1571144	1129577
私营股份有限公司	16600	16400	9944	9944
其他(内资企业)	15630	10765	18949	9191
港澳台商投资	340524	228672	332904	176946
外商投资	190323	117176	214092	199504

5-9 房地产开发企业、房屋建筑面积及价值（2013-2014年）

Floor Space and Value of Buildings in Real Estate Development (2013-2014)

项　　目	2013年			2014年		
	房屋建筑面积（平方米）		竣工房屋价值（万元）	房屋建筑面积（平方米）		竣工房屋价值（万元）
	施工面积	竣工面积		施工面积	竣工面积	
合　　计	28379534	2649359	1138633	35856561	4103542	1965068
内资	25888168	2143100	945690	32941746	3697116	1714896
国有	583813	39974	16105	85252		
集体	871230	46639	14896	963520	185893	44695
国有独资公司	331189	220063	105188	239886	123087	52881
其他有限责任公司	13884055	964213	348029	19234101	2308753	1062867
私营独资	252449	45061	21664	1000		
私营有限责任公司	9432885	713886	360523	11838164	1026830	520294
私营股份有限公司	235507	113264	79285	137587	52553	34159
其他(内资企业)	142638			141219		
港澳台商投资	1485561	227245	109239	1814197	328715	202845
外商投资	1005805	279014	83704	1100618	77711	47327

5-10 商品房屋销售情况（2014年）

Sale of Commercialized Buildings (2014)

项目	商品房屋销售建筑面积（平方米）	#住宅	商品房屋销售额（万元）	#住宅
合计	6436516	5562242	6266493	5092691
内资	6023532	5217695	5786293	4737333
国有	8196	7133	7531	6596
集体	226850	185970	166198	133702
国有独资公司	46110	4328	42261	4326
其他有限责任公司	3818991	3310226	3767868	3063019
私营独资	62976	59509	40281	35709
私营有限责任公司	1765375	1566946	1593390	1348600
私营股份有限公司	16533	16533	25232	25232
其他内资企业	26275	15475	31365	8634
港澳台商投资	183473	136258	266744	179197
外商投资	229511	208289	213456	176161

5-11 建筑施工企业主要指标（2013-2014年）

Main Indicators of Construction Enterprises (2013-2014)

指标	单位	2013年 合计	2013年 #国有单位	2014年 合计	2014年 #国有单位
企业单位数	个	503	1	536	1
年平均人数	人	73648	7952	76814	9222
自有固定资产原价	万元	355985	17327	332340	32207
自有固定资产净值	万元	178874	7970	173158	20734
自有施工机械设备年末总台数	台	12629	416	13129	477
自有施工机械设备年末净值	万元	65049	4606	73194	7053
自有施工机械设备年末总功率	万千瓦	25	2	28.1	1.9
建筑业总产值	万元	1881265	236746	2042058	289309
建筑工程产值	万元	1612562	235422	1748742	289309
安装工程产值	万元	229628	1324	245725	
其他产值	万元	39075		47591	
建筑业竣工产值	万元	1218317	165194	1428636	243559
建筑业增加值	万元	827325		876238	
房屋建筑施工面积	万平方米	790	6	1103	11
房屋建筑竣工面积	万平方米	392		506	6
利润总额	万元	98485	2838	104417	3138
利税总额	万元	164030	10185	168095	11355
劳动生产率(按总产值计算)	元/人	286159	318464	265845	313716
劳动生产率(按增加值计算)	元/人	125844		114073	
技术装备率	元/人	8832	5792	9529	7648
动力装备率	千瓦/人	3.4	1.9	3.7	2.0
房屋建筑面积竣工率	%	49.6		45.9	55.1
产值利润率	%	5.2	1.2	5.1	1.1
产值利税率	%	8.7	4.3	8.2	3.9

主要统计指标解释

Explanatory Notes on Main Statistical Indicators

固定资产投资额 是以货币形式表现的在一定时期内建造和购置固定资产的工作量以及与此有关的费用的总称。按构成可分为建筑工程、安装工程、设备工器具购置和其他费用。

房屋建筑施工面积 指报告期内施工的全部房屋建筑面积。包括本期新开工的面积和上期开工跨入本期继续施工的房屋面积，以及上期已停建在本期复工的房屋面积。本期竣工和本期施工后又停缓建的房屋，其建筑面积仍计入本期施工房屋面积中。

房屋建筑竣工面积 指在报告期内房屋建筑按照设计要求已全部完工，达到住人和使用条件，经验收鉴定合格(或达到竣工验收标准)，可正式移交使用的各栋房屋建筑面积的总和。

房屋建筑面积竣工率 指一定时期内房屋竣工面积占同期房屋施工面积的比率。它是从房屋建筑施工速度的角度反映投资效果和建筑业经济效益的指标。

固定资产交付使用率 指一定时期新增固定资产与同期完成投资额的比率。它反映各个时期固定资产动用速度、衡量建设过程中投资效果的一个综合性指标。

六、运输邮电

Transport, Postal and Telecommunication Services

6-1 主要年份运输邮电主要指标

Main Indicators of Transport, Postal and Telecommunication Services in Main Years

项　　目	单　位	1985年	1990年	1995年	2000年	2005年	2010年	2013年	2014年
公路通车里程	公里	1240	1325	2327	2519	2871	4751	5002	5145
#高速公路	公里				89	154	217	335	335
一级公路	公里		6	679	782	1315	2394	2507	2580
内河通航里程	公里	532	598	598	798	664	643	643	643
公路桥梁	座	211	267	338	538	826	1211	1548	1420
民用汽车	辆	7897	19394	88311	153684	406577	920766	1389103	1559588
#载客	辆	1878	7225	25366	69658	268918	772701	1225695	1405878
载货	辆	5980	12087	52242	80405	129298	143005	158298	148612
摩托车	辆	11786	47881	255591	482636	775838	423766	154568	88339
机动船	艘	2883	5885	5292	806	467	286	351	386
机动船净载重	吨位	80324	186056	259329	152661	148737	557846	1422747	1620323
邮电局(所)	处	52	53	273	594	702	555	611	715
邮路长度	公里	790	459	685	3550	6835	4667	4070	4552
局用交换机容量	万门	1.14	6.98	52.29	103.13	286.25	365.02	295.26	363.83
移动电话交换机总容量	万户			4.8	154.2	1059.1	1657.0	2646.4	2033.0
本地电话用户	万户	0.77	4.90	31.57	78.12	384.52	332.42	314.48	327.22
移动电话用户(含充值卡)	万户		0.05	4.77	123.68	1016.41	1607.60	1850.39	1763.09
互联网用户	万户			0.05	13.78	52.90	153.92	216.11	204.86
邮政业务收入	万元						63178	88635	108193
电信业务收入	万元						1490174	1669207	1586444
客运量	万人	2072	5758	10237	30697	33551	77446	78113	5555
#公路	万人	1940	5728	10210	30680	33510	77415	78082	5524
旅客周转量	万人公里	95237	322236	446230	1001906	1185290	1290692	1559856	854598
#公路	万人公里	90950	320690	444293	1000492	1182000	1288675	1557823	852594
货运量	万吨	2913	2701	4266	5431	6400	9312	12863	15375
#公路	万吨	1922	1571	2377	3440	4586	7640	9162	10915
货物周转量	万吨公里	171591	184700	264605	404678	424829	1090340	4322745	4480052
#公路	万吨公里	113038	72162	128026	246046	272500	510801	683889	755240
港口货物吞吐量	万吨	276	233	201	746	2280	5657	11187	12900

注：1. 2006年起公路通车里程含专用公路和村道，下同。
　　2. 2010年起，邮政业务相关指标不包括速递物流及邮政储蓄银行独立运营部分，下同。
　　3. 2014年客运量和旅客周转量不含城市客运量，数据与往年不可比，下同。

6-2 历年运输线路长度与公路密度

Length of Transportation Routes and Road Density over Years

年 份	公路通车里程（公里）	等级公路	#一级	等外公路	高级、次高级路面通车里程（公里）	内河通航里程（公里）	公路密度（公里/百平方公里）
1978	1259	287		972		530	51.08
1979	1225	355		870		603	49.70
1980	1225	355		870		603	49.70
1981	1225	845		380		415	49.70
1982	1225	845		380		115	49.70
1983	1225	872		353		132	49.70
1984	1240	896		344		132	50.30
1985	1240	490		750		132	50.30
1986	1248	977		271		274	50.63
1987	1261	991		270		598	51.16
1988	1302	1068	6	234		598	52.82
1989	1325	1091	6	234		598	53.75
1990	1325	1102	6	223	750	598	53.75
1991	1759	1226	6	533	1137	598	71.36
1992	2055	1431	151	624	1442	599	83.37
1993	2260	1673	315	587	1675	598	91.68
1994	2292	1868	599	424	1773	598	92.98
1995	2327	1930	679	397	1650	598	94.40
1996	2330	2087	689	243	1653	598	94.50
1997	2330	2087	690	243	1563	598	94.50
1998	2429	1897	714	480	1958	598	98.52
1999	2467	1935	717	480	2048	798	100.06
2000	2519	2339	782	91	2253	798	102.15
2001	2570	2393	845	78	2321	798	104.26
2002	2641	2464	908	78	2406	798	107.14
2003	2688	2508	967	75	2472	716	109.05
2004	2759	2609	1148	37	2637	798	111.93
2005	2871	2686	1315	31	2774	664	116.47
2006	3891	3619	1585	117	3823	664	157.85
2007	3924	3650	1591	116	3860	535	159.19
2008	4001	3884	1639	117	3864	643	162.31
2009	4713	4598	2389	115	4643	643	191.21
2010	4751	4637	2394	114	4681	643	192.74
2011	4828	4716	2420	112	4759	643	196.24
2012	4969	4861	2484	108	4800	643	201.98
2013	5002	4896	2507	106	4937	643	202.94
2014	5145	5058	2580	87	5093	643	208.72

注：公路密度数据来源于交通运输局，下同。

6-3 主要年份运输线路长度

Length of Transport Routes in Main Years

项　　目	单　位	1980年	1990年	1995年	2000年	2005年	2010年	2013年	2014年
公路通车里程合计	公里	1225	1325	2327	2519	2871	4751	5002	5145
#按等级分									
等级公路	公里	355	1102	1930	2339	2686	4637	4896	5058
高速公路	公里				89	154	217	335	335
一　级	公里		6	679	782	1315	2394	2507	2580
二　级	公里		65	361	684	703	1317	1335	1370
三　级	公里		60	135	310	297	178	205	254
四　级	公里	355	971	755	563	371	532	514	519
等外公路	公里	870	223	397	91	31	114	106	87
#按路面分									
有路面里程	公里		800	1808	2508	2858	4689	4945	5102
#高级、次高级	公里		750	1650	2253	2774	4681	4937	5093
无路面里程	公里		524	519	11	13	62	58	42
桥梁合计	座		267	338	538	826	1211	1395	1420
	延米				39956	112385	162767	267814	239363
公路密度	公里/百平方公里	49.70	53.75	94.40	102.15	116.47	192.74	202.94	208.72
#等级公路密度	公里/百平方公里	14.40	44.71	78.30	94.89	108.97	188.12	198.63	205.19
内河通航里程	公里	603	598	598	798	664	643	643	643

6-4 主要年份运输工具拥有量

Possession of Main Means of Transport in Main Years

项　　目	单　位	1985年	1990年	1995年	2000年	2005年	2010年	2013年	2014年
民用车辆拥有量									
汽车	辆	7897	19394	88311	153684	406577	920766	1389103	1559588
载客汽车	辆	1878	7225	25366	69658	268918	772701	1225695	1405878
	客位	23462	66361	302844	560155	2420591	5101240	7463470	8296490
载货汽车	辆	5980	12087	55000	81623	129298	143005	158298	148612
	吨位	20428	38010	133757	332621	243390	253879	294303	290894
其他汽车	辆	39	82	7945	2403	8361	5060	5110	5098
摩托车	辆	11786	47881	255591	482636	775838	423766	154568	88339
挂车	辆				8	2222	2983	3267	3510
民用运输船舶拥有量									
机动船	艘	2883	5885	5292	806	467	286	351	386
	净载重吨位	80323	186056	259329	152661	148737	557846	1422747	1620323
	客位	2056	776	1881	1054	604	902	589	550
#货船	艘	2866	5875	5259	796	465	283	349	384
	净载重吨位	80285	186038	259314	152661	148431	557236	1422442	1620018
客船	艘			26	10	2	3	2	2
	客位			1295	1054	604	902	589	550
期末机动车驾驶员	人	44186	118229	351947	563564	798086	1287738	1827929	2025514
#汽车驾驶员	人	10661	28768	94778	173865	428912	1110932	1737504	1956584

注：2002年起民用汽车拥有量按新的口径分类，部分指标数值与往年不可比。

6-5 历年客货运输量

Passenger and Freight Traffic over Years

年份	客运量(万人)	公路	水运	旅客周转量(万人公里)	公路	水运
1978	403	224	179	9425	5097	4328
1979	467	272	195	11162	6354	4808
1980	572	362	210	13584	8285	5299
1981	578	349	229	13845	7943	5902
1982	639	405	234	16026	9683	6343
1983	1281	1071	210	54075	47939	6136
1984	1287	1130	157	62107	56890	5217
1985	2072	1940	132	95237	90950	4287
1986	2304	2224	80	127458	124322	3136
1987	3359	3283	76	159117	156578	2539
1988	3223	3176	47	173335	171575	1760
1989	5288	5254	34	240999	239193	1806
1990	5758	5728	30	322236	320690	1546
1991	6749	6719	30	373284	371720	1564
1992	9267	9247	20	503973	502607	1366
1993	10907	10897	10	577800	576116	1684
1994	11234	11229	5	595134	594100	1034
1995	10237	10210	27	446230	444293	1937
1996	10749	10723	26	477466	476072	1394
1997	11300	11273	27	511592	509614	1978
1998	17485	17463	22	577452	575541	1911
1999	25404	25385	19	804278	802590	1688
2000	30697	30680	17	1001906	1000492	1414
2001	31220	31203	17	1031579	1030192	1387
2002	32100	32081	19	1091821	1090155	1666
2003	32588	32566	22	1126964	1125098	1866
2004	33240	33200	40	1166262	1163010	3352
2005	33551	33510	41	1185290	1182000	3290
2006	35182	35143	39	1213809	1210944	2865
2007	37182	37136	46	1264982	1261777	3205
2008	122468	122431	37	2248521	2246128	2393
2009	73324	73291	33	1053469	1051324	2145
2010	77446	77415	31	1290692	1288675	2017
2011	80337	80306	31	1458811	1456782	2029
2012	79739	79707	32	1568758	1566652	2106
2013	78113	78082	31	1559856	1557823	2033
2014	5555	5524	31	854598	852594	2004

6-5 续表 1

年 份	货运量(万吨)	公 路	#个体及联户	水 运	#个体及联户
1978	394	73		321	
1979	399	68		331	
1980	349	51		298	
1981	317	37		280	
1982	319	35		284	
1983	2366	1519	1515	847	535
1984	2738	1728	1710	1018	718
1985	3110	1922	1906	1188	814
1986	3296	2208	2190	1088	725
1987	2618	1304	1288	1314	928
1988	2685	1374	1358	1311	912
1989	3233	1516	1501	1717	1375
1990	2701	1571	1557	1130	837
1991	2456	1300	1286	1156	282
1992	2895	1703	1688	1192	902
1993	3256	1976	1960	1280	1011
1994	3646	2233	2222	1413	1147
1995	4266	2377	2368	1889	1599
1996	4451	2645	2636	1806	1556
1997	4644	2748	2740	1896	1622
1998	4776	2808	2808	1968	1678
1999	5016	3039	3039	1977	1653
2000	5431	3440	3440	1991	1660
2001	5527	3539	3539	1988	1659
2002	5857	4015	4015	1842	1504
2003	5877	4046	4046	1831	1496
2004	6054	4250	4250	1804	721
2005	6400	4586	4586	1814	1484
2006	5481	4930	4930	551	
2007	5676	5115	1194	561	75
2008	9273	8010	1273	1263	86
2009	8733	6944	1973	1789	159
2010	9312	7640	2080	1672	158
2011	10165	8210	2155	1955	133
2012	11191	8421	2310	2770	84
2013	12863	9162	2897	3701	80
2014	15375	10915	4033	4460	81

6-5 续表 2

年份	货物周转量（万吨公里）	公路	#个体及联户	水运	#个体及联户	港口货物吞吐量（万吨）
1978	15148	924		14224		293
1979	15390	636		14654		297
1980	16353	1479		14874		295
1981	15606	304		15302		272
1982	17185	252		16933		253
1983	108634	70723	70572	37911	20317	319
1984	140113	91774	91702	48339	29179	268
1985	171591	113038	113002	58553	31784	276
1986	126898	71392	71358	55506	27916	268
1987	174942	101285	101253	73657	41049	296
1988	169112	69014	68986	100098	82351	320
1989	186626	70942	70921	115684	82351	297
1990	184700	72162	72141	112538	83094	233
1991	194101	82555	82534	111546	82075	267
1992	232752	116698	116673	116054	85084	292
1993	248230	134918	134890	113312	87574	313
1994	273053	151108	148152	121945	93235	370
1995	264605	128026	127928	136579	105099	201
1996	267193	121625	121603	145568	118169	289
1997	278649	126336	126244	152313	122428	338
1998	285889	130378	130378	155511	123343	516
1999	300410	143465	143465	156945	119120	654
2000	404678	246046	246046	158632	119855	746
2001	406247	250121	250121	156126	118112	883
2002	420684	265908	265908	154776	115444	1611
2003	422822	268998	268998	153824	114812	2352
2004	423669	272220	272220	151449	48377	2600
2005	424829	272500	272500	152329	113249	2280
2006	336783	278566	278566	58217		1951
2007	356677	297223	50803	59454	6414	2017
2008	1747489	462797	38398	1284692	5598	3208
2009	1016490	452880	126052	563610	8787	3530
2010	1090340	510801	131929	579539	9399	5657
2011	1874802	531304	138976	1343498	9606	6848
2012	2967132	543633	147604	2423499	5941	9228
2013	4322745	683889	216590	3638856	5296	11187
2014	4480052	755240	389342	3724812	4103	12900

6-6 历年主要运输工具年末拥有量

Possession of Main Means of Transport at Year-end over Years

年 份	民用汽车(辆)	#客车	货车	摩托车(辆)	机动船(艘)	万人拥有公共汽(电)车数量(标台)
1978	623	78	506	134	2169	
1979	1115	178	1089	156	2034	
1980	2009	516	1457	170	1948	
1981	3039	751	2031	517	2107	
1982	3419	791	2724	1168	2285	
1983	4473	854	3580	1636	2313	
1984	6059	1243	4822	7060	2563	
1985	7897	1878	5980	11786	2883	
1986	8632	2245	6334	18006	4368	
1987	9983	2954	6973	21308	4884	
1988	13581	3456	8690	26995	4911	
1989	16340	4214	10434	36820	4901	
1990	19394	7225	12087	47881	5885	
1991	20734	5206	15423	65770	4405	
1992	32625	5753	25048	106013	4351	
1993	48145	8710	35421	153014	4379	
1994	61572	11550	43925	200543	4562	
1995	88311	25366	55000	255591	5292	
1996	90793	29430	54870	249492	5313	
1997	103425	40101	62507	287076	5064	
1998	113435	47769	64434	382010	456	
1999	127007	55715	69470	399324	690	
2000	153684	69658	82841	482636	806	
2001	183638	89677	91304	560310	536	
2002	220134	116783	102253	642034	483	
2003	255603	155206	97047	692562	392	
2004	319725	210531	105050	687651	417	
2005	406577	268918	129298	775838	467	
2006	489306	351265	131704	697175	440	
2007	608933	466999	134825	567002	393	
2008	701600	557359	136295	521118	326	
2009	795554	653273	137334	470818	293	
2010	920766	772701	143005	423766	286	
2011	1061373	906454	149635	352553	312	
2012	1207044	1047922	153655	276401	333	
2013	1389103	1225695	158298	154568	351	17.47
2014	1559588	1405878	148612	88339	386	18.36

6-7 主要年份邮电通信业务基本情况

Basic Statistics on Postal and Telecommunication Services in Main Years

项　　目	单位	1978年	1990年	1995年	2000年	2005年	2010年	2013年	2014年
邮电通信网									
邮电局、所	处	50	53	273	594	702	555	611	715
邮路长度	公里	513	459	685	3550	6835	4667	4070	4552
农村投递线路长度	公里	1985	1812	2057	8865	19722	13261	16048	21424
邮电通信工具									
邮政汽车	辆		7	10	35	192	131	200	208
移动电话交换机总容量	万户			4.8	154.2	1059.1	1657.0	2646.4	2033.0
移动电话用户(含充值卡)	万户				123.68	1016.41	1607.60	1850.39	1763.09
移动电话用户(不含充值卡)	万户		0.05	4.77	80.97	176.83	174.04	568.34	597.48
局用交换机容量	万门		6.98	52.29	103.13	286.25	365.02	295.26	363.83
本地电话用户	万户	0.20	4.90	31.57	78.12	384.52	332.42	314.48	327.22
市内电话用户	万户	0.04	1.50	9.78	19.69	68.30	85.76	58.52	63.20
农村电话用户	万户	0.16	3.40	21.80	58.43	316.22	246.66	255.97	264.02
数字数据用户(DDN)	端口				2741	2170	1098	890	384
互联网用户	万户			0.05	13.78	52.90	153.92	216.11	204.86
邮电业务量									
邮电业务收入	亿元						155.34	175.78	169.46
#电信业务	亿元						149.02	166.92	158.64
#移动通信业务	亿元						105.78	126.76	122.25
邮政特快专递	万件					292.17	183.00	114.00	88.00
函件	万件		3372	10407	8124	9430	4507	4316	4369

6-8 历年邮电通信业务主要指标

Main Indicators of Postal and Telecommunication Services over Years

年 份	邮 电 局、所 (处)	局用交换机容量 (万门)	本地电话用户 (万户)	移动电话用户 (万户)	邮电业务收入 (亿元)
1978	50		0.20		
1979	50		0.21		
1980	50	0.50	0.31		
1981	50		0.34		
1982	51		0.35		
1983	51		0.39		
1984	52		0.48		
1985	52	1.14	0.77		
1986	53		0.88		
1987	45		1.63		
1988	48		2.52		
1989	50		4.30	0.02	
1990	53	6.98	4.90	0.05	
1991	60	9.82	7.50	0.11	
1992	91	11.07	9.70	0.30	
1993	161	21.24	14.98	0.72	
1994	216	36.37	23.19	2.41	
1995	273	52.29	31.57	4.77	
1996	310	52.79	36.91	8.24	
1997	339	57.76	42.65	15.29	
1998	397	73.09	50.13	26.17	
1999	458	84.79	60.87	51.01	
2000	594	103.13	78.12	123.68	
2001	689	155.29	98.96	295.76	
2002	696	176.94	127.93	412.39	90.56
2003	846	220.28	206.11	660.86	105.12
2004	854	265.66	281.35	856.09	120.78
2005	702	286.25	384.52	1016.41	132.82
2006	560	299.19	461.31	1216.34	146.69
2007	567	329.50	469.17	1408.23	161.90
2008	547	340.71	439.41	1454.29	172.38
2009	546	347.15	378.40	1409.29	156.31
2010	555	365.02	332.42	1607.60	155.34
2011	626	357.00	319.55	1677.77	164.86
2012	595	364.00	330.79	1797.75	169.96
2013	611	295.26	314.48	1850.39	175.78
2014	715	363.83	327.22	1763.09	169.46

注：本地电话用户含小灵通用户。

6-9 邮电通信企业财务指标（2013-2014年）

Main Financial Indicators of Postal and Telecommunication Enterprises (2013-2014)

单位：万元

指　　标	2013年	2014年
年初存货	12404	10627
期末资产负债		
流动资产合计	124535	97578
#应收账款	64132	58643
存货	9972	8655
固定资产原价	3409603	3546891
本年折旧	256499	250695
资产总计	1618007	1634467
负债合计	824771	986662
所有者权益合计	793236	647805
损益及分配		
营业收入	1921928	1820720
#主营业务收入	1853708	1775157
营业成本	797636	767439
#主营业务成本	724455	725175
营业税金及附加	57145	28816
#主营业务税金及附加	55023	25983
销售费用	324927	282803
管理费用	51739	38794
#税金	2482	2914
财务费用	2378	2497
#利息收入	77	281
利息支出	3070	2575
投资收益(损失以“-”号记)		
营业利润	674380	691259
营业外收入	5955	5339
#补贴收入		31
营业外支出	8402	9149
利润总额	671887	687277
应交所得税	108544	109423
人工成本及增值税		
应付职工薪酬(本年贷方累计发生额)	130040	133682
应交增值税	43	44210
从事服务业活动的从业人员平均人数(人)	6451	10115

主要统计指标解释

Explanatory Notes on Main Statistical Indicators

公路里程 指在一定时点上实际达到交通部规定的公路技术等级标准，并经公路主管部门正式验收交付使用的公路里程数。包括大、中城市的郊区公路以及公路通过城镇（指县城、集镇）街道的里程数。但不包括大、中城市街道，厂矿、林区内部生产用道、农业生产用道，以及新建公路尚未进行验收交付使用的路段里程。公路按工程技术等级分为高速、一、二、三、四级公路；按公路是否铺设路面分为有路面和无路面公路；按公路通车情况分为晴雨通车里程和晴通雨阻里程。

货（客）运量 在一定时期内，各运输部门实际运送的货物（旅客）数量。货运按吨计算，客运按人计算。货物不论运输距离长短，货物类型，均按实际重量统计；旅客不论行程远近或票价多少，均按一人一次作为客运量统计。半价票，小孩票也按一人统计。货（客）运量反映运输业为国民经济和人民生活服务的数量，也是制定和检查运输生产计划，研究运输发展规模和速度的重要指标。

货物（旅客）周转量 指在一定时期内，由各种运输工具运输业运送的货物（旅客）数量与其相应运输距离的乘积，通常以吨公里和人公里为计算单位。计算货物周转量通常按发出站与到达站之间的最短距离，也就是计费距离计算。它是反映运输业生产总成果的重要指标，也是编制和检查运输生产计划，计算运输效率，劳动生产率以及核算运输单位成本的主要基础资料。

货物吞吐量 是指经由水运运进、运出港区范围，并经过装卸的货物数量。货物吞吐量分别按国内进口（装卸）、出口（装船），外贸进口、出口统计。货物吞吐量按货物实际重量吨统计，以货物交接清单或货单上记载的重量吨为准。如无实际重量吨，可根据船舶装载情况来推算。在本港区内的水运转口分别按进口和出口各计算一次吞吐量。货物吞吐量是衡量港口生产规模的一个主要数量指标。

邮电业务收入 是指邮电营运企业从事邮政、电信、移动及其他邮电业务所取得的营业收入。

局用交换机容量 指安装在本地电信运营商内用于接读本地固定电话的电话交换机容量，有倍增设备按倍增后的数量计数。包括现用和备用的人工或自动交换全部容量。

本地电话用户 是指接入本地电信运营商固定电话网上的电话用户。包括：住宅电话、单位用户、公用电话用户等。

移动电话用户 是指在移动通信部门办理登记手续，通过移动电话交换机进入移动电话网，占用移动电话号码的电话用户。

邮政局所 指经邮政部门审批许可，有固定的地址，领有上级发给的邮政日戳或邮政戳记，对外营业直接为用户办理邮政业务（至少办理出售邮票和收寄给据函件）的服务机构。邮政局所按经营方式分为自办局所和代办局所；按设置地点分为城市局所和农村局所。

七、国内贸易

Domestic Trade

7-1 历年社会消费品零售总额

Total Retail Sales of Consumer Goods over Years

年份	社会消费品零售总额		按城乡分	
	绝对值（万元）	增速（%）	城镇(万元)	乡村(万元)
1978	21269			
1979	24956	17.3		
1980	31595	26.6		
1981	40201	27.2		
1982	48126	19.7		
1983	52255	8.6		
1984	73930	41.5		
1985	93640	26.7		
1986	122420	30.7		
1987	150511	23.0		
1988	246518	63.8		
1989	270354	9.7		
1990	319738	18.3		
1991	364972	14.2		
1992	443464	21.5		
1993	636882	43.6		
1994	851556	33.7		
1995	1130081	32.7		
1996	1255311	11.1		
1997	1460396	16.3		
1998	1751551	19.9		
1999	2023008	15.5		
2000	2351634	16.2		
2001	2757143	17.2		
2002	3212436	16.5		
2003	3697814	15.1		
2004	4264704	15.3		
2005	5062917	18.7		
2006	5993201	18.4		
2007	7224491	20.5		
2008	8811519	22.0		
2009	10290420	16.7		
2010	12233380	18.9	11290960	942420
2011	14412451	17.8	13418775	993676
2012	16004124	11.0	14932002	1072122
2013	17866589	11.6	16684394	1182195
2014	19422889	8.7	18083947	1338942

注：本表1979-2003年数据根据东莞市第一次全国经济普查结果重新核定，2005-2008年数据根据东莞市第二次全国经济普查结果重新核定，2009-2013年数据根据东莞市第三次全国经济普查结果重新核定。

7-2 历年批发零售贸易企业与个体户数

Wholesale and Retail Trades Enterprises and Self-employed Individuals over Years

单位：个

年 份	单位数合计	国有经济	集体经济	其他经济	#私营个体经济
1979	2459	406	1918	135	135
1980	2613	395	1679	539	537
1981	4603	371	1954	2278	2274
1982	3323	373	1838	1112	1107
1983	8723	401	1539	6783	6783
1984	18917	431	6720	11766	11766
1985	16885	670	4543	11672	11671
1986	18547	823	3063	14661	14660
1987	23468	739	4102	18627	18626
1988	26247	665	4405	21177	21176
1989	28453	695	4196	23562	23561
1990	27931	709	3512	23710	23709
1991	29474	678	3934	24862	24862
1992	34465	803	4193	29469	29469
1993	43511	886	7640	34985	34985
1994	49706	633	11396	37677	37677
1995	56339	745	14492	41102	41101
1996	60078	670	15183	44225	44224
1997	48910	811	8477	39622	39546
1998	52543	1064	4046	47433	46615
1999	55925	1056	3843	51026	50172
2000	57474	1024	3581	5289	51914
2001	68909	866	2960	65083	63760
2002	89246	748	2424	86078	84614
2003	113531	530	2068	110933	109236
2004	149067	539	1941	146587	144304
2005	192525	393	1451	190681	188082
2006	236124	283	1090	234751	231930
2007	284109	268	930	282911	279524
2008	301996	288	833	300875	296613
2009	300088	256	744	299088	294753
2010	300668	239	654	299775	295166
2011	288904	223	629	288052	283209
2012	305784	227	594	304963	299666
2013	313612	197	555	312860	307352
2014	339933	183	513	339237	333920

7-3 批发零售业商品销售总额（2014年）

Total Sales of Commodities in Wholesale and Retail Trades (2014)

单位：万元

项　目	商品销售总额	批发额	零售额
合　计	48066916	30068809	17998107
按行业分			
批发业	29809942	29152673	657269
零售业	18256974	916136	17340838
按规模分			
限额以上企业和个体户	28350064	20243458	8106606
粮油、食品、饮料、烟酒类	2444404	1926740	517664
#粮油类	306730	189326	117404
肉禽蛋类	65956	23535	42421
水产品类	20104	402	19703
蔬菜类	46678	12032	34646
干鲜果品类	95148	27080	68068
饮料类	297409	217844	79565
烟酒类	1033342	981093	52250
服装鞋帽、针纺织品类	1840523	1502842	337681
#服装类	1119305	903821	215484
鞋帽类	169115	110082	59033
针、纺织品类	552103	488940	63163
化妆品类	77306	15365	61942
金银珠宝类	136866	106996	29869
日用品类	512728	377477	135251
#洗涤用品类	161713	93201	68513
儿童玩具类	45314	34068	11246
五金、电料类	510202	493660	16542
体育、娱乐用品类	28998	19220	9778
书报杂志类	23281	13018	10264
电子出版物及音像制品类	2135	618	1517
家用电器和音像器材类	981350	647379	333970
中西药品类	834812	610825	223988
#西药	341394	180930	160464
中草药及中成药	381811	326550	55261
文化办公用品类	269017	170801	98217
家具类	733543	727239	6305
通讯器材类	1966941	1847049	119892
煤炭及制品类	1493544	1489945	3599
木材及制品类	85802	85802	
石油及制品类	6020929	3965676	2055253
化工材料及制品类	2092449	2092449	
#化肥类	24021	24021	
金属材料类	1101052	1101052	
建筑及装潢材料类	222668	194248	28420
机电产品及设备类	406552	371645	34907
#农机类	822	822	
汽车类	4315649	318682	3996966
种子饲料类	4742	4742	
棉麻类	2		2
其它	2244569	2159988	84581
限额以下企业和个体户	19716852	9825351	9891501

注：限额以上分类别数据采用月报数据。

7-4 限额以上住宿业和餐饮业经营情况（2014年）

Business of Hotels and Catering Services above Designated Size (2014)

项　　目	法人企业（个）	从业人数（人）	营业额（万元）	客房收入	餐费收入	商品销售收入	其它收入
总　计	325	49695	670009	155313	463482	7783	43431
住宿业	171	31768	376283	152322	181535	2421	40005
按登记注册类型分							
内资企业	159	28040	332239	134830	158654	2419	36337
港、澳、台商投资企业	8	2203	29118	12301	14395	2	2421
外商投资企业	4	1525	14926	5191	8487	1	1247
按国民经济行业分							
旅游饭店	139	28854	353931	139104	174693	1889	38245
一般旅馆	25	2525	18592	10233	6184	454	1720
其它住宿服务业	7	389	3760	2984	658	79	40
餐饮业	154	17927	293726	2991	281946	5362	3426
按登记注册类型分							
内资企业	133	12509	178296	2672	168811	4977	1836
港、澳、台商投资企业	12	2029	27394	319	25138	367	1571
外商投资企业	9	3389	88036		87997	19	20
按国民经济行业分							
正餐服务业	124	11106	150220	2991	140133	3670	3425
快餐服务业	12	4633	110116		110116		
饮料及冷饮服务业	1	429	1421		124	1298	
其他餐饮服务业	17	1759	31969		31573	394	1

7-5 限额以上批发和零售企业财务状况（2014年）

Main Financial Indicators of Enterprises above Designated Size in Wholesale and Retail Trade (2014)

单位：万元

项目	法人企业数（个）	年末资产负债				
		流动资产合计	#存货	固定资产原价	累计折旧	#本年折旧
总计	1346	11210741	1859912	1386476	528776	94682
批发企业	821	6906243	1038768	737756	266961	40994
按登记注册类型分						
内资企业	763	6373425	936867	722302	261047	39492
港、澳、台商投资企业	41	450268	72353	13244	4776	930
外商投资企业	17	82551	29548	2210	1138	571
按国民经济行业分						
农、林、牧产品批发业	2	2710	223	188	7	5
食品、饮料及烟草制品批发业	53	592258	88899	90249	21941	3278
纺织、服装及家庭用品批发业	115	918714	98152	25984	13634	1562
文化、体育用品及器材批发业	29	243522	46721	9699	4816	808
医药及医疗器材批发业	27	328557	88416	22552	6280	1244
矿产品、建材及化工产品批发业	375	3531008	489808	466642	178029	24716
机械设备、五金交电及电子产品批发业	130	648517	148035	83751	29680	7101
贸易经纪与代理	33	315707	6308	8123	4757	619
其他批发业	57	325250	72205	30569	7818	1662
零售企业	525	4304498	821144	648720	261814	53688
按登记注册类型分						
内资企业	489	4045179	747124	521169	206041	45035
港、澳、台商投资企业	21	135169	37518	62897	24003	4005
外商投资企业	15	124150	36502	64655	31770	4648
按国民经济行业分						
综合零售业	77	275921	75772	141950	68283	10992
食品、饮料及烟草制品专门零售业	12	22526	9911	3664	2111	232
纺织、服装及日用品专门零售业	17	30519	17605	12610	2576	727
文化、体育用品及器材专门零售业	7	75046	41900	928	294	140
医药及医疗器材专门零售业	31	75946	24206	10679	4865	1083
汽车、摩托车、燃料及零配件专门零售业	300	3230928	507611	365545	153157	32604
家用电器及电子产品专门零售业	34	505323	130989	42413	10700	4808
五金、家具及室内装修材料专门零售业	12	15935	5466	5904	3860	298
货摊、无店铺及其他零售业	35	72355	7684	65027	15967	2805

7-5 续表 1

（2014年）

单位：万元

项目	年末资产负债				损益及分配	
	资产总计	负债合计	所有者权益合计	#实收资本	营业收入合计	#主营业务收入
总　计	13370494	10336966	3032869	1294382	26419223	26200157
批发企业	8304994	6925844	1378491	847879	18334986	18270453
按登记注册类型分						
内资企业	7736790	6571451	1164680	740605	16936105	16873160
港、澳、台商投资企业	478847	295594	183253	88668	1152903	1151467
外商投资企业	89356	58799	30558	18606	245979	245826
按国民经济行业分						
农、林、牧产品批发业	10154	5051	5103	5020	53214	53214
食品、饮料及烟草制品批发业	975278	644484	330794	88437	1712883	1688706
纺织、服装及家庭用品批发业	960592	869197	91395	61270	3386844	3383369
文化、体育用品及器材批发业	294734	266645	28088	19733	405582	405420
医药及医疗器材批发业	347901	302757	45145	25445	557999	557792
矿产品、建材及化工产品批发业	4268231	3630680	636893	497191	8568525	8538691
机械设备、五金交电及电子产品批发业	761749	600688	161061	99268	1711804	1706769
贸易经纪与代理	327709	296911	30798	23230	1105140	1104251
其他批发业	358644	309431	49214	28286	832994	832242
零售企业	5065500	3411122	1654378	446504	8084237	7929704
按登记注册类型分						
内资企业	4707177	3181523	1525654	337154	6877294	6753630
港、澳、台商投资企业	182866	110327	72539	50811	537451	522518
外商投资企业	175458	119273	56185	58539	669492	653556
按国民经济行业分						
综合零售业	457674	397500	60174	75432	934179	889596
食品、饮料及烟草制品专门零售业	25122	14860	10262	2550	29857	29462
纺织、服装及日用品专门零售业	43819	35208	8611	7542	44784	44774
文化、体育用品及器材专门零售业	80046	67576	12469	11250	83184	83175
医药及医疗器材专门零售业	87448	69878	17570	5250	201257	200969
汽车、摩托车、燃料及零配件专门零售业	3660550	2246849	1413702	259070	5650976	5576759
家用电器及电子产品专门零售业	562296	483087	79210	36780	822114	801619
五金、家具及室内装修材料专门零售业	19241	25027	-5786	8624	35530	31073
货摊、无店铺及其他零售业	129304	71138	58167	40007	282357	272278

7-5 续表 2

(2014年)

单位：万元

项目	损益及分配					
	主营业务成本	主营业务税金及附加	其他业务利润	销售费用	管理费用	#税金
总计	24500782	81138	127095	932032	399965	16015
批发企业	17279616	60980	52119	476522	228756	9041
按登记注册类型分						
内资企业	16004036	58797	51508	389143	205741	7983
港、澳、台商投资企业	1057070	1594	487	74311	13122	883
外商投资企业	218510	589	124	13067	9893	176
按国民经济行业分						
农、林、牧产品批发业	52577	3		423	139	
食品、饮料及烟草制品批发业	1416397	47759	2618	65581	42497	1817
纺织、服装及家庭用品批发业	3278845	1425	4300	58584	25591	1501
文化、体育用品及器材批发业	383696	483	4515	14713	5860	203
医药及医疗器材批发业	513706	800	414	13080	14911	257
矿产品、建材及化工产品批发业	8174422	5352	34789	237865	77965	3636
机械设备、五金交电及电子产品批发业	1597062	2769	3667	54219	39792	894
贸易经纪与代理	1081239	235	903	9002	8961	327
其他批发业	781672	2154	914	23056	13041	407
零售企业	7221166	20159	74976	455510	171209	6974
按登记注册类型分						
内资企业	6183782	16704	62847	374122	145141	6333
港、澳、台商投资企业	459665	1518	3600	35689	12425	158
外商投资企业	577720	1936	8530	45700	13643	483
按国民经济行业分						
综合零售业	744188	6446	22626	158659	22452	365
食品、饮料及烟草制品专门零售业	26348	92	201	1299	973	36
纺织、服装及日用品专门零售业	31004	182	132	10484	5444	48
文化、体育用品及器材专门零售业	70572	241	239	7561	3849	3
医药及医疗器材专门零售业	165335	502	353	19946	11907	130
汽车、摩托车、燃料及零配件专门零售业	5189255	9356	38119	167785	99674	4185
家用电器及电子产品专门零售业	730261	2367	6802	68852	15721	1994
五金、家具及室内装修材料专门零售业	28566	138	1418	5149	1556	39
货摊、无店铺及其他零售业	235636	835	5087	15776	9633	174

7-5 续表 3

(2014年)

单位：万元

项目	损益及分配				应付职工薪酬	应交增值税
	财务费用	营业利润	利润总额	应交所得税		
总计	179124	385867	413657	118010	461840	370656
批发企业	122347	237263	264609	87768	214247	252879
按登记注册类型分						
内资企业	119209	230526	254500	85546	187289	236007
港、澳、台商投资企业	3045	3132	6562	1316	20201	14603
外商投资企业	93	3605	3548	905	6758	2270
按国民经济行业分						
农、林、牧产品批发业	0	71	86	21	185	5
食品、饮料及烟草制品批发业	16100	147726	147294	35470	56644	47089
纺织、服装及家庭用品批发业	6735	15294	20240	3383	28065	84113
文化、体育用品及器材批发业	4909	4712	4856	412	5611	2130
医药及医疗器材批发业	6949	8065	7967	2105	12107	6359
矿产品、建材及化工产品批发业	72234	42188	63687	40676	59823	63047
机械设备、五金交电及电子产品批发业	8729	7838	8963	3623	36252	30175
贸易经纪与代理	3175	2172	2647	753	4138	849
其他批发业	3516	9197	8870	1325	11422	19114
零售企业	56777	148603	149048	30243	247593	117777
按登记注册类型分						
内资企业	50586	94510	92963	22497	205991	98588
港、澳、台商投资企业	3097	24726	26177	3234	17080	7219
外商投资企业	3094	29368	29908	4512	24522	11971
按国民经济行业分						
综合零售业	2865	1012	3990	4292	50297	16312
食品、饮料及烟草制品专门零售业	486	461	471	127	1448	387
纺织、服装及日用品专门零售业	66	-2229	-2334	65	4186	2321
文化、体育用品及器材专门零售业	110	832	409	196	6415	248
医药及医疗器材专门零售业	1610	2049	2148	796	14591	3140
汽车、摩托车、燃料及零配件专门零售业	44663	128048	130972	20478	119000	79931
家用电器及电子产品专门零售业	5378	-462	-229	1122	35828	10813
五金、家具及室内装修材料专门零售业	566	-463	-601	34	3165	684
货摊、无店铺及其他零售业	1034	19355	14222	3134	12663	3942

7-6 限额以上住宿和餐饮企业财务状况（2014年）

Main Financial Indicators of Enterprises above Designated Size in Hotels and Catering Services (2014)

单位：万元

项目	法人企业数（个）	年末资产负债				
		流动资产合计	存货	固定资产原价	累计折旧	本年折旧
总计	325	801585	37752	1056912	493494	80700
住宿业	171	565692	26310	962439	447513	75016
按登记注册类型分						
内资企业	159	476464	23192	840193	373154	70817
港、澳、台商投资企业	8	75945	2283	77893	54341	3185
外商投资企业	4	13283	835	44353	20018	1015
按国民经济行业分						
旅游饭店	139	550434	24842	923800	431169	73472
一般旅馆	25	14393	1325	36728	15320	1439
其它住宿服务业	7	866	143	1911	1024	105
餐饮业	154	235892	11443	94472	45982	5684
按登记注册类型分						
内资企业	133	203845	7477	42373	20923	3218
港、澳、台商投资企业	12	16804	456	24170	9036	1102
外商投资企业	9	15244	3510	27930	16023	1364
按国民经济行业分						
正餐服务业	124	54309	6319	62673	29421	3994
快餐服务业	12	164822	2807	28923	15775	1443
饮料及冷饮服务业	1	592	567	601	97	73
其他餐饮服务业	17	16169	1749	2275	688	173

7-6 续表 1

(2014年)

单位：万元

项目	年末资产负债				损益及分配	
	资产总计	负债合计	所有者权益合计	#实收资本	营业收入	#主营业务收入
总计	1641575	1516578	124997	271165	679766	674110
住宿业	1295314	1316316	-21002	203747	374853	369358
按登记注册类型分						
内资企业	1141355	1165247	-23892	154744	330623	325228
港、澳、台商投资企业	111967	115223	-3256	27382	29080	29080
外商投资企业	41992	35845	6147	21621	15150	15049
按国民经济行业分						
旅游饭店	1250078	1294520	-44441	189190	352463	347199
一般旅馆	41397	17861	23535	13757	18630	18398
其它住宿服务业	3839	3935	-96	800	3760	3760
餐饮业	346261	200262	145999	67419	304913	304753
按登记注册类型分						
内资企业	259123	164119	95004	38780	189476	189338
港、澳、台商投资企业	38604	25879	12725	13038	27394	27391
外商投资企业	48534	10264	38270	15601	88043	88023
按国民经济行业分						
正餐服务业	104623	68105	36518	36599	150607	150448
快餐服务业	219571	120036	99535	25364	110564	110564
饮料及冷饮服务业	1097	333	764	240	1421	1421
其他餐饮服务业	20971	11789	9183	5216	42321	42319

7-6 续表 2

(2014年)

单位：万元

项目	损益及分配					
	主营业务成本	主营业务税金及附加	其他业务利润	销售费用	管理费用	#税金
总计	272855	37724	7089	255808	157713	3525
住宿业	121207	22405	5378	151950	125555	2408
按登记注册类型分						
内资企业	106117	19886	5273	136231	108643	2323
港、澳、台商投资企业	9646	1620	1	8735	12140	60
外商投资企业	5444	899	104	6984	4772	25
按国民经济行业分						
旅游饭店	110948	21059	5158	144648	120814	2352
一般旅馆	8693	1117	220	6201	4138	56
其它住宿服务业	1567	228		1101	603	1
餐饮业	151648	15319	1711	103857	32158	1118
按登记注册类型分						
内资企业	101673	9315	1061	54777	24166	1053
港、澳、台商投资企业	10670	1478	7	10171	2886	64
外商投资企业	39305	4525	643	38909	5106	1
按国民经济行业分						
正餐服务业	74884	8156	1038	48202	18443	1091
快餐服务业	47833	5710	623	49251	8841	2
饮料及冷饮服务业	995	3		333	16	1
其他餐饮服务业	27935	1451	50	6072	4857	24

7-6 续表 3

(2014年)

单位：万元

项目	损益及分配				应付职工薪酬
	财务费用	营业利润	利润总额	应交所得税	
总计	36244	-82398	-72016	2047	167582
住宿业	36218	-83646	-73315	735	108089
按登记注册类型分					
内资企业	31135	-72334	-62707	735	95022
港、澳、台商投资企业	4383	-7443	-6815		8480
外商投资企业	700	-3869	-3793		4587
按国民经济行业分					
旅游饭店	35738	-81867	-71508	599	101675
一般旅馆	462	-1962	-1960	83	5302
其它住宿服务业	18	183	152	53	1112
餐饮业	27	1248	1299	1312	59493
按登记注册类型分					
内资企业	626	-1318	-590	888	41377
港、澳、台商投资企业	-35	2249	2256	235	5632
外商投资企业	-564	318	-367	189	12484
按国民经济行业分					
正餐服务业	594	142	1028	780	34642
快餐服务业	-581	-961	-1816	200	17012
饮料及冷饮服务业	1	75	75	19	790
其他餐饮服务业	12	1993	2012	313	7049

7-7 历年住宿餐饮企业与个体户数

Enterprises and Self-employed Individuals in Hotels and Catering Services over Years

单位：个

年 份	单位数合 计	国有经济	集体经济	其他经济	#私营个体经济
1979	147	22	115	10	10
1980	182	23	121	38	38
1981	622	24	283	315	315
1982	308	24	102	182	182
1983	2069	31	98	1940	1940
1984	4012	31	445	3536	3536
1985	2982	36	389	2557	2557
1986	3268	38	270	2960	2956
1987	2281	35	308	1938	1934
1988	2265	31	296	1938	1934
1989	2850	32	276	2542	2538
1990	3387	30	439	2918	2914
1991	3438	44	225	3169	3165
1992	4456	25	320	4111	4106
1993	7119	12	1851	5256	5232
1994	7819	12	1748	6059	6051
1995	8918	26	1802	7090	7082
1996	9708	9	1900	7799	7789
1997	9968	28	606	9334	9210
1998	11069	102	368	10599	10532
1999	11904	80	337	11487	11392
2000	8335	78	361	7896	7831
2001	9776	67	343	9366	9318
2002	15128	74	265	14789	14740
2003	17615	64	229	17322	17276
2004	19802	39	424	19339	19224
2005	25972	28	315	25629	25522
2006	27108	16	247	26845	26747
2007	38435	11	219	38205	38094
2008	40154	9	177	39968	39687
2009	38220	5	130	38085	37795
2010	36156	4	113	36039	35728
2011	29280	4	91	29185	28825
2012	29381	4	81	29296	28874
2013	31780	2	70	31708	31205
2014	36172	2	55	36115	35559

7-8 历年限额以上企业商品购进、销售、库存总额

Total Purchases, Sales and Stock of Commercial Enterprises above Designated Size over Years

单位：万元

年　份	商品购进总　额	商品销售总　额	批发总额	零售总额	年末库存总　额
1978	82347	74936	50207	24729	7576
1979	91074	82878	55528	27350	8378
1980	109147	99324	66547	32777	10041
1981	131797	119936	80357	39579	12125
1982	156730	142615	95552	47063	14418
1983	160485	146042	97848	48194	14764
1984	214364	195072	130698	64374	19721
1985	254458	231557	155143	76414	23410
1986	630988	283945	190243	93702	28706
1987	380242	346021	231834	114187	34982
1988	714661	650342	435729	214613	65749
1989	729163	663539	444570	218969	67083
1990	766549	697560	467365	230195	70523
1991	796488	672666	433991	238675	74092
1992	881697	743990	473014	270976	64939
1993	1141163	1063567	725979	337588	92249
1994	1323263	1296363	912457	383906	177377
1995	1584470	1556882	1044334	512548	143404
1996	1694496	1737121	1117111	620010	166267
1997	1857884	1922001	1212399	709602	175715
1998	779319	863214	696921	166293	91640
1999	1064070	1106048	875799	230249	73620
2000	1232026	1354640	1072929	281711	58304
2001	1312924	1405409	1080688	324721	67415
2002	1588853	1682579	1188961	493618	102657
2003	1712564	1805840	1138496	667344	107996
2004		5406921	3479209	1927712	251427
2005	4798504	5683548	3882222	1801326	322445
2006	5324450	6487742	4215562	227179	335108
2007	6706290	8102415	4875668	3226748	485401
2008	8349926	10772768	6604662	4168106	790691
2009	8689984	10167222	6137228	4029994	839175
2010	12846503	14271362	9046899	5224463	1002940
2011	15777469	18129917	11738336	6391581	1401733
2012	20036523	22307974	15515426	6792549	1699355
2013	26698507	29369393	21570487	7798906	3189454
2014	25329332	29033764	20733048	8300715	2551678

7-9 市场分类基本情况（2013-2014年）

Basic Statistics on Market Classification (2013-2014)

单位：个

项 目	2013年			2014年		
	合 计	城 市	农 村	合 计	城 市	农 村
合 计	815	185	630	779	146	633
消费品市场	763	216	547	729	185	544
消费品综合市场	160	43	117	146	39	107
农副产品市场	496	132	364	490	108	382
农副产品综合市场	486	130	356	480	128	352
农副产品专业市场	10	3	7	10	3	7
工业品消费市场	72	33	39	72	33	39
工业消费品综合市场	42	25	17	42	25	17
工业消费品专业市场	30	8	22	30	8	22
其他消费品市场	35	8	27	21	5	16
生产资料市场	52	16	36	50	16	34
生产资料综合市场	11	3	8	11	3	8
工业生产资料市场	23	5	18	22	5	17
机动车交易市场	6	2	4	6	2	4
钢材交易市场	2		2	2		2
煤炭交易市场						
木材交易市场	5	1	4	5	1	4
其他工业生产资料市场	10	2	8	9	2	7
其他生产资料市场	18	8	10	17	8	9

注：本表数据来源于市工商局。

7-10　历年城乡集市贸易

Statistics on Urban and Rural Trade Fairs over Years

单位：个

年　份	集贸市场 总　数	城　市	农　村
1978	35		35
1979	35		35
1980	35		35
1981	38		38
1982	40		40
1983	41		41
1984	43		43
1985	48		48
1986	57	7	50
1987	63	10	53
1988	66	12	54
1989	69	11	58
1990	73	10	63
1991	75	10	65
1992	53	7	46
1993	155	13	142
1994	162	12	150
1995	189	17	172
1996	219	20	199
1997	241	23	218
1998	252	25	227
1999	286	36	250
2000	308	29	279
2001	375	31	344
2002	495	28	467
2003	576	34	542
2004	610	35	575
2005	665	36	629
2006	812	39	773
2007	845	36	809
2008	871	228	643
2009	883	225	658
2010	792	194	598
2011	812	181	631
2012	816	186	630
2013	815	185	630
2014	779	146	633

注：2008年以前的城市集贸市场数只包括莞城的集贸市场，2008年起包括莞城、东城、南城和万江四大街道办的市场数。

主要统计指标解释

Explanatory Notes on Main Statistical Indicators

社会消费品零售总额 指企业（单位、个体户）通过交易直接售给个人、社会集团非生产、非经营用的实物商品金额，以及提供餐饮服务所取得的收入金额。个人包括城乡居民和入境人员，社会集团包括机关、社会团体、部队、学校、企事业单位、居委会或村委会等。

商品购进总额 指从本企业以外的单位和个人购进（包括从国外直接进口）作为转卖或加工后转卖的商品金额（含增值税）。本指标反映批发和零售业从国内外市场上购进商品的总价。

商品销售总额 指对本单位以外的单位和个人出售的商品金额（包括售给本单位消费用的商品，含增值税），本指标反映批发和零售业在国内市场上销售商品以及出口商品的总量。

期末库存 对于批发和零售业法人企业和个体经营户，是指取得所有权的全部商品金额（含增值税）；对于批发和零售业产业活动单位，是指期末实际在库且归属法人具有所有权的全部商品金额（含增值税）。这个指标反映批发和零售业的商品库存情况，以及对市场商品供应的保证程度。

批发额 指售给国民经济各行业企业（单位）用于生产、经营用的商品金额。

零售额 指售给城乡居民用于生活消费和社会集团用于公共消费的商品金额。

住宿和餐饮业零售额 指住宿和餐饮业单位因为提供就餐服务或销售商品取得的全部收入，包括餐费收入和商品销售收入（含增值税）。

流动资产合计 资产满足以下条件之一应归为流动资产：（1）预计在一个正常营业周期中变现、出售或耗用，主要包括存货、应收帐款等；（2）主要为交易目的而持有；（3）预计在资产负债表日起一年内（含一年）变现；（4）自资产负债日起一年内，交换其他资产或清偿负债的能力不受限制的现金或现金等价物。包括货币资金、应收票据、应收账款、存货等项目。根据会计“资产负债表”中“流动资产合计”项目的期末余额数填报。

固定资产合计 指企业为生产商品、提供劳务、出租或经营管理而持有的，使用寿命超过一个会计年度的有形资产。包括使用期限超过一年的房屋、建筑物、机器、机械、运输工具以及其他与生产、经营有关的设备、器具、工具等。固定资产合计是时点指标，表示固定资产经过扣减折旧、减值准备等后的期末余额。根据会计“资产负债表”中“固定资产”项目的期末余额数填报。

所有者权益合计 指企业资产扣除负债后由所有者享有的剩余权益。公司的所有者权益又称股东权益。包括实收资本、资本公积、盈余公积、未分配利润等。根据会计“资产负债表”中“所有者权益合计”项目的期末余额数填报。

营业税金及附加 指企业因从事生产经营活动按税法规定缴纳的应从经营收入中抵扣的税金和附加，包括营业税、消费税、城市维护建设税、教育费附加等。根据会计“利润表”中“营业税金及附加”项目的本期金额数填报。

利润总额 指企业在一定会计期间的经营成果，是生产经营过程中各种收入扣除各种耗费后的盈余，反映企业在报告期内实现的亏盈总额。根据会计“利润表”中“利润总额”项目的本期金额数填报。执行2006年《企业会计准则》的企业，利润总额为营业利润加上营业外收入，减去营业外支出后的金额；未执行2006年《企业会计准则》的企业，利润总额为营业利润加上投资收益、补贴收入、营业外收入，再减去营业外支出后的金额。

应交增值税 指企业按税法规定，从事货物销售或提供加工、修理修配劳务等增加货物价值的活动本期应交纳的税金。指企业在报告期应交增值税额。

计算公式 本年应交增值税＝销项税额－（进项税额－进项税额转出）－出口抵减内销产品应纳税额－减免税款＋出口退税

批发零售贸易、餐饮业统计限额标准

行业类别	统计指标名称	限额标准
批发业	年主营业务收入	2000万元
零售业	年主营业务收入	500万元
住宿业、餐饮业	年主营业务收入	200万元

说明：

1. 外贸企业包括在批发业中，其年销售额以外币计量的，应折合成人民币，按批发业标准执行。

2. 本限额标准对象为批发和零售业、住宿和餐饮业法人企业和个体经营户、非批发和零售业、住宿和餐饮业法人单位附营的批发和零售业、住宿和餐饮业产业活动单位。

八、价格指数

Price Indices

8-1 历年物价总指数（以上年价格为100）

General Price Indices over Years (Preceding Year=100)

年 份	商品零售价格总指数	#食品	#家用电器及音像器材	居民消费价格总指数	#食品	#服务项目	工业生产者出厂价格指数
1978	100.4	101.6					
1979	102.6	107.1					
1980	110.9	114.5					
1981	109.3	110.3					
1982	101.2	100.8					
1983	99.6	99.5					
1984	98.6	97.5		99.3	97.5	102.0	
1985	106.9	108.7		106.5	108.7	103.3	
1986	104.4	105.0		104.2	105.0	102.3	
1987	112.2	113.6		112.0	113.6	109.6	
1988	132.8	133.9		136.0	133.9	168.0	
1989	122.4	125.7		122.0	127.5	118.8	
1990	94.9	92.8		96.6	92.8	111.0	
1991	101.4	101.1		102.4	101.1	109.8	
1992	107.7	109.0		109.2	109.0	117.9	
1993	119.5	123.7		121.8	123.7	134.6	
1994	118.4	125.9	99.6	123.5	126.4	141.2	
1995	109.7	119.5	95.6	113.9	119.1	128.9	
1996	104.7	108.1	94.5	106.8	107.8	115.0	
1997	99.7	100.0	92.7	101.5	99.4	113.1	
1998	98.7	99.9	93.3	99.9	99.5	108.4	
1999	95.9	95.6	94.9	97.9	95.7	109.5	
2000	100.1	100.3	97.2	101.5	100.4	112.8	
2001	97.8	99.1	97.0	96.6	98.9	101.1	
2002	99.1	100.9	98.0	98.1	99.0	98.7	
2003	101.7	103.6	99.0	100.7	103.5	97.8	
2004	103.2	108.6	98.7	103.0	108.6	99.7	
2005	103.0	106.5	101.1	102.4	106.5	100.4	100.4
2006	102.8	100.1	100.5	101.2	100.1	101.6	100.7
2007	104.2	108.3	98.2	103.1	108.0	100.2	101.4
2008	107.9	115.6	100.4	105.5	115.1	100.1	101.7
2009	95.3	97.9	95.6	96.9	98.1	96.3	96.8
2010	103.2	104.8	95.6	102.8	104.6	102.6	102.6
2011	104.7	111.1	99.3	104.9	111.1	103.0	102.9
2012	102.4	106.4	95.2	102.9	106.1	101.1	99.8
2013	100.6	103.2	96.9	101.9	103.1	102.1	98.9
2014	101.2	106.1	95.9	102.3	106.0	101.4	99.0

8-2 居民消费价格分类指数（2014年，以上年价格为100）

Consumer Price Indices by Category (2014, Preceding Year=100)

项　　目	指 数	项　　目	指 数
居民消费价格总指数	102.3	袜子	100.3
非食品价格指数	100.4	帽子	105.7
服务项目价格指数	101.4	衣着加工服务费	102.1
扣除鲜菜鲜果总指数	102.1	家庭设备用品及维修服务	101.3
消费品价格指数	102.6	耐用消费品	100.0
食　品	106.0	家具	104.3
粮食	103.0	家庭设备	96.7
大米	103.2	室内装饰品	97.7
粮食制品	95.6	床上用品	100.2
淀粉及制品	96.1	家庭日用杂品	101.1
干豆类及豆制品	102.6	家庭服务及加工维修服务	104.2
油脂	97.2	医疗保健和个人用品	100.3
肉禽及其制品	104.3	医疗保健	100.5
蛋	105.3	中药材及中成药	99.6
水产品	109.8	西药	100.6
菜	99.3	医疗保健服务	100.0
鲜菜	98.1	个人用品及服务	100.0
干菜及菜制品	107.6	化妆美容用品	100.0
调味品	103.6	清洁类化妆品	101.5
糖	99.6	个人饰品	93.2
食糖	100.4	个人服务	103.5
糖果	103.1	交通和通信	98.3
茶及饮料	99.1	交通	97.8
干鲜瓜果	116.3	交通工具	96.2
鲜瓜果	119.5	市区公共交通费	100.0
糕点饼干面包	100.1	城市间交通费	100.4
液体乳及乳制品	104.9	通信	99.3
在外用膳食品	107.8	通信工具	94.2
主食	105.4	通信服务	100.0
炒菜	106.2	娱乐教育文化用品及服务	101.7
地方小吃	116.6	文娱用耐用消费品及服务	94.4
其他食品	107.7	教育	103.9
烟酒	100.4	教材及参考书	105.3
烟草	99.1	学前教育	108.0
酒	102.1	文化娱乐类	99.5
衣着	100.3	文化娱乐用品	98.7
服装	101.5	书报杂志	100.0
衣着材料	97.3	文娱费	99.8
棉布	96.9	旅游	105.3
化纤布	94.9	居住	100.8
毛线	100.3	建房及装修材料	104.3
其他	97.9	住房租金	101.6
鞋袜帽	97.2	自有住房	99.0
鞋	96.3	水、电、燃料	101.2

8-3 居民消费价格分月指数（2014年，以上年同月价格为100）

Consumer Price Indices by Month (2014, Same Month of Preceding Year=100)

项　　目	1 月	2 月	3 月	4 月	5 月	6 月
居民消费价格总指数	103.4	102.7	102.6	102.5	103.5	103.0
非食品价格指数	102.3	100.6	100.4	100.6	101.0	100.5
服务项目价格指数	105.6	101.8	101.7	101.6	101.8	100.9
扣除鲜菜鲜果总指数	103.0	101.9	102.2	102.5	103.2	102.6
消费品价格指数	102.6	103.0	103.0	102.9	104.2	103.8
食品	105.7	106.9	107.1	106.4	108.6	108.1
#粮食	101.5	102.9	103.6	102.2	103.1	104.8
肉禽及制品	103.0	99.8	100.1	104.3	109.1	107.7
蛋	96.1	95.3	98.5	100.0	108.6	112.3
水产品	112.7	112.4	118.8	117.7	113.9	111.6
菜	108.4	119.4	111.9	93.5	99.1	99.7
烟酒	101.5	101.1	100.7	100.5	100.0	99.4
#烟草	100.3	99.9	99.4	99.4	98.9	98.4
酒	103.2	102.9	102.5	102.0	101.5	100.7
衣着	97.8	97.9	98.2	98.0	99.6	99.9
#服装	99.8	100.1	100.5	100.1	100.8	101.0
家庭设备用品及维修服务	104.5	101.9	101.6	101.9	101.8	100.9
#耐用消费品	101.9	102.0	101.1	101.0	100.7	99.7
医疗保健和个人用品	100.9	99.5	99.9	100.0	100.3	100.3
#医疗保健	100.3	100.1	100.5	100.1	100.3	100.4
个人用品及服务	102.0	98.4	98.8	99.8	100.3	100.1
交通和通信	98.8	97.4	98.2	98.8	99.4	99.4
#交通	98.9	96.7	97.6	98.6	99.3	99.3
通信	98.7	98.7	99.1	99.2	99.6	99.6
娱乐教育文化用品及服务	104.3	101.2	101.4	101.6	103.1	103.3
#文娱用耐用消费品及服务	95.8	94.6	93.5	94.1	93.7	93.9
教育	103.8	103.8	103.0	103.7	103.7	103.7
文化娱乐类	99.3	99.5	99.4	99.7	99.5	99.5
旅游类	114.9	103.7	106.8	105.4	112.2	112.4
居住	104.9	103.3	101.7	101.8	101.3	99.7
#建房及装饰材料	106.2	106.6	105.8	106.4	106.5	105.8
住房租金	110.7	107.4	104.8	104.8	102.0	97.7
自有住房	105.6	102.2	99.4	99.4	98.1	95.9
水、电、燃料	102.2	101.8	101.6	101.6	102.7	102.2

8-3 续表

项　　目	7 月	8 月	9 月	10 月	11 月	12 月
居民消费价格总指数	102.5	101.6	101.4	101.8	101.6	100.8
非食品价格指数	100.5	100.2	100.0	100.0	99.7	99.2
服务项目价格指数	100.6	100.1	100.3	100.9	100.7	100.5
扣除鲜菜鲜果总指数	102.3	101.7	101.7	101.8	101.3	100.6
消费品价格指数	103.2	102.2	101.8	102.2	101.9	100.9
食品	106.6	104.4	103.9	105.4	105.4	103.9
#粮食	104.7	103.5	103.1	103.2	102.5	101.4
肉禽及制品	104.9	102.4	105.2	106.1	104.7	104.3
蛋	110.7	105.5	109.9	109.7	110.0	109.6
水产品	108.8	106.5	104.7	106.3	104.2	101.1
菜	98.9	90.0	85.2	95.0	101.1	98.6
烟酒	99.2	100.4	100.9	100.4	100.1	100.2
#烟草	98.4	98.4	99.0	99.0	99.0	99.0
酒	100.3	103.0	103.5	102.1	101.5	101.7
衣着	101.0	101.9	102.7	100.9	101.8	103.5
#服装	101.6	103.0	104.1	102.0	102.3	102.9
家庭设备用品及维修服务	101.0	101.0	100.4	99.9	100.5	100.5
#耐用消费品	100.0	99.5	98.7	98.3	98.3	99.1
医疗保健和个人用品	100.7	100.4	100.3	100.6	100.3	100.5
#医疗保健	100.4	100.6	100.6	100.9	100.9	100.7
个人用品及服务	101.4	100.0	99.6	100.1	99.1	100.1
交通和通信	99.6	99.0	98.2	97.8	97.2	96.3
#交通	99.3	98.6	97.5	96.9	96.1	94.5
通信	99.9	99.7	99.3	99.1	99.1	99.3
娱乐教育文化用品及服务	103.1	102.6	101.2	99.9	99.4	99.0
#文娱用耐用消费品及服务	93.3	95.0	95.1	95.2	94.4	93.7
教育	103.7	103.7	104.5	104.4	104.4	104.4
文化娱乐类	99.4	99.2	99.5	99.4	99.8	99.8
旅游类	111.7	108.8	102.1	97.5	95.6	94.7
居住	99.1	98.6	99.4	101.1	100.4	98.7
#建房及装饰材料	104.8	102.2	101.4	103.2	102.3	101.3
住房租金	96.3	96.0	97.0	101.9	101.9	100.9
自有住房	95.2	94.9	96.9	100.3	100.3	100.2
水、电、燃料	102.2	102.2	102.2	101.1	99.2	95.4

8-4 居民消费价格分月指数（2014年，以上月价格为100）

Consumer Price Indices by Month (2014, Preceding Month=100)

项　　目	1 月	2 月	3 月	4 月	5 月	6 月
居民消费价格总指数	101.0	100.5	99.8	100.3	100.2	99.7
非食品价格指数	100.5	99.1	100.1	100.1	100.0	99.7
服务项目价格指数	101.8	98.8	100.1	100.1	99.9	99.7
扣除鲜菜鲜果总指数	100.9	100.2	99.9	100.1	100.3	99.7
消费品价格指数	100.7	101.2	99.7	100.3	100.3	99.8
食品	102.1	103.2	99.2	100.6	100.6	99.8
#粮食	100.5	101.0	100.5	99.4	100.2	100.8
肉禽及制品	99.8	100.1	99.0	101.0	102.5	99.5
蛋	101.0	100.9	99.6	100.1	104.7	99.6
水产品	106.5	106.9	100.5	98.5	100.8	97.9
菜	98.2	106.4	97.8	101.8	95.0	102.0
烟酒	100.1	100.1	100.2	99.9	99.8	99.2
#烟草	100.0	100.0	100.0	100.0	99.5	99.5
酒	100.3	100.3	100.5	99.9	100.1	98.9
衣着	98.0	99.3	100.3	100.2	101.6	100.5
#服装	99.0	99.2	100.5	100.2	101.0	100.4
家庭设备用品及维修服务	102.2	98.9	99.3	100.6	100.1	99.4
#耐用消费品	99.5	100.2	100.4	100.3	100.0	99.7
医疗保健和个人用品	100.9	99.3	99.8	100.1	100.2	99.8
#医疗保健	100.0	100.0	100.1	99.8	100.2	100.0
个人用品及服务	102.5	98.0	99.2	100.7	100.4	99.5
交通和通信	100.0	99.3	100.2	99.9	100.0	99.9
#交通	100.1	99.1	100.2	99.9	100.0	99.8
通信	99.8	99.8	100.2	99.9	100.0	100.0
娱乐教育文化用品及服务	102.2	97.9	99.6	100.2	100.9	100.6
#文娱用耐用消费品及服务	100.4	98.4	99.2	99.7	99.5	99.7
教育	100.0	100.0	100.9	100.8	100.0	100.0
文化娱乐类	99.5	99.6	100.5	100.1	100.0	100.0
旅游类	108.4	94.0	97.4	99.8	103.5	102.2
居住	99.8	99.5	100.7	100.1	98.9	98.9
#建房及装饰材料	100.5	100.4	99.5	100.7	99.8	100.8
住房租金	99.4	101.7	102.3	100.0	97.3	97.2
自有住房	98.6	100.1	101.4	100.0	98.7	98.6
水、电、燃料	100.9	97.9	99.8	100.0	99.2	98.8

8-4 续表

项　　目	7 月	8 月	9 月	10 月	11 月	12 月
居民消费价格总指数	99.6	99.8	100.6	99.9	99.5	99.9
非食品价格指数	100.2	99.8	100.0	100.3	99.7	99.7
服务项目价格指数	100.6	99.8	99.8	100.9	99.5	99.5
扣除鲜菜鲜果总指数	99.8	99.9	100.3	100.1	99.6	99.8
消费品价格指数	99.2	99.8	100.9	99.5	99.5	100.0
食品	98.4	99.8	101.7	99.1	99.2	100.2
#粮食	99.7	99.5	100.4	100.1	99.2	100.2
肉禽及制品	98.5	100.8	103.5	100.1	99.7	99.8
蛋	99.4	101.8	104.1	99.3	99.6	99.5
水产品	96.1	99.4	100.2	98.6	96.7	99.6
菜	98.0	99.0	102.3	96.6	98.7	103.5
烟酒	99.5	100.7	100.5	99.9	100.1	100.1
#烟草	100.0	100.0	100.0	100.0	100.0	100.0
酒	98.8	101.6	101.1	99.8	100.2	100.2
衣着	99.6	100.0	100.9	100.2	101.7	101.1
#服装	99.6	100.0	101.1	100.2	101.3	100.3
家庭设备用品及维修服务	100.2	99.7	100.3	99.7	100.2	99.9
#耐用消费品	100.4	99.8	99.7	99.2	100.0	99.9
医疗保健和个人用品	99.9	100.3	100.1	100.4	99.7	100.0
#医疗保健	100.0	100.2	100.2	100.3	99.9	99.9
个人用品及服务	99.7	100.3	99.9	100.5	99.3	100.1
交通和通信	100.1	99.5	99.5	99.4	99.2	99.3
#交通	99.9	99.4	99.4	99.2	98.7	98.8
通信	100.3	99.8	99.7	99.8	99.9	100.1
娱乐教育文化用品及服务	101.2	99.1	99.0	100.0	98.9	99.5
#文娱用耐用消费品及服务	99.2	99.2	100.2	100.1	98.6	99.2
教育	100.0	100.1	102.6	100.0	100.0	100.0
文化娱乐类	100.0	99.8	100.1	99.4	100.9	100.0
旅游类	104.8	97.4	93.0	100.3	96.2	98.7
居住	100.1	100.0	100.4	101.4	99.7	99.3
#建房及装饰材料	100.4	99.1	99.7	100.5	99.9	100.0
住房租金	100.0	100.3	100.3	104.2	100.0	98.3
自有住房	100.0	100.3	101.0	102.3	100.0	99.2
水、电、燃料	100.0	100.0	100.0	100.0	99.2	99.4

8-5 居民消费价格分月指数（2014年，以上年12月价格为100）

Consumer Price Indices by Month (2014, December of Preceding Year=100)

项　　目	1 月	2 月	3 月	4 月	5 月	6 月
居民消费价格总指数	101.0	101.5	101.3	101.6	101.8	101.5
非食品价格指数	100.5	99.6	99.7	99.8	99.8	99.5
服务项目价格指数	101.8	100.5	100.7	100.8	100.7	100.4
扣除鲜菜鲜果总指数	100.9	101.1	101.0	101.1	101.5	101.1
消费品价格指数	100.7	101.9	101.6	101.9	102.3	102.0
食品	102.1	105.4	104.6	105.2	105.8	105.6
#粮食	100.5	101.5	101.9	101.3	101.5	102.4
肉禽及制品	99.8	99.9	98.9	99.9	102.4	101.8
蛋	101.0	101.8	101.4	101.5	106.2	105.8
水产品	106.5	113.8	114.4	112.7	113.6	111.3
菜	98.2	104.5	102.2	104.0	98.7	100.7
烟酒	100.1	100.2	100.5	100.4	100.2	99.4
#烟草	100.0	100.0	100.0	100.0	99.5	99.0
酒	100.3	100.5	101.1	100.9	101.1	99.9
衣着	98.0	97.4	97.7	97.8	99.4	100.0
#服装	99.0	98.3	98.7	98.9	99.9	100.3
家庭设备用品及维修服务	102.2	101.1	100.4	101.0	101.0	100.5
#耐用消费品	99.5	99.7	100.1	100.4	100.4	100.1
医疗保健和个人用品	100.9	100.2	100.0	100.1	100.3	100.1
#医疗保健	100.0	100.1	100.1	99.9	100.1	100.1
个人用品及服务	102.5	100.4	99.7	100.4	100.7	100.2
交通和通信	100.0	99.3	99.5	99.4	99.4	99.3
#交通	100.1	99.2	99.4	99.2	99.2	99.0
通信	99.8	99.6	99.8	99.7	99.7	99.7
娱乐教育文化用品及服务	102.2	100.1	99.7	99.9	100.7	101.3
#文娱用耐用消费品及服务	100.4	98.8	98.0	97.7	97.2	97.0
教育	100.0	100.0	100.9	101.7	101.7	101.7
文化娱乐类	99.5	99.1	99.6	99.7	99.6	99.6
旅游类	108.4	101.9	99.2	99.1	102.6	104.8
居住	99.8	99.3	100.0	100.1	98.9	97.8
#建房及装饰材料	100.5	100.9	100.5	101.2	100.9	101.8
住房租金	99.4	101.0	103.3	103.3	100.6	97.8
自有住房	98.6	98.7	100.1	100.1	98.8	97.4
水、电、燃料	100.9	98.8	98.6	98.6	97.8	96.7

8-5 续表

项 目	7 月	8 月	9 月	10 月	11 月	12 月
居民消费价格总指数	101.1	100.9	101.5	101.4	100.9	100.8
非食品价格指数	99.7	99.5	99.5	99.8	99.5	99.2
服务项目价格指数	100.9	100.7	100.6	101.4	101.0	100.5
扣除鲜菜鲜果总指数	101.0	100.8	101.2	101.3	100.8	100.6
消费品价格指数	101.2	101.0	101.8	101.3	100.9	100.9
食品	103.9	103.7	105.5	104.5	103.7	103.9
#粮食	102.0	101.5	101.9	102.1	101.2	101.4
肉禽及制品	100.3	101.1	104.7	104.8	104.4	104.3
蛋	105.1	107.0	111.4	110.6	110.2	109.6
水产品	107.0	106.3	106.5	105.0	101.6	101.1
菜	98.7	97.7	100.0	96.6	95.3	98.6
烟酒	98.9	99.6	100.1	100.0	100.1	100.2
#烟草	99.0	99.0	99.0	99.0	99.0	99.0
酒	98.8	100.4	101.5	101.3	101.5	101.7
衣着	99.6	99.6	100.5	100.7	102.3	103.5
#服装	99.9	99.9	101.0	101.3	102.6	102.9
家庭设备用品及维修服务	100.7	100.4	100.7	100.3	100.6	100.5
#耐用消费品	100.5	100.3	99.9	99.2	99.2	99.1
医疗保健和个人用品	100.1	100.3	100.4	100.8	100.5	100.5
#医疗保健	100.1	100.4	100.5	100.9	100.8	100.7
个人用品及服务	99.9	100.3	100.2	100.7	100.0	100.1
交通和通信	99.3	98.9	98.4	97.8	97.0	96.3
#交通	98.9	98.3	97.7	96.9	95.6	94.5
通信	100.0	99.8	99.5	99.3	99.2	99.3
娱乐教育文化用品及服务	102.5	101.6	100.6	100.5	99.5	99.0
#文娱用耐用消费品及服务	96.2	95.4	95.6	95.8	94.4	93.7
教育	101.7	101.8	104.4	104.4	104.4	104.4
文化娱乐类	99.6	99.4	99.5	98.9	99.8	99.8
旅游类	109.9	107.0	99.5	99.8	96.0	94.7
居住	97.9	97.9	98.3	99.7	99.4	98.7
#建房及装饰材料	102.2	101.3	101.0	101.5	101.4	101.3
住房租金	97.8	98.1	98.4	102.6	102.6	100.9
自有住房	97.4	97.8	98.8	101.0	101.0	100.2
水、电、燃料	96.7	96.7	96.7	96.7	95.9	95.4

8-6 商品零售价格分类指数（2014年，以上年价格为100）

Retail Price Indices by Category (2014, Preceding Year=100)

项　　目	指　数	项　　目	指　数
商品零售价格总指数	101.2	专业音像器材	96.9
食品类	106.1	文化办公用品	96.5
粮食	103.0	日用品	100.2
淀粉及制品	96.1	日用百货	98.7
干豆类及豆制品	102.6	日用杂品	103.6
油脂	97.2	洗涤用品	101.5
肉禽及其制品	104.3	其他日用品	98.2
蛋	105.3	体育娱乐用品	99.7
水产品	109.8	体育用品	101.0
菜	99.3	娱乐用品	98.4
调味品	103.6	交通、通信用品	97.1
糖	99.6	交通运输机械	98.8
干鲜瓜果	116.3	通信器材类	94.3
糕点饼干面包	100.1	家具	104.3
液体乳及乳制品	104.9	化妆品类	101.2
在外用膳食品	107.8	金银珠宝类	90.6
其他食品	107.7	中西药品及医疗保健用品类	100.5
饮料、烟酒	99.8	医疗器具及用品	100.2
茶及饮料	99.1	中药材及中成药	99.6
烟草	99.1	西药	100.6
酒	102.1	保健器具及用品	102.1
服装、鞋帽类	100.1	书报杂志及电子出版物类	102.0
服装	101.5	教材及参考书	105.3
鞋袜帽	97.2	书报杂志	100.0
其他	97.9	电子音像制品	98.0
纺织品类	98.7	燃料类	97.4
衣着材料	97.3	煤炭及制品类	100.0
床上用品	99.1	石油及制品类	97.4
家用电器及音像器材	95.9	建筑材料及五金电料类	101.4
家庭设备	96.7	建筑装璜材料	102.0
文娱用耐用消费品	94.1	五金电料类	99.9

8-7 工业生产者出厂价格指数（2013-2014年，以上年价格为100）

Producer Price Index (PPI) for Manufactured Goods

(2013-2014, Preceding Year=100)

项　　　目	2013年	2014年
工业生产者出厂价格指数	98.9	99.0
#轻工业	99.5	99.7
重工业	98.4	98.5
#农副食品加工业	97.5	92.2
食品制造业	99.5	100.8
酒、饮料和精制茶制造业	100.3	101.0
纺织业	99.6	101.6
纺织服装、服饰业	101.2	100.9
皮革、皮毛、羽毛及其制品和制鞋业	103.0	102.7
木材加工和木、竹、藤、棕、草制品业	98.8	99.7
家具制造业	101.2	101.1
造纸和纸制品业	95.6	99.2
印刷和记录媒介复制业	99.4	100.9
文教、美工、体育和娱乐用品制造业	99.0	100.7
石油加工、炼焦和核燃料加工业	97.5	95.7
化学原料和化学制品制造业	98.3	99.1
医药制造业	101.9	102.3
化学纤维制造业	97.0	98.3
橡胶和塑料制品业	98.9	99.3
非金属矿物制品业	102.1	97.2
黑色金属冶炼和压延加工业	93.7	93.8
有色金属冶炼和压延加工业	96.2	95.7
金属制品业	98.6	98.3
通用设备制造业	98.9	97.8
专用设备制造业	98.8	101.4
汽车制造业	98.1	97.0
铁路、船舶、航空航天和其他运输设备制造业	99.8	100.6
电气机械和器材制造业	99.5	98.8
计算机、通信和其他电子设备制造业	97.7	98.3
仪器仪表制造业	99.5	102.2
其他制造业	115.9	111.8
废弃资源综合利用业	98.9	96.3
金属制品、机械和设备修理业	97.0	105.5
电力、热力的生产和供应业	100.3	99.4
燃气生产和供应业	98.0	96.9
水的生产和供应业	101.5	101.4

主要统计指标解释

Explanatory Notes on Main Statistical Indicators

居民消费价格指数 是度量消费商品及服务项目价格水平随着时间而变动的相对数，反映居民家庭购买的消费品及服务价格水平的变动情况。它是宏观经济分析、决策、调控和价格总水平监测以及国民经济核算的重要指标。其按年度计算的变动率通常被用来作为反映通货膨胀(或紧缩)程度的指标。

商品零售价格指数 是度量市场商品零售价格水平变动趋势和变动程度的相对数，反映商品在流通过程中最后一个环节的价格即工业、商业、餐饮业和其他零售企业向城乡居民、机关团体出售生活消费品和办公用品价格水平的变动趋势。它可以为国家宏观调控和国民经济核算提供参考依据，并在此基础上派生其他价格指数。

工业生产者出厂价格总指数 是反映各工业部门主要工业产品出厂价格变动趋势和程度的相对数。编制该价格指数，用以观察和分析在生产环节中工业品价格变动对企业经济效益及宏观经济运行的影响，并为工业增长速度的科学计算提供重要的依据。

九、对外经济贸易与旅游

Foreign Trade and Tourism

9-1 主要年份对外经济与旅游业主要指标

Main Indicators of Foreign Trade and Economic Cooperation and Tourism in Main Years

指　　标	单 位	1985年	1995年	2000年	2005年	2010年	2013年	2014年
进出口总额	万美元		1539112	3204526	7437150	12133773	15307167	16253046
出口总额	万美元	17545	779867	1715927	4092905	6959751	9086371	9706918
进口总额	万美元		759245	1488599	3344245	5174022	6220796	6546128
新签利用外资协议(合同)数	宗	625	3077	1276	992	875	506	465
#“三来一补”项目	宗	514	2094	871	219	6		
“三资”项目	宗	111	983	405	773	869	506	465
利用外资增资项目宗数	宗				1138	1059	680	598
合同规定外商投资额	万美元	6815	330920	183633	475238	307282	415614	443973
“三来一补”项目	万美元	1870	97428	69302	166363	47542	11504	12514
“三资”项目	万美元	4945	233492	114331	308875	259740	404110	431459
合同规定外商增资项目	万美元				187422	180723	320106	291479
实际利用外资	万美元	2894	105665	164712	375139	316287	402935	462134
“三来一补”项目	万美元	1511	38418	55975	93023	43116	9160	9215
“三资”项目	万美元	1383	67247	108737	282116	273171	393775	452919
本年止累计“三来一补”企业投产宗数	宗	1592	8447	9917	8997	5688	1569	1264
年末“三来一补”企业从业人员	万人	9.82	59.44	72.89	126.49	81.00	28.20	23.84
本年止累计“三资”企业投产数	宗	51	2629	3908	6657	8338	9592	9806
年末“三资”企业从业人员	万人	0.64	25.01	87.17	145.50	163.53	195.48	197.01
当年来料加工企业转为三资或民营企业	家					1250	197	73
合同规定外商投资额(新口径)	万美元				298029	259740	404110	431459
实际利用外资(新口径)	万美元				146796	273171	393775	452919
全年接待旅游人数	万人次		89	291	1156	2251	2826	2791
#国际及港澳台旅游者	万人次		27	106	169	327	418	356
#外国人	万人次		6	15	70	109	138	122
国内旅客	万人次		62	185	987	1924	2408	2435
国际旅游收入	万美元		5679	7617	28189	67592	144981	157493
星级以上宾馆酒店客房数	间		7568	18024	18258	16631	18611	12855
宾馆酒店客房开房率	%		68.80	61.88	58.90	58.12	56.87	51.20

注：1. 对外经济部分除有注明新口径的以外均为旧口径，旧口径包括“三资”和“三来一补”，新口径不含“三来一补”且以验资作为统计标准，后同。
2. 2002年起旅游业指标采用旅游局口径，与往年数不可比。

9-2 主要年份进出口贸易

Total Imports and Exports in Main Years

单位：万美元

项　　目	1995年	2000年	2005年	2010年	2013年	2014年
进出口总额	1539112	3204526	7437150	12133773	15307167	16253046
出口总额	779867	1715927	4092905	6959751	9086371	9706918
按贸易方式分						
#一般贸易	23180	20937	175502	954098	2007791	2687709
来料加工装配	434646	834347	1611676	1955379	1070242	1102722
进料加工	320186	858409	2304325	3946227	5758315	5472315
其他	1855	2234	1402	104047	250023	444172
按经济类型分						
#国有企业	474304	867501	1139776	1102678	343322	292144
三资企业	305061	835611	2353253	4426236	6835927	6709114
集体企业	122	12259	37893	141561	17739	16589
民营企业			561650	1285124	1885059	2683874
进口总额	759245	1488599	3344245	5174022	6220796	6546128
按贸易方式分						
#一般贸易	5394	72475	236133	755349	1237293	1614999
来料加工装配	353138	645562	1216566	1424118	806988	775951
进料加工	259397	616319	1625629	2457194	3573281	3333100
其他	141316	154243	265917	537362	603235	822079
按经济类型分						
#国有企业	419827	764945	987421	1076821	333140	233935
三资企业	329164	706145	1882393	3028036	4546167	4447363
集体企业	243	10267	32167	78053	10723	9547
民营企业			439521	967472	1326849	1844320
贸易顺差	20622	227328	748660	1785728	2865575	3160789

9-3 历年进出口总额

Total Value of Imports and Exports over Years

单位：万美元

年 份	进出口总 额	出口总额	#一般贸易	来料加工装配	进料加工	进口总额	#一般贸易	来料加工装配	进料加工
1978		3938							
1979		5382							
1980		7737							
1981		9173							
1982		10879							
1983		11890							
1984		12966							
1985		17545							
1986		23280							
1987		26755							
1988		31781							
1989		34868							
1990	108229	56828				51401			
1991	317463	165159				152304			
1992	509007	260272				248735			
1993	675647	321137				354510			
1994	882997	429416				453581			
1995	1539112	779867	23180	434646	320186	759245	5394	353138	259397
1996	1784222	918683	16377	496833	405066	865539	8956	383988	309710
1997	2129885	1136768	18020	582863	535708	993117	7598	445237	420014
1998	2327324	1306055	15409	652853	636822	1021269	10406	462194	463450
1999	2846291	1515391	16347	759638	738191	1330900	51726	584224	582721
2000	3204526	1715927	20937	834347	858409	1488599	72475	645562	616319
2001	3445457	1898924	25945	940908	931766	1546533	68392	684323	656910
2002	4424706	2373646	34848	1171688	1167047	2051060	83522	922916	886699
2003	5210623	2800227	48988	1257934	1492723	2410396	144235	962367	1127404
2004	6451775	3519237	85056	1503757	1929967	2932538	222262	1090197	1402413
2005	7437150	4092905	175502	1611676	2304325	3344245	236133	1216566	1625629
2006	8422107	4737640	265784	1661399	2806910	3684467	259709	1265725	1879233
2007	10687290	6023212	357941	2235125	3398212	4664078	371073	1702595	2196521
2008	11329947	6553738	487193	2428365	3585619	4776209	455447	1712939	2206139
2009	9415458	5516861	571682	1823160	3055047	3898597	456075	1297315	1820882
2010	12133773	6959751	954098	1955379	3946227	5174022	755349	1424118	2457194
2011	13522382	7832871	1341146	1693479	4654300	5689511	988370	1174341	2881689
2012	14441587	8506606	1692301	1216525	5398579	5934981	1096531	901512	3322199
2013	15307167	9086371	2007791	1070242	5758315	6220796	1237293	806988	3573281
2014	16253046	9706918	2687709	1102722	5472315	6546128	1614999	775951	3333100

注：出口总额1990年以前为外经贸口径，1990年起为海关口径。

9-4 分国别(地区)进出口总值（2013-2014年）

Total Value of Imports and Exports by Countries (Regions) (2013-2014)

单位：亿美元

国别(地区)	实际出口		进口到货	
	2014年	2013年	2014年	2013年
亚洲	516.68	496.47	571.80	541.71
东南亚联盟	75.10	63.32	88.00	82.73
非洲	12.06	7.23	2.25	1.27
欧洲	159.22	137.26	29.71	29.34
欧盟	149.69	128.88	27.22	27.79
拉美洲	32.05	27.40	14.00	15.45
北美洲	237.32	229.43	33.84	29.89
大洋洲	13.36	10.84	2.68	4.16
美国	225.03	218.28	28.73	24.12
香港	266.12	262.39	3.74	3.59
日本	75.40	76.42	85.30	82.82
荷兰	28.16	24.95	1.71	2.42
德国	31.96	29.33	7.17	6.75
英国	25.01	21.28	3.64	3.87
韩国	46.10	52.60	90.57	92.68
台湾	17.42	17.56	112.22	103.40
法国	12.30	11.36	1.78	1.25
加拿大	12.29	11.15	5.12	5.76
澳大利亚	11.68	9.85	2.26	3.51
新加坡	9.94	8.49	12.18	10.77
马来西亚	10.50	7.99	24.41	22.70

9-5 主要商品类别出口总值（2009-2014年）

Total Export Value by Category of Main Commodities (2009-2014)

单位：亿美元

商 品 名 称	2009年	2010年	2011年	2012年	2013年	2014年
机电产品(包括本表已具体列名的机电产品)	387.52	494.83	556.16	607.69	658.05	696.25
高新技术产品	159.39	241.95	273.42	297.39	336.07	365.24
自动数据处理设备及其部件	42.26	52.82	61.21	61.42	74.50	79.76
服装及衣着附件	28.11	38.98	46.13	56.51	56.93	59.60
录、放像机	8.41	13.24	16.19	7.70	6.05	4.89
自动数据处理设备的零件	26.68	33.31	34.71	37.54	39.55	40.68
纺织纱线、织物及制品	13.68	15.21	16.43	16.71	15.28	16.16
玩具	12.28	16.32	17.20	18.62	20.00	22.56
鞋类	24.57	30.96	30.72	29.89	29.83	30.88
家具及其零件	24.26	32.09	34.00	39.58	39.64	44.08
录音机及收录(放)音组合机(包括整套散件)	7.46	8.85	9.42	9.95	8.19	7.43
塑料制品	9.10	11.37	12.71	14.21	16.68	18.61
静止式变流器	23.14	35.98	37.61	35.95	37.14	36.19
旅行用品及箱包	11.43	15.65	18.16	19.87	21.56	22.29
灯具、照明装置及类似品	7.84	10.37	11.74	14.00	17.03	19.41
电线和电缆	10.81	15.22	17.31	21.25	22.70	23.98
通断及保护电路装置	10.37	13.40	16.18	19.66	21.06	21.93
有线电话机(包括整套散件)	14.84	16.44	19.26	19.23	28.96	57.50
电视、收音机及无线电讯设备的零附件	12.59	16.12	14.42	13.37	13.32	12.97

9-6 主要商品进口数量与金额（海关口径，2013-2014年）

Main Import Commodities in Volume and Value (Custom Statistics) (2013-2014)

金额单位：万美元

商品名称	数量单位	2013年		2014年	
		数量	金额	数量	金额
谷物及谷物粉	万吨	9.14	4118	10.18	4183
食用植物油	万吨	8.85	7934	13.14	10808
食糖	万吨	15.91	6834	5.44	2328
天然橡胶(包括胶乳)	万吨	1.62	3656	3.28	5528
合成橡胶(包括胶乳)	万吨	6.07	17197	5.21	14788
原木	万立方	13.24	6227	15.02	7194
锯材	万立方	51.44	17617	54.23	21709
羊毛(包括羊毛条)	吨	1431	1204	1084	899
纺织用合成纤维	万吨	1.01	2346	0.86	2106
#聚酯纤维	万吨	0.79	1381	0.65	1221
人造纤维短纤	吨	85.79	28	372.14	117
成品油	万吨	9.43	10051	4.13	4836
合成有机染料	吨	1917.51	1601	1484.00	1544
初级形状的塑料	万吨	174.80	357973	166.20	354086
#初级形状的聚乙烯	万吨	14.68	22866	13.55	21955
初级形状的聚丙烯	万吨	25.33	40310	23.44	38025
初级形状的苯乙烯聚合物	万吨	49.91	100409	49.01	98291
初级形状的氯乙烯聚合物	万吨	21.37	23971	15.94	19047
初级形状的聚酯	万吨	16.64	54723	17.59	57462
牛皮革及马皮革	万吨	5.11	57940	6.32	68439
纸及纸板(未切成形的)	万吨	22.60	23105	21.33	23059
毛纱线	万吨	0.55	5971	0.63	7325
合成纤维纱线	万吨	3.88	17771	3.69	17742
棉机织物	万米	13647	25343	9666	19336
涂覆浸渍塑料的织物	万吨	2.30	13708	2.09	13725
针织或钩编织物	万米	15350	24780	15452	23882
钢材	万吨	84.28	100958	81.61	99362
#钢铁板材	万吨	6.90	15804	68.29	74017
未锻造的铜及铜材	万吨	17.39	141345	16.55	132124
#铜材	万吨	12.17	102980	11.43	96502
未锻造的铝及铝材	万吨	3.86	18587	3.13	15476
#铝材	万吨	2.54	15380	2.24	13176

9-6 续表

金额单位：万美元

商品名称	数量单位	2013年		2014年	
		数量	金额	数量	金额
钢材或铝制结构体及其部件	吨	722	287	768	281
蒸汽锅炉及过热水锅炉	台	1	3	1	2
液泵及液体提升机	万台	157.23	2414	184.37	2330
冷冻机和制冷设备	金额		274		121
机械提升搬运装卸设备及零件	金额		7973		6010
制造纸及纸制品用机械及零件	金额		2937		1562
印刷、装订机械及零件	金额		77516		82485
纺织机械及零件	金额		8192		4293
#针织机及缝编机	台	1639	6796	519	2822
纱线织物等后整理机器	台	145	582	147	464
工业用缝纫机	台	514	331	530	357
金属加工机床	台	2094	17627	11379	66290
橡胶或塑料加工机械及零件	金额		12572		13985
型模及金属铸造用型箱	金额		10068		9369
自动数据处理设备及其部件	万台	4573	124949	4638	126914
自动数据处理设备的零件	吨	16688	208749	14304	231728
电动机及发电机	万台	39560	39100	33080	29268
发电机组及旋转式变流机	台	53	2332	140	4320
电视、收音机及无线电讯设备的零附件	吨	4477	109343	5133	101804
通断及保护电路装置及零件	金额		191233		189409
二极管、晶体管及类似半导体	亿个	444.36	190676	1005.48	233466
电线和电缆	吨	29357	53446	29312	55084
计量检测分析自控仪器及器具	金额		38818		48472
塑料制品	吨	18982	18341	19880	18664

9-7 主要商品出口数量与金额（海关口径，2013-2014年）

Main Export Commodities in Volume and Value (Custom Statistics) (2013-2014)

金额单位：万美元

商品名称	数量单位	2013年		2014年	
		数量	金额	数量	金额
活猪(种猪除外)	万头	0.15	26	0.17	29
水海产品	万吨	0.35	1462	0.31	1364
谷物及谷物粉	万吨				
蔬菜	万吨	1.59	704	1.05	622
鲜、干水果及坚果	金额		1		
食用植物油(包括棕榈油)	吨	484.06	243	277.56	167
中药材及中式成药	吨	159	35		
锯材	立方米	100	2		
成品油	万吨	0.03	30	0.01	9
合成有机染料	吨	235	95		
医药品	吨	836	820	862	837
美容化妆品及护肤品	吨	3718	2243	3326	1980
洗衣粉	吨	25096	1781	22854	1966
烟花、爆竹	吨				
初级形状的聚氯乙烯	吨	9300	1435	9000	1382
家用或装饰用木制品	吨	10900	4674	11400	4833
纸及纸板(未切成形的)	万吨	9.22	6307	13.16	9933
纺织纱线、织物及制品	金额		152796		161603
#棉纱线	吨	15590	8105	13866	7582
亚麻及苎麻纱线	万米	12.87	36	1.85	7
棉机织物	万米	1794.24	4251	1355.79	3894
玻璃制品	金额		5423		7412
家用陶瓷器皿	吨	21500	5326	23600	10624
钢材	万吨	7.77	11206	3.30	8595
未锻造的铜及铜材	吨	22847	17651	34600	25782
未锻造的铝及铝材	吨	7800	3509	6500	3457
手用或机用工具	吨	16600	23203	19600	25801

9-7 续表

金额单位：万美元

商品名称	数量单位	2013年		2014年	
		数量	金额	数量	金额
电扇	万台	12395.47	38374	12026.07	41066
纺织机械及零件	金额		2685		3261
金属加工机床	万台	0.54	3414	1.71	4514
电子计算器	亿台	0.42	13871	0.32	12929
电动机及发电机	亿台	6.26	75288	5.39	71700
静止式变流器	亿个	6.69	371444	5.74	361863
原电池	亿个	16.30	16768	14.48	14866
蓄电池	亿个	0.04	6081	0.03	5361
电话机	万台	5694.67	289625	9403.14	575031
扬声器	亿个	2.19	73762	1.52	77041
收音设备(包括收录音组合机)	万台	4047.94	81970	3774.18	74271
电视机	万台	259.45	59851	223.43	74070
#彩色电视机	万台	259.45	59851	223.43	74070
电视、收音机及无线电讯零附件	万吨	5.47	133225	5.09	129735
电容器	万吨	1.30	98944	1.03	79020
通断及保护电路装置	金额		210585		219286
二极管及类似半导体器件	亿个	555.16	50851	1108.67	82321
电线和电缆	万吨	19.03	226993	19.75	239765
照相机	万架	727.40	42980	917.92	47835
医疗仪器及器械	金额		20920		25214
手表	亿只	0.43	16095	0.48	17035
#电动手表	亿只	0.42	15660	0.48	16557
家具	金额		396379		440795
灯具、照明装置及类似品	金额		170281		194056
箱包及类似容器	金额		215586		222882
服装及衣着附件	金额		569267		596005
#织物制服装	金额		504557		523903
裘皮服装	吨	75.04	860	88.78	930
帽类	万个	11818.25	16237	15515.96	19403
鞋	亿双	1.69	282337	1.61	289701
塑料制品	万吨	53.05	166814	56.82	186052
玩具	金额		200009		225640
贵金属或包贵金属的首饰	金额		10721		27333

9-8 历年新签利用外资协议(合同)宗数

Number of Signed Agreements or Contracts of Utilization of Foreign Capital over Years

单位：宗

年 份	新签协议(合同)数	“三来一补”企业	“三资”企业
1979	184	184	
1980	415	415	
1981	555	553	2
1982	470	468	2
1983	454	447	7
1984	551	508	43
1985	625	514	111
1986	618	559	59
1987	824	729	95
1988	2048	1839	209
1989	939	779	160
1990	1267	1075	192
1991	1636	1268	368
1992	2232	1374	858
1993	3118	1773	1345
1994	2678	1521	1157
1995	3077	2094	983
1996	1678	1343	335
1997	1685	1492	193
1998	1383	1051	332
1999	1362	1135	227
2000	1276	871	405
2001	1395	705	690
2002	1391	524	867
2003	1524	392	1132
2004	1423	391	1032
2005	992	219	773
2006	786	177	609
2007	790	82	708
2008	588	35	553
2009	601	22	579
2010	875	6	869
2011	1325	1	1324
2012	690		690
2013	506		506
2014	465		465

9-9 历年新签利用外资协议(合同)规定外商投资额

Amount of Signed Agreements or Contracts of Utilization of Foreign Capital over Years

单位：万美元

年　份	协议(合同)规定外商投资额	“三来一补”企业	“三资”企业
1979	476	476	
1980	1055	1055	
1981	806	784	22
1982	787	771	16
1983	1616	841	775
1984	3217	1013	2204
1985	6815	1870	4945
1986	3398	1593	1805
1987	18513	14082	4431
1988	62173	42507	19666
1989	23365	9268	14097
1990	30180	12346	17834
1991	64483	19348	45135
1992	208825	29720	179105
1993	355515	54823	300692
1994	349703	47700	302003
1995	330920	97428	233492
1996	208861	62811	146050
1997	121351	62114	59237
1998	163677	58709	104968
1999	147247	69756	77491
2000	183633	69302	114331
2001	209779	56833	152946
2002	248914	47285	201629
2003	325633	59538	266095
2004	413216	124089	289127
2005	475238	166363	308875
2006	552758	197836	354922
2007	625088	176903	448185
2008	393701	134952	258749
2009	203040	41420	161620
2010	307282	47542	259740
2011	370189	19353	350836
2012	415522	34491	381031
2013	415614	11504	404110
2014	443973	12514	431459

9-10 历年实际利用外资

Foreign Capital Actually Utilized over Years

单位：万美元

年份	累计实际利用外资	当年实际利用外资		
			"三来一补"企业	"三资"企业
1979	173	173	173	
1980	1107	934	934	
1981	1642	535	528	7
1982	2357	715	668	47
1983	3258	901	871	30
1984	5175	1917	1233	684
1985	8069	2894	1511	1383
1986	11111	3042	1553	1489
1987	22370	11259	9185	2074
1988	46496	24126	17717	6409
1989	71445	24949	16559	8390
1990	95764	24319	14309	10010
1991	121918	26154	11478	14676
1992	168510	46592	13716	32876
1993	261938	93428	14181	79247
1994	366750	104812	26938	77874
1995	472415	105665	38418	67247
1996	579979	107564	38061	69503
1997	701406	121427	33467	87960
1998	835219	133813	40780	93033
1999	980951	145732	48620	97112
2000	1145663	164712	55975	108737
2001	1327225	181562	66841	114721
2002	1542073	214848	68980	145868
2003	1798409	256336	80936	175400
2004	2101839	303430	89555	213875
2005	2476978	375139	93023	146796
2006	2910751	433773	98543	180789
2007	3415146	504395	94365	211759
2008	3737716	322570	77902	244668
2009	4031873	294157	34758	259399
2010	4348160	316287	43116	273171
2011	4353694	321821	16769	305052
2012	4725598	371904	34966	336938
2013	5128533	402935	9160	393775
2014	5590667	462134	9215	452919

9-11 主要年份“三资”企业利用外资

Utilization of Foreign Capital of Enterprises with Foreign Investment in Main Years

项　　目	计量单位	1990年	1995年	2000年	2005年	2010年	2013年	2014年
全部“三资”企业利用外资情况								
当年新签协议宗数	宗	192	983	405	773	869	506	465
本年止累计执行宗数	宗	591	2807	4012	6657	8338	9592	9806
#已投产	宗	454	2629	3908	5870	7469	9086	9341
项目(协议)终止宗数	宗	24	48	338	193	471	284	251
实际利用外资总额	万美元	18642	75853	115801	290553	277547	395270	452919
引进设备价值	万美元	6619	50267	80215	118401	63822	22586	57500
出口总值	万美元	13439	178351	835600	2353253	4426236	6835926	6709114
期末职工人数	万人	3.81	25.01	87.17	145.50	163.53	195.48	197.01
中外合作企业利用外资情况								
当年新签协议宗数	宗	72	195	19	2			
本年止累计执行宗数	宗	237	730	705	337	184	119	117
#已投产	宗	177	682	700	299	184	119	117
项目(协议)终止宗数	宗	15	12	130	25	23	8	2
实际利用外资总额	万美元	5072	15159	10045	13529	1345	66	253
引进设备价值	万美元	2411	9320	5033	4060	651		37
出口总值	万美元	2423	35718	92100	116157	117188	41045	45065
期末职工人数	万人	1.02	5.82	13.57	10.38	3.50	2.43	2.45

注：本表2000年起出口总值是海关口径。

9-11 续表

项目	计量单位	1990年	1995年	2000年	2005年	2010年	2013年	2014年
中外合资企业利用外资情况								
当年新签协议宗数	宗	93	378	29	31	18	29	25
本年止累计执行宗数	宗	338	1590	1690	712	507	463	474
#已投产	宗	251	1498	1650	668	489	434	449
项目(协议)终止宗数	宗	9	31	159	53	99		14
实际利用外资总额	万美元	13070	39659	23966	25672	36342	41229	41608
引进设备价值	万美元	3920	25557	14365	4060	28850	1796	909
出口总值	万美元	10934	90357	248800	289344	348622	315527	315998
期末职工人数	万人	2.69	13.51	24.68	17.95	11.60	9.43	9.50
外商独资企业利用外资情况								
当年新签协议宗数	宗	27	410	357	740	851	477	440
本年止累计执行宗数	宗	16	487	1614	5607	7641	8994	9215
#已投产	宗	8	449	1555	4903	6790	8517	8775
项目(协议)终止宗数	宗		5	49	115	349	276	235
实际利用外资总额	万美元	500	21035	79113	252194	239860	353632	
引进设备价值	万美元	288	15390	58140	91288	34321	32405	56554
出口总值	万美元	82	52276	494700	1947751	3960425	5937926	6348051
期末职工人数	万人	0.10	5.67	48.92	117.17	148.43	183.29	185.06

9-12 主要年份分方式、分国别（地区）实际利用外资

Foreign Capital Actually Utilized by Type and Countries (Regions) in Main Years

单位：万美元

项目	1990年	1995年	2000年	2005年	2010年	2013年	2014年
按引进方式分							
总计	10167	68438	164712	375139	316287	402935	462134
外商直接投资	10010	67247	108737	282116	273171	393775	452919
合资经营企业	5871	31314	18865	18195	32135	39734	42022
合作经营企业	3645	14983	8305	12669	1176	66	277
外资(独资)经营企业	494	20950	78890	251252	239634	353632	410372
外商投资股份公司			2677		226	343	248
外商其他投资	157	1191	55975	93023	43116	9160	9215
国际租赁							
补偿贸易							
加工装配	157	1191	55975	93023	43116	9160	9215
按国家和地区分							
总计	10167	67247	164712	375139	316287	402935	462134
香港	10167	58333	88950	185214	182600	185075	236826
澳门		13		44	442		482
台湾		3016	23722	130682	82674	119873	110805
日本		391	7476	25253	12861	39379	36228
泰国		96	33	20			14
新加坡		822	3511	3994	6094	9448	32609
德国		3	1884	487	1488	3014	2994
法国			89	20	688	27	2669
瑞士			546		127	1025	2607
加拿大		46	15	99	568	74	37
美国		3230	2391	8122	3309	16125	12971
澳大利亚		56	14	48	61	82	112
韩国			2362	6958	5955	10769	7155
利比亚			153				
英国		79		12	277		507
其他		1162	33566	14186	19143	18044	16118

注：1995年分国别地区的外商投资额是外商直接投资额。

9-13 外商直接投资分行业情况（2013-2014年）

Foreign Direct Investment by Sector (2013-2014)

单位：万美元

行业	2013年			2014年		
	项目个数(个)	合同外资金额	实际投资金额	项目个数(个)	合同外资金额	实际投资金额
总计	506	404110	393775	465	431459	452919
农、林、牧、渔业	4	427	357		164	2890
采矿业				1	21	34
制造业	301	313357	316209	201	312885	362095
#纺织业	13	6409	6499	7	10988	12886
化学原料及化学制品制造业	4	4989	3731	4	5175	5730
医药制造业	1	1181	20		1800	1550
通用设备制造业	11	12842	12098	6	9130	13548
专用设备制造业	17	19524	28893	15	24716	23876
通信设备、计算机及其他电子设备制造业	55	75900	80802	34	69641	90002
电力、燃气及水的生产和供应业	2	871	1857	1	6420	4796
建筑业	1	39	13	2	120	39
交通运输、仓储和邮政业	9	17217	8399	9	17306	11491
信息传输、计算机服务和软件业	1	781	38	1	74	2
批发和零售业	142	51973	51437	185	49567	41864
住宿和餐饮业	4	47	380	9	125	942
金融业		1989	489		3733	922
房地产业	2	2253	6201	2	29352	22618
#房地产开发经营	2	2253	6201	2	29352	22618
租赁和商务服务业	29	9289	2624	30	9424	3535
科学研究、技术服务和地质勘查业	6	1031	523	20	1571	890
居民服务和其他服务业	2	293	717	2	159	236
卫生、社会保障和社会福利业		4536	4536			
公共管理和社会组织						

9-14 主要年份宾馆酒店接待能力和接待人数

Capacity and Tourists Received by Hotels in Main Years

项目	单位	1990年	1995年	2000年	2005年	2010年	2013年	2014年
三星级以上宾馆(酒店)	家	3	16	30	63	82	75	58
三星级	家	3	16	23	27	35	29	18
四星级	家			6	22	25	24	19
五星级	家			1	14	22	22	21
客房(已评1星以上)	间	3793	7568	18024	18258	16631	18611	12855
床位(已评1星以上)	张	8531	15136	30895	25014	24841	24437	16921
开房率	%	60.2	68.8	61.9	58.9	58.1	56.9	51.2
全年接待人数	万人次	125	89	291	1156	2251	2826	2791
国际及港澳台旅游者	万人次	27	27	106	169	327	418	356
#外国人	万人次	1	6	15	70	109	138	122
港澳台同胞	万人次	26	21	89	99	219	280	234
国内旅客	万人次	98	62	185	987	1924	2408	2435
外出旅游人数	万人次					154	160	151
国内旅游人数	万人次					139	144	131
出国(境)游人数	万人次					15	18	19

9-15 历年旅游业情况

Basic Statistics on Tourism over Years

年份	三星级以上宾馆(酒店)(家)	客房(已评1星以上)(间)	床位(已评1星以上)(张)	开房率(%)	全年接待人数(万人次)	国际及港澳台旅游者	外国人	港澳台同胞	国内游客	国际旅游外汇收入(万美元)
1978										
1979										
1980										
1981										
1982										
1983										
1984										
1985										
1986					80	11		10	69	554
1987					107	19	1	18	87	453
1988		6435	7641	65.8	125	20		19	105	710
1989		3324	7376	64.8	115	18		18	97	504
1990		3793	8531	60.2	125	27	1	26	98	1025
1991		4004	8701	64.9	155	37	1	36	118	2443
1992		4042	8770	72.6	172	47	2	46	125	2473
1993		4258	8517	75.1	169	52	2	50	117	2888
1994		3542	7443	77.6	119	44	4	40	75	3464
1995	16	7568	15136	68.8	89	27	6	21	62	5679
1996	16	13409	26818	50.3	175	36	6	29	139	6464
1997	19	10420	19142	50.6	171	59	5	54	112	6778
1998	20	17428	31987	53.3	216	75	11	63	141	6601
1999	20	17931	25482	63.5	253	97	17	77	156	7055
2000	30	18024	30895	61.9	291	106	15	89	185	7617
2001	48	20572	32789	62.0	327	110	22	88	217	8200
2002	53	9427	14652	69.0	930	108	22	86	822	11847
2003	52	8170	12599	65.0	1086	80	24	56	1006	13825
2004	60	10530	14934	61.2	1131	149	66	83	982	23437
2005	63	18258	25014	58.9	1156	169	70	99	987	28189
2006	71	18258	25014	60.1	1363	193	81	112	1170	33180
2007	74	19023	26132	63.4	1725	248	102	146	1477	42702
2008	77	19510	26864	58.9	1872	268	103	165	1604	45614
2009	80	16332	24389	58.0	2037	286	104	182	1751	51756
2010	82	16631	24841	58.1	2251	327	109	219	1924	67592
2011	77	17899	24348	60.0	2615	357	121	236	2258	90975
2012	75	17254	23612	59.9	2744	415	135	280	2329	126924
2013	75	18611	24437	56.9	2826	418	138	280	2408	144981
2014	58	12855	16921	51.2	2791	356	122	234	2435	157493

注：国际旅游外汇收入1995年以前单位为万元(外汇券)，1995年起为万美元。

主要统计指标解释

Explanatory Notes on Main Statistical Indicators

海关进出口总额　指实际进出我国国境的货物（包括贸易和非贸易）的价值总和。主要包括对外贸易实际进出口货物，来料加工装配、补偿贸易、进料加工进出口货物，国家间及国际组织无偿援助物资和赠送品，华侨、港澳台同胞和外籍华人捐赠品，租赁期满归承租人所有的租赁货物，边境地方贸易及边境地区小额贸易进出口货物（边民互市贸易除外），中外合资、合作经营企业、外商独资经营企业进出口货物和公用物品，到、离岸价格在规定限额以上的进出口货样和广告品（无商业价值、无使用价值和免费提供出口的除外），从保税仓库提取在中国境内销售的进出口货物，以及其他进出口货物。海关进出口总额反映一个国家在对外经济贸易方面实际进出口货物的总规模。

贸易出口　指由外贸进出口公司、工农贸易进出口公司和地方性的进出口公司由国家统一安排的出口、代理出口和自营、联营出口，其中包括进料加工出口，以及各进出口公司在国内以外汇结算方式售给友谊商店、华侨商店、出国人员服务公司和中外合资、合作经营和外资企业等的出口商品。

“三来一补”出口　指来料加工装配出口按工缴费计算，中小型补偿贸易按金额计算。

“三资”企业出口　指三资企业自己出口的本企业产品。不包括委托外贸进出口公司出口的商品。

利用外资　指我国各级政府、部门、企业和其他经济组织通过对外借款、吸收外商直接投资以及向境外发行债券、股票等方式筹措的境外资金。

外资的形式可以是现汇、实物、工业产权或专有技术等有形资本和无形资本。

我国自有外汇如国家外汇、中国银行等金融机构用自有资金发放的外汇贷款等，华侨、港澳同胞的捐赠，联合国或其他国际组织的无偿赠送资金、无偿援建的项目均不属于外资范围。

利用外资的方式有：对外借款，外国（或港澳地区）企业和经济组织或个人在我国境内开办独资企业，与我国境内的企业或组织共同开办合资企业合作经营（企业）项目或合作开发资源，以及补偿贸易、国际租赁等。

外商直接投资　指外国企业和经济组织或个人（包括华侨、港澳同胞以及我在境外注册的企业）按我国有关政策、法规，在我国境内开办外商独资企业，与我国境内的企业或经济组织共同举办中外合资企业、合作经营企业或合作开发资源的投资以及外商从企业得到收益的再投资。

新口径合同利用外资　根据2003年修订的《利用外资统计制度》，明确指出合同外资的统计指外商直接投资（三资企业）企业设立时，根据合同（章程）规定，外方投资者应缴付的注册资本。

国际旅游（外汇）收入　指国内各部门为来我国旅游的外国人、华侨、港澳和台湾同胞提供商品和劳务而得到的外汇收入。包括供应商品、饮食和提供住宿、交通、邮电、文化娱乐、导游等各项服务所得的全部外汇收入。

十、财政、金融与保险

Finance, Banking and Insurance

10-1 主要年份财政收支主要指标

Main Indicators of Government Revenue and Expenditure in Main Years

单位：万元

项　　目	1978年	1980年	1985年	1990年	2000年	2005年
财政收入						
来源于东莞的财政收入	6604	6710	11118	35719	1035561	3319079
中央财政收入					617151	1935069
#关税和海关代征税					273972	483327
省级财政收入					113681	344330
市财政一般预算收入	6604	6710	11118	35719	304730	1039680
工商税收						
工商税收总额					867584	2923001
国税(不含关税)					607216	1849818
地税					260368	1073183
财政支出						
市财政一般预算支出	1792	2015	4999	22779	336102	1170427
#基本建设支出					27426	276646
企业挖潜改造支出		88	15	37	1584	9107
科技三项费用支出		7		140	9963	31572
农林水气部门事业费支出		304	1154	3261	40097	62181
工交部门事业费支出		2	7	180	192	20499
城市维护费支出		31	219	1350	41267	162370
科教文卫体事业费支出		1051	2139	7357	86737	210620
#科学事业费				404	936	3956
教育事业费		760	1504	3786	68194	171055
卫生事业费		185	262	743	12083	11469
体育事业费		18	50	827	1517	2860
抚恤和社会福利救济支出		75	132	368	2888	8335
行政管理费支出		293	320	1324	29817	102296
公检法司支出			92	740	46446	166055

注：1. 1995年及以前年份，来源于东莞的财政收入不含关税。
2. 从2007年起财政收支按新的分类项目，在10-1续表中反映。

10-1 续表

单位：万元

指　　标	2010年	2013年	2014年
来源于东莞的财政收入	7851003	9747062	10662149
财政总收入	6542697	9963650	11226068
#中央	2940745	4432671	5148379
省级	823548	1438081	1525570
市公共财政预算收入	2778404	4092897	4552119
#增值税	626301	1037248	1240962
营业税	458712	505285	476997
企业所得税	247986	333022	378775
个人所得税	110441	103505	122854
房产税	92706	155422	237527
契税	186994	330370	262557
罚没收入	78400	94364	64531
市公共财政预算支出	2898306	4446589	4576816
#一般公共服务	269505	394668	395318
公共安全	388243	521421	536873
教育	653090	1135943	1189383
科学技术	79830	170307	141031
社会保障和就业	264017	266626	289608
农林水事务	229613	236060	233467
交通运输	90609	500212	358750
税收总额	6887249	10853642	12370426
#国税	4394366	6841231	8109237
地税	2492883	4012411	4261189

注：1. 2009及以前年份，国税不含海关代征税。
2. 2010年及以前年份，地税不含契税和耕地占用税。
3. 2011年起，来源于东莞的财政收入含政府性基金和出口退税。

10-2 历年财政收入

Government Revenue over Years

单位：万元

年份	来源于东莞的财政收入	财政总收入	中央财政收入	省级财政收入	市公共财政预算收入	各项税收	工商税收	专项收入	其他收入
1978	6604				6604	6595	5826		9
1979	6634				6634	6625	5725		9
1980	6710				6710	6699	5785		11
1981	6823				6823	6805	5942		18
1982	8103				8103	8068	7184		35
1983	8578				8578	8501	7599		77
1984	8469				8469	8385	7442		84
1985	11118				11118	10998	9708		120
1986	16053				16053	15865	14574	45	143
1987	20221				20221	19989	18551	50	182
1988	27076				27076	26837	25309	76	163
1989	31888				31888	30997	29331	116	775
1990	35719				35719	33544	31911	686	1489
1991	44374				44374	41659	39302	913	1802
1992	56204				56204	52620	48272	1351	2233
1993	93828				93828	88920	83462	1947	2961
1994	130531				76940	70451	60889	2697	3792
1995	180051				115618	106388	95463	4070	5160
1996	283506				96541	85648	74323	4470	6423
1997	335044				114069	96980	85245	4794	12295
1998	472422				151012	123816	106700	5693	21503
1999	717847				182577	159873	134852	8759	13945
2000	1035561				304730	265565	248159	14709	24456
2001	1259961				450163	402668	381660	18356	29139
2002	1678848				552933	489780	467998	26438	36715
2003	2064052				674461	575342	536390	30710	68409
2004	2591086				826389	707954	655571	35273	83162
2005	3319079				1039680	879653	797038	36423	123604
2006	4065412	3358095	1638195	430455	1289445	1077152	990029	49285	163008
2007	5395362	4574778	2151906	558404	1864468	1652620	1291335	55863	155985
2008	6010642	5234746	2476902	665596	2092248	1682270	1555499	60590	349388
2009	6278114	5402140	2392927	697658	2311555	1822650	1618514	60007	428899
2010	7851003	6542697	2940745	823548	2778404	2217675	1950773	72153	488576
2011	8385226	7665371	3422151	1112580	3130639	2433937	2171228	133951	562751
2012	8456419	8624762	3777465	1284053	3563245	2792883	2514813	159582	610780
2013	9747062	9963650	4432671	1438081	4092897	3318201	2938124	221062	553634
2014	10662149	11226068	5148379	1525570	4552119	3651289	3364746	233430	667400

注：1. 1995年及以前年份，来源于东莞的财政收入不含关税。
2. 2011年起，来源于东莞的财政收入含政府性基金和出口退税。

10-3 历年财政支出

Government Expenditure over Years

单位：万元

年 份	预算内地方财政支出总额	#基本建设支出	科技三项费用	农林水气等部门事业费	城 市维护费	科教文卫体育事业费	教 育事业费	行 政管理费
1978	1792							
1979	1908		20	451	74	852	618	202
1980	2015		7	304	31	1051	760	293
1981	2139		4	341	36	1182	818	246
1982	2612		1	359	141	1346	912	336
1983	2804		1	413	28	1672	1004	287
1984	3013			264	48	1868	1309	340
1985	4999			1154	219	2139	1504	320
1986	9916			2541	1431	2887	1793	330
1987	12512			3479	1624	4759	1871	510
1988	17475		100	4094	1614	6950	3339	888
1989	21623		103	3509	2286	7958	3733	1159
1990	22779		140	3261	1350	7357	3786	1324
1991	27499		30	4938	866	7956	4720	1484
1992	38162		50	5637	567	17505	7682	2348
1993	72910	5400	1289	8882	5737	25716	14427	4002
1994	88984	14575	1496	12835	5254	20725	13552	6158
1995	124173	13736	441	15798	9947	31021	23110	8433
1996	124059	17285	1332	14962	5199	28927	21237	10384
1997	148510	16923	1479	15349	6258	36614	23262	11691
1998	179064	26144	1164	19255	7264	36710	25578	11082
1999	212641	40681	1429	26648	12994	40863	30631	12979
2000	336102	27426	9963	40097	41267	86737	68194	29817
2001	478646	119692	4113	28957	43706	105990	85544	28961
2002	649606	165283	28013	37348	64483	143225	120195	43678
2003	765190	201077	30062	41164	44240	193138	163390	50022
2004	941554	179039	27110	53855	164770	162573	139337	84798
2005	1170427	276646	31572	62181	162370	210620	171055	102296
2006	1478955	242829	87397	64911	205426	291467	244113	119034

注：从2007年起财政支出按新的分类项目，在10-1续表中反映。

10-4 税务登记情况及税种征收情况（2013-2014年）

Taxes (2013-2014)

指标	国税		地税	
	2013年	2014年	2013年	2014年
税务登记情况(户)	339849	385408	537300	587653
#国有企业	311	337	1168	1046
集体企业	2370	1986	7930	7494
私营企业	45374	62002	46711	66451
港澳台投资企业	7412	7481	13181	13232
外商投资企业	4301	4398	5194	5362
个体经营	199389	212579	339353	350108
工商税收总额(万元)	6841230	8109237	4012411	4261189
#国有企业	17819	14822	35071	36786
集体企业	27664	19891	194006	204429
私营企业	693350	898720	393070	518592
港澳台投资企业	1526505	1678260	619874	663086
外商投资企业	1128092	1392054	509169	558451
个体经营	470069	512017	518269	488241
#增值税	5527765	6634806		
消费税	52594	57284		
营业税			1267911	1214902
企业所得税	971169	1098533	730627	817296
个人所得税	103	11	517420	614260
房产税			155422	237526
印花税			87481	119675
城镇土地使用税			128469	172467
土地增值税			318537	370094
车船税			61766	67046
车辆购置税	287627	316574		
#第一产业	129	149	3320	5257
第二产业	4103704	4876932	1406495	1519869
#采矿业	1049	1190	1331	1093
制造业	3858694	4607530	1054973	1161063
农副食品加工业	18866	14488	9801	11044
食品制造业	85610	73303	68316	26939
酒、饮料和精制茶制造业	38860	37416	15881	13582
纺织业	164412	195781	19141	20440
纺织服装、服饰业	202533	231919	41955	50742
皮革、毛皮、羽毛及其制品和制鞋业	208988	221127	32253	34264
木材加工和木、竹、藤、棕、草制品业	18346	16486	4012	4316
家具制造业	153949	132983	24612	25135
造纸和纸制品业	157409	169322	35254	39739

10-4 续表

单位：万元

指　　标	国税		地税	
	2013年	2014年	2013年	2014年
印刷和记录媒介复制业	96160	96767	16020	19013
文教、工美、体育和娱乐用品制造业	155461	148871	25171	27259
石油加工、炼焦和核燃料加工业	9718	10027	1601	2178
化学原料和化学制品制造业	92588	96070	22892	20864
医药制造业	33899	40574	7612	8618
化学纤维制造业	4979	6202	409	617
橡胶和塑料制品业	326649	338016	65428	75990
非金属矿物制品业	72662	85399	13879	16938
黑色金属冶炼和压延加工业	1752	2152	1562	2197
有色金属冶炼和压延加工业	6750	6715	3648	3815
金属制品业	273150	308279	58324	64624
通用设备制造业	154231	185221	21664	25496
专用设备制造业	138883	167299	29450	33032
汽车制造业	42916	58983	8604	8720
铁路、船舶、航空航天和其他运输设备制造业	22516	13522	7963	5985
电气机械和器材制造业	346301	428345	84149	96867
计算机、通信和其他电子设备制造业	917270	1385433	353251	423771
仪器仪表制造业	48881	72045	12783	18725
其他制造业	64935	64785	69338	80153
电力、燃气及水的生产和供应业	236625	260501	40191	46940
建筑业	7336	7711	310000	310773
房屋和土木工程建筑业	1752	1485	82375	92941
建筑安装业	1946	2370	162735	157970
建筑装饰和其他建筑业	3638	3856	64890	59862
第三产业	2737397	3232155	2602596	2736063
#交通运输、仓储及邮政业	49721	61575	84887	79026
信息传输、软件和信息技术服务业	11407	55372	72580	61422
批发和零售业	611944	657067	173082	203848
住宿和餐饮业	1698	2196	89510	80508
金融业	175101	221762	377147	420670
房地产业	129607	101333	1253404	1273413
租赁和商务服务业	39202	51185	216435	308521
科学研究和技术服务业	25041	24581	25719	30594
居民服务、修理和其他服务业	19093	8111	206596	172891
教育	205	295	6246	8235
卫生和社会工作	931	732	6037	9848
文化、体育和娱乐业	817	1938	22374	20619
公共管理、社会保障和社会组织	72	39	49241	42331
其他行业	1672558	2045969	19338	24137

10-5 历年金融机构各项人民币存贷款余额

Balance of RMB Deposits and Loans over Years

单位：万元

年 份	各项存款余额	#城乡居民储蓄存款余额	各项贷款余额	#短期贷款	#中长期贷款
1978	10497	5409	19607	19607	
1979	14875	7184	21301	21301	
1980	26093	11718	30797	29669	403
1981	38003	20339	40243	38365	765
1982	45120	27650	45525	44081	690
1983	60547	38597	57618	56063	837
1984	110265	61823	121891	114522	3365
1985	134867	91941	142437	130716	6230
1986	195948	131352	206813	193501	9486
1987	284819	189654	312431	292104	7162
1988	380511	249134	415818	381957	12351
1989	468203	325670	493737	456504	12338
1990	680696	455140	630355	570324	13427
1991	949713	614737	783957	714848	17385
1992	1473354	815404	1059794	935064	23000
1993	1798346	1071715	1343103	923157	237985
1994	2497834	1515445	1734350	1246772	250806
1995	3836761	2329685	2548512	1645696	274157
1996	4896463	3180215	3128076	2053343	353298
1997	6711687	4258238	3826560	2737916	205486
1998	8640053	5337482	4427394	3666563	155295
1999	10408377	6163430	5243735	4628058	328875
2000	12286706	6720704	6308405	5313933	469249
2001	14586491	7991768	7501801	5341925	1436127
2002	17901799	10016909	9334054	5731973	2312883
2003	21267775	12310616	12067237	6918877	3730104
2004	24628693	14316777	14052461	7118671	5222504
2005	29334026	17282760	15005217	7341939	7007138
2006	33656508	20133979	17305554	7792175	8684306
2007	37518345	21207413	21547660	9245906	11427676
2008	43545340	26380433	23803585	10132902	12052974
2009	49866108	29045704	29037984	12604957	14519686
2010	59433885	33868535	33298244	12340319	19675448
2011	66093904	37109919	37160847	14804666	20698930
2012	74304570	42042032	41956074	17567188	22363544
2013	86307325	44764310	47742282	20372287	25350443
2014	90699213	46067942	53316348	20429023	30496989

10-6　保险行业主要指标（2008-2014年）

Main Indicators of Insurance (2008-2014)

指　　标	单位	2008年	2009年	2010年	2011年	2012年	2013年	2014年
保险公司	家	35	37	37	38	46	52	52
保险业从业人员	人	24771	27386	27281	28064	33449	40867	43886
保费收入	万元	902986	1150795	1597166	1636513	1776566	2071338	2580654
寿险类	万元	583983	797192	1129950	1085528	1166113	1355224	1731887
#传统寿险	万元	61255	63681	72494	72212	79299	110599	465876
分红险	万元	355674	572703	867738	813006	966343	1072335	1026853
万能险	万元	73233	85142	110035	18650	17032	16823	18354
投连险	万元	38195	18481	18953	805	724	680	768
意外险	万元	17188	17143	18718	23730	27899	37653	54475
健康险	万元	38438	40043	42012	57507	74816	117135	165561
财险类	万元	319010	353602	467216	550985	610453	716114	848797
#机动车险	万元	270082	301526	400405	460241	515282	612210	722660
企财险	万元	22626	24276	32123	34107	32135	35318	35246
家财险	万元	1373	1113	1832	1806	1476	1761	1482
货运险	万元	2819	3648	4576	6917	7164	5695	6218
责任险	万元	6571	7273	9772	10516	12930	16584	19837
短健险	万元	759	8058	4289	7222	6924	7268	7382
短意险	万元	13145	6184	11073	10271	11959	13650	14914
农业险	万元	17		55	35	61	130	25

主要统计指标解释

Explanatory Notes on Main Statistical Indicators

公共财政预算收入 国家财政参与社会产品分配所取得的收入，是实现国家职能的财力保证，主要包括：

（1）各项税收 包括增值税、营业税、消费税、土地增值税、城市维护建设税、资源税、城市土地使用税、印花税、个人所得税、企业所得税、关税、农牧业税和耕地占用税等。

（2）专项收入 包括征收排污费收入、征收城市水资源费收入，教育费附加收入等。

（3）其他收入 包括基本建设贷款归还收入、基本建设收入、捐赠收入等。

（4）国有企业计划亏损补贴 这项为负收入，冲减财政收入。

公共财政预算支出 国家财政将筹集起来的资金进行分配使用，以满足经济建设和各项事业的需要，主要包括：基本建设支出、企业挖潜改造资金、地质勘探费用、科技三项费用、支援农村生产支出、农林水利气象等部门的事业费用、工业交通商业等部门的事业费、文教科学卫生事业费、抚恤和社会福利救济费、国防支出、行政管理费、价格补贴支出等项目。

银行信贷存款 指企业、机关、团体或居民把货币资金存入银行或其他信用机构保管并取得一定利息的一种信用活动形式。根据存款对象的不同可划分为：企业存款、财政存款、机关团体存款、基本建设存款、城镇居民储蓄存款、农村存款等科目。它是银行信贷资金的主要来源。

银行信贷贷款 银行或其他信用机构根据必须归还的原则，按一定利率，为企业、个人等提供资金的一种信用活动形式。我国银行贷款，分流动资金贷款、固定资产贷款、城乡个体工商户贷款以及农业贷款等科目。

十一、人民生活

People's Living Conditions

11-1 主要年份人民生活主要指标

Basic Statistics on People's Living Conditions in Main Years

指　　　标	单位	1985年	1990年	1995年	2000年	2005年	2010年	2013年	2014年
全市职工年平均工资	元				7765	10639	16108	30067	36057
城镇在岗职工年平均工资	元	1456	3552	9682	14051	28253	46576	42870	47600
国有单位	元	1400	3600	9390	16371	37919	57275	75846	78384
城镇集体单位	元	1501	3507	7507	10475	15958	27391	38409	47024
其他各种单位	元	1571	3525	7891	14218	20882	37803	40776	45469
城镇常住居民人均可支配收入	元	791	2508	9588	14142	22882	35690	46594	36764
城镇常住居民人均消费性支出	元	689	2038	9220	12529	21768	25733	33251	27071
食品烟酒	元	493	1295	3644	4048	6035	8732	11704	9022
衣着	元	28	95	604	487	1285	1706	2280	1653
居住	元	58	184	1084	1218	1242	2089	3034	4550
生活用品及服务	元	48	153	694	623	1165	1771	2328	1932
医疗保健	元	14	42	258	431	811	1294	1619	1280
交通通信	元	4	25	1562	3309	7482	5925	6408	4712
教育文化娱乐	元	21	113	991	1517	3205	3443	4666	3200
其他用品和服务	元	23	131	383	896	543	773	1212	723
农村常住居民人均可支配收入	元	803	1542	4769	8484	13076	20486	27214	22327
农村常住居民人均消费性支出	元						11842	17003	18505
全体居民人均可支配收入	元								35712
全体居民人均消费性支出	元								26532

注：1. 2012年起城镇在岗职工含劳务派遣人员；2013年起，将原属于乡镇企业且符合城镇非私营单位条件的“四上”企业纳入城镇单位从业人员及工资统计的范围，下同。
2. 全市职工年平均工资调查范围为东莞市辖区内除农户以外各类经济实体。
3. 按照国家统计局的统一部署，自2012年12月起正式启动城乡住户调查一体化改革工作。在经历了为期一年的过渡期后，从2014年起正式对外发布全体居民人均可支配收入和消费支出指标。新口径指标将城市居民人均可支配收入改为城镇常住居民人均可支配收入，农民人均纯收入改为农村常住居民人均可支配收入，与往年数不可比，下同。

11-2 历年城镇在岗职工工资总额与平均工资

Total and Average Wage of Employed Persons in Urban Areas over Years

年份	工资总额（万元）	国有单位	城镇集体单位	其他单位	平均工资（元）	国有单位	城镇集体单位	其他单位
1978	4485	2911	1574		474	630	325	
1979	5869	3611	2258		650	708	574	
1980	7255	4210	3045		750	867	632	
1981	9416	5000	4416		887	979	801	
1982	11839	6440	5399		1095	1089	1102	
1983	12808	6834	5974		1197	1138	1273	
1984	14963	7002	7961		1383	1333	1431	
1985	17260	7619	9238	403	1456	1400	1501	1571
1986	20980	10336	10026	618	2616	1698	1525	1940
1987	27610	12300	14159	1151	2067	2028	2094	2166
1988	35007	17931	14854	2222	2757	2942	2588	2574
1989	42947	20340	20808	1799	3320	3355	3295	3236
1990	46780	22321	21012	3447	3552	3600	3507	3525
1991	54002	24456	23268	6278	3777	3841	3674	3933
1992	68360	30469	28886	9005	4531	4610	4404	4696
1993	107088	47088	40171	19829	6228	7007	5583	6044
1994	131160	61869	49323	19968	8360	9390	7507	7891
1995	171543	75157	51398	44988	9682	10802	8007	10367
1996	178968	83372	52581	43015	10382	11623	8658	10775
1997	175156	87890	47185	40081	10691	12160	8774	10610
1998	187636	98109	50302	39225	11422	13123	9362	10959
1999	204550	109437	52217	42896	12557	14601	9966	12062
2000	229404	125711	53903	49790	14051	16371	10475	14218
2001	261645	152564	52645	56436	16183	19869	11001	15238
2002	291778	165611	58907	67260	17804	22228	11640	17348
2003	362935	230464	55866	76605	22598	29773	12940	19140
2004	432893	282512	62898	87483	25326	35163	13954	19223
2005	518216	349572	70872	97772	28253	37919	15958	20882
2006	608670	413718	74637	120315	31135	41457	17174	23032
2007	707007	487826	74408	144773	35284	46197	18807	26218
2008	809893	570134	82432	157327	39516	51441	20833	28838
2009	944243	639161	76001	229081	42585	56129	22077	31195
2010	1029873	678673	96664	254537	46576	57275	27391	37803
2011	1229001	826777	104824	297400	50398	61504	30549	39591
2012	1434133	960274	126456	347404	57007	66857	35977	47726
2013	10499782	1138596	218818	9142369	42870	75846	38409	40776
2014	11319163	1189178	226508	9903477	47600	78384	47024	45469

11-3 城镇在岗职工工资总额及平均工资(2014年，按经济类型、行业分)

Total and Average Wage of Fully Employed Persons in Urban Areas (2014, by Status of Registration and Sector)

项目	工资总额(万元)	国有单位	城镇集体单位	其他单位	平均工资(元)	国有单位	城镇集体单位	其他单位
总计	11319163	1189178	226508	9903477	47600	78384	47024	45469
按企业、事业和机关分								
企业	10378230	293960	206003	9878267	46180	96292	45536	45489
事业	537625	534975	987	1663	77109	77309	48363	52135
机关	360243	360243			69299	69299		
按国民经济行业分								
农、林、牧、渔业	875	875			81037	81037		
工业	8689489	2992	76802	8609695	44393	50286	36954	44471
建筑业	140227	46062	24479	69687	41821	51032	41916	37338
交通运输、仓储和邮政业	174354	46976	386	126993	59614	90616	33267	53031
信息传输、软件和信息技术服务业	89190	14562		74628	116315	123306		115042
批发和零售业	286442	24166	6047	256228	47690	107548	39089	45536
住宿和餐饮业	98306		2428	95878	32198		31654	32212
金融业	328323	158144	50004	120175	117262	122678	79270	136562
房地产业	154781	125	3839	150817	65800	78000	47686	66433
租赁和商务服务业	198382	4373	33321	160688	49267	94039	43140	50093
科学研究、技术服务业	93969	9501	9660	74808	79132	89975	54978	82551
水利、环境和公共设施管理业	9584	3919	416	5249	47776	49054	39971	47586
居民服务、修理和其他服务业	43616	551	26	43039	31730	44452	51000	31607
教育	280124	238234		41889	78332	88228		47824
卫生和社会工作	325221	258381	18662	48177	74377	72019	80027	87325
文化、体育和娱乐业	36024	10581	440	25003	52559	67310	54259	48073
公共管理、社会保障和社会组织	369735	369735			69020	69020		
国际组织								

11-4 主要年份各种分组的城镇在岗职工平均工资

Average Wage of Employed Persons in Urban Areas by Item in Main Years

单位：元

项　　目	1985年	1990年	1995年	2000年	2005年	2010年	2013年	2014年
职工平均工资	1456	3552	9682	14051	28253	46576	42870	47600
按企业事业和机关分								
企　业			9316	13501	24152	43121	41399	46180
事　业			10872	15485	32203	46478	75153	77109
机　关			12171	15383	38441	57300	67183	69299
按经济类型分								
国有单位	1400	3600	10802	16371	37919	57275	75846	78384
城镇集体单位	1501	3507	8007	10475	15958	27391	38409	47024
其他单位	1571	3525	10367	14218	20882	37803	40776	45469
按国民经济行业分								
农、林、牧、渔业	1312	3639	12412	14000	37046	61606	59001	81037
工　业	1450	3481	8945	12316	18371	30418	39891	44393
建筑业	2052	3813	9125	9820	18385	31020	40877	41821
交通运输、仓储和邮政业					31989	40809	44788	59614
信息传输、软件和信息技术服务业					71801	110207	109747	116315
批发和零售业					28565	38986	44432	47690
住宿和餐饮业					18257	21955	29247	32198
金融业	1500	3303	13254	20560	40655	94569	102473	117262
房地产业	1779	4414	11184	17993	34805	53939	57209	65800
租赁和商务服务业					29824	47505	44600	49267
科学研究、技术服务业					37423	51017	73226	79132
水利、环境和公共设施管理业					34573	51426	67295	47776
居民服务、修理和其他服务业					44853	56776	31771	31730
教育					27255	37734	66980	78332
卫生和社会工作					37991	52867	78168	74377
文化、体育和娱乐业					37710	58317	52436	52559
公共管理、社会保障和社会组织	1519	3666	12347	15424	37888	56817	67048	69020
国际组织								

11-5 各种经济类型分行业城镇在岗职工工资总额、平均工资(2013-2014年)

Total and Average Wage of Employed Persons in Urban Areas by Status of Registration and Sector (2013-2014)

项　　目	国有经济		城镇集体经济		其他经济类型	
	2013年	2014年	2013年	2014年	2013年	2014年
职工工资总额(万元)	1138596	1189178	218818	226508	9142369	9903477
农、林、牧、渔业	3971	875				
工业	2048	2992	78647	76802	7999135	8609695
建筑业	35891	46062	26155	24479	70274	69687
交通运输、仓储和邮政业	30361	46976	2964	386	88721	126993
信息传输、软件和信息技术服务业	14190	14562			74201	74628
批发和零售业	25609	24166	6911	6047	240558	256228
住宿和餐饮业			2960	2428	109471	95878
金融业	163484	158144	34015	50004	85040	120175
房地产业	218	125	4107	3839	122838	150817
租赁和商务服务业	15589	4373	34688	33321	149534	160688
科学研究、技术服务业	9337	9501	8628	9660	59275	74808
水利、环境和公共设施管理业	5443	3919	415	416	8699	5249
居民服务、修理和其他服务业	767	551	451	26	39566	43039
教育	203939	238234			34423	41889
卫生和社会工作	290717	258381	18436	18662	37038	48177
文化、体育和娱乐业	14542	10581	441	440	23353	25003
公共管理、社会保障和社会组织	322493	369735				
国际组织						
职工平均工资(元)	75846	78384	38409	47024	40776	45469
农、林、牧、渔业	59001	81037				
工业	39605	50286	30767	36954	40008	44471
建筑业	45134	51032	36973	41916	40518	37338
交通运输、仓储和邮政业	56749	90616	36106	33267	42090	53031
信息传输、软件和信息技术服务业	145686	123306			104803	115042
批发和零售业	88154	107548	37154	39089	42431	45536
住宿和餐饮业			27659	31654	29292	32212
金融业	116916	122678	53847	79270	116942	136562
房地产业	218200	78000	47430	47686	57530	66433
租赁和商务服务业	93683	94039	39231	43140	43602	50093
科学研究、技术服务业	74455	89975	46286	54978	79778	82551
水利、环境和公共设施管理业	78086	49054	37369	39971	64196	47586
居民服务、修理和其他服务业	62382	44452	18420	51000	31731	31607
教育	74632	88228			41669	47824
卫生和社会工作	79344	72019	81038	80027	68934	87325
文化、体育和娱乐业	74496	67310	69921	54259	44096	48073
公共管理、社会保障和社会组织	67048	69020				
国际组织						

11-6 国有企、事业和机关单位城镇在岗职工工资总额及平均工资(2014年)

Total and Average Wage of Employed Persons in Urban State-owned Enterprises, Institutions and Government Agencies (2014)

项　　目	单位从业人员劳动报酬(万元)	在岗职工工资总额	其他从业人员工资总额	在岗职工平均工资(元)
总　计	1201553	1189178	12375	78384
按企事业机关分				
企　业	299480	293960	5520	96292
#地　方	248920	243400	5520	94697
事　业	538241	534975	3266	77309
#地　方	535843	532577	3266	77219
机　关	363832	360243	3590	69299
#地　方	363695	360105	3590	69290
按行业分				
农、林、牧、渔业	879	875	4	81037
工　业	3072	2992	80	50286
建筑业	46484	46062	422	51032
交通运输、仓储和邮政业	47676	46976	701	90616
信息传输、软件和信息技术服务业	18412	14562	3850	123306
批发和零售业	24269	24166	103	107548
住宿和餐饮业				
金融业	158381	158144	237	122678
房地产业	125	125		78000
租赁和商务服务业	4502	4373	129	94039
科学研究、技术服务业	9622	9501	120	89975
水利、环境和公共设施管理业	3949	3919	30	49054
居民服务、修理和其他服务业	551	551		44452
教育	238521	238234	287	88228
卫生和社会工作	260893	258381	2511	72019
文化、体育和娱乐业	10790	10581	209	67310
公共管理、社会保障和社会组织	373428	369735	3693	69020
国际组织				

11-7 工业、建筑业城镇在岗职工工资总额和平均工资（2013-2014年）

Total and Average Wage of Employed Persons in Urban Industrial and Construction Units (2013-2014)

项　　目	2013年		2014年	
	工资总额（万元）	平均工资（元）	工资总额（万元）	平均工资（元）
工业总计	8079830	39891	8689489	44393
按经济类型分				
国有单位	2048	39605	2992	50286
城镇集体单位	78647	30767	76802	36954
其他各种单位	7999135	40008	8609695	44471
按工业行业分(大类)				
农副食品加工业	25662	55306	27603	60229
食品制造业	54269	43769	42338	35323
酒、饮料和精制茶制造业	47410	69251	48026	67122
烟草制品业				
纺织业	139856	35014	134748	38104
纺织服装、服饰业	417113	36471	405354	39403
皮革、毛皮、羽毛及其制品和制鞋业	791615	34202	828301	40308
木材加工和木、竹、藤、棕、草制品业	6309	32254	4384	34818
家具制造业	213783	37237	250147	41923
造纸和纸制品业	169641	41159	193829	46844
印刷和记录媒介复制业	154339	41334	163140	43378
文教、工美、体育和娱乐用品制造业	563992	34034	592300	35851
石油加工、炼焦和核燃料加工业	1063	55354	1226	58651
化学原料和化学制品制造业	97473	53055	97229	62040
医药制造业	13190	55072	16577	61262
化学纤维制造业	3773	41831	5344	44385
橡胶和塑料制品业	535549	37805	665269	42498
非金属矿物制品业	58023	42297	60444	43794
黑色金属冶炼和压延加工业	19528	44656	20048	50677
有色金属冶炼和压延加工业	30354	40316	27936	43766
金属制品业	324174	42199	419472	45726
通用设备制造业	331193	43849	374078	47236
专用设备制造业	164854	45175	182871	48799
汽车制造业	93080	52817	103293	58252
铁路、船舶、航空航天和其他设备制造业	40594	55222	46023	56450
电气机械和器材制造业	783757	38748	849674	43356
计算机、通信和其他电子设备制造业	2638114	42036	2749674	47383
仪器仪表制造业	245160	42458	258427	49452
其他制造业	51423	41188	54977	43460
废弃资源综合利用业	221	40091	290	58000
电力、热力生产和供应业	35014	90498	34196	97898
燃气生产和供应业	7011	76785	8012	89023
水的生产和供应业	22297	51722	24259	54798
建筑业总计	132319	40877	140227	41821
国有单位	35891	45134	46062	51032
城镇集体单位	26155	36973	24479	41916
其他单位	70274	40518	69687	37338

11-8 历年城乡居民收入

Income of Households over Years

单位：元

年　份	城镇常住居民人均可支配收入	农村常住居民人均可支配收入	全体居民人均可支配收入
1978		149	
1979		188	
1980		272	
1981		463	
1982		567	
1983		618	
1984		691	
1985	791	803	
1986	1033	951	
1987	1247	1142	
1988	1778	1325	
1989	2282	1424	
1990	2508	1542	
1991	3068	1673	
1992	4026	2290	
1993	5970	2903	
1994	8270	3769	
1995	9588	4769	
1996	10824	5554	
1997	11032	6132	
1998	11506	6830	
1999	12954	7704	
2000	14142	8484	
2001	16938	9383	
2002	16949	10178	
2003	18471	11033	
2004	20526	11941	
2005	22882	13076	
2006	25320	14313	
2007	27025	15747	
2008	30275	16904	
2009	33045	18098	
2010	35690	20486	
2011	39513	22842	
2012	42944	24944	
2013	46594	27214	
2014新口径	36764	22327	35712

注：本表城镇居民人均可支配收入1997年以前是生活费收入口径，1997年起是可支配收入口径，下同。

11-9 历年城镇常住居民人均可支配收入

Income of Urban Households over Years

单位：元

年 份	可支配收入	工资性收入	经营净收入	财产净收入	转移净收入
1985	791	603			
1986	1033	974			
1987	1247	989			
1988	1778	1097			
1989	2282	1185			
1990	2508	1459	46	30	417
1991	3062	2160	226	55	534
1992	4026	2560	411	175	709
1993	5969	3684	749	889	319
1994	8270	5758	840	553	994
1995	9588	6260	1210	659	1329
1996	10824	8428	1127	455	1273
1997	11032	8024	625	349	1544
1998	11506	8334	884	319	1207
1999	12954	7910	1799	357	1541
2000	14142	8702	2740	895	720
2001	16938	11037	2643	895	1879
2002	16949	13050	1662	1076	1923
2003	18471	15282	1598	1210	1388
2004	20526	17153	1634	1553	1535
2005	22882	18524	2709	1894	1536
2006	25320	18318	4389	2504	1946
2007	27025	18930	3359	4849	2101
2008	30275	20872	4521	3527	3047
2009	33045	23723	4724	4209	3094
2010	35690	26799	4171	4771	3220
2011	39513	27272	4075	7481	4374
2012	42944	30518	3940	9099	3484
2013	46594	33051	4003	10136	3941
2014新口径	36764	28256	3993	6711	-2196

11-10 历年城镇常住居民人均消费性支出

Living Expenditure of Urban Resident over Years

单位：元

年 份	年人均消费性支出	食品烟酒	衣 着	居 住	生活用品及服务	医 疗保 健	交 通通 信	教育文化娱乐	其他用品和 服 务	恩格尔系 数(%)
1985	689	493	28	58	48	14	4	21	23	71.6
1986	883	588	43	66	84	15	6	46	35	66.6
1987	1174	709	64	79	128	55	9	106	24	60.4
1988	1583	977	64	136	171	22	12	124	77	61.7
1989	1980	1235	101	156	196	55	24	115	98	62.4
1990	2038	1295	95	184	153	42	25	113	131	63.5
1991	2481	1476	188	254	122	47	47	211	136	59.5
1992	3901	1834	259	369	263	94	587	331	164	47.0
1993	5533	2615	373	333	583	133	855	389	252	47.3
1994	7270	3172	420	761	925	192	850	714	236	43.6
1995	9220	3644	604	1084	694	258	1562	991	383	39.5
1996	8585	3682	706	674	660	225	990	847	802	42.9
1997	8309	3681	594	880	435	415	916	939	449	44.3
1998	8644	3785	457	659	612	455	1025	1074	577	43.8
1999	11348	3712	400	898	601	371	3398	1043	923	32.7
2000	12529	4048	487	1218	623	431	3309	1517	896	32.3
2001	14669	4572	648	1173	746	513	4258	1429	1330	31.2
2002	15157	4818	748	1060	611	529	4303	2660	428	31.8
2003	15446	4804	921	2966	1093	693	2062	2512	395	31.1
2004	18426	5041	1134	2517	925	811	4973	2673	352	27.4
2005	21768	6035	1285	1242	1165	811	7482	3205	543	27.7
2006	18995	6321	1238	2341	1229	809	3531	3001	525	33.3
2007	21545	6966	1213	1903	1342	860	5208	3515	538	32.3
2008	23208	7778	1349	2585	1539	1332	4462	3464	699	33.5
2009	24270	7972	1492	2232	1616	1400	5456	3326	776	32.8
2010	25733	8732	1706	2089	1771	1294	5925	3443	773	33.9
2011	27495	9513	1806	2128	1902	1251	6035	3886	974	34.6
2012	31369	11103	2121	2852	2173	1521	6108	4348	1143	35.4
2013	33251	11704	2280	3034	2328	1619	6408	4666	1212	35.2
2014新口径	27071	9022	1653	4550	1932	1280	4712	3200	723	33.3

11-11 历年农村常住居民人均收入

Per Capita Actual Income of Rural Households over Years

单位：元

年 份	可支配收入	工资性收入	经营净收入	财产净收入	转移净收入
2006	17676	8522	4195	4171	789
2007	19945	9446	4388	5191	920
2008	20622	9876	4326	5531	889
2009	22077	10442	4517	6210	908
2010	22537	11201	3629	6402	1305
2011	26460	13254	4150	7232	1822
2012	27008	14045	3829	7013	2121
2013	29399	15147	4171	7368	2713
2014新口径	22327	21030	2286	1846	-2836

11-12 历年农村常住居民人均消费性支出

Per Capita Consumption Expenditure of Rural Households over Years

单位：元

年 份	年人均消费性支 出	食品烟酒	衣 着	居 住	生活用品及服务	医 疗保 健	交 通通 信	教育文化娱乐服务	其他用品和 服 务
2006	9370	3380	448	1458	474	510	1543	932	625
2007	10771	3805	602	2001	581	494	1953	1029	306
2008	10887	3823	691	1500	622	545	1799	1198	709
2009	10598	3711	633	1485	471	565	1764	1223	746
2010	11842	4447	627	1877	480	569	2120	1082	640
2011	14055	5313	655	2345	574	665	2698	1225	580
2012	16103	5980	751	2817	771	765	2828	1533	659
2013	17003	6291	812	2744	752	748	3103	1769	784
2014新口径	18505	7154	1131	3191	817	471	3811	1684	245

11-13 城乡居民人均收入和支出(2014年)

Income and Expenditure of Households (2014)

单位：元

项　　目	全体常住居民	城镇常住居民	农村常住居民
年人均可支配收入	35712	36764	22327
工资性收入	27889	28256	21030
经营净收入	3862	3993	2286
财产净收入	6264	6711	1846
转移净收入	-2304	-2196	-2836
年人均消费支出	26532	27071	18505
食品烟酒	8955	9022	7154
衣着	1621	1653	1131
居住	4469	4550	3191
生活用品及服务	1836	1932	817
交通通信	4685	4712	3811
教育文化娱乐	3079	3200	1684
医疗保健	1209	1280	471
其他用品和服务	680	723	245

主要统计指标解释

Explanatory Notes on Main Statistical Indicators

可支配收入 指调查户在调查期内获得的、可用于最终消费支出和储蓄的总和，即调查户可以用来自由支配的收入。可支配收入既包括现金，也包括实物收入。按照收入的来源，可支配收入包含四项，分别为：工资性收入、经营净收入、财产净收入和转移净收入。计算公式为：

可支配收入 = 工资性收入 + 经营净收入 + 财产净收入 + 转移净收入

其中：经营净收入 = 经营收入 − 经营费用 − 生产性固定资产折旧 − 生产税

财产净收入 = 财产性收入 − 财产性支出

转移净收入 = 转移性收入 − 转移性支出

工资性收入 指就业人员通过各种途径得到的全部劳动报酬和各种福利，包括受雇于单位或个人、从事各种自由职业、兼职和零星劳动得到的全部劳动报酬和福利。

经营净收入 指住户或住户成员从事生产经营活动所获得的净收入，是全部经营收入中扣除经营费用、生产性固定资产折旧和生产税之后得到的净收入。

财产净收入 指住户或住户成员将其所拥有的金融资产、住房等非金融资产和自然资源交由其他机构单位、住户或个人支配而获得的回报并扣除相关的费用之后得到的净收入。财产净收入包括利息净收入、红利收入、储蓄性保险净收益、转让承包土地经营权租金净收入、出租房屋净收入、出租其他资产净收入和自有住房折算净租金等。

转移净收入 计算公式为：转移净收入 = 转移性收入 − 转移性支出

转移性收入 指国家、单位、社会团体对住户的各种经常性转移支付和住户之间的经常性收入转移。包括政府、非行政事业单位、社会团体对居民转移的养老金或退休金、社会救济和补助、惠农补贴、政策性生活补贴、救灾款、经常性捐赠和赔偿以及报销医疗费等；住户之间的赡养收入、经常性捐赠和赔偿以及在外（含国外）工作的本住户非常住成员寄回带回的收入等。

转移性支出 指调查户对国家、单位、住户或个人的经常性或义务性转移支付。包括缴纳的税款、各项社会保障支出、赡养支出、经常性捐赠和赔偿支出、外来从业人员寄给家人的支出以及其他经常转移支出等。

消费支出 指住户用于满足家庭日常生活消费需要的全部支出，包括用于消费品的支出和用于服务性消费的支出。根据用途不同，消费支出可划分为食品烟酒、衣着、居住、生活用品及服务、交通通信、教育文化娱乐、医疗保健、其他用品及服务八大类。根据来源不同，消费支出可划分为现金消费支出、实物消费支出（含自产自用、来自单位、来自政府和其他社会组织）。

职工工资总额 指各单位在一定时期内直接支付给本单位全部职工的劳动报酬总额。工资总额的计算原则应以直接支付给职工的全部劳动报酬为根据。各单位支付给职工的劳动报酬以及其他根据有关规定支付的工资，不论是计入成本的还是不计入成本的，不论是按国家规定列入计征奖金税项目的，还是未列入计征奖金税项目的，不论是以货币形式支付的还是以实物形式支付的，均包括在工资总额内。

职工平均工资 指企业、事业、机关单位的职工在一定时期内平均每人所得的货币工资额。它表明一定时期职工工资收入的高低程度，是反映职工工资水平的主要指标。计算公式为：职工平均工资=报告期实际支付全部职工工资总额/报告期全部职工平均人数。

十二、社会事业

Social Undertakings

12-1 主要年份社会事业主要指标

Main Indicators of Social Undertakings in Main Years

项　　目	单位	1985年	1990年	1995年	2000年	2005年	2010年	2013年	2014年
公有企事业单位科学技术人员数	人	9166	11629	16856		42593	40025	41812	42141
专利申请量	件		34	325	1653	6694	21654	29013	28432
专利授权量	件		30	262	1399	3114	20397	22595	20340
各类技术合同签订项目数	项		5	46	110	50	90	175	177
各类技术合同签订项目金额	万元		12	1804	3469	4058	18366	25960	11241
在校学生数									
普通高等学校	人			1628	3241	16645	38293	60877	69866
成人高等学校	人	403	531	1254	3642	12665	21703	17254	17476
中等职业技术学校	人	3363	8919	18737	23144	29487	47531	61011	64412
普通中学	人	46596	61188	92481	112418	191044	258276	278289	284648
小学	人	134421	162664	195063	272793	480923	552377	659138	687269
小学学龄儿童入学率	%	99.8	99.9	100.0	100.0	100.0	100.0	100.0	100.0
小学毕业生升学率	%	79.5	95.4	99.2	99.8	99.9	100.0	100.0	100.0
初中毕业生升学率	%	38.5	43.6	85.4	90.3	94.1	97.9	98.4	98.4
普通高中毕业生升学率	%	26.5	31.2	64.9	70.5	96.5	95.1	95.4	98.4
高考省线入围人数	人	285	224	809	2646	11196	13761	18405	18766
电影放映单位	个	60	114	218	192	70	46	66	60
艺术表演团体	个	1	7	2	1		4	10	16
文化馆(群众艺术馆)	个	1	1	1	1	1	1	1	1
公共图书馆	个	3	5	15	18	473	505	641	641
博物馆	个	2	2	2	3	16	30	31	33
档案馆	个	1	1	1	1	1	1	1	1
《东莞日报》发行量	万份		177	987	1578	2751	4563	3270	3266
广播电台	座		1	1	1	1	1	1	1
电视台	座	1	1	1	1	1	1	1	1
镇街文化广电服务中心	个						28	28	28
病床床位数	张	2323	3866	5798	7081	11972	19980	25736	26704
卫生技术人员数	人	3305	3902	5290	6915	16608	37487	42132	43091
#执业(助理)医师	人	1201	1721	2299	3309	6901	13214	14864	15081
举办全民健身活动	次							331	333
参加全民健身活动人数	万人次							17.76	18.87
律师人数	人	6	12	85	130	625	1366	1748	1878
公证人员数	人	6	10	19	20	48	96	110	116
人民调解委员会调解人员数	人	3603	3664	3664	3644	4556	17438	16161	14768
优抚收养单位收养人数	人		19	11	7	8	8	6	7
一般工业固体废物综合利用率	%	37.5	17.9	18.2	63.8	86.5	95.0	78.9	83.4
城市环境空气质量达标天数	天						357	266	254

注：1. 2010年起，公有企事业单位科学技术人员数只统计在编在岗人员数，与往年数不可比。
2. 中等职业技术学校包含市技工学校，不含一般成人中专。
3. 2004年起，卫生方面包含诊所、卫生所、医务室及村卫生室的数据，与往年数不可比。

12-2 科技活动基本情况（2014年）

Basic Statistics on Scientific and Technological Activities (2014)

项　　目	单位	2014年	项　　目	单位	2014年
科技企业			获专利授权数	件	176
企业数			营业收入	万元	176396
#国家高新技术企业	个	755	科技园区和基地		
省创新型试点企业	个	32	国家级高新区	个	1
省创新型企业	个	22	省级高新区	个	
省创新百强企业	个	10	专业镇	个	30
重点培育上市后备科技企业	个	76	#工业总产值	亿元	10754.32
科技合作			全镇科技投入	亿元	83.14
国际合作项目立项数	项	2	国家高新技术企业数	个	566
#国家立项数	项	2	火炬计划特色产业基地	个	9
省级立项数	项		#工业总产值	亿元	1668.96
国际科技合作示范基地	个	25	国家高新技术企业数	个	130
#国家级基地	个	4	科技企业孵化器/加速器	个	23
省级基地	个	21	#建筑场地面积	万平方米	80.27
产学研项目立项数	项	23	在孵企业数	个	634
资助金额	万元	2000	毕业企业数	个	261
科技特派员入驻数	人	587	工程中心		
省部产学研示范基地	个	31	国家级工程中心	个	1
省部产学研创新联盟	个	10	省级工程中心	个	92
科技机构			#工程中心职工总数	人	12553
机构数	个	50	经费收入	万元	174143
从业人员	人	8175	研究开发课题(项目)	项	746
#科技活动人员	人	6932	专利授权数	项	1211
#本科及以上	人	4639	研究与发展(R&D)人员	人	7415
科技经费筹集额	万元	148157	研究与发展经费	万元	153639
#政府拨款	万元	53763.6	市级工程中心	个	93
企业自筹	万元	94393.4	#工程中心职工总数	人	10465
科技经费内部支出	万元	124882	经费收入	万元	191055
项目(课题)数	项	403	研究开发课题(项目)	项	699
项目(课题)经费支出额	万元	99289.2	专利授权数	项	1215
论文数	篇	253	研究与发展(R&D)人员	人	7911
科技专著数	篇		研究与发展经费	万元	168180
专利申请数	件	666			

12-3 研究与试验发展(R&D)基本情况（2010-2013年）

Basic Statistics on Research and Development (R&D) (2010-2013)

指标	单位	2010年	2011年	2012年	2013年
R&D活动单位数	个	492	495	668	1489
R&D研究机构数	个	414	482	456	500
R&D项目(课题)数	个	2583	3208	3850	4846
R&D活动人员数	人	38330	45123	57333	60825
#研究人员	人	7507	8630	9648	12612
R&D人员折合全时当量合计	人年	27809	36038	46200	50112
#研究人员	人年	5161	6558	7243	10354
R&D经费内部支出	万元	516701	716221	830190	1099321
按执行部门分					
规上工业企业	万元	495099	612516	748347	983720
重点服务业企业					10714
科研机构	万元	12166	92239	68365	93791
高等院校	万元	3528	5556	7569	8284
其他企事业单位	万元	5908	5909	5909	2812
按活动类型分					
基础研究	万元	691	50653	23512	5999
应用研究	万元	18253	18719	18165	10071
试验发展	万元	497757	646850	788513	1083251
按资金来源分					
政府资金	万元	31237	85894	53970	44814
企业资金	万元	463927	613432	753387	1021510
境外资金	万元	10021	3083	5626	22692
其他资金	万元	11516	13810	17207	10305
按使用项目分					
日常性支出	万元	433603	539954	728069	958784
资产性支出	万元	83097	176266	102121	140537
R&D经费内部支出占GDP比重	%	1.22	1.51	1.66	2.00
R&D经费外部支出	万元	12383	14921	29557	54038
R&D产出情况					
专利申请数	件	4994	6060	8384	11588
#发明专利	件	1433	1323	2751	4685
专利授权数	件	205	112	194	302
#发明专利	件	25	25	73	81
有效发明专利数	件	2044	3457	2367	3663
专利所有权转让及许可数	件	170	552	152	113
专利所有权转让及许可收入	万元	9572	16763	10960	296
植物新品种权授予数	项	2		1	1
形成国家或行业标准数	项	181	63	219	189
发表科技论文数	篇	1205	1266	1370	1133
出版科技著作数	种	26	31	30	19
工业新产品产值	万元	5501675	6945494	8643848	11744374
工业新产品销售收入	万元	5391190	6373687	8385864	11951808

注：直至年鉴出版，国家未能反馈相关数据。

12-4 规模以上工业企业R&D活动及相关情况（2010-2014年）

The Main Index on R&D of Enterprises above Designated Size (2010-2014)

指　　标	单位	2010年	2011年	2012年	2013年	2014年
R&D企业情况						
有科技机构的企业数	家	314	351	321	372	563
有R&D活动的企业数	家	436	428	607	709	855
企业办科技机构情况						
机构数	个	376	468	417	476	716
在境外设立的机构数	个	4	29	7	8	8
机构人员合计	人	26376	29772	27060	29943	40012
机构经费支出	万元	330015	395075	440568	558771	746857
R&D项目情况						
全部R&D项目数	项	1955	2448	3083	3973	4307
#限额以上R&D项目数	项	1440	1624	2604	2764	3246
R&D活动人员情况						
R&D人员合计	人	36064	39400	51386	53258	58752
#研究人员	人	6095	5513	6807	9109	8707
R&D人员折合全时当量合计	人年	26634	31743	44335	43635	49457
#研究人员	人年	4542	4421	5999	7727	7432
R&D经费内部支出合计	万元	495099	612516	748347	983720	1150506
其中：①经常费支出	万元	420877	493831	676645	855711	1041473
②资产性支出	万元	74222	118686	71702	128009	109034
其中：①基础研究支出						
②应用研究支出	万元	9740	7790	348	183	3754
③试验发展支出	万元	485360	604726	747999	983537	1146753
其中：①政府资金	万元	20388	23729	16789	16012	11334
②企业资金	万元	455496	576732	720243	938785	1114200
③境外资金	万元	10021	3045	5626	22682	14807
④其他资金	万元	9194	9010	5690	6241	10165
R&D经费外部支出合计	万元	11050	13888	28331	49266	143368
#对境内研究机构支出	万元	6467	10703	4437	14379	120399
对境内高等学校支出	万元	2622	2577	2980	2142	1626
对境外支出	万元	982	225	1245	7380	13177
科技活动产出及相关情况						
自主知识产权情况						
专利申请数	件	4654	5746	8038	10946	9586
#发明专利	件	1301	1177	2574	4256	3819
有效发明专利数	件	1926	3320	2064	3217	5363
#境外授权	件	112	237	119	210	283
专利所有权转让及许可数	件	161	537	136	112	119
专利所有权转让及许可收入	万元	8640	15859	10584	2908	3733
新产品开发、生产及销售情况						
新产品开发项目数	项	2276	2534	3094	6376	5978
新产品开发经费支出	万元	589036	776818	765927	1232410	1497801
新产品产值	万元	5501675	6945494	8643848	11744374	22172598
新产品销售收入	万元	5391190	6373687	8385864	11951808	21901522
#出口	万元	1988713	3109605	3466739	3786174	8113170
其他情况						
发表科技论文	篇	205	340	309	209	190
拥有注册商标数量	件	2287	3047	3194	3580	4327
#境外注册	件	310	326	309	482	752
形成国家或行业标准	项	171	50	201	172	139

注：限额以上R&D项目是指项目经费支出10万元以上的项目。

12-5 主要年份公有企事业单位科学技术人员

Scientific and Technical Personnel in Public Enterprises and Institutions in Main Years

单位：人

项目	1990年	1995年	2005年	2010年	2013年	2014年
公有企事业单位科技人员数	11629	16856	42593	40025	41812	42141
#工程技术人员	1084	1718	1839	1438	1378	1552
农业技术人员	432	230	290	172	208	205
卫生技术人员	1430	1988	16188	11171	10613	10290
科学研究人员	21	52	77	16	17	19
教学人员	7524	11553	21717	24010	25707	25807
经济人员	278	329	636	1184	1678	1954
会计人员	581	484	1299	1454	1514	1628
统计人员	170	77	82	91	169	87

注：2010年起，公有企事业单位科学技术人员数只统计在编在岗人员数，与往年数不可比，下同。

12-6 主要年份三种专利申请量与授权量

Three Kinds of Patents Application Accepted and Granted in Main Years

单位：件

项目	1990年	1995年	2000年	2005年	2010年	2013年	2014年
申请量	34	325	1653	6694	21654	29013	28432
发　明	1	5	35	245	3143	6454	6912
实用新型	5	70	386	1971	7677	12746	11980
外观设计	28	250	1232	4478	10834	9813	9540
授权量	30	262	1399	3114	20397	22595	20340
发　明	1	8	4	24	442	1495	1624
实用新型	4	41	344	1116	7529	12080	10585
外观设计	25	213	1051	1974	12426	9020	8131

12-7 主要年份各类技术合同签订情况

Basic Statistics on Technical Contracts Signed by Type in Main Years

项目	1990年	1995年	2000年	2005年	2010年	2013年	2014年
技术合同项目数(项)	5	46	110	50	90	175	177
#技术开发合同	3		1	41	79	151	160
技术咨询合同				2			
技术转让合同	2	44	78	1	2	15	8
技术服务合同		2	31	6	9	9	9
技术合同金额(万元)	12	1804	3469	4058	18366	25960	11241
#技术开发合同			1000	1888	6878	14402	8290
技术咨询合同				80			
技术转让合同	12	1656	2007	2000	11046	11333	2737
技术服务合同		148	1362	90	442	225	214
技术合同实现金额(万元)	7	1623	2398	2522	17891	24610	10298
#技术开发合同			700	1427	6402	13052	7351
技术咨询合同				35			
技术转让合同	7	1535	1260	1000	11046	11333	2737
技术服务合同		88	438	60	442	225	210

12-8 主要年份高新科技发展情况

Basic Statistics on High-tech Development in Main Years

项目	单位	1995年	2000年	2005年	2010年	2013年	2014年
高新技术企业							
企业数	个	11	66	247	334	666	755
总产值	亿元	30.55	274.41	925.07	1240.59	1640.46	2324.01
总收入	亿元	26.76	266.49	927.72	1249.50	1627.95	2374.89
出口总额	亿美元	0.54	7.34	71.59	99.08	90.81	110.60
从业人员数	人	6400	36304	171812	246134	256243	250234
#科技活动人员	人	832	8663	34448	72833	60692	59451
高新技术产品							
企业数	家			543	924	978	937
产品	个	27	177	947	1430	1695	1748
总产值	亿元	31.43	186.00	1062.40	2353.70	4184.97	4742.72
#电子与信息技术	亿元			726.92	1407.39	3172.74	3285.25
生物技术	亿元			8.20	51.93	27.56	50.34
新材料技术	亿元			51.43	115.46	415.07	626.10
光机电一体化技术	亿元			146.94	153.74	363.85	326.86
新能源高效节能技术	亿元			32.71	95.52	157.20	143.42
环保技术	亿元			6.58	4.95	32.33	8.59
其他	亿元			89.63	524.70	16.22	302.16
销售收入	亿元			1033.64	2316.74	4100.14	4583.97
#出口销售收入	亿元			651.99	1510.87	2365.15	2393.44
实现利税	亿元			66.06	116.82	152.52	218.63

注：1. 高新技术企业情况2009年以前为省级高新技术企业情况，2009年起为国家级高新技术企业情况。
2. 高新技术产品情况从2010年起，统计口径为规模以上工业企业。

12-9 主要年份科学技术成果项数

Achievements for Scientific and Technological Research in Main Years

单位：项

项　目	1985年	1990年	1995年	2000年	2005年	2010年	2013年	2014年
获省级科技进步奖		1	4	6	3	8	9	8
市级科技进步奖	68	31	22	47	75	87	93	75
农业方面	30	8	3	13	9	7	7	8
一等奖	1	4		2	1	2	2	
二等奖	3	3		5	3	2	3	3
三等奖	18	1	3	6	5	3	2	5
四等奖	8							
工业方面	32	18	14	24	42	57	58	48
特等奖				1	2			
一等奖	1	3		5	7	13	18	7
二等奖	8	11	5	8	19	21	21	16
三等奖	10	4	9	10	14	23	19	25
四等奖	13							
医药卫生方面	6	5	5	10	25	23	28	14
特等奖								
一等奖			1			5	6	5
二等奖		1		2	4	6	9	6
三等奖	2	4	4	8	19	12	13	3
四等奖	4							
市长奖						5	4	
技术成果类						1	1	
荣誉类						4	3	

12-10 科技创新平台情况（2011-2014年）

Basic Statistics on Technology Innovation Platform (2011-2014)

单位：个

项　目	2011年	2012年	2013年	2014年
科技创新平台				
#公共科技创新平台	11	13	16	17
专业镇技术创新平台	12	12	12	12
企业创新平台				
#企业工程技术研究开发中心	124	124	161	186
#国家级	2	1	1	1
省级	42	45	76	92
市级	80	78	84	93
实验室				
#国家级				
省级	9	11	11	11
市级	31	31	35	37
#重点实验室	31	31	35	37

12-11　历年公有企事业单位科学技术人员数

Scientific and Technical Personnel in Public Enterprises and Institutions over Years

单位：人

年　份	科学技术人员	#工程技术人员	农业技术人员	卫生技术人员	科学研究人员	教学人员	经济人员	会计人员	统计人员
1980	6619	370	190	1076	19	4282		564	99
1981	7473	463	217	1166	23	4978		501	109
1982	7547	468	243	1241	28	4954		509	101
1983	8453	525	315	1699		5257		109	109
1984	9033	615	307	1791		5534		261	201
1985	9166	663	318	2319	6	5129		491	214
1986	9490	768	358	2398	5	5222		501	203
1987	10945	797	378	2426	6	6495		583	222
1988	12495	1014	359	3093	24	7064	72	590	197
1989	11306	960	388	1393	19	7394	281	632	181
1990	11629	1084	432	1430	21	7524	278	581	170
1991	15004	2170	405	3347	13	7843	308	558	153
1992	16809	2522	375	3690	18	8659	313	613	153
1993	18491	2871	264	4074	112	9511	290	916	141
1994	20198	3490	272	4513	57	9949	300	657	112
1995	23104	3944	255	4878	66	11613	329	750	171
1996	24693	4037	263	5356	51	12287	360	740	143
1997	26103	4258	294	5504	48	13371	418	882	280
1998	26582	4321	310	4862	48	14316	376	894	171
1999	28789	4620	288	5246	48	15604	416	946	152
2000									
2001	24677	795	121	5493	31	17309	252	273	40
2002	34168	5261	246	6538	28	18756	555	1319	184
2003	33070	996	159	11145	44	19614	314	741	57
2004	39398	1752	276	14541	141	20905	561	613	74
2005	42593	1839	290	16188	77	21717	636	1299	82
2006	46371	1913	462	18401	70	22434	763	1512	93
2007	49032	2037	492	19528	71	23364	892	1832	92
2008	51729	2375	343	20955	50	24063	1048	1827	100
2009	55097	2302	284	21679	43	26741	1129	1940	122
2010	40025	1438	172	11171	16	24010	1184	1454	91
2011	41370	1427	216	11117	21	25084	1393	1426	90
2012	41336	1426	217	10762	24	25412	1261	1556	79
2013	41812	1378	208	10613	17	25707	1678	1514	169
2014	42141	1552	205	10290	19	25807	1954	1628	87

12-12 历年三种专利与技术合同签订情况

Basic Statistics on Three Kinds of Patents and Technical Contracts Signed by Type over Years

年 份	三种专利申请量(件)	#发明	三种专利授权量(件)	#发明	技术合同签订项目数（项）	技术合同签订金额（万元）	技术合同实现金额（万元）
1990	34	1	30	1	5	12	7
1991	70	3	50	1	4	10	10
1992	102	5	78	2	3	23	10
1993	100	3	90	1	2	24	2
1994	104	4	100	2	14	2537	1756
1995	325	5	262	8	46	1804	1623
1996	333	3	312	4	133	4839	3756
1997	725	1	321		78	2036	800
1998					62	3048	2398
1999					20	1124	1077
2000	1653	35	1399	4	110	3469	2398
2001	2914	71	1753	5	89	1335	953
2002	3100	90	2680	10	91	766	730
2003	3865	93	2858	14	58	700	680
2004	4325	185	3167	26	69	4278	2726
2005	6694	245	3114	24	50	4058	2522
2006	9879	553	4872	28	25	13644	13402
2007	13842	876	6752	44	53	8510	8138
2008	14406	1188	8093	115	54	12838	3694
2009	19106	1593	12918	254	60	6996	6264
2010	21654	3143	20397	442	70	15760	15572
2011	24455	4214	19353	758	163	31966	29923
2012	29199	5568	20900	1381	152	14516	13577
2013	29013	6454	22595	1495	175	25960	24610
2014	28432	6912	20340	1624	177	11241	10298

12-13 历年科学技术成果项数

Scientific and Technological Achievements over Years

单位：项

年 份	获国家级科技进步奖	获省级科技进步奖	获市级科技进步奖	特等奖	一等奖	二等奖	三等奖	四等奖
1979			25			5	4	16
1980			27			2	11	14
1981			35		2	4	11	18
1982			62		1	3	21	37
1983			38		2	6	11	19
1984			35			11	11	13
1985			68		2	11	30	25
1986			86		5	14	27	40
1987			59		2	19	25	13
1988		1	37		6	10	16	5
1989		1	32		4	6	22	
1990		1	31		7	15	9	
1991		4	35	1	3	18	13	
1992		3	19		4	7	8	
1993			18	1	3	8	6	
1994		6	23		4	9	10	
1995		4	22		1	5	16	
1996		3	32		7	6	19	
1997		4	32		7	6	19	
1998		6	38	1	2	11	24	
1999		9	39		6	11	22	
2000		6	47	1	7	15	24	
2001		4	51		4	23	24	
2002		3	47		7	15	25	
2003		4	50		7	14	29	
2004		6	60	1	6	19	34	
2005		3	75	2	10	25	38	
2006		2	70	1	8	24	37	
2007		7	83	1	18	26	38	
2008		7	83		19	28	36	
2009		19	85		22	24	39	
2010		8	87		20	29	38	
2011		13	77		21	30	26	
2012		9	93		22	33	38	
2013		9	93		26	33	34	
2014		8	75		12	27	36	

12-14 主要年份各类学校情况

Basic Statistics on Schools by Type in Main Years

项　　目	单位	1985年	1990年	1995年	2000年	2005年	2010年	2013年	2014年
普通高等专业学校									
学校数	所			1	1	4	5	6	6
毕业生数	人			395	985	1439	8105	11630	12990
招生数	人			576	1440	7273	12660	20816	22830
在校学生数	人			1628	3241	16645	38293	60877	69866
教职工数	人			262	293	1761	3192	4146	4435
#专任教师	人			119	161	1081	2174	2952	3148
中等职业技术学校									
学校数	所	3	17	20	23	21	26	25	25
毕业生数	人	234	2210	4641	9554	9062	14028	16660	17521
招生数	人	1508	3866	8697	8759	10971	18477	24687	24524
在校学生数	人	3363	8919	18737	23144	29487	47531	61011	64412
教职员工数	人	217	619	1134	1608	2230	2996	3449	3643
#专任教师	人	150	434	859	1221	1621	2341	2677	2861
普通中学									
学校数	所	106	64	69	77	134	190	207	212
毕业生数	人	12317	18688	24165	30261	48935	73810	78364	82718
#高中生	人	2055	2527	3231	7120	12233	20816	24341	25180
招生数	人	16978	20441	33086	41488	70843	93196	100170	102112
#高中生	个	2915	3389	6099	9048	19540	24668	26039	26741
在校学生数	人	46596	61188	92481	112418	191044	258276	278289	284648
#高中生	人	6304	8572	13653	24677	52283	70398	77045	78053
教职员工数	人	3266	4001	5900	6012	12177	16946	20665	21663
#专任教师	个	2420	2963	4381	5027	9640	14572	16422	17148
小　学									
学校数	所	583	570	595	552	414	330	321	320
毕业生数	人	17901	18262	27257	33684	61173	77429	84641	86693
招生数	人	20264	26158	36702	53786	84784	108900	127237	125039
在校学生数	人	134421	162664	195063	272793	480923	552377	659138	687269
教职员工数	人	7009	7797	9560	9131	21964	28298	29527	31290
#专任教师	人	6017	6785	8060	7946	17478	23733	26681	28679

注：中等职业技术学校包含市技工学校，不含一般成人中专，下同。

12-14 续表

项　　目	单位	1985年	1990年	1995年	2000年	2005年	2010年	2013年	2014年
成人高等专业教育									
当年招生人数	人				1697	6387	6086	7211	6582
在校学生数	人	403	531	1254	3642	12665	21703	17254	17476
小学适龄儿童入学									
小学适龄儿童总数	人	103460	133011	177791	247555	423058	511439	629097	664388
小学已入学儿童数	人	103282	132934	177787	247539	423058	511439	629097	664388
小学学龄儿童入学率	%	99.8	99.9	100.0	100.0	100.0	100.0	100.0	100.0
小学毕业生升学									
小学毕业生人数	人	17901	18262	27257	33684	61173	77429	84641	86693
已升学人数	人	14235	17413	27166	33627	61095	77429	84641	86693
小学毕业生升学率	%	79.5	95.4	99.2	99.8	99.9	100.0	100.0	100.0
初中毕业生升学									
初中毕业生人数	人	10262	16161	20933	23141	36702	52994	54023	57538
已升学人数	人	3955	7134	17876	20896	34536	51881	53158	56617
初中毕业生升学率	%	38.5	43.6	85.4	90.3	94.1	97.9	98.4	98.4
普通高中毕业生升学									
高考省线入围人数	人	285	224	809	2646	6455	13761	18405	18766
高考录取人数	人	543	759	2095	5017	12461	20099	23346	23769
#高考升本科人数	人	274	250	697	1678	5161	11033	13464	14142
普通高中毕业生升学率	%	26.5	31.2	64.9	70.5	96.5	95.1	95.4	98.4
幼儿园									
幼儿园数	所	83	86	258	452	511	727	827	881
在园幼儿数	人	31382	47040	84263	111763	111330	208373	277777	290548
幼教职工数	人	984	1387	1427	7517	12567	22122	31523	35369
#专任教师	人	841	1160	1160	4618	7002	13947	17640	18748
全国各类大中专院校招生人数									
国家各大(学)专院校在我市招生人数	人				11680	35831	40795	47921	44765
全市教育经费投入总额	亿元				15.5	50.2	94.4	155.2	165.7

12-15 历年各类学校在校学生数

Number of Students Enrollment by Type of School over Years

单位：人

年份	普通高等学校	中等职业技术学校	#技工学校	普通中学	#高中	小学	幼儿园
1949		151		1960	318	52781	
1952		543		3394	296	70359	
1957		561		6652	848	88001	
1962		380		9736	1513	119998	
1965		358		10469	1397	160931	
1970				60150	9873	118128	
1975		689		49569	10847	168236	
1978		595		76025	12092	161114	18228
1979		450		62292	7010	158008	12774
1980		386		54829	6909	154871	7630
1981		450		43514	5755	150857	8103
1982		661		41683	4654	144754	14650
1983		967		42777	4798	135440	15436
1984		1070		46488	5766	134567	23702
1985		3363		46596	6304	134421	31382
1986		3891	60	49445	7880	140700	38195
1987		5847	117	54435	8367	144287	42569
1988		7120	229	59268	8201	150097	42845
1989		7878	293	61955	7687	155852	44110
1990		8919	582	61188	8572	162664	47040
1991		10938	915	60146	8725	170064	51051
1992		13161	1277	65171	9711	175203	57537
1993	1079	14176	1516	75305	10297	180114	65310
1994	1451	16084	2025	85827	11409	186244	72552
1995	1628	18737	2404	92481	13653	195063	84263
1996	1771	22614	2567	95150	16887	205957	85709
1997	2025	24821	2598	98005	20609	221838	100059
1998	2171	25588	2291	101202	22490	235787	103585
1999	2241	25073	2001	105518	23084	248759	109773
2000	3241	23144	1746	112418	24677	272793	111763
2001	3802	23638	2039	122115	28232	295384	112963
2002	5144	25363	2152	135256	32398	342804	108898
2003	6884	27664	2564	149656	38143	386890	104832
2004	9104	28487	2559	171336	45050	448296	112538
2005	16645	29487	2618	191044	52283	480923	111330
2006	22005	35403	2905	214638	57662	496828	118683
2007	25178	40429	3063	234578	61151	520684	130932
2008	28656	45419	3238	248442	63962	528644	156362
2009	33992	46538	3268	249464	66750	511160	176249
2010	38293	47531	2955	258276	70398	552377	208373
2011	45081	48159	2915	263076	73644	578279	227656
2012	52381	50092	2833	267918	75851	608118	255657
2013	60877	61011	13101	278289	77045	659138	277777
2014	69866	64412	14192	284648	78053	687269	290548

12-16 历年各类学校当年招收学生数

Number of New Students Enrollment by Type of School over Years

单位：人

年 份	普通高等学校	中等职业技术学校	#技工学校	普通中学	#高中	小 学
1949		102				
1952		285		1666	190	
1957		80		2516	259	
1962		45		3716	566	
1965		134		3656	476	
1970				45069	7919	
1975		188		28329	5930	
1978		250		29788	3436	30152
1979		200		25364	3900	28315
1980		186		24083	3906	26857
1981		266		16808	2594	26461
1982		162		17492	2317	23970
1983		573		18111	2344	19604
1984		1964		16609	2477	17644
1985		1508		16978	2915	20264
1986		1977	60	17944	2781	25867
1987		2883	64	21720	2665	28926
1988		2832	112	23280	2925	29437
1989		2966	124	21877	2686	27539
1990		3866	343	20441	3389	26158
1991		5008	445	21430	3266	27539
1992		5696	487	26161	3751	28804
1993	567	5835	633	29948	3944	31841
1994	569	7064	952	32229	4440	34495
1995	576	8697	996	33086	6099	36702
1996	711	10119	978	33576	7385	39689
1997	750	9718	798	35140	8273	42066
1998	750	9664	852	36423	8118	43802
1999	802	9060	665	38400	8199	47715
2000	1440	8759	527	41488	9048	53786
2001	1597	8850	1116	44729	10727	56521
2002	2190	9417	1153	49881	11852	65066
2003	3104	9809	874	55564	15147	71476
2004	3804	10618	1044	63085	17467	80525
2005	7273	10971	1100	70843	19540	84784
2006	8032	13357	1250	79985	20866	89663
2007	8519	16491	1297	85816	21146	92860
2008	10218	17475	1163	89808	22313	94641
2009	12863	15767	1598	88325	23631	92281
2010	12660	18477	2052	93196	24668	108900
2011	16837	17812	1180	95155	25647	114763
2012	20507	18269	1306	96348	25758	123290
2013	20816	24687	7069	100170	26039	127237
2014	22830	24524	5110	102112	26741	125039

12-17　历年各类学校当年毕业生数

Number of Graduates by Type of School over Years

单位：人

年　份	普通高等学校	中等职业技术学校	#技工学校	普通中学	#高中	小　学
1949				414	83	
1952		48		588	44	14349
1957		87		1365	203	59056
1962		209		2680	468	28418
1965		44		2363	393	32508
1970				15081	1954	26187
1975		374		20842	4937	25009
1978		244		43035	8533	30480
1979		244		33554	8004	28925
1980		250		19578	3096	27294
1981		191		13308	3046	27215
1982				10483	3004	27348
1983		260		10752	1940	26723
1984		230		10969	1404	17870
1985		234		12317	2055	17901
1986		660		13527	1271	17533
1987		819		13895	2296	23183
1988		1323		15322	2966	23054
1989		1960	60	15310	2716	20315
1990		2210	57	18688	2527	18262
1991		2634	112	19820	2559	19186
1992		2126	123	19323	2643	23308
1993	30	2915	390	18363	3020	26893
1994	197	5035	445	20360	2787	28500
1995	395	4641	541	24165	3231	27257
1996	560	5813	753	27675	3483	27156
1997	484	6745	691	28729	3834	27992
1998	556	8316	918	29839	5448	29794
1999	714	9044	796	30109	6585	31426
2000	985	9554	634	31291	7120	33684
2001	1019	7748	684	32409	7553	37077
2002	753	7171	542	34204	8277	40611
2003	1350	7217	509	39031	8784	45599
2004	1506	8630	917	43471	10676	51831
2005	1439	9062	777	48935	12233	61173
2006	2269	9422	677	55856	15486	70474
2007	5096	10061	754	60436	17354	74681
2008	6486	10728	821	66594	19315	78037
2009	7292	11927	962	71811	20550	78027
2010	8105	14028	956	73810	20816	77429
2011	9463	14774	831	76816	22095	80463
2012	12625	14099	993	79449	23398	87733
2013	11630	16660	2426	78364	24341	84641
2014	12990	17521	2834	82718	25180	86693

12-18 历年各级各类学校专任教师数

Number of Full-time Teachers by Level and Type of School over Years

单位：人

年 份	普通高等学校	中等职业技术学校	#技工学校	普通中学	#高中	小 学	幼儿园
1978		34		3641	638	5641	
1979		31		3367	369	6136	
1980		29		2996	370	6022	
1981		32		2343	344	6433	
1982		38		2210	284	6186	
1983		61		2361	296	5830	
1984		63		2352	309	5971	
1985		150		2420	354	6017	841
1986		168	5	2463	407	6515	720
1987		208	7	2709	490	6878	941
1988		306	9	3007	540	7112	967
1989		422	11	2949	462	6743	980
1990		434	12	2963	488	6785	1160
1991		513	15	3019	500	6831	1470
1992		600	17	3198	479	7164	1569
1993	99	737	16	3583	610	7314	1773
1994	113	767	26	4001	710	7610	1920
1995	119	859	34	4381	733	8060	1160
1996	119	924	40	4310	886	7410	2175
1997	123	1151	89	4404	991	7518	2753
1998	125	1338	93	4632	1065	7912	3247
1999	133	1205	92	4699	1149	7198	3715
2000	161	1221	84	5027	1310	7946	4618
2001	231	1286	121	5348	1411	8693	4701
2002	290	1445	125	6373	1769	10880	5351
2003	312	1548	124	7069	1976	12490	5505
2004	560	1531	134	8437	2367	15512	6218
2005	1081	1621	150	9640	2817	17478	7002
2006	1357	1801	122	10953	3215	18717	7919
2007	1569	1965	156	12272	3678	20511	9279
2008	1691	2218	161	12995	3976	21203	11072
2009	1890	2321	160	13598	4178	21130	12419
2010	2174	2341	171	14572	4541	23733	13947
2011	2435	2403	167	15262	4851	24787	15232
2012	2729	2448	180	15858	5026	25379	16689
2013	2952	2677	458	16422	5114	26681	17640
2014	3148	2861	628	17148	5291	28679	18748

12-19 历年各类学校入(升)学率与高考入围人数

Number of Passing College Entrance Examination and Proportion of Students Entering Schools over Years

年 份	学龄儿童入学率(%)	小学毕业生升学率(%)	初中毕业生升学率(%)	高中毕业生升学率(%)	高考入围人数(人)	#省线入围人数
1978	98.36	85.80	14.30	8.14	846	250
1979	98.70	76.00	16.00	6.71	566	166
1980	98.85	73.40	25.40	7.15	222	140
1981	98.72	50.56	27.40	8.64	239	154
1982	99.06	54.40	34.40	8.04	252	115
1983	99.75	57.60	37.40	12.34	245	150
1984	99.65	70.80	29.86	43.32	619	220
1985	99.83	79.52	38.54	26.50	534	285
1986	99.90	84.71	33.89	43.69	595	228
1987	99.94	83.60	40.10	27.09	644	297
1988	99.93	89.88	42.00	30.63	925	315
1989	99.92	96.18	43.30	32.92	977	284
1990	99.94	95.35	43.60	31.20	759	224
1991	99.92	96.18	45.20	26.22	861	268
1992	99.94	97.58	56.00	35.59	994	312
1993	99.95	97.79	68.50	39.23	1102	423
1994	99.96	98.94	79.02	62.75	1823	586
1995	99.99	99.16	85.40	64.90	2095	809
1996	99.98	96.45	86.70	66.80	2160	1093
1997	99.99	99.90	87.35	60.00	2212	1215
1998	99.99	99.86	88.25	47.69	2348	1315
1999	99.99	99.87	89.80	53.15	3501	1790
2000	99.99	99.83	90.30	70.50	5017	2646
2001	100.00	99.77	90.50	74.82	5651	3225
2002	100.00	99.80	91.10	83.00	6873	3759
2003	100.00	99.80	92.10	93.60	9167	4509
2004	100.00	99.90	93.30	96.70	10756	5452
2005	100.00	99.90	94.10	96.50	11196	6455
2006	100.00	100.00	94.80	82.90	11359	7652
2007	100.00	100.00	95.20	89.10	13275	9185
2008	100.00	100.00	96.60	91.00	15047	9987
2009	100.00	100.00	97.00	87.50	17487	12569
2010	100.00	100.00	97.90	95.10	18845	13761
2011	100.00	100.00	98.00	94.50	19588	15501
2012	100.00	100.00	97.80	95.90	22127	17316
2013	100.00	100.00	98.40	95.40	22840	18405
2014	100.00	100.00	98.40	98.37	23900	18766

12-20 历年文化艺术、文物事业机构数

Number of Institutions in Culture and Cultural Relics over Years

年 份	电影放映单位(个)	#影剧院	艺术表演团体(个)	群众艺术馆(个)	文化站(广电文化中心)(个)	公共图书馆(个)	公共图书馆藏书量(万册)	博物馆(个)	档案馆(座)
1978	167	5	1	1	33	1	11	2	1
1979	157	5	1	1	33	1	15	2	1
1980	65	5	1	1	33	1	16	2	1
1981	75	6	1	1	33	1	17	2	1
1982	53	6	1	1	33	1	19	2	1
1983	49	6	1	1	33	1	19	2	1
1984	65	6	1	1	33	1	24	2	1
1985	60	7	1	1	33	3	30	2	1
1986	61	9	2	1	33	3	30	2	1
1987	70	13	4	1	33	8	30	2	1
1988	78	15	5	1	33	3	30	2	1
1989	102	26	6	1	33	3	30	2	1
1990	114	26	7	1	33	5	30	2	1
1991	126	36	5	1	33	6	31	2	1
1992	150	50	2	1	33	8	37	2	1
1993	163	53	2	1	33	11	47	2	1
1994	193	63	2	1	33	14	58	2	1
1995	218	97	2	1	33	15	68	2	1
1996	225	111	4	1	33	16	73	2	1
1997	229	130	4	1	33	26	84	2	1
1998	233	147	4	1	32	26	106	3	1
1999	210	87	4	1	32	20	133	3	1
2000	192	87	1	1	32	18	97	3	1
2001	145	84	1	1	32	21	99	3	1
2002	162	81	2	1	32	24	109	3	2
2003	107	55	2	1	32	346	289	3	2
2004	88	78		1	32	397	631	6	2
2005	70	31		1	32	473	660	16	2
2006	51	34		1	33	1222	771	21	2
2007	51	34		1	33	1271	896	23	2
2008	40	34	1	1	33	387	515	23	1
2009	40	62	4	1	33	504	599	31	1
2010	46	62	4	1	33	505	701	30	1
2011	52	62	5	1	33	622	771	31	1
2012	59	11	6	1	33	649	1020	31	1
2013	66	11	10	1	33	641	1061	31	1
2014	60	11	16	1	33	641	996	33	1

12-21 主要年份广播电视事业发展情况

Basic Statistics on Radio and Television Industry in Main Years

项　　目	单位	1985年	1990年	1995年	2000年	2005年	2010年	2013年	2014年
广播电台	个		1	1	1	1	1	1	1
电视台	个	1	1	1	1	1	1	1	1
镇街文化广电服务中心	个						28	28	28

12-22 主要年份安全生产事故中火灾事故情况

Basic Statistics on Fire of Production Accidents in Main Years

项　　目	单位	1995年	2000年	2005年	2010年	2013年	2014年
发生起数	起	24	60	13	13	19	7
受伤人数	人	8	34	7	8	14	2
死亡人数	人	12	31	18	15	39	14
损失折款	万元	1596	1022	22	21	274	539
平均每起事故损失	万元	66.50	17.03	1.67	1.63	14.42	76.99

注：本表数据来源于市安监局。

12-23 主要年份交通事故发生情况

Basic Statistics on Traffic Accidents in Main Years

项　　目	单位	1995年	2000年	2005年	2010年	2013年	2014年
发生起数	起	2015	7386	7124	4874	4361	4215
受伤人数	人	2061	8217	8642	5355	4941	4671
死亡人数	人	692	903	921	528	484	483
损失折款	万元	685	1759	934	682	632	770
平均每起事故损失	元	3400	2382	1312	1400	1448	1827

注：本表数据来源于市安监局，含道路和水上交通事故。

12-24 各类卫生事业机构及床位、人员数（2014年）

Number of Health Care Institutions, Beds and Employed Personnel by Type of Institution (2014)

项　　目	机构数(个)	实有床位数(张)	卫生工作人员(人)	#卫生技术人员	#执业(助理)医师
总　　计	2194	26704	53013	43091	15081
医疗机构	2156	26704	52197	42549	14881
县及县以上及其他医院	83	25994	39756	32381	10571
#综合医院	59	23147	35869	29423	9683
中医医院	3	1113	1757	1496	479
专科医院	21	1734	2130	1462	409
社区卫生服务中心(站)	397		5643	4469	1687
村(社区)卫生站	811		1927	1383	737
门诊部（含18所分院个数）	327		2199	1976	917
诊所、卫生所、医务室	535		1369	1311	632
妇幼保健院	1	590	1025	835	279
专科疾病防治院	1	120	249	173	58
急救中心(站)	1		29	21	
采供血机构	1		110	87	9
疾病预防控制中心（防疫站）	1		166	136	82
卫生监督所	1		103	54	
健康教育所	1				
其他卫生机构	34		437	265	109

12-25 主要年份卫生事业机构各类人员数

Number of Personnel in Health Institutions in Main Years

单位：人

项　　目	1980年	1985年	1990年	1995年	2000年	2005年	2010年	2013年	2014年
卫生工作人员	3599	3945	4503	6149	9289	22127	46102	52325	53013
#卫生技术人员	2960	3305	3902	5290	8065	18757	37487	42132	43091
执业(助理)医师	1167	1201	1721	2299	3309	8130	13214	14864	15081
注册护士	584	643	1164	1751	2673	6303	14689	18123	18841
药剂人员	236	572	546	602	706	1281	2284	2666	2603
检验人员	120	147	152	216	367	781	1412	1561	1597
其　他	1040	766	316	395	350	2262	5888	4918	4969
其他技术人员	8		13	96	174	786	1217	1339	1234
管理人员	299	282	243	432	597	1080	2418	2206	2330
工勤人员	332	358	345	331	453	1504	4980	5759	5814

注：2004年起，卫生方面包含诊所、卫生所、医务室及村卫生室的数据，与往年数不可比。

12-26 医疗机构服务情况（2014年）

Services in Medical Institutions (2014)

指标名称	诊疗人数（人次）	#门、急诊	入院人数（人）	病死率（%）	健康检查人数(人次)
总　　计	65357077	65188676	895135	0.40	3548715
医院	35973424	35873242	863708	0.41	3497693
#综合医院	33781270	33697773	808624	0.44	3401588
中医医院	1405436	1401261	25747		47519
专科医院	786718	774208	29337	0.01	48586
#民营医院	5455523	5429308	211629	0.35	989279
社区卫生服务中心(站)	17154735	17115477			1428772
村卫生站	5634160	5613790			
门诊部(所)	4962983	4954392			
妇幼保健院(所、站)	1320716	1320716	30080	0.04	15983
专科疾病防治院(所、站)	210044	210044	1347		35039
其他医疗机构	101015	101015			

12-27 历年卫生事业机构、床位、人员数

Number of Health Care Institutions, Beds and Personnel over Years

年 份	机构数(个)	实有床位数(张)	卫生工作人员(人)	#卫生技术人员	#执业(助理)医 师
1978	82	2257	3242	2636	768
1979	81	2271	3466	2863	971
1980	83	2207	3599	2960	1167
1981	83	2210	3724	3091	1102
1982	83	2292	3886	3253	1097
1983	83	2098	3985	3335	1088
1984	83	2231	4005	3351	1132
1985	87	2323	3945	3305	1201
1986	88	3054	4084	3454	1179
1987	88	3393	4475	3490	1304
1988	87	3640	4582	3829	1537
1989	87	3677	4522	3874	1620
1990	85	3866	4503	3902	1721
1991	85	4085	4578	3946	1755
1992	83	4517	4705	4127	1832
1993	99	4940	5247	4524	2023
1994	98	5365	5689	4930	2221
1995	99	5798	6149	5290	2299
1996	99	5288	6712	5766	2449
1997	151	5505	7286	6283	2605
1998	171	5892	8306	7139	2955
1999	176	6241	8697	7575	3080
2000	174	7081	9289	8065	3309
2001	173	7474	9323	8064	3429
2002	178	8641	10692	9011	3523
2003	172	9820	11584	9807	3758
2004	944	10797	15058	13053	4870
2005	874	11972	22127	18757	8130
2006	1210	13293	27128	22904	8629
2007	1649	15227	34151	28758	10446
2008	2106	16778	40449	33113	11869
2009	2106	18080	43561	35766	12884
2010	2229	19980	46102	37487	13214
2011	2249	22814	48142	39582	13644
2012	2222	24617	49353	40597	14043
2013	2254	25736	52325	42132	14864
2014	2194	26704	53013	43091	15081

注：2004年起本表包含诊所、卫生所、医务室及村卫生室的数据，与往年数不可比。

12-28 历年体育运动情况

Basic Statistics on Sports over Years

年份	破（超）世界纪录（次）	破（超）亚洲纪录（次）	破（超）全国纪录（次）	在国际比赛中获得金牌总数（枚）	在全国比赛中获得金牌总数（枚）	在省级比赛中获得金牌总数（枚）	市级运动会参赛运动员人数（人）	为国家省输送运动员（人）
1978			9	1	7	26	2500	11
1979	2		2	1	7		2250	18
1980			12		2		2400	14
1981			11	4	19		2500	13
1982			14	4	30	15	2650	9
1983	1		7	5	6		2420	7
1984			1	16	5		2500	33
1985		2	1	5	2		1960	7
1986		7	4	7	4	52	2420	16
1987	1	1	8	35	9		2130	19
1988	3	1	4	14	25		2540	15
1989			27	5	43	92	6430	18
1990	13	5		4	6		2370	25
1991	2	1	8	12	14		4800	16
1992	2	3	21	10	6		15000	30
1993	2	8	5	12	9		10350	16
1994	34	2	24	6	23	157	2720	14
1995	10	1		5	37		1500	14
1996				3	16		7800	13
1997	10	9		1	6	36	6000	74
1998	2	4	28	4	28	87	1560	74
1999				4	33		6000	6
2000			3	4	91		4000	6
2001				13	22	48	8000	5
2002				2	35	58		11
2003		7		2	31	82		6
2004	3	4	4	49	34			18
2005				2	13	46	8564	44
2006				20	21	32	16000	
2007				3	25	46	2740	9
2008				3	16	49	630	17
2009		1	3	8	20	94	1550	17
2010				4	6	40	9895	16
2011				8	27	116	3300	25
2012					10	127	3400	16
2013					5	55	3600	
2014					8	113	3998	

12-29　主要年份体育比赛成绩

Basic Statistics on Sports Achievements in Main Years

项　　目	单位	1980年	1985年	1990年	1995年	2000年	2005年	2010年	2013年	2014年
破世界纪录	次			13	10					
获得国际赛冠军	个		5	4	5	4		4		
破亚洲纪录	次		2	5	1					
破全国纪录	次	12	1			3				
获国际比赛奖牌										
金牌	枚		5	4	5	4	2	4		
银牌	枚			4	3	2	1	2		
铜牌	枚						2			
获全国比赛金牌	枚	2	2	6	37	91	13	6	5	8

注:“获得国际赛冠军”及“获国际比赛奖牌”含地区赛。

12-30　主要年份群众体育活动情况

Basic Statistics on Activities of Mass Sports in Main Years

项　　目	单位	1980年	1985年	1990年	1995年	2000年	2005年	2010年	2013年	2014年
举办市级运动会	次	5	4	9	4	2	4	16	12	8
市级运动会参赛运动员人数	人	2400	1960	2370	1500	4000	8564	9895	3600	3998
举办全民健身活动	次								331	333
参加全民健身活动人数	万人次								17.76	18.87
为国家和省输送运动员人数	人	14	7	25	14	6	47	16		

12-31 主要年份治安案件情况

Basic Statistics on Public Security Cases in Main Years

项　　目	单位	2005年	2010年	2013年	2014年
治安案件受理数	起	13760	44979	76313	124203
扰乱公共秩序	起	2816	198	582	332
妨害公共安全	起	243	630	766	645
侵犯人身、财产权利	起	6044	24551	53382	95896
#盗窃	起	2599	10513	28651	56302
妨害社会管理秩序	起	4296	19600	21583	27330
#吸毒	起	2697	4455	7629	12443
卖淫、嫖娼	起	153	663	616	829
赌博或为赌博提供条件	起	942	10464	6402	9544
治安案件查处数	起	12490	37818	48785	60155
扰乱公共秩序	起	2797	186	545	279
妨害公共安全	起	237	583	533	510
侵犯人身、财产权利	起	4865	17687	26266	32914
#盗窃	起	2007	5476	9823	17000
妨害社会管理秩序	起	4246	19362	21441	26452
#吸毒	起	2665	4317	7608	12331
卖淫、嫖娼	起	147	659	611	819
赌博或为赌博提供条件	起	938	10408	6400	9520
查处违法人员数	人	20692	42815	47083	51113
扰乱公共秩序	人	4486	363	830	549
妨害公共安全	人	218	618	490	487
侵犯人身、财产权利	人	6769	14145	13047	9651
#盗窃	人	2676	3802	2945	2215
妨害社会管理秩序	人	8201	27689	32716	40426
#吸毒	人	3922	4885	8820	14151
卖淫、嫖娼	人	415	1506	1391	1945
赌博或为赌博提供条件	人	3179	17191	15146	20309

注：本表数据来源于市公安局。

12-32 主要年份刑事案件情况

Basic Statistics on Criminal Cases in Main Years

单位：起

项　　目	2005年	2010年	2013年	2014年
刑事案件立案数	44641	36965	112749	103598
危害公共安全	264	586	952	1223
破坏市场经济秩序	451	577	1041	1849
侵犯公民人身权利	3748	3587	3628	3166
#杀人	87	69	27	37
伤害	3071	2882	2843	2354
强奸	266	336	412	412
侵犯财产	39657	31251	105320	94550
#抢劫	9144	5045	8362	6494
抢夺	3736	3250	18740	15138
入室盗窃	4150	8779	24643	20747
盗窃机动车	16050	3526	2594	2299
诈骗	897	3203	13969	14742
妨害社会管理秩序	571	963	1805	2808
#毒品犯罪	215	587	1237	1752
刑事案件破案数	13682	16271	19801	20394
危害公共安全	161	550	911	1137
破坏市场经济秩序	439	388	443	1089
侵犯公民人身权利	2037	1933	1740	1456
#杀人	73	61	24	32
伤害	1586	1449	1288	1024
强奸	171	224	226	227
侵犯财产	10598	12534	15249	14502
#抢劫	3582	2531	1848	1410
抢夺	1525	1700	2961	2369
入室盗窃	1081	4182	3764	3972
盗窃机动车	1880	631	375	538
诈骗	202	536	980	1168
妨害社会管理秩序	490	866	1456	2209
#毒品犯罪	210	569	1075	1484

注：本表数据来源于市公安局。

12-33 主要年份道路交通违法情况

Basic Statistics on Traffic Offense in Main Years

项目	单位	2005年	2010年	2013年	2014年
处理违法起数	万起	61.04	282.48	325.66	214.09
#机动车	万起		280.44	324.62	213.32
非机动车	起		10084	10142	7738
行人和乘车人	起		10281	251	7
教育人次	人次		261411	168	1
#机动车	人次		253789	168	1
非机动车	人次		3479		
行人和乘车人	人次		4143		
罚款总额	万元	9991.70	44359.52	58019.12	39546.45
#机动车	万元		44355.07	57977.42	39506.24
非机动车	万元		2.80	41.67	40.20
行人和乘车人	元		16500	300	70

注：本表数据来源于市公安局。

12-34 主要年份律师、公证、基层司法及普法教育

Basic Statistics on Lawyers, Notarization, Grassroots Judicial Work and Law Education in Main Years

项目	单位	1990年	1995年	2000年	2005年	2010年	2013年	2014年
律师工作								
律师事务所	个	2	8	22	46	115	148	148
律师	人	12	85	221	625	1366	1748	1878
担任常年法律顾问	家	102	364	416	1426	2752	3383	3597
民事诉讼代理	件	145	343	1203	6543	12041	13841	14039
非诉讼法律事务	件	110	1162	2079	13391	19967	21877	22093
刑事辩护及代理	件	295	235	438	2496	2776	3641	3745
经济案件诉讼代理	件	107	348	1100	1801	1133	1664	1779
#涉外及港澳台	件	165	11	27	160	299	94	83
公证工作								
公证处	个	1	1	1	1	3	3	3
公证人员	人	10	19	20	48	96	110	116
办结公证总数	件	5347	11377	28910	60685	48296	70147	65780
#国内民事公证	件	113	2795	19607	19627	35104	54278	48949
国内经济公证	件	236	898	1776	34015	3536	2940	3023
涉外公证(含港澳台)	件	4998	7684	4809	4607	9656	7557	4094
基层司法工作								
法律服务所	个	24	29	32	32	32	32	32
法律服务工作者	人					58	104	90
担任法律顾问	家	62	482	695	1208	724	672	593
民事诉讼代理	件	26	568	1221	1790	1090	645	758
非诉讼代理	件	129	1045	3016	3837	1549	777	719
调解工作								
人民调解委员会	个	904	813	750	814	1552	1536	1573
调解人员	人	3664	3466	3644	4556	17438	16161	14768
调解民间纠纷	件	2005	2632	2642	15210	15239	15575	13925
参加普法教育人数	万人	79.9	170	79	571	288	592	883

12-35 历年计划生育情况

Basic Statistics on Family Planning over Years

年 份	已婚育龄妇女人数(人)	女性初婚人数(人)	#23周岁及以上	不足20周岁	落实各种节育措施	
					育龄夫妇(对)	节育率(%)
1978	130438	10974			103414	79.28
1979	134483	11914			104612	77.79
1980	136742	9270	8920		101190	74.00
1981	141079	13714			112956	80.07
1982	142324	8729			115302	81.01
1983	149928	12664			129035	86.06
1984	156444	9579			138785	88.71
1985	159985	11208			142974	89.37
1986	168611	13983	11899		150545	89.30
1987	176868	13492	11252		158857	89.80
1988	183022	12419	10072		164889	90.10
1989	196042	13691	10228	15	172799	88.20
1990	202505	13264	9670	29	177425	87.60
1991	211544	13790	10834	12	184254	87.10
1992	224624	15295	10375	13	190151	84.70
1993	235150	13932	9793	6	200673	85.30
1994	243456	13213	9833	9	208234	85.50
1995	252627	13921	10430	26	215339	85.20
1996	258873	13556	10114	20	221805	85.70
1997	263646	12968	9623	9	226674	85.98
1998	267982	12366	9260	7	233007	86.95
1999	280455	12114	8999	4	249368	88.92
2000	285244	11122	7050	14	249741	87.55
2001	295395	10903	6755	14	260077	88.04
2002	303134	11635	7082	8	268243	88.49
2003	306157	12441	7767	5	266832	87.16
2004	312941	13957	9318	2	273387	87.36
2005	317062	13251	9057	5	275685	86.95
2006	323479	12460	9117	3	279246	86.33
2007	331556	13621	10333	1	293733	85.29
2008	343051	14485	11053	1	291049	84.84
2009	352115	14450	11157	5	297559	84.51
2010	367607	14265	11019	4	309054	84.07
2011	380570	14899	11820	1	320135	84.12
2012	384854	14875	12049	12	320907	83.38
2013	391864	13549	10952	5	327002	83.45
2014	399044	14871	12118	6	333848	83.66

12-35 续表

年 份	领取独生子女证 累计（人）	领取独生子女证 领证率（%）	人口出生率（‰） 省计划指标	人口出生率（‰） 实际完成	政策生育率（%）	多孩率（%）
1978			13.0	18.73		
1979			12.0	24.13		
1980	423	1.84	13.0	24.41	69.72	23.38
1981			11.9	21.86		
1982			18.1	19.07		
1983			17.0	16.74		
1984			15.5	15.54		
1985	1954	1.22	15.3	15.37	88.94	4.27
1986	2029	1.20	16.5	16.44	92.45	2.93
1987	2257	1.28	16.0	16.11	93.16	1.97
1988	2408	1.32	17.0	16.75	93.58	2.14
1989	2116	1.10	17.0	17.06	92.35	2.54
1990	2288	1.13	17.5	17.07	89.08	3.71
1991	2514	1.19	20.0	17.91	89.55	3.65
1992	2335	1.04	19.8	19.31	86.08	4.44
1993	2905	1.24	20.0	18.38	87.29	4.50
1994	3245	1.33	19.2	17.88	86.50	4.71
1995	3389	1.34	19.3	17.76	85.09	4.33
1996	4028	1.63	18.3	17.05	83.83	4.87
1997	4514	1.71	18.0	16.50	83.98	4.68
1998	4971	1.85	16.6	15.31	90.01	2.92
1999	21228	7.57	15.8	14.55	89.31	2.92
2000	30921	10.84	15.3	12.11	90.17	1.77
2001	41636	14.10	14.9	11.16	91.75	1.57
2002	49188	16.23	14.3	10.35	91.80	1.31
2003	51814	16.92	12.5	10.34	92.45	1.24
2004	55425	17.71	12.5	10.86	93.48	1.14
2005	60426	19.06	11.5	10.62	94.32	0.80
2006	69507	21.49	11.6	10.14	94.69	0.71
2007	73766	22.25	11.0	10.39	95.48	0.63
2008	77919	22.71	11.0	10.77	96.28	0.54
2009	80738	22.93	11.0	10.67	96.75	0.75
2010	81736	22.23	11.5	10.90	96.97	0.99
2011	83312	21.89	12.5	10.92	98.65	0.90
2012	81341	21.14	12.0	13.32	84.23	3.42
2013	81215	20.73	13.4	11.79	83.52	3.65
2014	80769	20.24	10.2	11.20	89.21	2.57

注：领证率是期末已领取独生子女证人数除以全市已婚育龄妇女人数。

12-36 主要年份优抚和社会救济、福利事业

Basic Statistics on Special Care, Social Relief and Welfare in Main Years

项　　目	单位	1990年	1995年	2000年	2005年	2010年	2013年	2014年
优抚事业								
优抚收养性事业单位数	个	1	1	1	1	1	1	1
优抚收养性单位收养人数	人次	19	11	7	8	8	6	7
优抚事业费用	万元	340	213	412	2400	4555	331	345
社会救济								
社会救济人数	人次	4433	7273	19914	23886	36516	24020	21032
年末社会散居孤老残幼人数	人	2026	2444	1596	875	11	239	119
#定期救济对象	人	142	569	29	18	11	239	119
社会救济福利事业费	万元		190	993	6955	21199	18113	22444
自然灾害生活救助费	万元	4.6	70	50	744	139	584	467
社会福利								
社会福利事业单位数	个	1	1	3	36	38	34	37
#民政部门办	个	1	1	3	4	3	3	3
社会福利事业单位收养人数	人	363	351	406	2240	2609	2389	2724
#民政部门办	人	363	351	406	893	1715	1158	1121
社会福利企业单位	个	9	15	20	20	10	7	6
安排“四残”人员就业人数	人	199	239	393	351	321	314	685
社会福利事业单位费用支出	万元					9770	19130	22404
敬老院情况								
全市敬老院个数	个			32	31	35	31	34
年末敬老院供养人数	人			833	1347	894	1231	1603
“五保户”情况								
年末列入“五保户”户数	户			1545	1575	1254	907	847
年末列入“五保户”人数	人			1587	1575	1263	913	854
全年“五保户”费用支出	万元			2198	1594	1536	1882	2123
城乡基层社会保障								
建立社会保障网络镇街数	个	33	24	32	32	32	32	32

注：“五保户”人数及费用支出含敬老院供养人数及费用支出。

12-37 主要年份婚姻登记情况

Basic Statistics on Marriage Registration in Main Years

项　　目	单位	1985年	1990年	1995年	2000年	2005年	2010年	2013年	2014年
准予登记结婚	对	11870	13668	14170	10535	14293	11415	16976	18731
#涉外、华侨、港澳台同胞	对	638	709	510	213	113	79	156	143
准予登记离婚	对				448	1319	1856	1639	3697
#涉外、华侨、港澳台同胞	对						9	48	63

12-38 主要年份环境保护基本情况

Basic Statistics on Environmental Protection in Main Years

项　　目	单 位	1985年	1990年	1995年	2000年	2005年	2010年	2013年	2014年
废水									
废水排放总量	万吨	3100	5259	9681	40703	69049	87953	102937	117539
#工业废水	万吨	2686	4124	5511	11753	21355	29742	23463	28292
污水厂集中处理率	%						71.5	90.9	92.1
废气									
工业废气排放量	亿标立方	34	307	556	1318	1695	2340	3047	3175
一般工业固体废物									
固体废物产生量	万吨	16	112	108	149	284	313	540	549
固体废物处置量	万吨	8	2	1	5	12	15	111	91
固体废物处置率	%	48.2	1.8	0.9	66.9	99.8	4.8	20.6	16.5
固体废物综合利用率	%	37.5	17.9	18.2	63.8	86.5	95.0	78.9	83.4
城市环境质量及污染控制									
空气质量指数	范围值				21-87	24-123	14-108	20-201	23-209
交通干线噪声平均值	db				68.4	67.9	67.7	68.3	68.5
汽车尾气排放达标率	%				81.2	88.1	81.0	83.0	83.0
全市生活垃圾无害化处理率	%						37.3	67.6	66.4

12-39 主要年份社会保险事业情况

Basic Statistics on Social Insurance in Main Years

项　　目	单 位	1995年	2000年	2005年	2010年	2013年	2014年
参加各种社会保险人数	万人次	149.33	338.33	804.71	2726.37	2576.55	2748.28
#失业保险	万人次	6.49	17.84	177.78	279.90	322.44	392.59
养老保险	万人次	8.46	82.95	182.49	421.84	521.91	632.03
医疗保险	万人次	7.60	88.21	189.40	592.27	618.09	615.69
工伤保险	万人次	126.78	136.53	235.10	469.08	496.03	492.28
社会保险基金总收入	万元	18155	127964	491540	1544112	2568687	2870489
#失业保险	万元	60	2732	28954	27008	44983	75679
养老保险	万元	7697	85245	343429	976257	1758837	2085644
医疗保险	万元	2057	23488	82138	333342	643783	572906
工伤保险	万元	8341	15891	35073	62806	121084	136260
社会保险基金总支出	万元	10520	40454	217413	547470	1162430	1312216
#失业保险	万元	16	440	6676	9681	21193	29288
养老保险	万元	7450	24130	135958	194055	473077	622838
医疗保险	万元	1436	3694	51021	299975	572422	540487
工伤保险	万元	1618	11703	22220	41910	95738	119603

注：1. 1997年起养老保险因口径调整，与以前年份不可比。
　　2. 参加各种社会保险总人数包含生育保险人数。

12-40 主要年份最低生活保障情况

Basic Statistics on Minimum Income Relief in Main Years

项　　目	单 位	2005年	2010年	2013年	2014年
居民最低生活保障线	元/人月	320	440	510	510
村民最低生活保障线	元/人月	300	440	510	510
居民最低生活保障户数	户	1911	1599	3025	3062
居民最低生活保障人数	人	4885	3643	6584	6560
居民最低生活保障金支出	万元	790	673	3034	3351
村民最低生活保障户数	户	6705	12214	6768	6217
村民最低生活保障人数	人	17426	30785	15432	13939
村民最低生活保障金支出	万元	2318	5922	6539	7053

12-41 主要年份市政建设情况

Basic Statistics on Municipal Construction in Main Years

项　　目	单 位	1995年	2000年	2005年	2010年	2013年	2014年
水厂日供水能力	万立方米	66	187	480	700	757	748
年末供水管道总长度	公里	1580	2106	3680	16268	20063	19894
全年供水量	万立方米	18802	70046	155100	165607	160831	158864
#生活用水量	万立方米	7361	21433	51100	28560	40418	43222
园林绿地面积	万平方米	800	1396	10298	33092	39165	39000
#公园绿地面积	万平方米				9075	10075	10580
建成区绿化覆盖面积	万平方米	1885	1364	9436	35571	41841	41727
建成区土地面积	平方公里	82.00	147.68	657.17	798.48	902.95	922.02
公园数	个		273	931	1004	1071	1221
公园面积	公顷		1423	2887	11130	10691	14651

注：公园数和公园面积不含森林公园数及其面积。

12-42 主要年份液化石油气及天然气供应情况

Basic Statistics on Supply of Liquefied Petroleum Gas and Natural Gas in Main Years

项　　目	单 位	1995年	2000年	2005年	2010年	2013年	2014年
年末液化石油气用户数	户	63419	110172	144797	956018	934664	936827
#居民用户数	户	62246	106910	144035	870921	912392	882174
全年液化石油气供气量	吨	25935	58287	161930	344762	290356	286098
#家庭用量	吨	18948	22104	24354	188108	176761	222301
年末天然气用户数	户			5027	147047	528733	454127
#居民用户数	户			5000	116239	526230	446671
全年天然气供气量	万立方米			350	23414	62747	67672
#家庭用量	万立方米			45	1600	11661	18052
年末汽车天然气加气站	个				10	16	21
天然气汽车加气全年供应量	万立方米				5324	10762	13429

注：本表2000-2006年为市喜威液化石油气有限公司与市中液石油气有限公司的业务量,2007年起调整为市城市管理局统计口径。

12-43 历年环境保护基本情况

Basic Statistics on Environmental Protection over Years

年 份	降 水 PH均值	酸 雨 PH均值	酸雨频率 (%)	酸雨占 总 降 水 量 (%)	交通干 线噪声 平均值 (db)	工 业 废 水 排放量 (万吨)
1982						1842
1983						2068
1984	6.53					2127
1985						2686
1986					76.8	2416
1987	6.64	5.38		38.4	78.9	3501
1988	4.85	4.72	63.6	75.1	77.6	3029
1989	5.44	5.21	31.0	31.8	74.1	3976
1990	6.15	5.30	29.5	43.3	75.9	4124
1991	5.24	4.78	35.4	30.4	72.2	5506
1992	5.10	4.71	36.8	35.9	76.0	5849
1993	4.93	4.41	22.5	29.1	75.8	6500
1994	5.33	4.81	23.2	25.5	72.6	7057
1995	5.89	5.49	9.2	13.7	70.3	5511
1996	5.83	5.40	14.7	10.9	70.4	6033
1997	4.94	4.84	56.6	76.4	70.6	8930
1998	4.79	4.70	60.3	80.4	70.3	7989
1999	4.97	4.68	40.0	50.5	69.1	11719
2000	4.90	4.67	50.7	56.6	68.7	11753
2001	5.06	4.74	31.6	43.9	68.2	11694
2002	5.47	5.09	29.3	28.8	68.0	25587
2003	4.55	4.44	60.5	77.2	67.9	23389
2004	4.47	4.41	69.6	85.7	68.0	22501
2005	4.07	4.00	65.7	86.2	67.9	21355
2006	3.57-6.57	4.70	50.0	42.4	68.0	24134
2007	5.21	4.36-7.59	54.2	59.2	67.9	91260
2008	4.83	4.65	60.1	63.6	63.6	33359
2009	5.03	4.88	51.8	67.3	63.8	29960
2010	5.11	4.97	52.2	65.3	67.7	29742
2011	5.02	4.59	47.6	31.9	67.8	29091
2012	5.26	4.98	33.7	47.2	67.9	26909
2013	5.23	4.93	30.8	46.7	68.3	23463
2014	5.46	5.16	38.2	40.2	68.5	28292

注：2007年工业废水排放量统计口径变更，与往年不可比。

主要统计指标解释

Explanatory Notes on Main Statistical Indicators

工程技术人员 指在国民经济各行业从事工程技术工作的自然科学技术专业人员，包括：高级工程师、工程师、助理工程师、技术员和未评定职称的技术人员。

农业技术人员 指在国民经济各行业从事农业技术工作的自然科学技术专业人员，包括：高级农艺师、农艺师、助理农艺师、技术员和未评定职称的技术人员。

科学研究人员 指在国民经济各行业从事科学技术活动的科学技术专业人员，包括：正副研究员、助理研究员、研究实习员、技术员和未评定职称的技术人员。

专利申请量 指企业当年向国家知识产权局提出专利申请并被受理项数。

专利授权量 指企业当年获国家知识产权局授予专利权的项数。

发明 专利法及其实施细则所称的发明是指对有关产品、方法或其改进所提出的新的技术方案。

实用新型 专利法及其实施细则所称的实用新型是指对产品的形状、构造或者其结合所提出的适于实用的新的技术方案。

外观设计 专利法及其实施细则所称的外观设计是指对产品的形状、图案、色彩或者其结合所作出的富有美感并适于工业上应用的新设计。

毕业生数 毕业生数是指上学年内，具有学籍的学生学完教学计划规定的全部课程，考试及格，实际毕业的学生数。不包括结业生和肄业生。

招生数 招生数是指新学年开始时，按规定实际招收入学的新生数，不包括重读生和复学生（高等教育包括春秋两季招收的学生）。

在校学生数 是指具有学籍的注册学生总数。

学龄儿童入学率 指调查范围内已入小学学习的学龄儿童占校内外学龄儿童总数（包括弱智儿童在内，但不包括盲聋哑儿童）的比重。

电影放映单位 指具有放映机器设备、固定或不固定的放映场所与专职或兼职的放映技术人员，经有关部门登记批准，经常为一定的观众对象放映电影的机构。包括经批准对外开放进行营业，并与电影发行放映管理机构分帐的专用放映单位和军委系统租片单位。

公共图书馆藏书量 是指本馆已编目的古籍、图书、期刊和报纸的合订本、小册子、手稿，以及缩微制品、录像带、录音带、光盘等视听文献资料数量之和。

医疗机构 是指根据《医疗机构管理条例》的规定，经登记取得《医疗机构执业许可证》的机构。包括医院、社区卫生服务中心（站）、卫生院、门诊所、诊疗所、医务室、村卫生室、妇幼保健院（所、站）、专科疾病防治院（所、站）、急救中心、临床检验中心。

医院 指设有固定床位能收容病人住院并能为病人提供医疗、护理服务的医疗机构。包括县及县以上医院、农村乡卫生院、其他医院三部分。按所属性质分为卫生部门、工业及其他部门、集体经济单位三类。其中县及县以上医院按业务性质分为综合医院和专科医院。

实有床位 是指报告期末固定实有床位数，包括正规床、简易床、监护床、正在消毒和修理床位、因扩建或修理而停用的床位，不包括产科新生儿床、待产室待产床、库存床、观察床、临时加床和病人家属陪伴床。

诊疗人数 是指所有诊疗工作的总人数。包括病人来院就诊的门诊、急诊人次和出诊、下地段、赴家庭病床、到工厂、农村、工地、会议、集体活动等外出诊疗的人次数，以及外出进行的单项健康检查及健康咨询指导人次数。并包括本院职工的诊疗的人次数及局部的单项健康检查人数。

卫生技术人员 指卫生事业机构支付工资的全部固定职工和合同制职工中现任职务为卫生技术工作的专业人员。包括中医师、西医师、中西医结合高级医师、护师、中药师、西药师、检验师、其他技师、中医士、西医士、护士、助产士、中药剂士、西药剂士、检验士、其他技士、其他中医、护理员、中药剂员、西药剂员、检验员，其他初级卫生技术人员。

病死率 是指年内住院病人中死亡人数占出院人数的比例。

刑事案件立案 是指实施违反我国刑事法律的行为，构成犯罪的案件。根据《关于公安机关办理刑事案件程序规定》第一百六十二条，公安机关受理案件后，经过审查，认为有犯罪事实需要追究刑事责任，且属于自己管辖的，由接受单位制作《刑事案件立案报告书》，经县级以上公安机关负责人批准，予以立案。

刑事案件破案 根据《关于公安机关办理刑事案件程序规定》第一百六十六条的规定，刑事案件破案应当具备下列条件：（一）犯罪事实已有证据证明；（二）有证据证明犯罪事实是犯罪嫌疑人实施的；（三）犯罪嫌疑人或者主要犯罪嫌疑人已经归案。

治安案件查处 是指触犯了《中华人民共和国治安管理处罚条例》规定，给社会或个人造成一定危害，公安机关依照相关法律、法规和规定，应当给予处罚的行为事件。

律师 指受聘参加法律顾问处工作，担任法律顾问、刑（民）事代理人、刑事辩护人，办理非诉讼事件、解答法律询问，代写法律事务文书等主要从事律师业务的专职法律工作者和兼职律师。

公证人员 指在国家公证机关依法办理公证事务的司法人员。包括公证员、助理公证员和在公证处工作的其他人员。

调解人员 在人民调解委员会担负调解民间一般民事纠纷和轻微违法行为所引起的纠纷的工作人员。包括调解委员会的委员和调解小组的调解员。

社会保险基金收入 是指根据国家规定，由纳入基本社会保险范围的单位，按照国家规定的缴费基数和缴费比例缴纳的社会统筹基金，以及通过其他方式取得的形成基金来源的收入，包括：单位缴纳的社会统筹基金收入、财政补贴收入、利息收入、其他收入。

社会保险基金支出 是指按照国家政策规定的开支范围和开支标准从社会统筹基金中支付给参加基本社会保险人员个人的费用，以及由于保险关系转移、上下级之间调剂资金等原因而发生的支出。

社会福利事业单位 指集中收养社会孤老、残、幼的机构。包括由民政部门管理的社会福利院、儿童福利院、精神病人福利院和城镇集体办的福利院，以及农村集体举办的敬老院。

社会福利事业单位收养人数包括民政部门管理的和城镇及农村集体举办的社会福利事业单位中收养的老人、少年儿童、缺乏生活自理能力的残疾人员和精神病人。

废水排放总量 包括工业废水和生活污水。工业废水指工业企业在生产、科研过程中向企业外部排放的所有排放口的废水量总和。生活污水指居民或职工在饮用、洗涤、烹饪、清洁卫生等过程中排放的污水量。

十三、能　源

Energy

13-1 主要节能情况

Main Condition of Energy Conservation

单位：±%

年　份	单位生产总值能耗上升或下降	单位生产总值电耗上升或下降	单位工业增加值能耗上升或下降
2006	-4.86	-5.69	-10.66
2007	-5.36	-7.64	-10.07
2008	-5.11	-12.49	-10.94
2009	-4.48	-8.42	-0.26
2010	-2.02	2.84	-10.92
2011	-4.61	-3.40	-6.12
2012	-4.46	-2.85	-11.42
2013	-5.35	-6.17	-8.45
2014	-5.88	-1.50	-9.74

13-2 规模以上工业企业能源加工转换情况（2014年）

Energy Convertion of Industrial Enterprises Above Designated Size (2014)

能源名称	计量单位	工业生产消费量	#加工转换投入合计	火力发电	供热	加工煤制品	能源加工转换产出
原煤	吨	17284611	16718737	12740943	3909697	68097	
煤制品	吨	101491	65790	28908	36882		94010
天然气(气态)	万立方米	64866	62365	59399	2967		
柴油	吨	6359	3329	3329			
燃料油	吨	138	5	5			
润滑油	吨	105					
热力	百万千焦	53533606					64185826
电力	万千瓦时	915416					3436278
煤矸石用于燃料	吨						
城市垃圾用于燃料	吨	1608906	1608906	1608906			
能源合计	吨标准煤	16144979	12787067	10223300	2507579	56188	6462450

13-3 全市规模以上工业企业能源购进、消费及库存量（2014年）

Energy Purchases, Consumptton and Stock of Industrial Enterprises of Whole Municipality Above Designated Size (2014)

能源品种	单 位	购进量	消费量	#工业生产	年末库存量
原煤	吨	19003092	18996655	18990799	845100
煤制品	吨	98857	136498	136039	2902
焦炭	吨	7079	7232	7232	485
天然气(气态)	万立方米	108345	108354	107274	22
液化天然气(液态)	吨	1771	1826	1668	
汽油	吨	19199	19490	3213	149
煤油	吨	218	231	200	3
柴油	吨	88241	89184	61615	4992
燃料油	吨	41288	35702	34348	15380
液化石油气	吨	13576	13725	12438	303
润滑油	吨	322	323	323	13
溶剂油	吨	11	21	21	
石油焦	吨	693	720	720	18
热力	百万千焦	6380229	60088414	59924871	
电力	万千瓦时	2340598	3217490	3080077	
城市垃圾用于燃料	吨	1603735	1608906	1608906	20275
生物质废料用于燃料	吨	77330	76272	75932	163
其他燃料	吨标准煤	1139	1394	1366	

13-4 全市规模以上工业企业分行业能源消费量（2014年）

Total Energy Consumption of Industrial Enterprises Above Designated Size by Sector (2014)

行业	原煤（吨）	煤制品（吨）	焦炭（吨）	天然气（气态）（万立方米）	液化天然气（液态）（吨）	汽油（吨）
总计	18996655	136498	7232	108354	1826	19490
采矿业						
煤炭开采和洗选业						
石油和天然气开采业						
黑色金属矿采选业						
有色金属矿采选业						
非金属矿采选业						
开采辅助活动						
其他采矿业						
制造业						
农副食品加工业	191549	339		218		135
食品制造业	1803	83		1859		239
酒、饮料和精制茶制造业	731			1828	108	15
烟草制品业						
纺织业	699475			286	3	1024
纺织服装、服饰业	7366	3537		228		984
皮革、毛皮、羽毛及其制品和制鞋业	2385			413		1805
木材加工和木、竹、藤、棕、草制品业	2646					111
家具制造业	197			552		634
造纸和纸制品业	7808263	72472		406		866
印刷和记录媒介复制业	4969	27		107		524
文教、工美、体育和娱乐用品制造业	4546			411	93	631
石油加工、炼焦和核燃料加工业				199		
化学原料和化学制品制造业	66203		1868	730		841
医药制造业				326		71
化学纤维制造业	3692			10		19
橡胶和塑料制品业	77774	8255		549	46	1537
非金属矿物制品业	50978	51785		29384		249
黑色金属冶炼和压延加工业			4197	18	665	131
有色金属冶炼和压延加工业				1204		298
金属制品业			1168	1996	264	842
通用设备制造业				373	4	1494
专用设备制造业				340	28	783
汽车制造业				766	1	291
铁路、船舶、航空航天和其他运输设备制造业				51	528	10
电气机械和器材制造业	1929			1499	8	1690
计算机、通信和其他电子设备制造业				2116	77	3409
仪器仪表制造业				111		359
其他制造业	36850					101
废弃资源综合利用业						
金属制品、机械和设备修理业						
电力、热力、燃气及水生产和供应业						
电力、热力生产和供应业	10035299			62351		201
燃气生产和供应业				23		7
水的生产和供应业						191

13-4 续表 1

(2014年)

行业	煤油(吨)	柴油(吨)	燃料油(吨)	液化石油气(吨)	润滑油(吨)	溶剂油(吨)
总计	231	89184	35702	13725	323	21
采矿业						
煤炭开采和洗选业						
石油和天然气开采业						
黑色金属矿采选业						
有色金属矿采选业						
非金属矿采选业						
开采辅助活动						
其他采矿业						
制造业						
农副食品加工业		1581	419	5		
食品制造业		1316		162		
酒、饮料和精制茶制造业		1082	30			
烟草制品业						
纺织业		2790	1876	22		
纺织服装、服饰业	28	5046	786	327		
皮革、毛皮、羽毛及其制品和制鞋业		4437	1561	417		
木材加工和木、竹、藤、棕、草制品业		580				
家具制造业	1	1139	51	898		
造纸和纸制品业	9	11178	2206	242	4	7
印刷和记录媒介复制业		2372	71	5		
文教、工美、体育和娱乐用品制造业		4397	706	221		
石油加工、炼焦和核燃料加工业		12	198			
化学原料和化学制品制造业		3601	3077	41		
医药制造业		38				
化学纤维制造业		142				
橡胶和塑料制品业	3	4480	2427	303		
非金属矿物制品业		4026	19900	936		
黑色金属冶炼和压延加工业		67				
有色金属冶炼和压延加工业		2298	884	163		
金属制品业	57	5176	858	1563	86	
通用设备制造业	108	2926	41	1110	76	1
专用设备制造业	10	1628		31	15	
汽车制造业	4	859		1	6	
铁路、船舶、航空航天和其他运输设备制造业		3370		48		
电气机械和器材制造业	3	4919	482	3826		
计算机、通信和其他电子设备制造业	8	14096	131	3370	23	12
仪器仪表制造业		735		19		
其他制造业		1937			8	
废弃资源综合利用业						
金属制品、机械和设备修理业						
电力、热力、燃气及水生产和供应业						
电力、热力生产和供应业		2833		15	105	
燃气生产和供应业						
水的生产和供应业		124				

13-4 续表 2

(2014年)

行业	石油焦（吨）	热力（百万千焦）	电力（万千瓦时）	城市垃圾用于燃料（吨）	生物质废料用于燃料（吨）	其他燃料（吨标准煤）
总计	720	60088414	3217490	1608906	76272	1394
采矿业						
煤炭开采和洗选业						
石油和天然气开采业						
黑色金属矿采选业						
有色金属矿采选业						
非金属矿采选业						
开采辅助活动						
其他采矿业						
制造业						
农副食品加工业		1215502	37845		3843	
食品制造业		24380	20298		6416	
酒、饮料和精制茶制造业		300739	13718			
烟草制品业						
纺织业		4513555	76794		3651	
纺织服装、服饰业		30816	54594		18909	
皮革、毛皮、羽毛及其制品和制鞋业		688746	100365		1425	
木材加工和木、竹、藤、棕、草制品业			9247		5837	
家具制造业			57534		1854	
造纸和纸制品业	720	52312910	808598		6716	
印刷和记录媒介复制业			41154		904	
文教、工美、体育和娱乐用品制造业			100396			
石油加工、炼焦和核燃料加工业			344			
化学原料和化学制品制造业		503087	48056		1080	
医药制造业			2834		4108	
化学纤维制造业			8170		1688	
橡胶和塑料制品业		442171	259393		11152	
非金属矿物制品业			111329		4724	
黑色金属冶炼和压延加工业			10139			
有色金属冶炼和压延加工业			21339			
金属制品业			110732		925	
通用设备制造业			70310			
专用设备制造业			46820			255
汽车制造业			26522			
铁路、船舶、航空航天和其他运输设备制造业		55906	10909			
电气机械和器材制造业		285	202694		2269	1139
计算机、通信和其他电子设备制造业		317	665713		771	
仪器仪表制造业			40501			
其他制造业			11461			
废弃资源综合利用业			75			
金属制品、机械和设备修理业			50			
电力、热力、燃气及水生产和供应业						
电力、热力生产和供应业			209523	1608906		
燃气生产和供应业			1293			
水的生产和供应业			38741			

13-5 主要年份全社会用电量

Total Consumption of Electricity in Main Years

单位：万千瓦时

项　　目	2005年	2010年	2013年	2014年
全社会用电量总计	4198289	5619996	6225139	6609853
#各行业用电量合计	3855742	5036303	5504528	5793469
第一产业	9761	10279	23853	18316
第二产业	3397588	4317267	4602716	4884314
第三产业	448393	708757	877959	890839
城乡居民生活用电量合计	342547	583693	720611	816385
各行业用电分类				
农、林、牧、渔业	9761	10279	23853	18316
工　业	3374306	4262339	4537990	4829488
#轻工业	1357858	1821542	1697956	1977248
重工业	2016448	2440797	2876068	2852241
#采矿业	8112	8044	5265	3773
制造业	3044575	3953169	4177734	4463609
电力、燃气及水的生产和供应业	321619	301126	354991	362106
#电力、热力的生产和供应业	240737	183361	252465	253982
#电厂生产全部耗用电量	41656	51096	53108	52677
线路损失电量	190736	132265	199357	201305
燃气生产和供应业	654	1778	2604	1484
水的生产和供应业	80228	115987	99922	106640
建筑业	23282	54928	64726	54826
交通运输、仓储和邮政业	14425	26524	42436	45191
交通运输业	8614	16173	25795	26210
仓储业	2084	5774	11526	13949
邮政业	3727	4577	5115	5031
信息传输、计算机服务和软件业	15277	35085	52583	57879
商业住宿和餐饮业	282238	376037	477922	485423
批发和零售业	148555	194549	284327	309266
住宿和餐饮业	130153	181488	193595	176157
金融、房地产、商务及居民服务业	65223	117690	112448	101884
金融业	16158	14156	8547	7996
房地产业	21976	23489	25953	19693
租赁和商务服务、居民服务和其他服务	27089	80045	77948	74195
公共事业及管理组织	71230	153421	192570	200462
#科学研究、技术服务和地质勘查业	4550	2950	2312	2991
#地质勘查业	248	45	137	166
水利、环境和公共设施管理业	26633	56514	73884	69467
#水利管理业	12157	5208	12768	8843
教育、文化、体育和娱乐业	13596	29655	41562	47264
#教育	4793	8615	32979	37895
卫生、社会保障和社会福利业	12151	8964	26918	30151
公共管理和社会组织、国际组织	14300	55338	47894	50589

13-6 规模以上工业综合能源消费量（2013-2014年）

Overall Energy Consumpiton of Industrial Enterprises above Designated Size (2013-2014)

单位：万吨标准煤

指　　标	2013年	2014年
合　计	1452.58	1448.37
采矿业		
煤炭开采和洗选业		
石油和天然气开采业		
黑色金属矿采选业		
有色金属矿采选业		
非金属矿采选业		
开采辅助活动		
其他采矿业		
制造业	904.34	917.17
农副食品加工业	22.29	20.41
食品制造业	6.20	5.43
酒、饮料和精制茶制造业	5.46	5.25
烟草制品业		
纺织业	57.25	54.30
纺织服装、服饰业	8.99	8.93
皮革、毛皮、羽毛及其制品和制鞋业	17.25	14.81
木材加工和木、竹、藤、棕、草制品业	1.87	1.64
家具制造业	7.20	7.64
造纸和纸制品业	502.46	507.31
印刷和记录媒介复制业	3.90	5.51
文教、工美、体育和娱乐用品制造业	12.41	13.05
石油加工、炼焦和核燃料加工业	0.21	0.33
化学原料和化学制品制造业	13.88	14.11
医药制造业	0.93	0.98
化学纤维制造业	1.14	1.31
橡胶和塑料制品业	36.57	39.43
非金属矿物制品业	59.63	58.08
黑色金属冶炼和压延加工业	1.61	1.74
有色金属冶炼和压延加工业	5.44	4.60
金属制品业	13.21	16.28
通用设备制造业	6.80	9.10
专用设备制造业	5.15	5.99
汽车制造业	3.64	4.14
铁路、船舶、航空航天和其他运输设备制造业	1.84	2.08
电气机械和器材制造业	25.27	26.82
计算机、通信和其他电子设备制造业	77.12	81.65
仪器仪表制造业	4.24	4.48
其他制造业	2.40	1.73
废弃资源综合利用业	0.003	0.01
金属制品、机械和设备修理业		0.01
电力、热力、燃气及水生产和供应业	548.24	531.20
电力、热力生产和供应业	543.43	526.32
燃气生产和供应业	0.02	0.15
水的生产和供应业	4.79	4.73

主要统计指标解释

Explanatory Notes on Main Statistical Indicators

能源购进量　指能源使用企业（单位）在报告期购进、用于本企业（单位）消费的各种能源数量。本指标解释不涉及能源贸易企业的能源购进量。

工业企业能源消费量　指工业企业在工业生产活动和非工业生产活动中消费的能源，包括工业生产活动中作为燃料、动力、原料、辅助材料使用的能源，生产工艺中使用的能源，用于能源加工转换的能源；非工业生产活动中使用的能源。

工业生产能源消费量　指工业企业为进行工业生产活动所消费的能源。主要包括：

（1）用于本企业产品生产、工业性作业的能源，包括用作原料、材料、燃料、动力的能源；作为能源加工转换企业，还包括用作加工转换的能源。

（2）产品生产过程中作为辅助材料使用的能源。

（3）生产工艺过程使用的能源。

（4）新技术研究、新产品试制、科学试验使用的能源。

（5）为了工业生产活动而在进行的各种修理过程中使用的能源。

（6）生产区内的劳动保护用能等。

能源库存量　指能源使用企业（单位）在报告期的某时间点所拥有的、用于企业（单位）消费的各种能源的库存量。本指标解释不涉及能源生产企业的能源产成品库存和能源贸易企业的能源商品库存。

综合能源消费量　指企业（单位）在报告期内工业生产实际消费的各种能源（扣除能源加工转换和能源回收利用等重复因素）的总和。计算综合能源消费量时，需要将各种能源品种的消费量换算成按照标准计量单位（如：吨标准煤）计量的消费量。

能源加工转换投入　能源加工转换，指为了特定的用途，将一种能源（一般为一次能源），经过一定的工艺，加工或转换成另外一种能源（二次能源）。

火力发电的加工转换投入　指火力发电企业为发电而投入发电锅炉燃烧室的燃料数量。通常燃料主要有：煤炭、燃料油、天然气、焦炉煤气、高炉煤气、转炉煤气、生物质燃料、可燃废弃物和可燃垃圾等。

供热的加工转换投入　指热力生产企业为生产热力而投入供热锅炉燃烧室的燃料数量，以及热电联产机组按照热电产出比例分摊的用于供热的燃料投入量。

加工煤制品的加工转换投入　指煤制品生产企业，在不改变煤炭基本属性的情况下，为生产型煤（煤球、煤饼、蜂窝煤）、煤粉、水煤浆等煤制品而使用的原煤或其他煤炭产品的数量。

能源加工转换产出量　指一次能源经过加工转换产出的二次能源产品（包括不作能源使用的其他副产品和联产品）的数量，比如火力发电产出的电力，热电联产同时产出的电力、蒸汽、热水，原煤洗选产出的洗精煤、洗中煤、洗煤泥等，炼焦产出的焦炭、焦炉煤气和其他焦化产品（煤焦油、粗苯等），炼油和煤制油产出的汽油、煤油、柴油、燃料油、液化石油气、炼厂干气 、石脑油、润滑油、石蜡、溶剂油、石油焦、石油沥青等，制气（指煤气生产）产出的发生炉煤气、焦炭和其他焦化产品（煤焦油、粗苯等）。

十四、镇街主要指标

Main Indicators of Towns

14-1 镇街生产总值

Gross Domestic Product by Town

单位：万元

镇街	(1991年) 地区生产总值	第一产业	第二产业	第三产业	(1992年) 地区生产总值	第一产业	第二产业	第三产业
全市	959073	134523	503220	321330	1108922	144115	592701	372106
莞城	22046	174	16612	5260	28881	108	22263	6510
石龙	25154	907	17669	6578	29467	1026	21163	7278
虎门	44900	10059	16412	18429	56539	10336	24781	21422
东城	23500	7179	13793	2528	32770	7362	21392	4016
万江	18518	3874	11653	2991	27997	3968	18928	5102
南城	13339	2219	8181	2939	18147	1973	12681	3493
中堂	14889	3300	9065	2524	19902	4360	10669	4873
望牛墩	11950	2794	7394	1762	13789	2854	8683	2252
麻涌	24449	10489	11478	2482	26907	9797	14294	2816
石碣	12556	2686	7660	2210	16967	2888	11140	2939
高埗	11546	3352	5163	3031	14295	4017	6503	3775
道滘	15659	4540	9542	1577	19009	4805	12003	2201
洪梅	6492	3879	1872	741	6906	2441	3435	1030
沙田	12616	6467	4552	1597	16779	6511	7850	2417
厚街	31303	5679	22403	3221	38272	6064	28528	3680
长安	24850	7961	13185	3704	36298	8980	21883	5435
寮步	23700	9030	8979	5691	30083	9256	12627	8200
大岭山	10557	5918	3123	1516	16175	6342	4928	4905
大朗	19481	11277	4870	3334	24694	10104	9836	4754
黄江	20403	2765	15888	1750	28355	3244	22864	2247
樟木头	10515	10515	2107	6426	13972	2212	8536	3224
清溪	8673	2076	4428	2169	12742	2405	6936	3401
塘厦	17826	6128	9049	2649	30454	6300	19988	4166
凤岗	8676	2698	5550	428	12119	3257	8146	716
谢岗	9472	2019	5197	2256	7178	2339	4236	603
常平	38008	13134	14511	10363	45046	11625	20103	13317
桥头	14030	4083	8114	1833	22099	5429	10336	6334
横沥	11125	2499	6349	2277	15673	2710	[illegible]	[illegible]
东坑	16245	3544	11393	1308	22332	3368	[illegible]	[illegible]
企石	16155	3731	9575	2849	21159	4699	[illegible]	[illegible]
石排	16123	2350	10727	3046	18091	2704	[illegible]	[illegible]
茶山	13328	3385	7146	2797	16377	416[illegible]	[illegible]	[illegible]

注：各镇街合计不等于全市数，下同。

14-1 续表 1

单位：万元

镇街	(1993年) 地区生产总值	第一产业	第二产业	第三产业	(1994年) 地区生产总值	第一产业	第二产业	第三产业
全市	1570491	143953	873114	553424	2170340	174796	1194928	800616
莞城	41307		32838	8469	55021		43120	11901
石龙	34182	582	21188	12412	48891	216	32738	15937
虎门	74808	11281	37710	25816	103070	14350	51597	37123
东城	37567	4379	25901	7287	44963	5223	30065	9675
万江	39317	4818	26939	7561	45953	5499	31186	9268
南城	23341	2767	16312	4262	46416	2811	38511	5094
中堂	31352	7282	16982	7089	34819	6271	19472	9076
望牛墩	15717	2642	10196	2879	18449	2796	11974	3679
麻涌	34553	9305	22223	3025	42676	9160	27917	5599
石碣	23877	2542	16311	5024	34401	2816	24582	7003
高埗	17843	4751	8347	4745	22368	5495	10877	5996
道滘	24306	5086	15471	3749	37062	5698	27835	14072
洪梅	8069	2265	4292	1512	9020	2406	4756	1858
沙田	24446	6574	14434	3438	31950	6196	20646	5107
厚街	57912	6707	44408	6796	101289	7615	77637	16037
长安	49862	9995	31962	7905	68914	11024	46939	10951
寮步	46311	9423	21926	14962	63089	12428	30205	20456
大岭山	22611	6717	7660	8234	27722	6725	11258	9739
大朗	32720	10237	15152	7331	46550	13958	21052	11540
黄江	37008	3021	30171	3816	47096	3254	39031	4811
樟木头	18265	1361	13994	2910	23438	1680	18008	3750
清溪	19533	3299	12076	4158	30510	4230	20391	5889
塘厦	41635	4353	31001	6281	80870	6396	65620	8854
凤岗	16961	3282	12778	901	24520	4166	19054	1300
谢岗	12063	2367	8997	699	16093	3365	11143	1585
常平	67921	12564	34518	20839	100294	13561	62109	24624
桥头	27654	5023	15085	7546	40632	6225	22445	11962
横沥	23825	23825	2604	13815	33565	3922	17444	12198
东坑	33565	4073	25007	4485	36161	4245	26665	5251
企石	28573	5167	17684	5722	34915	6545	21854	6516
石排	25462	2992	17949	4521	31920	3699	21172	7049
[illegible]山	21196	4908	12096	4192	30233	6017	18221	5995

14-1 续表 2

单位：万元

镇 街	(1995年)				(1996年)			
	地区生产总值	第一产业	第二产业	第三产业	地区生产总值	第一产业	第二产业	第三产业
全 市	2962892	214306	1669723	1078863	3617502	248645	1994826	1374031
莞 城	69318		52710	16608	72335		50523	21812
石 龙	70501	318	46550	23633	72190	303	36303	35584
虎 门	130282	18388	68784	43110	158257	25193	85444	47620
东 城	85114	6208	57257	21649	100581	6744	66136	27701
万 江	55648	6705	37884	11059	63649	8488	40934	14227
南 城	83707	2938	63407	17362	103785	3667	79347	20771
中 堂	41537	6593	23358	11585	50533	7418	28908	14206
望牛墩	21961	3197	14061	4703	25963	3440	16512	6011
麻 涌	47340	11783	28584	6973	49764	15494	26884	7386
石 碣	46831	3332	33206	10293	66081	3495	45532	17054
高 埗	28324	6213	14403	7708	36274	6945	19348	9981
道 滘	47605	5698	27835	14072	55596	6031	35931	13634
洪 梅	15209	2667	6923	5619	16733	2908	7657	6168
沙 田	42922	7741	29376	5806	49023	10655	32354	6015
厚 街	118353	9670	90642	18041	140036	10906	83151	45979
长 安	93323	12505	65233	15585	131672	12882	97066	21724
寮 步	75398	14727	32311	28360	85876	15651	37022	33203
大岭山	39228	8485	17265	13478	49383	9773	21083	18527
大 朗	66807	17319	25844	23644	78506	16982	29641	31883
黄 江	61098	3708	46392	10998	63391	3929	46558	12904
樟木头	31914	2662	24710	4543	41323	3443	32232	5647
清 溪	52550	5721	35627	11202	82953	6083	55419	21451
塘 厦	112158	6909	90588	14661	139903	9900	112916	17087
凤 岗	37051	4767	30135	2149	48015	5521	39670	2824
谢 岗	18872	4356	12655	1861	25536	5213	18242	2081
常 平	135315	18444	87856	29015	146594	19303	86033	41258
桥 头	54012	7206	30626	16180	64694	8418	38393	17883
横 沥	44663	4484	23559	16620	54922	4717	29045	21161
东 坑	34654	5179	19727	9748	50965	5274	32218	13473
企 石	44588	7760	28861	7967	54066	8947	35535	9584
石 排	34349	4898	20547	8904	37946	5718	21459	10769
茶 山	41484	6017	18221	5995	51339	7159	24892	9433

14-1 续表 3

单位：万元

镇街	(1997年)				(1998年)			
	地区生产总值	第一产业	第二产业	第三产业	地区生产总值	第一产业	第二产业	第三产业
全市	4485981	256388	2432816	1796777	5579965	259437	3056779	2263749
莞城	80298		49962	30336	110076		49677	60399
石龙	95560	293	48361	46906	133953	116	77910	55927
虎门	246823	25799	130963	90061	362826	29535	176729	156562
东城	125730	5850	78959	40921	161819	5246	105142	51431
万江	69516	8749	42333	18434	82239	9424	50075	22922
南城	130392	3490	103126	23776	160524	3933	128850	27741
中堂	61741	7610	35991	18140	76980	7727	45359	23894
望牛墩	30854	3780	19390	7684	36531	3941	22769	9821
麻涌	52217	15965	29345	6907	62531	16443	35485	10603
石碣	85990	3782	54674	27534	109255	3852	70872	34531
高埗	46630	7586	26579	12465	60242	8235	36383	15624
道滘	69424	6383	47525	15516	80887	6756	54039	20092
洪梅	20052	4501	7602	7949	23134	4607	9569	8958
沙田	54881	11342	36602	6936	71203	16829	42167	12207
厚街	184205	11448	96880	75877	247177	12150	146229	88798
长安	180377	13111	134235	33031	245676	13562	183031	49083
寮步	103656	17341	45112	41203	129731	18768	60452	50511
大岭山	65246	10538	31884	22824	83268	9134	45040	29094
大朗	95301	19093	38996	37212	122409	15008	53085	54316
黄江	67618	4139	47073	16406	83585	4244	58492	20849
樟木头	55682	4725	43020	7936	71299	5333	51615	14351
清溪	120961	7519	84276	29166	160483	7802	115314	37367
塘厦	178757	11467	140870	26420	230580	12121	177569	40890
凤岗	63066	5925	51486	5655	79286	6187	65440	7659
谢岗	29488	6379	20521	2588	34881	6958	24888	3035
常平	185390	20195	98068	67127	231059	19811	131252	79995
桥头	79685	8523	51919	19243	96661	9712	61140	25809
横沥	67894	6411	34892	26591	81263	5364	45427	30472
东坑	63718	4810	44682	14226	78576	5726	54359	18491
企石	62625	9562	42240	10823	72065	9827	47551	14687
石排	43477	6463	23530	13484	53842	6606	28932	18304
茶山	63955	9321	39524	15110	77319	9878	47785	19656

14-1 续表 4

单位：万元

镇街	(1999年)				(2000年)			
	地区生产总值	第一产业	第二产业	第三产业	地区生产总值	第一产业	第二产业	第三产业
全市	6672386	257863	3670519	2744004	8202531	259087	4507072	3436372
莞城	131005		58104	72901	184225		67030	117195
石龙	157715	349	86171	71195	184256	189	98240	85827
虎门	442633	31013	213607	198014	532946	30479	263928	238539
东城	207432	4126	125159	78147	262854	4233	153667	104954
万江	97379	9435	59636	28308	138724	11604	85526	41594
南城	198820	2756	149678	46386	233013	3119	171413	58481
中堂	94412	7001	57217	30194	123213	7032	76571	39610
望牛墩	43303	4012	26738	12553	51516	4072	31399	16045
麻涌	75449	12466	44768	18215	90816	12213	45965	32638
石碣	137148	3866	88152	45130	175180	4021	111038	60121
高埗	78709	8792	50131	19786	102516	9155	67888	25473
道滘	93751	7151	61687	24913	109999	7569	67841	34589
洪梅	26118	4162	11872	10084	29921	4383	14095	11443
沙田	86339	12167	53505	20667	109128	12714	71503	24911
厚街	300721	12412	171495	116814	405317	12705	221947	170665
长安	332335	13820	240690	77825	419347	14256	299650	105441
寮步	161782	19944	82582	59256	202379	20732	110577	71070
大岭山	108469	9238	67662	31569	138789	9742	89991	39056
大朗	156427	16699	69193	70535	201504	17826	94065	89613
黄江	97621	4410	67206	26005	123331	5243	83748	34340
樟木头	94385	4225	64138	26021	147697	4639	71921	71138
清溪	206524	8790	151219	46515	303131	9984	231303	61844
塘厦	288110	12783	217897	57430	363971	13486	272234	78251
凤岗	100753	6267	61392	33094	128298	6336	79138	42824
谢岗	42142	3610	29017	9515	50174	3975	35779	10420
常平	302805	15703	166347	120755	395318	16116	218229	160974
桥头	111892	9062	69595	33235	130380	9093	82261	39026
横沥	97209	6178	55276	35756	116749	8593	62314	45842
东坑	101287	5363	65010	30913	118430	6241	76250	35940
企石	85313	10000	51789	23524	99467	11339	58897	29231
石排	69030	6772	37874	24384	87817	6913	48532	32372
茶山	90250	9514	55468	25268	105432	10712	64726	29994

14-1 续表 5

单位：万元

镇街	(2001年)				(2002年)			
	地区生产总值	第一产业	第二产业	第三产业	地区生产总值	第一产业	第二产业	第三产业
全市	9918905	260968	5405092	4252845	11869374	248791	6488109	5132474
莞城	222233		80203	142030	312742		76890	235852
石龙	215738	150	115691	99897	248664	144	135163	113357
虎门	618557	30469	304781	283307	717425	26838	350636	339951
东城	342044	3785	188628	149631	466960	2110	232502	232348
万江	175693	13015	90857	71821	213919	11026	106945	95948
南城	286473	2929	211622	71922	350029	2711	262431	84887
中堂	153366	7155	95677	50533	194263	5908	122819	65536
望牛墩	60921	3540	36872	20509	73104	3591	43299	26214
麻涌	127061	12298	74806	39957	173557	1002	120426	43079
石碣	243163	4139	150613	88411	340162	4141	209830	126191
高埗	133362	9477	90730	33155	173004	9701	120415	42888
道滘	128327	8011	76692	43624	153201	8479	87039	57683
洪梅	34245	4587	16543	13115	41756	4793	21676	15287
沙田	142060	13641	92266	36153	182363	13912	119778	48673
厚街	483117	13088	253149	216880	583689	13976	297707	272006
长安	529219	14496	371263	143460	679022	14622	469032	195368
寮步	252526	21246	143824	87456	314871	20276	182688	111907
大岭山	194021	10089	133489	50443	251078	5741	178811	66526
大朗	264929	17764	128283	118882	341930	15525	181234	145171
黄江	154595	5176	98438	50981	199781	5288	122001	72492
樟木头	176062	4460	84195	87407	210845	5545	101237	104063
清溪	393471	10517	302613	80341	501941	11106	382584	108251
塘厦	457175	13796	335872	107507	573947	13603	425078	135266
凤岗	162854	6400	97540	58914	205006	2035	126903	76068
谢岗	58323	4115	41585	12623	71092	5665	40790	24637
常平	493419	16451	272983	203985	557039	16077	310537	230425
桥头	151979	8366	98054	45559	179442	7245	118564	53633
横沥	140251	9252	74148	56851	168932	9380	90576	68976
东坑	132805	6013	84256	42535	149147	5438	92587	51122
企石	115314	12403	63421	39490	127616	9088	68807	49721
石排	107585	6925	61859	38801	131394	6967	75798	48629
茶山	123931	9801	75341	38789	153215	9801	91916	51498

14-1 续表 6

单位：万元

镇街	(2003年) 地区生产总值	第一产业	第二产业	第三产业	(2004年) 地区生产总值	第一产业	第二产业	第三产业
全市	14525187	228165	7981954	6315068	18060258	227087	10160382	7672789
莞城	415993		80802	335191	552370		94035	458335
石龙	287713	116	167126	120471	317521	51	186652	130820
虎门	905165	27106	462105	415954	1139827	27168	598000	514659
东城	652408	1657	314094	336657	897727	900	411172	485655
万江	269593	9622	129625	130346	329849	5617	156431	167801
南城	452911	2743	314752	135416	741609	1869	349496	390244
中堂	256251	7013	162945	86292	338808	5956	206693	126159
望牛墩	87872	3520	50846	33506	106086	3550	59709	42827
麻涌	234612	8769	177540	48303	292911	8664	226131	58116
石碣	463023	4253	290495	168275	590604	3649	381862	205093
高埗	224078	9891	157949	56238	282716	9943	202317	70456
道滘	178954	8975	100566	69413	217400	9499	119688	88213
洪梅	53960	5113	29668	19179	76686	4770	41140	30776
沙田	236769	13944	155438	67387	310921	13975	202383	94563
厚街	721188	12275	374482	334431	878666	12341	454284	412041
长安	887947	14863	603308	269776	1162826	15040	759582	388204
寮步	394322	13167	234806	146349	498253	5327	303435	189491
大岭山	322872	4937	226565	91370	447412	4571	313857	128984
大朗	443891	10640	240983	192268	574604	6986	325826	241792
黄江	258682	4567	152903	101212	331432	3294	187369	140769
樟木头	250877	4863	119145	126869	291893	4350	139729	147814
清溪	645553	11218	495035	139300	848426	9610	660589	178227
塘厦	710030	13565	526730	169735	882099	13700	653816	214583
凤岗	284608	2048	170574	111986	373309	2015	220434	150860
谢岗	91482	4266	51312	35904	119007	4328	69024	45655
常平	657385	12627	377679	267079	796109	10792	468642	316674
桥头	213712	5419	134937	73356	264849	4495	144282	116072
横沥	205872	9602	117554	78716	253887	9075	153884	90928
东坑	181394	8423	113270	59701	230057	7943	145998	76116
企石	142717	5216	72284	65217	167279	3848	80461	82970
石排	157729	7144	92020	58565	190127	7259	109953	72915
茶山	195098	8607	118895	67596	268473	7413	161070	99990

14-1 续表 7

单位：万元

镇街	(2005年) 地区生产总值	第一产业	第二产业	第三产业	(2006年) 地区生产总值	第一产业	第二产业	第三产业
全市	21831961	205546	12278624	9347791	26279791	120089	15065985	11093717
莞城	617849		153367	464482	712319		230144	482174
石龙	349301	141	194749	154411	384329	35	213392	170902
虎门	1283052	22937	668632	591483	1492628	11446	763086	718096
东城	1049758	480	473888	575389	1264850	427	571728	692694
万江	375471	4209	164099	207164	440346	4711	187932	247702
南城	1016644	1900	440431	574313	1229016	1995	508223	718798
中堂	424212	6122	276399	141691	507968	6428	332766	168774
望牛墩	126751	3511	73191	50049	156949	3480	87638	65831
麻涌	387211	8588	310275	68348	494018	7106	398466	88445
石碣	728816	3782	491498	233535	868731	3091	588622	277018
高埗	366593	10020	254017	102556	456695	6552	320225	129918
道滘	255589	8753	143285	103551	301036	9568	174820	116648
洪梅	102660	3939	61138	37583	123863	4082	77274	42507
沙田	364800	13695	240822	110283	442784	12585	293854	136345
厚街	1033929	11722	531019	491188	1199117	6929	609223	582965
长安	1339428	9492	917732	412204	1539236	7505	1042139	489592
寮步	598969	7765	364261	226943	739610	1136	451671	286803
大岭山	547734	4102	370108	173524	675091	2329	431260	241502
大朗	707369	14112	411161	282096	850356	1491	499588	349277
黄江	364377	3065	220654	140658	441152	741	276062	164349
樟木头	330537	3463	157434	169640	393688	600	185556	207532
清溪	984943	9036	761281	214626	1097986	8012	828219	261755
塘厦	1057175	13661	771724	271790	1186644	12312	830537	343794
凤岗	517427	1762	320177	195488	623929	1750	373375	248804
谢岗	148917	4467	91026	53424	192841	4795	118714	69332
常平	951464	10062	556932	384470	1119659	6338	644544	468777
桥头	287240	4495	168473	114271	388604	1387	210763	176454
横沥	304870	8593	195659	100619	373304	7274	242406	123624
东坑	261238	11543	165441	84254	295233	5703	194653	94877
企石	200581	3129	102183	95269	244027	2266	129255	112506
石排	234709	7268	128132	99308	294009	7283	154259	132467
茶山	305183	6652	190620	107911	384988	3215	245078	136695

14-1 续表 8

单位：万元

镇街	(2007年) 地区生产总值	第一产业	第二产业	第三产业	(2008年) 地区生产总值	第一产业	第二产业	第三产业
全市	31600489	118991	17546573	13934924	37036004	148251	19016068	17871685
莞城	897597		298250	599347	1015311		294311	721000
石龙	427216	10	235821	191385	475742	7	239943	235792
虎门	1846638	10373	936639	899626	2153489	11940	1093014	1048535
东城	1559123	377	699730	859017	1816793	339	773623	1042831
万江	520636	3405	221314	295917	604659	3702	262498	338459
南城	1425257	2015	583496	839747	1632407	1285	618209	1012913
中堂	588085	6553	379181	202351	659949	6760	419455	233734
望牛墩	193635	3462	105983	84190	236495	3359	127759	105377
麻涌	651344	5985	537412	107947	834681	7564	693959	133158
石碣	994532	3096	670790	320646	1082524	2795	694349	385380
高埗	568276	6530	384637	177109	690604	6526	442377	241701
道滘	362268	8202	211240	142826	439328	7218	240510	191600
洪梅	163384	4281	110958	48145	206785	4381	147969	54435
沙田	515106	12403	327706	174997	588063	12863	337140	238060
厚街	1420026	7270	719643	693113	1616483	7971	797404	811108
长安	1770272	7746	1152474	610052	2029075	4979	1158887	865209
寮步	886584	1118	531815	353650	1038493	2141	584767	451585
大岭山	822554	2241	502679	317634	960138	2248	554712	403178
大朗	1025864	2098	592111	431655	1100875	877	688340	411658
黄江	556305	740	347972	207593	721414	724	438204	282486
樟木头	461719	505	228647	232567	507743	311	253050	254382
清溪	1266762	6207	924401	336153	1417816	5170	966538	446108
塘厦	1365736	11206	903107	451422	1602945	10447	980030	612468
凤岗	747757	1752	409163	336843	901696	1725	472782	427189
谢岗	239771	5178	143093	91500	273944	9273	160217	104454
常平	1311744	6665	747353	557726	1495652	6058	796227	693366
桥头	467790	1326	242928	223536	536868	2692	254438	279737
横沥	443014	4350	275399	163265	522130	6972	300380	214778
东坑	320991	4532	204804	111654	372361	4017	231268	137076
企石	291765	2868	150052	138844	320630	2314	159252	159064
石排	360806	7308	187787	165711	417073	7313	216033	193727
茶山	476010	3131	293991	178888	593265	4327	353036	235902
松山湖					618635		297419	321216

14-1 续表 9

单位：万元

镇街	(2009年)				(2010年)			
	地区生产总值	第一产业	第二产业	第三产业	地区生产总值	第一产业	第二产业	第三产业
全市	37858259	147877	18360096	19350286	42782106	165719	21917828	20698558
莞城	1039596		304342	735255	1120356		302272	818084
石龙	504196	7	251309	252880	563812	18	304608	259186
虎门	2424929	12828	1214281	1197820	2712345	16705	1300263	1395378
东城	1972630	500	746158	1225972	2308515	656	963402	1344456
万江	608904	3390	242069	363446	681580	3222	271521	406837
南城	1838797	1284	700382	1137130	1996248	1269	503015	1491965
中堂	667852	7100	403004	257748	680472	7310	409239	263924
望牛墩	287776	3472	164372	119932	304774	3658	169114	132002
麻涌	936352	7862	783010	145479	1097963	8234	904031	185698
石碣	1086458	2648	641252	442558	1119051	3295	741995	373761
高埗	606138	5999	383433	216706	691277	5892	444102	241283
道滘	451406	8351	239202	203854	524691	8861	301184	214645
洪梅	259432	4740	193219	61473	341015	4887	262817	73311
沙田	611189	13163	359306	238720	671307	13446	415810	242050
厚街	1678345	8479	898569	771297	1900402	9339	1049787	841276
长安	2191401	4875	1290474	896052	2476284	5739	1522056	948489
寮步	1113184	1661	635046	476478	1331469	1897	785661	543911
大岭山	978589	2294	513473	462823	1065349	2490	541915	520944
大朗	1169527	1280	684678	483568	1380864	1436	828791	550638
黄江	759627	770	426511	332346	850323	852	478420	371051
樟木头	525108	370	253945	270793	550792	387	238952	311453
清溪	1355016	5502	890772	458742	1432701	6065	944468	482168
塘厦	1737670	11238	1072265	654167	1854479	11288	1148809	694383
凤岗	1019431	1233	520978	497220	1130971	1248	560451	569272
谢岗	295849	9452	170525	115872	364081	8230	226867	128984
常平	1527726	6940	797473	723314	1647385	7562	785535	854288
桥头	533939	3291	258057	272591	591569	4943	291724	294902
横沥	544391	6058	334338	203994	593004	3689	338669	250646
东坑	407774	1903	257886	147986	495426	1420	325976	168030
企石	317899	2160	178008	137731	330285	1973	196062	132250
石排	443189	7210	248863	187116	521559	6950	314768	199840
茶山	610347	4214	359288	246846	624169	2729	343837	277602
松山湖	807836		384075	423761	994690		473193	521497

14-1 续表 10

单位：万元

镇街	(2011年) 地区生产总值	第一产业	第二产业	第三产业	(2012年) 地区生产总值	第一产业	第二产业	第三产业
全市	47719336	178776	24175357	23365203	50392120	187556	24446097	25758468
莞城	1222655		345656	876999	1312960		336032	976928
石龙	629604	20	335392	294192	674289	28	351445	322817
虎门	3083685	16073	1354138	1713474	3449740	16086	1528888	1904766
东城	2549277	869	994680	1553728	2759681	1210	957773	1800698
万江	771560	2832	302715	466013	806233	2684	297329	506219
南城	2324783	1316	568939	1754528	2602379	1230	565615	2035535
中堂	759504	8362	452733	298409	759839	8500	438227	313112
望牛墩	362001	4049	203523	154429	372158	4493	193674	173991
麻涌	1225141	9587	949921	265633	1274486	10132	936615	327739
石碣	1120241	3031	737704	379506	1126839	3139	727501	396199
高埗	796174	5677	505676	284821	835235	5775	516211	313249
道滘	597487	10424	336278	250785	632178	11771	344767	275640
洪梅	367244	5430	271593	90221	368660	5029	267867	95764
沙田	722343	16062	420766	285516	770194	18396	369414	382384
厚街	2183188	10109	1238029	935050	2672266	10596	1612391	1049279
长安	2700394	5630	1623068	1071697	2997437	5850	1888651	1102936
寮步	1474860	1431	860989	612441	1585830	8556	906576	670698
大岭山	1230485	2592	604612	623281	1340909	2738	678908	659263
大朗	1519385	1701	889042	628642	1647461	2111	942467	702883
黄江	953803	936	511631	441236	1092088	1103	592122	498864
樟木头	626259	417	264935	360907	654566	328	272232	382006
清溪	1519387	6889	954224	558274	1554412	7990	941313	605109
塘厦	2136115	11593	1250805	873717	2296084	13283	1262674	1020128
凤岗	1338390	1414	655037	681939	1443889	1634	671346	770909
谢岗	429711	10748	273012	145951	482047	14028	315477	152542
常平	1863138	8627	884541	969971	2066421	9493	923396	1133532
桥头	636208	3917	319231	313060	754630	3897	412213	338520
横沥	654815	4617	367161	283037	713002	4492	394598	313912
东坑	624978	1621	425730	197628	704773	1549	473215	230010
企石	373472	2380	215989	155103	405816	2780	230741	172295
石排	550833	6716	311739	232378	554266	6839	309790	237638
茶山	696375	3086	355755	337534	737038	3438	396459	337141
松山湖	1322103		625162	696941	1507742		719184	788558

14-1 续表 11

单位：万元

镇街	(2013年)				(2014年)			
	地区生产总值	第一产业	第二产业	第三产业	地区生产总值	第一产业	第二产业	第三产业
全市	55174708	195518	26226700	28752490	58813173	203493	27944169	30665510
莞城	1339920		317520	1022401	1419815		316944	1102870
石龙	768510	40	411491	356979	828879	42	444840	383998
虎门	3824840	16924	1634600	2173316	4132811	17675	1745903	2369233
东城	3303629	1679	1229249	2072701	3456419	1753	1268004	2186663
万江	939750	2724	350319	586707	986999	2845	359822	624332
南城	3012235	1269	650744	2360222	3239733	1243	623104	2615386
中堂	793906	9280	435852	348775	833920	9688	460049	364183
望牛墩	486471	4921	251694	229856	520110	5139	262892	252078
麻涌	1470511	11042	1000864	458605	1535610	11510	1046529	477571
石碣	1152872	3046	754524	395302	1245249	3184	814839	427226
高埗	1023272	5958	649450	367864	1102860	6220	698804	397836
道滘	701067	13120	381843	306105	747656	13676	397045	336935
洪梅	432280	5536	313316	113428	501312	5782	353550	141980
沙田	889532	20113	393891	475528	977426	20998	425057	531371
厚街	2848938	11491	1553664	1283783	3029896	11978	1555886	1462032
长安	3404500	6274	2226636	1171590	3636575	6540	2378672	1251363
寮步	1872441	7996	1080016	784429	2006549	8335	1140825	857389
大岭山	1521845	2899	831833	687112	1633407	3026	883138	747243
大朗	1851180	2338	1009803	839039	2007114	2502	1075277	929335
黄江	1215390	1263	649602	564525	1256520	1317	661385	593819
樟木头	754398	344	320684	433370	795822	358	359653	435810
清溪	1806184	8817	1088267	709101	1923374	9221	1148214	765939
塘厦	2612946	13965	1577367	1021614	2788544	14754	1680339	1093451
凤岗	1749523	1734	849065	898724	1945158	1808	1007922	935428
谢岗	536402	12346	358653	165403	622337	12894	428006	181437
常平	2450935	10491	1136304	1304139	2599815	10935	1186883	1401996
桥头	907965	3873	497587	406505	1036247	4037	602304	429906
横沥	840177	4630	470940	364606	920083	4834	511149	404100
东坑	825806	1490	550685	273632	903038	1556	596840	304642
企石	467766	3258	263467	201041	496360	3396	279580	213384
石排	641382	7042	359996	274345	687253	7355	390947	288952
茶山	849677	3585	460233	385858	911046	3737	495466	411843
松山湖	1705264		816223	889041	2109233		1094934	1014299

注：2013年起，沙田镇地区生产总值含虎门港数据。

14-2 镇街第三产业增加值（2014年）

Value-added of the Tertiary Industry by Town (2014)

单位：万元

镇街	第三产业增加值	#交通运输及仓储业	批发和零售业	住宿和餐饮业	金融业	房地产业
全市	30665510	1996868	7352571	1472305	3708027	4457653
莞城	1102870	93916	264256	26186	230912	91806
石龙	383998	22138	116480	22695	51330	49454
虎门	2369233	228433	567672	141720	259706	372084
东城	2186663	126446	402428	119607	352050	279032
万江	624332	50903	149342	51287	85944	111207
南城	2615386	55027	491644	60707	517274	325260
中堂	364183	7283	98749	28031	41063	43158
望牛墩	252078	33718	54227	15287	27960	33486
麻涌	477571	168055	119245	14680	39324	49159
石碣	427226	11137	153830	33034	43871	55786
高埗	397836	29199	101742	34692	30816	82488
道滘	336935	16719	87801	24443	38390	86810
洪梅	141980	20138	56286	5849	12498	14663
沙田	531371	141305	136559	22290	24108	85488
厚街	1462032	39600	468246	120310	165511	297972
长安	1251363	29860	412877	93133	141449	166717
寮步	857389	81415	341173	47343	60228	105271
大岭山	747243	28639	230191	53823	65780	127803
大朗	929335	48055	301572	54006	101692	145143
黄江	593819	16592	254069	46072	62068	98216
樟木头	435810	28675	100352	34637	55552	88500
清溪	765939	29602	298903	60342	65225	108974
塘厦	1093451	39022	318354	97350	131903	219056
凤岗	935428	30160	211262	62009	101804	188145
谢岗	181437	10019	50926	15087	28651	29327
常平	1401996	48414	380632	101918	120197	224691
桥头	429906	4180	172227	31256	44379	52600
横沥	404100	19008	133356	41137	44695	69013
东坑	304642	14979	95857	15888	24719	53245
企石	213384	14351	48996	9873	27365	49925
石排	288952	13970	84098	25654	38978	50497
茶山	411843	21307	122934	31105	55242	62316
松山湖	1014299	4571	249936	12057	66098	272577

14-3 镇街户籍户数与人口数（2014年）

Population of Household by Town (2014)

单位：人

镇街	户数(户)	农业户	非农业户	人口数	按性别分 男	女	按农业、非农业分 农业人口	非农业人口	总人口中未落户籍的人口数
全市总计	558833	266943	291890	1913879	970181	943698	922138	991741	3338
莞城	40477	1	40476	179668	92036	87632	3013	176655	
石龙	21776	2379	19397	71940	35766	36174	8860	63080	956
虎门	35477		35477	131470	66553	64917	1	131469	1
东城	27260		27260	96377	49196	47181		96377	8
万江	26027		26027	81832	41622	40210		81832	205
南城	24014		24014	82991	42861	40130		82991	12
中堂	22539	16019	6520	77018	39138	37880	57349	19669	2
望牛墩	12114	10359	1755	47768	23742	24026	41228	6540	708
麻涌	22127	17804	4323	74478	37238	37240	63860	10618	176
石碣	15413	11659	3754	46137	23443	22694	38103	8034	11
高埗	11642	10883	759	38951	19623	19328	35960	2991	46
道滘	17221	12765	4456	57089	28598	28491	45212	11877	
洪梅	7040	6451	589	23241	11707	11534	21706	1535	392
沙田	13062	11540	1522	42828	21468	21360	8013	5049	11
厚街	29686	23717	5969	100166	50283	49883	86130	14036	
长安	13981		13981	47713	24635	23078		47713	
寮步	22741	14072	8669	74647	37758	36889	44205	30442	
大岭山	13710	11487	2223	47009	23681	23328	40152	6857	
大朗	19527	16732	2795	73492	37946	35546	63874	9618	3
黄江	8753	6023	2730	27133	13639	13494	19064	8069	
樟木头	8464		8464	29337	14834	14503		29337	5
清溪	12054	9428	2626	37192	18540	18652	29833	7359	
塘厦	18281		18281	50382	25364	25018		50382	13
凤岗	7561	4995	2566	26527	12911	13616	17988	8539	2
谢岗	5438	4306	1132	21181	10576	10605	17687	3494	163
常平	25654	18139	7515	77529	39968	37561	59144	18385	2
桥头	11875	4959	6916	36809	18539	18270	16604	20205	134
横沥	11950	8954	2996	38313	19623	18690	31176	7137	3
东坑	10775	9003	1772	30747	15874	14873	27516	3231	282
企石	13688	11572	2116	43455	22236	21219	37922	5533	15
石排	13395	11799	1596	44219	22277	21942	39831	4388	178
茶山	13825	11897	1928	45688	22946	22742	37941	7747	10
松山湖	1285		1285	10551	5559	4992		10551	

注：沙田镇户籍户数及人口数含虎门港数据，下同。

14-4 镇街户籍人口自然变动情况（2014年）

Population Household by Town (2014)

镇街	出生		死亡		自然增长	
	人数（人）	出生率（‰）	人数（人）	死亡率（‰）	人数（人）	自然增长率（‰）
全市总计	21383	11.20	10253	5.37	11130	5.83
莞城	1426	8.03	859	4.84	567	3.19
石龙	584	8.09	414	5.73	170	2.35
虎门	1402	10.55	824	6.20	578	4.35
东城	989	10.34	356	3.72	633	6.62
万江	874	10.60	392	4.76	482	5.85
南城	1125	13.93	245	3.03	880	10.90
中堂	868	11.30	479	6.24	389	5.07
望牛墩	565	12.00	262	5.56	303	6.43
麻涌	935	12.59	431	5.80	504	6.79
石碣	600	13.06	295	6.42	305	6.64
高埗	488	12.43	204	5.20	284	7.23
道滘	611	10.45	370	6.33	241	4.12
洪梅	293	12.82	126	5.51	167	7.30
沙田	470	11.06	289	6.80	181	4.26
厚街	1162	11.53	551	5.47	611	6.06
长安	631	13.38	247	5.24	384	8.14
寮步	836	11.32	403	5.46	433	5.86
大岭山	617	13.07	223	4.72	394	8.34
大朗	877	11.97	420	5.73	457	6.24
黄江	347	12.77	138	5.08	209	7.69
樟木头	339	11.37	131	4.39	208	6.97
清溪	436	11.83	244	6.62	192	5.21
塘厦	623	12.41	231	4.60	392	7.81
凤岗	330	12.21	152	5.63	178	6.59
谢岗	273	13.14	107	5.15	166	7.99
常平	804	10.39	433	5.60	371	4.79
桥头	443	11.96	229	6.18	214	5.78
横沥	401	10.46	231	6.03	170	4.44
东坑	311	10.19	177	5.80	134	4.39
企石	602	13.60	281	6.35	321	7.25
石排	488	11.09	238	5.41	250	5.68
茶山	443	9.70	266	5.82	177	3.88
松山湖	190	19.29	5	0.51	185	18.78

14-5 镇街人口迁移变动情况（2014年）

Population Migration by Town (2014)

单位：人

镇　　街	迁移总计	省　内	省　外	迁入总计	省内迁入	省外迁入	迁出总计	迁往省内	迁往省外
全市总计	36278	11212	25066	25530	8103	17427	10748	3109	7639
莞　　城	9634	901	8733	5480	593	4887	4154	308	3846
石　　龙	856	423	433	578	301	277	278	122	156
虎　　门	1161	499	662	837	376	461	324	123	201
东　　城	2456	860	1596	1912	699	1213	544	161	383
万　　江	1193	409	784	1044	342	702	149	67	82
南　　城	4355	1539	2816	3516	1171	2345	839	368	471
中　　堂	361	189	172	257	147	110	104	42	62
望 牛 墩	162	81	81	129	61	68	33	20	13
麻　　涌	457	199	258	319	138	181	138	61	77
石　　碣	607	208	399	415	135	280	192	73	119
高　　埗	144	76	68	105	52	53	39	24	15
道　　滘	282	124	158	236	102	134	46	22	24
洪　　梅	137	46	91	113	37	76	24	9	15
沙　　田	353	132	221	288	108	180	65	24	41
厚　　街	788	299	489	614	239	375	174	60	114
长　　安	1417	416	1001	1121	289	832	296	127	169
寮　　步	1431	498	933	1286	442	844	145	56	89
大 岭 山	487	196	291	388	154	234	99	42	57
大　　朗	652	233	419	551	209	342	101	24	77
黄　　江	689	300	389	617	273	344	72	27	45
樟 木 头	665	253	412	516	191	325	149	62	87
清　　溪	669	221	448	421	176	245	248	45	203
塘　　厦	1362	543	819	1127	465	662	235	78	157
凤　　岗	770	276	494	573	206	367	197	70	127
谢　　岗	207	104	103	131	77	54	76	27	49
常　　平	1203	410	793	944	329	615	259	81	178
桥　　头	287	98	189	171	70	101	116	28	88
横　　沥	348	121	227	277	105	172	71	16	55
东　　坑	197	55	142	120	42	78	77	13	64
企　　石	314	101	213	190	83	107	124	18	106
石　　排	268	85	183	149	71	78	119	14	105
茶　　山	290	96	194	176	86	90	114	10	104
松 山 湖	2075	1220	855	928	333	595	1147	887	260

注：本表按户籍人口统计。

14-6 镇街土地面积和人口密度（2014年）

Land Area and Population Density by Town (2014)

镇　街	土地面积（平方公里）	人口密度（人/平方公里）	
		户籍人口	常住人口
莞　城	11.2	16042	14946
石　龙	13.8	5213	10384
虎　门	166.5	790	3840
东　城	105.1	917	4711
万　江	48.5	1687	5120
南　城	56.6	1466	5345
中　堂	59.9	1286	2346
望牛墩	31.6	1512	2718
麻　涌	87.2	854	1386
石　碣	36.2	1275	6843
高　埗	34.6	1126	6286
道　滘	54.3	1051	2610
洪　梅	33.2	700	1756
沙　田	117.7	364	1524
厚　街	125.7	797	3484
长　安	89.4	534	7408
寮　步	72.5	1030	5789
大岭山	95.5	492	2945
大　朗	97.5	754	3219
黄　江	92.9	292	2524
樟木头	118.8	247	1136
清　溪	140.1	265	2255
塘　厦	128.2	393	3801
凤　岗	82.4	322	3867
谢　岗	91.0	233	1079
常　平	103.3	751	3780
桥　头	56.0	657	2954
横　沥	44.7	857	4602
东　坑	23.7	1297	5785
企　石	58.2	747	2113
石　排	48.7	908	3304
茶　山	45.4	1006	3465
松山湖	58.1	182	1910

注：1.土地面积数据来源于市国土局，不包括海域面积。
2.沙田镇土地面积含虎门港数据。

14-7 镇街常住人口（2013-2014年）

Permanent Population by Town (2013-2014)

单位：万人

镇　　街	2013年	2014年	镇　　街	2013年	2014年
莞　　城	16.58	16.74	寮　　步	42.29	41.97
石　　龙	14.34	14.33	大 岭 山	28.21	28.12
虎　　门	64.42	63.93	大　　朗	31.46	31.39
东　　城	49.68	49.51	黄　　江	23.41	23.45
万　　江	24.71	24.83	樟 木 头	13.46	13.49
南　　城	29.87	30.25	清　　溪	31.53	31.59
中　　堂	14.12	14.05	塘　　厦	48.70	48.73
望 牛 墩	8.62	8.59	凤　　岗	32.03	31.86
麻　　涌	11.99	12.09	谢　　岗	10.04	9.82
石　　碣	24.82	24.77	常　　平	38.95	39.05
高　　埗	21.81	21.75	桥　　头	16.83	16.54
道　　滘	14.38	14.17	横　　沥	20.70	20.57
洪　　梅	5.91	5.83	东　　坑	13.98	13.71
沙　　田	18.01	17.94	企　　石	12.29	12.30
厚　　街	44.25	43.79	石　　排	16.25	16.09
长　　安	66.92	66.23	茶　　山	15.74	15.73
松 山 湖	5.36	11.10			

注：2013年起，沙田镇常住人口含虎门港数据。

14-8 镇街外来暂住人口数（2013-2014年）

Migrant Population by Town (2013-2014)

单位：人

镇街	2013年			2014年		
	外来暂住人口	男	女	外来暂住人口	男	女
全市总计	4346839	2186786	2160053	4158580	2103624	2054956
莞城	49529	25473	24056	39963	21932	18031
石龙	55020	22745	32275	54514	22492	32022
虎门	379754	182179	197575	377490	183951	193539
东城	210360	121454	88906	188830	100714	88116
万江	65892	32704	33188	65139	33397	31742
南城	213169	111540	101629	135176	71605	63571
中堂	48772	27234	21538	49207	27439	21768
望牛墩	36471	18330	18141	30052	15210	14842
麻涌	35201	20330	14871	35315	21960	13355
石碣	95659	40267	55392	95222	44796	50426
高埗	129624	72159	57465	83622	47968	35654
道滘	54312	24705	29607	52634	23491	29143
洪梅	27351	13957	13394	27816	14222	13594
沙田	72183	37041	35142	72613	39120	33493
厚街	303542	141727	161815	315692	147728	167964
长安	397898	193079	204819	398952	189491	209461
寮步	186523	96132	90391	186823	98214	88609
大岭山	101612	56210	45402	103205	56960	46245
大朗	131285	62033	69252	127523	60255	67268
黄江	149137	74888	74249	108302	61736	46566
樟木头	107593	61751	45842	121659	66215	55444
清溪	145184	52842	92342	151560	58842	92718
塘厦	337694	176547	161147	308696	161387	147309
凤岗	225119	115821	109298	201018	108447	92571
谢岗	45812	22184	23628	50480	26089	24391
常平	217963	105295	112668	197706	97888	99818
桥头	84130	45114	39016	72915	39263	33652
横沥	100883	60188	40695	100416	60183	40233
东坑	71512	37510	34002	60208	26331	33877
企石	37761	19518	18243	37028	18661	18367
石排	92378	44361	48017	89983	43211	46772
茶山	79834	41106	38728	77925	42937	34988
其他单位	57682	30362	27320	140896	71489	69407

14-9 镇街计划生育情况（2014年）

Basic Statistics on Family Planning by Town (2014)

镇街	已婚育龄妇女人数（人）	女性初婚人数（人）	#23周岁及以上	落实各种节育措施 育龄夫妇（对）	节育率（%）	领取独生子女证 累计（人）	领证率（%）	政策生育率（%）	多孩率（%）
全市总计	399044	14871	12118	333848	83.66	80769	20.24	89.21	2.57
莞城	34988	1152	1068	29172	83.38	9042	25.84	92.92	1.61
石龙	13727	492	426	11047	80.48	3555	25.90	85.10	2.91
虎门	26666	950	762	21180	79.43	4386	16.45	85.59	2.92
东城	21913	654	586	18586	84.82	3843	17.54	86.65	3.03
万江	17506	568	487	15038	85.90	4238	24.21	89.24	2.29
南城	21583	687	619	17732	82.16	3454	16.00	89.60	0.80
中堂	14347	650	537	12079	84.19	3107	21.66	92.17	1.50
望牛墩	8759	405	330	7487	85.48	1669	19.05	91.68	2.12
麻涌	14628	768	659	12324	84.25	3855	26.35	92.41	2.14
石碣	9590	405	330	8155	85.04	2164	22.57	90.83	3.17
高埗	7583	336	264	6039	79.64	1564	20.63	89.75	3.28
道滘	10502	486	382	8522	81.15	2140	20.38	87.56	3.11
洪梅	4532	197	146	3878	85.57	887	19.57	90.44	1.37
沙田	9201	332	238	7799	84.76	2246	24.41	95.32	1.70
厚街	20009	754	618	16625	83.09	3593	17.96	81.07	5.08
长安	10972	457	372	9360	85.31	1516	13.82	92.55	2.38
寮步	15692	621	493	13407	85.44	2747	17.51	89.95	2.99
大岭山	10545	491	368	9110	86.39	1822	17.28	94.00	2.11
大朗	15123	574	408	12703	84.00	3407	22.53	88.71	2.51
黄江	6432	223	181	5260	81.78	1531	23.80	87.90	2.31
樟木头	7140	219	165	5827	81.61	797	11.16	90.27	3.54
清溪	8407	274	204	6987	83.11	1409	16.76	87.39	2.98
塘厦	11234	436	359	9007	80.18	2181	19.41	88.76	3.21
凤岗	6363	218	181	5378	84.52	714	11.22	84.55	4.85
谢岗	4629	189	145	3947	85.27	741	16.01	91.58	1.10
常平	15747	496	400	13157	83.55	3875	24.61	92.79	1.49
桥头	7880	305	244	6903	87.60	1840	23.35	85.33	4.06
横沥	7874	287	207	6932	88.04	1644	20.88	89.53	1.50
东坑	5640	218	172	4831	85.66	1279	22.68	90.68	1.61
企石	9155	322	221	7962	86.97	1521	16.61	83.72	3.16
石排	9156	346	265	7667	83.74	1929	21.07	89.55	3.48
茶山	9162	285	212	7874	85.94	1497	16.34	89.16	2.93
松山湖	2359	74	69	1873	79.40	576	24.42	97.37	1.05

注：沙田镇计划生育情况含虎门港数据。

14-10 镇街农林牧渔业总产值（2014年）

Gross Output Value of Agriculture by Town (2014)

单位：万元

镇　　街	农林牧渔业总产值	农业	林业	牧业	渔业	农林牧渔服务业
石　　龙	73				74	
虎　　门	26498	8789		6196	11514	
东　　城	2382	1602	317		464	
万　　江	4830	4129			702	
南　　城	1997	1996	1			
中　　堂	14071	12346	7	13	1706	
望 牛 墩	14640	14640				
麻　　涌	13893	11937	3		1953	
石　　碣	5282	4311			547	425
高　　埗	10396	9327			695	375
道　　滘	11230	6770	3	333	4065	60
洪　　梅	5477	1791		10	3676	
沙　　田	36003	12349	11	3134	16224	4286
厚　　街	21125	17712	44		3370	
长　　安	6846	1305	42	142	5358	
寮　　步	16264	14601	9		1655	
大 岭 山	6224	3546	51	508	2119	
大　　朗	4563	2862	3	971	727	
黄　　江	5240	1703	65	3048	425	
樟 木 头	609	439		127		44
清　　溪	15569	12117	144	3048	259	
塘　　厦	21156	14902	14	5534	705	
凤　　岗	2426	2271	11		144	
谢　　岗	22976	11907	128	1073	9869	
常　　平	12238	7550	60	2989	1639	
桥　　头	6698	4870	8	64	1756	
横　　沥	8181	2756		3781	1643	
东　　坑	1274	1029			245	
企　　石	11060	4078	4	5537	1441	
石　　排	8774	5193			3582	
茶　　山	10416	2258		5179	2980	

注：沙田镇农林牧渔业总产值含虎门港数据。

14-11 镇街主要农产品生产及产品产量（2014年）

Production and Output of Main Agricultural Products by Town (2014)

镇街	粮食播种面积（亩）	粮食总产量（吨）	稻谷播种面积（亩）	稻谷产量（吨）	蔬菜(含菜用瓜)播种面积（亩）	蔬菜(含菜用瓜)产量（吨）	水果总面积（亩）	水果总产量（吨）
石龙								
虎门	1452	481	569	216	18667	20496	6425	1273
东城	1326	600	1326	600	2409	4027	256	205
万江	1192	409	749	277	7422	12110	187	113
南城	850	212	38	13	330	401	1790	173
中堂	1584	530	1024	386	17584	26530	4801	7487
望牛墩	1683	428	348	124	2765	3662	6317	9351
麻涌	4607	1514	4277	1413	10822	11748	16430	20645
石碣	703	198	5	2	10200	12886	70	52
高埗	2100	691	414	166	15272	22771	100	204
道滘	2154	646	1086	378	11340	21027	38	89
洪梅	2405	832	1655	600	485	607	1628	2425
沙田	3378	1086	1323	478	23903	27925	1827	2170
厚街	1602	450			43384	48300	29381	3326
长安	362	80			1615	1481	4838	892
寮步	791	210			1646	2026	2668	529
大岭山	448	110			7758	7855	9865	1138
大朗	702	173			4209	3696	18174	1225
黄江	700	196			1560	2787	14200	791
樟木头	510	102			540	773	5120	210
清溪	863	230			12430	13406	11590	993
塘厦	1003	271			28751	34497	12106	1422
凤岗	720	175			4585	4342	11551	935
谢岗	2522	847	420	164	18320	26737	14250	1524
常平	1600	405			21170	35984	9681	314
桥头	1026	276	6	2	7250	10303	1946	421
横沥	700	185			6870	6533	3380	920
东坑	700	170			1342	1375	1827	470
企石	1154	327	473	146	6024	8598	3744	954
石排	1356	321			9882	11804	850	1907
茶山	1070	251			6020	5797	3248	317

注：沙田镇农产品生产及产品产量含虎门港数据，下同。

14-11 续表 1

(2014年)

镇街	香(大)蕉面积(亩)	香(大)蕉产量(吨)	荔枝面积(亩)	荔枝产量(吨)	林业用地面积(亩)	当年种植面积(亩)	生猪年末存栏量(头)	生猪出栏量(头)
石龙					119			
虎门	220	180	4622	508	33440		19849	41229
东城			106	120	12003			
万江	161	92	5	5				
南城			1050	123	13821			
中堂	4520	7055	42	9				1405
望牛墩	6180	9210						1571
麻涌	14468	18809						
石碣	20	45	50	7				
高埗								
道滘	38	39						2494
洪梅	1628	2425						
沙田	1454	1944	62	9	599			1071
厚街	62	40	25042	2466	52383	500		
长安			4700	850	19053	500	200	726
寮步	20	30	2200	281	14547			
大岭山			9000	906	54414		10755	5107
大朗			16287	981	30512		3050	5409
黄江			13140	550	76896	1346	9000	19800
樟木头			4470	160	54477	510		
清溪			9140	600	70872	2500	4446	21002
塘厦			10806	681	38468	500	9646	15500
凤岗			8448	715	44271	2500		
谢岗	750	126	13000	1363	61895	852		
常平	40	10	8388	165	25197	1160	2145	2208
桥头	176	140	720	26	8282			
横沥	240	450	3000	435	5471		18000	26000
东坑	125	300	1339	130	4323			
企石	1051	682	2323	206	11600		200	34000
石排	542	1806	45	24	1286			
茶山	9	6	2930	180	7764			30718

注：林业用地面积、当年种植面积指标采用林业局数据。

14-11 续表 2

(2014年)

镇街	三鸟年末存栏量(只)	三鸟出栏量(只)	畜牧总肉量(吨)	#猪肉	禽蛋产量(吨)	淡水养殖面积(亩)	水产品产量(吨)	#淡水产量
石龙						99	78	78
虎门	134000	595400	3662	2856	10	7433	11062	4586
东城						1320	601	601
万江						1620	776	776
南城								
中堂	860	3310	103	100		3525	1942	1942
望牛墩			119	119		2355	738	738
麻涌						3345	1751	1751
石碣						930	591	591
高埗						1712	811	811
道滘	150	150	167	167		6435	3977	3977
洪梅		3546	4			4552	2390	2390
沙田	196268	879205	1137	80	98	14445	11464	7135
厚街						5505	1881	1881
长安	4135	10469	66	54		2640	3511	478
寮步						1345	1428	1428
大岭山			255	255		1875	2215	2215
大朗	19497	40350	440	389	24	3351	892	892
黄江	3008	16500	1522	1485		4635	498	498
樟木头	4200	36353	44					
清溪	21743	34568	1511	1470		786	268	268
塘厦	341345	881450	2176	1110	553	2685	961	961
凤岗						225	180	180
谢岗	100240	395871	597			17550	9586	9586
常平	351425	912000	1219	126	421	4096	1988	1988
桥头	8140	11860	12		16	3750	2260	2260
横沥	13000	42000	1870	1820	8	2289	1419	1419
东坑						471	322	322
企石	300	142000	2669	2448		3045	1702	1702
石排						7500	3988	3988
茶山	3000	77270	2495	2365		2220	3120	3120

14-12 镇街农机总动力、机耕面积及农村用电量（2014年）

Basic Statistics on Total Power of Agricultural Machinery, Area of Tractor Ploughing and Electricity Consumption in Rural Areas by Town (2014)

镇　　街	农　机 总动力 (千瓦)	#耕作机械	排灌机械	农　　村 用 电 量 (万千瓦时)	化肥施用 实 物 量 (吨)	农　药 使用量 (吨)
石　　龙				1867		
虎　　门	31286	182	1235	485248	1639	58
东　　城	11307	341	8895		204	1
万　　江	442		200	82603	528	1
南　　城				262	38	1
中　　堂	11080	617	2199	160163	1512	36
望 牛 墩	1276	259	305	7187	568	14
麻　　涌	3741	581	175	9021	2139	45
石　　碣	1663	155	1289	172408	538	22
高　　埗	13063	2602	2165	131492	284	3
道　　滘	904	213	118	128056	870	45
洪　　梅	519	97	272	1240	307	15
沙　　田	38242	1514	1473	57905	1342	82
厚　　街	841		436		3305	86
长　　安	163		18	114068	358	3
寮　　步	130	4	126	28115	300	5
大 岭 山	4686	180	130	26552	950	22
大　　朗	820	524	144	281892	1303	38
黄　　江	46	7	3	75531	978	26
樟 木 头				100246	93	15
清　　溪	886	449	280	263987	1491	70
塘　　厦	386	30	136	44270	2230	24
凤　　岗	363	123	170	259526	782	8
谢　　岗	5720	329	1330	5360	1710	39
常　　平	210		58	385370	1750	8
桥　　头	1393	351	472	133430	1426	7
横　　沥	7340	520	6220	122938	397	5
东　　坑				54865	276	
企　　石	492	412	80	81998	586	1
石　　排	3243	282	1590		836	26
茶　　山	6629	760	400	151307	701	10

14-13 镇街农村集体(经联社、经济社两级合计)经济收益分配（2014年）

Income Distribution of Rural Economy by Town (2014)

单位：万元

镇　　街	经营总收入	经营总费用	经营纯收入
全市总计	1714711	676702	1038008
莞　　城	18457	5122	13334
石　　龙	19502	9007	10494
虎　　门	171662	66639	105023
东　　城	107830	43939	63890
万　　江	52909	21122	31787
南　　城	71844	23662	48182
中　　堂	76285	14417	61868
望 牛 墩	10406	3511	6895
麻　　涌	18615	7036	11579
石　　碣	69224	29753	39471
高　　埗	24490	9323	15167
道　　滘	25159	9594	15566
洪　　梅	6951	2975	3976
沙　　田	28011	11200	16812
厚　　街	124079	58351	65728
长　　安	162904	56816	106089
寮　　步	82452	38111	44341
大 岭 山	44523	16648	27875
大　　朗	69933	32410	37523
黄　　江	26028	8519	17509
樟 木 头	23368	15958	7411
清　　溪	57994	23149	34845
塘　　厦	75903	23720	52183
凤　　岗	77023	21967	55055
谢　　岗	10578	3477	7101
常　　平	76483	33283	43199
桥　　头	34096	15468	18628
横　　沥	27807	15424	12383
东　　坑	25850	10987	14863
企　　石	18143	9567	8576
石　　排	34069	15309	18760
茶　　山	42135	20238	21897

14-14 镇街规模以上工业企业主要经济指标（2014年）

Main Indicators of Industrial Enterprises above Designated Size by Town (2014)

单位：万元

镇街	企业单位数（个）	亏损企业	工业销售产值	工业增加值
莞城	31	7	1060010	259414
石龙	53	7	2212488	469699
虎门	366	40	4907430	1324708
东城	249	29	3793056	948333
万江	71	6	929850	250740
南城	63	12	1418400	489026
中堂	107	14	2137147	375701
望牛墩	100	12	958884	232987
麻涌	79	8	5475922	855834
石碣	150	12	4170815	850324
高埗	136	17	2270531	779350
道滘	134	15	1307560	302769
洪梅	52	7	1833236	348119
沙田	113	11	2059512	387329
厚街	299	36	7527863	1406608
长安	269	57	11693139	1781472
寮步	255	44	4880411	1108060
大岭山	208	28	3812365	826870
大朗	343	38	3282762	823822
黄江	127	18	2787154	560407
樟木头	92	21	1113475	294184
清溪	280	37	5163044	1099809
塘厦	349	40	6054288	1385150
凤岗	247	26	3340382	871436
谢岗	105	19	1026162	255519
常平	253	24	4345222	939495
桥头	145	12	2370916	465307
横沥	143	23	1640110	391763
东坑	99	12	2171684	461598
企石	128	16	1052998	233909
石排	111	14	1084372	285931
茶山	149	16	1967611	469129
松山湖	67	13	12898206	1744634

注：沙田镇规模以上工业企业各经济指标含虎门港数据，下同。

14-14 续表 1

(2014年)

单位：万元

镇街	资产总额	#流动资产	固定资产净值	负债总额
莞城	966292	474199	350943	559531
石龙	1394068	1089408	212481	689961
虎门	3965056	2832100	811992	2191559
东城	3180247	2105681	818076	1598884
万江	868616	557525	245456	548424
南城	1523762	1043551	383105	690341
中堂	2056758	1213450	637648	1421326
望牛墩	722391	512859	167418	510417
麻涌	5306130	2887222	2010170	2932319
石碣	2446522	1857356	486933	1422691
高埗	1672371	1175836	406196	1037310
道滘	1129796	803173	215351	541893
洪梅	1931360	1110582	714593	896530
沙田	1264111	898667	250411	752442
厚街	3608308	2734990	645148	1935219
长安	7305546	4734297	1735997	4321218
寮步	2906482	2103006	601213	1760138
大岭山	3917822	3242310	481350	2949499
大朗	3021775	2409746	423951	2141853
黄江	1817576	1265005	422697	992057
樟木头	904655	613270	198802	556049
清溪	3662032	2615736	788876	2014792
塘厦	4014473	2941379	774433	2306503
凤岗	3103095	1879169	950817	1670945
谢岗	783213	509219	216617	511225
常平	3080845	2295592	622820	1607084
桥头	1594409	1105419	243711	1160969
横沥	1412696	1022387	282873	901259
东坑	1365566	990582	302065	864361
企石	1080506	894367	132589	742665
石排	795788	540447	187953	435483
茶山	1388207	964236	327541	754404
松山湖	6787887	4846843	851532	5016343

14-14 续表 2

(2014年)

单位：万元

镇街	主营业务收入	主营业务税金及附加	利润总额	利税总额	本年应交增值税	全部从业人员平均人数（人）
莞城	1051907	4273	63107	89701	22027	16006
石龙	2210156	10247	153065	186753	23421	33862
虎门	4790888	22714	204681	327361	99740	163477
东城	3763741	28090	80063	208740	100561	102555
万江	924475	4017	21033	43203	18116	29790
南城	1444057	8393	93086	142168	40688	42958
中堂	2234193	9282	42611	108885	56938	29521
望牛墩	951233	3909	58417	88222	25895	21394
麻涌	5935606	8616	157516	259402	93185	38577
石碣	4170759	8726	138112	204087	56943	92479
高埗	2220078	7486	57778	90551	25257	102173
道滘	1307180	5080	47687	81697	28860	32418
洪梅	1839356	2272	26069	52902	23966	19469
沙田	2210602	5440	42291	68272	20320	34740
厚街	7548682	19160	221362	345711	105160	180000
长安	11795674	32136	458981	679902	188683	217202
寮步	4876713	12625	81358	185526	91342	124455
大岭山	3802397	8909	122048	239389	107652	84819
大朗	3164310	11176	49863	136387	74855	88994
黄江	2731075	11716	54475	104454	38131	78661
樟木头	1127341	4279	3147	39388	31945	35528
清溪	5124149	12917	104263	163359	45587	146971
塘厦	5787827	20712	165159	288064	102075	189331
凤岗	3206124	10544	141829	206600	54194	112204
谢岗	1025195	3438	6611	25114	15065	33486
常平	4355754	13158	120110	183383	50064	124076
桥头	2393156	7141	16608	39860	16100	58725
横沥	1630821	5743	53979	80923	20998	55978
东坑	2196146	5391	47236	64476	11847	62137
企石	1063991	3643	19295	41345	18382	35462
石排	1083033	4311	32980	48386	11083	47717
茶山	1923574	6735	56600	95910	32531	47424
松山湖	12867964	38319	354860	489317	96129	64079

14-15 镇街规模以上工业企业主要经济效益指标（2014年）

Main Indicators on Economic Benefit of Industrial Enterprises above Designated Size by Town (2014)

镇　街	工业增加值率 (%)	总资产贡献率 (%)	资产负债率 (%)	流动资产周转率 (次/年)	成本费用利润率 (%)	全员劳动生产率 (元/人)	产品销售率 (%)
莞　城	24.3	11.0	57.9	2.3	6.3	162073	99.3
石　龙	21.3	13.6	49.5	2.0	7.4	138710	100.1
虎　门	24.6	8.4	55.3	1.7	4.4	81033	91.2
东　城	23.6	6.7	50.3	1.8	2.2	92471	94.3
万　江	26.2	5.7	63.1	1.7	2.3	84169	97.0
南　城	33.7	9.5	45.3	1.4	7.2	113838	97.6
中　堂	16.7	7.4	69.1	1.9	1.9	127266	94.9
望牛墩	24.0	13.2	70.7	1.9	6.5	108903	98.7
麻　涌	15.5	5.2	55.3	2.2	2.6	221851	98.9
石　碣	20.1	8.3	58.2	2.3	3.4	91948	98.4
高　埗	34.1	6.0	62.0	1.9	2.6	76277	99.4
道　滘	23.0	7.7	48.0	1.6	3.8	93395	99.2
洪　梅	18.3	3.0	46.4	1.7	1.4	178807	96.2
沙　田	18.7	6.3	59.5	2.5	2.0	111494	99.4
厚　街	18.3	9.7	53.6	2.8	3.0	78145	98.1
长　安	15.3	9.2	59.2	2.5	4.0	82019	100.3
寮　步	22.2	7.0	60.6	2.3	1.7	89033	97.6
大岭山	21.4	6.7	75.3	1.2	3.3	97486	98.7
大　朗	23.9	4.7	70.9	1.3	1.6	92571	95.3
黄　江	19.5	5.8	54.6	2.2	2.0	71243	97.0
樟木头	26.6	5.4	61.5	1.8	0.3	82803	100.7
清　溪	20.8	4.5	55.0	2.0	2.1	74832	97.8
塘　厦	22.4	7.4	57.5	2.0	2.9	73160	97.9
凤　岗	24.9	7.2	53.9	1.7	4.5	77665	95.6
谢　岗	23.2	3.6	65.3	2.0	0.7	76306	93.3
常　平	21.3	6.1	52.2	1.9	2.8	75719	98.6
桥　头	19.4	3.4	72.8	2.2	0.7	79235	98.6
横　沥	23.1	6.3	63.8	1.6	3.4	69985	96.7
东　坑	21.3	5.0	63.3	2.2	2.2	74287	100.3
企　石	21.7	4.5	68.7	1.2	1.8	65961	97.8
石　排	26.0	6.5	54.7	2.0	3.1	59922	98.8
茶　山	22.6	7.5	54.3	2.0	3.0	98922	94.9
松山湖	13.5	7.3	73.9	2.8	2.7	272263	99.5

14-16 镇街规模以上工业企业R&D人员情况（2014年）

R&D Personnel of Industrial Enterprises above Designated Size by Town (2014)

镇 街	有R&D活动的工业企业数（个）	R&D人员合计（人）	#参加项目人员	#女性	#研究人员	#全时人员	非全时人员
全市总计	855	58752	54047	6912	8707	31302	27450
莞 城	10	698	657	76	126	246	452
石 龙	21	1703	1481	375	336	1365	338
虎 门	35	2053	1919	236	359	944	1109
东 城	45	2581	2386	223	555	1101	1481
万 江	34	1645	1570	236	263	789	855
南 城	16	619	565	41	93	126	493
中 堂	17	538	471	68	61	292	246
望牛墩	13	287	249	22	40	162	125
麻 涌	21	1938	1832	112	294	923	1015
石 碣	26	6948	6475	357	821	1756	5192
高 埗	17	911	905	193	136	911	
道 滘	18	711	644	50	72	363	348
洪 梅	8	1213	1167	47	65	456	757
沙 田	21	1118	990	108	150	540	578
厚 街	24	1677	1594	223	469	1000	677
长 安	35	4277	4036	704	258	2569	1708
寮 步	46	2462	2282	171	482	1389	1073
大岭山	37	1540	1386	190	361	973	567
大 朗	53	2215	2063	494	374	1542	673
黄 江	23	1276	1190	130	103	603	673
樟木头	18	363	334	96	82	205	158
清 溪	36	2786	2486	484	428	2212	574
塘 厦	49	4896	4463	581	404	2576	2320
凤 岗	28	2136	1965	235	312	943	1193
谢 岗	8	274	255	8	69	24	250
常 平	50	1814	1640	238	341	1124	690
桥 头	23	1091	982	29	92	262	829
横 沥	15	521	480	62	40	354	167
东 坑	18	838	809	28	194	174	664
企 石	12	384	365	28	52	167	217
石 排	17	1209	964	209	152	569	640
茶 山	18	572	529	101	66	320	252
松山湖	43	5458	4913	757	1057	4322	1136

注：沙田镇规模以上工业企业R&D相关数据含虎门港，下同。

14-17 镇街规模以上工业企业R&D人员全时当量情况（2014年）

R&D Personnel Full-time-equivalent of Industrial Enterprises above Designated Size by Town (2014)

镇　街	有R&D活动的工业企业数（个）	R&D人员全时当量（人年）	#研究人员	#应用研究人员	#试验发展人员
全市总计	855	49457	7432	15	49442
莞　城	10	684	127		684
石　龙	21	1084	226		1084
虎　门	35	1701	286		1701
东　城	45	2166	513		2166
万　江	34	1126	211		1126
南　城	16	501	52	15	486
中　堂	17	373	41		373
望牛墩	13	236	35		236
麻　涌	21	1535	254		1535
石　碣	26	6772	807		6772
高　埗	17	874	130		874
道　滘	18	558	51		558
洪　梅	8	1163	54		1163
沙　田	21	982	128		982
厚　街	24	1458	424		1458
长　安	35	3446	203		3446
寮　步	46	2006	449		2006
大岭山	37	1207	276		1207
大　朗	53	1855	308		1855
黄　江	23	861	70		861
樟木头	18	313	73		313
清　溪	36	2373	365		2373
塘　厦	49	4258	325		4258
凤　岗	28	1684	242		1684
谢　岗	8	242	62		242
常　平	50	1488	276		1488
桥　头	23	817	71		817
横　沥	15	444	30		444
东　坑	18	786	179		786
企　石	12	346	48		346
石　排	17	834	122		834
茶　山	18	335	35		335
松山湖	43	4949	961		4949

14-18 镇街规模以上工业企业R&D经费情况（2014年）

The R&D Funds of Industrial Enterprises above Designated Size by Town (2014)

镇街	R&D经费内部支出合计（万元）	按活动类型分组			按资金来源分组			
		基础研究支出	应用研究支出	试验发展支出	政府资金	企业资金	境外资金	其他资金
全市总计	1150506		3754	1146753	11334	1114200	14807	10165
莞城	13317			13317		12228		1089
石龙	32496			32496	857	30116		1523
虎门	54539			54539	234	54305		
东城	63880			63880	506	62932	57	384
万江	19035			19035	305	18389		340
南城	17944		3754	14190	2045	15899		
中堂	8964			8964	58	8906		
望牛墩	5181			5181		5181		
麻涌	58882			58882	376	58350		156
石碣	78483			78483		78483		
高埗	20363			20363	20	20343		
道滘	12910			12910	215	11217	1478	
洪梅	22751			22751	5	22746		
沙田	20074			20074	16	19950		108
厚街	53931			53931	16	42584	10351	980
长安	86406			86406	87	86005		314
寮步	41808			41808	177	41215	277	139
大岭山	26050			26050	108	25602		340
大朗	37743			37743	1747	35579		417
黄江	18304			18304	19	16315	190	1780
樟木头	6075			6075		6000	75	
清溪	37689			37689	610	36492	21	565
塘厦	57611			57611	243	56918		449
凤岗	25911			25911	168	25196	144	403
谢岗	5431			5431		3825	1606	
常平	34498			34498	257	33679		562
桥头	22555			22555		21862	607	85
横沥	9440			9440	19	9314		107
东坑	20775			20775	30	20660		85
企石	5945			5945	599	5346		
石排	10969			10969		10969		
茶山	8870			8870	19	8743		109
松山湖	211678			211678	2598	208852		229

14-18 续表

(2014年)

镇街	按使用项目分		R&D经费外部支出合计（万元）	对境内研究机构支出	对境内高等院校支出	对境外支出
	经常性支出	资产性支出				
全市总计	1041473	109034	143368	120399	1626	13177
莞城	12224	1093	16	16		
石龙	24880	7616	1631	1217	210	205
虎门	49810	4729	521	515		
东城	59960	3920	56	24	1	
万江	15957	3078	613	344	57	207
南城	15073	2871	39	39		
中堂	7955	1009	521	205	316	
望牛墩	4733	448				
麻涌	57076	1806	1297	932	16	339
石碣	75064	3419	87		1	
高埗	16995	3368	3			
道滘	11896	1015	63			
洪梅	22010	741	9		8	
沙田	17757	2318	825	100		417
厚街	48916	5014	234	71	4	5
长安	81778	4628	4363	8	8	292
寮步	36720	5088	132	9	100	
大岭山	23580	2470	50		38	
大朗	31878	5865	69	28	6	
黄江	15406	2898				
樟木头	5142	933	841			
清溪	32838	4851	151		141	
塘厦	53675	3936	960		72	701
凤岗	23974	1937	112		14	
谢岗	4677	754				
常平	29417	5082	72	23	46	1
桥头	19915	2639	15		10	
横沥	7196	2245	404		10	394
东坑	17825	2950	2372	10	271	
企石	4760	1185	11	11		
石排	8986	1984	40	40		
茶山	7883	987	65	65		
松山湖	195519	16159	127801	116744	298	10616

14-19 镇街规模以上工业企业全部R&D项目情况（2014年）

Basic Statistics on R&D Projects of Industrial Enterprises above Designated Size by Town (2014)

镇　街	项目数（个）	项目人员折合全时当量（人年）	全部项目经费内部支出（万元）
全市总计	4307	45603	1084522
莞　城	150	644	12625
石　龙	100	977	30903
虎　门	103	1590	51911
东　城	227	2003	59971
万　江	133	1072	16645
南　城	109	454	15786
中　堂	58	326	8743
望牛墩	43	205	4929
麻　涌	116	1448	57488
石　碣	253	6317	76695
高　埗	46	868	20258
道　滘	90	512	12425
洪　梅	60	1122	21876
沙　田	72	884	18973
厚　街	84	1394	52812
长　安	214	3230	77929
寮　步	131	1850	40842
大岭山	186	1088	23147
大　朗	234	1730	35362
黄　江	83	822	17331
樟木头	27	289	5295
清　溪	161	2114	34996
塘　厦	226	3874	54221
凤　岗	166	1542	24594
谢　岗	18	229	5258
常　平	210	1348	32515
桥　头	88	737	20563
横　沥	66	410	6993
东　坑	82	762	19220
企　石	36	330	5573
石　排	66	660	9774
茶　山	423	310	8522
松山湖	246	4461	200349

14-20 镇街规模以上工业企业办科技机构情况（2014年）

Basic Statistics on Scientific and Technological Institutions of Industrial Enterprises above Designated Size by Town (2014)

镇　街	有科技机构的工业企业数（个）	机构数（个）	机构人员合计（人）	#博士毕业	#硕士毕业	#本科毕业	机构经费支出（万元）
全市总计	563	716	40012	311	1446	15081	746857
莞　城	10	14	383	1	12	204	6126
石　龙	13	14	1048	13	43	550	26905
虎　门	21	26	1262	5	25	441	25993
东　城	44	53	2805	16	66	1320	59095
万　江	14	18	820	8	30	363	11851
南　城	5	5	106		5	83	3934
中　堂	4	4	200		8	66	1582
望牛墩	10	12	392	2	18	103	8144
麻　涌	13	17	1100	8	58	573	19919
石　碣	14	14	1123	4	15	382	16065
高　埗	9	9	642	4	12	400	14864
道　滘	12	14	626	6	11	222	8478
洪　梅	8	13	479	6	12	163	8427
沙　田	6	6	258	3	19	167	8315
厚　街	18	23	2936	7	78	1375	72359
长　安	22	25	2360	18	41	541	36909
寮　步	21	22	1938	12	48	670	29814
大岭山	29	30	1475	6	39	567	22708
大　朗	42	53	1982	19	42	828	38315
黄　江	13	14	697	4	22	245	14439
樟木头	7	7	182	2	1	62	3131
清　溪	28	50	2895	17	62	723	33781
塘　厦	35	42	3193	26	66	1024	47847
凤　岗	21	33	1678	6	35	512	22459
谢　岗	6	6	91		7	56	1502
常　平	30	34	1650	11	52	551	31122
桥　头	14	19	530		7	168	7283
横　沥	7	8	350	3	8	111	5846
东　坑	19	30	911	15	185	321	15430
企　石	18	23	909	10	28	428	14024
石　排	12	13	916	5	26	310	10841
茶　山	13	17	410	4	10	88	5551
松山湖	25	48	3665	70	355	1464	113799

14-21 镇街规模以上工业企业高新技术产品情况（2014年）

Basic Statistics on High-tech Products of Industrial Enterprises above Designated Size by Town (2014)

镇 街	生产高新技术产品企业数(家)	高新产品个数(个)	高新产品产值(万元)	高新产品销售收入(万元)	#高新产品出口销售收入	高新产品实现利税(万元)
全市总计	937	1748	47427215	45839724	23934352	2186316
莞 城	10	18	307919	308240	62210	40477
石 龙	19	34	1768436	1745640	1476267	149590
虎 门	61	85	1331470	1158600	541742	32043
东 城	28	70	1009178	790217	516378	-86782
万 江	24	38	259519	255868	53293	8155
南 城	24	36	460085	370545	213031	18595
中 堂	9	21	80535	78202	18176	2637
望 牛 墩	29	39	237727	233192	78672	13323
麻 涌	13	43	428784	418739	48780	8366
石 碣	37	57	2125004	2027804	1609035	113871
高 埗	24	31	500124	499227	301090	31780
道 滘	22	41	306127	311260	171969	22741
洪 梅	13	19	206149	204250	36511	5665
沙 田	21	39	786148	772451	179372	25357
厚 街	22	38	3055424	3011187	2902144	137302
长 安	53	164	7013583	6561336	1621998	617531
寮 步	53	94	2712824	2655504	2251648	50242
大 岭 山	53	109	2085967	2040014	1021853	63023
大 朗	33	70	555262	520454	286644	27813
黄 江	19	44	1127753	1102182	695152	21611
樟 木 头	5	6	97816	97825	63215	474
清 溪	52	86	2472327	2428934	2135759	52757
塘 厦	49	84	1474583	1468200	740440	63677
凤 岗	22	54	725969	682399	162405	152597
谢 岗	21	28	230507	226374	114966	2420
常 平	51	107	3803674	3791606	1570576	66420
桥 头	14	22	867616	758124	652688	101003
横 沥	29	50	401585	366245	235759	21701
东 坑	35	45	928883	919517	556860	25582
企 石	16	32	138686	137885	35308	3329
石 排	10	21	173251	173602	39949	3096
茶 山	32	42	629497	600557	214065	27067
松 山 湖	34	81	9124806	9123546	3326400	362856

14-22 镇街固定资产投资总额（2014年）

Total Investment in Fixed Assets by Town(2014)

单位：万元

镇街	固定资产投资	#第二产业	#工业	第三产业	#民营
莞城	202210	35200	35200	167010	151565
石龙	219873	38649	38649	181224	44102
虎门	1067910	236458	236458	831452	934180
东城	781403	88093	88093	693310	746977
万江	287832	46272	46272	241560	158183
南城	437269	26221	26221	411048	359208
中堂	153927	35891	35891	118036	146269
望牛墩	267378	236314	236314	29264	234744
麻涌	434794	244595	244595	190199	266724
石碣	244602	121496	121496	123106	174908
高埗	179045	64053	64053	114737	161126
道滘	183805	111819	111819	71986	180347
洪梅	136998	66600	66600	70398	101872
沙田	413096	97276	97276	315820	192395
厚街	785597	65435	65435	720162	688017
长安	495844	190666	190666	305178	367505
寮步	552383	82648	82648	469735	529766
大岭山	295362	76336	76336	218996	260449
大朗	507609	141858	141858	365751	418726
黄江	325232	68391	68391	256841	278932
樟木头	190541	37687	37687	152854	101637
清溪	373363	228276	228276	145087	272311
塘厦	585240	97016	97016	487540	447632
凤岗	625039	200330	200330	424709	372496
谢岗	117822	100731	100731	17091	87929
常平	402053	83486	81686	318567	348875
桥头	222183	139210	139210	82973	201300
横沥	106752	48853	48853	57899	81381
东坑	241009	122129	122129	118880	201252
企石	116350	55676	55676	60674	92710
石排	173703	93606	93606	80097	127343
茶山	195769	76350	76350	119419	127801
松山湖	838954	279484	279484	559470	636698

注：沙田镇固定资产投资总额含虎门港数据。

14-23 镇街邮电局、所通信能力及服务网点（2013-2014年）

Communication Capacity and Service Establishments of Telecommunication Offices by Town (2013-2014)

镇街	邮电局(所、综合营业厅)(处)		服务网点(含报刊亭)(处)		固定电话用户(含小灵通)(户)	
	2013年	2014年	2013年	2014年	2013年	2014年
全市总计	611	715	4269	4652	2643671	2736680
市区	65	74	708	771	530682	520972
石龙	9	11	74	82	61453	92281
虎门	44	49	315	346	217669	210726
中堂	12	14	62	66	51141	51546
望牛墩	5	7	41	46	23556	24772
麻涌	8	10	41	44	32993	30551
石碣	15	17	149	162	64056	72674
高埗	11	13	76	82	45971	51786
道滘	7	8	75	82	40952	40465
洪梅	4	6	36	37	17460	14165
沙田	10	13	74	79	45163	44802
厚街	34	39	269	298	157411	160151
长安	49	53	221	244	195105	187269
寮步	20	21	176	188	100552	100006
大岭山	24	26	131	142	63127	74091
大朗	24	29	151	166	112019	122039
黄江	18	22	141	156	69733	75499
樟木头	15	18	115	125	66491	68846
清溪	22	26	171	191	70452	81565
塘厦	41	47	247	270	121671	126858
凤岗	25	30	166	163	79549	86530
谢岗	7	10	53	55	29947	37095
常平	41	45	214	231	146203	155251
桥头	19	23	122	134	47039	51176
横沥	19	23	110	122	51012	58776
东坑	10	13	70	80	34822	36507
企石	12	15	47	51	37120	38424
石排	13	16	114	127	52235	57766
茶山	24	30	85	94	56515	54857
松山湖	4	7	15	18	21572	9234

注：市区指莞城、南城、东城、万江四个街道。

14-24 镇街商贸情况（2014年）

Statistics on Commerce by Town (2014)

单位：万元

镇 街	社会消费品零售总额	批发和零售业销售额	住宿和餐饮业营业额
莞 城	1078951	3528185	55633
石 龙	350485	767821	36831
虎 门	1670776	2350012	188039
东 城	1147359	4105437	132226
万 江	452063	1273446	51197
南 城	1720871	5400502	150779
中 堂	282638	819071	36072
望 牛 墩	97331	410275	9602
麻 涌	130130	811215	20301
石 碣	349748	684129	33202
高 埗	235903	543029	27493
道 滘	164014	326866	21911
洪 梅	59056	120376	10471
沙 田	237516	4140206	28695
厚 街	1352407	1919607	128161
长 安	1062783	2492236	96713
寮 步	2013218	2906549	56304
大 岭 山	562766	2317129	53636
大 朗	741015	1285171	52172
黄 江	372242	2073356	40353
樟 木 头	521814	2084598	38662
清 溪	397040	457215	53723
塘 厦	826149	1034905	66634
凤 岗	455773	689126	40198
谢 岗	116306	291253	16682
常 平	1001610	2265715	133082
桥 头	255348	310406	32706
横 沥	240742	267843	37706
东 坑	172498	272788	15739
企 石	154043	222687	13390
石 排	225143	330264	22973
茶 山	265316	452712	26070
松 山 湖	44540	585512	30072

注：1.沙田镇商贸情况含虎门港数据。
2.本表数据根据第三次全国经济普查资料进行修订。

14-25 镇街注册工商企业及个体户数（2014年）

Registered Industrial & Commercial Enterprises and Self-employed Individuals by Town (2014)

单位：户

镇街	总户数	#内资企业	外资企业	三来一补	私营企业	个体户
全市总计	629333	14424	11932	1715	180829	419584
莞城	17655	616	223	5	6036	10729
石龙	11002	247	110	5	1505	9126
虎门	57135	850	739	55	13830	41625
东城	43772	1178	696	53	14131	27619
万江	21072	391	200	11	6976	13488
南城	34164	1393	605	15	16584	15419
中堂	11070	295	95	15	2229	8427
望牛墩	3805	145	92	4	900	2661
麻涌	6237	281	76	6	1038	4819
石碣	15962	290	244	39	3579	11803
高埗	9511	183	163	7	2076	7073
道滘	7883	173	160	12	2188	5347
洪梅	2807	100	78	1	577	2047
沙田	9384	369	221	9	2319	6451
厚街	33286	551	586	42	8347	23692
长安	56356	889	1111	244	20670	33329
寮步	29994	612	450	17	8802	20100
大岭山	22308	429	347	31	7136	14352
大朗	29414	533	465	74	7090	21242
黄江	14878	358	369	50	4498	9584
樟木头	15592	336	241	34	4524	10435
清溪	17175	326	600	120	4543	11576
塘厦	32452	531	920	206	10655	20116
凤岗	20069	478	574	205	5235	13570
谢岗	6178	139	218	45	1311	4453
常平	28419	616	693	149	7740	19128
桥头	11870	303	328	50	2718	8464
横沥	13917	308	397	63	3495	9642
东坑	7483	264	161	26	1498	5529
企石	8934	257	180	32	1851	6611
石排	13868	301	235	43	2769	10515
茶山	13589	296	242	47	2830	10172
松山湖	2092	386	113		1149	440

注:本表数据来源于市工商局。

14-26 镇街集市贸易市场数及私营个体户注册资金额(2013-2014年)

Fair Trades and Registered Capital of Private Enterprises & Self-employed Individuals by Town (2013-2014)

镇　　街	集市贸易市场数(个)		个体工商户注册资金额(万元)		私营企业注册资金额(万元)	
	2013年	2014年	2013年	2014年	2013年	2014年
全市总计	815	779	988046	1098675	18385430	28377133
莞　城	28	24	22745	24695	950621	1206107
石　龙	16	16	16042	18444	209732	298225
虎　门	76	80	89419	99419	1125667	1699942
东　城	64	57	55335	61242	1805289	2966347
万　江	51	34	29977	31941	653887	1063903
南　城	42	31	34132	38984	2880557	4642419
中　堂	21	25	22055	24594	307551	355368
望牛墩	6	6	7694	8725	157535	225604
麻　涌	13	14	10235	11873	204906	299680
石　碣	21	24	27226	31405	211076	357605
高　埗	19	13	17538	20098	305039	432410
道　滘	11	11	13642	14795	222519	376692
洪　梅	4	4	4740	5079	219783	194326
沙　田	18	19	15352	17574	311556	517025
厚　街	49	46	58004	60185	1011026	1277414
长　安	41	40	75023	78108	1003255	1842263
寮　步	35	34	42377	46579	756921	1248372
大岭山	20	20	33284	38190	481055	748158
大　朗	25	24	56711	68593	607991	1039539
黄　江	24	23	22904	25772	329308	525766
樟木头	23	21	23921	26960	290043	516321
清　溪	22	22	26764	30337	307902	528472
塘　厦	29	30	39584	44457	949598	1379179
凤　岗	21	17	33866	37696	341422	535006
谢　岗	11	11	13446	15802	136347	186266
常　平	38	38	58642	63056	704826	1109386
桥　头	15	17	21477	24581	275031	396153
横　沥	11	14	25186	28768	254372	412904
东　坑	14	16	14320	15787	192596	241936
企　石	13	14	19260	22033	223790	312552
石　排	13	14	29202	31252	204474	306824
茶　山	19	18	24959	28222	242439	378991
松山湖	2	2	2983	3427	507316	755984

注:本表数据来源于市工商局。

14-27 镇街来料加工装配签约宗数、出口值及引进设备价值(2014年)

Contracts of Processing and Assembling of Import Materials, Export Value and Value of Equipments Imported by Town (2014)

镇　　街	累计投产宗数(宗)	出口值(万美元)	引进设备价值(万美元)
莞　　城	9	366	
石　　龙	4	247	
虎　　门	58	2209	1
东　　城	45	4530	2055
万　　江	8	909	
南　　城	12	390	
中　　堂	13	1817	1
望 牛 墩	2	2	
麻　　涌	2		
石　　碣	31	1751	
高　　埗	2	1284	
道　　滘	9	1342	
洪　　梅	1	25	
沙　　田	3	57	
厚　　街	25	10261	1
长　　安	213	217476	6134
寮　　步	33	301	
大 岭 山	21	14743	282
大　　朗	42	2255	
黄　　江	34	96509	122
樟 木 头	37	4668	
清　　溪	89	22369	2096
塘　　厦	150	28151	2831
凤　　岗	100	5971	
谢　　岗	30	2306	144
常　　平	71	3131	1
桥　　头	30	2058	
横　　沥	42	4947	
东　　坑	14	12004	
企　　石	21	1497	
石　　排	30	1608	
茶　　山	19	6035	

14-28 镇街“三资”企业签约、实际利用外资及出口值(新口径)(2014年)

Contracts, Foreign Capital Actually Utilized and Export Value of Enterprises with Foreign Investment by Town (2014)

镇　街	签约宗数(宗)	投产企业宗数(宗)	协议(合同)规定外商投资总额(万美元)	外商实际投资总额(万美元)	出口值(万美元)
莞　城	6	89	7916	3888	38370
石　龙	1	68	4791	7869	208443
虎　门	17	593	13048	19003	243474
东　城	37	428	29970	35199	225403
万　江	3	145	2484	3920	23850
南　城	34	274	33884	18430	92176
中　堂	1	83	280	635	26643
望牛墩	1	87	1297	3343	20181
麻　涌	2	62	40637	34272	137484
石　碣	7	224	7989	8857	375211
高　埗	5	135	3403	11170	121119
道　滘	2	147	2082	2997	40082
洪　梅	5	70	11226	8614	34535
沙　田	8	199	13911	9932	92857
厚　街	33	423	6608	9131	852928
长　安	41	860	25535	33958	555021
寮　步	17	402	2849	16203	492474
大岭山	8	293	6117	6028	139194
大　朗	17	405	16840	21907	116303
黄　江	14	321	17087	18113	279724
樟木头	9	192	2917	1584	66692
清　溪	19	538	23793	13692	480004
塘　厦	34	835	17083	30398	393058
凤　岗	19	500	52313	44948	228226
谢　岗	9	206	10901	5785	59275
常　平	29	576	23453	24039	477987
桥　头	7	301	3754	9844	288256
横　沥	15	341	8999	8134	129908
东　坑	5	151	7094	9426	160051
企　石	7	164	1684	3434	40172
石　排	7	216	8212	6879	64791
茶　山	8	200	7316	10808	71203
松山湖	30	111	10389	7510	113873

14-29 镇街进出口总额（2013-2014年，海关口径）

Total Value of Exports and Imports by Town (2013-2014, Custom Statistics)

单位：万美元

镇街	2013年			2014年		
	进出口总额	进口	出口	进出口总额	进口	出口
莞城	167263	56708	110555	182465	57764	124702
石龙	289031	95747	193284	319004	106843	212160
虎门	494159	161836	332323	420459	147244	273214
东城	527475	171338	356137	557307	142400	414907
万江	56924	18794	38130	61024	16653	44372
南城	734754	386386	348368	683795	224209	459587
中堂	79949	52825	27124	87533	54707	32826
望牛墩	50659	16199	34460	42061	14379	27683
麻涌	418469	255887	162582	434267	287171	147097
石碣	598473	221326	377147	614345	223140	391205
高埗	210176	71978	138198	218533	76574	141959
道滘	84848	37329	47519	79236	30757	48479
洪梅	181218	141529	39689	148507	111215	37292
沙田	208757	104840	103917	527830	229856	297974
厚街	1553619	576769	976850	1432689	508049	924639
长安	1562396	710861	851535	1765915	865495	900420
寮步	1093497	459128	634369	1132265	481447	650818
大岭山	426308	191152	235156	468680	196858	271822
大朗	333409	89962	243447	355254	93996	261257
黄江	734421	284451	449970	670074	273464	396610
樟木头	116377	41932	74445	126676	48746	77930
清溪	924896	378838	546058	912189	368025	544164
塘厦	706379	223993	482386	730142	222735	507408
凤岗	462165	144822	317343	559770	215919	343852
谢岗	104984	33249	71735	90278	26784	63493
常平	876765	336078	540687	844621	310502	534118
桥头	536786	220691	316095	512007	207915	304092
横沥	207715	66513	141202	221614	67107	154507
东坑	332346	131535	200811	316393	121364	195029
企石	60045	14976	45069	82773	16895	65878
石排	105726	23324	82402	118677	24283	94394
茶山	150538	71086	79452	162025	69299	92727
松山湖	570956	376859	194097	1166862	633678	533184

14-30 镇街实际利用外资（2013-2014年）

Foreign Capital Actually Utilized by Town (2013-2014)

单位：万美元

镇　街	2013年	2014年	镇　街	2013年	2014年
莞　城	4971	3888	寮　步	14837	16203
石　龙	5144	7869	大岭山	5555	6028
虎　门	15692	19003	大　朗	18668	21907
东　城	18250	35199	黄　江	14339	18113
万　江	3214	3920	樟木头	3462	1584
南　城	11354	18430	清　溪	19656	13692
中　堂	2924	635	塘　厦	28990	30398
望牛墩	2291	3343	凤　岗	29037	44948
麻　涌	25928	34272	谢　岗	5192	5785
石　碣	7473	8857	常　平	20006	24039
高　埗	18782	11170	桥　头	8582	9844
道　滘	2552	2997	横　沥	7453	8134
洪　梅	6556	8614	东　坑	8087	9426
沙　田	5077	9932	企　石	3196	3434
厚　街	18238	9131	石　排	5454	6879
长　安	28980	33958	茶　山	10143	10808
松山湖	4639	7510			

14-31 镇街税收总额（2013-2014年）

Taxes by Town (2013-2014)

单位：万元

镇街	2013年			2014年		
	税收总额	国税	地税	税收总额	国税	地税
莞城	274172	86487	187684	297838	101102	196736
石龙	147170	78741	68428	161704	91196	70509
虎门	580772	335674	245098	616672	371317	245354
东城	717802	316439	401363	758289	351930	406359
万江	184654	94395	90259	190450	105922	84528
南城	914215	285124	629092	898492	318552	579940
中堂	120925	84906	36018	136006	96099	39907
望牛墩	74020	59311	14709	85799	68793	17006
麻涌	261312	169922	91391	248419	148921	99498
石碣	217668	141551	76117	295981	177689	118292
高埗	132007	91803	40204	158225	115907	42318
道滘	124483	88483	36000	136093	95092	41001
洪梅	64148	43472	20676	72457	53549	18908
沙田	154693	86987	67706	201172	123697	77475
厚街	438205	213394	224811	511568	248078	263490
长安	639372	414713	224659	750099	500985	249114
寮步	381337	223966	157370	406016	248372	157644
大岭山	244483	158773	85710	278085	181586	96499
大朗	237545	149238	88307	273673	180852	92821
黄江	181830	101942	79887	211619	123600	88019
樟木头	116626	59259	57367	145421	70448	74972
清溪	282414	205422	76992	325530	237320	88210
塘厦	493380	277234	216146	602788	341153	261635
凤岗	274578	148918	125660	333097	177925	155171
谢岗	72345	53778	18568	83304	62890	20414
常平	324040	173004	151036	329145	183970	145175
桥头	124727	81714	43013	144090	100782	43308
横沥	128607	94272	34335	142088	104672	37416
东坑	100299	68303	31997	113908	75689	38219
企石	75410	52202	23208	90504	61646	28859
石排	90228	61964	28264	106145	76366	29779
茶山	126798	87008	39790	146002	101399	44603
松山湖	311251	134912	176339	428884	227613	201271

注：沙田税收(国税、地税)总额含虎门港数据。

14-32 镇街本级可支配财政收入和财政支出（2013-2014年）

Disposable Government Revenue and Expenditure by Town (2013-2014)

单位：万元

镇街	可支配财政收入		财政支出	
	2013年	2014年	2013年	2014年
莞城	69640	73431	61549	65209
石龙	67554	72450	67040	72140
虎门	225958	227971	208193	226773
东城	202190	209036	200052	207022
万江	73532	73086	70047	72291
南城	169378	171625	166271	107807
中堂	66593	69586	65996	71551
望牛墩	46894	50660	46644	50409
麻涌	78310	90622	78305	90589
石碣	63347	69683	61326	67854
高埗	55722	63608	55537	63460
道滘	62502	68806	62303	68604
洪梅	37284	37390	37252	37353
沙田	117149	107363	106234	136672
厚街	176574	304663	160787	276701
长安	186269	220228	179769	213700
寮步	117330	130082	117161	129960
大岭山	106804	105867	97842	106399
大朗	86723	95451	86650	90929
黄江	147444	126031	149196	107944
樟木头	75305	77984	73959	77889
清溪	82495	118555	80869	115870
塘厦	189279	180093	162012	184707
凤岗	118351	184594	118434	185241
谢岗	40801	44048	40690	43363
常平	129349	142296	122522	159399
桥头	62511	67283	61237	65826
横沥	73083	79986	70059	83785
东坑	65460	62887	63197	62508
企石	39607	47566	39601	45592
石排	49363	53910	51542	58314
茶山	61365	72595	60484	73158
松山湖	113027	201474	145809	191145

注：沙田镇本级可支配财政收入和财政支出含虎门港数据。

14-33 镇街各项人民币存贷款余额与城乡居民储蓄存款余额（2013-2014年）

Balance of Deposits and Loans by Town and Savings Deposit of Urban and Rural Household (2013-2014)

单位：万元

镇　街	年末各项存款余额		年末各项贷款余额		年末城乡居民储蓄存款余额	
	2013年	2014年	2013年	2014年	2013年	2014年
莞　城	9994948	11572596	3967650	4228796	2097387	2027096
石　龙	1727497	1759294	825702	921560	1131933	1139044
虎　门	6266356	6387868	3060000	3437642	4589828	4627977
东　城	7563735	7753739	5389686	5640689	3643572	3704206
万　江	1809034	1832714	1181825	1276305	1223059	1286142
南　城	15072762	15872116	11245498	13307606	3493445	3513345
中　堂	1103103	1099944	813614	922720	767014	806150
望牛墩	516814	528295	254179	254230	350956	364171
麻　涌	986595	1047500	372072	463162	490114	491266
石　碣	1756276	1813265	636578	660292	1164959	1207248
高　埗	852386	886058	311267	349798	605755	647470
道　滘	827093	874521	417199	431502	590315	620215
洪　梅	327903	319671	258867	347550	198305	208031
沙　田	1084794	1070677	586079	586177	601489	615987
厚　街	4324393	4427479	2999937	3481753	2731276	2811184
长　安	5750285	5963129	2209172	2380408	3382771	3557554
寮　步	1982272	2013728	964289	1096122	1386568	1471880
大岭山	1487020	1586831	800871	821527	1022240	1095686
大　朗	2707877	2779206	1397976	1666197	1826737	1921560
黄　江	1621125	1545464	630589	675268	1076025	1121875
樟木头	1356175	1438944	803648	898040	991529	1010324
清　溪	1674100	1708220	555194	604119	1140655	1192221
塘　厦	3182514	3230830	1920106	2314123	1922981	1958116
凤　岗	2066219	2276806	1278820	1513352	1284834	1351120
谢　岗	552610	722254	226567	337492	380028	400252
常　平	3316937	3245683	1496750	1493839	2327021	2360496
桥　头	1033474	1057808	527985	574688	777356	787527
横　沥	1025086	1092939	411530	425918	783295	843373
东　坑	694291	710287	337258	370454	504085	539924
企　石	729949	793143	430318	397005	539463	571245
石　排	1006274	1111983	347993	391034	747494	788967
茶　山	1179959	1195252	431036	436557	845436	869679
松山湖	727468	980971	652025	610422	146389	156612

注：本表数据来源于市人民银行。

14-34 镇街普通中学情况（2014年）

Basic Statistics on Regular Secondary Schools by Town (2014)

镇街	学校数(所)	毕业生数(人)	#普通高中	招生数(人)	#普通高中	在校学生数(人)	#普通高中	教职工数(人)	#专任教师
全市总计	212	82718	25180	102112	26741	284648	78053	21663	17148
莞城									
石龙	4	1345		1459		4296		303	269
虎门	10	3251	336	4895	402	13304	1163	1417	834
东城	12	3100	9	4762	653	12028	1065	945	682
万江	6	1923		1889		6146		496	404
南城	9	2921	673	3586	689	10428	2072	771	661
中堂	7	2082	160	2638	220	7172	629	594	420
望牛墩	3	1400		1197		3770		266	224
麻涌	2	949		686		2402		262	215
石碣	8	1689		2341		6336		489	387
高埗	5	823		1206		3322		235	196
道滘	4	1661	459	2092	457	5878	1390	477	335
洪梅	1	201		309		628		73	58
沙田	4	1440	355	1985	574	5680	1693	709	393
厚街	10	2365		3215		8648		703	494
长安	5	2213		2756		7518		434	376
寮步	7	2459		3188		8953		585	493
大岭山	6	1796	315	2384	300	6400	877	455	363
大朗	7	2922	504	3977	513	10517	1547	726	541
黄江	3	855		1222		3353		226	190
樟木头	3	926		1273		3442		242	201
清溪	7	1451		2237		5741		449	329
塘厦	4	2458	315	3591	543	9561	1439	567	471
凤岗	10	2186	280	3227	318	8589	947	640	451
谢岗	3	719		882		2480		157	140
常平	11	2557		3504		9594		578	474
桥头	5	1736	456	2375	625	6287	1497	690	426
横沥	5	1043		1576		4104		246	209
东坑	6	1030		1731		4205		389	218
企石	3	1035		1177		3482		247	208
石排	5	932		1383		3581		263	237
茶山	7	1748	357	3496	1121	8128	2250	577	467
松山湖	2	177		812	419	1736	735	203	156
市直属	28	29325	20961	29061	19907	86939	60749	6249	5626

14-35 镇街小学情况（2014年）

Basic Statistics on Primary Schools by Town (2014)

镇街	学校数(所)	毕业生数(人)	招生数(人)	在校学生数(人)	教职工数(人)	
						#专任教师
全市总计	320	86693	125039	687269	31290	28679
莞城	9	2033	2258	13007	826	785
石龙	5	1555	1942	10523	520	469
虎门	22	5382	8216	42089	2077	1810
东城	14	5181	7734	40421	1700	1630
万江	16	3375	4931	25731	1132	1056
南城	10	3228	4775	26588	1304	1273
中堂	9	2458	2776	16379	804	765
望牛墩	4	914	1051	6286	387	361
麻涌	8	784	1168	6181	441	385
石碣	8	2941	3719	21698	928	892
高埗	6	1629	2310	12849	551	504
道滘	7	1774	2035	11230	516	495
洪梅	3	299	360	1801	129	112
沙田	4	1338	2219	11725	505	463
厚街	15	3957	6250	34601	1558	1402
长安	23	4455	8347	44331	1939	1743
寮步	16	3884	5299	31004	1365	1207
大岭山	9	2588	3697	19741	805	754
大朗	18	4330	6067	34663	1425	1220
黄江	9	1746	3152	16263	767	628
樟木头	7	1862	2823	14773	597	546
清溪	8	2781	3527	22574	1059	962
塘厦	13	3869	6024	33284	1526	1340
凤岗	14	3784	5642	30656	1377	1284
谢岗	3	1004	1212	7401	329	313
常平	18	4624	6352	36376	1493	1403
桥头	8	1988	2377	14509	725	675
横沥	5	2064	3412	18119	702	675
东坑	5	1884	2921	15124	605	546
企石	7	1413	1884	11031	476	429
石排	8	1917	2881	15161	715	657
茶山	5	2389	3343	18905	910	869
松山湖	2	511	1056	4900	283	262
市直属	2	2752	3279	17345	814	764

14-36 镇街卫生事业机构、床位及人员数（2014年）

Number of Health Care Institutions, Beds and Personnel by Town (2014)

镇街	机构数(个)	#医院	病床床位(张)	卫生工作人员(人)	#卫生技术人员	#执业(助理)医师	注册护士	药剂人员	检验人员
全市总计	2194	83	26704	53013	43091	15081	18841	2603	1597
莞城	56	4	387	1107	856	289	337	65	27
石龙	21	3	1778	2582	2077	710	907	137	71
虎门	176	7	2112	4249	3461	1170	1502	220	128
东城	180	9	3234	6344	5080	1707	2249	304	213
万江	65	4	2969	5157	4403	1395	2151	218	152
南城	109	6	1116	3323	2613	972	1117	130	119
中堂	50	2	902	1026	863	273	418	43	26
望牛墩	31	1	150	362	284	90	111	31	13
麻涌	32	2	442	567	456	163	190	37	22
石碣	33	1	270	882	751	273	341	65	23
高埗	60	2	333	777	612	212	241	40	23
道滘	59	1	200	518	406	144	156	48	18
洪梅	14	1	139	337	256	76	97	27	13
沙田	47	2	217	620	491	185	185	33	15
厚街	110	2	1055	2448	2058	706	962	86	72
长安	123	5	1357	2625	2111	817	973	130	70
寮步	126	3	1047	1981	1567	576	698	83	51
大岭山	87	2	430	1144	964	393	386	70	35
大朗	96	3	1152	1900	1535	511	648	81	52
黄江	53	2	666	1174	960	362	402	66	39
樟木头	31	2	510	1166	926	299	402	49	35
清溪	74	2	604	1381	1113	406	448	71	54
塘厦	79	4	823	2146	1781	637	742	127	78
凤岗	67	3	1019	1766	1411	501	627	84	62
谢岗	22	1	180	360	304	123	127	19	8
常平	120	3	1234	2050	1674	631	733	93	55
桥头	47	1	500	886	768	288	313	37	25
横沥	62	1	420	959	763	289	312	43	21
东坑	42	1	350	646	530	194	220	26	19
企石	39	1	448	875	705	204	268	47	18
石排	40	1	360	858	664	243	300	39	18
茶山	40	1	300	731	605	227	263	46	20
松山湖	2			66	43	15	15	8	2

14-37 镇街优抚和社会救济基本情况（2014年）

Basic Statistics on Special Care and Social Relief by Town (2014)

镇 街	敬老院个数（个）	敬老院供养人数（人）	最低生活保障户数（户）	最低生活保障人数（人）	最低生活保障费支出（万元）
全市总计	31	853	8991	19461	5744.90
莞 城	1	26	296	604	186.32
石 龙	1	20	262	593	171.93
虎 门	1	22	277	591	232.27
东 城	1	19	15	27	9.99
万 江	1	45	553	1129	368.65
南 城			49	97	29.17
中 堂	1	30	656	1587	420.89
望牛墩	1	65	383	947	336.35
麻 涌	1	17	1151	2186	780.60
石 碣	1	31	47	122	33.70
高 埗	1	15	256	661	150.29
道 滘	1	38	475	1087	318.13
洪 梅	1	32	482	904	253.56
沙 田	1	27	831	1391	191.84
厚 街	1	38	367	811	238.26
长 安	1	30	6	11	2.25
寮 步	1	41	169	391	80.82
大岭山	1	27	160	399	129.94
大 朗	1	27	432	917	202.56
黄 江	1	30	99	203	67.81
樟木头	1	38	71	164	65.61
清 溪	1	46	104	242	120.31
塘 厦	1	25	92	188	46.46
凤 岗	1	8	17	28	9.75
谢 岗	1	13	153	483	122.05
常 平	1	21	145	282	130.18
桥 头	1	41	80	169	52.73
横 沥	1	6	221	509	148.51
东 坑	1	17	198	430	123.12
企 石	1	26	286	665	219.69
石 排	1	12	452	1038	368.95
茶 山	1	20	206	605	132.21

14-38 镇街专利申请与授权数（2014年）

Basic Statistics on Patents Application Accepted and Granted by Town (2014)

单位：件

镇　街	专　利 申请数	#发明	实用新型	外观设计	专　利 授权数	#发明	实用新型	外观设计
全市总计	28432	6912	11980	9540	20340	1624	10585	8131
莞　城	356	90	147	119	306	49	144	113
石　龙	173	82	62	29	138	31	75	32
虎　门	1315	302	689	324	943	53	566	324
东　城	1972	418	952	602	1566	186	656	724
万　江	739	181	391	167	570	52	363	155
南　城	1168	260	632	276	880	80	503	297
中　堂	209	70	110	29	167	19	127	21
望牛墩	266	74	100	92	155	17	114	24
麻　涌	160	25	69	66	127	20	67	40
石　碣	647	112	297	238	596	35	296	265
高　埗	237	49	105	83	180	22	97	61
道　滘	428	103	224	101	288	20	172	96
洪　梅	134	35	46	53	113	16	49	48
沙　田	439	66	168	205	393	18	195	180
厚　街	2058	106	316	1636	1611	25	278	1308
长　安	3128	1413	1218	497	1562	219	940	403
寮　步	1126	222	463	441	878	90	412	376
大岭山	1095	120	309	666	769	42	320	407
大　朗	772	155	409	208	611	35	387	189
黄　江	848	150	284	414	629	23	311	295
樟木头	622	88	245	289	442	13	213	216
清　溪	1029	115	611	303	777	46	477	254
塘　厦	1606	267	898	441	1214	71	801	342
凤　岗	772	97	384	291	453	12	263	178
谢　岗	150	36	62	52	103	4	56	43
常　平	1134	213	482	439	879	48	468	363
桥　头	522	99	205	218	405	11	184	210
横　沥	666	165	304	197	544	14	372	158
东　坑	357	55	194	108	318	9	208	101
企　石	301	49	136	116	273	13	139	121
石　排	561	59	237	265	537	34	253	250
茶　山	499	136	214	149	332	35	161	136
松山湖	2930	1497	1009	424	1572	261	912	399
其　它	13	3	8	2	9	1	6	2

14-39 镇街总用电量和总售水量（2013-2014年）

Gross Comsumption of Electicity and Water by Town (2013-2014)

镇街	总用电量（万千瓦时）		总售水量（万吨）	
	2013年	2014年	2013年	2014年
莞城	49433	51707	1961	1785
石龙	71067	75045	1883	1898
虎门	405989	421271	9977	8804
东城	289123	298813	10261	10279
万江	127433	134270	3787	4224
南城	106193	110598	4972	4705
中堂	305228	346338	2346	2261
望牛墩	70313	74128	1364	1296
麻涌	126227	134009	2201	2334
石碣	163253	172408	3480	3506
高埗	127832	132212	2381	2698
道滘	122403	128020	2209	2454
洪梅	56063	59255	1310	1267
沙田	117883	133000	2980	3055
厚街	322975	336025	8125	7893
长安	569302	605602	11409	10316
寮步	241448	258810	6069	6014
大岭山	183024	197181	3612	3418
大朗	255167	281950	6498	6577
黄江	169016	177786	3137	3208
樟木头	95249	100246	2268	2380
清溪	244487	263874	5056	5132
塘厦	353751	383099	7532	7648
凤岗	234021	259526	4253	4434
谢岗	83082	89121	1707	1772
常平	288493	300209	7339	6935
桥头	154734	161999	3003	3020
横沥	136667	148688	3459	3543
东坑	87630	94607	1983	2036
企石	81917	89893	1672	2043
石排	125930	139190	2136	2634
茶山	138728	151307	3681	3733
松山湖	82505	101618	1806	1952

注：2013年起，沙田镇总用电量及总售水量含虎门港数据；总售水量数据来源于市水务局。

十五、村（居）委会主要指标

Main Indicators of Villagers' (Neighborhood) Committees

15 村(居)委会主要指标（2014年）

Main Indicators of Villagers'(Neighborhood) Committees (2014)

村(居)委会	土地面积(平方公里)	户籍人口(人)	外来暂住人口(人)	全部企业及个体户数(个)	#工业企业	资产总额(万元)	负债总额(万元)	资产负债率(%)	村组两级经营纯收入(万元)
莞　城									
市桥社区	0.9	32266	1697	2003	2	507	15	3.0	
东正社区	1.7	21560	3288	1020	15	603	15	2.5	
罗沙社区	1.8	15657	6250	1765		411	146	35.5	
西隅社区	0.6	11914	180	310	3	838	166	19.8	
北隅社区	1.1	28304	9650	1620	4	860	67	7.8	
博厦社区	1.0	9272	940	250	3	210	10	4.8	
兴塘社区	2.6	14032	10917	4109	20	265	100	37.7	
创业社区	1.5	21800	6284	2349	31	296	8	2.7	
罗沙联合社						24439	1123	4.6	9258
博厦联合社						6327	265	4.2	1245
细村联合社						18212	1587	8.7	2830
石　龙									
忠维村	0.8	1016	3016	277	18	8006	1970	24.6	702
林屋村	0.7	668	1988	524	5	4309	1402	32.5	594
新维村	0.6	555	1935	997	75	15376	1716	11.2	2045
蒲溪村	0.7	640	340	4		3412	842	24.7	617
西湖村	3.5	2873	4520	2382	126	80532	6369	7.9	4023
王屋洲村	3.2	1599	7213	612	39	13085	655	5.0	833
黄家山村	2.5	1962	4380	565	51	34303	12738	37.1	228
中山东社区	0.5	19549	12082	777	11	955	329	34.5	
中山西社区	0.5	19692	3761	1073	25	1013	145	14.3	
兴龙社区		18583	7754	2731	9	3313	1006	30.4	
虎　门									
树田社区	4.0	1524	8200	817	532	11591	4230	36.5	1223
怀德社区	13.8	6357	27405	1505	235	59902	3545	5.9	9195
居岐社区	1.6	1325	13350	489	59	15389	1304	8.5	1406
村头社区	1.3	825	8000	220	60	12856	4289	33.4	1119
陈村社区	1.3	799	3870	63	31	6259	776	12.4	526
黄村社区	0.9	576	4625	86	31	3512	1209	34.4	396
大宁社区	5.4	2853	25600	650	300	183035	20450	11.2	13463
北栅社区	5.9	4735	38800	2070	347	33910	5005	14.8	6210
龙眼社区	3.0	2903	45500	1480	580	103084	7175	7.0	7242
赤岗社区	7.5	4396	4600	211	80	51111	2903	5.7	2793
博涌社区	5.9	7382	29000	3600	295	73601	15636	21.2	9082
新联社区	4.0	1203	6950	550	85	8050	1617	20.1	825
白沙社区	7.8	7223	11000	1100	153	49885	13265	26.6	3153
镇口社区	1.8	3176	12218	1514	179	21147	1865	8.8	3243
金洲社区	4.8	4041	25000	1450	85	91471	18752	20.5	5431

注：村（居）委会主要指标为镇、村自报数据。

15 续表 1

(2014年)

村(居)委会	土地面积(平方公里)	户籍人口(人)	外来暂住人口(人)	全部企业及个体户数(个)	#工业企业	资产总额(万元)	负债总额(万元)	资产负债率(%)	村组两级经营纯收入(万元)
小捷滘社区	2.0	912	5330	293	82	15448	3908	25.3	1458
南栅社区	8.2	5464	39929	1688	373	98335	19878	20.2	10449
东风社区	2.8	1790	7420	352	50	15979	4990	31.2	1292
宴岗社区	1.3	1139	5500	186	26	8734	1679	19.2	1042
路东社区	5.6	3248	23000	852	223	60098	7234	12.0	8194
沙角社区	11.2	5810	21500	1245	423	43463	13298	30.6	4471
虎门寨社区	2.0	7717	9500	6900	32	23909	2227	9.3	7982
九门寨社区	2.6	1487	5500	35	30	15539	6133	39.5	978
南面社区	7.3	2829	3560	339	25	21061	2038	9.7	1301
北面社区	5.5	2641	3845	83	52	8339	3829	45.9	959
武山沙社区	2.9	2329	4800	185	60	7552	3521	46.6	744
东方社区	0.7	9100	3450	706	4	654	124	19.0	21
则徐社区	1.2	15736	10750	2028	50	1259	269	21.4	21
新湾社区	1.0	10885	3785	201	24	7032	250	3.6	883
东　城									
温塘社区	11.6	9766	48000	650	65	25548	1424	5.6	13053
桑园社区	4.0	3766	25000	440	125	11632	919	7.9	4133
周屋社区	2.8	2394	8000	365	61	6423	616	9.6	1689
余屋社区	2.0	1672	3480	285	63	5696	182	3.2	1483
鳌峙塘社区	2.0	1056	2369	149	77	4462	1534	34.4	515
峡口社区	1.6	1229	2300	237	221	7281	1271	17.5	1275
柏洲边社区	1.0	1099	3850	217	60	6874	382	5.6	1581
上桥社区	1.0	1377	3600	227	45	3170	190	6.0	1425
下桥社区	2.0	2477	5300	924	47	7875	1487	18.9	3475
樟村社区	3.0	3178	3995	529	42	22053	6600	29.9	3193
梨川社区	1.0	1650	1290	289	72	7299	354	4.9	2586
堑头社区	1.5	3114	1550	296	32	9291	257	2.8	3664
主山社区	6.6	6136	13500	1163	88	19149	395	2.1	8590
石井社区	6.7	2076	2980	145	60	11008	4830	43.9	3054
同沙社区	4.6	2472	4410	405	128	16254	692	4.3	2536
光明社区	1.9	1445	2240	177	36	9240	191	2.1	1231
牛山社区	11.0	4169	10791	818	83	13216	2234	16.9	3228
立新社区	2.5	3092	5790	521	44	5561	472	8.5	4205
火炼树社区	1.2	1378	12800	468	405	7262	1820	25.1	2888
岗贝社区	1.7	14558	9780	2029		1942	198	10.2	
花园新村社区	0.8	1344	1100	667		2301	360	15.7	
东泰社区	1.4	16203	12053	1321		4250	276	6.5	
星城社区	2.7	9688	23461			382	68	17.8	
万　江									
万江社区	2.6	4230	3149	79	62	14457	2326	16.1	2722
石美社区	2.5	4159	3364	230	80	12701	1080	8.5	2843
莫屋社区	1.0	1502	1715	168	80	5541	936	16.9	974
拔蛟窝社区	1.3	2250	1867	222	66	19577	1186	6.1	729

15 续表 2

(2014年)

村(居)委会	土地面积(平方公里)	户籍人口(人)	外来暂住人口(人)	全部企业及个体户数(个)	#工业企业	资产总额(万元)	负债总额(万元)	资产负债率(%)	村组两级经营纯收入(万元)
黄粘洲社区	0.3	805	1283	38	20	3800	770	20.3	178
蚬涌社区	2.0	2039	2168	243	96	4628	1188	25.7	1376
谷涌社区	2.0	3138	1647	245	22	21771	1125	5.2	2363
小享社区	3.8	5024	2561	215	115	19449	727	3.7	2003
滘联社区	2.1	3456	1545	83	34	7053	6158	87.3	45
金泰社区	1.0	2174	1473	132	28	4788	604	12.6	2064
曲海社区	1.2	1585	622	33	2	15626	161	1.0	1192
牌楼基社区	1.6	1616	1576	265	38	19198	535	2.8	957
大莲塘社区	0.8	1015	410	73	35	9052	352	3.9	687
水蛇涌社区	1.5	2377	2254	150	38	13063	843	6.5	404
共联社区	1.3	2037	7287	158	62	6141	471	7.7	1441
新谷涌社区	1.4	2203	936	90	38	12273	1365	11.1	948
坝头社区	1.4	1578	1350	18	12	12847	3405	26.5	1655
胜利社区	0.9	956	5625	30	24	3067	253	8.3	1013
官桥滘社区	1.9	1769	1676	80	49	10411	620	6.0	802
简沙洲社区	1.6	1719	2694	141	110	3598	4639	128.9	725
新和社区	3.7	2728	8324	186	112	10223	908	8.9	2141
上甲社区	1.4	2451	1155	76	66	8971	2671	29.8	-10
严屋社区	1.0	1123	528	39	29	4867	1028	21.1	364
大汾社区	2.6	3388	1463	315	65	16349	760	4.7	1695
新村社区	5.8	8090	1723	426	163	15004	2677	17.8	1524
流涌尾社区	2.5	2354	1046	62	47	5071	1232	24.3	952
万江墟社区	1.0	6873	1564	233	27	3741	2157	57.7	216
新城社区		8675	3143	1122		731	358	49.0	
南　　城									
胜和社区	4.0	6714	21533	3321	2	33275	8774	26.4	14763
亨美社区	0.5	1921	5000	220	14	33436	5895	17.6	1760
三元里社区	0.2	1147	1392	31	9	34091	1973	5.8	2165
篁村社区	1.0	3069	6974	763	14	30877	2969	9.6	2456
新基社区	2.0	2857	5233	1548	26	102668	926	0.9	4062
周溪社区	5.0	4044	6869	273	19	48228	934	1.9	4149
袁屋边社区	2.1	2012	8032	367	12	129952	1203	0.9	5668
白马社区	4.0	3376	10572	2030	40	35268	550	1.6	3144
石鼓社区	2.0	1819	5000	243	25	35466	2319	6.5	2751
蛤地社区	8.0	2802	3738	101	23	26367	7500	28.4	2287
西平社区	3.9	3158	6187	635	11	94395	17759	18.8	1779
水濂社区	6.0	2117	3850	118	33	18677	8919	47.8	1753
雅园社区	1.8	2509	6685	303	120	30479	3248	10.7	937
元美社区	0.4	2662	3211	381	13	11288	2192	19.4	608
鸿福社区		13200	40080						
宏远社区	1.2	12989	15320	1443	1				
新城社区	2.2	3029	2261	2298					
宏图社区		6999	110000						

15 续表 3

(2014年)

村(居)委会	土地面积(平方公里)	户籍人口(人)	外来暂住人口(人)	全部企业及个体户数(个)	#工业企业	资产总额(万元)	负债总额(万元)	资产负债率(%)	村组两级经营纯收入(万元)
中　　堂									
潢涌村	9.3	9693	5972	936	129	306251	9994	3.3	41485
三涌村	4.0	3842	1815	490	101	8657	4046	46.7	1225
湛翠村	1.8	2401	1200	193	64	5461	2110	38.6	209
袁家涌村	4.0	5673	2093	581	147	8679	1859	21.4	1013
吴家涌村	3.4	2797	1888	442	82	9031	2443	27.1	916
凤冲村	1.3	1667	822	109	45	3214	1541	48.0	332
鹤田村	2.2	2265	2200	370	131	3493	1142	32.7	260
东泊社区	2.9	3821	4402	695	206	17031	4256	25.0	1138
中堂村	1.1	1993	916	202	47	2833	589	20.8	638
一村村	0.7	1837	6273	509	34	7223	432	6.0	1211
东向村	2.4	3340	2190	371	109	3721	737	19.8	750
斗朗社区	2.5	2663	890	216	54	7640	1768	23.1	1164
江南社区	2.1	2500	4698	1053	193	13891	235	1.7	2158
蕉利村	4.6	5003	2740	552	176	6361	2055	32.3	1463
槎滘村	9.4	10274	4690	582	211	32954	4614	14.0	2825
下芦村	1.3	1235	463	62	37	7701	1543	20.0	572
马沥村	1.9	2025	499	65	19	10836	1519	14.0	1448
四乡村	4.2	3302	449	87	16	3339	687	20.6	2943
红锋社区	0.1	797	53	25	3	3016	2333	77.4	175
中心社区	0.7	8907	5453	2031	21	1842	1385	75.2	
望牛墩									
李屋村	0.6	662	950	80	33	2834	448	15.8	198
望东村	1.4	2126	1453	212	21	2843	1138	40.0	323
扶涌村	0.6	929	1592	72	11	2905	855	29.4	195
赤滘村	1.9	3094	1668	45	38	9685	4385	45.3	649
五涌村	1.4	1561	1412	69	35	2926	1037	35.4	281
下漕村	3.5	4410	4250	98	42	6036	3433	56.9	426
上合村	1.9	3084	1621	46	34	3822	1662	43.5	470
聚龙江村	0.7	1034	2364	220	18	7297	908	12.4	512
望联村	2.8	5254	1372	424	24	3917	1050	26.8	487
洲湾村	1.6	1946	362	45	16	3653	1458	39.9	185
洲涡村	1.9	2678	716	42	22	5283	829	15.7	269
寮厦村	1.4	1460	1080	37	12	5101	1735	34.0	445
官桥涌村	0.7	1007	1171	22	14	3564	327	9.2	357
芙蓉沙村	0.8	1069	1315	30	15	3346	1092	32.6	396
杜屋村	1.8	2476	758	92	30	7110	1228	17.3	415
横沥村	1.8	2316	1382	36	7	4461	1382	31.0	181
福安村	0.6	1104	417	36	5	3932	670	17.0	216
官洲村	1.0	1074	576	40	13	2780	1293	46.5	211
石排村	0.4	648	960	16	7	2041	860	42.1	215
朱平沙村	2.7	3452	2564	48	14	11990	3475	29.0	268
锦涡村	2.2	1609	836	38	7	5813	778	13.4	196
望牛墩社区		4775	1233						

15　续表 4

(2014年)

村(居)委会	土地面积(平方公里)	户籍人口(人)	外来暂住人口(人)	全部企业及个体户数(个)	#工业企业	资产总额(万元)	负债总额(万元)	资产负债率(%)	村组两级经营纯收入(万元)
麻　　涌									
麻一村	4.0	4147	730	308	23	8326	1857	22.3	387
麻二社区	6.8	3647	651	152	27	12909	5012	38.8	891
麻三村	3.7	3852	1676	1435	52	10518	1175	11.2	621
麻四村	4.5	4896	760	240	23	16787	9707	57.8	280
大步村	10.7	7376	2496	854	38	25011	1305	5.2	965
东太村	4.8	4565	1413	385	21	8149	1341	16.5	633
新基村	4.4	5744	3374	419	37	11403	529	4.6	1087
川槎村	3.0	3990	2009	297	29	660	591	89.6	781
鸥涌村	2.8	3906	4115	354	17	794	411	51.8	1218
黎滘村	1.3	1362	514	80	15	2857	925	32.4	358
华阳村	5.5	5359	962	278	16	13844	3602	26.0	536
南洲村	3.4	2834	1521	214	18	10888	749	6.9	539
大盛村	6.9	3012	12750	797	28	25349	2246	8.9	2209
漳澎村	29.6	12787	2344	421	39	52458	25904	49.4	1073
麻涌社区		6964							
石　　碣									
唐洪村	1.0	1803	2102	428	45	13168	3452	26.2	1350
水南村	2.8	3632	5753	1556	148	18249	4199	23.0	4915
石碣村	4.6	5367	10250	1704	211	16457	5222	31.7	6455
刘屋村	4.9	4638	4723	553	128	9164	2456	26.8	2936
横滘村	1.6	2032	6228	1021	111	12457	5102	41.0	2448
鹤田厦村	2.5	1979	4665	285	25	10086	3125	31.0	1528
四甲村	4.0	4732	6288	858	136	16412	2418	14.7	4954
沙腰村	4.0	3623	3493	318	73	16389	1528	9.3	2299
梁家村	2.0	2484	1840	150	60	13013	6347	48.8	675
桔洲村	1.2	1487	9987	443	76	39569	1512	3.8	3432
单屋村	2.3	1323	2410	193	96	17016	3423	20.1	973
涌口村	1.6	1783	3738	465	130	18160	6349	35.0	832
西南村	2.6	2008	6500	1044	82	47943	2483	5.2	5358
黄泗围村	1.2	713	2153	454	80	12008	665	5.5	1316
城中社区		8533	5868	1451	143	7286	7289	100.0	45
高　　埗									
冼沙村	7.5	7672	32951	453	137	12566	10884	86.6	2912
卢溪村	2.3	1725	5249	50	35	4558	625	13.7	480
宝莲村	0.7	1046	1417	41	15	1913	330	17.3	108
塘厦村	2.7	1955	3497	105	19	2602	752	28.9	931
草墩村	0.8	822	1698	24	22	3778	1285	34.0	439
护安围村	1.9	1171	2350	95	43	5731	810	14.1	412
保安围村	2.3	2414	3370	112	55	22303	16078	72.1	-949

15 续表 5

(2014年)

村(居)委会	土地面积(平方公里)	户籍人口(人)	外来暂住人口(人)	全部企业及个体户数(个)	#工业企业	资产总额(万元)	负债总额(万元)	资产负债率(%)	村组两级经营纯收入(万元)
三联村	2.1	1374	2612	28	5	3426	1933	56.4	317
横滘头村	0.9	1107	2145	16	8	4358	820	18.8	467
低涌村	2.2	2900	21431	400	21	6065	2395	39.5	1529
朱磡村	1.0	1508	905	35	18	1898	774	40.8	315
欧邓村	0.7	946	7432	27	9	3209	1790	55.8	192
芦村	1.3	1744	4073	57	19	3215	591	18.4	249
高埗村	2.1	3372	48376	281	63	6207	2741	44.2	3406
凌屋村	1.2	1272	7255	80	7	4987	2140	42.9	217
上江城村	1.9	2331	18139	116	13	10383	4896	47.2	1215
下江城村	1.5	1562	6690	125	25	5881	2649	45.0	2073
新联村	1.3	1724	1540	148	9	1594	885	55.5	854
新创社区									
道滘									
南城村	7.1	4384	3311	582	119	17842	1339	7.5	2149
闸口村	5.2	2838	4310	438	38	14453	1404	9.7	1296
北永村	6.3	3787	3332	249	109	21844	3211	14.7	1215
永庆村	3.1	1677	2515	168	105	9387	512	5.5	920
厚德村	4.2	2511	4619	195	48	11913	558	4.7	571
蔡白村	5.5	4833	3638	317	65	25693	5349	20.8	826
南丫村	6.8	4229	11843	453	140	27313	4014	14.7	2194
九曲村	4.6	3153	2396	170	53	9560	1717	18.0	702
大罗沙村	4.5	2985	3617	65	35	8010	617	7.7	668
小河村	6.1	5803	3477	209	79	13711	3421	25.0	1508
昌平村	3.8	3560	2530	165	42	12382	5397	43.6	1198
大岭丫村	4.1	3719	4162	321	112	26190	6043	23.1	1878
大鱼沙村	1.7	1737	1571	210	33	5201	338	6.5	441
兴隆社区		11873	1189			348	283	81.3	
洪梅									
洪屋涡村	14.1	7019	5200	329	145	18462	1906	10.3	870
新庄村	1.0	888	3282	89	24	4192	1304	31.1	328
梅沙村	3.5	4074	1750	124	20	8592	2327	27.1	581
金鳌沙村	2.3	1368	580	41	12	4700	1677	35.7	482
乌沙村	3.7	2267	2700	44	22	10793	1098	10.2	427
尧均村	0.9	603	2850	82	11	2713	1125	41.5	160
夏汇村	1.0	740	200	10	6	2576	1116	43.3	248
氹涌村	1.6	2024	2000	117	7	6695	2133	31.9	230
黎洲角村	1.6	2715	6450	487	10	10102	1899	18.8	607
洪梅社区	5.0	1151	2731	469	3				
沙田									
中围村	3.2	1843		30	2	16899	1826	10.8	1460
和安村	6.7	3317		29	4	12912	2965	23.0	810

15 续表 6

(2014年)

村(居)委会	土地面积(平方公里)	户籍人口(人)	外来暂住人口(人)	全部企业及个体户数(个)	#工业企业	资产总额(万元)	负债总额(万元)	资产负债率(%)	村组两级经营纯收入(万元)
大流村	4.2	2139		92	7	14590	6214	42.6	1076
泥洲村	6.6	4017		34	4	15802	7902	50.0	1296
杨公洲村	3.9	1965	3326	768	306	9552	3088	32.3	1314
阁西村	5.4	2299	6283	853	134	34056	9751	28.6	1824
民田村	5.2	2676	8530	925	250	12461	3228	25.9	1139
大泥村	4.4	1899	7534	1151	583	10461	1632	15.6	845
福禄沙村	4.8	2012	2156	296	82	8392	1589	18.9	689
西大坦村	6.8	2150		170	12	9115	3280	36.0	424
穗丰年村	6.0	2828	3106	407	166	22355	5217	23.3	1562
齐沙村	3.8	2092	7086	617	186	14052	2624	18.7	1377
稔洲村	4.7	2516	12485	1402	489	18035	10471	58.1	937
义沙村	5.1	1934	11556	388	442	10960	2133	19.5	776
西太隆村	4.5	2070	7215	747	355	7567	3056	40.4	776
横流社区	1.0	3948	3215	1432	110	6243	1181	18.9	273
先锋村	0.6	2054	121	72	28	5803	1054	18.2	232
滨港社区		1025							
厚街									
厚街社区	5.7	9140	23002	6538	987	42106	13364	31.7	2707
珊美社区	2.0	2536	14138	2261	91	40175	10057	25.0	2789
寮厦社区	3.4	2477	9984	2625	275	29729	3686	12.4	2798
河田社区	10.1	6353	23078	2316	333	50753	9759	19.2	3701
汀山社区	4.7	1978	19299	1137	458	36690	1784	4.9	1476
环冈社区	5.0	2116	8406	415	111	19900	6070	30.5	544
三屯社区	3.5	2731	19084	1513	343	88017	10222	11.6	6930
宝屯社区	3.1	2602	9539	1274	501	31906	10785	33.8	3069
陈屋社区	2.5	1537	9191	1589	265	28373	1486	5.2	3175
赤岭社区	6.2	3733	27574	1663	443	64850	27539	42.5	4858
桥头社区	11.7	8170	14205	2036	573	78925	16188	20.5	4556
南五社区	1.2	1553	7631	731	211	16175	3810	23.6	1067
溪头社区	4.5	3889	19129	901	231	70338	9298	13.2	5840
沙塘社区	1.4	2071	4364	263	108	16542	4272	25.8	1720
宝塘社区	1.7	1610	7685	575	173	24352	4731	19.4	1692
下汴社区	6.0	1771	7434	807	279	21544	2275	10.6	1769
白濠社区	5.5	5425	22757	1743	718	50182	6094	12.1	4907
新塘社区	4.4	5725	16661	1782	401	77622	29611	38.2	5557
双岗社区	4.5	6960	7549	1238	401	24178	5381	22.3	2186
涌口社区	3.7	5570	14931	1281	335	53600	5332	10.0	3070
大迳社区	13.2	3669	3189	251	108	11979	2717	22.7	813
新围社区	17.6	4514	3419	360	145	11538	1882	16.3	506
竹溪社区		14036	5929	1		4958	424	8.6	93
长安									
涌头社区	3.8	1778	26476	1173	205	30829	12135	39.4	4632

15 续表 7

(2014年)

村(居)委会	土地面积(平方公里)	户籍人口(人)	外来暂住人口(人)	全部企业及个体户数(个)	#工业企业	资产总额(万元)	负债总额(万元)	资产负债率(%)	村组两级经营纯收入(万元)
霄边社区	8.3	3517	44865	3184	65	135011	8643	6.4	6432
咸西社区	4.0	1314	26198	1053	160	66286	6238	9.4	3197
锦厦社区	8.2	4411	61917	4222	286	140930	30966	22.0	20423
新安社区	8.5	3519	46323	3089	242	48049	6059	12.6	7970
乌沙社区	11.3	3952	99409	5276	705	56260	6899	12.3	26128
新民社区	2.4	958	29956	1148	187	40734	23957	58.8	1643
沙头社区	13.4	6456	70375	994	303	111955	19783	17.7	8869
上沙社区	7.4	2959	50938	3117	372	67691	8758	12.9	9087
厦岗社区	8.7	3291	42636	2125	562	50353	2580	5.1	5399
厦边社区	4.7	2539	25427	2590	301	25043	4683	18.7	5828
上角社区	3.2	1361	44407	1128	197	54741	15071	27.5	6469
长盛社区	0.8	8962	45709	4141	27	12660	3587	28.3	
寮　步									
塘边社区	0.7	1677	3000	250	30	5149	5577	108.3	1837
西溪村	4.5	4708	8235	716	350	14941	2256	15.1	1828
凫山村	4.0	6148	8100	562	95	12370	1051	8.5	4534
石步村	4.7	4646	7500	380	98	20950	2123	10.1	1920
良边村	2.7	3247	4550	334	250	6246	1548	24.8	1892
富竹山村	3.5	2034	4936	288	39	12905	2330	18.1	1190
塘唇村	3.4	2365	3125	423	50	23538	2588	11.0	2667
向西村	2.9	2628	4250	476	86	10360	5232	50.5	517
下岭贝村	1.8	1608	5321	249	41	14366	2157	15.0	2666
岭厦社区	0.9	1032	4000	152	59	17761	514	2.9	1897
新旧围社区	1.4	1022	1200	280	213	8327	729	8.8	804
霞边村	1.3	912	1500	97	20	9597	662	6.9	709
横坑社区	5.9	4999	24430	506	406	114295	4841	4.2	7405
竹园村	1.5	918	1896	138	42	6901	2500	36.2	272
上屯村	4.5	3449	3990	415	45	16410	2318	14.1	2067
石龙坑村	1.9	3703	4850	427	210	9711	257	2.7	2097
牛杨社区	1.2	1576	6800	298	109	12724	3309	26.0	1310
泉塘社区	2.3	1579	6000	54	29	6914	2087	30.2	1147
坑口社区	1.6	1237	4512	470	32	11465	2879	25.1	902
浮竹山村	3.4	1582	3000	163	33	14837	3179	21.4	1061
上底村	2.0	1514	1192	103	21	4540	1773	39.1	581
刘屋巷村	1.6	575	826	55	29	5907	1089	18.4	360
药勒村	2.4	1168	2900	175	65	23367	2107	9.0	852
陈家埔村	1.6	970	1800	203	40	10824	3254	30.1	603
缪边社区	1.6	1229	3000	158	35	11427	554	4.9	1164
寮步社区	1.7	8723	4700	2400	18	5795	988	17.1	439
小坑村	1.5	836	1500	48	16	6378	383	6.0	359

15 续表 8

(2014年)

村(居)委会	土地面积(平方公里)	户籍人口(人)	外来暂住人口(人)	全部企业及个体户数(个)	#工业企业	资产总额(万元)	负债总额(万元)	资产负债率(%)	村组两级经营纯收入(万元)
长坑村	1.5	994	600	26	19	9531	426	4.5	666
井巷村	1.1	934	1150	47	44	6749	1770	26.2	695
良平社区									
大岭山									
马蹄岗村	0.8	2246	6000	254	122	6325	2498	39.5	1048
大塘朗村	3.0	1651	3000	78	46	4988	1905	38.2	716
新塘村	2.0	2263	7026	278	102	9566	1218	12.7	1981
元岭村	0.3	1003	2310	120	3	14906	512	3.4	582
金桔村	4.3	3736	8500	534	60	24277	4670	19.2	1263
鸡翅岭村	4.5	1353	2012	185	25	6141	1861	30.3	712
大沙村	3.0	1901	2392	285	268	9297	2061	22.2	1347
旧飞鹅村	3.1	484	1300	20	13	5222	106	2.0	347
连平村	7.2	3004	13650	277	77	6469	1434	22.2	2485
梅林村	1.5	580	7600	142	69	3342	708	21.2	996
下高田村	0.5	478	835	61	39	2960	529	17.9	227
大环村	2.0	633	1500	65	28	3600	924	25.7	374
太公岭村	2.2	1749	4700	232	62	5050	743	14.7	935
百花洞村	4.8	1335	7100	283	65	12080	3337	27.6	702
大片美村	2.6	1025	4862	227	17	4435	235	5.3	826
矮岭冚村	5.5	3785	20000	1876	924	15361	6493	42.3	3034
大岭村	7.0	2411	705	88	76	5022	1347	26.8	682
农场社区	1.0	773	3780	468	15	7841	262	3.3	1812
水朗村	4.5	1413	2805	50	16	14700	325	2.2	861
大塘村	8.5	3371	20000	428	200	14286	2868	20.1	2064
杨屋村	12.0	5015	14500	640	150	11597	1219	10.5	4020
颜屋村	3.0	780	6680	209	116	5851	823	14.1	571
大岭山社区	10.0	6020	7550	1910	18	577	217	37.6	290
大朗									
竹山社区	1.3	1667	2764	366	174	13664	1068	7.8	671
高英村	1.7	1825	4098	427	205	15943	4531	28.4	514
巷头社区	3.5	4514	14186	4176	894	101512	17085	17.0	4276
巷尾社区	1.6	2011	6235	1397	389	41902	6289	15.0	2116
求富路社区	1.4	1478	6162	806	176	29364	3920	13.4	2285
长塘社区	2.7	4913	10486	2071	420	78225	32890	42.1	4449
大井头社区	4.1	5880	7508	3026	550	77311	9126	11.8	4010
圣堂社区	0.9	1636	2489	1769	119	28409	1036	3.7	2013
蔡边村	6.1	4298	4961	1631	594	46043	13042	28.3	1521
水口村	3.3	3048	6607	1121	461	27457	4451	16.2	1580
洋乌村	2.1	1728	2821	645	335	17740	2828	15.9	1367
洋坑塘村	1.1	1113	5541	580	248	12850	2532	19.7	709
松柏朗村	2.5	4282	4708	782	301	17066	7630	44.7	692

15 续表 9

(2014年)

村(居)委会	土地面积(平方公里)	户籍人口(人)	外来暂住人口(人)	全部企业及个体户数(个)	#工业企业	资产总额(万元)	负债总额(万元)	资产负债率(%)	村组两级经营纯收入(万元)
黄草朗社区	1.5	2411	4622	1050	538	16611	6354	38.3	527
黎贝岭村	1.9	2295	3435	781	299	17819	1408	7.9	1062
佛子凹村	1.1	2493	1027	420	137	11127	1339	12.0	1088
佛新社区	0.6	901	597	301	133	14457	1494	10.3	411
松木山村	2.7	2701	7220	1014	518	23279	4535	19.5	1530
犀牛陂村	8.0	3402	8155	1740	1033	18136	1396	7.7	2298
水平村	7.9	1940	4545	729	295	22665	3869	17.1	815
屏山社区	2.3	530	392	114	53	5978	536	9.0	361
宝陂村	0.5	737	116	89	24	12343	5291	42.9	462
石厦村	8.0	3074	5030	1031	521	17509	1581	9.0	855
杨涌村	1.5	1413	3726	541	198	4008	328	8.2	394
沙步村	3.1	2317	3361	1088	498	1126	875	77.7	695
新马莲村	6.6	1629	3736	605	260	3456	1650	47.7	822
大朗社区	0.3	6433	2358	679	25	3022	346	11.5	245
长富社区	1.5	2823	637	519	36				
黄江									
田美社区	11.4	4679	137773	1509	401	33743	3590	10.6	5261
宝山社区	4.9	2779	22839	618	165	34605	2160	6.2	3615
北岸社区	5.9	1618	15120	282	70	10717	816	7.6	1710
三新社区	16.0	2891	12240	772	148	21938	1072	4.9	1581
梅塘社区	18.2	4977	31936	1247	363	43854	5142	11.7	3856
长龙社区	18.0	2580	8000	280	68	11474	2930	25.5	1366
新市社区	1.6	7609	10697	1893		1429	427	29.9	148
樟木头									
圩镇社区	4.3	10810	9653	2279	187	18592	11954	64.3	67
樟罗社区	6.8	3595	15064	2962	72	32870	9367	28.5	2654
百果洞社区	2.4	979	6000	1280	26	14718	4915	33.4	355
樟洋社区	13.5	2482	27485	1872	45	18479	5284	28.6	842
石新社区	7.3	2363	9564	1724	136	41348	23539	56.9	1599
柏地社区	6.6	1444	7200	930	94	16826	6869	40.8	286
官仓社区	3.0	1135	2750	285	38	7337	2566	35.0	290
裕丰社区	10.0	2093	13834	569	102	10635	4108	38.6	882
金河社区	14.0	1772	9682	863	210	9678	2768	28.6	458
清溪									
罗马村	7.0	1889	7550	350	53	3895	1826	46.9	1670
长山头村	4.3	1181	5000	79	32	12990	4378	33.7	1519
荔横村	3.4	1545	12600	274	60	9590	7979	83.2	3460
浮岗村	3.0	1947	7300	520	45	16742	5297	31.6	1717
松岗村	3.9	1250	3030	86	46	2010	778	38.7	917
上元村	4.3	951	3500	225	29	4249	1712	40.3	1059
重河村	8.4	2718	8000	350	40	11294	3516	31.1	3339

15 续表 10

(2014年)

村(居)委会	土地面积(平方公里)	户籍人口(人)	外来暂住人口(人)	全部企业及个体户数(个)	#工业企业	资产总额(万元)	负债总额(万元)	资产负债率(%)	村组两级经营纯收入(万元)
清厦村	2.3	1588	6825	570	40	5912	3481	58.9	1581
铁松村	5.6	2582	9568	197	90	12204	4390	36.0	1997
铁场村	7.4	804	268	23	6	6645	3163	47.6	614
九乡村	7.5	1705	3000	200	62	7427	5519	74.3	1126
大埔村	1.8	727	3200	95	33	3069	1261	41.1	331
大利村	9.6	2687	11856	885	61	13538	3287	24.3	3465
渔樑围村	2.5	1123	18400	350	72	9918	1525	15.4	2296
三星村	2.5	1086	4300	115	28	2492	1849	74.2	1034
厦坭村	1.7	921	6210	339	30	10846	7885	72.7	416
土桥村	1.2	597	6800	256	42	9256	5186	56.0	1068
谢坑村	3.2	802	4620	98	52	6396	1579	24.7	930
三中村	9.0	1790	58312	673	135	13015	5965	45.8	3360
青皇村	6.5	1149	3300	60	36	2693	342	12.7	1420
清溪社区	7.0	8150	13927	3038	20	4903	3036	61.9	1527
塘厦									
林村社区	21.0	5761	44510	1842	249	88852	8057	9.1	12173
莲湖社区	9.0	2270	19875	562	222	18784	5656	30.1	2665
石潭埔社区	6.8	1644	10150	145	68	40692	1101	2.7	2615
横塘社区	4.0	1166	8600	104	93	10823	1461	13.5	1717
莆心湖社区	6.1	2160	17500	206	75	34718	1469	4.2	3233
诸佛岭社区	2.4	1157	10598	291	50	29895	5055	16.9	3217
振兴围社区	2.4	1019	13200	225	45	17704	820	4.6	1658
四村社区	4.0	1130	9910	931	39	17153	4095	23.9	1569
蛟乙塘社区	4.9	1475	9905	321	100	29419	1334	4.5	2494
沙湖社区	4.0	612	7743	103	85	13155	586	4.5	1420
大坪社区	13.0	1412	12532	88	78	46327	1147	2.5	2168
田心社区	4.5	910	9800	101	90	16682	1974	11.8	1814
龙背岭社区	8.2	1004	10000	257	73	12960	626	4.8	806
石鼓社区	6.4	2657	17000	287	103	31721	1910	6.0	4030
石马社区	2.7	501	6000	180	60	7061	1413	20.0	551
清湖头社区	4.1	1462	19800	202	156	23360	2095	9.0	3906
平山社区	4.8	828	10000	141	108	25628	4462	17.4	1902
桥陇社区	2.8	1049	11921	166	73	11393	2658	23.3	1259
凤凰岗社区	3.5	1378	10326	365	80	18751	2183	11.6	1985
塘厦社区	0.9	3889	46000	2130	340	2663	199	7.5	1049
三局社区		2780							
塘新社区		14010							
凤岗									
雁田村	21.8	3815	58982	3397	398	289413	55871	19.3	21700
官井头村	10.4	1977	18233	1474	165	134499	5112	3.8	4958
油甘埔村	6.9	2058	20327	519	415	37660	8930	23.7	5806
凤德岭村	3.4	1291	5348	464	134	16607	4657	28.0	3042

15 续表 11

(2014年)

村(居)委会	土地面积(平方公里)	户籍人口(人)	外来暂住人口(人)	全部企业及个体户数(个)	#工业企业	资产总额(万元)	负债总额(万元)	资产负债率(%)	村组两级经营纯收入(万元)
塘沥村	6.7	1938	26538	300	80	8875	1053	11.9	4158
黄洞村	11.7	2267	13185	311	120	13810	2276	16.5	2699
竹塘村	5.7	1305	12384	380	91	10798	4963	46.0	3205
竹尾田村	1.5	754	5356	244	37	8490	619	7.3	1065
三联村	3.4	1500	13589	1386	36	5292	715	13.5	3299
五联村	5.6	1358	15772	375	179	17925	6425	35.8	2528
天堂围村	4.2	1134	8678	639	85	21564	2092	9.7	1758
凤岗社区	1.1	7130	2626	486	18				838
谢岗									
黎村村	12.8	3880	4105	158	58	12876	1843	14.3	1111
南面村	31.6	1542	788	33	20	4712	548	11.6	187
窑山村	1.0	534	1650	104	35	2849	525	18.4	245
大龙村	5.9	1058	2035	60	44	3033	1572	51.8	335
大厚村	6.3	1058	6780	199	65	10379	314	3.0	729
谢山村	3.9	642	3500	251	26	8449	184	2.2	419
谢岗村	10.4	2999	2984	158	82	12349	713	5.8	995
赵林村	7.1	1728	5547	136	76	10903	1175	10.8	1178
曹乐村	7.1	2227	10018	473	142	7164	2249	31.4	1093
五星村	1.8	1345	4289	120	30	1871	1589	84.9	299
稔子园村	2.4	659	2240	72	43	8509	318	3.7	511
泰园社区	0.8	3509	6544	1437	108	571	746	130.6	33
常平									
常平社区	0.7	18385	4750	872	32	313	53	16.9	
下墟村	0.8	856	2019	152	35	25567	7212	28.2	2465
岗梓村	3.0	2574	4807	113	74	7922	3459	43.7	879
桥梓村	1.8	2500	5471	320	155	19894	2539	12.8	1783
塘角村	1.2	968	6212	165	135	9666	1541	15.9	871
苏坑村	2.6	3694	5801	208	206	6947	1019	14.7	1638
袁山贝村	4.9	3650	10641	515	315	20039	4323	21.6	2299
金美村	3.1	2502	12778	310	145	33921	3955	11.7	3809
还珠沥村	5.1	2842	10376	581	153	12721	4714	37.1	1684
朗贝村	3.3	2041	8136	278	73	6452	578	9.0	2232
板石村	2.7	2041	6889	610	38	3892	697	17.9	2012
桥沥村	9.3	3590	15104	784	296	12509	1213	9.7	3463
卢屋村	2.4	858	4035	161	161	2556	1277	50.0	540
土塘村	6.7	2900	19380	1524	169	23423	1811	7.7	2298
麦元村	2.3	1100	7720	665	23	10542	1282	12.2	905
九江水村	7.5	1478	6742	236	76	25072	414	1.7	1255
朗洲村	6.4	627	1811	112	29	6130	560	9.1	253
陈屋贝村	2.7	1124	4432	166	41	11771	483	4.1	856
司马村	7.1	2827	12770	616	84	21037	3433	16.3	2352

15　续表 12

(2014年)

村(居)委会	土地面积(平方公里)	户籍人口(人)	外来暂住人口(人)	全部企业及个体户数(个)	#工业企业	资产总额(万元)	负债总额(万元)	资产负债率(%)	村组两级经营纯收入(万元)
霞坑村	1.7	755	4520	222	23	8454	2371	28.0	592
漱旧村	1.6	1127	1832	135	30	5996	628	10.5	643
漱新村	2.4	1277	2273	561	100	8786	4228	48.1	1236
黄泥塘村	1.0	894	1760	98	46	2855	1610	56.4	103
元江元村	2.1	1491	3348	217	85	7804	1166	14.9	662
横江厦村	5.0	2809	3085	231	85	13477	5866	43.5	603
田尾村	2.1	1565	3000	56	36	4332	2027	46.8	331
白花沥村	1.2	704	350	12	12	2837	849	29.9	205
沙湖口村	1.3	1032	2980	95	20	4040	2138	52.9	211
白石岗村	4.1	3795	5214	100	94	6436	3673	57.1	1252
松柏塘村	2.8	2397	4405	84	34	7540	3333	44.2	469
上坑村	1.3	955	3020	112	35	8832	1983	22.5	634
木棆村	3.2	2171	8261	694	58	36037	3330	9.2	4666
桥　头									
东江村	4.8	2438	2308	189	42	7708	3568	46.3	596
山和村	2.5	982	2500	135	35	7292	1906	26.1	514
屋厦村	2.0	715	2125	87	35	5608	1338	23.9	534
岗头村	0.6	485	2635	50	30	3778	1159	30.7	266
李屋村	2.3	1625	2478	57	39	15572	4537	29.1	493
邓屋村	2.7	1906	10960	53	38	20500	1203	5.9	1852
朗厦村	4.1	1628	4700	78	78	16658	1333	8.0	1455
邵岗头村	1.3	886	1720	41	35	5108	2235	43.8	435
桥头社区	1.0	1356	4362	297	48	24676	1763	7.1	3068
迳联社区	1.5	1804	3195	115	50	24007	6015	25.1	1503
田新社区	2.2	2210	3268	357	200	20207	5404	26.7	1211
岭头社区	1.3	1154	3684	265	55	14041	588	4.2	1259
石水口村	7.8	4580	7500	442	140	32453	8298	25.6	2802
大洲社区	4.6	3277	3400	166	80	17041	2790	16.4	1273
禾坑村	1.5	996	2580	72	22	6275	476	7.6	742
田头角村	1.2	756	1769	86	52	6250	1092	17.5	625
莲城社区	14.6	9937	55340						
横　沥									
石涌村	3.7	1807	6179	1105	112	15106	2619	17.3	1410
隔坑村	2.2	2749	5691	851	70	12332	3932	31.9	1874
半仙山村	2.2	1629	3661	956	16	14291	9717	68.0	625
横沥村	4.6	2971	3200	1104	51	13942	7068	50.7	1389
田头村	4.1	2560	7814	1114	54	12472	2732	21.9	1427
田坑村	4.8	2870	4503	1680	70	8215	2780	33.8	1601
村头村	3.5	2351	5750	793	90	13159	4040	30.7	419
长巷村	2.1	1688	896	98	12	5248	1951	37.2	201
田饶步村	2.8	1838	1554	360	67	14276	7344	51.4	-97

15 续表 13

(2014年)

村(居)委会	土地面积(平方公里)	户籍人口(人)	外来暂住人口(人)	全部企业及个体户数(个)	#工业企业	资产总额(万元)	负债总额(万元)	资产负债率(%)	村组两级经营纯收入(万元)
六甲村	1.4	1108	3117	248	65	7210	2917	40.5	236
村尾村	2.7	1501	3810	744	45	13783	4436	32.2	417
水边村	4.0	2859	6328	458	46	9099	2813	30.9	525
新四村	2.9	2103	6375	538	115	1884	1344	71.3	1271
山厦村	2.3	1075	2002	265	64	13088	820	6.3	477
月塘村	0.5	1132	1020	197	28	12346	1173	9.5	363
张坑村	1.0	628	2031	104	34	7296	1872	25.7	245
恒泉社区	0.2	7340	1684	1864	25	1400	696	49.7	64
东坑									
东坑村	2.0	3093	11000	1237	81	26007	5945	22.9	2315
黄麻岭村	0.8	1111	1837	259	73	7514	2780	37.0	265
长安塘村	1.3	1898	3100	359	146	15388	6401	41.6	958
寮边头村	0.8	1600	2995	326	46	6837	2486	36.4	546
塔岗村	2.1	1793	4600	333	98	15070	1548	10.3	859
坑美村	2.2	1993	3118	339	130	9857	1097	11.1	739
新门楼村	2.1	1733	6983	411	18	14715	5150	35.0	757
井美村	1.9	2515	5000	746	81	17812	1999	11.2	1643
初坑村	2.8	2517	7500	841	94	2532	689	27.2	2580
凤大村	0.3	751	589	136	21	5724	1517	26.5	381
丁屋村	1.1	1112	2880	165	15	4630	1389	30.0	569
彭屋村	2.1	1924	3148	300	13	5694	796	14.0	1232
黄屋村	2.0	2008	4600	1135	44	13795	3409	24.7	952
角社村	2.4	3468	6030	563	116	25610	978	3.8	1067
草塘社区	0.1	2993	325	192	7				
骏达社区	0.1	238	39620	68	13				
企石									
铁岗村	5.7	2559	2433	54	34	11782	3912	33.2	448
深巷村	4.1	2310	2130	150	50	6396	2187	34.2	181
湖美村	1.0	798	574	32	16	4575	1874	41.0	149
博夏村	6.7	3622	1000	78	35	9043	1130	12.5	226
上洞村	5.3	2735	1500	103	26	6811	1342	19.7	196
清湖村	4.6	2059	3200	56	37	7207	2156	29.9	255
江边村	5.0	3014	1380	48	21	5990	1068	17.8	243
旧围村	3.8	2016	1050	60	35	5318	833	15.7	273
东平村	1.5	748	2304	210	32	4395	3300	75.1	205
上截村	0.8	1189	3000	59	10	5750	4185	72.8	206
下截村	1.2	1487	1200	50	18	6961	2764	39.7	649
东山村	6.2	4402	5835	706	120	30751	7566	24.6	2451
铁炉坑村	3.4	3248	2451	122	64	11611	1495	12.9	441
企石村	1.5	1461	559	40	19	7034	2437	34.7	239
杨屋村	0.8	668	680	60	12	4182	2037	48.7	127
莫屋村	1.0	1250	610	66	21	3667	1653	45.1	161
霞朗村	1.0	912	1736	265	28	13268	3923	29.6	1353

15 续表 14

(2014年)

村(居)委会	土地面积(平方公里)	户籍人口(人)	外来暂住人口(人)	全部企业及个体户数(个)	#工业企业	资产总额(万元)	负债总额(万元)	资产负债率(%)	村组两级经营纯收入(万元)
新南村	2.8	2190	1765	329	49	8835	2189	24.8	574
南坑村	1.5	1254	1517	75	40	9471	1641	17.3	197
宝石社区	0.5	5533	6700	500		161	76	47.2	30
石排									
石排村	2.4	3686	10200	598	35	3313	952	28.7	1671
下沙村	3.4	2615	4000	510	140	4498	1099	24.4	2473
庙边王村	3.7	2428	7740	652	213	4983	1021	20.5	1676
福隆村	5.6	6015	10023	1133	272	17197	6196	36.0	1785
沙角村	3.4	2590	4648	148	36	3848	844	21.9	599
黄家壆村	2.4	1951	2500	145	30	8510	752	8.8	492
赤坎村	3.2	1428	3300	330	80	9341	2301	24.6	674
向西村	2.0	1208	5617	478	61	6521	861	13.2	776
水贝村	3.5	3325	4213	309	79	5901	782	13.3	1061
田寮村	3.3	1982	1500	130	40	5050	690	13.7	419
横山村	3.8	2059	6105	165	45	3087	1247	40.4	1199
谷吓村	3.0	1905	3850	168	105	6230	1980	31.8	958
埔心村	2.2	1590	11000	877	695	9819	496	5.1	2702
塘尾村	0.9	1094	3000	220	59	9875	1955	19.8	439
李家坊村	0.9	932	2750	201	55	5535	1148	20.7	274
田边村	4.2	2136	4470	183	70	3937	1627	41.3	865
中坑村	3.2	2329	3110	225	33	13146	1281	9.7	549
燕窝村	4.3	1779	4680	387	110	8675	790	9.1	1005
太和社区		3033				1829	544	29.7	157
茶山									
上元村	5.1	3198	3121	694	105	2422	803	33.2	1250
茶山村	2.3	1751	3537	610	60	11854	3790	32.0	1065
下朗村	1.8	1443	2053	242	32	22697	8533	37.6	1293
横江村	4.3	3128	4563	416	210	10972	3473	31.7	863
卢边村	3.6	2786	3653	365	95	11584	1754	15.1	657.3
寒溪水村	1.3	974	1895	125	120	3680	1059	28.8	538
增埗村	6.3	7352	14973	668	360	10217	5862	57.4	4432.9
南社村	4.1	3633	7807	450	225	29798	2559	8.6	1791
塘角村	2.8	3024	5974	367	128	13747	666	4.8	3606
京山村	4.2	2507	6082	345	48	16106	3386	21.0	2737.3
博头村	0.9	669	1798	34	26	5069	813	16.0	243
冲美村	0.7	781	1232	93	39	7841	360	4.6	605
粟边村	2.2	2037	2500	222	80	9881	768	7.8	655.1
刘黄村	1.5	1004	3619	182	64	6870	2059	30.0	523.4
孙屋村	0.8	719	1050	46	25	2402	889	37.0	146
超朗村	3.3	2925	10110	188	78	15743	3108	19.7	1490.7
茶山圩社区	0.3	6737	3958	672	18				
茶溪社区		1020							

十六、历年国民经济和社会发展主要指标

Main Indicators of National Economy and Social Development over Years

16 历年国民经济和社会发展主要指标

Main Indicators of National Economy and Social Development over Years

年 份	户 籍 人 口 (万人)	常 住 人 口 (万人)	外来暂住人口 (万人)	户籍人口自然增长率 (‰)	外来暂住从业人员 (万人)	城镇在岗职工人数 (万人)	城镇在岗职工平均工资(元)
1949	68.24						
1952	71.68						
1957	77.48					3.90	400
1962	79.64					2.93	552
1965	86.46			29.60		3.17	524
1970	98.56			20.60		3.29	534
1975	107.94			14.51		3.80	577
1978	111.23			13.81		8.20	474
1979	112.04			19.00		9.68	650
1980	112.70			19.31		9.86	750
1981	114.46			16.57		10.66	887
1982	116.19			14.14		11.41	1095
1983	117.59			11.53		11.59	1197
1984	118.95			10.60		11.76	1383
1985	120.85			10.83		12.30	1456
1986	123.01		15.62	11.56	10.41	13.27	2616
1987	124.86		25.29	11.67	18.03	13.67	2067
1988	126.76		36.89	12.09	29.25	12.71	2757
1989	128.76		47.19	12.39	40.53	13.10	3320
1990	131.85	175.62	65.59	12.31	57.20	13.16	3552
1991	133.65	200.01	80.58	13.34	70.20	14.59	3777
1992	136.06	227.78	114.48	14.50	107.10	15.47	4531
1993	138.92	259.41	121.70	13.41	112.68	17.66	6228
1994	141.40	295.43	139.09	13.37	124.18	16.09	8360
1995	143.65	336.45	142.18	12.75	126.54	17.87	9682
1996	145.25	383.17	143.32	11.97	127.66	17.50	10382
1997	147.12	436.38	144.68	12.09	130.73	16.50	10691
1998	148.77	496.97	199.11	10.86	183.19	16.40	11422
1999	150.82	565.98	244.81	10.22	216.15	16.39	12557
2000	152.61	644.84	254.72	7.52	244.84	16.41	14051
2001	153.89	654.43	457.82	7.01	449.68	16.42	16183
2002	156.19	654.84	433.65	5.91	426.01	16.42	17804
2003	158.96	655.25	440.45	5.65	432.73	16.60	22598
2004	161.97	655.66	486.95	5.96	473.39	17.54	25326
2005	165.65	656.07	584.98	6.02	553.42	18.86	28253
2006	168.31	685.66	586.76	5.86	566.98	19.99	31135
2007	171.26	717.02	557.80	5.98	538.95	20.56	35284
2008	174.87	750.60	552.50	6.23	530.30	20.72	39516
2009	178.73	786.08	429.96	6.31	413.46	22.60	42585
2010	181.77	822.48	411.47	6.23	391.23	22.63	46576
2011	184.77	825.48	413.62	6.13	394.71	24.61	50398
2012	187.02	829.23	416.74	8.10	397.94	25.02	57007
2013	188.93	831.66	434.68	7.18	412.80	239.82	42870
2014	191.39	834.31	415.86	5.83	389.33	234.25	47600

注：2012年起城镇在岗职工含劳务派遣人员；2013年起，将原属于乡镇企业且符合城镇非私营单位条件的“四上”企业纳入城镇单位从业人员及工资统计的范围。

16 续表 1

年份	地区生产总值(亿元)	第一产业	第二产业	第三产业	#工业	#建筑业	人均地区生产总值(元)
1978	6.11	2.72	2.68	0.71			553
1979	6.62	2.65	2.92	1.05			593
1980	7.22	2.63	3.33	1.26			643
1981	9.11	3.28	4.30	1.54			802
1982	11.43	3.73	5.81	1.89			991
1983	13.03	3.98	6.90	2.15			1115
1984	15.96	4.57	7.81	3.59			1350
1985	22.60	6.15	11.66	4.80			1885
1986	30.02	8.14	13.57	8.30	10.54	3.03	2462
1987	39.29	9.82	17.72	11.74	14.24	3.49	3170
1988	55.46	11.89	28.28	15.29	25.05	3.23	4408
1989	60.92	12.66	27.97	20.29	27.22	0.75	4768
1990	80.44	13.28	40.53	26.63	39.18	1.34	6173
1991	95.91	13.45	50.32	32.13	48.34	1.98	5095
1992	110.89	14.41	59.27	37.21	56.63	2.64	5038
1993	157.05	14.40	87.31	55.34	82.89	4.42	5850
1994	217.03	17.48	119.49	80.06	110.77	8.72	6357
1995	296.29	21.43	166.97	107.89	154.19	12.78	7421
1996	361.75	24.86	199.48	137.40	187.85	11.63	8444
1997	448.60	25.64	243.28	179.68	230.79	12.50	9747
1998	558.00	25.94	305.68	226.37	290.69	14.99	11265
1999	667.24	25.79	367.05	274.40	349.53	17.52	12494
2000	820.25	25.91	450.71	343.64	430.45	20.25	13679
2001	991.89	26.10	540.51	425.28	517.03	23.48	15268
2002	1186.94	24.88	648.81	513.25	621.86	26.96	18131
2003	1452.52	22.82	798.20	631.51	757.18	41.01	22174
2004	1806.03	22.71	1016.04	767.28	968.01	48.03	27554
2005	2183.20	20.55	1227.86	934.78	1173.23	54.63	33287
2006	2627.98	12.01	1506.60	1109.37	1441.69	64.91	39173
2007	3160.05	11.90	1754.66	1393.49	1681.83	72.83	45057
2008	3703.60	14.83	1901.61	1787.17	1819.22	82.38	50471
2009	3785.83	14.79	1836.01	1935.03	1754.46	81.55	49273
2010	4278.21	16.57	2191.78	2069.86	2109.42	82.37	53913
2011	4771.93	17.88	2417.54	2336.52	2339.75	77.79	57913
2012	5039.21	18.76	2444.61	2575.85	2366.49	78.12	60907
2013	5517.47	19.55	2622.67	2875.25	2542.60	86.69	66440
2014	5881.32	20.35	2794.42	3066.55	2709.00	91.35	70605

注：1. 本表按当年价格计算。
2. 人均生产总值1990年及以前年份按年平均户籍人口计算，1991年起按年平均常住人口计算。

16　续表 2

(上年＝100)

年　份	地区生产总值指　数	第一产业	第二产业	第三产业	#工　业	#建筑业	人均地区生产总值指　数
1979	99.5	86.5	107.0	146.4			98.6
1980	102.7	90.3	117.3	113.9			102.0
1981	116.6	115.0	122.1	110.8			115.4
1982	116.9	105.3	131.0	117.6			115.1
1983	110.4	104.8	115.7	111.3			108.9
1984	114.2	109.0	107.0	140.9			112.9
1985	132.3	118.9	144.5	132.7			130.5
1986	126.1	111.9	110.3	174.7			124.0
1987	122.5	111.6	127.7	126.0	125.8	147.0	120.5
1988	115.7	90.6	143.7	103.0	151.4	77.9	114.0
1989	107.1	99.8	106.2	113.7	106.4	103.7	105.5
1990	123.2	104.4	127.6	128.0	130.6	76.4	120.8
1991	117.5	103.1	121.5	118.6	121.8	113.2	108.8
1992	108.3	100.0	112.6	105.1	113.7	78.0	92.6
1993	127.9	79.4	139.2	129.0	138.5	168.1	104.8
1994	122.5	107.2	124.7	122.3	124.3	138.5	96.3
1995	127.4	110.5	135.1	116.8	135.3	128.3	108.9
1996	117.5	109.4	115.5	123.5	116.2	91.2	109.5
1997	119.6	104.5	119.8	121.8	120.1	106.1	111.3
1998	121.8	100.9	122.1	124.5	122.2	115.1	113.1
1999	119.7	102.3	120.6	120.3	120.7	115.2	111.0
2000	119.7	99.8	120.7	120.0	120.9	110.5	106.6
2001	119.9	103.0	121.6	118.9	122.0	113.0	110.7
2002	120.5	97.6	122.6	119.1	123.0	114.1	119.6
2003	120.5	90.2	122.3	119.7	121.4	143.5	120.4
2004	121.0	90.0	125.6	115.8	126.5	106.8	120.9
2005	119.5	102.3	120.0	119.3	120.2	113.5	119.4
2006	119.2	58.9	121.9	117.1	122.0	118.7	116.6
2007	118.3	89.9	114.8	123.3	115.0	108.7	113.1
2008	114.0	110.6	106.1	124.0	106.4	100.9	109.0
2009	105.3	102.3	100.3	110.8	100.1	104.7	100.6
2010	110.3	101.6	117.1	103.7	118.0	97.1	105.4
2011	108.0	100.5	107.4	108.7	108.1	87.8	105.4
2012	106.1	100.0	106.1	106.2	106.4	98.5	105.7
2013	109.8	100.1	111.9	107.7	112.1	104.5	109.4
2014	107.8	102.8	109.1	106.3	109.3	103.3	107.4

注：本表按可比价格计算。

16 续表 3

年　份	固定资产投资总额(亿元)	地方公共财政预算收入(亿元)	地方公共财政预算支出(亿元)	居民消费价格指数(上年=100)	商品零售价格指数(上年=100)	农林牧渔业总　产　值(亿元)	农林牧渔业总产值指数(1978年=100)
1949						0.54	
1952		0.28	0.02			0.66	
1957		0.32	0.04			0.78	
1962		0.31	0.07			0.76	
1965		0.47	0.07			1.28	
1970		0.48	0.08			1.47	
1975		0.65	0.11			2.53	
1978	0.23	0.66	0.18		100.4	4.24	100.0
1979	0.16	0.66	0.19		102.6	4.15	96.5
1980	0.24	0.67	0.20		110.9	4.19	98.0
1981	0.38	0.68	0.21		109.3	5.04	102.1
1982	1.81	0.81	0.26		101.2	5.59	117.6
1983	1.84	0.86	0.28		99.6	5.64	117.4
1984	3.01	0.85	0.30	99.3	98.6	7.02	126.7
1985	7.06	1.11	0.50	106.5	106.9	9.12	138.9
1986	11.52	1.61	0.99	104.2	104.4	12.30	174.6
1987	14.19	2.02	1.25	112.0	112.2	14.84	186.4
1988	16.55	2.71	1.75	136.0	132.8	20.37	182.1
1989	5.01	3.19	2.16	122.0	122.4	22.11	181.9
1990	7.51	3.57	2.28	96.6	94.9	23.64	195.3
1991	13.75	4.44	2.75	102.4	101.4	24.26	199.5
1992	18.88	5.62	3.82	109.2	107.7	27.13	211.3
1993	32.76	9.38	7.29	121.8	119.5	28.45	175.5
1994	140.76	7.69	8.90	123.5	118.4	34.75	188.4
1995	63.14	11.56	12.42	113.9	109.7	42.69	207.8
1996	67.62	9.65	12.41	106.8	104.7	49.72	216.3
1997	65.89	11.41	14.85	101.5	99.7	51.44	225.0
1998	77.00	15.10	17.91	99.9	98.7	53.60	227.3
1999	88.32	18.26	21.26	97.9	95.9	53.74	242.8
2000	102.89	30.47	33.61	101.5	100.1	54.64	243.3
2001	125.49	45.02	47.86	96.6	97.8	55.93	246.3
2002	191.57	55.29	64.96	98.1	99.1	53.67	263.2
2003	319.39	67.45	76.52	100.7	101.7	49.02	209.7
2004	454.87	82.64	94.16	103.0	103.2	44.19	213.5
2005	597.24	103.97	117.04	102.4	103.0	42.05	222.2
2006	705.45	128.94	147.90	101.2	102.8	21.26	121.0
2007	841.21	186.45	193.10	103.1	104.2	19.98	105.6
2008	944.34	209.22	218.26	105.5	107.9	25.53	118.3
2009	1094.08	231.16	232.62	96.9	95.3	25.31	122.2
2010	1114.98	277.84	289.83	102.8	103.2	28.31	126.2
2011	1079.31	313.06	351.92	104.9	104.7	30.66	126.1
2012	1180.35	356.32	385.58	102.9	102.4	32.01	126.9
2013	1383.94	409.29	444.66	101.9	100.6	33.15	125.1
2014	1427.11	455.21	457.68	102.3	101.2	33.94	126.4

注：农林牧渔总产值1952−1970年按1957年不变价计算，1975年按1970年不变价计算，1978年起按当年价计算。

16 续表 4

年 份	农作物总播种面积(千公顷)	#粮食	粮食产量(万吨)	油料产量(万吨)	水果产量(万吨)	肉类产量(万吨)	水产品产量(万吨)
1949	141.26	127.26	21.07	0.15			0.32
1952	167.61	149.68	26.95	0.35			0.34
1957	188.98	165.53	28.80	0.33			0.42
1962	155.97	138.18	33.12	0.38			0.63
1965	158.97	121.64	43.71	0.72	4.54		0.99
1970	174.60	127.25	45.08	0.96	6.95		1.62
1975	202.00	137.03	50.72	1.11	3.68		2.19
1978	190.63	138.15	53.23	1.42	2.65	2.69	3.09
1979	172.36	129.16	53.53	1.91	2.33	2.92	2.23
1980	162.41	117.12	52.94	2.90	2.37	2.77	2.55
1981	151.17	107.13	44.75	3.55	4.69	2.80	2.49
1982	146.96	106.68	54.33	2.99	5.82	3.30	2.77
1983	146.21	109.02	56.12	1.97	7.72	3.57	3.03
1984	144.35	105.12	55.82	2.31	10.59	3.33	3.25
1985	130.01	93.05	48.87	2.10	18.94	3.33	3.26
1986	119.41	83.81	45.52	2.01	30.77	4.33	4.65
1987	119.73	83.40	46.28	1.70	36.31	4.61	6.57
1988	119.53	82.42	46.09	1.51	26.37	5.61	6.81
1989	122.27	85.61	48.76	1.37	22.14	5.86	6.23
1990	123.25	85.74	49.43	1.34	28.24	6.22	6.85
1991	119.42	81.77	47.37	1.15	34.32	6.88	6.90
1992	104.10	64.26	36.81	0.93	34.48	6.80	7.32
1993	71.20	36.74	20.21	0.56	27.13	7.66	6.50
1994	67.30	35.75	20.24	0.37	26.49	8.54	6.74
1995	71.89	39.90	22.74	0.37	24.32	9.76	7.48
1996	72.23	41.89	24.32	0.31	20.63	11.61	8.11
1997	72.17	41.61	24.69	0.29	16.50	12.90	9.19
1998	73.46	41.63	24.72	0.26	11.41	15.35	9.69
1999	72.59	41.77	24.73	0.22	13.63	15.99	9.40
2000	65.73	35.18	20.41	0.20	12.94	17.90	9.51
2001	56.95	22.56	12.84	0.16	15.01	19.84	8.96
2002	42.28	9.88	5.37	0.09	18.93	18.88	8.24
2003	33.97	5.65	3.05	0.04	14.64	15.46	7.58
2004	30.82	5.41	3.04	0.02	17.54	14.62	7.15
2005	27.38	4.14	2.00	0.01	15.13	17.17	6.74
2006	22.26	2.29	1.00	0.01	13.96	3.49	4.71
2007	21.37	2.15	0.99	0.01	13.16	2.03	4.73
2008	23.48	2.72	1.19	0.01	10.15	2.41	7.23
2009	24.72	2.77	1.19	0.01	9.15	2.55	7.33
2010	24.62	2.79	1.25	0.01	7.55	2.88	7.63
2011	24.46	2.76	1.29	0.01	7.39	2.60	7.82
2012	24.83	2.75	1.25	0.03	6.49	2.67	7.70
2013	24.52	2.74	1.24	0.02	6.11	2.28	7.45
2014	24.41	2.75	1.24	0.02	6.25	2.01	7.27

16 续表 5

年份	工业企业单位数(个)	工业增加值(亿元)	工业增加值指数(上年=100)	规模以上工业增加值(亿元)	总供电量(亿千瓦时)	全社会用电量(亿千瓦时)	建筑业总产值(亿元)	建筑业增加值(亿元)
1949	1							
1952	23							
1957	262							
1962	280				0.08			
1965	260				0.36			
1970	220				0.71			
1975	324				1.24			
1978	1290				1.64			
1979	1250				1.93			
1980	1293				2.17			
1981	1479				2.22			
1982	1862				2.69			
1983	1964				3.15			
1984	2329				3.26			
1985	4187				3.82			
1986	5949	10.54		4.28	3.93			3.03
1987	8106	14.24	125.8	5.67	6.43			3.49
1988	8408	25.05	151.4	7.93	9.48			3.23
1989	8757	27.22	106.4	9.36	12.09		1.03	0.75
1990	9892	39.18	130.6	12.25	18.01	18.01	1.27	1.34
1991	10094	48.34	121.8	17.63	24.05	24.05	2.19	1.98
1992	11639	56.63	113.7	25.66	32.00	32.00	3.19	2.64
1993	12449	82.89	138.5	35.05	43.62	43.62	5.39	4.42
1994	14086	110.77	124.3	56.61	58.58	58.58	7.99	8.72
1995	15215	154.19	135.3	64.99	68.00	68.00	9.49	12.78
1996	15326	187.85	116.2	84.14	80.03	80.03	9.66	11.63
1997	16857	230.79	120.1	103.90	94.93	94.83	28.73	12.50
1998	16406	290.69	122.2	168.71	109.48	109.48	35.92	14.99
1999	16877	349.53	120.7	232.15	132.78	134.37	40.73	17.52
2000	16975	430.45	120.9	259.44	178.03	179.66	40.45	20.25
2001	18094	517.03	122.0	290.67	207.72	209.17	50.13	23.48
2002	21313	621.86	123.0	466.61	258.55	259.86	65.84	26.96
2003	21935	757.18	121.4	595.48	321.65	323.53	76.48	41.01
2004	22156	968.01	126.5	800.45	372.84	375.85	77.01	48.03
2005	21868	1173.23	120.2	1062.42	415.66	419.83	84.35	58.61
2006	22447	1441.69	122.0	1318.58	464.45	472.01	94.58	64.91
2007	22587	1681.83	115.0	1430.60	507.89	515.40	112.87	72.83
2008	25656	1819.22	106.4	1602.98	507.35	514.16	108.81	82.38
2009	31160	1754.46	100.1	1453.37	488.85	495.58	99.40	81.55
2010	38273	2109.42	118.0	1708.31	556.89	562.00	122.06	82.37
2011	46413	2339.75	108.6	1642.45	579.35	586.07	130.85	77.79
2012	57808	2366.49	106.4	1978.13	600.58	604.28	157.58	78.12
2013	67332	2542.60	112.1	2425.62	617.20	622.51	188.13	86.69
2014	80567	2709.00	109.3	2490.84	655.72	660.99	204.21	91.35

16 续表 6

年　份	公路通车里程(公里)	民用汽车拥有量(万辆)	旅客周转量(万人公里)	货物周转量(万吨公里)	邮电业务收入(万元)	本地电话用户(万户)	移动电话用户(万户)
1949	204	0.002					
1952	219	0.002	1350	139			
1957	373	0.005	2100	195			
1962	598	0.007	4120	293			
1965	882	0.010	4725	457			
1970	1134	0.012	2800	900			
1975	1173	0.025	3890	694			
1978	1259	0.06	9425	15148	686	0.20	
1979	1225	0.11	11162	15290	790	0.21	
1980	1225	0.20	13584	16353	927	0.31	
1981	1225	0.30	13845	15606	962	0.34	
1982	1225	0.34	16026	17185	940	0.35	
1983	1225	0.45	54075	108634	1018	0.39	
1984	1240	0.61	62107	140113	1263	0.48	
1985	1240	0.79	95237	171591	1560	0.77	
1986	1248	0.86	127458	126898	2015	0.88	
1987	1261	1.00	159117	174942	3410	1.63	
1988	1302	1.36	173335	169112	5728	2.52	
1989	1325	1.63	240999	186626	9620	4.30	0.02
1990	1325	1.94	322236	184700	17555	4.90	0.05
1991	1759	2.07	373284	194101	27733	7.50	0.11
1992	2055	3.26	503973	232752	42155	9.70	0.30
1993	2260	4.81	577800	248230	65699	14.98	0.72
1994	2292	6.16	595134	273053	102238	23.19	2.41
1995	2327	8.83	446230	264605	152761	31.57	4.77
1996	2330	9.08	477466	267193	207573	36.91	8.24
1997	2330	10.34	511592	278649	284278	42.65	15.29
1998	2377	11.34	577452	285889	376708	50.13	26.17
1999	2467	12.70	804278	300410	515916	60.87	51.01
2000	2518	15.37	1001906	404678	724593	78.12	123.68
2001	2570	18.36	1031579	406247	1225474	98.96	295.76
2002	2641	22.01	1091821	420684	1816802	127.93	412.39
2003	2688	25.56	1126964	422822	1051220	206.11	660.86
2004	2759	31.97	1166262	423669	1207778	281.35	856.09
2005	2871	40.66	1185290	424829	1328172	384.52	1016.41
2006	3891	48.93	1213809	336783	1466871	461.31	1216.34
2007	3924	60.89	1264982	356677	1619048	469.17	1408.23
2008	4001	70.16	2248521	1747489	1723829	439.41	1454.29
2009	4713	79.56	1053469	1016490	1563077	378.40	1409.29
2010	4751	92.08	1290692	1090340	1553352	332.42	1607.60
2011	4828	106.14	1458811	1874802	1648579	319.55	1677.77
2012	4969	120.70	1568758	2967132	1699619	330.79	1797.75
2013	5002	138.91	1559856	4322745	1758017	314.48	1850.39
2014	5145	155.96	854598	4480052	1694637	327.22	1763.09

注：1. 公路通车里程2006年起含专用公路和村道。
2. 邮电业务收入2003年以前为邮电业务总量，按1990年不变价计算，2003年起为邮电业务收入。
3. 2014年客运量和旅客周转量不含城市客运量，数据与往年不可比。

16 续表 7

年 份	社会消费品零售总额(亿元)	进出口总额(亿美元)			协议(合同)规定外商投资额(亿美元)	实际利用外资(亿美元)	
			出口总额	进口总额			#外商直接投资
1957			0.02				
1962			0.04				
1965			0.08				
1970			0.10				
1975			0.25				
1978	2.13		0.39				
1979	2.50		0.54		0.05	0.02	
1980	3.16		0.77		0.11	0.09	
1981	4.02		0.92		0.08	0.05	0.001
1982	4.81		1.09		0.08	0.07	0.005
1983	5.23		1.19		0.16	0.09	0.003
1984	7.39		1.30		0.32	0.19	0.07
1985	9.36		1.75		0.68	0.29	0.14
1986	12.24		2.33		0.34	0.30	0.15
1987	15.05		2.68		1.85	1.13	0.21
1988	24.65		3.18		6.22	2.41	0.64
1989	27.04		3.49		2.34	2.49	0.84
1990	31.97	10.82	5.68	5.14	3.02	2.43	1.00
1991	36.50	31.75	16.52	15.23	6.45	2.62	1.47
1992	44.35	50.90	26.03	24.87	20.88	4.66	3.29
1993	63.69	67.56	32.11	35.45	35.55	9.34	7.92
1994	85.16	88.30	42.94	45.36	34.97	10.48	7.79
1995	113.01	153.91	77.99	75.92	33.09	10.57	6.72
1996	125.53	178.42	91.87	86.55	20.89	10.76	6.95
1997	146.04	212.99	113.68	99.31	12.14	12.14	8.80
1998	175.16	232.73	130.61	102.13	16.37	13.38	9.30
1999	202.30	284.63	151.54	133.09	14.72	14.57	9.71
2000	235.16	320.45	171.59	148.86	18.36	16.47	10.87
2001	275.71	344.55	189.89	154.65	20.98	18.16	11.47
2002	321.24	442.47	237.36	205.11	24.89	21.48	14.59
2003	369.78	521.06	280.02	241.04	32.56	25.63	17.54
2004	426.47	645.18	351.92	293.25	41.32	30.34	21.39
2005	506.29	743.72	409.29	334.42	47.52	37.51	14.68
2006	599.32	842.21	473.76	368.45	55.28	43.38	18.08
2007	722.45	1068.73	602.32	466.41	62.51	50.44	21.18
2008	881.15	1132.99	655.37	477.62	39.37	32.26	24.47
2009	1029.04	941.55	551.69	389.86	20.30	29.42	25.94
2010	1223.34	1213.38	695.98	517.40	30.73	31.63	27.32
2011	1441.25	1352.24	783.29	568.95	37.02	32.18	30.51
2012	1600.41	1444.16	850.66	593.50	41.55	37.19	33.69
2013	1786.66	1530.72	908.64	622.08	41.56	40.29	39.38
2014	1942.29	1625.30	970.69	654.61	44.39	46.21	45.29

注：1. 出口总额1990年起为海关口径，1990年以前为外经贸口径。
2. 外商直接投资2004年起为新口径，是以验资作为统计标准，与往年数不可比。

16　续表 8

年　份	国际及港澳台旅游者（万人次）	旅游总收入（亿元）	国际旅游外汇收入（万美元）	接待国内游客人　次（万人次）	各项人民币存款余额（亿元）	＃城乡居民储蓄存款余额	各　项人民币贷款余额（亿元）
1952						0.003	0.004
1957						0.02	0.26
1962					0.08	0.04	0.75
1965					0.16	0.09	0.81
1970					0.39	0.16	0.87
1975					0.96	0.41	1.39
1978					1.05	0.54	1.96
1979					1.49	0.72	2.13
1980					2.61	1.17	3.08
1981					3.80	2.03	4.02
1982					4.51	2.77	4.55
1983					6.05	3.86	5.76
1984					11.03	6.18	12.19
1985					13.49	9.19	14.24
1986	11		554	69	19.59	13.14	20.68
1987	19		453	87	28.48	18.97	31.24
1988	20		710	105	38.05	24.91	41.58
1989	18		504	97	46.82	32.57	49.37
1990	27		1025	98	68.07	45.51	63.04
1991	37		2443	118	94.97	61.47	78.40
1992	47		2473	125	147.34	81.54	105.98
1993	52		2888	117	179.83	107.17	134.31
1994	44		3464	75	249.78	151.54	173.44
1995	27		5679	62	383.68	232.97	254.85
1996	36		6464	139	489.65	318.02	312.81
1997	59		6778	112	671.17	425.82	382.66
1998	75		6601	141	864.01	533.75	442.74
1999	97		7055	156	1040.84	616.34	524.37
2000	106		7617	185	1228.67	672.07	630.84
2001	110	39.80	8200	217	1458.65	799.18	750.18
2002	108	72.51	11847	822	1790.18	1001.69	933.41
2003	80	79.92	13825	1006	2126.78	1231.06	1206.72
2004	149	85.70	23437	982	2462.87	1431.68	1405.25
2005	169	90.72	28189	987	2933.40	1728.28	1500.52
2006	193	96.01	33180	1170	3365.65	2013.40	1730.56
2007	248	118.88	42702	1477	3751.83	2120.74	2154.77
2008	268	128.69	45614	1604	4354.53	2638.04	2380.36
2009	286	151.49	51756	1751	4986.61	2904.57	2903.80
2010	327	191.32	67592	1924	5943.39	3386.85	3329.82
2011	357	249.37	90975	2258	6609.39	3710.99	3716.08
2012	415	306.35	126924	2329	7430.46	4204.20	4195.61
2013	418	346.43	144981	2408	8630.73	4476.43	4774.23
2014	356	374.60	157493	2435	9069.92	4606.79	5331.63

16　续表 9

<table>
<tr><th rowspan="2">年　份</th><th colspan="3">在校学生数（万人）</th><th rowspan="2">小学学龄儿童入学率(%)</th><th rowspan="2">高考入围人数（人）</th><th rowspan="2">#省线入围人数</th></tr>
<tr><th>普通高等学校</th><th>普通中学</th><th>小学</th></tr>
<tr><td>1949</td><td></td><td>0.20</td><td>5.28</td><td></td><td></td><td></td></tr>
<tr><td>1952</td><td></td><td>0.34</td><td>7.04</td><td></td><td></td><td></td></tr>
<tr><td>1957</td><td></td><td>0.67</td><td>8.80</td><td></td><td></td><td></td></tr>
<tr><td>1962</td><td></td><td>0.97</td><td>12.00</td><td></td><td></td><td></td></tr>
<tr><td>1965</td><td></td><td>1.05</td><td>16.09</td><td></td><td></td><td></td></tr>
<tr><td>1970</td><td></td><td>6.02</td><td>11.81</td><td></td><td></td><td></td></tr>
<tr><td>1975</td><td></td><td>4.96</td><td>16.82</td><td></td><td></td><td></td></tr>
<tr><td>1978</td><td></td><td>7.60</td><td>16.11</td><td>98.36</td><td>846</td><td>250</td></tr>
<tr><td>1979</td><td></td><td>6.23</td><td>15.80</td><td>98.70</td><td>566</td><td>166</td></tr>
<tr><td>1980</td><td></td><td>5.48</td><td>15.49</td><td>98.85</td><td>222</td><td>140</td></tr>
<tr><td>1981</td><td></td><td>4.35</td><td>15.09</td><td>98.72</td><td>239</td><td>154</td></tr>
<tr><td>1982</td><td></td><td>4.17</td><td>14.48</td><td>99.06</td><td>252</td><td>115</td></tr>
<tr><td>1983</td><td></td><td>4.28</td><td>13.54</td><td>99.75</td><td>245</td><td>150</td></tr>
<tr><td>1984</td><td></td><td>4.65</td><td>13.46</td><td>99.65</td><td>619</td><td>220</td></tr>
<tr><td>1985</td><td></td><td>4.66</td><td>13.44</td><td>99.83</td><td>534</td><td>285</td></tr>
<tr><td>1986</td><td></td><td>4.94</td><td>14.07</td><td>99.90</td><td>595</td><td>228</td></tr>
<tr><td>1987</td><td></td><td>5.44</td><td>14.43</td><td>99.94</td><td>644</td><td>297</td></tr>
<tr><td>1988</td><td></td><td>5.93</td><td>15.01</td><td>99.93</td><td>925</td><td>315</td></tr>
<tr><td>1989</td><td></td><td>6.20</td><td>15.59</td><td>99.92</td><td>977</td><td>284</td></tr>
<tr><td>1990</td><td></td><td>6.12</td><td>16.27</td><td>99.94</td><td>759</td><td>224</td></tr>
<tr><td>1991</td><td></td><td>6.01</td><td>17.01</td><td>99.92</td><td>861</td><td>268</td></tr>
<tr><td>1992</td><td></td><td>6.52</td><td>17.52</td><td>99.94</td><td>994</td><td>312</td></tr>
<tr><td>1993</td><td>0.11</td><td>7.53</td><td>18.01</td><td>99.95</td><td>1102</td><td>423</td></tr>
<tr><td>1994</td><td>0.15</td><td>8.58</td><td>18.62</td><td>99.96</td><td>1823</td><td>586</td></tr>
<tr><td>1995</td><td>0.16</td><td>9.25</td><td>19.51</td><td>99.99</td><td>2095</td><td>809</td></tr>
<tr><td>1996</td><td>0.18</td><td>9.52</td><td>20.60</td><td>99.98</td><td>2160</td><td>1093</td></tr>
<tr><td>1997</td><td>0.20</td><td>9.80</td><td>22.18</td><td>99.99</td><td>2212</td><td>1215</td></tr>
<tr><td>1998</td><td>0.22</td><td>10.12</td><td>23.58</td><td>99.99</td><td>2348</td><td>1315</td></tr>
<tr><td>1999</td><td>0.22</td><td>10.55</td><td>24.88</td><td>99.99</td><td>3501</td><td>1790</td></tr>
<tr><td>2000</td><td>0.32</td><td>11.24</td><td>27.28</td><td>99.99</td><td>5017</td><td>2646</td></tr>
<tr><td>2001</td><td>0.38</td><td>12.21</td><td>29.54</td><td>100.00</td><td>5651</td><td>3225</td></tr>
<tr><td>2002</td><td>0.51</td><td>13.53</td><td>34.28</td><td>100.00</td><td>6873</td><td>3759</td></tr>
<tr><td>2003</td><td>0.69</td><td>14.97</td><td>38.69</td><td>100.00</td><td>9167</td><td>4509</td></tr>
<tr><td>2004</td><td>0.91</td><td>17.13</td><td>44.83</td><td>100.00</td><td>10756</td><td>5452</td></tr>
<tr><td>2005</td><td>1.66</td><td>19.10</td><td>48.09</td><td>100.00</td><td>11196</td><td>6455</td></tr>
<tr><td>2006</td><td>2.20</td><td>21.46</td><td>49.68</td><td>100.00</td><td>11359</td><td>7652</td></tr>
<tr><td>2007</td><td>2.52</td><td>23.46</td><td>52.07</td><td>100.00</td><td>13275</td><td>9185</td></tr>
<tr><td>2008</td><td>2.87</td><td>24.84</td><td>52.86</td><td>100.00</td><td>15047</td><td>9987</td></tr>
<tr><td>2009</td><td>3.40</td><td>24.95</td><td>51.12</td><td>100.00</td><td>17487</td><td>12569</td></tr>
<tr><td>2010</td><td>3.83</td><td>25.83</td><td>55.24</td><td>100.00</td><td>18845</td><td>13761</td></tr>
<tr><td>2011</td><td>4.51</td><td>26.31</td><td>57.83</td><td>100.00</td><td>19588</td><td>15501</td></tr>
<tr><td>2012</td><td>5.24</td><td>26.79</td><td>60.81</td><td>100.00</td><td>22127</td><td>17316</td></tr>
<tr><td>2013</td><td>6.09</td><td>27.83</td><td>65.91</td><td>100.00</td><td>22840</td><td>18405</td></tr>
<tr><td>2014</td><td>6.99</td><td>28.46</td><td>68.73</td><td>100.00</td><td>23900</td><td>18766</td></tr>
</table>

年 份	医疗机构病床床位数(张)	卫生机构技术人员数(万人)	#执业(助理)医师	每万人口拥有		年末参加基本养老保险人数(万人)	年末参加基本医疗保险人数(万人)
				床位数(张)	执业(助理)医师(人)		
1949	219	0.02		3.21			
1952	179	0.01		2.50			
1957	403	0.03		5.20			
1962	1376	0.13		17.28			
1965	1308	0.16		15.13			
1970	1476	0.17		14.98			
1975	1970	0.23		18.25			
1978	2257	0.26	0.08	20.29	6.90		
1979	2271	0.29	0.10	20.27	8.67		
1980	2207	0.30	0.12	19.58	10.35		
1981	2210	0.31	0.11	19.31	9.63		
1982	2292	0.33	0.11	19.73	9.44		
1983	2098	0.33	0.11	17.84	9.25		
1984	2231	0.34	0.11	18.76	9.52		
1985	2323	0.33	0.12	19.22	9.94		
1986	3054	0.35	0.12	24.83	9.58		
1987	3393	0.35	0.13	27.17	10.44		
1988	3640	0.38	0.15	28.72	12.13		
1989	3677	0.39	0.16	28.56	12.58		
1990	3866	0.39	0.17	22.01	9.80		
1991	4085	0.39	0.18	20.42	8.77		
1992	4517	0.41	0.18	19.83	8.04		
1993	4940	0.45	0.20	19.04	7.80		
1994	5365	0.49	0.22	18.16	7.52	7.55	7.77
1995	5798	0.53	0.23	17.23	6.83	8.46	7.60
1996	5288	0.58	0.24	13.80	6.39	9.16	7.65
1997	5505	0.63	0.26	12.62	5.97	7.53	8.29
1998	5892	0.71	0.30	11.86	5.95	7.84	9.05
1999	6241	0.76	0.31	11.03	5.44	8.35	9.95
2000	7081	0.81	0.33	10.98	5.13	82.95	88.21
2001	7474	0.81	0.34	11.42	5.24	83.01	84.99
2002	8641	0.90	0.35	13.20	5.38	103.19	105.19
2003	9820	0.98	0.38	14.99	5.74	104.13	105.90
2004	10797	1.31	0.49	16.47	7.43	104.44	105.95
2005	11972	1.88	0.69	18.25	10.52	182.49	189.40
2006	13293	2.29	0.86	22.21	12.58	204.08	212.16
2007	15227	2.88	1.04	21.24	14.57	227.98	236.32
2008	16778	3.31	1.19	22.35	15.81	262.63	513.25
2009	18080	3.58	1.29	23.00	16.39	315.81	536.57
2010	19980	3.75	1.32	24.29	16.07	421.84	592.27
2011	22814	3.96	1.36	27.64	16.53	481.05	602.41
2012	24617	4.06	1.40	29.69	16.93	513.29	616.86
2013	25736	4.21	1.49	30.95	17.87	521.91	618.09
2014	26704	4.31	1.51	32.01	18.08	632.03	615.69

注：每万人口拥有床位数、执业(助理)医师数按常住人口计算。

16 续表 11

年 份	专 利 申请量 (件)	专 利 授权量 (件)	城镇居民最低生活保障人数 (人)	城镇常住居民人均可支配收入 (元)	农村常住居民人均可支配收入 (元)
1978					149
1979					188
1980					272
1981					463
1982					567
1983					618
1984					691
1985				791	803
1986				1033	951
1987				1247	1142
1988				1778	1325
1989				2282	1424
1990	34	30		2508	1542
1991	70	50		3068	1673
1992	102	78		4026	2290
1993	100	90		5970	2903
1994	104	100		8270	3769
1995	325	262		9588	4769
1996	333	312		10824	5554
1997	725	321		11032	6132
1998	890	709		11506	6830
1999	1221	819		12954	7704
2000	1653	1399	1825	14142	8484
2001	2914	1753	2003	16938	9383
2002	3100	2680	2711	16949	10178
2003	3865	2858	2876	18471	11033
2004	4325	3167	4968	20526	11941
2005	6694	3114	4885	22882	13076
2006	9879	4872	6091	25320	14313
2007	13842	6752	3129	27025	15747
2008	14406	8093	3653	30275	16904
2009	19106	12918	3770	33045	18098
2010	21654	20397	3643	35690	20486
2011	24455	19352	9415	39513	22842
2012	29199	20900	6598	42944	24944
2013	29013	22595	6584	46594	27214
2014	28432	20340	6560	新口径36764	新口径22327

十七、东莞与全国、全省、三角洲城市及港澳台主要指标比较

Comparison of Main Indicators between Dongguan and China, Guangdong Province, the Cities of the Pearl River Delta Hong Kong Macao Taiwan

17-1 主要年份全国国民经济与社会发展指标

Main Indicators on National Economy and Social Development of China

指　　标	单 位	1980年	1990年	1995年	2000年	2005年	2010年	2013年	2014年
人口与劳动力									
年末总人口	万人	98705	114333	121121	126743	130756	134091	136072	136782
年末就业人员人数	万人	42361	64749	68065	72085	74647	76105	76977	77253
#城镇就业人员	万人	10525	17041	19040	23151	28389	34687	38240	39310
经济总量									
国内生产总值	亿元	4546	18668	60794	99215	184937	401513	588019	636463
第一产业增加值	亿元	1372	5062	12136	14945	22420	40534	55322	58332
第二产业增加值	亿元	2192	7717	28680	45556	87598	187383	256810	271392
第三产业增加值	亿元	982	5888	19979	38714	74919	173596	275887	306739
人均国内生产总值	元	463	1644	5046	7858	14185	30015	43320	46652
农业									
主要农产品产量									
粮食	万吨	32056	44624	46662	46218	48402	54678	60194	60703
水果	万吨	679	1874	4215	6225	16120	21401	25093	26142
肉类	万吨		2857	5260	6014	6939	7926	8535	8707
水产品	万吨	450	1237	2517	3706	4420	5373	6172	6462
工业									
工业增加值	亿元	1997	6858	24951	40034	77231	160722	217264	227991
主要工业产品产量									
机制纸及纸板	万吨	535	1372	2812	2487	5404	9833	11514	11786
彩电	万台	3	1033	2058	3936	8283	11830	12745	14129
发电量	亿千瓦时	3006	6212	10070	13556	24747	42072	54316	56496
钢材	万吨	2716	5153	8980	13146	39692	80277	108201	112557
运输邮电									
货运量	亿吨	54.65	97.06	123.49	135.87	186.21	324.18	409.89	438.11
货物周转量	亿吨公里	12027	26208	35909	44321	80258	141837	168014	185398
客运量	亿人	34.18	77.27	117.26	147.86	184.70	326.95	212.30	220.94
旅客周转量	亿人公里	2281	5628	9002	12261	17467	27894	27572	30096
邮电业务总量	亿元	39	156	989	4793	12029	31979	18432	21846
年末固定电话用户	万户	214	685	4071	14483	35045	29434	26699	24943
年末移动电话用户	万户		1.8	363	8453	39341	85900	122911	128609

注：1.城镇就业人员1998年起为城镇在岗职工人数。
2.2014年客运量和旅客周转量不含城市客运量，数据与往年不可比。

17-1 续表

指　　标	单　位	1980年	1990年	1995年	2000年	2005年	2010年	2013年	2014年
固定资产投资									
固定资产投资总额	亿元	911	4517	20019	32918	88774	278122	446294	512761
#房地产开发	亿元		253	3149	4984	15909	48259	86013	95036
商业									
社会消费品零售总额	亿元	2140	8300	20620	39106	67177	156998	242843	271896
物价总指数									
商品零售价格指数	上年=100	106.0	102.1	114.8	98.5	100.8	103.1	101.4	101.0
居民消费价格指数	上年=100	107.5	103.1	117.1	100.4	101.8	103.3	102.6	102.0
外贸外经									
海关进出口总额	亿美元	381	1154	2809	4743	14219	29740	41590	43030
进口总额	亿美元	200	533	1321	2251	6599	13962	19500	19603
出口总额	亿美元	181	621	1488	2492	7620	15778	22090	23427
实际利用外资	亿美元		35	375	407	603	1057	1176	1196
财政、金融									
公共财政收入	亿元	1160	2937	6242	13395	31649	83102	129210	140350
公共财政支出	亿元	1229	3084	6824	15887	33930	89874	140212	151662
各项人民币存款余额	亿元		13943	53882	123804	287170	718238	1043847	1138645
各项人民币贷款余额	亿元		17511	50544	99371	194690	479196	718961	816770
人民生活									
在岗职工平均工资	元	762	2140	5500	9371	18364	37147	52379	57346
城镇居民人均可支配收入	元	478	1510	4283	6280	10493	19109	26467	28844
农村居民人均可支配收入	元	191	686	1578	2253	3255	5919	9430	10489
城乡居民人民币储蓄存款余额	亿元	400	7120	29662	64332	141051	303302	447602	485261
教育									
在校学生数									
普通高等学校	万人	114	206	291	556	1562	2232	2468	2548
普通中学	万人	5508	4586	5371	7369	8581	7703	6876	6785
小学	万人	14627	12241	13195	13013	10864	9941	9361	9451
卫生									
医院床位数	万张	120	187	206	217	245	339	458	496
卫生技术人员	万人	280	390	426	449	456	588	721	759
#执业(助理)医师	万人	115	176	192	208	204	241	280	289

注：实际利用外资不含对外借款，2005年起为实际使用外商直接投资口径。

17-2 主要年份广东省国民经济与社会发展指标

Main Indicators on National Economy and Social Development of Guangdong Province

指　　标	单　位	1980年	1990年	1995年	2000年	2005年	2010年	2013年	2014年
人口与劳动力									
年末常住人口	万人		6347	7387	8650	9194	10441	10644	10724
年末就业人员人数	万人	2368	3118	3551	3989	5023	5752	6118	6183
#城镇就业人员	万人	564	785	912	759	904	1119	1967	1973
经济总量									
地区生产总值	亿元	250	1559	5933	10741	22557	46036	62475	67810
第一产业增加值	亿元	83	385	864	986	1428	2287	2977	3167
第二产业增加值	亿元	103	616	2900	5000	11357	22822	28994	31420
第三产业增加值	亿元	64	559	2168	4755	9773	20928	30503	33223
人均地区生产总值	元	481	2484	8129	12736	24647	44758	58833	63469
农业									
主要农产品产量									
粮食	万吨	1682	1896	1803	1822	1395	1317	1316	1357
水果	万吨	29	329	415	644	832	1129	1369	1438
肉类	万吨	63	202	305	324	384	441	435	429
水产品	万吨	63	208	354	593	695	729	816	837
工业									
工业增加值	亿元	90	523	2449	4463	10490	21270	26895	29144
主要工业产品产量									
机制纸及纸板	万吨	31	104	288	260	691	1435	1911	2071
彩电	万台	1	262	764	1532	4090	4495	6691	7040
发电量	亿千瓦时	109	344	821	1293	2163	3101	3796	3870
成品钢材	万吨	45	134	247	406	1366	2919	3385	3447
运输邮电									
货运量	万吨	14201	85809	111063	119216	133992	205034	305833	352926
货物周转量	亿吨公里	1413	2599	4643	3065	3917	5934	12496	15014
客运量	万人	21444	78046	130998	164791	161357	467049	636816	193299
旅客周转量	亿人公里	114	453	936	1219	2043	3342	4852	3967
邮电业务总量	亿元	2	26	205	757	2122	4833	2508	3394
年末固定电话用户	万户		113	591	1415	3443	3169	3100	2949
年末移动电话用户	万户		1	99	1357	6407	9710	14706	14943

注：1.2010年年末人口数为第六次全国人口普查数据。
2.2014年客运量和旅客周转量不含城市客运量，数据与往年不可比。

17-2 续表

指　标	单　位	1980年	1990年	1995年	2000年	2005年	2010年	2013年	2014年
固定资产投资									
固定资产投资总额	亿元	38	381	2327	3234	7164	16113	22829	25928
#房地产开发	亿元		33	564	859	1592	3660	6490	7638
商业									
社会消费品零售总额	亿元	118	667	2478	4380	7916	17458	25454	28471
物价总指数									
商品零售价格指数	上年=100	108.5	95.6	111.6	99.9	101.8	103.3	101.0	101.4
居民消费价格指数	上年=100		97.5	114.0	101.4	102.3	103.1	102.5	102.3
外贸外经									
海关进出口总额	亿美元	26	419	1040	1701	4280	7849	10918	10767
进口总额	亿美元	4	197	474	782	1898	3317	4555	4305
出口总额	亿美元	22	222	566	919	2382	4532	6364	6462
实际利用外资	亿美元	2	20	121	146	152	210	250	269
财政、金融									
地方公共财政预算收入	亿元	38	131	382	911	1807	4517	7081	8065
地方公共财政预算支出	亿元	27	151	526	1070	2289	5422	8411	9153
各项人民币存款余额	亿元		1577	7090	16908	35784	78286	111881	118908
各项人民币贷款余额	亿元		1704	5496	11204	20745	46099	66889	76096
人民生活									
在岗职工平均工资	元	789	2929	8250	13823	23959	40358	53611	59827
城镇常住居民人均可支配收入	元	473	2303	7439	9762	14770	23898	29537	32148
农村常住居民人均可支配收入	元	274	1043	2699	3654	4690	7890	11068	12246
城乡居民人民币储蓄存款余额	亿元	30	752	3885	8667	19051	36219	49288	52411
教育									
在校学生数									
#普通高等学校	万人	4	10	15	30	87	143	171	179
中等职业教育学校	万人	6	45	67	66	71	155	141	128
普通中学	万人	252	234	339	461	612	709	625	591
小学	万人	749	747	883	930	1067	849	808	832
卫生									
医院及卫生院床位数	万张	8	11	14	16	19	28	35	37
卫生技术人员	万人	14	19	23	26	30	45	55	58
#执业(助理)医师	万人	6	8	10	11	12	17	20	21

17-3 主要经济指标东莞占全国、全省的比重（2014年）

Proportion of Main Indicators of Dongguan to China and Guangdong Province (2014)

指　　标	单 位	绝 对 值			东莞占全国的比重(%)	东莞占全省的比重(%)
		全 国	全 省	东 莞		
人口						
年末常住人口	万 人	136782	10724	834.31	0.61	7.78
经济总量						
地区生产总值	亿 元	636463	67810	5881.32	0.92	8.67
第一产业增加值	亿 元	58332	3167	20.35	0.03	0.64
第二产业增加值	亿 元	271392	31420	2794.42	1.03	8.89
第三产业增加值	亿 元	306739	33223	3066.55	1.00	9.23
工业						
工业增加值	亿 元	227991	29144	2709.00	1.19	9.30
主要工业产品产量						
机制纸及纸板	万 吨	11786	2071	1545.59	13.11	74.64
彩电	万 台	14129	7040	546.86	3.87	7.77
发电量	亿千瓦时	56496	3870	344.03	0.61	8.89
农业						
主要农产品产量						
粮食	万 吨	60703	1357	1.24	0.002	0.09
水果	万 吨	26142	1438	6.25	0.02	0.43
肉类	万 吨	8707	429	2.01	0.02	0.47
水产品	万 吨	6462	837	7.27	0.11	0.87
固定资产投资额						
固定资产投资总额	亿 元	512761	25928	1427.11	0.28	5.50
运输邮电						
货物周转量	亿吨公里	185398	15014	448.01	0.24	2.98
旅客周转量	亿人公里	30096	3967	85.46	0.28	2.15
年末固定电话用户	万 户	24943	2949	327.21	1.31	11.10
年末移动电话用户	万 户	128609	14943	1763.09	1.37	11.80
财政、金融						
公共财政收入	亿 元	140350	8065	455.21	0.32	5.64
公共财政支出	亿 元	151662	9153	457.68	0.30	5.00
各项人民币存款余额	亿 元	1138645	118908	9069.92	0.80	7.63
各项人民币贷款余额	亿 元	816770	76096	5331.63	0.65	7.01
外经外贸						
进出口总额	亿美元	43030	10767	1625.30	3.78	15.09
进口总额	亿美元	19603	4305	654.61	3.34	15.21
出口总额	亿美元	23427	6462	970.69	4.14	15.02
实际利用外资	亿美元	1196	269	45.29	3.79	16.86
商业、物价						
社会消费品零售总额	亿 元	271896	28471	1942.29	0.71	6.82
商品零售价格指数	上年=100	101.0	101.4	101.2		
居民消费价格指数	上年=100	102.0	102.3	102.3		
人民生活						
城镇在岗职工年平均工资	元	57346	59827	47600		
城镇常住居民人均可支配收入	元	28844	32148	36764		
农村常住居民人均可支配收入	元	10489	12246	22327		
城乡居民人民币储蓄存款余额	亿 元	485261	52411	4606.79	0.95	8.79

17-4 主要经济指标东莞占全国、全省的比重（2013年）

Proportion of Main Indicators of Dongguan to China and Guangdong Province (2013)

指标	单位	绝对值			东莞占全国的比重(%)	东莞占全省的比重(%)
		全国	全省	东莞		
人口						
年末常住人口	万人	136072	10644	831.66	0.61	7.81
经济总量						
地区生产总值	亿元	588019	62475	5517.47	0.94	8.83
第一产业增加值	亿元	55322	2977	19.55	0.04	0.66
第二产业增加值	亿元	256810	28994	2622.67	1.02	9.05
第三产业增加值	亿元	275887	30503	2875.25	1.04	9.43
工业						
工业增加值	亿元	217264	26895	2542.60	1.17	9.45
主要工业产品产量						
机制纸及纸板	万吨	11368	1911	1201.60	10.57	62.88
彩电	万台	12745	6691	695.68	5.46	10.40
发电量	亿千瓦时	54316	3796	348.00	0.64	9.17
农业						
主要农产品产量						
粮食	万吨	60194	1316	1.24	0.002	0.09
水果	万吨	25093	1369	6.11	0.02	0.45
肉类	万吨	8535	435	2.28	0.03	0.52
水产品	万吨	6172	816	7.45	0.12	0.91
固定资产投资额						
固定资产投资总额	亿元	446294	22829	1383.94	0.31	6.06
运输邮电						
货物周转量	亿吨公里	168014	12496	432.28	0.26	3.46
旅客周转量	亿人公里	27572	4852	155.98	0.57	3.21
年末固定电话用户	万户	26699	3100	314.48	1.18	10.14
年末移动电话用户	万户	122911	14706	1850.39	1.51	12.58
财政、金融						
公共财政收入	亿元	129210	7081	409.29	0.32	5.78
公共财政支出	亿元	140212	8411	444.66	0.32	5.29
各项人民币存款余额	亿元	1043847	111881	8630.73	0.83	7.71
各项人民币贷款余额	亿元	718961	66889	4774.23	0.66	7.14
外经外贸						
进出口总额	亿美元	41590	10918	1530.72	3.68	14.02
进口总额	亿美元	19500	4555	622.08	3.19	13.66
出口总额	亿美元	22090	6364	908.64	4.11	14.28
实际利用外资	亿美元	1176	250	39.38	3.35	15.78
商业、物价						
社会消费品零售总额	亿元	242843	25454	1786.66	0.74	7.02
商品零售价格指数	上年=100	101.4	101.0	100.6		
居民消费价格指数	上年=100	102.6	102.5	101.9		
人民生活						
城镇在岗职工年平均工资	元	52379	53611	42870		
城镇常住居民人均可支配收入	元	26467	29537	46594		
农村常住居民人均可支配收入	元	9430	11068	27214		
城乡居民人民币储蓄存款余额	亿元	447602	49288	4476.43	1.00	9.08

17-5 主要经济指标人均水平东莞与全国、全省的比较（2014年）

Comparison of Per Capita Level of Main Economic Indicators between Dongguan and China, Guangdong Province (2014)

指标	单位	人均水平			东莞相当于全国(%)	东莞相当于全省(%)
		全国	全省	东莞		
地区生产总值	元	46652	63469	70605	151.3	111.2
财政收入	元	10288	7544	5465	53.1	72.4
出口总额	美元	1717	6049	11653	678.6	192.7
各项人民币存款余额	元	83245	110880	108712	130.6	98.0
居民储蓄存款余额	元	35477	48872	55217	155.6	113.0
固定资产投资总额	元	37585	24268	17132	45.6	70.6
社会消费品零售总额	元	19930	26648	23317	117.0	87.5
实际利用外资	美元	88	252	544	620.4	216.2
城镇在岗职工年平均工资	元	57346	59827	47600	83.0	79.6
城镇常住居民人均可支配收入	元	28844	32148	36764	127.5	114.4
农村常住居民人均可支配收入	元	10489	12246	22327	212.9	182.3
粮食产量	公斤	445	127	1	0.3	1.2
水产品产量	公斤	47	78	9	18.4	11.1
水果产量	公斤	192	135	8	3.9	5.6
工业发电量	千瓦时	4141	3622	4130	99.7	114.0
医院卫生院床位数	张/千人	3.63	3.47	3.12	85.9	89.9
卫生技术人员数	人/千人	5.55	5.38	5.16	93.1	96.0

注：本表人均指标时点数按常住人口计算，时期数按年平均常住人口计算。

17-6 主要经济指标人均水平东莞与全国、全省的比较（2013年）

Comparison of Per Capita Level of Main Economic Indicators between Dongguan and China, Guangdong Province (2013)

指标	单位	人均水平			东莞相当于全国(%)	东莞相当于全省(%)
		全国	全省	东莞		
地区生产总值	元	43320	58833	66440	153.4	112.9
财政收入	元	9519	6668	4929	51.8	73.9
出口总额	美元	1627	5993	10942	672.3	182.6
各项人民币存款余额	元	76713	105112	103777	135.3	98.7
居民储蓄存款余额	元	32894	46306	53823	163.6	116.2
固定资产投资总额	元	32879	21498	16665	50.7	77.5
社会消费品零售总额	元	17891	23970	21514	120.3	89.8
实际利用外资	美元	87	235	474	547.3	201.4
城镇在岗职工年平均工资	元	52379	53611	42870	81.8	80.0
城镇常住居民人均可支配收入	元	26467	29537	46594	176.0	157.7
农村常住居民人均可支配收入	元	9430	11068	27214	288.6	245.9
粮食产量	公斤	443	124	1	0.3	1.2
水产品产量	公斤	45	77	7	16.2	9.6
水果产量	公斤	185	129	8	4.2	6.1
工业发电量	千瓦时	4002	3575	4191	104.7	117.2
医院卫生院床位数	张/千人	3.37	3.29	3.01	89.4	91.5
卫生技术人员数	人/千人	5.30	5.17	5.07	95.6	98.0

注：本表人均指标时点数按年末常住人口计算，时期数按年平均常住人口计算。

17-7 珠江三角洲国民经济和社会发展主要指标（2014年）

指　　标	单 位	广州市	深圳市	珠海市
综合				
行政区域土地面积	平方公里	7249	1997	1724
年末常住人口	万人	1308.05	1077.89	161.42
年末户籍人口	万人	842.42	346.60	110.22
地区生产总值	亿元	16706.87	16001.82	1867.21
第一产业增加值	亿元	218.70	5.58	43.94
第二产业增加值	亿元	5590.97	6812.02	938.71
第三产业增加值	亿元	10897.20	9184.22	884.57
人均生产总值(按常住人口计算)	元	128478	149495	116537
农村经济				
农林牧渔业总产值	亿元	398.30	12.92	83.56
粮食产量	万吨	44.31	0.01	4.25
水果产量	万吨	45.66	0.21	7.30
水产品产量	万吨	47.85	4.29	28.15
工业				
规模以上工业企业数	个	4767	6355	1008
规模以上工业增加值	亿元	4364.66	6252.09	881.04
规模以上工业企业主营业务收入	亿元	16892.43	23985.79	4176.70
规模以上工业企业利润总额	亿元	1076.69	1496.16	293.96
规模以上工业产品销售率	%	97.3	97.4	95.1
固定资产投资				
固定资产投资总额	亿元	4889.50	2717.42	1135.05
#房地产开发投资额	亿元	1816.15	1069.49	388.30
商品房屋销售面积	万平方米	1540.02	532.57	349.04
商品房屋销售额	亿元	2420.70	1316.69	408.29
交通、邮电				
民用汽车拥有量	万辆	222.77	311.15	34.56
年末固定电话用户数	万户	502.93	529.51	78.45
年末移动电话用户数	万户	2905.44	2959.77	363.96
全年总用电量	亿千瓦时	765.85	779.93	134.32

Main Indicators of National Economy and Social Development of the Pearl River Delta Economic Zone (2014)

佛山市	惠州市	肇庆市	江门市	东莞市	中山市
3798	11346	14891	9505	2460	1784
735.06	472.66	403.58	451.14	834.31	319.27
385.61	348.52	433.73	393.39	191.39	156.06
7441.60	3000.37	1845.06	2082.76	5881.32	2823.01
133.75	141.09	270.19	168.02	20.35	66.99
4602.17	1697.01	923.61	1021.62	2794.42	1560.76
2705.68	1162.27	651.26	893.12	3066.55	1195.26
101617	63657	45795	46237	70605	88682
270.47	228.61	408.64	308.21	33.94	113.70
9.84	59.21	115.58	95.27	1.24	7.52
4.38	68.36	143.53	24.92	6.25	17.52
61.26	16.16	40.17	74.59	7.27	34.29
5883	1815	1083	1961	5377	2963
4138.71	1475.02	924.53	847.29	2490.84	1209.10
17953.59	6720.44	3729.56	3314.61	11890.43	5651.33
1365.33	306.00	216.05	170.84	365.98	291.15
97.4	98.3	97.6	94.3	97.9	95.7
2612.45	1606.71	1138.73	1111.65	1427.11	903.66
832.70	667.30	188.89	313.01	588.06	429.66
1061.14	983.94	494.17	360.59	643.65	764.07
940.37	588.81	248.22	214.55	626.65	464.02
153.85	47.09	26.54	45.70	155.96	63.98
294.71	120.20	61.20	115.20	327.21	102.75
1265.12	546.59	329.49	507.21	1763.09	610.18
564.13	276.41	156.24	227.87	660.99	237.64

17-7 续表

(2014年)

指　　标	单 位	广州市	深圳市	珠海市
金融、贸易、财政				
年末金融机构本外币存款余额	亿元	35469.29	37350.50	4570.67
年末金融机构本外币贷款余额	亿元	24231.71	27922.13	2426.24
社会消费品零售总额	亿元	7144.45	4919.00	815.71
地方公共财政收入	亿元	1243.10	2082.73	224.31
地方公共财政支出	亿元	1436.22	2166.18	275.90
对外经济				
进出口总额	亿美元	1306.00	4877.65	549.98
进口总额	亿美元	578.85	2033.62	259.44
出口总额	亿美元	727.15	2844.03	290.54
合同利用外资金额	亿美元	80.40	108.95	29.96
实际利用外商直接投资	亿美元	51.07	58.05	19.31
人民生活、物价				
在岗职工年平均工资	元	74245	72651	62729
城镇常住居民人均可支配收入	元	42955	40948	35287
城镇常住居民人均消费支出	元	33385	28853	26638
农村常住居民人均可支配收入	元	17663		18395
农村常住居民人均消费性支出	元	12868		14303
居民消费价格总指数(以上年为100)	%	102.3	102.0	103.1
教育、卫生				
学校数				
中等职业技术学校	所	86	16	8
普通中学	所	500	325	67
小学	所	938	331	115
在校学生数				
中等职业技术学校	人	245434	36870	21756
普通中学	人	532870	378690	90546
小学	人	900072	793178	140593
医院医疗机构数	个	2668	661	3185
#医院	个	224	57	127
医院床位数	张	68685	11378	29068
执业(助理)医师	人	40284	6324	27081

佛山市	惠州市	肇庆市	江门市	东莞市	中山市
11275.63	3394.60	1679.26	3587.64	9323.28	4149.69
7595.79	2436.97	1172.51	2024.51	5562.36	2644.90
2400.58	968.70	559.90	923.35	1942.29	981.80
501.19	300.75	139.13	177.20	455.21	251.74
525.01	372.97	241.71	236.10	457.68	261.46
688.18	594.12	78.42	203.75	1625.30	369.61
220.98	230.81	32.25	52.87	654.61	90.81
467.20	363.31	46.17	150.88	970.69	278.80
37.32	30.55	33.31	13.01	43.15	8.86
26.56	19.66	13.33	8.54	45.29	6.81
55679	53576	49045	48168	47600	53123
36555	27300	21726	24976	36764	34304
26043	20065	15215	16762	27071	22944
20094	14364	12642	12746	22327	22166
13474	11008	7996	9191	18505	15189
102.3	102.1	102.7	102.7	102.3	102.2
36	24	20	23	25	11
193	234	174	185	212	102
406	453	219	313	320	206
76322	61765	64359	46441	64412	25189
307769	276309	266168	222952	284648	147485
474382	472152	332450	299322	687269	267907
692	502	1383	380	2194	948
38	54	101	25	83	33
12738	15601	25994	4908	25994	9528
8296	10591	14344	4475	15081	8471

17-8 长江三角洲国民经济和社会发展主要指标（2014年）

指　　标	单位	上海市	南京市	苏州市	无锡市	常州市	镇江市
综合							
行政区域土地面积	平方公里	6341	6587	8488	4627	4372	3847
年末常住人口	万人	2425.68	821.61	1060.40	650.01	469.64	317.14
年末户籍人口	万人	1429.26	648.72	661.08	477.14	368.64	272.07
地区生产总值	亿元	23560.94	8820.75	13760.89	8205.31	4901.87	3252.38
第一产业增加值	亿元	124.26	223.96	227.91	138.13	138.46	122.15
第二产业增加值	亿元	8164.79	3671.45	7034.10	4095.89	2458.17	1662.55
第三产业增加值	亿元	15271.89	4925.34	6498.88	3971.29	2305.24	1467.68
农村经济							
农林牧渔业总产值	亿元	322.07	384.62	392.49	253.76	256.81	213.90
工业							
规模以上工业增加值	亿元	7163.40	2999.44	6227.87	3017.50	2460.44	1883.20
规模以上工业企业主营业务收入	亿元	35169.85	12863.55	30417.16	14429.56	11276.93	7856.45
规模以上工业企业利润总额	亿元	2661.13	755.60	1425.16	866.67	607.36	509.68
固定资产投资							
固定资产投资总额	亿元	6016.43	5460.03	6230.67	4634.21	3310.05	2142.34
#房地产开发投资额	亿元	3206.48	1125.49	1764.44	1269.48	681.53	319.05
交通、邮电							
民用汽车拥有量	万辆	255.19	172.19	240.37	152.29	87.30	38.50
年末固定电话用户数	万户	840.18	261.13	268.69	187.19	144.43	98.70
年末移动电话用户数	万户	3292.74	1097.00	1661.00	941.40	491.33	340.20
金融、贸易、财政							
年末金融机构本外币存款余额	亿元	73882.45	20733.39	22832.53	12315.01	6980.70	3598.68
年末金融机构本外币贷款余额	亿元	47915.81	16448.55	18427.41	9029.64	4897.39	2730.19
社会消费品零售总额	亿元	8718.65	4167.18	4061.11	3054.75	1804.19	976.56
地方公共财政收入	亿元	4585.55	903.49	1443.82	768.01	433.88	277.76
地方公共财政支出	亿元	4923.44	920.90	1304.80	784.06	426.92	313.30
对外经济							
进出口总额	亿美元	4666.22	572.21	3113.06	741.70	288.10	103.07
进口总额	亿美元	3402.43	245.93	1301.28	299.39	74.46	37.05
出口总额	亿美元	2102.77	326.28	1811.78	442.31	213.64	66.02
实际利用外商直接投资	亿美元	181.66	32.91	81.20	31.16	24.09	12.95
人民生活、物价							
常住居民人均可支配收入	元		37283	39780	36471	32662	28850
城镇常住居民人均可支配收入	元	47710	42568	46677	41731	39483	35752
农村常住居民人均可支配收入	元	21192	17661	23560	22264	20133	17617
居民消费价格总指数(以上年为100)	%	102.7	102.6	102.1	102.2	102.2	102.0

注：1.扬州、杭州民用机动车拥有量为全市机动车拥有量，无锡为全社会拥有车辆。

Main Indicators on National Economy and Social Development of the Yangtze River Delta Economic Zone (2014)

南通市	扬州市	泰州市	杭州市	宁波市	嘉兴市	湖州市	绍兴市	舟山市	台州市
8001	6591	5787	16596	9816	3915	5820	8279	1440	9411
729.80	447.79	463.86	889.20	781.10	457.00	293.00	495.60	114.60	601.50
767.63	461.34	508.51	715.76	583.80	348.14	263.78	443.04	97.49	597.10
5652.69	3697.89	3370.89	9201.16	7602.51	3352.80	1955.96	4265.83	1021.66	3387.51
367.11	240.00	209.25	274.36	275.18	145.14	120.96	194.25	100.82	215.62
2873.83	1886.26	1727.45	3858.90	3935.57	1811.31	1001.58	2213.51	430.07	1588.88
2411.76	1571.63	1434.19	5067.90	3391.76	1396.35	833.42	1858.07	490.77	1583.01
631.90	432.30	361.94	419.41	431.60	249.12	211.40	296.96	199.48	379.34
2864.24	2145.68	2169.70	2805.25	2540.18	1328.26	700.60	1517.92	316.56	831.50
12308.30	9083.47	9331.76	12462.36	12354.65	6862.16	3915.40	9448.25	1114.68	3657.95
936.42	616.95	716.79	876.28	648.14	366.19	231.66	525.70	2.06	195.09
3896.39	2416.66	2200.19	4952.70	3989.46	2221.21	1242.92	2304.68	960.88	1765.93
678.92	360.44	288.39	2301.08	1328.10	525.72	342.70	631.51	225.80	496.05
99.66	83.63	47.03	269.63	159.72	65.27	47.15	85.12	17.11	103.95
231.10	125.81	119.88	311.14	270.00	135.23	90.62	150.94	40.44	140.55
791.38	487.81	405.18	1561.71	1267.00	614.60	383.00	532.31	163.88	758.62
8508.32	4323.54	4061.82	24450.51	13890.10	5684.10	2813.71	6666.73	1624.05	5671.03
5258.93	2766.18	2854.53	21316.83	14569.78	4641.26	2363.04	6006.70	1453.70	5039.37
2166.10	1232.00	937.17	3838.73	2992.00	1347.02	871.20	1487.14	376.58	1646.32
550.00	295.19	277.95	1027.32	860.61	307.07	167.84	317.27	101.02	265.21
650.00	374.67	367.55	961.18	1000.86	334.90	224.57	346.44	188.19	371.47
316.47	100.12	108.93	679.98	1047.04	337.34	99.89	346.84	123.35	220.79
91.67	23.30	47.15	188.32	315.95	100.83	11.83	49.32	65.59	27.28
224.80	76.82	61.78	491.66	731.09	236.51	88.06	297.51	57.76	193.51
23.05	13.88	9.39	63.35	38.11	24.96	9.84	6.71	2.00	2.42
25340	24157	23833	39237	38074	34318	31510	35335	35330	30950
33374	30322	31346	44632	44155	42143	38959	43167	41466	39763
15821	15284	15076	23555	24283	24676	22404	23539	23783	19362
102.1	102.1	102.1	102.0	101.9	102.0	102.3	102.1	101.7	102.3

2.数据为初步统计数。

17-9 中国香港特别行政区主要社会经济指标

Main Statistical Indicators of Hong Kong Special Administrative Region

指　　标	单　位	1990年	2000年	2010年	2013年	2014年
人口及生命统计						
年中人口	万人	570.4	666.5	702.4	718.8	724.2
粗出生率	‰	12.0	8.1	12.6	7.9	8.6
粗死亡率	‰	5.2	5.1	6.0	6.0	6.2
劳动、就业						
劳动人口	万人	274.8	337.4	363.1	385.9	387.6
劳动人口参与率	%	63.2	61.4	59.6	61.2	61.1
失业率	%	1.3	4.9	4.3	3.4	3.3
就业不足率	%	0.9	2.8	2.0	1.5	1.5
实际工资指数（1992年9月=100)		100.2	112.5	113.5	118.7	115.7
本地生产总值						
按2012年环比物量计算						
本地生产总值年增长率	%	3.8	7.7	6.8	2.9	2.3
本地生产总值	亿港元	8702	12822	19110	20961	21446
人均本地生产总值	港元	152545	192371	272058	291626	296152
按当年价格计算						
本地生产总值年增长率	%	11.7	4.0	7.1	4.7	5.3
本地生产总值	亿港元	5993	13375	17763	21318	22457
人均本地生产总值	港元	105050	200675	252887	296599	310113
政府收支、货币、金融						
政府收入总额	亿港元	895	2251	3765	4553	4707
政府支出总额	亿港元	856	2329	3014	4335	3971
货币供应量M3	亿港元	12880	36928	71563	100852	110497
居民消费物价指数						
(2009年10月至2010年9月=100)						
综合消费物价指数		57.3	96.5	100.7	115.1	120.2
本地居民总收入(按当年价格计算)						
本地居民总收入	亿港元		13482	18139	21723	23065
人均本地居民总收入	港元		202287	258240	302236	318505

注:本表数据由香港特别行政区政府统计处提供，国家统计局整理编辑。1996年及以前年份数据均指原香港地区。

17-9　续表

指　　标	单　位	1990年	2000年	2010年	2013年	2014年
工业生产						
工业生产指数(2008年=100)				95.0	95.0	94.6
工业电力消费量	万亿焦耳	24934	17769	11080	11190	11281
工业煤气消费量	万亿焦耳	583	982	917	1612	1673
房屋及物业						
已登记物业买卖合约涉及的价值	亿港元		2225	6895	4563	5475
住宅	亿港元		1684	5607	2989	4334
非住宅	亿港元		541	1288	1573	1140
建筑工程完成名义总值	亿港元	613	1221	1113	1766	1986
新落成房屋委员会租住单位	个	32619	55492	13672	14057	9938
运输、通讯						
进出香港的货运车辆	万辆	473.35	940.22	834.57	755.99	722.46
进出香港的货物						
总卸下	万吨	6076	13035	17282	17942	20090
总装上	万吨	2997	8692	12882	12632	12558
集装箱吞吐量	万标准集装箱单位	510	1810	2370	2235	2223
领牌车辆	万辆	37	52	61	68	70
电话服务	万条操作线路	245	395	426	432	432
对外商品贸易						
港产品出口	亿港元	2259	1810	695	544	553
转口	亿港元	4140	13917	29615	35053	36175
进口	亿港元	6425	16580	33648	40607	42190
旅　游						
访港旅客	万人次	658	1306	3603	5430	6084
酒店入住率	%	79	83	87	89	90
教　育						
小学学生人数	人	526720	493979	331112	320918	329300
中学学生人数	人	453423	466710	452581	397215	374797
大学教育学生人数	人	57824	78295	166018	195147	187714

17-10 中国澳门特别行政区主要社会经济指标

Main Statistical Indicators of Macao Special Administrative Region

指　　标	单　位	1990年	2000年	2010年	2013年	2014年
人口及生命统计						
年中人口	万人	33.5	43.1	53.7	59.2	62.2
出生率	‰	20.5	8.9	9.5	11.1	11.8
死亡率	‰	4.4	3.1	3.3	3.2	3.1
劳动力						
劳动人口	万人	16.9	20.9	32.4	36.8	39.5
劳动力参与率	%	66.6	64.3	72.0	72.7	73.8
失业率	%	3.2	6.8	2.8	1.8	1.7
就业不足率	%	2.3	3.0	1.7	0.6	0.4
本地生产总值						
以2012年环比物量计算						
本地生产总值实际增长率(支出法)	%	8.0	5.7	27.5	10.7	-0.4
本地生产总值	亿澳门元	653.9	851.2	2594.2	3801.1	3787.7
人均本地生产总值	亿澳门元	19.5	19.8	48.3	64.1	61.0
按当年价格计算						
本地生产总值名义增长率(支出法)	%	20.4	2.7	33.4	19.3	8.1
本地生产总值	亿澳门元	254.6	516.3	2269.4	4099.6	4433.0
人均本地生产总值	亿澳门元	7.6	12.0	42.3	69.2	71.4
政府收支、货币、金融						
政府总收入	亿澳门元	60.2	153.4	884.9	1759.5	1560.7
政府总开支	亿澳门元	55.1	150.2	383.9	513.9	657.8
货币供应（广义货币供应量M2)	亿澳门元	307.4	849.2	2430.5	4414.1	4875.9
消费价格指数						
(2013年10月至2014年9月=100)						
综合消费价格指数			64.82	80.50	95.35	101.11
工业生产						
工业电力消耗量	亿千瓦小时		1.6	1.6	1.8	1.9

注：本表数据由澳门特别行政区政府统计暨普查局提供，国家统计局整理编辑。1998年及以前数据均指原澳门地区。

17-10 续表

指　　标	单　位	1990年	2000年	2010年	2013年	2014年
建　筑						
建成的私人楼宇单位数目	个	11574	3146	4527	1316	3001
建成的私人楼宇总建筑面积	万平方米	105.7	37.0	127.2	56.2	44.0
新动工的私人楼宇单位数目	个		1167	870	2241	1900
新动工的私人楼宇总建筑面积	万平方米		20.3	18.4	239.6	223.9
楼宇单位买卖数目	个	8463	10211	29617	19237	13230
不动产买卖契约数目	宗	8559	12484	12707	10527	10279
不动产按揭贷款数目	宗	6610	7367	15127	17093	32193
房屋（期末值）						
公共房屋	个	4871	9084	8174	12221	11344
运输、通讯						
进出澳门货运车辆数目	万辆	26.4	45.4	35.8	31.1	35.7
领牌车辆	万辆	5.1	11.4	19.7	22.8	24.0
电话线	万条	9.6	17.7	16.8	15.8	15.4
对外商品贸易						
出口	亿澳门元	136.4	203.8	69.6	90.9	99.1
本地产品出口	亿澳门元		170.8	23.9	20.1	20.2
转口	亿澳门元		33.0	45.7	70.8	78.9
进口	亿澳门元	123.4	181.0	441.2	810.1	899.5
旅　游						
访澳旅客	万人次	594.2	916.2	2496.5	2932.5	3152.6
酒店入住率	%	69	58	80	83	87
教　育						
幼儿教育学生	人	20814	14978	10804	13395	14552
小学生	人	34972	45474	23785	22862	24252
中学生	人	17601	38156	37224	32054	30088
高等教育学生	人	7425	8358	25539	29521	30771

17-11 中国台湾省主要社会经济指标

Main Statistical Indicators of Taiwan Province

指　　标	单　位	1995年	2000年	2010年	2013年	2014年
人口						
户籍登记人口数	万人	2136	2228	2316	2337	2343
人口自然增加率	‰	9.90	8.08	0.91	1.85	1.98
人口密度	人/平方公里	590	616	640	646	647
劳动、就业						
劳动力人口	万人	921	978	1107	1145	1154
劳动参与率	%	58.7	57.7	58.1	58.4	58.5
失业率	%	1.8	3.0	5.2	4.2	4.0
国民经济核算						
本地居民生产总值	新台币亿元	71291	101716	145489	156462	166214
本地生产总值	新台币亿元	70179	100320	141192	152212	160818
人均本地居民生产总值	新台币元	336042	459729	628706	670226	710407
物价年涨跌率						
批发	%		1.82	5.46	-2.43	-0.56
消费者	%		1.26	0.96	0.79	1.20
工　业						
受雇者劳动生产力指数(2011年＝100)				97.1	99.4	103.1
工业生产指数（2011年＝100）				95.8	100.4	106.8
工业生产总值	新台币亿元	71609	91425	149384	149453	155480
运输、旅游						
铁路客运人数	亿人	1.6	4.6	7.8	9.7	10.2
公路客运人数	亿人	12.0	11.0	11.1	12.2	12.4
航空						
省内	万人	2874	2665	973	1055	1056
国际	万人	1499	1978	3111	3939	4440
港埠货物装卸量	万收费吨	42017	56695	65540	70575	74861
出岛旅客	万人次	519	733	942	1105	1184
来台湾旅客	万人次	233	262	557	802	991
对外贸易						
出口	亿美元	1117	1520	2746	3054	3137
进口	亿美元	1036	1407	2512	2701	2740
财政、金融及景气						
赋税实征净额	新台币亿元	12323	19298	16222	18341	19761
货币供应量M2	新台币亿元	128054	188978	309544	355189	376968
存款	新台币亿元	131309	193087	310063	350624	371339
放款与投资	新台币亿元	121003	166220	228037	267206	281106

注：本表数据来源于台湾统计月报。

第三部分　基本单位情况

Part Three　Basic Units

1-1 按行业分的法人单位、产业活动单位数（2014年）

Number of Corporate Units and Industrial Establishments by Sector (2014)

项　　目	法　人 单位数 （个）	单 产 业 法人单位	多 产 业 法人单位	产业活动 单 位 数 （个）	#多产业法 人单位的 产业活动 单　　位
合　　计	134066	131394	2672	150000	18606
采 矿 业	13	13		14	1
煤炭开采和洗选业					
石油和天然气开采业					
黑色金属矿采选业					
有色金属矿采选业					
非金属矿采选业	12	12		13	1
开采辅助活动	1	1		1	
其他采矿业					
制 造 业	62928	62499	429	63471	972
农副食品加工业	322	315	7	329	14
食品制造业	514	503	11	526	23
酒、饮料和精制茶制造业	123	117	6	129	12
烟草制品业					
纺织业	1814	1802	12	1826	24
纺织服装、服饰业	3689	3655	34	3703	48
皮革、毛皮、羽毛及其制品和制鞋业	3322	3307	15	3339	32
木材加工和木、竹、藤、棕、草制品业	612	609	3	620	11
家具制造业	2020	1996	24	2038	42
造纸和纸制品业	2941	2935	6	2949	14
印刷和记录媒介复制业	2092	2086	6	2098	12
文教、工美、体育和娱乐用品制造业	2834	2813	21	2843	30
石油加工、炼焦和核燃料加工业	70	68	2	77	9
化学原料和化学制品制造业	1888	1868	20	1901	33
医药制造业	56	52	4	64	12
化学纤维制造业	101	101		103	2
橡胶和塑料制品业	7355	7327	28	7384	57
非金属矿物制品业	1151	1145	6	1170	25
黑色金属冶炼和压延加工业	309	306	3	312	6
有色金属冶炼和压延加工业	470	469	1	477	8
金属制品业	7059	7036	23	7095	59
通用设备制造业	4182	4136	46	4219	83
专用设备制造业	5483	5448	35	5522	74
汽车制造业	268	265	3	272	7

1-1 续表 1

(2014年)

项目	法人单位数(个)	单产业法人单位	多产业法人单位	产业活动单位数(个)	#多产业法人单位的产业活动单位
铁路、船舶、航空航天和其他运输设备制造业	161	160	1	166	6
电气机械和器材制造业	5280	5237	43	5319	82
计算机、通信和其他电子设备制造业	6669	6616	53	6727	111
仪器仪表制造业	941	931	10	949	18
其他制造业	913	911	2	916	5
废弃资源综合利用业	63	60	3	159	99
金属制品、机械和设备修理业	226	225	1	239	14
电力、燃气及水的生产和供应业	216	212	4	298	86
电力、热力生产和供应业	43	43		53	10
燃气生产和供应业	26	24	2	65	41
水的生产和供应业	147	145	2	180	35
建筑业	4226	4125	101	4929	804
房屋建筑业	429	407	22	684	277
土木工程建筑业	359	349	10	529	180
建筑安装业	869	842	27	957	115
建筑装饰和其他建筑业	2569	2527	42	2759	232
批发和零售业	30810	30380	430	36412	6032
批发业	17152	16996	156	18290	1294
零售业	13658	13384	274	18122	4738
交通运输、仓储和邮政业	2541	2428	113	3590	1162
铁路运输业	26	26		35	9
道路运输业	873	847	26	1008	161
水上运输业	79	75	4	86	11
航空运输业	9	7	2	15	8
管道运输业				2	2
装卸搬运和运输代理业	1150	1098	52	1474	376
仓储业	182	179	3	190	11
邮政业	222	196	26	780	584
住宿和餐饮业	1847	1692	155	2621	929
住宿业	821	727	94	911	184
餐饮业	1026	965	61	1710	745
信息传输、软件和信息技术服务业	1853	1807	46	2283	476
电信、广播电视和卫星传输服务	79	68	11	366	298
互联网和相关服务	414	408	6	465	57
软件和信息技术服务业	1360	1331	29	1452	121
金融业	406	354	52	2072	1718
货币金融服务	123	102	21	1390	1288
资本市场服务	137	133	4	199	66
保险业	82	55	27	404	349

1-1 续表 2

(2014年)

项目	法人单位数(个)	单产业法人单位	多产业法人单位	产业活动单位数(个)	#多产业法人单位的产业活动单位
其他金融业	64	64		79	15
房地产业	4244	4019	225	4924	905
房地产业	4244	4019	225	4924	905
租赁与商务服务业	13049	12738	311	14737	1999
租赁业	255	253	2	286	33
商务服务业	12794	12485	309	14451	1966
科学研究、技术服务业	1847	1801	46	2067	266
研究和试验发展	212	207	5	219	12
专业技术服务业	1296	1260	36	1500	240
科技推广和应用服务业	339	334	5	348	14
水利、环境和公共设施管理业	480	465	15	544	79
水利管理业	67	64	3	77	13
生态保护和环境治理业	102	101	1	122	21
公共设施管理业	311	300	11	345	45
居民服务、修理和其他服务业	2368	2312	56	2615	303
居民服务业	890	869	21	1045	176
机动车、电子产品和日用产品修理业	749	731	18	798	67
其他服务业	729	712	17	772	60
教育	2183	2137	46	2849	712
教育	2183	2137	46	2849	712
卫生和社会工作	965	899	66	1546	647
卫生	848	783	65	1427	644
社会工作	117	116	1	119	3
文化、体育和娱乐业	1729	1709	20	1879	170
新闻和出版业	19	18	1	18	
广播、电视、电影和影视录音制作业	108	104	4	136	32
文化艺术业	259	258	1	266	8
体育	114	113	1	123	10
娱乐业	1229	1216	13	1336	120
公共管理、社会保障和社会组织	2361	1804	557	3149	1345
中国共产党机关	60	60		60	
国家机构	862	810	52	1434	624
人民政协、民主党派	12	12		12	
社会保障	14	14		25	11
群众团体、社会团体和其他成员组织	775	758	17	915	157
基层群众自治组织	638	150	488	703	553
国际组织					
国际组织					

1-2 按注册类型分的法人单位、产业活动单位数（2014年）

Number of Corporate Units and Industrial Establishments by Registration Status (2014)

项目	法人单位数（个）	单产业法人单位	多产业法人单位	产业活动单位数（个）	#多产业法人单位的产业活动单位
合计	134066	131394	2672	150000	18606
内资	123180	120764	2416	137655	16891
国有	1759	1643	116	3466	1823
集体	2398	2299	99	3138	839
股份合作	525	515	10	663	148
国有联营	10	8	2	16	8
集体联营	75	72	3	96	24
国有与集体联营	13	12	1	32	20
其他联营	189	185	4	220	35
国有独资公司	72	64	8	86	22
其他有限责任公司	39629	38952	677	44148	5196
股份有限公司	1846	1779	67	3532	1753
私营独资	13828	13755	73	14361	606
私营合伙	3950	3920	30	4062	142
私营有限公司	47256	46586	670	50129	3543
私营股份有限公司	1673	1643	30	1797	154
其他	9957	9331	626	11909	2578
港澳台商投资	7813	7665	148	8437	772
与港澳台商合资经营	362	339	23	463	124
与港澳台商合作经营	215	210	5	246	36
港澳台商独资	6844	6726	118	7243	517
港澳台商投资股份有限公司	185	183	2	218	35
其他港、澳、台商投资	207	207		267	60
外商投资	3073	2965	108	3908	943
中外合资经营	250	230	20	429	199
中外合作经营	68	66	2	93	27
外资企业	2540	2459	81	3066	607
外商投资股份有限公司	106	103	3	128	25
其他外商投资	109	107	2	192	85

1-3 按地域分的法人单位、产业活动单位数（2014年）

Number of Corporate Units and Industrial Establishments by District (2014)

项目	法人单位数（个）	单产业法人单位	多产业法人单位	产业活动单位数（个）	#多产业法人单位的产业活动单位
全市	134066	131394	2672	150000	18606
莞城街道	5665	5440	225	6544	1104
石龙镇	1346	1295	51	1695	400
虎门镇	8480	8389	91	9376	987
东城街道	8324	8063	261	9658	1595
万江街道	3988	3889	99	4421	532
南城街道	8470	8197	273	9803	1606
中堂镇	2312	2258	54	2645	387
望牛墩镇	1096	1067	29	1254	187
麻涌镇	1417	1380	37	1702	322
石碣镇	3720	3660	60	4057	397
高埗镇	1946	1897	49	2181	284
道滘镇	2214	2163	51	2423	260
洪梅镇	733	710	23	869	159
沙田镇	2543	2495	48	2816	321
厚街镇	6009	5919	90	6807	888
长安镇	11214	11104	110	12303	1199
寮步镇	7955	7799	156	8673	874
大岭山镇	4404	4351	53	4807	456
大朗镇	6767	6669	98	7388	719
黄江镇	3276	3224	52	3651	427
樟木头镇	4082	4012	70	4601	589
清溪镇	4180	4113	67	4539	426
塘厦镇	8140	8046	94	8781	735
凤岗镇	3896	3831	65	4303	472
谢岗镇	1421	1397	24	1592	195
常平镇	6289	6144	145	7257	1113
桥头镇	2508	2472	36	2830	358
横沥镇	2691	2658	33	2964	306
东坑镇	1579	1536	43	1814	278
企石镇	1615	1569	46	1840	271
石排镇	2406	2364	42	2638	274
茶山镇	2516	2469	47	2798	329
松山湖管委会	846	796	50	948	152
东莞生态园	18	18		22	4

注：沙田镇法人单位、产业活动单位含虎门港数据。

1-4 星级酒店名单(2014年)

List of Star-ranking Hotels (2014)

酒店名称	星级	电话	地址
凤岗名冠金凯悦大酒店	五星	87759888	凤岗镇凤深大道158号
东莞豪门大饭店	五星	85117888	虎门镇虎门大道
嘉华大酒店	五星	85928888	厚街镇家具大道1号
东莞富盈雅高美爵酒店	五星	85888888	厚街镇赤岭路段
索菲特东莞御景湾酒店	五星	22698888	东城区迎宾路8号
长安莲花山庄酒店	五星	85538388	长安镇莲峰北路77号
长安海悦花园大酒店	五星	85318888	长安镇霄边管理区二环路
柏宁长安国际酒店	五星	85333333	长安镇德政路222号
石龙名冠金凯悦大酒店	五星	86188888	石龙镇莞龙路西湖路段
东莞喜来登大酒店	五星	85988888	厚街镇S256省道莞太路段
新都会怡景酒店	五星	87883888	塘厦镇环市东路6号
太子酒店	五星	83363333	黄江镇江北路32号
塘厦三正半山酒店	五星	87299333	塘厦镇迎宾大道
汇华国际饭店	五星	83938888	常平镇常平大道2号
帝豪花园酒店	五星	83122222	大朗镇美景中路769号
丰泰花园酒店	五星	85708888	虎门镇S358省道大板地路段
华尔登国际酒店	五星	81028888	桥头镇广场路3号
悦莱花园酒店	五星	81118888	寮步镇香市路8号
欧亚国际酒店	五星	82838888	常平镇常东路8号
东莞虎门美思威尔顿酒店	五星	82888888	虎门镇虎门大道黄河商业城
厚街国际大酒店	五星	85088888	厚街镇东风路与S256省道交汇处
东莞宾馆	四星	22222222	莞城区东正路11号
江龙大酒店	四星	85838888	厚街镇S256省道莞太路段
新都会酒店	四星	87713333	樟木头镇维多利商业大道38号
宏远酒店	四星	22418888	南城区宏远路1号
汇美酒店	四星	83918888	常平镇中元路9号
东莞市花园酒店	四星	87799888	樟木头镇南城广场
长安酒店	四星	85532388	长安镇中心S358省道旁
新世纪酒店	四星	83338888	常平镇常平大道8号
厚街海悦花园大酒店	四星	85885888	厚街镇厚街大道东
汇源美爵酒店	四星	85244888	虎门镇虎门大道

1-4 续表

(2014年)

酒店名称	星级	电话	地址
业丰大酒店	四星	83113888	大朗镇莞樟路金朗大道23号
方中假日酒店	四星	86866666	茶山镇茶山大道西28号
常平半岛酒店	四星	83988888	常平镇北环路
波尔顿华禧酒店	四星	85383888	长安镇S358省道沙路段
嘉辉会酒店	四星	87563388	凤岗镇官井头嘉辉路
美怡登酒店	四星	83028888	常平镇中元路
天悦酒店	四星	81812222	石碣镇崇焕路18号
华庭花园酒店	四星	81633333	厚街镇广东现代国际展览中心南侧
新都会璜玛酒店	四星	87633338	谢岗镇花园大道73号
石龙宾馆	三星	86613333	石龙镇绿化中路2号
广彩城酒店	三星	22402088	南城区莞太路
石碣豪华大酒店	三星	86633333	石碣镇新城区
金湖粤海酒店	三星	87869888	塘厦镇塘厦大道南99号
黄江假日酒店	三星	83362888	黄江镇黄江大道3号
西湖大酒店	三星	22822888	南城区西平板岭
明苑大酒店	三星	85122918	虎门镇金龙大道南
宝石大酒店	三星	86662188	企石镇振华路1号
恒丰酒店	三星	83343333	桥头镇恒丰新村2号
嘉福海港酒店	三星	88682888	沙田镇中心区港口大道17号
中明酒店	三星	88883368	中堂镇新兴路1号
东逸酒店	三星	85396388	长安镇莲峰路103号
鸿茂酒店	三星	83999388	常平镇常黄路
宏信假日酒店	三星	87363888	清溪镇香芒西路
天鹅湖酒店	三星	83338388	常平镇天鹅湖路8号
中青旅山水	三星	21988888	东城区东纵大道189号
亚都酒店	三星	85343888	长安镇长中路115号
金沙亚都酒店	三星	85413888	长安镇靖海中路36号
耀豪酒店	二星	88865333	沙田镇中心区
盈丰酒店	二星	83333333	常平镇振兴路中段
海霞酒店	二星	82822888	常平镇板石霞村路段
冠城酒店	二星	82804888	常平镇中元街常平广场
海月酒店	二星	85926888	厚街镇港口大道涌口路段

1-5 高新技术企业名录（2014年）

List of High-tech Enterprises (2014)

企业名称	所在镇街	行业类别
广东智通人才连锁股份有限公司	莞城街道	职业中介服务
东莞市政创软件科技有限公司	莞城街道	信息系统集成服务
东莞市捷联科技有限公司	莞城街道	互联网信息服务
广东华盈光达科技有限公司	莞城街道	信息系统集成服务
广东慧讯计算机网络工程有限公司	莞城街道	信息系统集成服务
广东宏达工贸集团有限公司	莞城街道	其他建筑安装业
东莞市圣火网络科技有限公司	莞城街道	软件开发
东莞市鼎立软件有限公司	莞城街道	信息系统集成服务
东莞恩斯克转向器有限公司	莞城街道	汽车零部件及配件制造
东莞市彩丽建筑维护技术有限公司	莞城街道	工程和技术研究和试验发展
广东玉兰装饰材料有限公司	莞城街道	其他纸制品制造
东莞市乐琪光电科技有限公司	莞城街道	绘图、计算及测量仪器制造
东莞市光华实业有限公司	石龙镇	电力电子元器件制造
东莞泽龙线缆有限公司	石龙镇	电线、电缆制造
泰阳电子(东莞)有限公司	石龙镇	燃气、太阳能及类似能源家用器具制造
东莞市广安电气检测中心有限公司	石龙镇	质检技术服务
广东开普互联信息科技有限公司	石龙镇	软件开发
东莞市石龙富华电子有限公司	石龙镇	其他仪器仪表制造业
广东华南药业集团有限公司	石龙镇	化学药品制剂制造
广东众生药业股份有限公司	石龙镇	中成药生产
东莞市龙基电子有限公司	石龙镇	电子元件及组件制造
广东巨龙信息技术有限公司	石龙镇	软件开发
日本电产三协电子(东莞)有限公司	石龙镇	电子元件及组件制造
东莞市龙信数码科技有限公司	石龙镇	软件开发
东莞天意电子有限公司	石龙镇	计算机整机制造
东莞市精航科技有限公司	石龙镇	其他未列明金属制品制造
东莞高仪电子科技有限公司	虎门镇	灯用电器附件及其他照明器具制造
信义汽车玻璃(东莞)有限公司	虎门镇	其他玻璃制造
广东银禧科技股份有限公司	虎门镇	初级形态塑料及合成树脂制造
东莞市科达计算机系统工程有限公司	虎门镇	信息系统集成服务
东莞中探探针有限公司	虎门镇	其他电子设备制造
东莞市联升电线电缆有限公司	虎门镇	电线、电缆制造
东莞康源电子有限公司	虎门镇	印制电路板制造
信义玻璃工程(东莞)有限公司	虎门镇	其他玻璃制造
东莞令特电子有限公司	虎门镇	电子元件及组件制造
兴科电子(东莞)有限公司	虎门镇	电子元件及组件制造
东莞市平波电子有限公司	虎门镇	电子元件及组件制造
东莞市妙达电动工具制造有限公司	虎门镇	风动和电动工具制造
虎彩印艺股份有限公司	虎门镇	包装装潢及其他印刷
广东福德电子有限公司	虎门镇	电子工业专用设备制造
东莞市瑞辉机械制造有限公司	虎门镇	金属切削机床制造
东莞市万锦电子科技有限公司	虎门镇	家用清洁卫生电器具制造
东莞市鸿金顺机械制造有限公司	虎门镇	其他机械设备及电子产品批发
东莞市怡合达自动化科技有限公司	虎门镇	其他金属加工机械制造
东莞宝根精密模塑有限公司	虎门镇	其他电子设备制造
东莞长联电线电缆有限公司	虎门镇	电线、电缆制造
东莞常禾电子有限公司	虎门镇	音响设备制造

1-5 续表 1

(2014年)

企业名称	所在镇街	行业类别
东莞市晋诚机械有限公司	虎门镇	其他金属加工机械制造
东莞市精铁机械有限公司	虎门镇	电工机械专用设备制造
东莞市康祥电子有限公司	虎门镇	电力电子元器件制造
东莞市康庄电路有限公司	虎门镇	集成电路制造
东莞市力生机械设备有限公司	虎门镇	其他通用设备制造业
东莞市易辉自动化机械有限公司	虎门镇	其他通用设备制造业
东莞市科美斯制冷设备有限公司	虎门镇	制冷、空调设备制造
东莞市励晶电子科技有限公司	虎门镇	电子元件及组件制造
东莞市连威电子有限公司	虎门镇	其他电子设备制造
东莞市热恒注塑科技有限公司	虎门镇	塑料加工专用设备制造
广东奥其斯科技有限公司	虎门镇	照明灯具制造
东莞市伟煌试验设备有限公司	东城街道	其他通用设备制造业
东莞市伟旺达电子有限公司	东城街道	电子元件及组件制造
东莞市新铂铼电子有限公司	东城街道	电子元件及组件制造
东莞市奕东电子有限公司	东城街道	电子元件及组件制造
东莞市星曜光电照明科技有限公司	东城街道	照明灯具制造
东莞市创业电气设备有限公司	东城街道	配电开关控制设备制造
东莞万德电子制品有限公司	东城街道	电子元件及组件制造
东华机械有限公司	东城街道	塑料加工专用设备制造
东莞科威医疗器械有限公司	东城街道	假肢、人工器官及植(介)入器械制造
东莞市百分百科技有限公司	东城街道	光电子器件及其他电子器件制造
广东晖速通信技术有限公司	东城街道	通信系统设备制造
东莞美维电路有限公司	东城街道	印制电路板制造
东莞市安拓普塑胶聚合物科技有限公司	东城街道	再生橡胶制造
广东宏远集团药业有限公司	东城街道	化学药品原料药制造
东莞市凯格精密机械有限公司	东城街道	电子工业专用设备制造
东莞市大忠电子有限公司	东城街道	变压器、整流器和电感器制造
广东建邦计算机软件有限公司	东城街道	软件开发
东莞市嘉腾仪器仪表有限公司	东城街道	光学仪器制造
东莞通华液晶有限公司	东城街道	其他电子设备制造
东莞市鸿宝锂电科技有限公司	东城街道	其他专用设备制造
广东长天精密设备科技有限公司	东城街道	电子工业专用设备制造
广东东日环保有限公司	东城街道	环境保护专用设备制造
广东立佳实业有限公司	东城街道	其他仪器仪表制造业
广东红旗家具有限公司	东城街道	木质家具制造
东莞市正新包装制品有限公司	东城街道	塑料薄膜制造
东莞丝丽雅电子科技有限公司	东城街道	汽车零部件及配件制造
东莞市旗丰消声器有限公司	东城街道	汽车零部件及配件制造
东莞市台工电子机械科技有限公司	东城街道	包装专用设备制造
东莞市天勤仪器有限公司	东城街道	光学仪器制造
广东守门神电子科技有限公司	东城街道	电子工业专用设备制造
东莞市港润机械科技有限公司	东城街道	汽车零部件及配件制造
德科摩橡塑科技(东莞)有限公司	东城街道	橡胶加工专用设备制造
广东咏华实业有限公司	东城街道	电线、电缆制造
东莞市鸿铭机械有限公司	东城街道	包装专用设备制造
东莞市普凯塑料科技有限公司	东城街道	其他塑料制品制造
东莞市普密斯精密仪器有限公司	东城街道	工业自动控制系统装置制造

1-5 续表 2

(2014年)

企业名称	所在镇街	行业类别
东莞市博世机电设备有限公司	东城街道	金属切割及焊接设备制造
东莞市德瑞精密设备有限公司	东城街道	锂离子电池制造
东莞市合通电子有限公司	东城街道	印制电路板制造
广东戈兰玛汽车系统有限公司	东城街道	汽车零部件及配件制造
长园高能电气股份有限公司	东城街道	绝缘制品制造
东莞市劲升无尘涂装科技有限公司	东城街道	日用塑料制品制造
东莞市骏宏电子科技有限公司	东城街道	社会公共安全设备及器材制造
东莞科视自动化科技有限公司	东城街道	电子工业专用设备制造
东莞市天唯智能科技有限公司	东城街道	信息系统集成服务
东莞市贝尔试验设备有限公司	东城街道	电子工业专用设备制造
东莞市大能环保科技有限公司	东城街道	热力生产和供应
东莞市冈田电子科技有限公司	东城街道	电子工业专用设备制造
广东智华计算机科技有限公司	东城街道	信息系统集成服务
东莞市力星激光科技有限公司	东城街道	其他非金属加工专用设备制造
东莞市利瀚机械有限公司	东城街道	其他机械设备及电子产品批发
东莞市菱锐机械有限公司	东城街道	其他日用品生产专用设备制造
东莞市嘉准电子科技有限公司	东城街道	电子元件及组件制造
东莞市金沃实业有限公司	东城街道	其他橡胶制品制造
岭南园林股份有限公司	东城街道	其他未列明建筑业
东莞博力威电池有限公司	东城街道	锂离子电池制造
东莞大同数控机械有限公司	东城街道	金属成形机床制造
东莞市同涞节能设备有限公司	东城街道	燃气、太阳能及类似能源家用器具制造
东莞市信誉通计算机科技有限公司	东城街道	软件开发
东莞市邦臣光电有限公司	东城街道	灯用电器附件及其他照明器具制造
东莞市伟盈汽车科技有限公司	东城街道	汽车零部件及配件制造
广东罗尔科技有限公司	东城街道	工业自动控制系统装置制造
东莞市博晟电子科技有限公司	东城街道	信息系统集成服务
广东至诚化学工业有限公司	万江街道	涂料制造
广东五星太阳能股份有限公司	万江街道	燃气、太阳能及类似能源家用器具制造
东莞市康源节能科技有限公司	万江街道	燃气、太阳能及类似能源家用器具制造
东莞基业电气设备有限公司	万江街道	其他输配电及控制设备制造
东莞市恒生机械制造有限公司	万江街道	其他通用设备制造业
东莞市铭丰包装品制造有限公司	万江街道	皮箱、包(袋)制造
东莞市安默琳节能环保技术有限公司	万江街道	机床附件制造
东莞市爱克斯曼机械有限公司	万江街道	纺织专用设备制造
广东广视通科教设备有限公司	万江街道	其他家具制造
广东硕源科技股份有限公司	万江街道	其他未列明制造业
东莞华尔泰装饰材料有限公司	万江街道	轻质建筑材料制造
东莞埃欧热能技术有限公司	万江街道	其他通用设备制造业
东莞市派乐玛新材料技术开发有限公司	万江街道	密封用填料及类似品制造
东莞利扬微电子有限公司	万江街道	集成电路制造
东莞市中诺质检仪器设备有限公司	万江街道	轻小型起重设备制造
东莞市吉川机械设备有限公司	万江街道	其他原动设备制造
东莞市西奥计算机智能科技有限公司	万江街道	软件开发
东莞市长盛刀锯有限公司	万江街道	切削工具制造
东莞市多贺自动化科技有限公司	万江街道	其他通用设备制造业
东莞市鸿企机械有限公司	万江街道	铸造机械制造

1-5 续表 3

(2014年)

企业名称	所在镇街	行业类别
东莞市金澜电工材料有限公司	万江街道	有色金属合金制造
东莞市明天纳米科技有限公司	万江街道	涂料制造
东莞市耐斯机械制造有限公司	万江街道	其他非金属矿物制品制造
东莞市中大科技网络有限公司	南城街道	信息技术咨询服务
东莞市爱玛数控科技有限公司	南城街道	皮革、毛皮及其制品加工专用设备制造
东莞市杉杉电池材料有限公司	南城街道	其他未列明制造业
广东万维博通信息技术有限公司	南城街道	软件开发
东莞市凯诺德软件科技有限公司	南城街道	信息技术咨询服务
东莞市领航通通信科技有限公司	南城街道	信息系统集成服务
东莞市佛尔盛机电科技有限公司	南城街道	风机、风扇制造
东莞新科技术研究开发有限公司	南城街道	工程和技术研究和试验发展
广东益翔自动化科技有限公司	南城街道	电工机械专用设备制造
东莞市开创精密机械有限公司	南城街道	其他金属加工机械制造
广东开源环境科技有限公司	南城街道	水污染治理
广东大榕树信息科技有限公司	南城街道	软件开发
东莞市钜大电子有限公司	南城街道	锂离子电池制造
广东天新软件科技有限公司	南城街道	软件开发
东莞市上川自动化设备有限公司	南城街道	其他机械设备及电子产品批发
东莞市斯宇自动化设备有限公司	南城街道	其他专用设备制造
东莞市伟光照明电器工程有限公司	南城街道	其他未列明建筑业
东莞市相思鸟软件科技有限公司	南城街道	软件开发
东莞市信测科技有限公司	南城街道	信息技术咨询服务
广东技安网络工程有限公司	南城街道	信息系统集成服务
广东迪科思信息科技有限公司	南城街道	信息技术咨询服务
广东凌康科技有限公司	南城街道	信息系统集成服务
广东盛世商潮网络科技有限公司	南城街道	其他互联网服务
广东融正资讯科技有限公司	南城街道	信息系统集成服务
东莞市创锐电子技术有限公司	南城街道	计算机、软件及辅助设备批发
广东优信通信有限公司	南城街道	信息系统集成服务
广东沃杰森环保科技有限公司	南城街道	水污染治理
东莞市银雁金融配套服务有限公司	南城街道	其他未列明服务业
东莞市正太合赢自动化设备有限公司	南城街道	其他通用设备制造业
东莞方天软件科技有限公司	南城街道	软件开发
东莞市宏山自动识别技术有限公司	南城街道	信息系统集成服务
东莞市思特电子技术有限公司	南城街道	软件开发
东莞市唯一网络科技有限公司	南城街道	互联网接入及相关服务
东莞市富默克化工有限公司	南城街道	化学试剂和助剂制造
东莞市艺博达实业有限公司	南城街道	缝制机械制造
东莞市华恒工业自动化集成有限公司	南城街道	其他未列明电气机械及器材制造
东莞市骏翼电子科技有限公司	南城街道	软件开发
东莞市力拓网络科技有限公司	南城街道	软件开发
广东宏泰照明科技有限公司	南城街道	灯用电器附件及其他照明器具制造
东莞市崴泰电子有限公司	南城街道	其他电子设备制造
东莞市鑫利机电有限公司	南城街道	家用厨房电器具制造
东莞市希贝实业有限公司	中堂镇	其他橡胶制品制造
广东广益科技实业有限公司	中堂镇	食品及饲料添加剂制造
东莞理文造纸厂有限公司	中堂镇	机制纸及纸板制造

1-5 续表 4

(2014年)

企业名称	所在镇街	行业类别
东莞爱屋氏日用品有限公司	中堂镇	其他日用化学产品制造
东莞建泰生物科技有限公司	中堂镇	化学试剂和助剂制造
东莞兆舜有机硅新材料科技有限公司	中堂镇	有机化学原料制造
东莞市铖泰制罐设备有限公司	中堂镇	电子工业专用设备制造
东莞日之泉蒸馏水有限公司	中堂镇	瓶(罐)装饮用水制造
广东金达照明科技股份有限公司	望牛墩镇	照明灯具制造
东莞市亚美精密机械配件有限公司	望牛墩镇	电子工业专用设备制造
东莞市华清净水技术有限公司	望牛墩镇	化学试剂和助剂制造
东莞市精诚电能设备有限公司	望牛墩镇	电子工业专用设备制造
东莞市科力钢铁线材有限公司	望牛墩镇	金属丝绳及其制品制造
东莞市今联实业有限公司	望牛墩镇	广播电视接收设备及器材制造
东莞智源彩印有限公司	望牛墩镇	包装装潢及其他印刷
东莞佳鸿机械制造有限公司	望牛墩镇	其他未列明制造业
广东南方宏明电子科技股份有限公司	望牛墩镇	电子元件及组件制造
东莞市奥思睿德世浦电子科技有限公司	望牛墩镇	光电子器件及其他电子器件制造
东莞玖龙纸业有限公司	麻涌镇	机制纸及纸板制造
东莞市贝特利新材料有限公司	麻涌镇	油墨及类似产品制造
广东信力材料科技有限公司	麻涌镇	合成橡胶制造
东莞太平洋博高润滑油有限公司	麻涌镇	原油加工及石油制品制造
广东省东莞电机有限公司	麻涌镇	电动机制造
广东中远船务工程有限公司	麻涌镇	金属船舶制造
东莞市汇美淀粉科技有限公司	麻涌镇	淀粉及淀粉制品制造
广东康达尔农牧科技有限公司	麻涌镇	饲料加工
东莞超盈纺织有限公司	麻涌镇	化纤织物染整精加工
东莞南玻工程玻璃有限公司	麻涌镇	平板玻璃制造
东莞市山力高分子材料科研有限公司	麻涌镇	密封用填料及类似品制造
东莞市天球实业有限公司	麻涌镇	其他电池制造
东莞南玻光伏科技有限公司	麻涌镇	光伏设备及元器件制造
东莞南玻太阳能玻璃有限公司	麻涌镇	平板玻璃制造
东莞地龙纸业有限公司	麻涌镇	纸和纸板容器制造
东莞市志基电子有限公司	石碣镇	半导体分立器件制造
东莞泉声电子有限公司	石碣镇	电子元件及组件制造
东莞广发制药有限公司	石碣镇	中成药生产
东莞市智高文具有限公司	石碣镇	文具制造
东莞市盈聚电子有限公司	石碣镇	其他电子设备制造
东莞市金源电池科技有限公司	石碣镇	锂离子电池制造
东莞市维尔霓斯照明科技有限公司	石碣镇	照明灯具制造
东莞市五株电子科技有限公司	石碣镇	印制电路板制造
东莞天龙阿克达电子有限公司	石碣镇	塑料零件制造
东莞市冠晔电子科技有限公司	石碣镇	其他未列明信息技术服务业
东莞市焊宏爱法电子科技有限公司	石碣镇	电子工业专用设备制造
东莞市科磊实业有限公司	石碣镇	塑料板、管、型材制造
东莞市宏达聚氨酯有限公司	高埗镇	有机化学原料制造
广东顺力工业设备有限公司	高埗镇	金属结构制造
东莞市唯美陶瓷工业园有限公司	高埗镇	建筑陶瓷制品制造
东莞康特尔云终端系统有限公司	高埗镇	广播电视接收设备及器材制造
东莞精锐电器五金有限公司	高埗镇	切削工具制造

1-5　续表 5

(2014年)

企业名称	所在镇街	行业类别
东莞市峄董塑胶科技有限公司	高埗镇	其他塑料制品制造
东莞东美食品有限公司	高埗镇	其他未列明食品制造
东莞市精研粉体科技有限公司	高埗镇	锻件及粉末冶金制品制造
东莞市德方斯电器科技有限公司	高埗镇	家用厨房电器具制造
东莞市沁鑫热能科技有限公司	高埗镇	家用厨房电器具制造
东莞市雄林新材料科技股份有限公司	道滘镇	初级形态塑料及合成树脂制造
东莞洲亮通讯科技有限公司	道滘镇	通信系统设备制造
东莞市恒宇仪器有限公司	道滘镇	其他专用仪器制造
东莞市群跃电子材料科技有限公司	道滘镇	印制电路板制造
广东瑞星新能源科技有限公司	道滘镇	制冷、空调设备制造
东莞市亿鑫丰精密机械设备科技有限公司	道滘镇	金属切割及焊接设备制造
东莞市易升电池有限公司	道滘镇	锂离子电池制造
东莞诺华家具有限公司	道滘镇	木质家具制造
东莞市广华化工有限公司	道滘镇	其他基础化学原料制造
东莞市国祥空调设备有限公司	道滘镇	制冷、空调设备制造
东莞市金瑞五金制品有限公司	道滘镇	其他未列明金属制品制造
银禧工程塑料(东莞)有限公司	道滘镇	初级形态塑料及合成树脂制造
广东理文造纸有限公司	洪梅镇	机制纸及纸板制造
东莞市汇星染织有限公司	洪梅镇	化纤织物染整精加工
东莞市绿通高尔夫观光车有限公司	洪梅镇	五金产品批发
台玻华南玻璃有限公司	洪梅镇	平板玻璃制造
东莞市海新金属科技有限公司	洪梅镇	家用厨房电器具制造
广东福利龙复合肥有限公司	洪梅镇	复混肥料制造
广东大众农业科技股份有限公司	洪梅镇	复混肥料制造
东莞市亚洲制药有限公司	洪梅镇	中成药生产
东莞井上五金橡塑有限公司	沙田镇	其他橡胶制品制造
东莞市虎门港网络系统有限公司	沙田镇	信息系统集成服务
东莞井上建上汽车部件有限公司	沙田镇	塑料零件制造
东莞市南星电子有限公司	沙田镇	其他电子设备制造
东莞庞思化工机械有限公司	沙田镇	其他专用设备制造
东莞市邦泽电子有限公司	沙田镇	其他文化、办公用机械制造
广东华坤新能源股份有限公司	沙田镇	电线、电缆制造
东莞市松燊塑料科技有限公司	厚街镇	塑料零件制造
东莞威信运动用品有限公司	厚街镇	其他体育用品制造
东莞市南兴家具装备制造股份有限公司	厚街镇	木材加工机械制造
东莞市金银丰机械实业有限公司	厚街镇	皮革、毛皮及其制品加工专用设备制造
东莞市力凯科技发展有限公司	厚街镇	软件开发
东莞市利拿实业有限公司	厚街镇	其他通用设备制造业
东莞朗诚微电子设备有限公司	厚街镇	电子工业专用设备制造
东莞市星士达电子有限公司	厚街镇	电子元件及组件制造
东莞市翔龙能源科技有限公司	厚街镇	照明灯具制造
东莞栢能电子科技有限公司	厚街镇	计算机零部件制造
东莞市名菱工业自动化科技有限公司	厚街镇	缝制机械制造
东莞市长泰尔电子有限公司	厚街镇	电子元件及组件制造
东莞乔登节能科技有限公司	厚街镇	锂离子电池制造
东莞市辉煌龙腾机械有限公司	厚街镇	管道和设备安装
东莞市铝美铝型材有限公司	厚街镇	铝压延加工

1-5　续表 6

(2014年)

企业名称	所在镇街	行业类别
东莞市巨冈机械工业有限公司	长安镇	其他金属加工机械制造
东莞市胜大光电科技有限公司	长安镇	其他玻璃制品制造
东莞市盛雄激光设备有限公司	长安镇	其他通用设备制造业
东莞市思拓达光电科技有限公司	长安镇	照明灯具制造
东莞市台科精密机械有限公司	长安镇	金属切削机床制造
东莞市爱加照明科技有限公司	长安镇	灯具零售
东莞市东元新能源科技有限公司	长安镇	其他未列明服务业
东莞五方光电科技有限公司	长安镇	光电子器件及其他电子器件制造
东莞市东阳光电容器有限公司	长安镇	电子元件及组件制造
广东万濠精密仪器股份有限公司	长安镇	其他仪器仪表制造业
东莞钜升塑胶电子制品有限公司	长安镇	其他塑料制品制造
先锐模具配件(东莞)有限公司	长安镇	模具制造
东莞劲胜精密组件股份有限公司	长安镇	电子元件及组件制造
东莞市奥普特自动化科技有限公司	长安镇	其他未列明电气机械及器材制造
东莞市汇乐清洁设备有限公司	长安镇	其他机械设备及电子产品批发
东莞福泰电子有限公司	长安镇	其他未列明制造业
东莞鸿图精密压铸有限公司	长安镇	有色金属铸造
广东冠辉科技有限公司	长安镇	建筑、家具用金属配件制造
东莞市胜蓝电子有限公司	长安镇	电子工业专用设备制造
东莞市扬明精密塑胶五金电子有限公司	长安镇	电子元件及组件制造
东莞市长原科技实业有限公司	长安镇	其他医疗设备及器械制造
东莞市星河精密压铸模具有限公司	长安镇	其他未列明金属制品制造
广东欧珀移动通信有限公司	长安镇	通信终端设备制造
东莞市三姆森光电科技有限公司	长安镇	信息系统集成服务
东莞市奥源电子科技有限公司	长安镇	电子元件及组件制造
广东小天才科技有限公司	长安镇	软件开发
东莞市亿辉光电科技有限公司	长安镇	光学仪器制造
环球石材(东莞)股份有限公司	长安镇	建筑用石加工
维沃移动通信有限公司	长安镇	软件开发
祥鑫科技股份有限公司	长安镇	汽车零部件及配件制造
东莞市铱伦实业有限公司	长安镇	阀门和旋塞制造
必诺机械(东莞)有限公司	长安镇	塑料加工专用设备制造
东莞市运通环保科技有限公司	长安镇	固体废物治理
东莞市珍世好电子科技有限公司	长安镇	其他金属加工机械制造
东莞市正旭新能源设备科技有限公司	长安镇	燃气、太阳能及类似能源家用器具制造
东莞明泰彩色包装印刷有限公司	长安镇	包装装潢及其他印刷
东莞捷荣技术股份有限公司	长安镇	模具制造
东莞市凯登能源科技有限公司	长安镇	电子工业专用设备制造
东莞市信诺橡塑工业有限公司	长安镇	初级形态塑料及合成树脂制造
东莞市雷洋电子科技有限公司	长安镇	音响设备制造
东莞市长信模具有限公司	长安镇	其他未列明金属制品制造
东莞市长江超声波机有限公司	长安镇	其他专用设备制造
东莞市广正模具塑胶有限公司	长安镇	其他塑料制品制造
东莞市龙顺自动化科技有限公司	长安镇	电子工业专用设备制造
东莞市汇鼎实业有限公司	长安镇	其他金属加工机械制造
东莞市蓝光塑胶模具有限公司	长安镇	其他塑料制品制造
东莞市维峰五金电子有限公司	长安镇	电子元件及组件制造

1-5 续表 7

(2014年)

企业名称	所在镇街	行业类别
东莞市盟拓光电科技有限公司	长安镇	光学仪器制造
东莞市其利模具有限公司	长安镇	其他未列明金属制品制造
东莞市长安上名模具科技有限公司	长安镇	灯用电器附件及其他照明器具制造
东莞市盛丰机械有限公司	寮步镇	其他日用品生产专用设备制造
东莞快灵通卡西尼电子科技有限公司	寮步镇	其他仪器仪表制造业
东莞市百味佳食品有限公司	寮步镇	其他调味品、发酵制品制造
东莞市丞冠橡塑制品有限公司	寮步镇	其他橡胶制品制造
东莞宇球电子股份有限公司	寮步镇	电子元件及组件制造
东莞三联热缩材料有限公司	寮步镇	其他塑料制品制造
广东宏磊达光电科技有限公司	寮步镇	光电子器件及其他电子器件制造
东莞市蓝冠环保节能科技有限公司	寮步镇	燃气、太阳能及类似能源家用器具制造
东莞市永强汽车制造有限公司	寮步镇	汽车整车制造
东莞市开关厂有限公司	寮步镇	配电开关控制设备制造
康达新能源设备股份有限公司	寮步镇	发电机及发电机组制造
广东佳景科技有限公司	寮步镇	油墨及类似产品制造
东莞市新泽谷机械制造股份有限公司	寮步镇	电子工业专用设备制造
东莞市骏泰精密机械有限公司	寮步镇	锂离子电池制造
东莞日进电线有限公司	寮步镇	电线、电缆制造
东莞唯佳电子有限公司	寮步镇	电子元件及组件制造
东莞长联新材料科技股份有限公司	寮步镇	油墨及类似产品制造
东莞市瑞必达科技有限公司	寮步镇	技术玻璃制品制造
广东永强奥林宝国际消防汽车有限公司	寮步镇	改装汽车制造
东莞电力设计院	寮步镇	工程勘察设计
东莞市汇星厨具有限公司	寮步镇	家用厨房电器具制造
东莞汇海光电科技实业有限公司	寮步镇	其他电子设备制造
东莞市科锐机电设备有限公司	寮步镇	其他专用设备制造
东莞市美之尊电子科技有限公司	寮步镇	音响设备制造
东莞市琅菱机械有限公司	寮步镇	其他通用设备制造业
东莞市得力仕机械科技有限公司	寮步镇	其他金属加工机械制造
东莞市国一精密机械有限公司	寮步镇	其他通用设备制造业
东莞市开源塑化科技有限公司	寮步镇	塑料薄膜制造
东莞市凯金新能源科技有限公司	寮步镇	石墨及碳素制品制造
东莞市美塑塑料科技有限公司	寮步镇	其他塑料制品制造
东莞市星火通讯科技有限公司	寮步镇	通信终端设备制造
东莞市嘉龙皮革机械有限公司	寮步镇	缝制机械制造
东莞优诺电子焊接材料有限公司	大岭山镇	化学试剂和助剂制造
东莞光群雷射科技有限公司	大岭山镇	塑料薄膜制造
东莞大宝化工制品有限公司	大岭山镇	涂料制造
东莞市瑞德丰生物科技有限公司	大岭山镇	生物化学农药及微生物农药制造
东莞市新时代新能源科技有限公司	大岭山镇	家用制冷电器具制造
东莞市奥达铝业有限公司	大岭山镇	铝冶炼
东莞市汇成真空科技有限公司	大岭山镇	泵及真空设备制造
东莞市宇佳电子实业有限公司	大岭山镇	其他电子设备制造
东莞金太阳研磨股份有限公司	大岭山镇	其他未列明制造业
东莞市莲盈无纺科技有限公司	大岭山镇	化纤织造加工
东莞锦弘精密机械有限公司	大岭山镇	锯材加工
东莞市台盛环保科技有限公司	大岭山镇	环境保护专用设备制造

1-5　续表 8

(2014年)

企业名称	所在镇街	行业类别
广东拓斯达科技股份有限公司	大岭山镇	其他专用设备制造
东莞市祺龙电业有限公司	大岭山镇	其他塑料制品制造
东莞市西特新能源科技有限公司	大岭山镇	锂离子电池制造
广东佳居乐厨房科技有限公司	大岭山镇	木质家具制造
东莞市亚星半导体有限公司	大岭山镇	电子元件及组件制造
宏达光电玻璃(东莞)有限公司	大岭山镇	光学玻璃制造
东莞龙冠真空科技有限公司	大岭山镇	其他塑料制品制造
东莞泰硕电子有限公司	大岭山镇	电子元件及组件制造
东莞优邦材料科技有限公司	大岭山镇	密封用填料及类似品制造
东莞华威铜箔科技有限公司	大岭山镇	其他机械设备及电子产品批发
东莞市宝瑞电子有限公司	大岭山镇	音响设备制造
东莞市龙健电子有限公司	大岭山镇	音响设备制造
东莞市中崎机械有限公司	大岭山镇	印刷专用设备制造
永发印务(东莞)有限公司	大岭山镇	包装装潢及其他印刷
东莞市智高化学原料有限公司	大岭山镇	专项化学用品制造
东莞崧崴电子科技有限公司	大岭山镇	木质家具制造
东莞亿东机器有限公司	大岭山镇	塑料加工专用设备制造
东莞市迈科科技有限公司	大朗镇	镍氢电池制造
东莞信易电热机械有限公司	大朗镇	塑料加工专用设备制造
东莞市迈科新能源有限公司	大朗镇	锂离子电池制造
东莞市中一合金科技有限公司	大朗镇	有色金属合金制造
东莞市台冠起重机械设备有限公司	大朗镇	起重机制造
大宝(东莞)模具切削工具有限公司	大朗镇	切削工具制造
东莞市飞新达精密机械科技有限公司	大朗镇	其他机械和设备修理业
东莞市毅豪电子科技有限公司	大朗镇	信息系统集成服务
东莞市润华光电有限公司	大朗镇	通信终端设备制造
东莞市升微机电设备科技有限公司	大朗镇	环境保护专用设备制造
东莞市耀安塑胶机器有限公司	大朗镇	其他非金属加工专用设备制造
广东良研冷暖设备科技有限公司	大朗镇	制冷、空调设备制造
广东伯朗特智能装备股份有限公司	大朗镇	其他通用设备制造业
东莞市冲宝模具有限公司	大朗镇	模具制造
东莞市缝神机械有限公司	大朗镇	缝制机械制造
东莞市海拓伟电子科技有限公司	大朗镇	锂离子电池制造
东莞金准电器有限公司	大朗镇	灯用电器附件及其他照明器具制造
环球工业机械(东莞)有限公司	大朗镇	金属切削机床制造
东莞钜鼎照明有限公司	大朗镇	照明灯具制造
东莞市安德丰电池有限公司	大朗镇	锂离子电池制造
东莞市立旺电子塑胶有限公司	大朗镇	其他电子设备制造
东莞市东升压铸模具有限公司	大朗镇	其他金属加工机械制造
东莞市东思电子技术有限公司	大朗镇	电子元件及组件制造
东莞市隆盛压铸设备有限公司	大朗镇	其他原动设备制造
东莞欧德雅装饰材料有限公司	大朗镇	其他塑料制品制造
东莞市雅思电子有限公司	大朗镇	家用美容、保健电器具制造
东莞富强鑫塑胶机械制造有限公司	大朗镇	塑料加工专用设备制造
东莞市永兴电子科技有限公司	大朗镇	光电子器件及其他电子器件制造
东莞市成功幕墙建材有限公司	大朗镇	建筑装饰搪瓷制品制造
丽清电子科技(东莞)有限公司	黄江镇	电子元件及组件制造

1-5 续表 9

(2014年)

企业名称	所在镇街	行业类别
鹏驰五金制品有限公司	黄江镇	其他未列明金属制品制造
广东欧科空调制冷有限公司	黄江镇	制冷、空调设备制造
东莞泰德照明科技有限公司	黄江镇	照明灯具制造
广东惠伦晶体科技股份有限公司	黄江镇	电子元件及组件制造
东莞新东方科技有限公司	黄江镇	合成橡胶制造
东莞市宏德电子设备有限公司	黄江镇	电子工业专用设备制造
泓凯电子科技(东莞)有限公司	黄江镇	计算机外围设备制造
广东兴锐电子科技股份有限公司	黄江镇	橡胶零件制造
广东保迪环保电镀设备有限公司	黄江镇	其他专用设备制造
东莞市天晖电子材料科技有限公司	黄江镇	光电子器件及其他电子器件制造
东莞盛世科技电子实业有限公司	黄江镇	电子元件及组件制造
东莞泰欣照明有限公司	黄江镇	照明灯具制造
东莞爱旺电子科技有限公司	黄江镇	计算机外围设备制造
东莞正隆纸制品有限公司	黄江镇	纸和纸板容器制造
东莞市科盛实业有限公司	黄江镇	其他橡胶制品制造
东莞市精诚厨具实业有限公司	黄江镇	金属制厨房用器具制造
东莞正扬电子机械有限公司	黄江镇	汽车零部件及配件制造
东莞市兰光光学科技有限公司	黄江镇	光学玻璃制造
东莞市纳川盈海照明有限公司	黄江镇	照明灯具制造
东莞市童星玩具制品有限公司	樟木头镇	玩具制造
东莞市张力机电科技有限公司	樟木头镇	微电机及其他电机制造
东莞市兄奕塑胶制品有限公司	樟木头镇	塑料板、管、型材制造
东莞市启天自动化设备有限公司	樟木头镇	其他通用设备制造业
广东广海大实业有限公司	樟木头镇	塑料家具制造
东莞积信制造有限公司	樟木头镇	家用厨房电器具制造
东莞市德诚塑化科技有限公司	樟木头镇	其他塑料制品制造
东莞永洪印刷有限公司	樟木头镇	包装装潢及其他印刷
东莞市摩尔达电器科技有限公司	樟木头镇	家用美容、保健电器具制造
东莞华明灯具有限公司	清溪镇	照明灯具制造
广东粤林电气科技股份有限公司	清溪镇	计算机外围设备制造
快意电梯股份有限公司	清溪镇	电梯、自动扶梯及升降机制造
东莞建玮电子制品有限公司	清溪镇	计算机外围设备制造
东莞龙杰电子有限公司	清溪镇	其他电子设备制造
模德模具(东莞)有限公司	清溪镇	金属表面处理及热处理加工
广东光阵光电科技有限公司	清溪镇	光电子器件及其他电子器件制造
东莞市联思电子有限公司	清溪镇	计算机零部件制造
健富塑胶五金制品(东莞)有限公司	清溪镇	卫星传输服务
东莞泰星五金制品厂有限公司	清溪镇	其他金属加工机械制造
东莞清溪华晖电器有限公司	清溪镇	家用厨房电器具制造
东莞市垠星科技发展有限公司	清溪镇	原油加工及石油制品制造
广东天元印刷有限公司	清溪镇	装订及印刷相关服务
东莞麦可龙医疗科技有限公司	清溪镇	其他医疗设备及器械制造
东莞市鸿德电池有限公司	清溪镇	锂离子电池制造
东莞市捷和光电有限公司	清溪镇	光电子器件及其他电子器件制造
东莞市华源光电科技有限公司	清溪镇	太阳能发电
东莞市万华电子有限公司	清溪镇	其他电子设备制造
东莞市联臣电子科技有限公司	清溪镇	其他电子设备制造

1-5 续表 10

(2014年)

企业名称	所在镇街	行业类别
东莞市普赛达密封粘胶有限公司	清溪镇	密封用填料及类似品制造
东莞市嘉鼎五金模具有限公司	清溪镇	金属结构制造
东莞市金铮自动冲压设备有限公司	清溪镇	金属切削机床制造
东莞市荣烨五金制品有限公司	清溪镇	其他金属加工机械制造
东莞永钜电子有限公司	清溪镇	其他通用设备制造业
东莞宜安科技股份有限公司	清溪镇	金属结构制造
实盈电子(东莞)有限公司	清溪镇	电子元件及组件制造
东莞市帝信光电科技有限公司	清溪镇	其他未列明制造业
东莞市冠佳电子设备有限公司	塘厦镇	其他电子设备制造
东莞立德电子有限公司	塘厦镇	电子元件及组件制造
广东升威电子制品有限公司	塘厦镇	电子元件及组件制造
东莞丰裕电机有限公司	塘厦镇	其他通用设备制造业
广东志成冠军集团有限公司	塘厦镇	电子工业专用设备制造
广东坚朗五金制品股份有限公司	塘厦镇	其他未列明金属制品制造
东莞市乐科电子有限公司	塘厦镇	电子元件及组件制造
东莞市千岛金属锡品有限公司	塘厦镇	锡冶炼
东莞市三友联众电器有限公司	塘厦镇	电力电子元器件制造
东莞启益电器机械有限公司	塘厦镇	变压器、整流器和电感器制造
东莞市锦润电子有限公司	塘厦镇	光电子器件及其他电子器件制造
东莞领航电子有限公司	塘厦镇	电子元件及组件制造
广东合科泰实业有限公司	塘厦镇	电子元件及组件制造
东莞市升丰电子有限公司	塘厦镇	光电子器件及其他电子器件制造
东莞市澳星视听器材有限公司	塘厦镇	幻灯及投影设备制造
金龙机电(东莞)有限公司	塘厦镇	光电子器件及其他电子器件制造
东莞市宙辉电子科技有限公司	塘厦镇	其他通用零部件制造
东莞阳天电子科技有限公司	塘厦镇	通信系统设备制造
东莞永湖复合材料有限公司	塘厦镇	其他体育用品制造
东莞市锐祥智能卡科技有限公司	塘厦镇	工业自动控制系统装置制造
东莞市现代精工实业有限公司	塘厦镇	光电子器件及其他电子器件制造
东莞市鑫惠展机电有限公司	塘厦镇	微电机及其他电机制造
东莞市鑫聚光电科技有限公司	塘厦镇	其他塑料制品制造
广东星河生物科技股份有限公司	塘厦镇	食用菌种植
东莞福泽尔电子科技有限公司	塘厦镇	影视录放设备制造
东莞市中汇瑞德电子有限公司	塘厦镇	电子元件及组件制造
东莞星晖真空镀膜塑胶制品有限公司	塘厦镇	日用塑料制品制造
东莞永安科技有限公司	塘厦镇	其他未列明金属制品制造
东莞永胜医疗制品有限公司	塘厦镇	医疗诊断、监护及治疗设备制造
东莞市俊知自动机械有限公司	塘厦镇	其他通用设备制造业
东莞市中控电子技术有限公司	塘厦镇	其他电子设备制造
东莞市华世邦精密模具有限公司	塘厦镇	模具制造
东莞市凯华电子有限公司	塘厦镇	电子元件及组件制造
东莞市凯昶德电子科技股份有限公司	塘厦镇	电线、电缆制造
东莞市君凯电子有限公司	塘厦镇	电子工业专用设备制造
东莞市凯鹏复合材料有限公司	塘厦镇	石墨及碳素制品制造
东莞市力嘉电池有限公司	塘厦镇	锂离子电池制造
东莞市力王电池有限公司	塘厦镇	其他电池制造
东莞市纬迪实业有限公司	塘厦镇	电子元件及组件制造

1-5 续表 11

(2014年)

企业名称	所在镇街	行业类别
东莞市雅康精密机械有限公司	塘厦镇	电工机械专用设备制造
东莞市亚通光电有限公司	塘厦镇	光电子器件及其他电子器件制造
广东曙光自动化设备股份有限公司	塘厦镇	其他未列明电气机械及器材制造
东莞格力良源电池科技有限公司	塘厦镇	锂离子电池制造
东莞市吉铼升电机有限公司	塘厦镇	微电机及其他电机制造
东莞市艺展电子有限公司	凤岗镇	电子元件及组件制造
东莞奥美佳电子有限公司	凤岗镇	照相机及器材制造
东莞宇宙电路板设备有限公司	凤岗镇	电子工业专用设备制造
东莞康佳模具塑胶有限公司	凤岗镇	模具制造
广东楚天龙智能卡有限公司	凤岗镇	集成电路设计
东莞永腾电子制品有限公司	凤岗镇	计算机外围设备制造
东莞市旭通达模具塑胶有限公司	凤岗镇	模具制造
广东福聚多节能科技有限公司	凤岗镇	灯用电器附件及其他照明器具制造
东莞市伊斯诺电池有限公司	凤岗镇	锂离子电池制造
东莞市振华新能源科技有限公司	凤岗镇	锂离子电池制造
东莞联洲电子科技有限公司	凤岗镇	计算机整机制造
东莞诚兴五金制品有限公司	凤岗镇	汽车零部件及配件制造
东莞市恒德光电设备制造有限公司	凤岗镇	农副食品加工专用设备制造
东莞康佳电子有限公司	凤岗镇	电视机制造
东莞市林积为实业投资有限公司	凤岗镇	汽车零部件及配件制造
东莞市科隆电机有限公司	凤岗镇	其他传动部件制造
东莞市海迪精机有限公司	凤岗镇	机械零部件加工
东莞市利赛奥新能源科技有限公司	凤岗镇	锂离子电池制造
东莞奥托泰电器制品有限公司	凤岗镇	其他通用设备制造业
东莞市科维电子科技有限公司	凤岗镇	导航、气象及海洋专用仪器制造
东莞市润星机械科技有限公司	谢岗镇	金属切削机床制造
东莞市华轩幕墙材料有限公司	谢岗镇	金属结构制造
东莞市天圣厨具实业有限公司	常平镇	家用厨房电器具制造
东莞勤上光电股份有限公司	常平镇	照明灯具制造
智嘉通讯科技(东莞)有限公司	常平镇	电力电子元器件制造
东莞市华立实业股份有限公司	常平镇	其他家具制造
东莞运城制版有限公司	常平镇	包装装潢及其他印刷
东莞东运机械制造有限公司	常平镇	印刷专用设备制造
东莞市世通国际快件监管中心有限公司	常平镇	其他仓储业
东莞市国研电热材料有限公司	常平镇	特种陶瓷制品制造
东莞东海龙环保科技有限公司	常平镇	照明灯具制造
东莞龙昌数码科技有限公司	常平镇	玩具制造
东莞欧达电子有限公司	常平镇	光学仪器制造
东莞市维信电脑科技有限公司	常平镇	信息系统集成服务
永泰电子(东莞)有限公司	常平镇	电子元件及组件制造
快捷达通信设备(东莞)有限公司	常平镇	通信系统设备制造
东莞市宇洁新材料有限公司	常平镇	其他仪器仪表制造业
广东宏展科技有限公司	常平镇	工业自动控制系统装置制造
东莞市欣隆光电材料有限公司	常平镇	灯用电器附件及其他照明器具制造
东莞市星擎电子科技有限公司	常平镇	其他电子设备制造
东莞金杯印刷有限公司	常平镇	书、报刊印刷
东莞英铭化工有限公司	常平镇	初级形态塑料及合成树脂制造

1-5 续表 12

(2014年)

企业名称	所在镇街	行业类别
迅得机械(东莞)有限公司	常平镇	其他未列明制造业
东莞市吉鑫高分子科技有限公司	常平镇	其他塑料制品制造
五川音响电子科技(东莞)有限公司	常平镇	音响设备制造
东莞市瀛通电线有限公司	常平镇	电线、电缆制造
东莞市嘉悦电子有限公司	常平镇	通信终端设备制造
东莞市麦蒂科技有限公司	常平镇	软件开发
广东富林木业科技有限公司	常平镇	胶合板制造
东莞市鼎聚光电有限公司	常平镇	照明灯具制造
东莞市宝达模具有限公司	常平镇	铸造机械制造
广东新一信通信发展有限公司	桥头镇	通信系统设备制造
东莞兴博精密模具有限公司	桥头镇	电子元件及组件制造
东莞新爱荣机械自动化设备有限公司	桥头镇	其他通用设备制造业
东莞市汇林包装有限公司	桥头镇	其他纸制品制造
东莞市玖木通实业有限公司	桥头镇	其他电子设备制造
东莞市汉维新材料科技有限公司	桥头镇	有机化学原料制造
东莞市吉之晟电子科技有限公司	桥头镇	电子元件及组件制造
东莞市技塑塑胶科技有限公司	桥头镇	其他塑料制品制造
东莞市井田自动化设备有限公司	桥头镇	风动和电动工具制造
东莞市凯成环保科技有限公司	桥头镇	包装装潢及其他印刷
东莞市美盈森环保科技有限公司	桥头镇	其他纸制品制造
东莞市鑫诠光电技术有限公司	桥头镇	灯用电器附件及其他照明器具制造
东莞泰克威科技有限公司	桥头镇	其他电子设备制造
东莞市日新传导科技股份有限公司	桥头镇	电线、电缆制造
东莞市鑫品模具有限公司	横沥镇	模具制造
东莞市森斯电子机械科技有限公司	横沥镇	电子工业专用设备制造
东莞市天桉硅胶科技有限公司	横沥镇	其他橡胶制品制造
东莞市天倬电器有限公司	横沥镇	家用厨房电器具制造
东莞市天倬模具有限公司	横沥镇	汽车零配件批发
东莞精恒电子有限公司	横沥镇	其他电子设备制造
东莞旭光五金氧化制品有限公司	横沥镇	金属表面处理及热处理加工
东莞台一盈拓科技股份有限公司	横沥镇	金属切削机床制造
广东明家科技股份有限公司	横沥镇	其他未列明电气机械及器材制造
忠信制模(东莞)有限公司	横沥镇	模具制造
意拉德电子(东莞)有限公司	横沥镇	潜水及水下救捞装备制造
东莞市金鸿盛电器有限公司	横沥镇	家用空气调节器制造
广东天誉飞歌电子科技有限公司	横沥镇	导航、气象及海洋专用仪器制造
东莞雷笛克光学有限公司	横沥镇	灯用电器附件及其他照明器具制造
广东正茂精机有限公司	横沥镇	塑料加工专用设备制造
鑫贺精密电子(东莞)有限公司	横沥镇	其他电子设备制造
东莞市盛光电子有限公司	横沥镇	变压器、整流器和电感器制造
东莞市泰晶新能源有限公司	横沥镇	光伏设备及元器件制造
东莞市万丰科技有限公司	横沥镇	电线、电缆制造
东莞市中泰模具股份有限公司	横沥镇	模具制造
东莞市准光半导体照明有限公司	横沥镇	电光源制造
博莱特光电科技(东莞)有限公司	横沥镇	照明灯具制造
东莞和汇电子有限公司	横沥镇	汽车零部件及配件制造
东莞虹日金属科技有限公司	横沥镇	其他金属工具制造

1-5 续表 13

(2014年)

企业名称	所在镇街	行业类别
东莞市凯恩电子科技有限公司	横沥镇	电力电子元器件制造
东莞市擎洲光电科技有限公司	横沥镇	灯用电器附件及其他照明器具制造
东莞市博恒达模具有限公司	横沥镇	汽车零部件及配件制造
东莞市和永包装有限公司	横沥镇	泡沫塑料制造
东莞市恒和节能科技有限公司	横沥镇	其他非金属矿物制品制造
东莞巨扬电器有限公司	横沥镇	照明灯具制造
东莞市久森新能源有限公司	横沥镇	锂离子电池制造
天钺电子(东莞)有限公司	横沥镇	计算机外围设备制造
东莞爱美达电子有限公司	横沥镇	电子元件及组件制造
东莞市龙钢模胚钢材有限公司	横沥镇	其他未列明金属制品制造
东莞市安达自动化设备有限公司	横沥镇	电子工业专用设备制造
东莞市尼的科技股份有限公司	横沥镇	塑料薄膜制造
东莞市托普莱斯光电技术有限公司	东坑镇	电视机制造
广东中德电缆有限公司	东坑镇	电线、电缆制造
东莞市华胜展鸿电子科技有限公司	东坑镇	照明灯具制造
东莞市艾炜特电子有限公司	东坑镇	电视机制造
东莞市维美德电子材料有限公司	东坑镇	其他未列明金属制品制造
广东泰卓光电科技股份有限公司	东坑镇	电光源制造
广东迅扬电脑科技股份有限公司	东坑镇	计算机外围设备制造
东莞市康德威变压器有限公司	东坑镇	变压器、整流器和电感器制造
东莞市金禄电子科技有限公司	东坑镇	其他电子设备制造
广东友通工业有限公司	企石镇	其他未列明制造业
广东若天新材料科技有限公司	企石镇	化学试剂和助剂制造
广东启光钢结构有限公司	企石镇	金属结构制造
东莞市铁生辉制罐有限公司	企石镇	金属包装容器制造
广东亿健绿色住宅材料工业有限公司	企石镇	轻质建筑材料制造
东莞美信科技有限公司	企石镇	变压器、整流器和电感器制造
东莞市中镓半导体科技有限公司	企石镇	光电子器件及其他电子器件制造
东莞山多力汽车配件有限公司	企石镇	汽车零部件及配件制造
东莞市贺喜光电有限公司	企石镇	电光源制造
东莞毓华电子科技有限公司	企石镇	变压器、整流器和电感器制造
东莞市台电环保科技有限公司	企石镇	其他通用设备制造业
东莞市新望包装机械有限公司	企石镇	包装专用设备制造
东莞联宝光电科技有限公司	企石镇	电子元件及组件制造
东莞市恒明光电科技有限公司	企石镇	照明灯具制造
东莞市智乐堡儿童玩具有限公司	石排镇	玩具制造
东莞市方振塑胶电子制品有限公司	石排镇	橡胶零件制造
东莞铭普光磁股份有限公司	石排镇	光电子器件及其他电子器件制造
广东谷麦光电科技有限公司	石排镇	其他电子设备制造
广东凯德能源科技有限公司	石排镇	锂离子电池制造
广东星弛光电科技有限公司	石排镇	平板玻璃制造
东莞乐域光电科技有限公司	石排镇	电子元件及组件制造
东莞市悠悠美居家居制造有限公司	石排镇	日用塑料制品制造
东莞市立敏达电子科技有限公司	石排镇	电子元件及组件制造
东莞市德颖光电有限公司	石排镇	电光源制造
东莞市旭业光电科技有限公司	石排镇	光电子器件及其他电子器件制造
东莞市佳禾电子有限公司	石排镇	计算机外围设备制造
东莞市三肯电子制造有限公司	茶山镇	电子元件及组件制造

1-5 续表 14

(2014年)

企业名称	所在镇街	行业类别
特新微电子(东莞)有限公司	茶山镇	其他未列明信息技术服务业
东莞市悠派智能展示科技有限公司	茶山镇	其他未列明制造业
东莞市贻嘉光电科技有限公司	茶山镇	照明灯具制造
东莞市英科水墨有限公司	茶山镇	油墨及类似产品制造
广东紫光电气有限公司	茶山镇	变压器、整流器和电感器制造
东莞森玛仕格里菲电路有限公司	茶山镇	印制电路板制造
广东百顺纸品有限公司	茶山镇	其他纸制品制造
东莞市威得客自动化科技有限公司	茶山镇	其他金属加工机械制造
东莞市闻誉实业有限公司	茶山镇	其他有色金属压延加工
东莞市奥能工程塑料有限公司	茶山镇	初级形态塑料及合成树脂制造
东莞市箭冠汽车配件制造有限公司	茶山镇	汽车零部件及配件制造
东莞市风火轮热能科技有限公司	松山湖	其他原动设备制造
东莞市中之光电科技有限公司	松山湖	照明灯具制造
东莞市迪凯精密管材有限公司	松山湖	其他医疗设备及器械制造
广东大普通信技术有限公司	松山湖	电子元件及组件制造
东莞安尔发智能科技股份有限公司	松山湖	其他通用设备制造业
东莞润赢电力科技有限公司	松山湖	信息系统集成服务
东莞市艾斯迪新材料有限公司	松山湖	其他未列明制造业
广东纳明新材料科技有限公司	松山湖	其他合成材料制造
东莞市微模式软件有限公司	松山湖	软件开发
广东盈达信息科技股份有限公司	松山湖	信息系统集成服务
东莞市中科教育电子有限公司	松山湖	电子乐器制造
东莞市万科建筑技术研究有限公司	松山湖	工程和技术研究和试验发展
领亚电子科技股份有限公司	松山湖	计算机外围设备制造
广东正业科技股份有限公司	松山湖	电子测量仪器制造
广东东阳光药业有限公司	松山湖	化学药品制剂制造
广东康菱动力科技有限公司	松山湖	发电机及发电机组制造
广东生益科技股份有限公司	松山湖	电子元件及组件制造
广东易事特电源股份有限公司	松山湖	计算机外围设备制造
东莞市科磊得数码光电科技有限公司	松山湖	照明灯具制造
东莞新能源科技有限公司	松山湖	锂离子电池制造
广东雨林木风计算机科技有限公司	松山湖	互联网信息服务
广东电子工业研究院有限公司	松山湖	其他未列明信息技术服务业
广东华南工业设计院	松山湖	专业化设计服务
东莞市劲威智能冲压成套设备有限公司	松山湖	其他通用设备制造业
东莞易步机器人有限公司	松山湖	助动自行车制造
广东三凯新材料股份有限公司	松山湖	其他橡胶制品制造
东莞市安美润滑科技有限公司	松山湖	其他未列明制造业
广东奥美格传导科技股份有限公司	松山湖	电线、电缆制造
东莞思谷数字技术有限公司	松山湖	工程和技术研究和试验发展
东莞市松庆智能自动化科技有限公司	松山湖	其他通用设备制造业
东莞市依时利科技有限公司	松山湖	信息技术咨询服务
广东中实金属有限公司	松山湖	其他有色金属压延加工
广东荣文能源科技集团有限公司	松山湖	节能技术推广服务
广东大族粤铭激光科技股份有限公司	松山湖	金属切削机床制造
广东世纪网通信设备股份有限公司	松山湖	通信终端设备制造
广东科硕机械科技股份有限公司	松山湖	电工机械专用设备制造
广东高标电子科技有限公司	松山湖	电力电子元器件制造

1-5 续表 15

(2014年)

企业名称	所在镇街	行业类别
东莞市荣文照明电气有限公司	松山湖	照明灯具制造
东莞市拓荒牛自动化设备有限公司	松山湖	包装专用设备制造
广东易凌信息科技有限公司	松山湖	软件开发
东莞市贝特电子科技股份有限公司	松山湖	电子元件及组件制造
东莞市威特隆仓储设备有限公司	松山湖	电工机械专用设备制造
东莞市远峰科技有限公司	松山湖	其他电子设备制造
广东聚光电子科技有限公司	松山湖	其他电子设备制造
广东威迪科技股份有限公司	松山湖	环境保护专用设备制造
泰斗微电子科技有限公司	松山湖	电子元件及组件制造
广东阿尔派新材料股份有限公司	松山湖	其他电力生产
广东百圳君耀电子有限公司	松山湖	电子元件及组件制造
东莞市亚聚电子材料有限公司	松山湖	其他合成材料制造
华为终端(东莞)有限公司	松山湖	通信终端设备制造
优利德科技(中国)有限公司	松山湖	电工仪器仪表制造
东莞市科旺科技有限公司	松山湖	变压器、整流器和电感器制造
东莞东石新材料开发有限公司	松山湖	玻璃纤维增强塑料制品制造
东莞市天域半导体科技有限公司	松山湖	半导体分立器件制造
东莞市新球清洗科技有限公司	松山湖	石油及制品批发
东莞市凯欣电池材料有限公司	松山湖	其他专用化学产品制造
东莞市新东方光电技术有限公司	松山湖	通信系统设备制造
广东洛贝电子科技有限公司	松山湖	家用厨房电器具制造
东莞劲芳生物医药孵化器有限公司	松山湖	生物药品制造
东莞市玮孚电子科技有限公司	松山湖	锂离子电池制造
东莞华贝电子科技有限公司	松山湖	通信终端设备制造
东莞市百大新能源股份有限公司	松山湖	非金属废料和碎屑加工处理
东莞市绿微康生物科技有限公司	松山湖	其他未列明制造业
广东阿尔派电力科技股份有限公司	松山湖	其他输配电及控制设备制造
东莞钜威新能源有限公司	松山湖	其他未列明制造业
广东一一五科技有限公司	松山湖	互联网信息服务
广东科创工程技术有限公司	松山湖	其他水的处理、利用与分配
广东中科遥感技术有限公司	松山湖	其他未列明信息技术服务业
东莞市华科制造工程研究院有限公司	松山湖	工程和技术研究和试验发展
东莞市帕马智能停车服务有限公司	松山湖	其他未列明信息技术服务业
东莞市锐源仪器股份有限公司	松山湖	电工仪器仪表制造
东莞瑞柯电子科技股份有限公司	松山湖	汽车零部件及配件制造
东莞市升力智能科技有限公司	松山湖	其他专用仪器制造
广东泰通农业发展集团有限公司	松山湖	其他农业
东莞市腾威电子材料技术有限公司	松山湖	集成电路制造
广东亨通光电科技有限公司	松山湖	光纤、光缆制造
广东志成华科光电设备有限公司	松山湖	其他电子设备制造
国云科技股份有限公司	松山湖	其他未列明信息技术服务业
东莞市尚睿电子商务有限公司	松山湖	互联网零售
广东瓦力网络科技有限公司	松山湖	互联网信息服务
东莞市意普万尼龙科技股份有限公司	松山湖	初级形态塑料及合成树脂制造
东莞市嘉宏有机硅科技有限公司	松山湖	有机化学原料制造
东莞爱尚菇食品科技有限公司	松山湖	其他未列明食品制造
广东普赛特电子科技股份有限公司	松山湖	光电子器件及其他电子器件制造
东莞市苏普尔电子科技有限公司	松山湖	光电子器件及其他电子器件制造

中国统计出版社最新图书简目

(仅供参考,以实际出版为准)

统计资料

中国统计年鉴　中国统计摘要　中国发展报告
中国经济普查年鉴2013　国际统计年鉴　金砖国家联合统计手册
中国-东盟国家统计手册　中国区域经济统计年鉴　中国县域统计年鉴
中国城市统计年鉴　中国农村统计年鉴　中国地区经济监测报告
中国贸易外经统计年鉴　中国对外直接投资统计公报　中国商品交易市场统计年鉴
大中型批发零售和住宿餐饮企业统计年鉴　中国零售和餐饮连锁企业统计年鉴　中国住户调查年鉴
中国价格统计年鉴　中国农产品价格调查年鉴　全国农产品成本收益资料汇编
中国环境统计年鉴　中国能源统计年鉴　国外资源、能源和环境统计资料汇编
中国工业统计年鉴　中国建筑业统计年鉴　中国房地产统计年鉴
中国城市建设统计年鉴　中国城乡建设统计年鉴　中国第三产业统计年鉴
中国证券期货统计年鉴　中国科技统计年鉴　中国高技术产业统计年鉴
工业企业科技活动资料　中国劳动统计年鉴　中国人口和就业统计年鉴
中国人才资源统计报告　中国社会统计年鉴　中国文化及相关产业统计年鉴
文化及相关产业统计概览　中国教育经费统计年鉴　中国民政统计年鉴
中国民族统计年鉴　中国工会统计年鉴　中国残疾人事业统计年鉴
中国妇女儿童状况统计资料（英）　中国乡镇街道行政区域简册

省级综合统计年鉴系列

北京 天津 河北 山西 内蒙古 辽宁 吉林 黑龙江 上海 江苏 浙江 安徽 福建 江西 山东 河南 湖北 湖南 广东 广西 海南 重庆 四川 贵州 云南 西藏 陕西 甘肃 青海 宁夏 新疆 新疆生产建设兵团

市(县)级综合统计年鉴系列

天津滨海新区 石家庄 唐山 邯郸 保定 沧州 邢台 廊坊 承德 衡水 秦皇岛 张家口 太原 大同 阳泉 长治 晋城 朔州 晋中 运城 忻州 临汾 呼和浩特 呼和浩特新城区 鄂尔多斯 包头 沈阳 大连 长春 四平 哈尔滨 齐齐哈尔 黑龙江垦区 上海浦东新区 南京 无锡 徐州 常州 苏州 南通 连云港 淮安 盐城 扬州 镇江 泰州 宿迁 江阴 丹阳 杭州 宁波 温州 嘉兴 绍兴 金华 衢州 舟山 台州 丽水 合肥 安庆 马鞍山 福州 厦门 宁德 南昌 九江 上饶 新余 抚州 济南 青岛 枣庄 滕州 郑州 洛阳 平顶山 三门峡 南阳 商丘 济源 武汉 十堰 荆州 宜昌 荆门 咸宁 长沙 广州 深圳 惠州 东莞 南宁 柳州 桂林 来宾 海口 三亚 成都 贵阳 昆明 西安 兰州 庆阳 银川 乌鲁木齐 兵团一师 兵团十师

调查年鉴系列

天津 山西 内蒙古 辽宁 吉林 上海　福建 河南 湖北 湖南 广西 重庆　四川 云南 甘肃 宁夏 新疆

“十二五”规划教材

统计学（经济管理类专业本科适用，单薇 等）　抽样调查理论与方法（冯士雍 等）
贝叶斯统计（茆诗松 等）　统计学（黄良文 等）　试验设计（茆诗松 等）
统计学：从数据到结论（吴喜之）　医学统计学（于浩）　统计学（经济、管理类专业基础教材，张小斐）
概率论与数理统计三十三讲（魏振军）　概率论与数理统计三十三：学习指导与习题解答（魏振军）
非参数统计（吴喜之 等）　统计学：经济与管理中的数据分析（李慧云 等）
卫生管理统计学（新编医学院校基础课教材，尚磊）　医院统计学（新编医学院校基础课教材，徐天和 等）
社会统计学（蒋萍 等）　现代金融投资统计分析（李腊生 等）
国民经济核算初级教程（经济类、统计类、管理类专业适用，蒋萍 等）

重点图书

图解中国经济2015　新编英汉汉英统计大词典　中华医学统计百科全书
挑大学选专业2016—考研择校指南　挑大学选专业2015—高考志愿填报指南